SH
401
M 4

41184

McNally, Tom

Fishermen's Bible

DATE DUE		
JAN 12	OCT 10	AUG - 7 1995
NOV 3 0 197	MAR 2 0 199	APR 1 4 1999
JUL 1 2 1978	JUL 19 198	AUG 2 0 2001
MAY 7 19		
APR 1 5 198	APR 0 3 1991	
OCT 1 4 198		
NOV 1 9 199	APR 2 8 1992	
MAR 2 4 199	MAY - 3 1993	
SEP 1 5	JUN 0 1 1993	
MAR 1 6 93		
APR 1 3 199	SEP 2 1 1994	

RENEW BOOKS BY
TELEPHONE
466-4811   EXT. 303

Waubonsee Community College

Ban the Bulldozer and Channelization

Each year hundreds of miles of America's prime rivers and streams are destroyed for the sake of what some, mostly politicians, call "progress."

The straightening, channelization, diking and leveeing of waterways is needlessly killing many of this country's most scenic, most important, most irreplaceable rivers and streams.

"Pork barrel projects"—which accomplish little good other than to enrich politicians and certain "business-men"—usually are to blame for the destruction, if only partial, of valued rivers and streams. But other despoilers are the "highwaymen," or road builders, most of whom couldn't care less that the stream they ravage with their bulldozers was, formerly, a world-renown trout stream.

In most instances road-builders do not hesitate to launch bulldozers into rivers and streams, where their powerful earthmoving monsters swiftly and efficiently gouge, tear, gut, *and destroy* the streambed.

The ecological life-blood of any river, stream, or creek is in its bottom. *Ravage a streambed, and you ravage the stream!*

It is on the floor of a river that life in the river begins. Indiscriminate bulldozing of a stream bed kills the nymphal stage of all of the stream's aquatic life in the area bulldozed. It alters the natural flow of the stream and drastically changes its current, and greatly decreases the oxygen content of the water. Bulldozing, or "channel-ization," causes siltation that consumes a river. Bull-dozing devours rapids, bends, eddies, pools, islands, riffles—and the destruction is *permanent!*

Few American waterways have gone unaffected by "road building" or "channelization." To name just a few of the country's most famous rivers and streams that have been at least partially slaughtered through indiscrimi-nate, unnecessary bulldozing, there is Wyoming's Snake River, Montana's Yellowstone and Big Hole rivers and prized Spring Creek (Lewistown), New York's famed Beaverkill, Pennsylvania's Brodhead, Utah's Logan River, and Florida's Kissimminee.

The reckless launching of bulldozers into our rivers and streams continues daily. At times, of course, the channelization, straightening, and bulldozing of a stream's floor is unavoidable, but most of the time such destructive work is totally unnecessary since equally effective alternate projects could be engineered.

In most instances the stated purpose of channel-ization is to control or prevent floods by speeding the surface runoff of rainwater that falls on a watershed. But what this usually accomplishes is the destruction of the natural features of the land which serve to *retard runoff*, so the channelization actually increases down-stream flooding and erosion, as well as destroying the biological productivity of the original water course and its adjacent flood plains.

Following channelization of a portion of Utah's Logan River, the Utah Division of Wildlife Resorces reported that the Logan River, "once a high quality habitat for wild brown trout, has been torn completely apart and destroyed by ditching, and 1971's brown trout and whitefish reproduction may have been completely eliminated, and the recreational fishing potential of the area has been lost." The Army Corps of Engineers sub-sequently ordered a halt to "work" on the Logan River —but the damage had been done.

The bulldozing and channelization of rivers and streams is, unfortunately, common to all areas. Every state has suffered, with many miles of natural streams converted into ditches. Georgia, for example, has only a few streams remaining in a natural state. Alabama and Ohio have rebelled against channelization and declared moratoriums on such projects. Ohio discovered there were plans to "improve," via channelization, 149 of its 309 watersheds. On one Ohio river alone, 190 miles of stream channelization had been planned at an estimated cost of $7,800,000 to *federal taxpayers*.

Stream channelization is conducted primarily by three agencies: the Bureau of Reclamation (in the West), the Army Corp of Engineers, and the U.S. Soil Conservation

(continued on back cover)

Tom McNally's
Fishermen's
Bible 2nd edition

Follett Publishing Company / Chicago

About the front cover:
On the cover of this second edition is a silhouette color photo of the author's eldest son, Bob McNally, with a 24 pound lake trout Bob caught at the Wolverine River in far northern Manitoba.

Library of Congress Catalog Card Number: 73-99591
ISBN 0-695-80352-2

Contents

How Buck Perry's "System" Cracks The Bass Barrier

Master spoonplugger Elwood ("Buck") Perry makes a cast to underwater "structure" . . .

Years ago if someone had told me he could catch bass anywhere at anytime, I'd have marked him for a beginning fisherman, a braggart, or a fool. Largemouth black bass, I once believed, are moody fish that sometimes hit and sometimes don't—and can't be caught consistently even by experts. Nonsense!

There is no such thing as a bass that won't hit if you locate him, and if you fish for him in the right way. And one system of bass fishing is almost faultless—developed by Elwood ("Buck") Perry of Hickory, North Carolina.

If you already can catch bass every time you go fishing, this story is not for you. However, if you catch bass only some of the time—then discard all your old beliefs, study what follows, practice the system set forth, and start catching bass like crazy.

Disbelievers and scoffers to the contrary, there is no disputing the effectiveness of spoonplugging for bass.

Spoonplugging is a *system* of fishing. Perry developed it over a period of thirty years and at a personal cost of $40,000. Perry's system runs contrary to all the old theories on bass fishing, and ruins all those old excuses

of weather, time of year, water temperature, angling pressure and so on. Yet it consistently puts fish in the boat.

However, spoonplugging isn't something you just go out and do. Neither is it based on a *miracle* lure, which is what fishermen everywhere always look for but never find. Spoonplugging is a *technique* that must be studied, understood, and—to be effective—must be followed according to formula. It's a system based on the complete understanding of the habits of black bass, and their migrations. Unless you decide to become a rigid perfectionist, following Perry's system to the letter, you might just as well save your time and stay in that school of plugcasters who simply chuck, and reel, and hope.

Many fishermen have been exposed to spoonplugging. Most of them were shocked at the results. In several southern states spoonplugging produced bass that made fishermen's eyes pop and their hearts pound!

Buck Perry is a quiet, gentle, unassuming ex-college professor. He once taught engineering at the University of North Carolina, and this background helped him develop the spoonplugging system.

Buck started spoonplugging in the Tar Heel State, and

. . . then sets the hook hard as a bass strikes!

began spreading the system throughout the South. Word of Perry's success at catching bass spread like wildfire. Fisherman from all over the country flocked to him for more information. Some of them learned the technique, then went out and caught bass as never before. But there were other fishermen—particularly those who had a hand in the manufacture of other lures and tackle—who proclaimed Buck Perry a fraud.

The scoffers haven't made Perry's road an easy one. It seems to be the way of some people never to accept anything new, or to admit that someone else has come up with something original and worthwhile. Buck once had set the Georgia fishing world on end with takes of phenomonal bass. An unfriendly, jealous character decided to try to discredit Buck publicly. There'd been talk that Buck caught his fish illegally, perhaps with nets or traps, or that he may even have been buying them from hatcheries. This fretful fellow arranged a fishing date with Buck, and when Buck turned up at the lake he found more than 20 newspaper reporters, magazine writers, and newsreel cameramen waiting. To save face, Buck was going to have to produce—but good!

Buck and his doubting companion went out in one boat, the newsmen and photogs in a couple of others. As luck would have it, Buck located a school of bass promptly. In thirty-three casts—all under the watchful "eyes" of the news-cameras—Buck hooked and landed thirty-three bass!

"It wasn't easy, though," Buck recalls. "I knew I'd better not miss. I trolled until I located a school of bass down deep, then I started casting. *Wham!* First cast, I had me a fish. About four pounds. Some eyebrows went up at that. I cast again. It was a big school of fish, and I wanted one on every cast. *Wham* again! It went on like that cast after cast, but every once in a while a bass would strike, get hooked, then shake off. I wouldn't let on that I'd lost one. I'd just let my plug settle down again, start bringing it back, and hook another bass. That way I made a perfect record of one fish boated for each cast."

There is all kinds of testimony to the effectiveness of the spoonplugging system. It isn't my intent here to *sell anything;* only to convince fishermen of the effectiveness of spoonplugging as a system, so they'll take the necessary time to learn the technique, and then catch bass regularly, under varied conditions.

Ray Bergmann, former Fishing Editor of *Outdoor Life Magazine,* called spoonplugging "a sure way to catch bass." Al McClane, Fishing Editor of *Field and Stream,* once devoted a column to the system.

Ray Bergmann has written that "Spoonplugging has a way of digging bass out, whether you have to scrape them off the bottom in deep water or gouge them out of weeds in the shallows." Jack Elliott, once mayor of Covington, Georgia, fished with Buck and said, "His system is astounding. I saw it, but I still can't believe it." George X. Sand, well-known outdoor writer, said of spoonplugging: "the big difference between Perry's system and others is that Perry uses a lure that finds fish." Joe Stearns, a southern syndicated outdoor columnist, reported to his readers that "the angler who masters the instructions on spoonplugging will start catching more bass than he ever caught in his life. Spoonplugging is a

fisherman's dream come true."

In one of his *Miami Herald* stories, when he was Outdoor Editor of that paper, Allen Corson wrote: "Would you like to make 30 casts and catch 30 black bass? That feat was performed by Buck Perry before 200 witnesses." This was *not* the day told about earlier, when Buck performed before a group of newsmen and photographers. Jay Johnson, president of a fly-tying materials company in Evanston, Illinois, went spoonplugging with Don Nichols of Riverside, Illinois one day on a lake thirty miles from Chicago. Afterward Jay remarked that "spoonplugging is the best system for locating bass that's ever been developed."

Hundreds of other outdoor writers, both in the magazine and newspaper fields, and thousands of fishermen, acclaim spoonplugging the greatest bass killer yet devised. And in my experience, as a fisherman and a writer, *I've seen nothing else that teaches a man so much about bass in so short a time.*

I first fished with Buck Perry more than a dozen years ago. When the trip was over I did a story on the spoonplugging system, for the *Chicago Tribune.* It upset the Midwest. There were telegrams, long-distance phone calls, letters, postcards, personal visits.

Only one Chicago sporting goods store was stocking Spoonplugs at the time. By 3:00 P.M. the day after my story appeared, they'd sold their 5,000th Spoonplug. A few days later, sales had reached 35,000. Fishermen lined up outside each of the firm's four stores to buy lures and to talk to clerks experienced at spoonplugging. Spoonplugs were rationed the way cigarettes were during World War II.

Television and radio stations flashed the news about spoonplugging. Other newspapers started running stories on the system, and *Sports Illustrated Magazine* added to the excitement by following up with a short piece on Perry and spoonplugging.

As generally happens when Buck Perry creates a stir, thousands of Chicago area fishermen bought Spoonplugs and rushed out to area lakes. They thought that at last a miracle lure had been discovered, and all they had to do was tie one on, make a cast, then stand back while the bass rushed in. They fished the Spoonplugs just like any other lure, and paid no attention to advice about the spoonplugging *system.* Naturally some of these people caught fish, but most failed miserably. Some admitted they "just didn't know how to spoonplug," but others hollered "fraud." A few wrote blistering letters, claiming they'd outfish Perry any old day. Perry has a standard reply for such correspondence: "Put up $100, and we'll see." There never has been a taker.

However, out of that great army of obvious misfits, a few fishermen arose who did try the spoonplugging system intelligently and persistently. I'll always remember one letter I received, from Angelo Vecchio, of 8043 Milwaukee Road, Niles, Illinois. It read, in part:

"I have read about spoonplugging. Believe me, it's true. I have fished a lake near here for over 20 years, and never believed that it held so many large bass. I was just an average fisherman, until I started to use this wonderful system, which is unbelieveable. The first time I spoonplugged I caught three bass, each about

*four pounds. Since then I have been skunked only once
. . . which is not bad fishing around Chicago.*"

For some years before meeting him I had been re-
motely aware of Buck Perry and spoonplugging. Occasionally, in my fishing travels around the country, I'd
pick up a paper and run across a story about Buck. Then
one day many years ago Don Nichols, whom I mentioned
earlier, sent me a photo of an immense string of large
bass and said he'd caught them spoonplugging at Lake
Marie, about thirty-eight miles from Chicago. At that
time I hadn't met Don, nor Perry. But I was attuned
to spoonplugging, and I knew that Perry—whoever he
was—apparently had found something new in the bass-
catchin' department. But I wasn't sure the Perry drum-
beating I heard and read wasn't just more of the seasonal
fishing hub-bub that pops up annually. I certainly wasn't
going to go out of my way to meet Perry and find out
about his new "bass fishing miracle".

Then, one July day, the telephone buzzed. It was
Perry.

"How'd you like to go out and catch some bass?" he
drawled. "I'll guarantee a mess of baking size." This
was my first contact with Buck.

"You'll *guarantee* them?" I asked.

"Sure will, son," Buck kidded. "You come with me
and we'll murder those little devils." I smelled a story.
Bass or no bass, I figured, any trip starting this way would
make good reading. But even so, I was hesitant. I didn't
want to waste a day, and I knew that fishermen working
lakes of the Chicago area had been doing poorly.

"How are we going to catch these fish?" I sparred.
"You sound awfully sure."

"We'll get 'em by a new system I've developed," Buck
replied. "It really breaks 'em up."

"You mean bass bugs?' I said. "Nothing takes largemouths like popping bugs if the fish are in the shallows."

"That's right," Buck agreed, "but I'll show you how
to take them when they're down deep, too." I agreed to
go fishing the next day.

The following morning our party—Don Nichols and
Bob Mummert of Chicago, Perry and I—met in a res-
taurent a few miles from Pistakee Bay on Fox Lake, one

TYPICAL CROSS SECTION OF "STRUCTURE" IN A LAKE

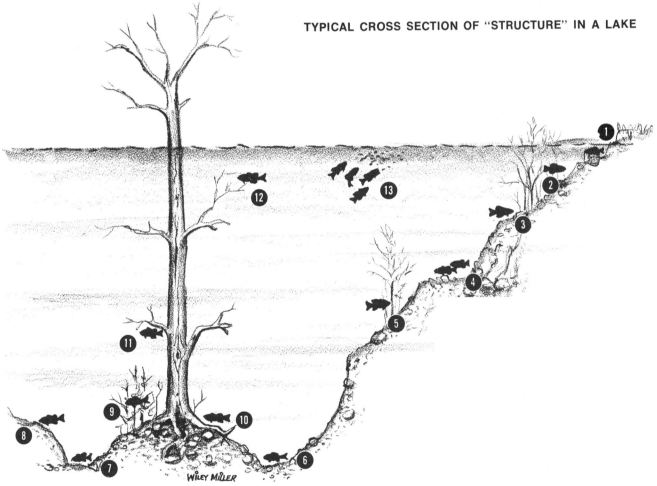

WILEY MILLER

(1) Shallow water bank fishing.
(2) Brushy point. Fish sitting in the midst of the heaviest brush.
(3) Fish sitting on drop-off at the edge of brush on a brushy point.
(4) Bass school sitting on stair-step ledge on a hard bottom in deeper water.
(5) Bass sitting in deep brush on steep drop off.
(6) Fish lying in gully or ditch.

(7) Fish sitting in base of creek bed.
(8) Fish sitting on bank of creek bed.
(9) Fish on brushy bank of creek bed.
(10) Fish sitting at the base of a large tree, on a knoll rise.
(11) Fish "suspended" in deep branches.
(12) Fish "suspended" in shallow branches.
(13) A school of bass running a school of shad off structure.

of many lakes about thirty-five miles northwest of Chicago. This is one of the most frequently fished lakes I know. Resorts and summer homes clutter its shores, and speedboats and water-skiers clutter its surface. On most summer days the lake is whipped into foam by speedboats, skiers, and swimmers. It isn't the sort of place I like to fish, nor the kind of spot where I'd expect to get many bass.

This day even the weather was kicking up a fuss to make prospects worse. A chilling, driving rainstorm was beating down from the northeast, tearing in from Lake Michigan. The temperature fell to about 40 degrees. We weren't in any rush to leave the restaurant, so we belted down several cups of coffee.

"There's no need to hurry," Buck grinned. "One of the nice things about my system is that you can catch bass any time, not just in the morning and evening."

It was 10:30 when we finally drove up to the dock. I stepped out of the car into the teeth of the wind, and jumped right back in. The rain was coming in sheets, and the wind was turning the lake upside down. Whitecaps were rolling over Pistakee Bay the way the surf slams into Maine's rocky coast. "Brother," I thought. "Nobody could catch many bass on a day like this. Every largemouth in the lake will be scratching his belly on bottom."

The other guys were donning woolens and rain parkas and readying their fishing gear. I dug into my duffle bag and put on all the clothing I had. Then I rigged a bugging rod and a casting rod, and a few minutes later Buck and I were in a boat chugging out across the lake. Don and Bob were following in another skiff. The rain slowed, finally petered out, but the wind came on, biting and kicking up a fuss. Soon I began to feel silly, full of a "why-n-hell-am-I-here?" sort of feeling.

For nearly two hours Buck and I trolled around Pistakee Bay. Everytime I looked up to check on Don and Bob, I saw them doing the same. To me they seemed like two rigid, wind-swept stumps, sitting motionless in their boat, seeming to troll aimlessly.

We were using only Buck's lures, the Spoonplugs, in various sizes and colors. Our rods were short, stiff trolling rods mounted with light salt water reels holding yards of twenty-five pound test monofilament line. The Spoonplugs—metal lures that look as though they'd been stepped on by a horse—dug along the bottom putting vibrations into our rod tips. No matter how fast or slow we trolled, the lures continued to gouge along the bottom. I thought that if Buck Perry had done nothing else, he had developed the first lure that would go down to a given depth, according to the lure's size, and stay down. Even a lead jig, with all its density, will plane in the water at a certain trolling speed.

We caught nothing, except an occasional small white bass. All this time Buck, still confident, explained his spoonplugging system. He said he'd learned that bass spend most of the time in deep water "sanctuaries," and that they leave these holes only a few times a day on the average. To catch largemouths consistently, Buck said, it is necessary to locate the sanctuaries and to know the migration routes the fish use in leaving these holes for shallows where they feed. We were trolling, Buck explained, because that was the fastest way to cover a lot of water

and to locate fish. Once a school of bass was found in a sanctuary, or individuals located as they moved up a migration route, we'd anchor and start casting. The sanctuaries, Buck claimed, usually were at the drop-offs of bars leading from a shallow point to deep water. Most of our trolling had been over two bars.

We ran parallel to the bars, our lures scraping deep, then crossed them, then criss-crossed. We made so many passes over these bars that our digging spoonplugs must have furrowed them like cornfields.

Finally, after the wind had dropped slightly, I noticed a weed bed inside a sheltered cove. I suggested we go go over and I'd try a popping bug. Buck agreed, and began paddling around the weeds as I cast. After five or six throws with a big yellow bug, I had a bass. He came out of a pocket in the grass. I set the hook hard, and the bass ducked back into the weeds. Then he came up again, hoisted himself out heavily, and went walking over the surface on his tail, rocking and rolling from side to side. A few minutes later I drew the fish in, a three-pounder, and released him. I turned to Buck.

"Looks as though they want bugs," I said.

"Uh-huh," Buck smiled. "But maybe that one was a straggler. Let's see you get another." I continued laying the bug up close to the weeds while Buck paddled. An hour passed, and I didn't catch another bass. We went back to trolling over the deepwater bars.

We buzzed along at varying speeds, the outboard kicking us fast then slow as Buck manipulated the throttle with one hand, held his trolling rod with the other. Suddenly it happened! Buck's rod jumped, and a bass broke water seventy yards astern. Buck's bass hardly had time to fall back when something tried to yank my rod out of my hand, and I looked back to see another leaping largemouth.

Buck cut the motor as we fought our fish close. Soon Buck grabbed a net and scooped up his bass, and then mine. Each was about four pounds. We motored back to within casting range of where Buck figured the fish had hit our trolled Spoonplugs. Anchors were dropped over at the bow and at the stern, and we started casting. Here we were in open water, nearly in the middle of the lake, casting "blind."

"This only looks like blind casting," Buck said. "It isn't really. There're fish out there now, moving right along up that bar that we can't see. Before, the bass had been sitting in a sanctuary too deep for our lures, but now they're coming up. Make a long cast, let the Spoonplug sink to bottom, then crawl it right over that bar."

I did, and a bass hit before I'd turned the reel handle three times. "Fish on," I said. "Here too," Buck said.

Don and Bob, seeing our arching rods, came roaring in from the other bar across the lake. They anchored opposite us and began casting. Soon I heard a *"whoop"* and looked up to see Don tied into a bass. Then Bob caught one. Then Buck had another and I don't know what the routine was after that. I was too busy hooking fish, or watching someone else's fish rocking around on his tail. It went that way for perhaps fifteen minutes—casting, getting a strike, losing a bass or landing one. Then it ended just as suddenly as it began.

"The school has dispersed," Buck explained. "The fish

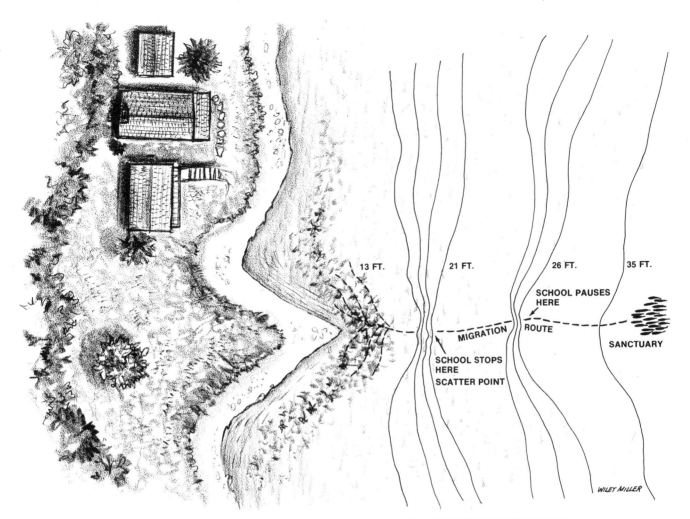

TOP VIEW OF UNDERWATER "STRUCTURE" AND FISH MIGRATION ROUTE

probably are in the shallows feeding on minnows now. We can catch more by going inshore."

"There's no need," I said. "We couldn't get more on the stringer."

I spent the next several minutes making photos of Buck, Don, and Bob with the fish, then we released most of them. After that we headed for the dock, stowed our gear, and spent the balance of the afternoon at a bar where I learned more about spoonplugging.

Buck said that it all began many years ago, when he first took up bass fishing. He'd go to some lake, and ask the dock man how fishing was. Invariably the answer was that the fish had been hitting like mad the day before, or the week before, or the month before—or they would be a day hence, or a week hence, or a month hence. They never seemed to be "hitting like mad" when Buck was ready to go fishing. Buck simply grew weary of being told the fish "ain't biting today."

"Finally I decided to give up fishing until I learned enough about bass to be able to catch them regularly," Buck said. "I just couldn't believe that sometimes fish would 'bite' and sometimes they wouldn't."

Buck went to libraries and read every available book on bass and bass fishing. He studied largemouths until he knew enough about them to write a biological thesis on the species. He learned the water temperatures bass prefer; what they feed on and how; the kind of bottom they like; the influences of weather on bass fishing; and even the bass's spawning habits. To learn still more, Buck went to work for a time at a bass hatchery. After some years, he decided he knew what made black bass tick. Buck became convinced that whenever he could locate bass, he could catch them.

After long years of study and research, Buck Perry finally went back to fishing. Before long he was enjoying what most anglers would consider exceptional sport. But it wasn't good enough for Buck, because there were a lot of "empty" days—days when he'd catch only a few bass, or perhaps none at all. Buck wasn't satisfied. He figured no fish was smarter than a man, so an exhaustive study of lure manufacture and design began. His engineering education was handy here.

Buck tried every lure available, and found all of them lacking in something. What Buck wanted was a lure that would work at certain depths, regardless of the speed of the retrieve. And the lure must have a tantalizing wiggle that would induce bass to strike whether they were hungry or not. Buck wanted a lure that would make it possible for him to "control" his fishing, completely eliminating luck. The result was the Spoonplug.

Spoonplugs are made in five sizes. But this isn't so that a fisherman can match a Spoonplug of proper weight to

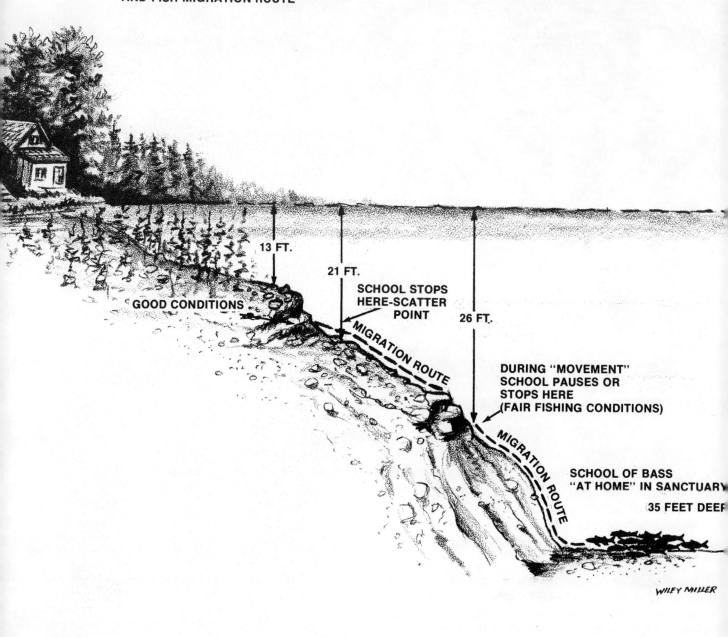

13 FT.

GOOD CONDITIONS

21 FT.

SCHOOL STOPS
HERE-SCATTER
POINT

MIGRATION ROUTE

26 FT.

DURING "MOVEMENT"
SCHOOL PAUSES OR
STOPS HERE
(FAIR FISHING CONDITIONS)

MIGRATION ROUTE

SCHOOL OF BASS
"AT HOME" IN SANCTUARY

35 FEET DEEP

WILEY MILLER

his spinning or casting tackle. Spoonplugs are made in different sizes because it is the size of the lure that determines the depth at which it operates. The smaller ones are for shallow water; the larger run from around ten to fifteen feet; and the largest size goes down to about twenty-one feet. Spoonplugs are ingeniously designed to run at their proper depths regardless of the speed of the retrieve.

Take a Spoonplug and cast it 100 feet. Let it sink to the bottom. Start reeling, and the lure will lift up on its nose and crawl across the bottom until it's directly under your boat. Then, by reeling harder, it will rise straight up to the side of the boat. I know of no other lure that will do this.

Take a Spoonplug and cast it out. Let it sink. Crank up your outboard and go tearing across the lake—at any speed from very fast to very slow. Even with the throttle wide open, the Spoonplug will not rise to the surface. It will stick to the bottom like it's been glued there. This is one of the things Buck strived for in designing his Spoonplug. He wanted a bait that would go down and stay down—down where the fish are so much of the time. Not even a lead jig can be trolled at a fast pace and not rise partially in the water.

Buck's whole theory of spoonplugging is based on *finding* fish. You can't catch them, he insists, until you locate them! Buck maintains that most of the time bass fishermen are casting over "empty" water.

When Buck Perry arrives at a strange lake, the first thing he does is ask a native about the fishing. "Are the bass biting?" he asks. Usually the answer is "No." Buck then asks, "Where were they catching them when they were biting last?" The guy generally points out some cove or shoreline. Buck knows, then, that the area indicated has a largemouth sanctuary or two nearby. Fishing's good when the bass are out of the sanctuary and are prowling along shore, where most fishermen can get at them. Bass are most vulnerable when they're in the shallows. After learning the general area where bass are, Buck's problem is to locate the specific spot or spots where they hole up.

He rigs a short, stiff trolling rod and attaches a midget, shallow-running Spoonplug. He outboards to the cove or shoreline indicated by the native, and begins trolling almost against the bank. He'll cruise back and forth, constantly altering trolling speed from very fast to very slow. As a general rule, the colder the day the slower Buck trolls; the warmer, the faster. This is the direct opposite of what most bass fishermen have done for years. Always we've assumed bass are lethargic in warm water, frisky in cold. Buck says it isn't so—and has proved it.

"Fish are cold-blooded critters," he explains. "When the water's cold, their metabolism slows. When it's warm, they're happy. In cold water a minnow moves sluggishly, but in warm water he goes like a bullet. That's the way I make my Spoonplugs behave."

If trolling near the bank fails, Buck moves out to depths of eight or twelve feet. Another size Spoonplug is used there, because the smaller ones won't run that deep. Always the lure is operated on bottom, scraping over the sand or mud.

Only on rare occasions, Buck says, has he found largemouths preferring a "free running" lure—one that isn't brushing bottom. Most of the time bass tip up on their noses and snatch a Spoonplug right off the bottom. On occasions they dig into the mud after it. Fishing with Buck or Don Nichols, I've caught bass whose mouths were edged with mud, or found them with a bit of weed hanging from their jaws, indicating the fish had grabbed the Spoonplug while it was half-buried in muck.

During his trolling runs, Buck constantly changes his Spoonplugs. He'll fish one of brass, then gold, then yellow, black, white, red, and many color combinations. There are times, he says, when one color out-produces another. However, the depth fished and speed of retrieve usually are the most important factors.

While "checking out" a lake, Buck studies shoreline topography. A hill falling off into a point jutting into the lake may indicate a bar, and there could be a hole or sudden drop-off at its end holding bass. Buck is sure to work such an area carefully. Throughout his trolling he is searching for holes and bars, checking the type bottom, whether sand, gravel or mud and mentally pigeon-holing each weed bed.

If necessary, Buck checks out all depths down to about twenty-one feet, which is nearly the maximum running depth of the largest Spoonplug. Usually he'll locate fish sometime during trolling. When he does, the boat is anchored and Buck casts because this is more sport than trolling and is less apt to spook the bass. Bass can be caught anywhere from the shallows to their sanctuary, but it's the holes where they school that are the real

"hot spots." Here the fish are concentrated, and Buck says he has found tiny sanctuaries in some lakes that held hundreds of largemouths. "Sometimes I think they must line up shoulder-to-shoulder down there," he said.

Anytime Perry is in an area that he knows bass frequent, yet isn't catching any, he assumes they are in a sanctuary too deep for him to fish. It could be sixty feet down. Even a Spoonplug won't work that deep. What to do then? Buck simply keeps working the general area, particularly the migration route the bass take from their deep hole to the shallows—if he knows the fish's highway, or migration route. Sooner or later the bass will move out of the hole, work along the migration route, and come face-to-face with a Spoonplug. One will hit, and Buck will then quickly fill his stringer.

Once Don, Jay Johnson, John Buoy, and I fished Lake Marie, one of the Fox Chain of Lakes, northwest of Chicago. This lake—like Fox Lake that I mentioned earlier—long had been considered almost "fished out."

We trolled from two boats for about three hours without a strike. Finally Don, Jay, and I went ashore to a dock-side restaurant for coffee. John stayed on the lake, anchored at a bar he figured was a bass migration route. When we left John he was casting repeatedly over the bar.

We were into our second coffee when a fisherman came barreling up to the dock in his outboard-powered skiff. Breathless, he rushed into the restaurant, and said John had sent him to tell us the "bass are moving."

We raced out of the restaurant, into our boat, and across the lake to John. He had five bass, one a six-pounder. *The first four he had caught in four casts!* But it was all over. Though all of us continued casting over the bar, no more bass were caught. The explanation? The migration that had taken place was a small one, and the bulk of the bass really hadn't moved from the sanctuary. However, this incident (and several others like it on later trips) proved that it's hitting the major migrations that really puts bass in the boat. Otherwise, with fish in a sanctuary too deep to reach, only jig fishing likely would take many bass.

It is difficult to condense Perry's complete bass fishing theories in limited space. Remember that the spoonplugging system is based on the fact that largemouths are school fish that spend most of their time in deep water, and occasionally migrate from deep holes along habitual routes into shallows where they feed. Everyone catches them in the shallows using nearly any lure or bait *when the fish are there*. But to take them consistently, you must locate the migration routes (usually bars) and use a lure that will scrape the bottom, stay there during the retrieve, and behave tantalizingly.

Buck Perry himself is quick to emphasize that spoonplugging is a *system* of fishing and that the Spoonplug is not a miracle lure that you can tie on, fish helterskelter, and catch bass with. Buck uses his own lure because it does the things he knows are necessary if fish are to be taken consistently.

"Don't let people tell you I'm an expert," says Buck. "Anyone can do the same thing if they want to take the time to study fish and develop a system to fit their habits." That's all there is to it!

A Spoonplugging Lesson
by "Buck" Perry

Many fishermen express their desire to go with me on a personal fishing trip. This is impossible, of course, but I can do the next best thing; relate some of my experiences to you, and ask you to accompany me on an imaginary trip—one that typifies a normal fishing day.

One of my most impressive experiences happened some years ago in a neighbor state. A very valuable lesson was learned, one that has never been forgotten. Later experience showed that it was not applicable to that geographical area alone.

I was driving through the state one day, and around noon came to a lake. Since I had never fished this particular lake, I decided that now was a good time to check it out.

I made haste, and was on the lake shortly after noon. It was one of those hot, mid-summer days, and very few fishermen had braved the heat to go fishing.

After checking several areas which had been suggested to me, without any results, I decided to go back up the lake. I had observed a point, and had mentally filed this as a spot that might have possibilities, one that should be worked before the day was over.

This proved to be a wise move. Small fish were in the shallows and a school of nice bass was on the bar at about the twelve foot depth. After the action was over on this bar, I checked and re-checked several more areas. The lake proved to be a real bonanza for fish.

By late afternoon, I had caught fifty-five bass. Since ten was the legal limit, the smaller ones were culled and ten beauties were put on the stringer. These were carried to the ice house for safe keeping during the night.

There was a small town near the lake, and the following morning I thought it appropriate to stop by the local sporting goods store, to see if the string of fish could generate any interest in the lures I'd used. During the course of conversation with the owner of the store, I made the statement that I had caught fifty-five bass the previous afternoon. The man looked me straight in the eyes and said, "You are a liar."

"Well," I replied, "I have ten of them up in the ice house."

There was nothing equivocal in his reply. He stated emphatically, "I still don't believe you!"

Any fisherman who has ten nice bass on a stringer is not going to let a man make a liar out of him, so I went to the ice house and got the fish. I returned to the store, and slung the fish down the entire length of his nice clean floor. To make a long story short, I left the store with a date to go fishing with him the next morning. He had gone to great lengths to explain to me that during this time of year, the only way they caught fish was to use top water lures early in the morning or late in the afternoon. I wanted him to have a satisfactory fishing trip, so I proceeded to row the boat for four hours while he churned the top of the water with a top water lure.

Finally he flopped down in the boat and said, "The fish just are not biting."

"Now," I asked, "Will you go SPOONPLUGGING with me?"

In the next three and one-half hours we caught sixty-five bass—ten more than I had caught two days before.

After leaving the lake, we went back to his sporting goods store, and I asked, rather expectantly, "All right, how about placing an order for some of my Spoonplugs?"

He turned, looked at me, and said, "Buck, they will never go over here."

"What do you mean they will never go over here?" I asked.

He replied, "Well, we just don't fish that way."

Perhaps that sporting goods store operator had another meaning in mind than the one I got. If so, I have not, to this day, gotten it. But to me, he was saying that while my ideas, method of fishing, and lures might produce, they were not in the accepted or old established manner; and, that he was not going to change his ways or ideas, even though a change could be for the better. I regret to say that this is still one of the main problems faced today; generations of habits are not easily displaced.

As we begin to make our imaginary fishing trip, the first thing to note is that our efforts are going to be directed toward largemouth bass. Some of you may not primarily fish for this species, but this is the rascal we must learn to catch. If we do, we will catch not only bass, but other species as well. My fishing over the country has shown me that any lack of interest in largemouth bass fishing is due mainly to the difficulties encountered in catching them consistently.

Even in saltwater there must be a procedure for catching fish. Just recently, while I was fishing for saltwater stripers in California, a man asked me: "How did you catch them?"

I replied, "I caught them while fishing for largemouth bass."

Of course, not knowing spoonplugging, he didn't know what I was talking about. But, whether fishing in fresh water or salt water, for small fish or large fish, for smallmouth, northern, white bass, walleye, or a variety of fish, the technique will be the same.

Figure No. 1 is looking down on a section of water which could represent a lake, pond, or stream.

Most likely when we arrive at the dock and ask the operator, "How's fishing?" his reply will be, "You should have been here last week."

We are not interested in last week's fishing; we're interested only in fishing today. Despite the negative

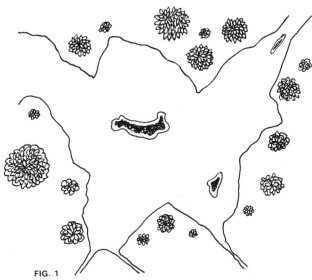

FIG. 1

information given that the fish may not be biting, there is one thing I know about the fish in this water. I know where the fish are. They are either in the shallows, in the deepest water in the area, or somewhere between. Now that always brings a howl of laughter, and it must sound stupidly amusing—but later on you should get the point of that statement. If you don't, then you will have missed the meaning of spoonplugging.

"Professor" Buck Perry (center) and friends Terry O'Malley (left) and Vic Saunders show lunker bass taken on a spoonplugging sortie.

To find out which areas fish are in, it is important to know a little something about 1) the fish and their habits; and 2) how to catch them.

The full understanding of spoonplugging includes knowledge of the fish, his habits, habitat, and reaction to certain stimuli. But it also involves presentation of lures in the correct manner. By controlling lures to take advantage of your knowledge of fish habits and reactions, fish can then be located, made to strike, and put on the stringer.

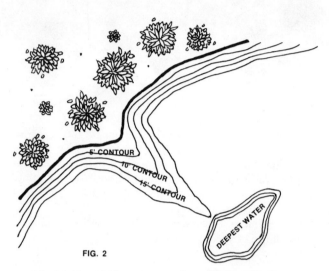

FIG. 2

Figure No. 2 is another view looking down on a lake, showing a bottom section with both shallow water and deep water. Shallow water is defined as the water that extends from the shoreline, or zero feet, out to a depth of eight to ten feet. Any water that extends to a depth greater than eight to ten feet is referred to as deep water. For consistent, successful fishing, a distinction must be made between shallow and deep water. Only in doing this can a correct presentation of lures be made.

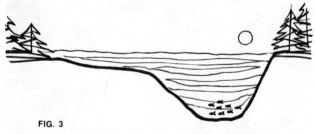

FIG. 3

Figure No. 3 is a cross-section view of this water. This view defines more clearly the statement made previously concerning the fish being either in the shallows, the deepest water in the area, or some place between. Deep water is the home of fish. It is important that this fact be kept in mind at all times. The older a fish gets, and the bigger he becomes, the tighter he schools and the more reluctant he is to leave the deep water; however, periodically he will move toward the shallows and sometimes into the shallows.

You will note that in the deepest water a group of dots has been placed to represent a school of bass. This school of bass can be most any weight—two and one-half pounders, four pounders, or up to approximately six

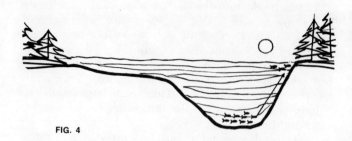

FIG. 4

pounders. The position of the fish, as shown, is in the deepest channel or hole. This is mainly the winter position of fish. While there is not much fishing nor movement of the fish during the winter or colder parts of the season, we must place them here to start with, so as to know what is to be expected during the very early part of the season. During the early or cold part of the season, there will be short, scattered migrations from the deep channel up toward the steep, deep shoreline as shown in Figure No. 4. These movements may not occur very often and not all of the fish will move at one time. This makes the movement very unpredictable, but during early spring fishing, these shores should be checked thoroughly.

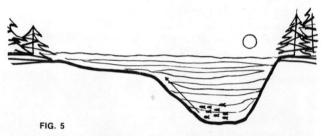

FIG. 5

Figure No. 5 shows the direction of bass movements during most of the year, and certainly during what we call the fishing season—spring, summer and early fall. During this warmer season, the movements of fish from deep water toward the shallows will be toward the shallow, sloping sides of the area. While a few small, scattered fish may be found along the steep, deep shores during this time, it would actually be a waste of effort to spend time here. These small or scattered fish are not what we are interested in.

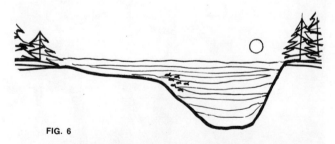

FIG. 6

Figure No. 6 brings these fish out of the deepest water position and shows them in a spot that is their "home" or "sanctuary." This is the place where they take up housekeeping for the summer or for the fishing season. This is the area where they now spend most of their time. If there is water deeper than twenty feet available, the home is always below this twenty foot depth. If it were possible to state the approximate depth fish will be on a normal fishing day, it could be around twenty-seven feet. Keep this in mind, because a little later on, when we start the presentation of lures and try to locate fish, this depth means trouble.

It's a shame this home area isn't in shallower water, because most fishermen lose control when fishing deeper than twelve to fifteen feet. There are lures and procedures that will certainly allow the fisherman to go beyond this depth, but it is then difficult to know where the lure is and what it is doing. Control is lost, and it is not likely that the school of fish can be located and made to strike.

You are beginning to see some of the difficulties involved, and might well ask, "Then how are we going to catch our fish?"

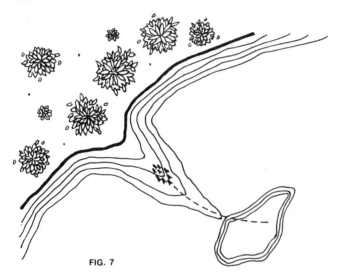

FIG. 7

Figure No. 7 shows how, once or twice a day, on a *normal* fishing day, fish will move from deep water toward the shallows. The key as to how we are going to catch the fish is knowing that this movement from deep water is not haphazard. When these fish move, they proceed toward the shallows along well established paths or migration routes. These migration routes are structures—bottom structures—with characteristics that serve as guides or signposts which fish are able to see and follow so that their position is known at all times. These migration routes, or structures, have characteristics or features that readily make them distinguishable from the surrounding area.

In most lakes, migration routes are represented by gradual sloping bars that extend out from points in the shoreline. They could, also, be reefs or underwater islands; but, however these routes are represented, they are structures different from the surrounding area, and they are always accessible to the deepest water in the area. These are the things we will look for.

As previously stated, on a normal fishing day there will be one or two movements or migrations of fish toward shallow water. There is no way to determine just when these movements will occur as they will usually change from day to day. If there is an early morning movement, another one should occur later in the afternoon or just before dark, if there is no drastic weather change.

Let's say we go fishing early in the morning, and are on the lake shortly after daybreak. Action is pretty good for a couple of hours, then rather abruptly the fish quit. We continue to fish hard all day, but do not get any more solid action until late in the afternoon. This is a situation many fishermen have experienced. What is the explanation? We caught fish early because they had moved into the shallows or into a reachable depth. We were fishing where the fish were. The fish then moved back down into deep water, out of reach of our lures, and did not move back within reach until the later period. It is impossible to catch fish if you are fishing where they "ain't."

Now let us assume that in our early morning fishing no movement occurs. There is one thing that we will not do, and that is leave the lake between ten o'clock and two o'clock, because we can almost win a bet that a movement will occur during these hours. My personal experience has been that this period produces some of the finest movements of fish. Whenever the movement occurs, early or late, in the middle of the day or night, it does not necessarily mean that any two movements or migrations will be for the same distance or for the same length of time.

Figure No. 8 shows the migration route of fish as they move toward the shallows. This path may not always be straight, as the structure may turn to the right or to the left. When migration occurs, the fish move up these structures on the bottom, in a group or school. If conditions are good, they move up to the eight to ten foot depth. If conditions are very good, they will then scatter into the shallows. When fish scatter into the shallows along the shoreline, the fisherman is aware of it, as this is when he says, "The fish are biting."

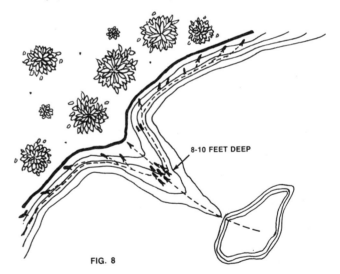

8-10 FEET DEEP

FIG. 8

At certain times of the year, most frequently in spring, fish may remain for some time in the shallows, and they may move as far as the bays, coves, and flats. However, most of the season they are in the shallows in quantity for only a short period of time, and the distance they scatter will not be very great—thus, the productive shoreline can be very short.

The first fish to appear in the shallows will always be the smaller "yearling" fish. If yearling bass are caught in the shallows this usually means a movement, and the larger fish should be at a reachable depth, on structure, in the near area. Usually, though, the migration of the larger fish does not extend quite to or past the scatter point (eight to ten ft.). This is particularly true if the school consists of the biggest bass in the area.

Never expect this entire school of large fish to move into the shallows and scatter at the same time. In all of my years of fishing, I have never seen more than two or three big bass move in at one time. I know that you have fished the shoreline at some time and found the fish were really biting. But how many of these big bass did you catch? The reason you caught only a few, or none, perhaps was not particularly due to any fault of yours, nor was it due to the fact that the fish were not there.

North or south, some fish live longer, grow faster, and obtain a final weight above the average, but normally largemouth bass will die off by the time they reach six pounds. In most areas of the country, the average life span in relation to the average growing rate will normally produce some schools whose average weight is slightly under six pounds. But whatever the average final weight, if any "lunkers" exist in the area, they will be with this group.

I have often been asked how fast fish move or travel along structure. This can never be pre-determined. The existing conditions and the species of fish will determine this. Another point that perhaps should be mentioned here is concerning the length of migration routes. They vary. Some are quite short, while others are quite long. But, whatever their length, they do have one thing in common—they extend from the shallows to the deepest water in the area.

There is no set length of time fish stay up before they drop back into the deeper water. The period of time they stay depends entirely upon the conditions that exist—weather and water temperatures, for example, and water conditions. At times it could be for minutes, while at other times it could be for hours. For an average though, I would have to say it is minutes rather than hours that bass remain in shallows.

Keeping Figure No. 8 in mind, let us assume fish have scattered into the shallows. This is when the shoreline fisherman scores, so these areas become known as "hot-spots." It is always important to know where these hot-spots are located, as they indicate this is potentially good water, and they also serve as a key to finding the migration routes. The shoreline is never the factor that determines whether or not an area is a hot-spot. It is a hot-spot only because the structure fish use, as they move from deep to shallow water, just happens to lead to this particular area.

Fishermen in every section of the country seem to have varied ideas as to the why's and wherefore's of fishing. Many seem to think that the behavior of bass found in the South or North differs from that of bass found in the East or West. Nothing could be farther from the truth. There is one mistaken thought or idea, though, that is universal, and that is this: in order to catch largemouth bass, the shoreline *must* have weeds, brush, pads, or growth of some kind, because this is the bass' home and this is where he spends all of his time. If he is not being caught it's because he's not in a biting mood.

Joe Stearns, former Educational Director of the

Georgia Game and Fish Commission, put it very aptly in an article he wrote after having had a spoonplugging lesson. "Up until I was introduced to spoonplugging, I always thought when I dropped a popping bug by an old log and didn't get a strike—the fish were not biting. Now I know better."

What is the basis of this belief and what are the facts? The facts are that while fish are reluctant and hesitant to go into shallows, they will do so more readily and stay for a longer period of time if, at the end of a migration route, cover is available. This being so, the shoreline fisherman has naturally caught bass more often around growth, and has decided that growth is a *must*. It does have the advantage of offering fish some cover, but such cover spots should never mistakenly be called the fish's home. Some of the finest hot-spots I have found do not have as much cover as a single blade of grass.

Quite a lot could be said about weather and the effect it has upon fishing, and particularly bass fishing. But actually, the only weather condition that fishermen should be greatly concerned with is a *cold front*. Local newspaper weather maps and T.V. reports can be used to learn of the approach, location, and character of cold fronts.

Figure No. 9 shows the reaction of fish to the passing of a cold front. The fish drop off into their winter position —becoming quite dormant, making little or no movements. This condition could exist for several days, depending on the severity of the front.

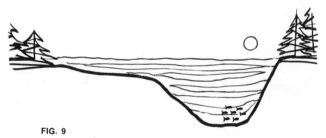

FIG. 9

Movements of the fish will be good until after the actual front goes through. After it passes, the finest fisherman could be "skunked," even though weatherwise it is bright, clear and a most beautiful day—the kind of day most any fisherman would choose as a perfect day to go fishing. The good movements will not occur again until the temperature starts to rise, the sky shows some haze, or high cirrus clouds are observed. Normally by the third day after the front passes, fishing will change for the better.

Figure No. 10 shows a cross-section view of a bass migration, or movement, of a group of fish along structure to a depth of eight to ten feet. I consider this a rather shallow movement for fish above two to two and one-half pounds.

Conditions would have to be excellent for these fish to continue into the shallows, in mass, and scatter. Unless this further movement occurred, it would mean that the average fisherman, and especially the shoreline fisherman, would never make contact with the fish, and therefore catch none.

Figure No. 10, however, would be an ideal condition for spoonpluggers. The fish are schooled, immediately

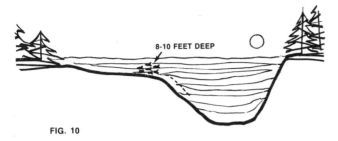

FIG. 10

available at a good reachable depth for lure control, and the action will be fast and furious. That is what every fisherman dreams of, but something only spoonpluggers consistently accomplish.

All of these comments, and Figures 1 through 10, might appear to have taken considerable time just to show the movements of fish. But the expected movements, or habits, must be known and understood if consistent catches are to be made.

Regardless of the water fished, or for whatever species, it must be remembered that: 1) the home of fish is deep water; 2) the home area is usually too deep for lures to be presented effectively; and 3) the fish, in this deep position, are inactive but will, on a normal fishing day, move into range. When, how, and where are items each fisherman must learn and work out in the waters being fished. The information given here, if applied properly, will enable any spoonplugger to find the answers.

For consistent limit catches, not only is an understanding of the movements of fish necessary, but there are certain factors that are involved. I prefer to think of these factors as controls. Luck should not be considered a factor, and it certainly is not controllable, so let's throw out the element of luck in the beginning so that we don't depend on it to any degree. And while we're at it, let's do away with the old saw of "biting or not biting" too. Let's replace this thinking with the fact that a gamefish can be made to strike when he is not feeding, but first he must be located.

We must control our fishing to overcome as many of the effects of water and weather conditions that exist as possible. With respect to control, many items might quickly come to mind, but if analyzed carefully, they would fall under these headings: 1) depth control; 2) speed control; 3) size of lure; 4) color; and 5) action.

These basic controls still present quite a number of things to be considered, so we should reduce them still further. Some of the controls can be quickly eliminated, as shown in Figure No. 11.

The first we will eliminate is *action*. Most manufacturers have built action into their lures and little can be done to change it. Spoonplugs were designed with the knowledge that it is impossible to state that any given action is best. The size, speed, and depth the lure is running would have to be considered, thus the actions were built into each size so that if the lure passed a fish at the correct speed, he would strike it.

Color can be eliminated by a simple rule of thumb. If conditions are bright, such as a bright day, clear water, use bright lures such as silver, white, or red-head. If conditions are dark, such as a cloudy day or dingy water, go to the darker lures such as copper or orange-black.

The golds, yellows, and brass would be considered more or less neutral and would work under either condition.

This rule will locate fish as far as color is concerned, and if there is a color preference it can be determined only after the fish have been located. With this rule in mind, you can never go wrong in having more than one color in your tackle box.

In eliminating *size*, I am always reminded of the remark so many fishermen make when looking at the large size Spoonplugs: "The fish I catch wouldn't even look at a lure that size." In thinking of the size of a lure, just remember that a fish, such as bass, will try to eat anything as big as he is—maybe bigger. I'm always catching small fish on a large lure, and often the fish is smaller than the lure. You can get big fish on a small lure or you can catch little fish on a big lure. Lure size is more important from the standpoint of getting better depth control. In most situations it is practically impossible to work down effectively to fifteen feet or more with a small lure, whereas it would be difficult to take a large deep-running lure and work the shallows where only a foot or so of water existed. If there is any size preference, it would be according to depth; that is, the deeper the fish the larger the lure.

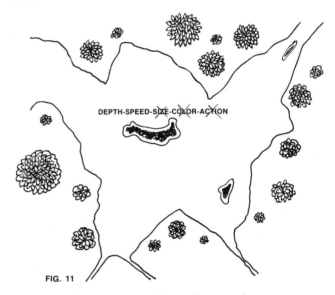

DEPTH-SPEED-SIZE-COLOR-ACTION

FIG. 11

You will note that we have eliminated, to a great extent, *action, color,* and *size,* and only two controls now remain (Figure 11). They are *speed* and *depth,* and of all the controls these are, by far, the most important. Most people buy lures for action, color, and size only, but I found long ago that these were not sufficient to achieve the desired results. Since the lures that were available did not allow sufficient control of speed and depth to be effective, it was necessary to design a lure to do this. The Spoonplug is the result, and while it has been described as looking like a "tromped on shoe horn," just remember that it was designed not for looks, so as to entice fishermen to buy it, but rather to perform so that it could be used to locate fish and entice them to strike.

Perhaps you have never thought of *speed* as being a very important part of fishing. In my talks and writings, I have stressed that many fishermen fish too slow under most conditions, particularly when working shallow water. Some have gotten the idea they should go racing helter-skelter over the lake. Speed is important, but in the proper areas and under certain conditions.

What are the areas and conditions that affect speed?

Weather and water temperatures are the primary conditions that determine speed. As weather and water temperatures go up, the speed goes up (increases); as weather and water temperatures go down, the speed goes down (decreases).

The different areas—shallow water and deep water—influence speed. Faster and more varied speeds are used in the shallows than are used when working the bottoms of the sanctuaries or migration routes.

Primary emphasis on fast speed is directed toward a free running lure when working the shallows. During the summer the speed needed here could be considerable. But, whatever speed is found necessary, when the lure makes contact with the bottom, speed is reduced so that the lure can "walk," not plow.

You can throw all of the action, color, and size lures found in your tackle box along a particular shoreline, but if you don't consider the speed of the lure, or the velocity with which it moves through the water, the shore has not been properly fished.

When working bottoms in deep water, the importance of speed is reduced to a minimum. The controlling factor here is the "walking" or bumping of the lure on the sanctuary or migration route. The speed needed is just enough to produce a steady walk or bump. The deeper you fish and the colder the water, the slower the walk or bump required.

From all this you can see that it is impossible to state that one particular speed is the one needed to do the job. The speed needed on any one day can be determined only at that particular time of fishing. Always start out with speed that is sufficient to give the lure some action, and increase at intervals. Keep in mind that maximum speed will be needed during the summer fishing, and less speed as weather and waters cool, reaching the minimum during the cold parts of the season. Only by varying the speed can the most productive one be found. If the same trolling or retrieving speed is used in August as was used in April, then chances for success are greatly decreased. Fish are quite sluggish during the colder parts of the season, but when hot summer arrives, they become quite active. That April speed needs more zip in it in August.

We now come to our last control factor, *depth*. This is the one thing that we are going to have to control, by some means, as effectively as possible. A fisherman can fish the top of the water and he can fish the bottom. But what about all the depths in-between? If we catch fish at one of these in-between depths, how can we get back to that particular depth? The only effective way that I know it can be done is to let the lures do it. If you have wondered why there are different size Spoonplugs, the answer should now be obvious. Each size lure was designed to run at a certain depth and maintain that depth, regardless of the trolling speed. This is a "tool" that is going to enable us to fish from the shallowest water to as deep as conventional fishing tackle will take us, and somewhere—in the shallow water, in the deep water, or

somewhere between—we are going to find fish.

In working out a lake to determine where the fish are, I like to begin by trolling with a motor. Trolling has many advantages. It allows a greater portion of the water to be covered quickly, allows for a greater speed variance, and in many situations will locate and catch fish where it would be practically impossible to do by any other means.

Since most casting rigs are no good for trolling, I use a short, stiff rod, rigged with a line that not only is heavy and stiff, but is metered so that I will know how much line is out at all times. With a rig of this type, I will be aware of what is going on at the other end of the line.

I am often asked if spoonplugging requires additional and special equipment, or can the fisherman do with what he has.

Before we finish this fishing trip you should begin to realize that successful fishing is purely mechanical. Any job can be done more easily and better if proper tools are available.

A few states do not allow motor trolling, or allow it only on certain lakes. In this case you'll have to check the water by casting. Do this in the same manner; that is, use different size lures to check the different depths, the bottom structure, and using varied retrieve speeds. It will take a longer period of time to work out the waters, but once this has been done and the specific areas to fish are known, casting can be, in many instances, more effective than trolling. Casting is discussed in detail a little later on.

Let's assume that the lake we have selected is one that we have never fished before. What should we do first? How do we start? How do we use the lures?

When fishing a lake I've never been on before, there is one thing I try to find out before leaving the dock area. That is where the hot spots are located. This information will expedite our work. Let's say we are on an imaginary lake, and someone tells us that at the northern end of the lake a lot of fish are caught at certain times. This is always good news to a spoonplugger, for he knows that somewhere in that area there is potentially good water. We will waste no time in getting to that end of the lake. In looking at the shoreline, the north end appears to be

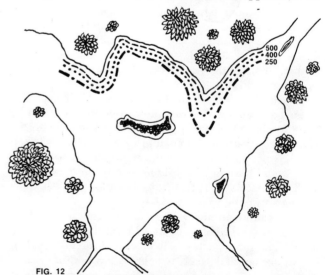

FIG. 12

about a mile long, more or less. We were not told where on this north end fish had been caught, so every lure we use for testing the shallows will be kept on until the total length of shore has been covered.

To begin our fishing, the first lure we're going to use is the small, 500 Series, Spoonplug. Figure 12 shows the path and the position of this size lure, as well as the other series we'll use in checking the shallows.

The amount of line let out will affect the depth the lure runs. The 500 Series has a depth range of from two to four feet. Shorter line lengths will give the minimum depth and the maximum depth will be reached with a line of 100 to 130 feet. Normally around eighty to ninety feet is enough line to run during this trolling.

We will start our troll with just enough speed to be sure that the lure has good action. At intervals, the speed will be increased.

The worst mistake most fishermen make is not keeping their lures in position; that is, each size lure running in its proper place. This north shore, like most lakes, will have sections where the bottom slopes off gradually with a lot of shallow water, while other sections will have steep banks where the bottom drops off rapidly with deep water close to shore. Our trolling procedure must be done in such a way so as to keep each size lure in its proper position, even though the bottom contour may be changing constantly.

In the section where the bottom slopes off gradually, we want to get our 500 lure as close to shore as possible so that the lure will be bumping bottom at times. If this area contains bushes, or has standing trees, we will get the lures back in among them, if at all possible. In the section that has the steep banks, where the bottom drops off rapidly, we will run this lure "jam-up" against the bank, or skipping along the rocks, or whatever the bottom might be. In some waters, the shallow sections contain weeds. Where this condition exists, we will get the lures as close to the weeds as possible, and maneuver the boat so that we are not continually fouled. If we are continually fouled, either we are not following the contour of the weed line, or we are in too close. However, if we never foul, we are possibly too far away.

It seems pertinent to add here that the Spoonplugs were designed to come to the top of the water when fouled. Most of the time the lures can be cleaned of weeds with a quick jerk of the rod.

After the entire length of the north shoreline has been covered with the 500 Series, and no strikes produced, we now change to the next size lure. It is important to use the different sizes in sequence, as this will allow the water to be "strained" thoroughly, leaving no section or control unchecked.

The next size lure we will use is the 400 Series. This lure runs at a depth of four to six feet. We will fish this lure along the same shoreline, as shown in Figure 12. It would be unwise to check another depth along a different shoreline. Again, we must keep the lure in its proper position. This is done by maneuvering the boat. To maneuver the boat we first move in toward shore until the lure starts bumping the bottom; then very slowly we head the boat toward the deeper, or open, water. As soon as the lure starts running free, we slowly head the boat back toward the shoreline until the lure is bumping again. By continuing to maneuver the boat in this manner, the contours of the bottom will be followed, regardless of shape.

After checking speeds, and varying the length of line with the 400 size lure, and still no strikes, we proceed to the next size, which is the 250 Series. The 250 Series runs from six to nine feet. We will fish this size in the exact manner as the previous two sizes, and along the same shoreline. The lure will be kept in position by maneuvering the boat as previously explained. Its position is shown in Figure 12.

If any fish are caught along this shoreline with any of these three sizes, as soon as the fish is caught, the immediate area would be checked thoroughly at that time by casting or by additional trolling to determine if other fish are in the area. When I say thoroughly, I mean depths, speeds, and colors. If weeds exist, and fish are caught along the weed line, it could mean fish are back in the weeds, and these should be checked with weedless or top-water Spoonplugs.

But, we didn't catch any fish. What next?

First, let's look at what we have accomplished in our fishing thus far. From the standpoint of catching fish, it would appear we have wasted our efforts. This is not true. In trolling the three sizes of lures in the manner described, three important things were accomplished:

1) We eliminated all of the shallow water in the area. We caught no fish, so we *must* assume that the fish are not in the shallows at this time. Since we have eliminated the shallows, we have only the in-between and the deep water left.

2) We would have noted the types of structure or bottom conditions in the area. Any sloping bar or possible migration route should have been found. Normally the contour of the shore itself would indicate such a structure. In Figure 12, the point of land as shown not only suggested such a structure, but the lures confirmed that here was the only underwater bar on the north shore.

3) Thus we have established the only potential migration route in the area. So, now, instead of fishing a mile or more of shoreline, we have come down to a narrow structure, or path, leading into deep water.

Figure 13 shows the point of land and the underwater

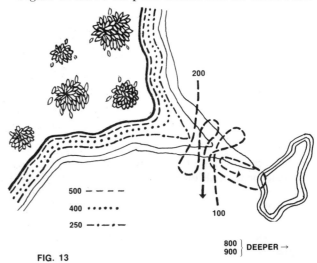

200

500 – – – –
400 • • • • •
250 — · — · —

100

800
900 } DEEPER →

FIG. 13

bar upon which we now concentrate our efforts. It also shows the series of lures to be used.

At this point, we make a definite change in our presentation. From now on, our main purpose is to work the bottom. This is done by keeping the lures walking or bumping right on the bottom. When bass are in the shallows, they may strike a free running lure, but when they are schooled together in this deeper water, the fisherman must never expect this to happen. A free, or swimming, lure can pass within a few inches of a school and there will be no strike, but a walking lure will cause all of the fish in the school to try to get it. All of the controls become insignificant here in comparison to the importance of walking or bumping the lure on structure.

The next size lure we will try is the 200 Series, and we are going to bump or walk it on the structure we have found. In order to cover all of the contours in this structure, we'll make trolling passes in several directions across it. On each pass, as soon as the lure runs off structure and begins to run free, we'll immediately turn the boat around and make another pass so that the lure will be back on the bottom. This size lure will reach bottom depths of eleven to twelve feet. We must make enough passes to feel reasonably sure that we've reached as much of the structure as possible with this size lure.

When working this bottom structure by trolling, maximum line can and should often be used. On the final passes, as much as eighty to ninety yards might be needed to allow the lures to reach their maximum depth.

If the 200 Series does not produce any strikes, the next series Spoonplug will be used so that we can work deeper on the structure. This size is the 100 Series, and will take us down to fourteen or fifteen feet. The 100 Series will be used in the same manner as the 200. Trolling passes will be made in several directions, and the lure kept bumping bottom as far out as possible on the structure.

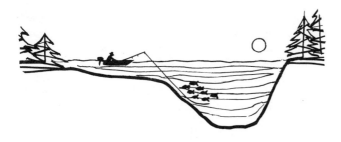

FIG. 14

As stated previously, we start running into difficulties with controls at this depth, so we have come to the point where we must assume that fish were not caught, or fish were caught. If no fish were caught, it means the fish are deeper than we are fishing. There are several possibilities that are now open to us: 1) we can exercise patience and wait for the fish to move up; or 2) if we are rigged properly with a short, stiff rod and with a stiff, monofilament trolling line, we can take the 800 and 900 Series Spoonplug and work down deeper to try to find the fish; or 3) we can go to another section of the lake that shows, judging by the shore, likely spots that could have structure, and proceed to work those areas by following exactly the same procedures as before. If we decide to move, then we should return periodically to the first area and re-check it to determine if any movement of fish has occurred.

If we decide to exercise patience and stay on this structure until the fish move, our efforts would now be concentrated as deep on it as we could effectively reach. This could be done more efficiently by casting.

Let us now assume that while working the structure with our 100 or 200 Series Spoonplugs, we picked up a bass. It was caught in deep water, and this means a school is there. We immediately want to position our boat for casting.

At the time of the strike, we quickly note the position of the boat with reference to the shore. This is important, because the fish are schooled, the area they cover is not too large, and we must get our lures back to the same spot. Sometimes this is a little difficult to do unless an additional pass or two is made or a marker thrown out to serve as a guide.

Figure 14 shows the position we will assume for casting to the school of bass.

We want to anchor the boat in water just as shallow as possible, but yet near enough to allow our cast to reach immediately beyond the fish. If we anchor over water too deep, we'll have difficulty in keeping the lure on the bottom for its walk through the school of fish, as the steep angle of retrieve will pull the lure up.

The size lure we cast will depend on the depth of water under the boat. If we are able to anchor in three or four feet of water, it might be possible to use the 250 Series Spoonplugs. If we find it necessary to anchor over six, seven, or eight feet of water, we will by necessity have to use the larger 100 or 200 Series.

We make our cast to reach just beyond the school of bass, and wait for the lure to sink to the bottom. This can be determined by noting the line. When the line stops sinking and the slack appears, the lure is on bottom. A slow turn or two of the reel handle is made to remove the slack line. This is followed by a few quick turns which will get the lure up on its nose in a walking position. From then on—a fast, steady retrieve will keep the lure walking the bottom and through the school of fish.

While casting to a school of fish, there are a few do's and don'ts involved.

When a strike is made and after the hook is set, remove the fish from the school quickly. You don't want him floundering around in the school to spook the fish. In fact, we don't want to play him around too long at any stage of the battle. Other fish in a school have a tendency to follow a hooked fish, and should they do so and see the boat, the school will spook. They will drop back into the deep hole again since depth is the only escape fish have.

These are deep fish and schooled fish, so they can be large. We want to do everything possible to keep from losing any of them. Too often, if the biggest fish of the school is hooked and lost, or if too many are lost, the school will be spooked. When we get into one of these schools, don't be surprised if you seem to have all thumbs and start to shake like a leaf on a tree in a wind storm. Just play it as cool as possible, and keep 'em coming.

Today's school of bass may be four-pounders, the school found tomorrow could hold close to six pounds. No fisherman has really lived until he has been into a school of these big beauties, where each successive cast puts one on the stringer. A stringer full of six-pound bass is truly a memorable experience.

Finding fish migration routes takes time, effort, and patience. It may be difficult at first, but as experience is gained and additional knowledge is had, this becomes just a routine part of fishing, and it becomes increasingly easy. Finding these routes, however, is well worth the time and effort. Once they have been found you can tell your grandchildren the exact spot to anchor the boat and where to concentrate their casts. Once these home areas and migration routes have been established they will remain so until a water level or bottom change is great enough to cause a change in the fish's habits.

After a lake has been worked out and the migration routes of the fish are known, these can be checked out by casting alone, if desired.

By anchoring the boat rather close to shore, long casts can be made along the shoreline. In this manner, the lure is fishing the shoreline for the entire length of the retrieve. It is also possible to check different depths efficiently from this position. If the shallows do not produce, long casts can be made on the migration route, but remember that this is the area for bottom fishing and the lure must be sunk. To work farther out on the migration route, progressively move the boat farther out so that the casts will come as near as possible to the drop-off. By casting all sections in this manner, you can determine if any fish are on the move. Figure 15 shows the best boat position for doing this.

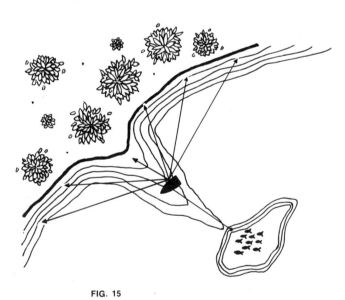

FIG. 15

Had our fishing trip been to a newly constructed lake, we would not be too concerned with time periods and specific areas. Normally new lakes have an abundance of young, growing fish. For the first couple of years successful fishing is not too difficult. Fish seem to be all over the lake and they seem to hit most any time. But by the fourth or fifth year fishing begins to get tough. The usual explanation given for the small or non-catches is that the lake has "gone bad." There are two main reasons, or explanations, for this: 1) The fish have adapted themselves to the lake and have eliminated all undesirable areas. They have established their own home areas, and instead of being scattered over many acres, they are now inhabiting only a few. 2) Another reason, and perhaps the major one, is that the fish are now older and much larger, and are reluctant to leave their deep home areas. Since most people are shoreline fishermen only, it's little wonder that fishing in this new lake is no longer considered to be any good. It will take some spoonplugging to work out such a lake and find the fish.

I have tried to cover the main points of spoonplugging to show how consistent, successful fishing can be accomplished. Fishing, like any sport, is perfected only by experience and knowledge. While it is impossible to gain experience other than by doing, I hope that my sharing with you some of the things learned from many years of fishing will be beneficial, and that it will help you to have some of the memorable experiences that come to those who learn the art of spoonplugging.

It is not possible to run into every situation on one short fishing trip as described here. In fact, a whole season would not bring exposure to all of the conditions and situations that could exist. You might wonder why, in this imaginary fishing trip, catching fish at some particular stage was not stressed. This was deliberate and for a purpose. My years of demonstrations with hundreds of fishermen, some experienced and some green horns, have proved to me that few absorb anything other than the operation and controls that were present when contact was made with the fish. In spite of my efforts to explain that this exact situation and combination of controls may not exist again for some time, it seldom makes an impression. Some fishermen fail because they forget about fish movements, and about how to fish different depths. They remember only that a specific lure produced at a particular place, and in a certain way. They assume where fish will be, and that kind of thinking results in failure.

It is quite easy to describe the proper procedures or steps for presentation of lures, and this does not require any particular skill, but it is impossible to show the exact combination of controls that bring success on each individual fishing trip. It is necessary to study and approach each day's fishing with an open mind as to how, where, and what is going to locate fish and put them on the stringer.

On the imaginary trip I've described, it was possible for fish to have been caught at any stage. The intent was to point out the necessary steps and what should be done if fish were or were not caught. By not emphasizing that fish were caught at any particular place or in a specific manner, it was hoped that the impression would be given that no one step or technique is favored over another. All of the steps are necessary for the orderly elimination of unproductive water. A fisherman must never believe that a particular presentation, depth, speed, or color of lure is best. Being open-minded in every respect on every trip is a must. Only after fish have been located is it safe to say that something appears best, but certainly not before, nor on future trips.

A Spoonplugger's Glossary

BOW—Excess line, in the form of a curve, which occurs between the rod tip and lure.

BREAK IN STRUCTURE—Where structure is no longer uniform, due to dips or quick drop in depths, rocks, stumps, etc.

CHECKED—When an area has been thoroughly fished correctly.

CONTROL—To present lures in an orderly and correct manner.

CONTROLS—Factors to be considered and used for successful fishing.

COLD FRONT—A weather condition. (Description and position obtainable from daily weather maps and reports.)

DROP-OFF—The place on structure where there is a sudden or rapid drop into deeper water, such as a hole or channel. (Do not confuse with "break" in a structure.)

DEEP WATER—Water that has a depth greater than eight to ten feet.

ELIMINATED WATER—Water that has been fished correctly and has produced no fish.

FAN CAST—A series of casts that covers the water in an arc.

FREE-SWIMMING LURE—A lure moving through open water.

GAMEFISH—Any fish considered worthy of pursuit, either for its pugnacious disposition or for its edibility.

HOME—The deep water areas where fish spend most of their time.

HOT-SPOT—An area where fish are caught consistently when fish are said to be "biting."

MIGRATION—Movement of fish from one section of water to another. Normally used when speaking of a change of depth.

MIGRATION ROUTE—The path fish take as they move from deep water to shallow water, or vice versa.

MOVEMENT—Closely associated with migration, but also, meaning that fish have become active (opposite of dormant.)

OPEN WATER—Water free from vegetation and away from shoreline.

POINT—An extrusion in the shoreline that extends out into and under the water.

SANCTUARY—The section of water, in the "home" area, where fish spend most of the time.

SCATTERPOINT—The depth on the bottom where fish start to separate and scatter, and are no longer schooled together.

SCHOOL OF FISH—A number of fish grouped close together.

SCHOOLING—A school of fish feeding on the surface, visably tearing up the water.

SHALLOW WATER—Water less than eight to ten feet in depth.

SIZE OF LURE—Normally the length of the lure in inches rather than by weight.

SPOOKED—Fish that have become alerted or scared. Their reaction is to drop into deeper water to escape or to become very inactive.

STRAGGLERS—An occasional fish, usually found apart from the others. (Yearlings are often in this category.)

STRUCTURE—A portion of the bottom of a lake extending from shallow water to deep water, with some unusual features that distinguish if from the surrounding bottom area.

TRAFFIC—The amount of fishing pressure, or water skiers, large boats and motors, and fast boats found in a given area.

WALKING OR BUMPING—A lure moving along the bottom and actually coming into contact with it and then "walking" along.

YEARLINGS—One to three year old fish.

"Buck" Perry's Spoonplugger's Quiz

NOTE: This Buck Perry spoonplugger's quiz was adapted by Perry to test fisherman "students" who attended Perry Spoonplugging clinics he conducted at various points around the country. Most knowledgeable fishermen can answer most of the questions correctly whether or not they ever attended a Perry Spoonplugging clinic. Too, a fisherman ought to be able to score highly on the quiz after reading the preceeding two articles "How Perry's System Cracks The Bass Barrier," and "A Spoonplugging Lesson"—Tom McNally.

Mark TRUE or FALSE

1. T   F   Spoonplugging is the only way a fish can be caught.

2. T   F   The Spoonplug is one of the few magic lures on the market today.

3. T   F   In learning how to catch fish, the largemouth bass is a good fish to start with.

4. T   F   The "home" of fish is deep water.

5. T   F   There is little difference between shallow water fishing and deep water fishing.

6. T   F   A fisherman should not expect largemouth bass to be deeper than fifteen feet.

7. T   F   Trolling for bass is a waste of time and indicates a lazy fisherman.

8. T   F   The white bass (striper) is a "school" fish.

9. T   F   The larger the bass, the more he becomes a "lone ranger," picking out some log or stump or rock to make his home, and running off all poachers.

10. T   F   As the water cools off, fish become more active and fight better.

11. T   F   After a fisherman has found a good fishing hole, he should do everything possible to keep it a secret, as other fishermen will soon fish it out.

12. T   F   The spoonplugger is a fisherman who understands the habits of fish, (what to expect) and goes about his fishing in an orderly manner to locate the fish, and present his lures in the best way possible.

13. T   F   The spoonplugger is normally a fisherman who holds no secrets and is usually eager to teach others.

14. T   F   A wise fisherman picks out waters that are clear and deep rather than those cloudy (dingy) or slightly muddy.

15. T   F   The best time to go fishing is right after a spell of rough weather when the day is clear and beautiful.

16. T   F   Good fishermen are "born."

17. T   F   The action of the lure determines whether a fish strikes or not.

18. T   F   Fishermen should use small lures for small fish, large lures for large fish.

19. T   F   The color of a lure may be important, but a fisherman should not rely on color alone to put fish on the stringer.

20. T   F   As the weather and water warms and the fish become sluggish, the fisherman should slow his retrieve and trolling speed.

21. T   F   A fisherman must constantly check different depths of water to locate fish.

22. T   F   Most of the time larger fish will be not deeper than ten feet.

23. T F When anchoring in high wind, the fisherman should drop and tie his anchor at the stern of his boat.

24. T F In trolling, each size Spoonplug should be kept "in position"—that is, it should be run at the depth for which it was designed.

25. T F When anchoring and casting to a school of bass, the boat should be anchored in as shallow water as possible.

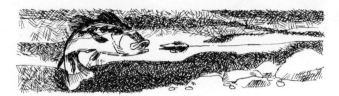

26. T F Trolling lines should be of a hard, stiff monofilament with stretch removed so that the fisherman will not lose his lure when a heavy strike occurs.

27. T F A long, limber, flexible rod is no good for trolling.

28. T T In most instances, a fisherman should immediately use deep running lures.

29. T F If a fisherman finds the fish today in a certain spot, he should normally expect to find them there tomorrow at the same time of day.

30. T F Most of the time a fisherman should use a heavy wire leader when fishing for walleyes.

31. T F Fish are color blind, so it is a waste of money to have more than one color lure.

32. T F The action of a lure may be important but it alone will never put fish on the stringer.

33. T F If there should be a lure size preference, it would normally be according to depth.

34. T F A fisherman should check all sizes of lures when working to find fish.

35. T F The speed used in trolling could vary as the depth increases.

36. T F When fishing deep water for bass the fisherman should work the bottom whenever possible.

37. T F Where tall weeds exists, the fisherman should assume that all the fish will be back in the weeds.

38. T F Where there's brush, the spoonplugger should never run the 500 Series so shallow as to get snagged.

39. T F Shallow water that contains weeds, which extend for some distance underwater, should only be tested with topwater or weedless lures.

40. T F Where the bottom of a lake contains muck or a mossy condition, the fisherman should never use large lures that would dig down into this material.

41. T F When trolling, the spoonplugger should always observe the path of the troll whether he has caught a fish or not.

42. T F Hot spots should be marked in some fashion, so the fisherman can return to them at a later date.

43. T F The best way to use a depth indicator is to cruise about a lake and look for schools of fish that might show up on the dial.

44. T F If a lake has clear water in one arm, and dingy water in another, the fisherman should always pick the dingy section.

45. T F It would be better for a fisherman to be a lone ranger in his fishing, rather than to seek the co-operation of others who may not be catching any more fish than he is.

46. T F There is more to fishing than just catching a fish.

47. T F A fisherman can have a good fishing trip without catching any fish.

48. T F A fisherman should never feel proud and show off his catch when other fishermen on the lake have not caught any.

49. T F It would be better to fish the upper reaches of a body of water, rather than near a dam, especially if the water is deep and clear there.

50. T F Little time should be spent in fishing areas that do not show weeds, brush or pads, etc.

51. T F The rocky rip-rap found along dams and road beds should always be checked.

52. T F It should be against the law for a fisherman to use live bait.

53. T F Some species of fish may require a different speed control than others.

54. T F After using all sizes, colors, and types of lures, and working all depths, and the fisherman has not caught a fish, he should quit and come back at a later date.

55. T F A fisherman can actually become as good a fisherman as he desires.

56. T F Little can be learned about successful fishing except by "doing."

57. T F Trolling correctly can be as important as casting.

58. T F At times, a fisherman should practice using his tackle, without being primarily concerned with catching fish.

59. T F Lots of casts are lost by the spin-caster, due to the tumbling effect this type casting imparts to the lure.

60. T F When fishing deeper water the fisherman should concentrate his efforts at "breaks."

61. T F Normally an area can be "checked" by using one lure.

62. T F   The lure the fisherman uses may often determine how much control he has of his fishing.

63. T F   To control his fishing, a fisherman should have several sizes of lures and should use them both casting and trolling.

64. T F   Weather reports are of little value to the well-trained spoonplugger.

65. T F   Normally the "drop-off" is shallower than the "home" of the fish.

66. T F   Deep water should be classified as water that is deeper than eight or ten feet.

67. T F   Contour maps of a lake bottom are of little use to the spoonplugger.

68. T F   Your favorite throttle setting while trolling should be the same regardless of the number of fishermen in the boat.

69. T F   Sometimes just moving the boat a few feet can make deep water casting productive or not.

70. T F   So far as successful fishing is concerned, a shoreline is useful for locating or positioning a fisherman and for holding water in a lake.

71. T F   Since fish spend most of the time in deep water, a fisherman should check that water first.

72. T F   Children should be ten or twelve years old before they go fishing for big fish.

73. T F   Casting skill is a must for successful fresh water bass fishing.

74. T F   If a person waits until retirement age before taking up fishing, he should not expect to become very good at it.

75. T F   Spoonplugging is a family sport.

76. T F   Most fishing clubs fail or do not grow because of competition among its members.

77. T F   Being able to exercise patience is the greatest asset to the spoonplugger.

78. T F   Spinning gear, while helping many fishermen to cast a lure reasonably well, is in most cases inadequate to do the whole job of fishing.

79. T F   A fisherman who does not use the larger lures (Spoonplugs), constantly is not likely to find a school of large fish.

80. T F   The movements, or migrations, of fish are triggered by the moon.

81. T F   After a spoonplugger has found the most productive structures, much time should be spent in learning the details of each.

82. T F   In most cases, a fisherman standing on shore can work deep water successfully.

83. T F   During extremely hot weather, fishermen should concentrate on fishing steep, deep, cliff-like shorelines.

84. T F   The average fisherman will never catch lots of big fish.

85. T F   Romantic tales and gimmick fishing tackle are the main reasons people do not catch more fish.

86. T F   A landing net should never be used by an experienced fisherman.

87. T F   Depth and lure speed are the two most important controls for successful fishing.

88. T F   Some waters require much use of topwater and weedless lures.

89. T F   Fishermen should get off a lake during an electrical storm, especially those in a metal boat.

90. T F   The only way that interest in fishing can be maintained is by catching fish.

91. T F   Most laws governing fishing were instigated by fishermen who griped about poor fishing.

92. T F   The best way to improve fishing is to pass more laws restricting the number and size of fish that may be caught, etc.

93. T F   It has been proven that it is unnecessary to have a stocking program on most game fish found in most lakes.

94. T F   Monies collected through the sale of fishing licenses should be used to improve fishing conditions, rather than allotting some of them for teaching fishermen how to fish.

95. T F   Frequently wind makes it impossible to fish lures correctly.

96. T F   Most likely the correct lure speed control will be different for different species of fish.

97. T F   Lakes that have walleyes and northern pike should be fished differently from those that contain bass.

98. T F   When the wind is from the east, a fisherman might as well stay at home.

99. T F A spoonplugger normally expects a migration movement of fish on the front side of a low pressure period, and on the backside of a high pressure period.

100. T F Heavy haze with high cirrus clouds could indicate there may be an exceptional movement of fish.

101. T F Some of the better movements or migrations of fish can occur at high noon.

102. T F An early morning movement of fish means there will be another later in the afternoon.

103. T F A clear blue sky could mean there will be very little movement or migration of fish.

104. T F After a cold front goes through white, snow-ball type clouds may form 4,000 to 5,000 feet on the second day after the front. This indicates that the effects of the cold front are over.

105. T F There may be several weeks following fish spawning when there will be little or no migration of fish to the shallows.

106. T F At times there can be "movement" but no migration.

107. T F The greatest asset to a spoonplugger is sharing his knowledge.

108. T F Shallow lakes in the South are normally better than shallow lakes in the northern part of the country.

109. T F Use of the term "fishing hole" by generations of fishermen has been a major factor, or cause, for lack of fishing success.

110. T F Most fishing in salt water should be done differently from that in fresh water.

111. T F Fishing guides generally know where to fish in deep water.

112. T F When trolling, the same length of line should be used on different size lures.

113. T F A fisherman should never stand up in his boat while casting.

114. T F The moment a fisherman puts his hopes and faith in size, color, and action of a lure, he is a dead duck.

115. T F A fisherman should always locate his fishing spot in open water by sighting two objects on opposite shores.

116. T F When fishing a "new" lake it is wise to spend some time driving around the lake observing the make-up of the shoreline and the condition of the water.

117. T F Most fish "counts" by biologists are a waste of time, effort, and money.

118. T F A fish that remains uncaught to grow to "lunker" size must give credence to the fact he is too "smart" for the average fisherman.

119. T F The bass fisherman should note shoreline cover such as brush, weeds, pads, stumps, etc. and confine his fishing to these areas.

120. T F Yearling "stripes" could be found in most any section of a lake.

121. T F Fish migrate to shallow water due only to hunger and their need to feed.

122. T F Constant use of the free-running, bottom-bumping Spoonplugs is a "must" to maintain depth and speed control.

123. T F Most lures will not catch fish.

124. T F The majority of fishermen fish too slow in cold weather.

125. T F It is impossible for a fisherman to get to the point where he can make no further progress or improvement.

126. T F Schools of small, migratory fish such as white bass, trout, walleyes, etc. may be located in any section of a lake, but to consistently catch lunker fish of these species, a fisherman must work structure.

127. T F A spoonplugger should always be aware of "breaks" in structure.

128. T F There is more migration among fish in cold water than in warm.

129. T F Weather and water conditions play an important part in the success or failure of a fishing season.

130. T F The slow period of fishing following the spawning of fish is primarily due to the time necessary for the water to warm to greater depths.

131. T F The major reason for fish going deep is temperature and atmospheric pressure.

132. T F At times a wire or leaded line is necessary to reach fish.

133. T F A wise fisherman should concentrate his efforts on one lake or one section of water until he knows it backwards and forwards.

134. T F After checking a structure thoroughly, it is not necessary to check it at a later period.

135. T F Most fishermen who catch fish at times consider themselves experts.

136. T F If a fisherman limits himself to only topwater lures, it is primarily an excuse for not catching fish.

137. T F When visiting or fishing strange waters, it is wise to find out about and purchase the lures being used at that time.

138. T F Most published fishing reports should be taken with a grain of salt.

139. T F Correct use of live bait is a good way to fish.

140. T F The two main factors in successful fishing is to know what makes fish tick, and the proper use of fishing gear.

141. T F In the colder part of the fishing season steep shorelines should be worked with all sizes of lures.

142. T F Most fishermen lose control of their lures below fifteen feet, thus most catches will be made after fish migrations.

143. T F Deeper portions of a structure can be worked more thoroughly by trolling.

144. T F Most migrations of fish from deep water to shallow occur in ditches or gullies.

145. T F Weather and water conditions will determine how shallow a fish migration goes and also how long it will last.

146. T F The fisherman who fishes in the early morning hours will miss many fine fish migrations.

147. T F The average fisherman pays too much attention to shorelines.

148. T F Most fish migration routes will be the same length.

149. T F The weedline in a lake could be the fish scatter-point regardless of its depth.

150. T F With no major weather changes a fisherman could expect about the same type of migration from fish every day.

151. T F The path a group of fish takes on migration is a straight line.

152. T F Migrating or "moving" fish always move up to at least the "scatter" point.

153. T F Lunker fish are hesitant to move shallower than eight to ten feet.

154. T F Most of a season the coves or bays in a lake will not be productive for most game fish.

155. T F Catching yearling fish is of no importance to the spoonplugger.

156. T F If a lunker fish is found in shallow water, a fisherman should expect a school of lunkers to be at the same depth.

157. T F Fish move about one-fourth mile per hour when migrating.

158. T F The spoonplugger should waste no time when fish movements occur, as the migration may last only a few minutes.

159. T F "Hot spots" are important to a spoonplugger, even though the fish may not be "biting."

160. T F A spoonplugger should not expect a good catch if the migration of fish does not extend to water eight to ten feet deep.

161. T F When a migration of fish does not occur, a fisherman should spend a great deal of time in channels or holes looking for deep fish.

162. T F Before leaving a structure it is wise to check the area with a "jump" type lure.

163. T F It is impossible to catch a fish unless it is feeding.

164. T F If a spoonplugger will use the different size spoonplugs and keep them "in position," his main concern then will be speed control.

165. T F The best lure action to use would be one that wiggles like something trying to swim.

166. T F The fish in some waters seem to have a color preference.

TAGGING FISH

167. T F Bright lures are usually sufficient to locate fish, so far as color is concerned.

168. T F A good reminder to the spoonplugger when considering lure size preference of fish, is that a game fish will try to eat anything that's not bigger than he is.

169. T F A troller should usually reduce speed when his lure starts hitting the bottom.

170. T F It is not necessary to bump the bottom when working shallow water.

171. T F When fishing some lakes for some species of fish, it is not necessary to check the speed of the lure.

172. T F In fishing cold water, it is better to keep the retrieve steady and fast.

173. T F The best way to check the trolling speed desired by fish is to start fast and then slowly retard the the throttle back to dead slow.

174. T F The wise spoonplugger always starts with large lures.

175. T F Normally trolling is not a good way to check shorelines longer than one-quarter mile.

176. T F Most of the time your casting gear will serve adequately for trolling.

177. T F When on a strange lake, fish it first by casting.

178. T F When working a shoreline by trolling, a fisherman should never fish more than 100 yards at a given depth.

179. T F The troller should not get too close to bushes, weeds, or rocks, as there is danger of fouling or damaging his motor.

180. T F When a fish is caught trolling, it is best to continue on around the lake using the same lure.

181. T F If a fisherman has been successful with a certain size lure but desires to work deeper with a larger size, he should use the same color and use it in the same manner.

182. T F After a spoonplugger has run all size lures but has caught no fish, there is little that can be done while he waits for fish to move.

183. T F A shoreline always indicates possible fish migration routes.

184. T F When casting over a bar, the fisherman should limit his casts to the very crown of the bar.

185. T F Some species of fish may hit a free-swimming lure deeper than will largemouth bass.

186. T F Some species of fish are not considered good eating; therefore fishermen should not fish for them.

187. T F Many times it is easy to find fish in their "home" area.

188. T F When about to fish a strange lake, it is wise to ask about hot spots.

189. T F "Migration" normally means a movement of fish along the bottom in specific areas.

190. T F It is possible to clean migration routes of brush and snags when a lake is drawn down.

191. T F A spoonplugger should never expect the same type of fish movement to occur consecutively.

192. T F Many fishermen fear lakes that have lots of open water.

193. T F Many times a "point" in the shoreline could indicate an underwater migration route.

194. T F A deep water sanctuary of fish will always be at the same depth.

195. T F Normally the "scatter point" on a migration route remains constant.

196. T F Each time a fish is caught, a spoonplugger should be sure to check the area for additional fish, regardless of the size of the fish landed.

197. T F Shallow water is water that contains weeds or brush.

198. T F The size of a lure can be determined by its weight.

199. T F It is impossible to spook a school of fish when they are feeding.

200. T F The spoonplugger should work for "straggler" fish if he is unable to locate a large school.

201. T F Where good bottom structure does not exist, it is impossible for a fisherman to do anything to improve the situation.

202. T F A good spoonplugger will exercise a great deal of patience waiting for fish to move.

203. T F A fisherman should spend a lot of time fishing over large "flats."

204. T F Boat traffic can, under some conditions, affect the migrations of fish.

205. T F A fisherman should strive, always, not to allow his lures to hit the bottom.

206. T F Most bass fishermen do their fishing in such a way that they catch mostly yearling fish.

207. T F The best way to fish a shoreline is to move out to a good castable distance and slowly move along the shoreline, making casts in toward the shore.

208. T F When two fishermen are fishing from a boat, they should always use the same size and color lure.

209. T F Underwater islands or humps are usually good fishing spots.

210. T F Frequently more fish can be caught by casting to a deep-water school than can be by trolling.

211. T F It is better to use a light test line when casting into a school of fish, as a heavier line may be seen and thus spook the fish.

212. T F When casting toward a group of fish in deep water, the retrieve should always be slow.

213. T F It is never wise to "horse in" a hooked fish.

214. T   F   Most lakes become hard to fish four or five years after they are built because they are usually "fished out" by that time.

215. T   F   Generally speaking, a fisherman should not expect to catch fish exactly the same way any two days running.

216. T   F   Experience tells us that once a fisherman has learned the procedures for successful fishing, he will not slip back into his old angling ways.

217. T   F   Beginning fishermen could save a lot of time, effort, and money if they would hire a teacher instead of a guide.

218. T   F   The test, or diameter, of a line can often determine whether or not a particular size lure is productive.

219. T   F   Many trollers fail to run enough line before changing lure sizes.

220. T   F   The rod tip should always be held high when trolling.

221. T   F   When casting, it is best to retrieve with the rod tip high and pointed toward the lure.

222. T   F   When using a level-wind casting reel, one should make each cast with a lot of snappy wrist action.

223. T   F   Accuracy in casting the shorelines will determine how successful a fisherman will be.

224. T   F   When casting deep on structure that has a mucky, soft bottom or is covered with moss, trash, etc., the fisherman should switch to a "jump" type lure if the "walking" lure fouls too often.

225. T   F   Detailed study of high water migration routes can be made when bottom structure is exposed by a drop in a lake's water level.

226. T   F   If a trolling fisherman has a depth meter, there is no need for him to study lake structure maps.

227. T   F   Throwing out floating markers to locate the shape of a bar or to show the edge of a weedline is of great importance to the troller.

228. T   F   If a fisherman uses an electronic depth-finder to follow the bottom contours his lures will be in position for best results.

229. T   F   For a fisherman to thoroughly locate himself on a body of water he should pick out shoreline sightings, if possible.

230. T   F   When fishing strange water, a lot of fish-hunting time can be saved by observing the surrounding terrain.

231. T   F   A fisherman should not carry too many floating markers, as they are costly.

232. T   F   Weedlines and breaklines can be located only with a depth meter.

233. T   F   Throwing markers along a weedline enables a troller to keep his lures in better position.

234. T   F   In "delta" type lakes, often the best spots are some distance from the shorelines.

235. T   F   Fishermen will find, in fishing rivers, that most of the "breaks" will be found on the outside of a bend.

236. T   F   The "inside" of a bend in a river will usually have a long, smooth sand bar with very few breaks.

237. T   F   In fishing a reservoir that previously covered a forested area, it is best for a fisherman to scout and study the lake to determine if any former farm land was inundated.

238. T   F   When fishing a lake formed by a dam on a large river, the fisherman should keep in mind areas where side feeder streams previously entered the main channel.

239. T   F   It is better for a fisherman to have no instruction, than to be given the wrong information.

240. T   F   A fisherman should always have floating markers to help him locate and fish correctly various structure and breaks.

241. T   F   It is difficult for a fisherman to get correct fishing information secondhand.

242. T   F   Many fishing trips will have to be made on a particular body of water before all of the details of structure and fish migrations will be known.

243. T   F   Cold fronts can be used too much as an excuse for not catching fish.

244. T   F   Most of the time failure in fishing is due to the fisherman not putting forth enough effort.

245. T   F   At times, catching a few fish can be more satisfying than getting a lot under better circumstances.

246. T   F   As our population grows, education in fishing becomes increasingly more important.

247. T F Big fish do not move constantly nor consistently, so a fisherman must be patient, and check and recheck structures for a movement of fish.

248. T F A fisherman should study weather forecasts before selecting the place for a fishing trip.

249. T F There is little a fisherman can do to offset the effects of a cold front.

250. T F The fisherman who does not understand how a fish migrates or moves around, and who does not understand the proper ways to go about catching fish will never become an expert angler.

To determine your Buck Perry Quiz score, count 1 for each mistake made and subtract total from 100. Passing is 70.

Answers
Buck Perry True, False Fishing Quiz

1. False	43. False	85. True	127. True	169. True	211. False
2. False	44. True	86. False	128. False	170. False	212. False
3. True	45. False	87. True	129. True	171. False	213. False
4. True	46. True	88. True	130. True	172. False	214. False
5. False	47. False	89. True	131. False	173. False	215. True
6. False	48. False	90. True	132. True	174. False	216. False
7. False	49. True	91. True	133. True	175. False	217. True
8. True	50. False	92. False	134. False	176. False	218. True
9. False	51. True	93. False	135. True	177. False	219. True
10. False	52. False	94. False	136. True	178. False	220. False
11. False	53. True	95. True	137. False	179. False	221. False
12. True	54. False	96. True	138. True	180. False	222. False
13. True	55. True	97. False	139. True	181. False	223. False
14. False	56. False	98. False	140. True	182. False	224. True
15. False	57. True	99. True	141. True	183. False	225. True
16. False	58. True	100. True	142. True	184. False	226. False
17. False	59. True	101. True	143. False	185. True	227. True
18. False	60. True	102. False	144. False	186. False	228. False
19. True	61. False	103. True	145. True	187. False	229. True
20. False	62. True	104. False	146. True	188. True	230. True
21. True	63. True	105. True	147. True	189. True	231. False
22. False	64. False	106. True	148. False	190. True	232. False
23. False	65. True	107. True	149. False	191. True	233. True
24. True	66. True	108. True	150. False	192. True	234. True
25. True	67. False	109. True	151. False	193. True	235. True
26. False	68. False	110. False	152. False	194. False	236. True
27. True	69. True	111. False	153. True	195. True	237. True
28. False	70. True	112. False	154. True	196. True	238. True
29. False	71. False	113. False	155. False	197. False	239. True
30. False	72. False	114. True	156. False	198. False	240. True
31. False	73. False	115. False	157. False	199. False	241. True
32. True	74. False	116. True	158. True	200. True	242. True
33. True	75. True	117. True	159. True	201. False	243. True
34. True	76. True	118. False	160. False	202. True	244. True
35. True	77. True	119. False	161. False	203. False	245. True
36. True	78. True	120. True	162. True	204. True	246. True
37. False	79. True	121. False	163. False	205. False	247. True
38. False	80. False	122. True	164. True	206. True	248. True
39. False	81. True	123. False	165. False	207. False	249. False
40. False	82. False	124. False	166. True	208. False	250. True
41. True	83. False	125. True	167. False	209. True	
42. True	84. True	126. True	168. True	210. True	

4

Basic Flies for Trout Fishing

There's no need to be a walking fly shop, toting hundreds of patterns. To score on trout consistently all you really need is a representative assortment of flies.

Dry flies . . . hundreds of them . . . but what specific "patterns" are really needed by the average trout fisherman?

One warm summer evening I stood near the tail of a flat pool on the Boardman River in Michigan and watched my white marabou streamer wiggling along the bottom. I had pinched a BB split-shot sinker on at the hook-eye, so the fly came crawling back *hippety-hop* as I retrieved. With each twitch of the rod tip the fly rose a couple inches, then nosed down and bumped bottom. Each bump sent up a tiny puff of sand, which I could see clearly in the six-inch deep water.

My cast had been across and downstream. The marabou had danced beside a brush pile before it slid into the shallows, but the brown trout that followed from the brush didn't really lose his marbles until the fly started that bump-and-grind routine along the gravel. I saw the fish nose down and inhale the streamer the way a bonefish sucks a crab off the bottom.

Another summer day I crouched beside a ledge on Pennsylvania's lovely little Dwarfskill River, on the stretch then maintained by the Fifty Club, and fished first dry flies then wet flies then streamers, but couldn't raise a fish. I switched to nymphs—casting a short line upstream and allowing the fly to drift down naturally with the current—and suddenly the ledge seemed like an apartment house for trout. I guided several different nymph patterns through the current that curled beneath the ledge, and the trout loved every one of them.

Still another time John Daley, of Baltimore, and I knelt on the shoulder of Big Hunting Creek near Thurmont, Maryland, at a spot known as the "Swimming Pool." The water was clear and cool as a martini, and we could see three small rainbows that had positioned themselves to pick black gnats from the surface. John floated a size 10 Deer Hair fly to the nearest trout, which clobbered it. He withdrew the fish quickly, released it, then I sent a size 14 Royal Coachman to the second trout, which *ate it!* When I released that one John cast a bulky Badger Spider to the farthest rainbow, which swallowed it so fast he nearly choked.

All of which points up that it is not so much the fly pattern you use, as it is the fly type and the method employed in fishing it!

While there are times that trout everywhere can be as selective in feeding as you must be with tax deductions, it is axiomatic that the average angler is overly concerned about trout fly patterns. "Matching the hatch" sometimes is not only desirable but necessary if many fish are to be creeled; but more often exact duplication of the natural insect with an artificial is relatively unimportant.

Once at an Inn at Phoenicia, New York—hard by the Esopus and the Chichester—I listened while one fisherman expounded to a group of attentive trouters how he had finally taken a limit of brown trout that day on the Lady Beaverkill dry. He had virtually gone through "every dry fly in his box," catching nothing, he said, until finally he tried the Lady Beaverkill—which, truly, had "saved the day!" Even the Beaverkill, this "expert" claimed, had not worked, although the major difference between these two flies is only a yellow "egg sac" (tag) sported by Milady Beaverkill.

I would hesitate to imply that a fellow fisherman was relating fiction, but assuredly it is a rare day indeed when

The size and "profile" of a dry fly, and how it is fished, can be more important than the specific pattern.

trout take or refuse a dry fly depending on the presence or absence of a yellow chenille tag not much larger than a pin-head.

Most experienced, intelligent, and honest trout fly fishermen agree that, at best, they hope only to *suggest* more natural insect, minnow, or other trout food with their *unnatural* flies. Even the *most perfectly modeled artificial fly* cannot compare favorably with the genuine morsel it is meant to duplicate!

This is not to say that a bivisible dry fly will produce as well as an artificial May fly on a day when green drake naturals are filling the air like snowflakes. Representative imitation of genuine insects is of more import to the dry fly angler than to the man fishing wet flies, streamers, or nymphs.

If trout are picking midges from the surface film, surely you should fish a midge fly. But whether your artificial is black or dusty brown probably will matter little to the trout. If the trout are feasting on the corpses of spent flies, then you will do better with a representative spent-wing dry fly than you would with, say, a Hairwing Coachman.

The *size* of the dry fly selected can be important at a given moment, as can its *profile* or its *type*. These factors are far more important than the *specific pattern* of fly. A properly stocked dry fly box should hold standard upright wing dry flies, a few fan wings, bivisibles, variants, spiders, some quill body types, high-floating deer hairs such as the Irresistible, midges, several May fly types, grasshopper imitations like Joe's Hopper, the Michigan Hopper, or Muddler Minnow, spinners or spent-wings, and some hair-wing patterns.

Except during those short periods when large May flies are present, small dry flies usually score best on Midwest and Eastern streams. From the opening of the trout seasons until about mid-July, dry flies in sizes 10, 12, and 14 seem to score most consistently on trout waters east of the Mississippi. From late July to the end of the season, dries in sizes 14, 16, 18, 20, and even 22, often are best. There are exceptions, of course, and a hatch of large mayflies becomes a major exception, but as a rule small dries produce best during low, clear water periods in the eastern half of the United States.

In the Far West large dry flies have become standard, just as Westerners have come to dote on oversized streamers, wet flies, and nymphs. A bushy, heavily-winged size 6 or 8 dry fly is a popular tool on western rivers, and rare is the Montana angler, for example, who will very often drop down to dry flies smaller than size 10. The tendency toward using big dry flies in the West is partly due to the large size of the rivers . . . and of the fish. The average Westerner long ago agreed to the old angling adage of *"big flies for big fish."*

While I've tried to stress that fly fishermen should be chiefly concerned with acquiring a representative assortment of flies, following are some dry fly patterns that serve well on most trout streams: Irresistible, Adams, Hendrickson, Quill Gordon, Mosquito, Light Cahill, Blue Dun, Joe's Hopper, Muddler Minnow (greased), Brown Bivisible, Dark Brown Cranefly, Gordon Spinner, Green Drake, Multi-colored Variant, Badger Spider, Olive Spent-Wing, Grey Wulff, and Brown and Black Midges.

The matter of specific patterns is even less important in selecting wet flies and streamers. Most anglers fish wet flies rarely, feeling that either nymphs or streamers will serve as well or better than wets. More often than not trout mistake wet flies for nymphs, anyway, so why not offer them a fly tied to a nymph? The wet fly fisherman of old is fading from the modern angling scene, yet there still are a few addicted wet fly anglers around, especially on our western rivers. These fishermen, however, are chiefly dedicated to the *system* of fishing wet flies, and not so much to the wet fly patterns. Fact is, artificial nymphs can be fished down-and-across stream in typical wet fly fashion—even in pairs—with devastating effect.

It is sometimes fun, of course, to fish wet flies for experiment, practice, or just as a change-of-pace. Drab wet fly patterns are preferred, in sizes 10 or 12 for eastern waters, and sizes 4 to 8 for the western rivers. Popular wet dressings are the Black Gnat, March Brown, Hare's Ear, Hendrickson, Dark and Light Cahill, Brown Hackle, Adams, and Western Bee.

Wet flies should be tied on extra heavy wire hooks, and as a rule the sparser ties are best. If you tie your own, make some weighted patterns by wrapping fine

The selection of specific "patterns" is probably least important in choosing wet flies. It's probable that wet flies are most commonly mistaken by fish to be nymphs.

A well-filled fly book should contain streamer fly patterns of marabou, bucktail, impala, and saddle-hackle winging.

"Attractor" type nymphs—ones that can be easily mistaken by trout for a multitude of real nymphs—are the ones to stock in your fly box.

lead wire over the hook shank before tying in the body material.

In general, most streamer flies have either saddle hackle (chicken feathers), bucktail, impala, or marabou winging. A well-filled streamer fly book should contain several of each, and they should be selected according to size, basic color, and type. It is doubtful if, under most conditions, a Black Ghost Marabou is any more effective than a plain White Marabou, but a Yellow Marabou might work wonders under certain light and water conditions that make a piker out of a White or Black Marabou.

A very excellent streamer is the plain White Marabou. Wrap lead wire over a 3X-long No. 6 or 8 hook, add the marabou winging, and that's that. All the fly consists of, really, is the hook and the marabou. No fancy trimmings. It's so effective, though, that if certain conservation departments knew what certain fishermen accomplish with that fly, they'd set up road blocks on the by-ways leading to our trout streams.

Yellow Marabou, Yellow and Red, White and Red, and Black all are good streamers. Trout sometimes chop short in striking marabou, missing the hook, so occasionally it is profitable to shorten the winging material. Do this by chewing or tearing the fibers, not by snipping. Marabou loses much of its action when it is trimmed or clipped with scissors or a nail clipper.

Thousands of saddle hackle type streamer patterns are available, and the same is true of bucktail patterns. Just remember that it is primarily the fly winging that is important, the fly's size, and its over-all silhouette. All trout fishermen should have some standard hackle-

wing streamers, and some with "breather" style winging, and plenty with silver or gold tinsel bodies.

Brown and white bucktails, with "optic" heads (a big-eyed, pea-size head), are deadly little killers. So is the Black-Nose Dace. So also is the Muddler Minnow which, although usually most effective fished dry, is demolishing to trout when stripped along just beneath the surface so that it creates a "V" wake, or when worked deep with the aid of split-shot or a sinking line.

In choosing nymphs, concentrate on "attractor" types—ones that reasonably suggest a multitude of genuine nymphs but which do not perfectly represent any specific natural insect larvae.

The best nymphs frequently are fur-bodied, made either of gray under-belly muskrat fur, or under-belly fur from a red fox. Otter and mink are other good furs with which to spin nymph bodies. With a few exceptions, dark colors are best, and nymph sizes 10 and 12 generally are superior on eastern streams, sizes 4, 6, and 8 on the western rivers.

Only the basic fly types and a few of the patterns have been discussed here. However, colors and sizes have been included that will form the nucleus of a stock of flies that will keep the angler happy on most trout streams most of the time. With experience you'll be able to add and deduct specific patterns according to seasonal conditions on your favorite stream. But you'll discover too (if you haven't already), that it isn't so much the pattern that counts as it is the fly type, its presentation, and method of fishing it.

Five Experts Tell About Their Favorite Spots

These famous fishermen give the details about places they like to fish the most.

ART WALLSTEN is a former Chicagoan now living in Boca Raton, Florida. He is a tackle manufacturer, and his Cisco Kid line of lures are popular with anglers around the world. Wallsten has fished in many areas and is particularly familiar with midwestern and Canadian waters. Following is his report on lakes he prefers to fish.

One of my favorite fishing spots in the Chicago area is Lake Geneva in southern Wisconsin. For the last few years it has given exceptional smallmouth bass fishing, and the walleyes have been hitting good too, as well as nice northerns.

I like to work the "flats" off the Lake Geneva Country Club, drifting and casting the weed beds. That's the "fish bowl" of the whole lake. Williams' Bay is sometimes good, though, and

so is the area off the pavillion right in the town of Lake Geneva.

Diamond Lake near Mundelein is a great largemouth spot, and Brown's Lake at Burlington, Wisconsin also can be very good, particularly in early spring and in late fall. Fishing at Diamond holds up good through summer, with morning and evening the best time.

In Canada, Big Vermilion Lake at Sioux Lookout is hard to beat. This is muskie water, but it's also loaded with smallmouths and northern pike, though there are no walleyes. Vermilion isn't fished too hard, and I once took a twenty-seven pound muskie there while fishing out of Deerfoot Camp. Bigger ones are there, however, and I know of one that went forty-five pounds.

BILL LAURENT, another former Chicagoan, now lives in Kalamazoo, Michigan. As an executive with the Shakespeare Tackle Company, he fishes a great deal, frequently with angling experts, and has wet lines in widely scattered areas. In his report, he discusses three of his favorite spots.

The best place to go fishing, of course, is the place you can get to—and the best time to go is when you have the chance. But when you have fished around a lot, certain places keep coming to mind as *the* very best.

Take North Manitou Island, for example. I guess I've been on little Lake Manitou on this island in northern Lake Michigan fifteen or twenty times. But it's still my favorite fresh water fishing spot. The reason: I've caught more big smallmouth bass here than anywhere else I've fished. And besides, the island itself is a beautiful hardwood wilderness full of deer and other wildlife, and it has an atmosphere that's simply disappeared from any other place I know of in the Midwest.

Operated as a fishing club by the North Manitou Island Association, Leland, Michigan, the island is open to the public on a reservation basis and boats, motors, rooms, and meals are available. You can fly in to a lighted landing strip in a private plane or take the mail boat out of Leland.

First time I visited the island I used ultralight spinning gear and hooked a five-and-one-half pound smallmouth on a small plastic worm—in twelve feet of water, and in the midst of tough pencil weeds. It was a battle to remember, and every time I go back I fish the same spot again. The lake (about 100 acres) is now stocked with rainbow trout, too. The fishing is never easy at Lake Manitou but there's always the chance of getting a really big smallmouth.

Deep Water Cay Club is situated on the East End of Grand Bahama Island. You fly from the Florida mainland to West End, Grand Bahama, then take a charter plane from there to the landing strip at the club. This is a private spot too, but open to the public with reservations through Deep Water Cay Club, P. O. Box 1145, Palm Beach, Florida, 33480. The club has comfortable lodgings, fine food, guides (a must), boats, motors, and tackle available.

Here I found the best bonefishing I've ever seen. On a decent day you'll cast to many big schools of tailing or mudding fish. Big bones, too! Last trip we saw some tails that belonged to bonefish well over ten pounds. Most are in the six to eight pound class. It's ideal fly fishing water and you'll seldom see another angler. You can travel the creeks and bays on the East End for miles and miles and be in good fishing water almost all the time. You can wade, or fish from your boat.

As an added attraction permit fishing is available, too. And while most of it is done with live crabs, a recent fly rod permit record was taken in Club waters.

And speaking of permits, I guess more are taken from the Content Keys area in the Florida Keys (along with Key West) than any other spot. This racehorse of the flats has a personal jinx on me as I'm still trying for my first. I headquarter in Marathon, Florida for this fishing and among the many great guides there I've fished most often with Capt. Arlin Leiby. He's put me on permit every time we've gone out but something has always gone wrong. (Last time I finally made a perfect cast to a tailing permit and darned if a bonefish didn't sneak in and take the jig!)

While you're in the Keys you've got to do some tarpon fishing on the flats. Marathon is good but I've had more fish on out of Islamorada farther up the island chain. Stake out on a good bank in Florida Bay in June and you're sure to see some pods of fish in the over-100-pound class come drifting through the channel while you stand ready to cast. As far as I'm concerned it's the biggest thrill in fishing! You'll jump maybe one fish out of six you cast to and bring maybe one out of six of these to the boat. To be released, of course!

Islamorada is stocked with great tarpon guides. Capt. Jim

Brewer is a fine one. He fishes hard, hard, hard!

These are my favorite fishing holes, out of a lot of waters that have gone under the boat in the last thirty-five years. And I didn't even touch Lake Norfork in Arkansas, the Isthmus off Catalina Island, Great Bear Lake, Lake Okeechobee, Greer's Ferry Lake, the Current River, and—

I'm just thankful I got to fish them all.

Tom Thompson, of LaCrosse, Wisconsin, is a Zebco Tackle Company representative and veteran Tribune Fishing School instructor. He's been a fisherman since boyhood, and has wet lines from far northern Canada to Mexico, Hawaii, The Bahamas and Norway, which are only some of the places he's fished. Here he describes three of his favorite spots.

For anyone who has fished in many places for fifty years, it is a delightful task to relive fishing experiences all over the globe. In trying to determine which, indeed, are my favorite fishing spots, my thoughts return to a catch of tuna off the coast of Hawaii, to blue marlin fishing off Puerto Rico, to bonefishing in the Florida Keys and the out-islands of The Bahamas, to Atlantic salmon fishing in the Reisa River in Norway, to snook fishing around Marco Island, Florida, to big northern pike at Saskatchewan's Cree Lake, to giant lake trout at God's Lake in northern Manitoba, to coho salmon in Lake Michigan, and to Pacific sailfish out of Alcapulco, Mexico.

All of those trips, all of that fishing, has been super–great, but for three all-time favorite spots I'd have to select Manitoba's Winnipeg River; Ontario's Little Vermillion Lake; and backwater areas of the Mississippi River near LaCrosse, Wisconsin.

For smallmouth bass, good northern pike, and fine walleyes, I suggest the Winnipeg River at Point Du Bois, Manitoba. Vic

Burgess' camp, called Pine Island Lodge, is the place to stay and to fish out of.

The Winnipeg is a fine, clear-flowing stream, so big, so broad that it is like fishing a typical Canadian wilderness lake. The bass are shallow here almost all season long, so fishing with fly rod poppers or streamer flies usually take fish. The accommodations, food, boats, guides—all are excellent at Vic's camp.

I suspect I have had about seventy-five muskies hooked and perhaps boated half of them, all thirty inches long or longer at Ontario's Little Vermillion. Few experiences surpass the thrill of a "follow" from a four-foot-long muskie, not knowing, but hoping, he will strike your lure before he comes too close to the boat so the figure "8" retrieve must be used. Every strike I have ever had, unfortunately, while using the figure "8", I failed to hook the fish.

Honestly, four and even five-foot muskies are quite prevalent at Little Vermillion Lake, and I recommend fishing it out of Fireside Lodge, Sioux Lookout, Ontario, Canada. Little Vermillion must be the best muskie lake in all of Canada. On one trip there every member of our fishing group—twelve strong—had muskies on. First-time muskie fisherman Tom Carlson, president of the Redhead Brand Corporation of Dallas, Texas, boated three. Those muskies hit in the morning, during the day, and at dusk. Incidentally, the season there usually opens about the third week in June.

Little Vermillion is about a six-hour drive from Duluth, Minnesota, with good roads all the way to camp. Camp owners will meet planes at the Sioux Lookout airport. Best bait, incidentally, for these Little Vermillion muskies, is a No. 3000 Jointed Creek Chub Pikie Minnow, and a Squirrel-Tail Spinner is great, too.

Another very favorite spot of mine, easy to reach for millions of fishermen, is the Mississippi River near LaCrosse, Wisconsin.

Some species of fish can always be caught in the Mississippi. It has walleyes, sauger, catfish, northern pike, largemouth and smallmouth bass, rock bass, crappies, sunfish, and roughfish such as carp, buffalo, and sheepshead.

After a few warm days in June, popper fishing with a fly rod for crappies and sunfish is great fun and very productive. The inveterate Mississippi fisherman, however, the real pro angler, is the guy after walleyes. Most such Mississippi fishermen are good because they fish all the time. They learn when to fish, and when not to. They can tell by the water temperature, river level, air temperature, barometer, river current—and a whole combination of other things when *the* time has arrived to go fishing.

Even average fishermen, however, can do really well on the Mississippi, just by experimenting. It's best to fish below the big dams and on the wing dams, and such fishing is almost certain to produce something. Something else that makes this area attractive to most fishermen is that it is readily accessible, there are lots of hotel-motel accommodations, and many boat rentals and guides available. For guides, I recommend Joe and Mike Abraham, 513 Copeland Avenue, LaCrosse, Wisconsin, 54601. They know the river and when to fish it.

E. L. "BUCK" PERRY, of Hickory, North Carolina, is known to millions of fishermen for his remarkable feats of "spoonplugging" bass, and is the manufacturer of the famed Spoon-plug line of lures. Perry probably has fished more bass waters than any other fisherman, and he has a large store of angling experience to draw upon in selecting favorite spots.

When asked to pick my five favorite fishing spots, my first thought was, "This is going to be a snap. All I have to do is sweep the country and recall a lifetime of fishing that has taken me to every state."

I would remember the great fishing trips to the New England states for bass, trout, and landlocked salmon. Then I'd swing on down the eastern seaboard states to the coastal sounds and sloughs, the great inland lakes of the Carolinas and Georgia, and on through Florida with it's streams, swamps, sloughs, canals, coastal and highland ridge lakes. A swing through the southern states east of the Mississippi, through the Delta and inland reservoirs, would recall the deep South with it's long seasons and beautiful water colors. In memory, I'd recollect the thousands of miles of shoreline in the vast TVA system that stretches from the highland reservoirs of Kentucky, Tennessee, and the Carolinas to the flatlands of the Mississippi basin.

While looking at the Great Lakes, from the Thousand Islands to Duluth, I would have to ponder a while on the smallmouth bass fishing in Lake St. Clair, and on the salmon fishing in Lake Michigan. But Wisconsin and Minnesota would recall, for me, hundreds of lakes full of bass, walleyes, northerns, and muskies—fishing at it's best. The Dakotas and the great waters of the Missouri, whose northern pike still create a tingle in me. The Ozarks, Oklahoma, Missouri, Arkansas, and Texas are referred to by many as the "heart" of this country's fishing. It would require some thought to pick out a particular water or spot in this area that I considered better fishing or more enjoyable than others. I'd spend some moments in recalling the uniqueness of Louisiana and the Mississippi backwaters and sloughs.

Fishing the remote streams and lakes of the eastern Rockies, all the way to the Canadian border, was a pleasant part of my fishing career. The great reservoirs of the Colorado River Basin, from the peaks of Colorado to the deserts of Mexico, help convince me that my fishing experience has been among the best. I can taste again the thrill of the Pacific Coast—the variety of fish in the Sacramento drainage to the high lakes of the Sierras to the arid regions of the lower peninsula. Having experienced such a vast amount of fishing, I felt there would be no chore in selecting five great fishing spots for this article.

DON NICHOLS, of La Grange Park, Illinois, is an airlines captain who does more than one man's fair share of fishing. He is an excellent bass fisherman, particularly skillful at deep-water techniques, and he has fished extensively through the Midwest and elsewhere.

When I go fishing I want to catch fish; that's the primary reason for going. However, in selecting some favorite fishing spots, many things besides catching fish consistently enter into my decision.

Scenery, types of water, the variety of fish, variety of types of fishing, lack of speedboat traffic, and convenience in being able to reach good fishing areas quickly—all these factors enter into my enjoyment of fishing. All the waters I am listing feature these characteristics in addition to being consistently good fish-producers.

My favorite fishing spot is Minaki Lodge on the Winnipeg River, about twenty-five miles northwest of Kenora, Ontario. The Winnipeg in this area has a large variety and quantity of fish. There are great numbers of smallmouth bass, northern pike, walleye, crappie, perch, and rock bass. There is also a fair number of muskie in the area.

I especially enjoy the fly rod popping bug fishing for smallmouth bass, which is unsurpassed in the Winnipeg the last two weeks of June. Fly rod streamer fishing for northern pike can be great at times. Good fly fishing is only a couple of minutes by boat from the dock.

It is excellent spoonplugging water and, when the fish are deep, working a Spoonplug at the drop-offs is deadly. Underwater structure throughout the area is very good and consistently produces.

Crappie, rock bass, large yellow perch, as well as walleye, are excellent targets for ultra-light spinning tackle, using small jigs.

It is easy to get away from all boat traffic at Minaki so you can enjoy complete solitude while also enjoying the beautiful natural surroundings characteristic of Ontario.

The best time of year to fish this area is during the last three weeks of June when the smallmouth bass are almost sure to be in the shallows. All other species will also be readily available at

that time. A second choice of fishing time would be late August and early September.

A midwestern lake that I especially enjoy fishing is Crab Orchard, located near Carbondale, Illinois. There are other lakes that contain more largemouth bass and have more lunkers, but Crab Orchard has enough. It also contains a large population of white bass.

I like Crab Orchard because it is a great spoonplugging lake with clean underwater structures that are ideal to fish. Good casting positions are plentiful and the many rip-rap areas along the dam and highways provide very enjoyable small lure and light tackle fishing. Water color is on the dingy side, making it possible to score well on the lake even after a cold front passes through.

Though I haven't done any camping at Crab Orchard, there are beautiful camp grounds and picnicking areas on the shores surrounding the lake. Because it is a state park there aren't any real estate developments around the lake to detract from the natural beauty of the area. Speedboat traffic is very light.

My favorite time to fish Crab Orchard is from the middle of September to the middle of October. A second choice would be the month of June.

Lake Pepin, one of my all-time favorite fishing spots, is actually part of the Mississippi River and is located at Lake City, Minnesota. The scenery along the river is very picturesque, with Mississippi river barges part of the scene at times. Speedboat traffic is practically nil.

Lake Pepin has a good variety of fish including largemouth bass, smallmouth bass, northern pike, walleye, white bass, channel catfish, and fresh water drum—all of which readily strike an artificial lure. The size of the northern pike, walleye, and white bass caught are above average.

All types of fishing from fly fishing to plug-casting are productive here. It is a very good spoonplugging lake too, with a clean rock and sand bottom, with great underwater structure everywhere. Various types of water from swift-flowing to calm can be fished only minutes apart.

Fishing is exceptional during May but remains good all through the summer months with August a prime time for schooling white bass and good migrations of smallmouth bass. October can also be excellent though a little inconsistent.

The James River Arm of Table Rock Reservoir in Missouri is a great favorite of mine for a number of reasons.

Many of the large reservoirs in Missouri and Arkansas are quite deep with water so clear that fishing conditions have to be ideal for a fisherman to do well on them. The James River Arm on Table Rock, however, is an exception.

The upper end of the James River Arm has fairly dingy water and, with maximum depth of the water only fifty feet in this area, good movements of bass out of the deep sanctuaries are frequent. There is excellent underwater structure in this area and, in direct contrast to most of the reservoirs in the Ozarks, the structures are relatively free of brush and other hangs.

There is an abundant supply of largemouth bass here, along with Kentucky bass, white bass, and crappie. Types of fishing are as varied as you could wish for with deep, timbered coves and rocky shores providing fine casting areas. There is swift water stream fishing at the extreme upper end of this section where the James River enters the lake.

Then it finally hit me, I was not asked to name five good fishing holes, nor where I felt the best catches could be made. I was asked, rather, to name *my* five *favorite* fishing spots.

Over the years many fishermen have asked me; "Where do

you find the best fishing?" My standard answer has been: "Wherever I happen to be fishing."

As I write this, however, I don't seem to remember a lake in terms of all the lunker fish I caught from it. I seem inclined, instead, to dwell on other aspects of fishing I experienced there; feelings that are warm, and leave me with a desire to go fishing there again.

In naming my favorite fishing spots, my choice is colored by water traffic, water skiing, big boats and their non-caring skippers. The affects of water pollution, the take over of shorelines by vacation cottages and weekend homes, all those factors affect my choice of fishing spots, and dampen my desire to return to certain areas.

The five specific waters I have chosen as favorite spots could not be classified as ones holding more favor than others, but they represent waters that I would be happy to spend my last fishing days upon.

Santee-Cooper Reservoir, in South Carolina, is one of my choice spots. The double lake system there, with it's many water colors, the mass of different underwater structures, the choice of working the rip-rap of the long dam, the big, clean underwater structures of the lower lake to the moving waters of the canal, the remote forest areas of the upper impoundment, and the quality and quantity of bass and land-locked striped bass, plus year-round fishing—all these are qualities I enjoy.

I could spend many a happy day on Florida's Lake Panasoffkee. This is a shallow lake, with a mucky bottom, and one that most people would consider a panfish lake. But much of the appeal to me in fishing Panasoffkee is the warmness of a winter day there, the absence of churning waters from passing speedboaters, and the variety of waters and the challenges they create. The grunt of a 'gator, the silent stare of a water snake, and the flapping wings of birds all are ingredients that add interest.

The mass of fish found in the clear-water springs of the back areas of the lake are undisturbed by civilization. A short drainage canal leading to the Withlacoochee River provides fishing waters unbelievably wild. All of this, coupled with bass—my favorite fish, which can be had in numbers and size, on any desired presentation from fly rod and popping bugs to soaking a shiner, and all in a jungle-like setting.

The great challenges and pleasures of the TVA system lakes would have to be a second choice for me. Kentucky Lake, huge and containing a variety of fighting fish for both winter and summer fishing, provides peaceful and satisfying fishing. The headwaters of Pickwick Reservoir, the area below Muscles Shoals, are great. From the swift waters below the dam, to the quite waters of upper Pickwick, there are record smallmouth bass, lunker largemouth, jumping Kentuckies, shad, big white bass, walleyes and sauger, and channel cats. A real day of fishing would be in store for anyone there.

The Mississippi River would have to be named as one of my favorite fishing spots. As I think of the river, from it's beginning in northern Minnesota to its passage through the marshes of Louisiana, I would pause at Lake Pepin at Lake City, in southern Minnesota. The great white bass and walleye run there in early May, and from the wing dam, near Red Wing, Minnesota down to the mouth of the Chippewa River, would supply smallmouth, great northern pike, and sauger that would indeed gladden any fishermen's heart. Farther down this great river are the old river channels and sloughs of the lower Mississippi. The best time here is in the early fall after the high waters of spring and summer have receded. A day on one of these so-called "cut-offs" could be described as one of peace and contentment.

An excellent Mississippi area is the Tunica Cut-off at Tunica, Mississippi. I would pass up the great early spring crappie fishing when the ole Mississippi was flowing through at the highwater stage, and would wait for the water to drop and a sixteen-mile area of the old channel was completely isolated from the river. I suspect this area would provide the finest bass fishing to be found anywhere. I'd pass beyond the levee, through the jungles to the isolation of the cut-off.

Here boat facilities are excellent and the courtesy of the people unmatched anywhere in this country. The scenery is the same as that seen by captains of the old stern–wheelers that plied these waters so many years ago. Here you can watch wild turkeys and deer as they come down to drink, and listen to the bark of an excited fox squirrel. I like to grab again for a bass as he jumped into the boat when crowded close on a trolling pass.

My next choice fishing spot would be in the great basin of the Southwest. Salton Sea, in southern California, is it. I could be assured that fishing there in late spring or early summer would give as big a thrill as fishing can produce. Set in the desert with snow-covered peaks in the background for a great part of the year, this huge body of water sets far below sea level. It is full of lunker Corvina—twenty pounds or better, which become suckers for the skills of a bass fisherman. These fish were introduced years ago from the Gulf of Mexico, and are one of the finest-eating fish to be found anywhere, in my opinion. Facilities are great all over the Salton Sea area, but my preference is the west shore. Desert Shores, a resort, is located near great a underwater structure that can provide a limit catch. You ain't lived until you've tied into a school of these lunker corvina.

Spring and fall in the Ozarks not only provide the finest fishing but also the best of scenery. Dogwood blossoms in the spring and the changing colors of the trees in the fall make this area an unusually attractive place to fish.

My favorite time to fish the James River Arm of Table Rock Reservoir is the last two weeks of April, with the last two weeks of October a close second choice.

I will include Lake Wisconsin, on the Wisconsin River flowage, among my favorite fishing spots although I seldom fish it anymore.

Lake Wisconsin is the best lake for large walleyes that I have ever fished. Over the years this lake has consistently produced limit catches of walleyes over seven pounds with many fish of ten pounds and up caught each year. The lake is easy to fish with good structure and dark, cypress-type water that encourages fairly shallow migrations of fish.

In addition to the large population of walleyes in Lake Wisconsin, it also has some largemouth bass and northern pike. Occasionally a few muskies are caught. Large white bass, bluegills, and crappie are plentiful, too.

Lake Wisconsin is a pretty lake to fish and speedboat traffic is light. The best time to fish it is May 15 to August 1. October can be very good but the fishing then is not consistent.

Water pollution, which plagues so many of our fresh water lakes and streams, has become a problem at Lake Wisconsin. I no longer like to keep any of the fish that I catch from its waters. As a result I don't fish Lake Wisconsin as often as I used to, and instead, I've been concentrating on my favorite bass lakes. The walleye is a great table fish but certainly rates poorly compared to a large mouth or smallmouth bass for fighting qualities. However, if you want to catch some truly lunker walleyes, I know of no other body of water where your chances are as good as they are on Lake Wisconsin.

6

Big Game Fishing Guide

The productivity of big-game fishing areas can change drastically year-to-year. Here's the latest report on the world's outstanding deep-water angling grounds.

SALINAS, ECUADOR: This is not the world's cleanest town, but it has friendly people. Striped marlin off this port average 150 pounds, but there are some going over 200. Black marlin to 575 pounds are available, along with occasional Pacific sailfish. Sails are never abundant, but they are *large* . . . averaging 140 pounds, and some have been taken commercially that weighed 250 pounds!

The best time for striped marlin is November to April, but good numbers of fish are here year-around. The black marlin start arriving in mid-April and are plentiful through June. Sailfishing is best April through June.

Fishermen can live like kings in Salinas on $25 a day.

For reservations and details write: Knud Holst, Pesca Tours, Box 487, Guayaquil, Ecuador.

VENEZUELA: Without doubt this is one of the world's *best* white marlin spots. Fishing is best out of La Guaira, and top season is July through September.

Blue marlin averaging 225 pounds are present in these waters year-around. Broadbill swordfish are caught frequently off La Blanquilla. How good is the fishing off Caracas? Last season a party aboard a cruiser owned by Dr. Ruben Jaen, of Caracas, boated *23 white marlin in a single day!* Best time for white marlin out of this port is August-September, and blue marlin fishing seems to peak in December.

A typical Venezuelan fishing tour covers seven days and six nights, plus all transfers to and from hotels, any domestic air fare, a double room with bath, meals, and the charter boat (3 days) for about $350 per person (minimum of two). There are excellent boats with good captains and mates available.

The Macuto-Sheraton Hotel, in Caracas, offers excellent accommodations and good food, but mighty aggravating service. Details: From Viasa Airlines, Caracas.

BAZARUTO ISLAND, MOZAMBIQUE: Now a spanking new fishing area, this is probably *the* best place for giant black marlin *today*. Marlin between 600-800 pounds are fairly common and already at least one has been taken that weighed over 1,000 pounds. All existing East African black and blue marlin records were scored here. The best fishing period is September to mid-December, and the peak month usually is October.

Sailfish running 80-100 pounds are common in the area, as are varieties of tuna. There is great sports fishing potential at Mozambique, but it is badly undeveloped thus far. There are 12 charter boats at this writing,

A typical day's marlin catch off Mozambique. Fish at left weighed 885 pounds.

Fishing off Columbia is untapped, offers spectacular sailfish angling.

ranging good to bad, and available for $50-$100 per day.

The Santa Carolina Hotel, on Bazaruto, is fairly comfortable, and rates are $14-$20 per person daily, with meals included.

PARADISE ISLANDS, MOZAMBIQUE: Chicagoan Jim Chapralis, a well-traveled sportsman and travel agent, feels this area offers the world's best in black marlin fishing. "It is my opinion that the waters of Mozambique offer the best possibility for huge black marlin," he said. "This is based on the fact that the area offshore of Cabo Blanco, Peru, has not made a good recovery from the days when thousand pound marlin were taken there regularly."

For years, he added, Rhodesian and South African anglers have been enjoying great sport with big Mozambique black marlins.

The largest black marlin registered thus far out of Paradise Islands was a lunker of 1,800 pounds. It was finally boated in violation of International Game Fish Association rules, however, so was not eligible for record status.

Best months to fish Paradise Islands area are September, October, and November. Marlin are caught year-around here, but seem most plentiful in the months indicated. Striped marlin, sailfish, and occasional blue marlin also are taken.

There's a very comfortable hotel on Santa Carolina Island, one of the Paradise chain. The hotel has nine big-game fishing cruisers, and entre to three others. However, all of them are only fair . . . slow but dependable. Each has fighting chairs and a "gin pole." Getting boat reservations is most difficult, however.

Additional information on Paradise Islands big-game fishing can be obtained from Jim Chapralis, Safari Outfitters, 8 South Michigan Avenue, Chicago, Illinois, 60603.

CABO BLANCO, PERU: Once famous for 1,000-pound plus black marlin, Cabo Blanco fishing is virtually finished today, mostly due to changes in current, but for other reasons, too. Hopefully good fishing may return here. Meanwhile, if you want big blacks, go elsewhere.

PUNTA CARNERO, ECUADOR: November-May period is best for fine striped marlin fishing. May-August period is the best time for black marlin. Blacks to 1,440 pounds have been taken here. And dolphin fishing, incidentally, is superb.

The plush new Carnero Inn offers a five-day angling "package"—6 nights, 5 days of fishing, all meals, and double occupancy, for only $495. A charter fleet of 10 sportsfishermen operates out of Carnero Inn.

MAZATLAN, MEXICO: There are more billfish boated here annually than anywhere else on earth—due to heavy fishing pressure and an excellent fish population. About 5,000 sailfish and marlin are caught yearly out of Mazatlan. Striped marlin come in around November and stay through April, with the top months being January, February, and March. Four to 6 hook-ups with striped marlin can be common on a good day.

Sailfish are present from April through November. Summer fishing is best, with hooking 10 sails daily not unusual. For best of black marlin and Pacific blue marlin, try to fish in July and August.

Curious seals cavort around fishermen working waters off Guaymas.

Excellent accommodations here. The Hotel Playa offers 2 meals daily for about $10 (double occupancy). Fishing trips can be easily arranged there. Two anglers sharing boat and hotel room can fish for about $40 each per day at the peak of the winter season, and for around $32 per day each in summer. The charter boats provide all tackle and bait. For full details contact Aviles Brothers, P.O. Box 224, Mazatlan, Sinaloa, Mexico.

Another of many excellent hotels in Mazatlan is the Hotel De Cima, Mazatlan, Sinaloa, Mexico.

GUAYMAS, MEXICO: This is a very good summer spot for Pacific sailfish and dolphin. But it is not too much in the winter, except for the many Pacific yellowtails in the 20-pound class. Charter boats only fair, but there are several available.

Guaymas is an interesting town, featuring scenic countryside, fine winter weather, and superb accommodations and food.

With the arrival of new sport fishing cruisers at a recently established marina on Cozumel Island, Mexico, some really fast sailfishing and marlin fishing has become available. Previously only inadequate native craft and guides were on hand.

For complete details contact Raul Gonzales, Hotel Cabanas Del Caribe, Quintana Roo, Isla de Cozumel, Mexico.

NEW ZEALAND: Mayor Island, off New Zealand's North Island and the focal point of New Zealand's deep-sea fishing, offers black, striped, and Pacific blue marlin, plus broadbill swordfish and mako sharks. There may be faster fishing at some other big-game fishing areas, but the average fish here run very large. The average striped marlin for example, will be over 200 pounds, and the New Zealand record is 465 pounds! Many black marlin weighing upwards of 700 pounds have been taken in these waters, and a Pacific blue marlin of over 1,000 pounds was caught here.

The best months are January through May. The available charter boats are generally very good and rates are about $70-$100 per day. Many fishermen headquarter at Tauranga, New Zealand.

The Mayor Island Fishing Club, on Mayor Island, offers a very good deal. Its special rates are: boats, $50-$90 a day, room-meals, $12-$16 per day per person. Write to the Hunting and Fishing Office, P.O. Box 527, Rotorua, New Zealand.

CONCEPTION BAY, NOTRE DAME BAY, NEWFOUNDLAND: These are two of the world's

Pacific yellowtails in 20-pound class are "incidental" catches at Guaymas, Mexico.

Good boats, skippers are available for Venezuela fishing.

top spots for bluefin tuna, although the newer Notre Dame Bay fishery is easily the best. Most of the fish go well over 400 pounds! The best sport is in August and September, but some bluefins are caught in late July and in early October.

Charter boats run about $100 per day, and the fish caught are generally considered to be the property of the boat captains. Accommodations are good at St. Johns. Try the Holiday Inn.

BAJA CALIFORNIA: The angling is excellent here for Pacific sailfish, and marlin. June through September is the best time for marlin and sailfish. Good charter boats and guides are the rule. With bait included, rates are around $70-$90 daily.

Cabo San Lucas has fine resorts catering to fishermen, such as the swank hotels, Cabo San Lucas and Hotel Pamilla. Rates are about $26 per day with meals.

South of La Paz there's very good striped marlin fishing from March through July, and good sailfishing from July to November, particularly out of Rancho Bueno Vista Lodge. Rancho Lodge is not too plush but it is more than adequate and it's clean. Boats run $60-$65 per day. Figure $20 per day, per person, for room and meals. Write Rancho Buena Vista Lodge, Buena Vista, Baja California Sur, Mexico, or their American agent, Charles Walters, P.O. Box 1486, Newport Beach, California, telephone (714) OR 3-4638.

PINAS BAY, PANAMA: This has to be one of the world's best spots for black marlin and Pacific sailfish, plus dolphin, roosterfish, and other species. Black marlin are plentiful from winter through spring but they are smallish, ranging 200-300 pounds on the average. Here a 500 pound fish is considered quite large.

Striped marlin are here in fair quantities beginning in early April. Pacific sailfish are present year-around and in amazing quantities. An experienced angler may at times hook and release 10 or 15 sails in a single day.

The only accommodations available are at Tropic Star Lodge, which was formerly the Club de Pesca de Panama, founded by the late Ray Smith, a Texas oilman and trucking magnate. Rates at last report were $1,095 per person (double occupancy), for a week-long package trip from Panama City. That includes everything—boat, guide, round-trip flight from Panama City to lodge, but there is a $30 additional charge if club tackle is used, which is normal.

For details and reservations contact: Tropic Star Lodge, c/o International Inn, 1808 Wellington Avenue, Winnipeg, Manitoba.

HAWAII: The Kona Coast of Hawaii is *the* place today for giant Pacific blue marlin, fish that may exceed 1,000 pounds. These giants are scarce, however, and even when found they are not easily taken.

Large dolphin, yellowfin tuna, wahoo and other good

game species are regularly available and in all seasons.

There are varying accommodations, from the ordinary to the super swank, and, of course, prices reflect quality. Kona Inn and the King Kamehameha Hotel seem to be favored by the majority of visiting anglers. Hotels here will arrange fishing charters, and prices range $85-$125 per day.

COSTA RICA: Prospects appear excellent in this Central American republic for offshore blue-water fishing (white marlin, Atlantic sailfish, wahoo, dolphin, etc.), but no ocean cruisers are yet available at Casa Mar or Parismina fishing camps on the east coast. Fishing at both camps now is primarily for giant tarpon (100-pound class) and big snook. The best time for all fishing, normally, is from mid-January to mid-May.

Rates: Parismina—$50 per person daily, all included; Casa Mar—set up for 5 days fishing, 6 men, $1,500. Details: Carlos Barrantes, P.O. Box 2816, San Jose, Costa Rica, C.A.

Costa Rica's excellent fishing is well known, but until recently, accommodations there for visiting fishermen were practically nil. Things are changing, however. The Casa Mar houseboat (Casa Mar Fishing Club, Ltd.) began operations along Costa Rica's Pacific Coast not long ago. This is a 43 foot deluxe, fiberglass houseboat powered by twin Diesel engines and it has a range of 375 miles. There's air conditioning, lighting, refrigerator— all conveniences—plus skiffs with new Johnson outboards. Winter through spring the boat operates near Puerto Cortes, fishing around the Terraba and Sierpe Rivers and Isla del Cano. Summer through fall the boat will locate in the Papagayo area, near the Costa Rica-Nicaraguan border.

The important fishing here is for snook, roosterfish, dolphin, wahoo, Pacific sailfish, corvina, snapper, grouper and various other reef fishes. Five-day bookings are requested, 2 couples preferred or 6 men. Total cost, $1,500 for each 5 day period, to be shared by all guests. Bookings can be made through Jim Chapralis, Safari Outfitters, Inc., 8 South Michigan Avenue, Chicago, Illinois, 60603.

Costa Rica has still another new fishing lodge. It's Blue River Lodge, operated by Jerry Thornhill of Texas.

The lodge, which consists of a main building and three cabins, will accommodate a total of 12 persons. It is located on the Pacific Coast near the Rio Grande de Terraba River.

The rates aren't fixed definitely but are expected to be about $30 per person daily for room and board, and about $50 daily (2 persons) for fishing skiff, outboard motor, and guide. A 6-day fishing trip is the normal plan.

LACSA Airlines flies from Miami to San Jose, Costa Rica. Flight details can be procured from LACSA, 238 Biscayne Boulevard, Miami, Florida. Full details on the camp and fishing can be had by writing Blue River Lodge, Inc., Apartado 2469, San Jose, Costa Rica, C.A.

The fishing there is primarily for snook (trophy size), various snappers, corvina, machaca, and guapote. The last two are excellent fresh water gamefish.

COLUMBIA: There is untapped fishing potential here, yet there are modern comforts. The best fishing areas are around Barranquilla and Santa Marta. Excellent sailfish, tarpon, snook, barracuda, and kingfish. Mid-December to mid-May is the best period. An all-expense, 8-day trip—Miami to Columbia and back—hotels, meals, boats, transportation, airline tickets included, can be arranged for about $800 for each person. For details write; Hal G. Hoham, P.O. Box 228, Auburn, Indiana, 46706, telephone (219) 925-3400.

AUSTRALIA: New South Wales. South coast fishing is the thing, about 250 miles south of Sydney. Headquarter at the towns of Bermagui, Bega, Merimbula, or Eden. There is excellent deep sea fishing in this section for striped marlin, swordfish, tuna, and very large sharks. North coast fishing 500 miles north of Sydney is good. Headquarter at the towns of Byron Bay or Tweed Heads. Really fine deep sea fishing around here.

Queensland. Here's the Great Barrier Reef, running offshore from Gladstone for 1,000 miles north to Cooktown. Some of the many good places to headquarter are Rockhampton, Mackay, Townsville, and Cairns. Giant black marlin over 1,000 pounds have been taken out of Cairns, as well as trophy class Pacific blue marlin. September, October, November are the best months, but

Baja California offers hundreds of miles of productive, big-game fishing grounds.

Black marlin in Pinas Bay, Panama struggles at boatside.

even then much patience is required since strikes from these deep-water monsters do not come frequently. Boats around Cairns run $100-$125 per day per party, and they are scarce.

South Australia. Giant sharks and snapper are the targets here. Main centers are Port Lincoln (a one hour flight from Adelaide), Streaky Bay, and Ceduna on Eyre Peninsula. Seven-day game fishing cruises operate from Port Adelaide, starting on Fridays at 7:00 P.M., $90 per person, everything included. Details: South Australian Government Tourist Bureau, Adelaide.

Typical lodging costs over most of Australia: a motel room with private shower, toilet, breakfast, $4 per person; hotel, 1st class, private shower, toilet, all meals, $6.50 per person; guest house, room with no facilities, all meals, $3 per person; country hotel, room with facilities, all meals, $5 per person.

BRITISH HONDURAS: Bill Haerr's Turneffe Islands Lodge (off the coast of British Honduras) advertises great salt water fishing and other features, including a "chip and putt" nine hole golf course. If you're a serious golfer, forget the golf course. It's a farce—just some holes dug and golf flag poles stuck in grassy surroundings.

The fishing, however, is superb. Most anglers work on the bonefish, which are smallish, but some tarpon are available, as well as barracuda, snook, various reef fishes and, offshore, white marlin, wahoo, and Atlantic sailfish.

Accommodations, boats, guides, etc. are excellent. For details write Bill Haerr, Turneffe Islands Lodge, Post Office, Belize, British Honduras, C.A.

BAY ISLANDS, HONDURAS: Possibly the newest fishing lodge in the Caribbean is the "Reef House," built by veteran American skipper-yachtsman, Capt. Bill Kepler, at Roatan, in the scenic Bay Islands group off the coast of Honduras. Roatan is about 30 miles offshore and is the center of a beautiful and undeveloped chain of islands.

Fishing around the islands is excellent for both light tackle and deep sea anglers. Kepler's operation is the first of its kind in this area.

Reef House is a new, screened building with modern plumbing, refrigeration, and good water. Four guests, 2 per room, can be accommodated.

The fishing craft available include a 52-foot offshore cruiser with twin Deisel engines, outriggers, etc., and there is room for a party of four to live aboard. At Reef House there are three 16-foot fiberglass skiffs with 20 h.p. outboards.

The chief fishing through the winter season, deep sea, is for white and blue marlin, Atlantic sailfish, kingfish, wahoo, and the usual reef fishes such as snappers, grouper, and amberjack. Inshore there is excellent bonefishing but the fish are on the small side, and there is sport with various jacks and barracuda, available.

A 3-day fishing package, all included, costs about $225 per person. The "extra day" rate is $50 per day per person. Air fare, via TAN, Miami to San Pedro Sula, Honduras, thence to Bay Islands, is about $155 round trip. Details: Capt. Bill Kepler, Oak Ridge Harbor, Roatan Island, Honduras, C.A.

Tarpon are available year-round in Honduras.

7

Best Ways to Bug Bass

By Bob McNally

Fly rod poppers are deadly on bass, but there are right and wrong ways of fishing them.

Bass bugs are most effective when fished in shallow, clear water, provided the bass are there.

If I had to choose one outfit for all of my bass fishing, it would be a fly rod and popping bugs. No other way of fishing catches more bass when the fish are shallow, and no other way of fishing provides more fun.

Popping bugs have taken bass for me from Florida's Lake Okeechobee to Ontario's Rainy Lake, and from Arizona's Lake Havasu to the ponds on Maryland's Eastern Shore. Having a wide-ranging outdoor writer for a dad (Tom McNally), I've been lucky enough since boyhood to fish a lot of places, and in the process I've learned there's no bass water where, at least some of the time, bass cannot be taken on bugs!

Many anglers don't realize just how deadly fly fishing with popping bugs is. For example, I remember a day some years ago, on Wisconsin's Lake Geneva, when I fished with the late Bart Mullins of Fox Lake, Illinois. As we loaded our fly tackle into a boat two fishermen outboarded up to the dock. One stepped out of the boat carrying a stringer holding four nice smallmouths. He was grinning like a Cheshire cat.

"Very nice!" I said. "What'd you catch 'em on?"

"Crayfish," he said proudly. "Spinning with crayfish. That's the *only* way to catch bass."

There's no denying spinning with crayfish, particularly the softshell variety, is an effective way of taking a few smallmouths. But Bart and I stuck to fly rod bugs that day, and between us we boated and released thirty-seven bass. They ranged from one-half to two and a half pounds on the average, although Bart got one beauty close to four pounds.

Fly rod poppers are killers, and there's something about them bass can't resist! Bass of all sizes hate bugs so much they'll knock the paint off them and tear up their hackles. I've taken quite a few largemouths over seven pounds on fly rod poppers, and smallmouths to six and a half pounds. *And I've seen days when a party of bug fishermen caught and released more than one hundred bass!!*

Bass bug fishing originated in America. In 1700 Florida's Seminole Indians were using deer-hair bugs to take largemouths, and in 1925 Joe Messinger developed the first hair frog—a bug still popular and productive today. Early outdoor writers turned out many stories promoting bug fishing—poppers have long received plenty of publicity. Yet each season millions of fishermen go blissfully along casting spoons, spinners, jigs, and plugs never pausing long enough to learn about and try bugs.

There are many reasons for the effectiveness of bass bugs. For one, bass quickly notice the loud surface popping commotion they make. (In clear water I've seen bass come fifty feet to a popper, drawn by its sputtering and splashing.) And bugs are light, hitting the water softly. They don't scare fish. A dragonfly, grasshopper or frog—all are small, light, and when hurt, struggle weakly over the surface. Thus artificial bugs readily imitate natural baits. On the other hand, a large, heavy lure, while it takes bass, cannot imitate real bug life.

I think a lot of the "fish-getting-appeal" of bugs is due to their lifelike action, too. Owing to their light, high-floating qualities, an angler can do things with poppers that will "bug" the shrewdest bass. Bugs talk a language bass understand.

It's worth noting too, that the bass bug fisherman

Hook points on bass bugs should be kept sharp as possible. Honing of points with a fine file or stone ensures fewer missed strikes.

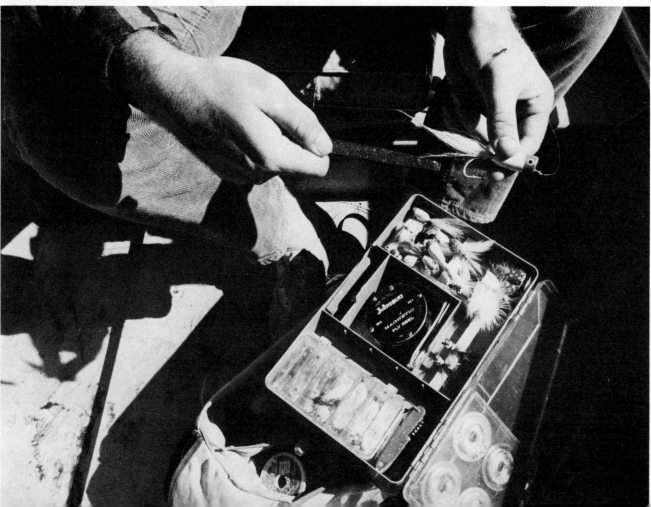

doesn't need a closet full of tackle. All he needs is a good rod, reel, line, leaders and bugs. The bugging rod should be eight to nine and a half feet long, weighing around five ounces, and of "heavy" action. The line should be torpedo tapered, size WF8-F (GBF) or WF-9F (GAF). Leaders should be at least nine feet, tapered to six to ten pound tippets.

Most experienced bass bug fishermen, prefer single-action reels, primarily because they are light and have interchangeable spools. With an extra spool and line, you can quickly switch to a fresh line in mid-day, after several hours of fishing have caused your first line to sink.

The bugging artist's most important piece of equipment, however, is his bugs. Well-designed commercial bugs are hard to find, so most experienced bug fishermen make their own. Making poppers is easy. You can buy pre-shaped cork bodies, as well as long-shank hooks and other necessary materials from tackle shops or fly-tyer supply houses.

A good bug has a cork body mounted on a hook long enough to easily hook striking bass. The cork faces of bugs should be flat or slanted upwards and out so that the bugs pick up easily on long casts yet "pop" well. A good bug will have no unnecessary hair or feathers, since too much hackling or bucktail causes extra wind resistance and makes a bug difficult to cast. Always hone bug hook points to needlelike sharpness, and strike hard and quickly when a bass hits.

I never use weedless bugs. Most of them are not only weedless but are "bassless" as well. Their hooks are so well protected with wire or heavy nylon that it's almost impossible to hook a bass with them.

Most bug fishermen aren't much concerned about the color of their bugs. But some fishermen prefer yellow, green, white, black, or brown poppers. And some bass bug enthusiasts merely coat their poppers with clear varnish, and they take a lot of fish on them, too.

My favorite bass bug is a cork-bodied frog. It's mounted on a size 1/0 or 2/0 (3X long) hump-shank hook. In making it I'm careful to mount the hook at a downward angle. It's length and downward slant guarantee that I'll hook most of the bass that strike.

I fit pieces of matchsticks into this bug's cork body to form "eyes," and the frog's "legs" are made from bunches of green bucktail. The body is painted green, with small yellow and black spots dabbed on, and I finish it with a white belly.

Most of the time I work the frog slowly by letting it "rest" for a few seconds after it hits the water, then I raise the rod tip to make the bug "pop" gently. Next I let the frog sit motionless while its legs flutter. Finally, I pop it in steadily, just fast enough to make its legs open and close.

My father originated this green frog popper more than twenty years ago, and in that time it has probably accounted for more bass for the two of us than any other single fly rod lure. Bugs exactly like the green frog we use are tied commercially by Jim Poulos of Wheeling, Illinois but most fly-tyers will find such frogs easy to make.

Bass bug fishermen who don't make their own bugs probably can shop around and find some commercially-made frog poppers that are good. Just be sure to get ones

Fishing an Illinois pond, author Bob McNally selects a bass bug.

with long-shank hooks, and whose legs will have action and plenty of "flutter" on the water.

Another of my favorite poppers is a simple, easy to tie, yellow bug. It also is tied on a 1/0 or 2/0 (3X long) hook. Its yellow hackles are mounted in an outward fashion so they "breathe" in the water. The wiggling action of the bug's hackles makes the bug look alive. There are no extra frills or "dressing" on this bug, so it casts like a charm.

I usually cast this bug out and "rest" it, then pop it by raising the rod tip with a swift, jerking motion. Next I yank the bug over the top of the water for about a yard. This is done by pointing the rod at the bug and stripping in line. This makes the bug skitter and bounce over the surface—much like a wounded minnow.

When a bug falls to the water near a bass, the fish swims off a few feet and watches it with hungry curiosity. While the bug lies motionless the bass builds up enough courage to swim back under the bug for a closer look. So now you lift your rod gently, and lightly "pop" the bug. KAPOW . . . the bass hits fast and hard!

That's the way 75 percent of bass take bugs . . . but for the other 25 percent you need a different kind of retrieve to get them to hit.

One day Tim Host of Stevens Point, Wisconsin, and I were fishing a small pond near Tim's home. The pond was full of weed beds and over-hanging willow trees. Tim was working one of my yellow poppers as we entered a small bay. A huge log, half in, half out of the water, lay at one end of the bay. The spot looked bassy, so Tim cast his bug to the log a half-a-dozen times, fishing it back with slow, gentle "pops" but with no results.

"Sputter it!" I said. "Fish it fast, and see if you can make any bass in there get mad!"

McNally makes a cast, gets a strike, hooks a fish, and, moments later . . .

Tim made a perfect cast to the log, got that popper dancing on its hackles right away, and *that quick* a bass swatted the bug. A few minutes later Tim released a plump two-pounder.

The fast, skipping retrieve frequently works bass into a frenzy. Many times when other methods failed I just skittered a bug across the surface and had better action right away.

Bill Gallasch, a Richmond, Virginia fly-tyer, makes a bug he calls the "Skipping Bug," which he designed for a fast, scooting retrieve. I fish it very fast, with a jerking, hopping, erratic action, and often I've caught bass that way after having fished a spot with a conventional, slow retrieve and getting nothing.

Bill's "Skipping Bug," fished with a fast retrieve, can be especially effective on windy days when bass seem to have a tough time spotting bugs on the surface. I also use the "Skipping Bug" a lot in the fall when bass prefer a fast-moving bug.

Many fly fishermen don't realize it, but big salt water bugs are great for good-size largemouths, and small-mouths too. Big bass want a big mouthful, and these bugs take a lot of bass from three pounds up.

Normally I fish these large bugs fairly fast, so they look like a wounded, flopping, darting minnow. I strip the line in with two to three foot hauls, and at times a flat water bug worked this way will stir bass up so much two or three will chase the bug at one time.

Most bugs designed for salt water fishing are three or four inches long, and mounted on ²/o or ³/o long-shank hooks. Those colored white, black, blue, and yellow, with bucktail or saddle hackles for tailing, are good. Because of their great size and wind resistance, salt water poppers can be difficult to cast, and as a rule only an experienced fly caster can handle them effectively, for long hours of fishing, without fatigue. But it pays to learn to use these salt water poppers, and to be able to get one out there *fast* whenever you're thinking of *big* bass!

My favorite bug for snag-filled, weedy water is an oversized, bushy, hairy thing my father stumbled onto years ago. It's a deer hair bug that's completely weedless, yet I don't miss bass strikes with it. It's especially productive when bass are in extremely shallow, weedy areas.

The bug resembles a bivisible dry fly, and it's tied on a short-shank ²/o hook. It's made with bunches of deer hair flaring out all over the hook, and these scraggly, untrimmed hairs make it possible to crawl the bug over weeds and brush without fouling. Yet when a bass hits this deer hair bug he "chomps" down on soft hairs and the hook's barb finds its mark.

This bug casts easily, and its weedless qualities make it the fly-rodder's answer to such places as the "hay fields" of Lake Okeechobee, in Florida. There the bass are in "flats" that look like flooded wheat fields, and unless you can get a lure or bug in there where the fish are you might as well go home. In other great bass areas, such as Back Bay, Virginia and Currituck Sound, North Carolina, weeds can spoil a day's fishing unless you've got weed-proof deer hair bugs.

Once Steve Gentry, of Golf, Illinois and I were fishing for bass at Bull Valley Lake, in northern Illinois. The muskrat grass was so thick we could hardly row the boat, but there were lots of small holes and openings in the weeds.

We fished slowly, Steve working a regular popper, I a big fluffy deer hair. I'd drop my bug into an open spot and dance it through the grass, and I took several bass that way. But Steve kept hanging up with his regular popper, getting weeds on almost every cast. Finally I convinced him to try a deer hair bug. He dropped it into a pocket, skittered it across the surface, and the lake just parted around that bug as a six and a half-pounder inhaled it!

... admires the plump two-pounder that hit his bug.

That was Steve's best bass of the season.

Another fine bass bug is the Marm Minnow. This is an old, proven bug, used regularly by southern bass fishermen. Fished conventionally, this great bug has taken countless bass for me, that is, just popping it along. But I've taken many more bass with this bug while fishing it in an unorthodox way. I tie three Marm Minnows on my leader, instead of just one, and fish them simultaneously. While three bugs on a single leader are difficult to cast, it nonetheless is worth the effort so far as results are concerned.

I space the bugs six to eight inches apart on my leader, and to bass they look like a small school of minnows when I skip them across the surface. Many times I've had several fish follow my phoney minnow school, and now and then I've even had two or three bass hooked at the same time. Normally I fish this "Marm Minnow school" fast, with an erratic retrieve, because that way it best represents a darting, scooting pod of frightened minnows.

A type of fly rod bug fishing that is also excellent on bass is one similar to the "nodding technique" used in fishing plugs. This kind of bugging might be called fishing with a "dead retrieve." It's particularly effective in the summer or when bass are sluggish and won't hit a bug retrieved normally.

The trick is to fish a bug as slowly as you can. When the bug hits the water let it rest for several minutes, then *lightly* twitch it, let it rest several more minutes, twitch it again . . . and so on. The slower the retrieve the better. It should take *twenty minutes* or longer to "fish out" a single cast!

Once Chris Riley, of Glenview, Illinois and I were fishing Yellowstone Lake in southwestern Wisconsin. By fishing our poppers the usual way along the brushy shoreline, we were able to pick up a bass here-and-there. But Yellowstone is crawling with bass, and I knew we

should have been getting lots more. Finally I made a cast to a log, but just then I kicked over my bug box. I grumbled while Chris laughed, then I put my rod down and started to stuff bugs back into the box. Chris continued fishing, while my bug floated idly out there by the log. Suddenly the lake opened up around my popper and Chris yelled for me to grab the rod. I did, and a few minutes later landed my best bass of the day—a three and a half-pounder.

After that we both used the "dead retrieve," and in two hours we caught twenty-three largemouths, including one by Chris that weighed just over five pounds! That day's fishing proved to me that at times *nothing* is more effective for bass than fly rod poppers fished *slow . . . slow . . . slow . . .* and then *slower.*

Some fishermen cast bugs onto rocks and logs, letting them bounce off the log or rock and onto the water. They claim that bass see the bug bounce off, and so are convinced the bug is a real frog, mouse or some other live creature, and so strike unhesitatingly. So far as I'm concerned, such ideas are nonsense. I find it difficult to believe that a bass lying by a log or rock sees any difference between a bug landing directly on the water, and one hitting the water after bouncing off a log. I doubt that bass very often see bugs flying through the air, so I don't think it makes a bit of difference whether a bug is cast directly beside a log or rock, or cast to hit the log or rock and bounce off. In my opinion, about all you can expect from casting your bugs at rocks and logs is to knock the paint off and dull the bug's hook.

Casting poppers onto lily pads, however, is a different matter. When a bug lands on a big lily pad it makes a *splat,* and the pad moves and puts rings out in the water. This disturbance—both the *splat* of the bug hitting the pad and the movement of the pad—alerts any nearby bass to the fact that *something*—maybe a frog—has landed on the lily pad. The bass hovers nearby, waiting, and when the bug is pulled off the pad he wallops it—*hard!*

Whenever a bass hits your bug but isn't hooked, don't cast back to him immediately. Wait five or ten minutes, and then toss a different bug to the bass, or if you're fishing with a friend who's using a different kind of bug have him cast to the fish. Frequently a bass that hits one bug but isn't hooked won't come back to that same bug, but he'll rise to a different kind of bug. Sometimes, too, an interested bass will rise to a popper but not hit it. You're working your bug along, and suddenly the water humps up near it, there's no strike. You force yourself to "rest" the bug, then twitch it, and again there's a big, heart-stopping swirl. The bass is there all right, and he's plenty excited, but just doesn't strike. Here again, if you offer the fish a different bug, he'll probably hit.

Be careful not to make a hasty, sloppy pick-up of the bug in your rush to change to another, or you'll spook the bass for sure. Fish the first bug back slowly and easily, then make a clean pick-up. And when you change to another bug, be sure to select a completely different one. If you'd been fishing, say, a "Green Frog," then next offer the bass a yellow "Skipping Bug." A complete "change of pace" is frequently needed to put these hard-to-catch bass in the boat.

Many fly rod anglers miss getting bass because they

are afraid to fish some of the best places. For example, they won't toss a bug over a log because they might get hung up, therefore they can't fish for a bass lurking behind a log or some other obstruction. These same fishermen never fish beneath over-hanging limbs because they don't know how to cast under tree limbs, and that's where many large bass lie. Actually, fishing bugs behind logs, rocks, or under tree limbs is quite simple.

It's easy to cast beyond a log, work the bug along, and then jump it right over the log. All you need do is cast your bug into a pocket behind a log, work it normally, then as it nears the log lower your rod tip, take up slack in the line, then jerk the rod tip up with a quick, backward sweep. This will make the bug "jump" or "hop" into the air and over the log.

If you hook a bass after casting over a log or rock, raise your rod high, and try to sweep the bass quickly along the surface and slide him over the obstruction. If you do this fast enough you usually can get the bass over the obstacle and into open water. Of course some bass are lost this way too, but I think it's more fun to hook a bass and lose it than to hook none at all.

When fishing along banks with over-hanging limbs, use

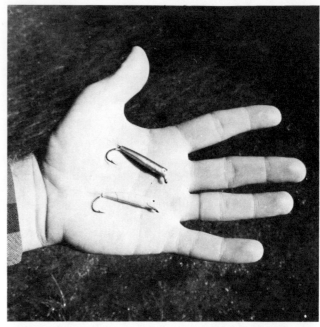

Two unusual but very effective bugs . . . the "Marm Minnows."

One evening's catch of largemouth's from Willow Slough, Indiana . . . all on bugs.

the "tight-bow" cast to get your bug under the limbs. This is an easy cast to execute, but few fishermen know about it.

A "tight bow" cast is one in which the forward cast is made with a very small, or "tight" loop, rather than a wide loop as on a normal cast. To throw a tight loop, and thus get your bug low to the water and up under over-hanging limbs, delay the start of the forward cast as long as possible, then lean forward, bending low at the waist, at the same time pushing forward hard with your rod to start the fly line into the forward cast. Snap the rod tip into the cast, bringing the rod low to the water, and at the same time tug downward on the line with your left hand. Properly delivered, a "tight bow" cast drives a bug a long way yet the fly line will be no more than four of five feet above the water, thus the bug can be "shot" right up under those over-hanging tree limbs. A "tight bow" cast,

incidentally, is also the one to use when casting into a strong wind.

Most bass bug fishermen simply do not give enough attention to lure play. Usually it's best to allow your bug to rest *dead still* after it strikes the water. If the bug moves only two or three inches many bass will ignore it and swim away. Let your bug lie *perfectly motionless* for at least fifteen seconds, then give it a good solid *pop*. Rest it again, *pop* it, then pause. Now give it a series of short, *punchy* "pops" and stop. If a bass still doesn't swat the bug, work it steadily back until it's close enough to pick up for another cast.

After some experience at bass bugging you'll discover you can get more bass on bugs, and often bigger bass, than by fishing other ways. And, finally, there's nothing more exciting than a surface strike—especially when it's a five-pounder slamming into a tiny cork bug.

Perfect bass-bugging water—provided the bass are in the shallows.

8

Hot New Fishing Area

. . . .It's the Louisiana Gulf Coast, where offshore oil rigs
and unusual currents are providing spectacular fishing
anyone can enjoy.

Louisiana's bayou country provides some exceptional largemouth bass fishing. This is in the Thibodaux area.

Board a boat at one of Louisiana's Gulf ports, such as Grand Isle, on any day of the year, which is likely to be a bright and sunny one, go out into the blue Gulf of Mexico, drop a baited hook over—then steady yourself and be prepared for anything.

Out there in the lovely Gulf beyond Louisiana's shores is the Yucatan Current, and a place called Desota Canyon, and they are the cause of some of the wildest "hot" new fishing to be found anywhere. The angler dropping a baited hook over or trolling a lure can reasonably expect to catch anything from wahoo to sailfish, from broadbill swordfish to marlin, and from snappers to bluefish—which is to name just a very few of this ultra new fishing ground's populous species.

Sport fishermen were unaware of the potential of Gulf fishing until the United States Fish and Wildlife Service conducted a survey to determine whether or not Gulf waters might support commercial fishing. The survey showed that the Gulf was, indeed, quite stiff with fish—including such spectaculor gamesters as Allison, bluefin and blackfin tuna, Atlantic sailfish, dolphin, swordfish, Atlantic spearfish, white marlin and, even, blue marlin.

The Desota Canyon is a deep trench in the northeastern part of the Gulf, and the Yucatan Current is a strong, persistent flow that comes into the Gulf from the south, passing between Mexico's Yucatan Peninsula and the western edge of Cuba. Where the Yucatan Current meets the Mississippi Delta flow, part of the current turns eastward and develops a clockwise movement around the DeSota Canyon. The resultant concentration of plankton there attracts small fish, which attract big fish, which attract anglers. Experts now believe that the area will prove to be one of the most productive fisheries in the Western Hemisphere.

The offshore, big-game Gulf fishing is done chiefly by trolling rigged baits, which might be small squid, bluefish, ladyfish, mackerel, or strips of fish flesh. The tackle used is generally heavy—big rods with big reels and a lot of line—and such outfits can be a bit expensive. But the fisherman who doesn't have his own big-game fishing outfit for a Gulf fishing trip needn't worry; complete fishing rigs, baits, etc. are provided by charter boat captains at no extra cost.

A lot of fishing skill isn't needed, either, for a Gulf fishing excursion. The captain or his mate will rig the tackle, put the baits over, then troll in likely areas and keep sharp eyes peeled for fish. When a strike comes, the mate or captain will even hook the fish for beginners who don't know how. Skilled blue-water anglers, however, will insist on hooking, and playing out, their own fish.

As fishing trips go, offshore charter trips into the Gulf can be a bit expensive, running anywhere from around $100 minimum to $140 for a day's fishing. But that price set-up is for a party of four, which brings the per-fisher-

Angling for giant kingfish in the winter months is exceptional out of Louisiana Gulf ports.

Big tarpon frequent Gulf Coast waters but receive little attention from local anglers.

Gulf waters are famous for the fishing at offshore oil rigs.

man rate down to around $25 or $35, and this isn't much for a day's fishing that might result in a 400-pound blue marlin on the dock, plus a couple sailfish and wahoo.

Out beyond Louisiana's Mississippi River passes, beyond Plaquemines Peninsula, beyond Chandeleur Sound and the Chandeleur Islands, is still another kind of special Gulf fishing. It's "fishing the platforms"—the oil rig structures that in recent years have blossomed all over the Gulf, and have created some remarkable angling for many kinds of fish—including the gourmet's delight, the delectable pompano.

When crude oil deposits were discovered lying far below the bottom of the Gulf of Mexico, oil companies built drilling rigs smack out in the open Gulf, in places where the water was 250 feet deep. There always were plenty of fish out in those areas, but as most anglers know, new structure in open water areas attracts and congregates fish. This is what the oil rigs have done. Their pilings, footings, and supports drew minute aquatic life, which in turn attracted small fish, which brought bigger fish. Some of the many kinds of fish to be taken, almost year-around, at these off-shore "platforms" in addition to pompano are bluefish, red-snappers, sea trout, grouper, Spanish mackerel, ladyfish, blue runners, and on occasion, even kingfish and cobia.

Over 2,100 oil structures dot the Gulf from 10 to 50 miles seaward along the coastal shelf, and each one of those platforms is a veritable marina of sport fishes of all kinds.

These oil rigs, and in some cases natural gas drillings, have brought another kind of unusual fishing to the Louisiana coast; it's "flare fishing."

Waste gases are produced from drillings, and since it must be disposed of, burning as it escapes from huge pipes above the surface of the water is about the only practical means of disposal available. The huge "flares" of burning gases can be seen for miles at night, and the flames attract bugs. The insects, warmed by the heat,

New state record kingfish was caught in the winter of '71 by Monty Thrailkill of Minden, La. The big king was taken from Capt. Charles Sebastian's cruiser "Sea Hawk," and weighed 67 pounds, 12 ounces.

Channel bass (redfish) haunt the tidal flats.

The close-in Yucatan Current is a recently discovered billfish grounds.

fall to the water and, naturally, start a food cycle—with small fish feeding on them, larger ones on the small fish, and so on. So good is this "flare fishing" of a night that many Cajun fishermen consider it a mighty bad trip indeed if, on returning to dock, every icebox on board is not filled with good-eating fish.

Visitors to the Pelican State can enjoy "oil rig fishing trips" any time of year, at comparatively small cost. Charter boats at the towns of Grand Isle and Empire make regular trips, with some boats accommodating as many as 15 anglers.

A party of eight persons can share the cost of a day's oil-rig fishing, which averages about $100. Party boats that are certified by the Coast Guard to take more than eight fishermen will cost a bit more, but the per capita charge is less.

Incidentally, there's a unique fact about this "oil rig" fishing—whether by night or by day—that should be noted. This is that fully 90 percent of all the fish caught in the Gulf of Mexico off the Louisiana shoreline are caught within 150 feet of those more than 2,100 oil structures mentioned earlier. Those oil rigs turn out to be, in effect, "fish attractors," just as are brushpiles and log jams in fresh water creeks and lakes.

This fishing is the sort that can appeal to both the novice and expert angler. The novice will enjoy it because, among other things, he needn't even bring tackle; the skipper will provide that, too. If you know nothing about the game but want to go fishing and catch fish, all you need do is pay your money and go on out—it's just that simple.

Now for the serious angler, the sportsman who spends all his free time at fishing, oil rig fishing remains a challenging, interesting sport. Such a fisherman should bring his own tackle, fly, bait-casting, or spinning gear. Fly rods should be on the heavy side, say 9-foot, taking a size GAF (WF-9) line, and mounted on a heavy-duty, single-action reel with a good drag, and with suitable capacity for at least 100 yards of Dacron 18 pound test backing line. Bait-casting outfits should be medium-heavy, with quality reels with good drags filled with 15 or 20 pound test monofilament or braided line. Spinning rods should be stout, 6 to 7½ feet, with 10, 12, or 15 pound test mono line.

9

How to Tie Dry Flies and Nymphs

You'll enjoy fishing even more when your own flies start fooling them.

Fly tying is an angler's most profitable spare-time activity. You can save money by tying flies, and you can build the special patterns you need that are unobtainable at sporting goods stores. But best of all, fly tying shortens long winter evenings, and it imparts a special kick to your fishing when the fish you land are fooled by your self-made flies.

All the tools and materials needed for fly tying can be purchased at sporting goods stores, or by mail from fly tying materials houses. (Check this book's "Departments" section). Except for a few basic tools and materials, many of the materials needed can be found around any farm yard or poultry house—chicken feathers, duck, turkey, and goose quills, etc. If you hunt—or have friends who do—you'll be well supplied with rabbit, fox, and squirrel fur, as well as with grouse, quail, and pheasant feathers. Accumulating a large supply of materials is no problem and even if you buy them, the cost is small and the materials will produce thousands of flies.

The basic tools are a vise, scissors, hackle pliers, razor blades, and perhaps a bobbin to hold the winding thread. Basic materials include thread, cement, books, chenille, tinsel, peacock herl, silk floss, and duck and chicken feathers.

Before starting to tie a fly, prepare your working area by placing a sheet of white cardboard under the vise, and arranging the tools and materials that you will use. Always have a bright lamp to work by.

Nymphs, representing the larvae of aquatic insects, are among the easier flies to tie. To make one, mount your vise at a comfortable height and place a size 10 hook in it. Apply a generous portion of cement to the hook, then start winding tying thread (size 00 nylon) from the eye to the bend of the hook. The cement helps hold the thread to the hook shank and also waterproofs the thread. Tie in three places of peacock herl (Figure A) or some similar material at the hook bend to form the nymph's tail. Next tie in a small section cut from a turkey or duck quill to form the nymph's back (Figure B). A short length of tinsel and some wool yarn, floss, or chenille are put on next (Figure C). Now wind the tying thread back-and-forth over the hook shank to give bulk to the fly's body, then wind on the body material (wool or floss, etc.) and top it by spiraling the tinsel forward to the hook eye, finally tying down the tinsel and other material just behind the hook eye (Figure D).

The quill section should now be brought forward over

Basic tools needed in fly tying include bobbin, vise, hackle pliers, razor, and scissors.

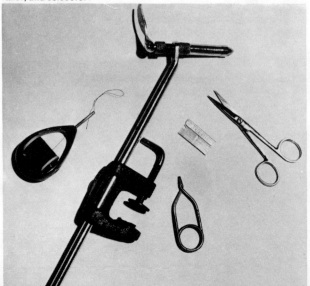

the top of the hook and fastened behind the hook eye, with any surplus trimmed off. Final step is to tie in several fibers from a webby chicken feather just under the hook eye. These simulate "legs," and give a waving fluttering action in the water. The tying thread now must be wrapped over the materials at the hook eye (Figure E) to build up a "head," then it is knotted and cemented.

After some practice at turning out several dozen nymphs, you may want to try dry flies. These are a bit more complicated to tie, but with practice you'll learn to turn out perfect, high-floating dries.

The materials used in dry flies are water repellent, since the mark of a good dry fly is its high-floating qualities. Chenille takes on water, so is never used in a good dry fly. High quality rooster neck hackles should be used for the tail and hackling since these are the parts that float a dry fly. Good dry fly body materials include deer hair, various furs, quill, herl, and floss.

To make a simple dry fly, start the tying thread as usual, winding it back-and-forth down the hook shank, coming back to the hook eye and letting the thread hang while weighed down with the hackle pliers, or bobbin. Next, cut a narrow section from each side of a duck quill and place the sections together. Holding them firmly between the thumb and forefinger, place them on the hook behind the eye, taking several tight turns over them with tying thread (Figure 1).

Still holding the sections firmly between the fingers, raise them erect and bring the tying thread in front of them, making enough turns around them to keep them upright (Figure 2). Spread the wings and wrap thread between, criss-crossing back-and-forth between the wings and around the hook until the wings stand upright and well apart. Go down the hook shank with the tying thread and tie in some hackle fibers or boar hairs or some similar stiff, hard material for a tail (Figure 2). Next tie in some silk floss and bring the thread back to the hook eye (Figure 3). Wind the floss around the hook up to the wings, and tie off. With the body, tail, and wings completed, tie a hackle feather in at the hook eye (Figure 4), then take the tip of the hackle between your fingers and turn it a couple times around the hook behind the eye. Catch the hackle tip with tying thread and bind it down. Cut off all surplus, finish the fly with a small neat head, and lacquer the head. Your first dry fly is now completed (Figure 5).

Simplest dry fly to build is the "bivisible," which also is a great fish-catcher. It's made by winding neck hackles along the shank of a hook so that they flare outwards, in what is known as "Palmer style." The hackles are tied off at the hook eye, and that's all there is to it. Being ultra-light and fluffy, the bivisible floats exceptionally well.

Streamer flies and wet flies are made with the same basic techniques used in tying nymphs and dry flies. The big difference is in the materials used and the sizes of the flies. Once you've mastered tying dry flies and high-quality nymphs, you'll be able to tie any fly, even complicated salmon flies. Don't attempt difficult flies, however, until you've had experience at tying simple kinds, and always tie on large hooks during the learning period.

Beginning is the hardest part of fly tying, so if you can

HOW TO TIE DRY FLIES AND NYMPHS

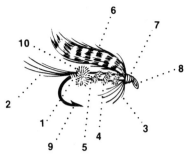

PARTS OF A FLY

1. Tag	6. Wing
2. Tail	7. Head
3. Hackle	8. Hook eye
4. Body	9. Hook
5. Ribbing	10. Butt

Fig. 1. To start dry fly, hook shank is wrapped with thread and wings tied on.

Fig. 2. Wings are brought upright and held by turns of tying thread, then tail fibers are tied down.

Fig. 3. Floss is tied in, wound forward to wings and tied down with thread.

Fig. 1.

Fig. 2.

Fig. 3.

Fig. 4. Hackle feather is tied in butt first and wound around hook.

Fig. 5. Winding thread ties off parts behind hook eye, and fly head is lacquered.

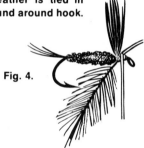

Fig. 4.

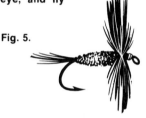

Fig. 5.

Fig. A. Tail of a peacock herl is fastened at hook bend in start of nymph fly.

Fig. B. Section of turkey feather, to form back of nymph, is tied in.

Fig. C. Next strand of body material and tinsel are tied in, and thread is brought forward.

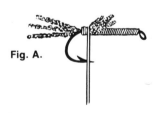

Fig. A.

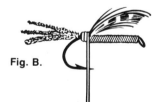

Fig. B.

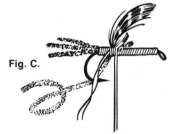

Fig. C.

Fig. D. With body material wrapped full around hook, tinsel follows in ribbing effect; then both are tied firmly at head of fly.

Fig. E. Wing is tied down, hackle added, and thread is tied off to form head.

Fig. D.

Fig. E.

Flies such as these, mostly streamers and wet flies, can be turned out quickly by a skilled tyer.

get an experienced tyer to help you in the early stages you'll progress much more rapidly. Turning out that first dozen flies is the most difficult part of fly tying. After a little experience though, you'll be able to make a fine streamer in 10 minutes, and a good dry fly or nymph in less time than that.

While learning, try to duplicate standard fly patterns, rather than attempting to design your own "killers."

There'll be plenty of time to come up with something new and startling *after* you've learned to make the time-proven, fish-getting patterns.

It takes time to get the skill and speed of an accomplished tyer. But once you have it, like swimming or riding a bike or double-hauling a fly line, it stays with you forever. And so will the fly tying bug, whose nip imparts an everlasting disease.

Fly-tying Equipment and Materials

The following tables outline the tools and materials needed to tie flies. There are three groups. Group one lists the essential things; group two secondary items; and group three some of the fancy things that can be used.

ESSENTIALS	SECONDARY	SUPPLEMENTARY
Tools		
Vise, razor blades, wax	scissors (curved blades)	soft wax for dubbed bodies
Scissors (straight blade)	thread bobbin	whip-finisher
Spring clothespin, bodkin	black thread: sizes 00, 0000	wing-cutter
Hackle pliers	tongs	thread: various sizes and colors
1 spool of "A" black thread	head cement and lacquer	small brush
1 bottle of clear lacquer	(various colors)	
Hooks		
Streamer #10 (long shank)	streamer #6-8-12	humped shank hooks for
Wet fly #12	wet fly #8-10-14	bass bugs
Dry fly #12	dry fly #14-16-18	
Body Materials		
1 Card each medium chenilles: black, white, red, yellow	chenille: other colors and the essential four colors in fine and heavy sizes	moose mane deer hair
1 spool each of floss: black, white, yellow, red	floss: other colors	embossed, oval and wire tinsels
1 each medium flat tinsel: silver, gold	fine and large tinsels flat: silver, gold	spun fur: various colors
1 peacock feather with eye	golden pheasant tippets	matched duck wings from
1 card of red yarn	silver pheasant tippets	which you make your own
1 each calf tails; white, yellow, red, brown, black	red fox fur muskrat fur	matched pair of quills
1 package each marabou feathers: white, yellow	mink fur peacock herl	
1 gray squirrel tail	assortment of yarn polar bear hair:	
1 pair each matched duck quills: white, gray or slate	red, white, yellow marabou: assorted colors	
	fox squirrel tail black squirrel tail matched quills: black, red, yellow	
	mallard side feathers teal side feathers natural and dyed bucktails	
Hackle Feathers		
1 package each saddle hackles: white, black, grizzly	selected neck hackles	complete necks: white, dark brown, ginger, black badger, grizzly
Note: Arrange with your duck hunting friends to save all the wings (in pairs) and flank feathers from the ducks they bag. Get them to save the squirrel tails, too. The ones with the white edging are the best for streamer flies and hair flies.	When in the country or a poultry market, keep your eyes open for roosters that have good shiny necks. Buy the whole bird and kill so that no blood gets on the neck. Then skin out the neck up to the head to get the tiny hackles that are so difficult to buy. Stretch the neck on a board and salt the skin.	Take all the long saddle hackles from such birds.

Complete Ultralight Spinning

Quite a few years ago ultralight spinning arrived on the angling scene. It involved the use of "scaled down" tackle—light rods and reels, hair-fine lines testing only a few pounds, and mini lures. Thousands of fishermen, and fishing writers, hailed the new ultralight as the fish-catchingest stuff around, and proclaimed it the sportiest tackle on earth.

Well, UL gear properly used certainly accounts for a lot of fish, and there's no denying its sporting aspects, but when UL surged to popularity too many tackle manufacturers marketed too much junk they wrongly claimed to be "ultralight." As a consequence, unknowing fishermen were trying to use what was supposed to be "ultralight" tackle, but found they couldn't cast properly, couldn't hook or hold fish, and couldn't keep from losing lures. They quit trying "ultralight" in disgust. As a result UL fell into disrepute among some fishermen.

Happily, though, many thousands of anglers *were* properly introduced to ultralight, and they continue to use and enjoy threadline gear and techniques today.

So it is that ultralight spinning is still very much around, and many fishermen recognize it for it's true worth—one of the most efficient ways to catch trout in small, clear streams; a superb technique for taking panfish; frequently the *only* way to catch wary fish of any species; and the *one* angling method that may provide maximum sport.

For those thousands of fishermen who, through no fault of their own, got off to bad starts with ultralight, and for the many thousands of newcomers who perhaps have never even heard of UL spinning, here is a complete book covering the tackle, tricks, and techniques of ultralight spinning. What follows is the only detailed work ever done on UL spinning. It can serve as a refresher course for the experienced threadliner, or as an encyclopedia and guidebook to the beginner. (T.McN.)

I—Ultralight Is Versatile

One of the many reasons for the tremendous popularity of ultralight spinning is that it makes big fish out of little

ones! A rod weighing only a hair over one ounce; line so fine it's hard to see; a tiny lure that weighs as little as $1/32$ of an ounce, is the outfit that's providing angling's newest kick—effectively converting small fish into lunkers. Ultralight spinning is a deadly fishing technique that offers a special challenge to spinning enthusiasts everywhere. And, best of all, it more than doubles the old pleasures of spinning.

For the experienced angler, ultralight spinning is like a shot in the arm. Let's assume you've been fishing for 20, 30, or 40 years. You've done your share of stillfishing, trolling, bait-casting. You're an expert fly fisherman. Ordinary spinning is as easy for you as falling off the proverbial log. Fishing has lost none of its appeal, but much of the excitement is gone. There seems to be nothing left to conquer, no new fields to explore, no different or interesting techniques to master. If you've reached this kind of angling "age," ultralight spinning will open to you a whole new world of fishing fun. It provides a

Finally boated, scales show fish to be only four pounds . . . small as lake trout go but plenty big enough on ultralight.

L spinning makes big fish out of little ones. Note the bend in this UL ngler's rod as he fights a small Manitoba lake trout.

real fishing kick, makes old men young, and young men kittenish.

Hairlining, however, isn't something you just go out and do. You need the right tackle, as well as a new casting technique. Your angling skills must be polished ever finer. Even modest trout and bass will test your accumulated stream and lake savvy, and larger fish will—when you land them—rekindle that long-lost and wonderful feeling of triumph.

For beginners, ultralight spinning provides thrills from the very first because those small fish that generally fall to the newcomer seem large. Also, hairlining helps beginners catch more fish. While a neophyte starting with standard heavy bait-casting, spinning, or fly rod gear will miss fish because of sloppy lure or line work, hairlining immediately solves the problems of gentle presentation. The fine monofilament line used is nearly invisible to fish, and settles to the water like a wisp of cobweb. And the baby baits drop to the water like flakes of silver. There is no fish-scaring plunk of lure nor slap of line.

On some waters for some fish under some conditions, ultralight makes all other tackle and techniques seem out of place. And on many waters for many fish under many conditions, hairlining will hold its own (or do better) than regulation gear and methods. On any water for any fish under any condition, it will always provide more fun—and that's what fishing is *for!*

There's just no denying that featherweight lures are remarkable fish-getters. They drop to the surface with almost no impact. They wiggle and wobble and shake and shimmer. They literally break fish up.

In shallow, clear water—where trout are educated and spooky—nothing demolishes them like ultralight lures. Even a skilled fisherman using live natural bait on standard gear can be out-fished by a hairliner fishing artificial lures. Why? Because you can toss a midget lure into paper-thin water and fish it back without fouling rocks or bottom snags. Some fingernail-size spinners seem to "float" in the current, winking, wobbling, weaving. No healthy trout can resist them. I can't think of a deadlier way to catch trout from hard-fished streams, or to take mantel-filling, wise old trophy browns.

With UL gear, you can fish narrow, shallow streams where standard spinning tackle would be clumsy. Those hard-to-reach spots that flyrodders can't touch are the hairliner's meat, his ace-in-the-hole. Often I have caught trout and smallmouth bass by hairlining that I couldn't have taken any other way.

There's no better way to introduce a youngster to fishing than by ultralight. UL gear is scaled down to a child's size. A UL rod, with mounted reel and line, weighs a total of less than 9 ounces. This is featherlight even to a youngster. It's absurd to present children with cumbersome gear when, today, there is tackle available that is tailored to their needs. Too, the important thing in fishing to a boy or girl is results. What kids want is fish, any fish, and lots of them. Ultralight puts fish in the pan for them like nothing else can.

In addition to its pleasant delicacy and its usefulness to junior anglers, ultralight spinning is assured a lasting place as a separate method of angling because it catches more fish under some conditions. Certain fishing conditions that are adverse situations for the fly fisherman, standard spin-fisherman, or bait-dunker are meat-and-potatoes for the ultralight man.

Generally speaking, ultralight is at its best on small trout streams. Clear-water streams and ponds that are pounded daily by an army of fishermen can be really hard fishing under bright, summer conditions. Yet UL spinning can bring you action with brooks, browns, and rainbows.

Once on Wisconsin's Pine River I met two fishermen leaving in disgust. They said they were quitting because the water was so low "even a dry fly bumps bottom," and the river was so clear that trout "spooked a mile ahead" of them.

It was a blistering August day. The water averaged only ankle deep. Everything about the river seemed dead. I picked out a rock 30 feet upstream, and flipped my spinner 4 feet above it. The spinner was a nearly weightless job—only 1/32 ounce—about the size of my little fingernail. It slipped silently into the water and twinkled down with the current. I watched the twirling blade blinking in the sun as it passed the rock, then something stopped it dead.

I raised the rod gently, and a fine little brown trout went skipping back and forth across the creek. In that shallow water the fish seemed to be trying to walk rather than swim. I was forced to pay out plenty of the thin, 1/2-pound test line when the trout zipped past me and hurried off downstream. I followed him, and when finally he wore himself to a frazzle I slid him gingerly onto a gravel bar, *30 yards from where I'd hooked him.* He measured only 13 inches, but that trout seemed like big game on my UL outfit!

I caught 14 trout that day on the Pine, under conditions other fishermen considered hopeless. There were several reasons UL produced. For one, I could make long casts and work trout from a distance without letting them see me. My wispy line was nearly invisible in the clear water. There was no disturbance on my casts, not even from the tiny spinner plinking to the surface. Finally, while other fishermen using heavier gear consistently hung bottom, my tiny spinners never fouled even in just inches of water. That day not even dry flies could have produced the way ultralight did. The water was so shallow and clear a falling fly line would have spooked the fish no matter how gentle and perfect the cast.

Often nothing is as effective as ultralight spinning tackle on very small trout streams. For example, many of our most popular trout streams average less than 10 feet across. They're deep, slow-moving, over-grown. Even expert fly rod anglers have difficulty fishing these creeks. But they're easy pickin's for the ultralight man. I've waded right down the center of such streams, using UL gear, and caught trout I couldn't possibly have taken by fly fishing. The short UL rod is a dream to handle in confined quarters; the UL spinners and spoons explore the cut-away banks where trout hide; and simple "catapult" or "underhand" casts flip UL lures straight out under the overhang.

Air-clear lakes frequently are a fly rodder's Waterloo, and only the most expert fly fisherman can take trout consistently under such difficult conditions. One August

I made a pack trip into Montana's Spanish Peaks country. We camped on Thompson Lake, and fished it for cutthroats and nearby Diamond Lake for rainbows. The water was so clear at both lakes, the fish so easily spooked by a fly line, that I found it necessary to fish a 22-foot leader, tapered to 6X. Strong winds whipped across those high lakes constantly, making casting with the long leader especially difficult. Others in the party couldn't handle casts long enough to turn over a 22-foot leader, and until I dug out two UL outfits, most of them caught only a few small fish that cruised near shore. But with ultralight tackle they were able to cast spinners, tiny spoons, and minute, inch-long plugs far out on hair-fine line. The half-pound test monofilament was nearly invisible to the fish, and they rushed for the UL lures as if they hadn't eaten in days.

One bright afternoon at Diamond Lake I spent several hours fishing with streamers and nymphs. I tried all the old favorites like Muddler Minnows and gray, furbodied nymphs, but nothing worked. Obviously the fish were deep. I kept adding split-shot sinkers to my leader, but the best I could do was sink my nymphs to 10 or 15 feet, and it was a long, painful process to wait for the nymph to get down after each cast.

I returned to camp and grabbed a UL outfit. Then, using 1/8-ounce spinners and spoons, I soon caught four good 'bows. The ultralight outfit made it possible for me to get my lures deep in a hurry, without adding fish-scaring lead weight. The compact lures and small diameter monofilament line put me down to 25 feet where the trout had dropped to avoid the sun. Also, I was able to cover more water more thoroughly with the ultralight than I had been by fly fishing.

In clear lakes it is the transparency factor—the depth to which sunlight penetrates—that usually determines the location of fish. Hence the depth at which you fish is vital, and with ultralight it's possible to work almost any depth satisfactorily.

Most fishermen now recognize lead-head "jigging" as one of the most effective methods yet for taking bass, walleyes, trout, and northern pike when the fish are deep. Jigging with UL tackle, with satisfactory jigs in UL size, is equally deadly.

Ice fishing is another field that has been explored extensively by UL fans. With the mounting popularity of ice fishing, ultralight tackle is putting new kicks into this old game. Most ice fishermen use fly rod tip-sections for jigging or bait rods, or merely handline their fish. However, UL rods and reels (and lures) are now used to put real *sport* into ice fishing.

A condition directly the opposite of low, clear water angling is, of course, early spring conditions of high, murky water. But here again UL is surprisingly effective. Most fly fishermen can't sink flies deep enough to take trout in roily water, but the heavier UL lures go down and stay down. Also, the twinkling, sparkling brass or chrome lures of the UL angler show up better than flies in heavy, discolored water. Nothing in the artificial line of lures seems to belt early season trout harder than wobbling spoons or flashing spinners.

Ultralight is especially effective for "pocket" water fishing. Many eastern mountain streams are strewn with rocks and boulders. Late in the season such creeks drop

'way down, and trout congregate in the pockets. Such places are hard to reach with flies, but with UL tackle you can pitch a spinner, plug, or small spoon into these holes with ease.

The miniature jointed plugs available to the ultralight angler are especially effective for large brown trout. Use them after dark on good brown trout water, and likely you'll discover that you have been missing some trophy trout by fishing over them with flies during the daylight hours. Large browns feed almost exclusively on minnows, and these fry-size wiggling plugs imitate natural bait perfectly. The largest brown I've taken so far on UL was a 4-pounder I caught an hour after dark one evening on Montana's Big Hole River, near Twin Bridges. Earlier I'd worked the pool carefully with streamers and nymphs, but what the brown wanted all the time was a one-inch plug served up after dark.

Fishing "natural" or real baits with ultralight tackle is unbelievably effective, too. On Maryland's Susquehanna River below Conowingo Dam you'll find some of the finest smallmouth bass fishing in the East. The fish average around a pound, but there are plenty of them. Late in the season, when the flow of water through the dam is reduced, the lower river drops down. Boulders as big as autos pop up. The current curls around 'em, and smallmouths lay up under the boulders catching tidbits coming down with the current. With UL gear you can stand on rocks, bait up with a single hellgrammite or crawfish, and by fishing the current edges along the rocks rack up one smallmouth after another.

A single nightcrawler or smaller dew worm, fished with ultralight on the average trout stream, is devastating too. Using plastic floating "bubbles," it's even possible to fish insects such as grasshoppers, Mayflies, western salmon flies, spiders, bees, crickets and so on. The plastic bubbles need not be filled with water, or even partially filled, in order to cast them well with ultralight. They're heavy enough for UL spinning even when empty. Using dry flies with these bubbles is another effective fishing method with ultralight, as is popping bug fishing, both of which will be discussed in some detail later.

In these days when many anglers must be satisfied with catching small, stocked trout, no tackle or system seems more appropriate or effective than ultralight. The midget lures are a perfect bite-size for trout under one pound, and the gear makes even these modest fish feel like giants. Also, stocked trout means heavy angling pressure, and this is a condition under which UL shines brightest.

II—Ultralight Is Different

The importance of properly matched and balanced tackle cannot be overly impressed on the beginning UL fisherman. Unless rod, lure, line, and reel are right, attempting to fish the ultralight way will be difficult if not impossible. Line that is too light used on a rod that is too stiff means breakage and loss of fish and lures. Unless the line test is appropriate to the weight of the lure used, you may flip the lure away on your very first cast. The tiniest of swivels must be used in order to permit the light UL lures complete freedom of action. Choose snap swivels that have an easy, free-swiveling action. For UL use, best sizes are 0, 1, 2, and 3. Some ultralight anglers change line when it becomes twisted, instead of using swivels, but this seems like an unnecessary and time-consuming operation.

Under various conditions of fishing with ultralight, the size, shape, or weight of the lure compared to the line used can mean the difference between success and failure. If the wrong kind of line is used, it probably will fail to "give" or stretch some when a fish hits and you're out of a good fish *and* another lure. For the same reason, the UL rod must be right. If it doesn't give a bit, with bending action right to the butt, you'll suffer excess line breakage.

The UL reel is important, too, for a matched, properly balanced ultralight spinning outfit. The UL reel must have a smooth, faultless drag. This is important since a faulty drag may hesitate or grab on a running fish, and again you'll be faced with line breakage.

Generally speaking, true ultralight tackle starts with a rod weighing from 1½ to 2½ ounces and measuring from 4½ to 5½ feet. A rod 4½ feet, weighing 1½ ounces, is the ultimate for ultralight fishing. Most fresh water spinning rods weigh in the neighborhood of 4 to 6 ounces, even more. The majority of fresh water spinning reels weigh 10 to 12 ounces. A UL reel should not weigh more than 7 ounces, and the best weigh between 5 and 6 ounces, some even less.

Line diameter and lure weight also are scaled down proportionately in assembling a genuine ultralight outfit. Line testing greater than 3 pounds is not considered truly ultralight, nor are lures weighing more than ⅛ ounce. Using monofilament line that "mikes" from .0031 inch to .0055 in diameter, rods measuring 54 inches and weighing 1½ ounces, and lures weighing as little as ¹⁄₃₂ of an ounce, is the ultimate in spinning. It would not be possible to refine this method of angling further. The line used in true ultralight fishing is, for example, so fine you can't feel it balanced on a finger, or see it leaving

your rod tip. Drop a loose end of it, and it floats slowly to the floor like a feather.

However, lightness alone isn't enough in a good ultralight outfit.

Some people still think that if you have a short, light rod you're all set for hairlining. Length of the rod is actually unimportant; it's the action of the rod that counts. It's conceivable that it would be possible to make a 4-foot broom handle out of some ultralight material, such as balsa or plastic, and it would weigh less than 2 ounces, but it would still have the "action" of a broom handle.

Manufacturers and sporting goods stores that push off the wrong merchandise to unsuspecting customers are not only performing a disservice to fishermen but also to themselves. Thousands of fishermen are wild over the idea of ultralight angling, but they give up fast when they try this fishing with the wrong kind of gear. Ultralight is a separate and distinct system of fishing, filling a longtime gap between angling methods, but it will be squelched by buck-hungry tackle manufacturers if they continue to peddle the wrong kind of gear.

The sportsman who wants to fish ultralight must buy a complete new spinning outfit—rod, reel, line, swivels, lures. Nothing he now owns will do, with the possible exception of a few tiny lures. Several major tackle firms, because they've been equipped for rod production for years, are now making excellent ultralight spinning rods. But only a few American firms now offer a complete matched and balanced UL line—rods of three lengths (4½, 5, and 5½ feet); lines testing from 3 pounds down to ½ pound; reels that fit into your shirt pocket; tiny snap swivels; and an assortment of lures ranging from the world's tiniest jointed plug (1 inch long, ¹⁄₁₆ ounce, hook size 14) to midget spinners weighing only ¹⁄₃₂ of an ounce.

When you buy your first UL outfit, examine the rod and reel carefully, making sure they'll give you what is needed. Get the right kind of line, and a good selection of the proper lures. Be sure the snap swivels you buy are the smallest, lightest, strongest, and best you can find.

Then, with your matchstick rod, hair-like line, light-weight reel, and midget lures, you'll be all set to enjoy spinning's biggest thrill.

III—The Perfect UL Reel

In no kind of fishing is the reel more important than in ultralight spinning. When fishing with hairline the reel assumes a vital role. Since most fish you will catch with UL gear feel and act like monsters, the reel must respond promptly and smoothly to their runs.

One of the smallest UL reels is the "Mignon," which is called "the tiniest spinning reel in the world." I doubt if it's possible to produce a smaller spinning reel that would still be practical and serviceable.

The housing of this reel measures a fraction over two inches. It fits in the palm of my hand. It weighs 5¾ ounces and balances perfectly with my 54-inch, 1½-ounce glass rod. Because the spool diameter is so small, the reel has a souped-up gear ratio of 5.2 to 1. If it didn't, it would take forever to work a lure back on even a mod-

A quality UL reel must have a smooth, faultless drag. One shown is the Italian made "Cargem Mignon 33," a 5¾ oz. giant.

erate cast, and it would not be possible to work a lure properly in the water.

One thing about a UL reel that must be thoroughly understood if you want to fish with a hair: the reel must have the smoothest, finest drag possible or you'll suffer a staggering loss of fish. Even with an extremely fine drag, it's best to set it very light and control the line by dropping your forefinger down on the rim of the spool. With regulation spinning gear this is not necessary as heavy line is used, and if the reel's drag should falter slightly you're not likely to lose a fish. Hairline, however, may part at the first hesitation of the drag.

To adjust the drag of an UL reel I merely turn the wingnut clockwise to tighten, counter-clockwise to loosen. The Mignon has a built-in drag, so you can change spools without resetting the drag. The spool release is push-button type, as with the Garcia "Mitchell" and some other reels, which allows instant change.

Since 100 yards of line is more than you'll need for most fishing, the reel spool should be filled to within about a quarter-inch of the rim with good backing line. This will leave plenty of room for 100 yards of fine-diameter monofilament. Without backing, a "Mignon" reel holds 230 yards of 2 pound test monofilament. Whatever size of line you use, be sure to put enough backing on the spool to bring the line to within 1/8 inch of the spool's lip.

The basic mechanics of casting with an ultralight reel are no different from those used with standard tackle. You simply reverse the reel handle until line comes under your forefinger, lift the line with the fingertip, then wind the bail to the top of the reel case. With the left thumb, push the bail down gently until it clicks into the open position for casting. That's all there is to it!

IV—The Perfect UL Rod

There is no standard length for an ultralight rod, so length alone is not a reliable yardstick for selecting a good UL rod. Neither is weight. While a UL rod naturally cannot be too long or too heavy, a rod that is ultra *short* and ultra *light* is not necessarily a good tool for casting tiny lures and playing fish on gossamer line. In fact, a rod can be very short and very light and still be all wrong for ultralight spinning. It's the rod's *action* that's important in UL fishing.

Since weight, length, taper, and the material used are what really determine rod action, we can set down a general guide for selecting the ideal ultralight rod. The best UL rods weigh no more than 2¼ ounces. My favorite weighs 1½ ounces with all fittings. Although weight alone is not the measure of a good UL rod, ounces should be shaved when possible just to keep overall tackle weight down, and in proportion to the kind of fishing for which ultralight spinning is designed.

Fiber-glass construction has made it possible to get maximum strength with minimum weight in rods of all types. Nearly all UL rods now available in this country are made of tubular glass for reasons of lightness, strength, and resiliency. While some manufacturers (particularly in France) are still turning out UL bamboo

rods, getting a good ultralight stick of cane is difficult and expensive.

My pet 1½ ounce UL rod measures a whopping 54 inches. Although a hollow, 5½-foot glass rod weighing 2¼ ounces is appropriate under some angling conditions, I find that the little 4½-footer answers my UL fishing needs nicely most of the time. For some forms of lake fishing, and when spinning the broad rivers of the West, I sometimes use a rod an extra 6 or 12 inches long. Slightly longer casts are possible with it, and under certain stream conditions the longer rod gives better control of the lure. A longer rod also makes it easier to handle hooked fish when the fish is romping around some distance away.

Actually, the compleat UL angler should equip himself with at least two rods, one 4½ feet, the other 5½. The eastern or midwestern angler likely will use the 4½-footer most often. This length is perfect for hairlining the brush-covered brooks, meadow streams, and willow-hung farm ponds and lakes. Under any conditions involving close-quarters casting, the shorter rod is the proper tool. This 54-inch job is so short I can hold the grip in one hand, and easily touch the tip with the other.

The most important feature of a UL rod is springiness. You need swift tip action, graduating all the way to the butt, to cast light lures and hair-fine line, and to hook and hold fish. If you use hairline on a rod that's too stiff, fish will break off on the strike.

Some fishermen starting out with UL gear criticize properly designed rods which they consider "too soft." Once an experienced fisherman examined one of my UL outfits. He flexed the rod and snickered. "With this rod," he grinned, "you couldn't sink a hook into the kind of trout I fish for." Fact is, ultralight lures have such needle-sharp hooks that there's no need to strike back hard and fast when a fish hits, as usually is necessary with conventional tackle. And these slow-tapered ultralight rods are ideal for fishing small streams. Their softness is no handicap even when fishing long casts where the strik-

The ideal UL rod must have good flex and "soft" action so that it bends under strain evenly from tip to butt.

ing fish grabs your lure 80 feet away.

The UL rod must have a very fast, flexible tip for chucking lures that may weigh as little as 1/32 of an ounce, and it *must* give instantly under the impact of a fish's strike. This action must continue all the way to the butt, if comparatively large fish are to be fought and tired out successfully. As a hairliner brings his fish close, the elasticity of the line naturally decreases. It's at this critical moment that resilient rod action becomes important. The extremely flexible rod yields easily to each rush of the fish, thus maintaining constant pressure and preventing the fish from pitting its weight and strength directly against the fine line. Today's willowy, tough glass makes ultralight matchstick rods exceptionally efficient angling tools.

Some UL fans, striving for the *perfect* rod, make their own by mounting spinning guides on discarded, glass fly rod tip sections. I've made rods this way, and while some were serviceable, most are not up to the quality of a factory-made, properly-designed ultralight rod because most fly rod tips have action that is too slow. Oddly enough, the first glass fly rods that appeared some 25 years ago had tips that would have made up into quite good UL spinning rods. But those early glass fly rods had a "wet noodle" kind of action, and the criticisms of fly casters soon forced the manufacturers to stiffen the tips.

The best ultralight rod has featherweight ferrules of strong metal. The ferrules of a two-piece rod must be made of the lightest, toughest metal or the rod's action will be deadened above and below the ferrule. Guides should be of flexible design, and foul-proofing guide supports are essential. The best 4½-foot rods have one piece tips which fit into female ferrules mounted in the rod handle. Handles 8 inches long are the most comfortable, and reel-seat rings should be of wide design to hold the reel-foot securely, and they should also be of durable, lightweight metal.

V—Selecting UL Line

The compleat UL angler needs monofilament lines of ½, 1, 1½, and 2 pound test.

It is line diameter that makes it possible to cast lures of given weight properly, yet if the line test is too light for the lure weight, breakage results. This is one reason so many UL beginners toss lures away during their first attempts at ultralight fishing. Thus it is vital to select lines of minimum diameter per pound test or, put another way, to choose the line that gives the greatest strength for its diameter.

The best nylon monofilament for ultralight spinning comes in the following diameters per pound test:

Diameter: .0031 .0039 .0047 .0055 .0063 .0071
Pound test: ½ 1 1½ 2 2½ 3

Strictly speaking, true ultralight spinning lines test 2 pounds or less; but lines to 3 or even 3½ pound test may be used where heavier lures are needed for large fish under difficult conditions. With these lines and lures, standard ultralight rod and reel may be used.

The monofilament used most often in ultralight work is so fine that it's hard to see it when you cast, even where it comes out of the rod tip. Stroking the line between your fingers is like trying to feel a wisp of spider web. These ultra-fine diameters make it possible to cast lures no larger than the nail on your little finger, and not much thicker than newsprint.

As a general guide, which will vary some according to the manufacturer, 2 pound test monofilament is about right for lures weighing from 1/8 to 1/12-ounce. For most lures under 1/16-ounce, the line should test 1½ pounds or less.

One-pound mono serves very well for most ultralight angling conditions, and is fine enough in diameter to cast any UL lure satisfactorily. Of course there are variations depending on the compactness of the lure, or its wind resistance. A tiny spoon may weigh only 1/10 ounce and cast well even with a fairly heavy line, while a melon-shaped, wind-resistant spinner considerably heavier may not cast well even with line miking less than .0055. Thus the relationship of lure weight and design to line diameter is important. Using the finest mono (½ pound, .0031 diameter), I've cast ordinary weighted streamer flies, fly rod lures and even worms.

Most fishermen will find 2-pound line suited to average trout fishing conditions. This line handles a wide variety of ultralight lures, is heavy enough for most fish the average UL angler encounters, and eliminates some of the problems faced when using finer line.

As the UL beginner progresses, however, he'll likely scale his lures and line down even further, enhancing his sport *and* the weight of his creel. One season, just for my own amazement, I seldom used line testing more than 1 pound and frequently dropped to ½ pound.

Properly made ultralight monofilament has enough elasticity to absorb some of the shock of a fish's strike, and to "give" when a hooked fish moves suddenly. Yet its recovery is such that the line snaps back to its original diameter and strength instantly. A good mono line is "limp" enough to spool evenly on the reel, and to pass its loops through the first rod guide on the cast with a minimum of friction or "impact" that might slow the flight of the lure. Uniformity of diameter is more important with UL line than with ordinary spinning mono, for obvious reasons. Whenever line and tackle are scaled down and refined, all imperfections are magnified.

It is wise to carry a couple of spare spools of line in different tests, ranging from ½ to at least 2 pounds. With these you'll be prepared to alter lure weights and fishing methods when conditions dictate a change. And if you do much ultralight angling, you'll hang the occasional fish that will at least partially strip your reel before breaking off; or for reasons of wind, or some personal or mechanical malfunction, you'll get a king-size snarl and need to snap in a fresh spool and line.

In ultralight diameters, mono is virtually invisible to fish—even to crafty brown trout, which are so often credited with telescopic eyesight. For this reason the color of the line used in UL spinning is comparatively unimportant, but good mono has no sheen or gloss and reflects a minimum of sunlight.

The knots used in hairline spinning differ little from those used in any other form of fishing. The *improved clinch knot* is generally popular for attaching lure or swivel to line. This differs from the ordinary clinch knot in that the end of the line is passed back through the loop created when the line end is brought forward toward the hook eye. The *blood knot* is used to join two pieces of nylon; it gives a straight pull in both directions, and is the strongest joining knot known. The *running loop,* a slip-type knot, is used for attaching the line to the reel spool. This loop can be thrown over the reel spool two or three times, drawn up tight, and it will never slip or slide when spooling line. The *shocker knot* can be used for attaching a heavier "shocker" length of strong nylon to the casting line which is desirable when fishing for hardmouthed or toothy fish. (See knots section.)

A trick often used by spinfishermen is to touch the end of a nylon knot with a lighted cigarette. The cigarette melts the line end, and forms a small ball which is not likely to work through the knot.

VI—UL Lures

Ultralight lures weigh from $\frac{1}{8}$ to $\frac{1}{32}$ of an ounce, with the majority weighing about $\frac{1}{10}$ or $\frac{1}{12}$ ounce. A few years ago the number of ultralight lures available in this country was limited; today almost *any type* of spinning lure is available in ultralight sizes. There are spinners, spoons, baby plugs, jigs, spinner-fly combinations, wobblers, and spinner-and-bead rigs being manufactured for the ultralight fan. Newest arrival in the field is an ultra-

Heavy "shock" tips or lengths of nylon must be attached to standard UL line when fishing for hardmouthed or toothy species such as northern pike.

Spoons are easily the best-casting of all UL lures and it was a spoon that knocked out this St. Johns River (Fla.) largemouth.

light, weedless surface plug—the first surface lure of its size in America. It resembles the famed "Jitterbug" in body shape and mouthpiece. However, it has a double, upturned hook at the rear, and trails a forked piece of plastic material that looks and acts like pork-rind in the water.

Probably the most unusual UL lure to date is the "Rocky Jr.," a tiny jointed plug that tips the postage scale to exactly ¹/₁₆ ounce, has two sets of size 14 treble hooks, and measures just one inch long. The "Rocky" is reputedly the smallest and lightest jointed plug made. It has proven so popular that it spawned a cousin known as "Rocky Sr." The Senior is armed with size 10 hooks, weighs ⅛ ounce, stretches 1½ inches over-all, and is deadly on larger trout and bass.

For early season trout fishing, when water is likely to be high and murky, tiny UL spoons and plugs produce well. The spoons get down in high water, and have fish attracting sparkle. They give best action when reeled at moderate speeds, which is another advantage when fishing in dingy water. Early season trout are apt to be sluggish and deep, and an inch-long wobbler twitched over the bottom can save the day. Since minnows form a large part of a trout's diet early in the season, before insects start hatching, the baby plugs should not be over-looked. They're especially attractive to large brown trout, but brookies and rainbows love 'em too!

Spoons are the best-casting of all UL lures, and they are the preferred baits when casting into wind, or when it's desirable to send lengthy casts sailing out across a broad river. Spoons are also good for lake fishing because they sink well and cover a lot of water. In stream fishing the current influences both the depth and speed of your lure, and while some spinners are excellent under some conditions, they may not fish deep enough in high, fast water. However, spoons knife through current, and so go deeper than do spinners at average retrieving speed.

Most ultralight spoons have unusually thick blades for their length. Thus they have great density and small surface, causing them to cast well and sink fast. In calm water UL spoons can be fished effectively to depths of around 25 feet, and in moving water (depending on current flow) to about 10 feet. By "effectively" I mean without excessive loss of time in waiting for the lure to sink following each cast.

When fishing conditions call for accurate, "spot" casting, I always use the micro-wobbler spoons. Their castability is such that you can shoot a straight, flat cast —and bullet them to the target. They weigh ¹/₁₀ ounce and are available with gold, nickel, red and white, pearl silver, pearl gold, or black zebra finishes. I keep my lure box stocked with two or three of each finish. I do not know why it should be, but I've experienced days when fish refused my gold and silver spoons, but clobbered the black. These micro-spoons are "hot" lures for rainbow trout, and even for small lake trout. Baby northern pike (under 5 pounds), and pickerel also have a passion for micro-spoons. I begin nearly every day of ultralight fishing by first probing the depths with these spoons, unless the water I am on is notoriously stacked with brown trout or bass; then I begin with a midget plug.

The UL surface plug mentioned earlier is a worthy addition to the ultralight tackle box. Its primary useful-ness, of course, is for bass living in weedy lakes, but it also takes brown trout at night. This is one of the heavier UL lures, weighing ⅙ ounce, but it hits the water with a bug-like "splat," then wobbles and wiggles, shimmers and shakes across the top, giving all the noise and telltale "V" wake of some small critter that's in big trouble.

For most trout, panfish, and small bass fishing, UL spinners and spinner-fly combinations are deadly. Under mid-summer fishing conditions of low, clear water it would be difficult to find any lure more effective than a twinkling, dime-size spinner. There's no refuting that these light lures, falling gently as a snowflake to the water, are deadly on hard-fished trout. These UL spinners will take selective-feeding trout that wouldn't look at standard flies or spinning lures. The fish seem to lose all hold on themselves when confronted with a tiny spinner that winks and blinks along, seemingly unattached to any line.

Spinners, as everyone knows, do not always cast well. They catch on the wind, twist and slide through the air, and the slightest breeze may carry one several feet off target. But their fish-catching qualities surmount the comparatively minor difficulties of casting them. Once the hairliner has mastered the straight, low-trajectory cast he'll have little serious trouble in casting even broad-bladed spinners.

Tiny UL spinner-fly combinations are death on small panfish and modest-size trout. Many weigh only $1/32$ of an ounce, yet their effectiveness on hard-pummeled trout living in low, clear streams is surprising. Fish them on $1/2$-pound test line, and with that fine mono you'll have some exciting angling. These lures seem to "float" in the water, and a good way to work them is to cast upstream and let them wash down naturally, giving them an occasional nudge with the rod tip. The blades of most UL

spinner-fly combos rotate so smoothly they give perfect action even on upstream casts.

The spoons and jointed plugs have it over other UL baits in salt water. As I write this, I am at the Cat Cay Club, near Bimini, in the Bahamas. A few hours ago, when the tide was full, Don McCarthy and I strolled to a coral point a hundred yards from my cottage. Don had a standard salt water spinning outfit, and each time he cast a covey of baby jacks followed his jig. When Don lifted the jig from the water, the little jacks scooted around, searching hungrily for the missing jig. I'd cast my $1/10$-ounce spoon with my UL outfit only when Don had a bunch of jacks scurrying at his feet, and in this way I managed a perfect score of one fish per cast. When a larger jack finally crashed the party and made off with my spoon, I tried spinners with 50 per cent less success. Jointed plugs, however, were nearly as good as the spoons.

Ultralight spinning, incidentally, has an interesting and provocative future in salt water fishing. Obviously only the smaller salt water fish are legitimate opponents for UL anglers, but even baby jack crevalle, grunts, pinfish, and such are wild fighters when hooked on a hair and a matchstick rod. It's hoped that the field of ultralight lures will be broadened considerably in the near future with a special line of jigs, spoons, and plugs specifically designed for salt water use.

VII—Casting And Playing Fish With UL Gear

Hairline tackle is so fine and delicate that it poses special problems to beginners. One does not just pick up an ultralight outfit and start casting a country mile, or with the usual degree of accuracy. When most people first try UL tackle, they flub their first few casts. Probably you will too. UL line is so light that a gentle breeze can foul it around the reel or rod tip unless you have control of it at all times. And you will be very conscious of the "weightlessness" of the lures you are casting.

Because UL lures are so light, you'll lose a few yards of casting distance, too. But after some practice you'll get the "feel" of spinning-with-a-hair and become as proficient with it as with standard spinning tackle. Best of all, you'll ultimately improve in over-all accuracy and fish-catching "lure presentation."

The only trick in attaining maximum distance and accuracy with UL is the careful matching of lure weight to line test, or diameter. Through experience you'll learn which lures cast best, and which line diameters are most suitable for different lures. Obviously, the lighter the lure and/or the more air-resistant it is, the finer the line you must use to cast well.

With light lures, let them hang about 10 inches from the rod tip before starting a cast. The heavier lures should be reeled almost to the rod tip. By allowing a light lure to hang well down, it will swing almost in pendulum style at the start of the cast and give the leverage needed to flex the rod tip and bring out the rod's action.

Learning to cast without the usual feel of lure weight at the rod tip is perhaps the most difficult aspect of

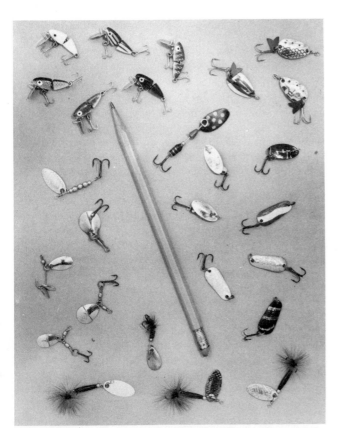
Ultralight lures include fish-catching spinners, spoons, and midget plugs.

Standard overhead cast is most commonly used by UL angler.

The backhand cast is ideal when there is little room for long, sweeping swings with the rod.

ultralight casting. Normally, a much faster backcast and forward cast is needed to get satisfactory distance with UL. Also, it's best to halt the backcast at 12 o'clock, which will allow the rod to slide to 1 o'clock, where the tip will be in position to snap forward with maximum thrust. This rule holds whether the cast is vertical or horizontal.

Probably because of the short rod, and its lightness, the UL caster has a tendency to allow the rod to "fade" far back on the backcast. Even some experienced casters swoop the rod all the way back to 4 o'clock when trying UL for the first time. Just remember to double your old rod speed, and to keep the tip working in the 12 to 1 o'clock zone.

If a breeze is at your back, or quartering in from either side, maximum distance is obtained with a high throw. Chuck your lure up where the breeze can catch it and carry it out. Do just the opposite when casting into the wind; shoot the cast low, with as flat a trajectory as possible, to get under the wind. This, of course, is done by not releasing the lure until the rod tip is snapped down to about the 9 o'clock position. A fast, short forward snap of the rod is the correct delivery for casting into a breeze. The sidearm cast, though often inaccurate, is another way to gain maximum distance against the wind.

Developing tea-cup accuracy is chiefly a matter of practice with correctly balanced UL tackle. Controlling the line with the fingertip, which slows or halts the flight of the lure by retarding the line as it spirals off the spool, is probably the most important single factor in casting accurately.

Incidentally, if you should have a break in the skin of your forefinger tip, or a callous, it may catch or break the cob-web UL line when you cast. Get some "New-skin" at the drug store, or clear nail polish, and coat your finger with it. Either will keep that important finger tip smooth!

Some UL fishermen aim their casts to points slightly

beyond target, then drop the fingertip to the reel spool to halt the flight of the lure suddenly, thus pulling the lure back and dropping it onto the target. This sometimes plunks the lure into the water heavily, but some casters can turn this plunk into a gentle plink. Others prefer to arch a cast in a gradually rising plane which curves swiftly downward when nearing the target. As it nears the target, they begin slowing the line with the finger, which drops the lure on target with a minimum of disturbance.

Many spin fishermen still use the bail to stop a cast. As the lure nears the target they give the reel handle a quick half turn to close the bail, which halts the flight of the lure instantly and engages the line for the retrieve. However, this method does not give you as much control over the lure as your forefinger does, and with the light lines used in UL fishing, it can sometimes cause breakage.

Regardless of the method used, a lure should be slowed considerably or stopped entirely just before it hits the water. This keeps the lure from fouling the line as it strikes the water, since stopping the cast causes the lure to straighten from the pull of centrifugal force and drop to the water flat.

There are a half-dozen casts used regularly in UL fishing. They are the *overhead, swipe, flip, bow-and-arrow, catapult,* and *backhand* casts. The overhead cast is standard for spin-fishing (and bait casting too) and *usually* is the most accurate cast. Certainly it is the safest cast to use when fishing from a boat with companions, and it provides good distance. In this cast, as in most of the others, the flexibility and power of the rod does the work. The rod bends and stores energy during the back cast, and releases it on the forward cast. The cast starts with the rod at 10 o'clock. You bring it sharply up and back to 1 o'clock, then snap it forward smartly, always moving the rod smoothly and in a vertical plane. Release the lure by letting the line slip off the forefinger as the rod reaches 10 o'clock on the forward cast, and follow through by lowering the rod gradually to about 9 o'clock. By following through as the lure flies out, friction of the line on the rod guides is reduced to give you more distance. You can slow the lure by letting the line slap your extended forefinger as it comes whipping off the reel, and stop it altogether by dropping the forefinger to the reel's spool. Actually, the overhead cast can be troublesome when using matchstick tackle. Because of the light lure and line, wind often plays havoc with a high, overhead toss.

The so-called "swipe" or side-arm cast keeps the lure much flatter in flight. You make a swipe cast by holding the rod at your side, tip near the water or at waist level, and casting the lure with a quick forward movement of the rod tip. Though not 100% accurate, this cast is useful in putting lures beneath over-hanging branches. Inci-

dentally, the swipe cast also can be made from the left side of the body by right-handed casters using a back-handed wrist movement. This is a difficult toss to learn, however, and quite often another kind of cast will get a lure out much better.

When you must cast from shore with trees and branches on either side and behind you, the flip, bow-and-arrow, or catapult casts are best.

To make a flip cast, hold the rod vertically in front of you, tip down. The cast is made with a slight flip forward so that, at the moment you release the line, the rod is aimed at the target. The bow-and-arrow and catapult casts are useful in tight places. For the bow-and-arrow cast take the lure in your left hand and, pointing the rod at the target, pull the lure back to bend the rod, then release it so the lure shoots out. In the catapult cast draw the lure back toward your waist instead of your

The "swipe" cast keeps a lure in low flight and is just right to toss baits beneath overhanging tree limbs.

Using a 54-inch rod, Mignon 33 reel, and 2 pound test line, Tom McNally plays a scrappy bass. Note author's finger on reel-spool to control drag.

head. All of the casts I've discussed are easy with UL tackle because of the short rod used.

While a fisherman using conventional tackle must usually strike back hard to set his hooks when a fish hits, the UL angler hasn't much of a problem in hooking fish. The hooks of UL lures are so sharp that fish nearly always hook themselves; about all the angler has to do is tighten the line with a slight wrist movement. When a fish hits on a very short line, the stretch in the monofilament line is reduced, so the shock of the strike alone usually is enough to hook him solidly on the tiny, needle-pointed UL hooks. A fish hitting on an average cast will be hooked when you just tighten the line, but if you get a strike on a long cast, you may have to raise the rod tip 'way back to set the hooks. Bear in mind that the farther the fish is away from you, the more "give" there is to the line. Always hold the rod nearly vertical when retrieving, so the flexible tip can absorb most of the shock of a fish's strike. If the rod is held low, the line has to take most of the jolt and . . . pop!

When hairlining, be sure to set the drag very light. This is a "must"! When you have a fish on, control the revolving spool by applying slight pressure with the forefinger. Until I learned this, I lost enough trout to fill a hatchery and enough lures to stock a tackle shop. A sensitive forefinger is the hairliner's most valuable asset.

By pressing against the reel spool when it is revolving

under pressure of a fish, you get the same kind of control you get in thumbing the spool of a bait-casting reel when fighting a bass. Both systems are excellent because they allow instantaneous changes of pressure.

Many spin fishermen using standard tackle turn the drag on their reels to a heavy setting, then reduce it considerably when they hook a fish, and apply tension by dropping their forefinger to the reel spool. The idea of a heavy drag initially is that the fish hits against solid tension and is hooked. The trick then is to reduce the drag swiftly before the fish gets his jets operating and snaps the line. Setting and re-setting the drag is unnecessary in UL fishing, however, partly because of the needle-sharp hooks and partly because you'll develop an uncanny awareness of tensions in your finger-tip resting on the reel's spool.

I turn the drag on my UL reel almost completely off —probably to less than a half-pound of resistance. When I cast, my forefinger drops to the spool just before the lure touches the water. I then raise the rod tip sharply so that the lure starts coming my way under tension the instant I close the bail of the reel. *Even if a fish hits before the bail closes, there is resistance and he's hooked.* Thereafter the fingertip applies whatever pressure is necessary to brake the nearly free-running spool. If the fish heads for a submerged log or weed bed, I simply apply fingertip pressure up to the breaking point of the line, adjusting the pressure (which you can't do conveniently with a mechanical brake) according to the weight and speed of the fish.

In playing a fish with UL tackle, never make a forceful attempt to horse the fish out of the water. *Play* him! With cobweb line, you *have* to. This time the odds aren't so heavily in your favor, and even a small fish can bust off and leave you feeling foolish.

Many fishermen hold their rods stationary when fighting fish, and merely reel. This, in effect, is playing the fish directly from the reel, and the fish's resistance is applied mainly to the line. With hairline this can be disastrous. The proper technique to work a fish in is to lower the rod tip, at the same time spooling line. With the tip low, press the forefinger against the reel spool to prevent outgoing line, then raise the rod slowly but firmly to about 12 o'clock. The action of raising the rod gradually "pumps" the fish close and allows you to take in line. With UL, "pumping" must be gentle. As long as the fish is fresh and full of scrap, take your time. Let him have his way unless, of course, he heads for a snag. Then hold him up as best you can, taxing your line and tackle to the limit. Try to maneuver your fish into the open. If he heads for brush, for example, perhaps you can wade to that area before the fish reaches it, thus keeping him out of trouble.

Reeling against a dead weight will twist a monofilament line. "Pumping" the rod eliminates line twist and also lets you spool the line when it is "relaxed," rather than stretched tight.

Most fish are lost on jumps because they fall back against a tight line. The line snaps, or the weight of the fish striking the line tears the hooks out. Lowering the rod tip swiftly the instant a hooked fish clears the surface slackens the line, so that if the fish does fall on it the line won't break, and the lure can't pull out. This way a leaping fish can free itself on the jump only by shaking out the lure, and if this happens the fish was not securely hooked and you'd probably have lost him later anyway. However, the small needle-sharp hooks on light UL lures generally bite deep and hold, so thrown lures are rare.

In the final phase of playing a fish with UL gear, some hairliners tighten the reel's drag enough so that the line doesn't slip out. Others leave the mechanical drag alone and use only finger pressure to prevent the fish from pulling line out. I much prefer the finger-tip method because so many fish make a last-minute flurry, and I can give them instant slack by reducing pressure on the spool.

The moment of beaching, gilling, or netting your UL-caught fish is the most dangerous time, just as it is with conventional gear. The difference is that with a line not much stronger than a hair, the danger of losing a fish at the net is greater.

More fish are probably lost during the landing operation than at any other time. If the fish is a good one the experienced angler often tries to rush the landing job, bringing a fish that's still strong up close on a tight line. A fish flopping on the surface, or trying to dive under your boots or your boat, and pulling against a short, tight line, is the one most likely to rip free. Because of the close quarters, your rod will not be able to absorb many of the fish's rapid-fire rushes, either.

Be sure your fish is properly played out before bringing him near. Any fish that is still "green" may swim your way soon after you hook him, but once he spies you he'll make every effort to sprint or jump clean out of the county. Even fish that appear beaten often have just enough left in reserve for a final spurt when they sense that the moment of truth is at hand. Even a small trout can bust fine, UL line on a final, sudden flurry unless you have absolute finger-tip control. If you dislike using a net, as I do, don't grasp the cobweb line above the lure and hope to haul your fish out. The line will part for sure. Instead, grab the lure and lead your fish out by the nose, or clamp your thumb and forefinger on his lower jaw. Eventually you'll discover that you lose fewer fish when hairlining than you do by other methods, simply because you play them more carefully and never try to land one that's "green." You'll also discover that you enjoy catching fish more than ever, because you have to fight the fish under conditions that make it a challenge to your skill.

If you try hairlining in water that holds trout or bass exceeding a few pounds, you may have to become a "trotter." You can't allow hooked fish to take out too much line, so you trot after those that head downstream.

Remember, too, that you can reel a fish too close. Never bring in a fish so close that the line still out of the rod tip is shorter than the rod. You can't bring a fish to you unless you have at least a foot or two more line out than the rod length. Then you can draw the fish to you by raising the rod and bending it back past your ear. The fish will slide to you, and you won't have to do any stretching.

When I first started UL fishing I expected to lose a barrel of fish. I lost some, then I quickly found myself

Murray Crowder of Spring Valley, Ill. blitzed this farm pond bass on U L tackle. In such open water bass of this size are fair game for the UL angler.

In this photo series Bob McNally shows how to land a big UL-hooked brown trout. The fish is carefully played out and drawn close . . .

. . . then Bob reaches gingerly and grabs trout by the lower jaw.

A quick hoist, and big brown is secured between lower jaw and gill cover.

enjoying the added thrill of rarely—but rarely—losing a fish. The niceties of UL spinning were giving me the extra fun of seeing how skillfully I could play each fish hooked, no matter how small, with the result that a lost fish brought the same sensation of flubbing a long-sought date with the curvy blonde in the office next door.

UL tackle is impractical, however, for large fish in excessively weedy or brushy water. While a few bass may be snaked out occasionally on 2-pound line, most fish hooked under such conditions on finer line will go their merry way. Even a 1-pound bass, or trout, would be difficult to hold on ½-or 1-pound line if the fish is hooked close to weeds or brush. While such a fish may be fair game for the ultralight angler in open water, he suddenly becomes a monster when in proximity to good cover. Thus the UL angler fishing weedy, brushy lakes must be prepared to lose some fish and kiss some lures good-bye. However, there's one trick all veteran fishermen use to cope with the problem of saving a large fish that is hooked close to weeds or brush. At the instant of the strike, the angler raises his rod smartly and hauls backward in one fast, smooth movement, reeling swiftly and lowering the rod to repeat the maneuver if necessary. If you react fast enough following the strike, you'll be able to skitter or slide many fish across the surface and away from weeds or brush. The fish is so surprised by this sudden tactic that he doesn't have a chance to dig in his heels before you get him away from his shelter.

Ultra-fine tackle is peculiarly suited to fishing fast, tiny brooks, and is perhaps deadliest in the warmer months when the water is low and clear as plate glass. Here, however, is where the threadliner's educated finger-tip becomes really important. In handling the light UL lures, check your casts over the target by dropping your finger tip to the reel spool. Then raise the rod sharply to give the lure forward momentum before engaging the line with the pickup bail. This takes all the slack out of the line, gets the lure moving even before it hits the water, and makes fouling nearly impossible even in inch-deep water. It also accounts for more fish. Experienced bass fishermen know that a plug that is moving with a lively wiggle the instant it hits the water will take more fish than a "dead" plug. Reasons are obvious. If the lure drops lifelessly, sinks a few feet, then begins moving, the bass has time to recognize the lure for what it is—just a piece of plastic, wood or metal. But the same bass is likely to be triggered into an instant strike when the quiet surface is suddenly dented by what appears to be a lively, swimming, or perhaps injured, minnow.

Distance casting is seldom important in small stream spinning. The average cast is well under 25 feet. But because of the clarity of the water and the angler's proximity to the fish, lure presentation is vital. For work on small streams, fast or slow water, the tiny UL spinners are preferred. They grab in the current and "float" along near the surface, and their free-swiveling blades are sensitive enough to work even in flat, slow water. The spinners hit the water with virtually no disturbance, and sink very slowly.

On slow meadow streams the ¹/₃₂-ounce spinners are excellent, although the ¹/₁₆-ounce wobbling plug, and

Comparatively large fish such as this can be taken by the persevering, skilled (and lucky) UL angler.

some 1/16-ounce spinners can be deadly. When cast with the finger-tip control method these lures barely make a dimple when dropped on flat water.

Current and cover spots that possibly hold fish determine how you will cast and retrieve a UL lure. Many fishermen just cast to the spot where they think a fish lies, plunking the lure right down on top of the fish. It's much better to put the lure well away from the spot you feel may hold a fish, then try to swim your lure tantalizingly into the fish's cone-of-vision.

With a tiny feather-light spinner, put your first cast into the shallow tail of a pool, delivering the cast from a point near the pour-in. Then guide the lure slowly among the rocks and brush of the deep bank, twitching it, allowing it to sink back, darting it forward. If there is a fast current, let the spinner hang momentarily in spots you feel may hold fish. Should a trout make a wide pass

at the spinner and miss, don't reel in to make another hasty cast. Instead, twitch the spinner repeatedly in that spot, and tease the trout into coming back and clobbering it.

Broad, deep rivers are far less difficult to fish than small streams. The rivers are a threadliner's delight, and the only stream savvy required, really, is the tactics of fishing your lure. Pick the heavier lures and cast up and across stream to swing a lure deep. Make the lure "work" by twitching the rod tip as the bait angles across the bottom.

Trolling and still-fishing with ultralight is a simplified game, and varies little from methods used with conventional gear. The trolling methods that pay off are first finding the fish, then offering the right lure at the proper depth. With UL, it's necessary to match lure and line test to the size of the fish you hope to catch and to the shock that your gear must weather on the strike.

VIII—UL Fishing Techniques

No fish is quite so vulnerable to ultralight methods as trout. Brown trout, often credited with super-intellect, become relatively minor problems to the expert UL spin-fisherman; rainbows become a snap; and brook trout are pushovers. These observations, of course, are based on the successes of the advanced and fully experienced UL angler, and of a period of fishing under varied conditions in many different areas. The point is that ultralight spinning is peculiarly adaptable to trout and trout fishing. Once you get the hang of UL spinning, and learn some of the "tricks" in ultralight fishing, you'll take trout as never before.

For example, with ultralight spinning tackle you can fish "hardware" upstream. As any experienced worm-dunker, wet fly man or nymph fisherman will agree, upstream fishing is about twice as effective as downstream fishing. Yet obviously it is difficult, if not impossible, to fish heavy spinning lures upstream because their weight promptly carries them to the bottom and hangs them there. So the man with orthodox spinning gear must turn his back to the current and fish downstream or across and down. That way, the force of the current and the rate-of-retrieve of his reel help to keep his lure off bottom and moving.

But the ultralight spin-fisherman has got it made. Spinning lures are so light, and require so very little water resistance to perform, that you can retrieve them at almost current speed, perhaps just a bit faster, without danger of hanging bottom or of destroying the lure's natural action. And this upstream casting is a deadly way to fish.

With ultralight tackle, you've got several things going for you. First, the lure is so light it does not sink quickly. Secondly, an ultralight spinner will spin, and an ultralight wobbler will wobble, against very light resistance, so you can bring it along with the current and keep it working throughout the retrieve. Riding with the current, the blade of an ultralight lure just sort of flutters, and fish seem to like it fluttering better than when it's twirling like crazy against the current.

In addition, the UL angler has a very light, sensitive rod that transmits to his hand the very "feel" of a stream—the gentle scrape of a lure against a rock, the tug of a twirling eddy, the lightest mouthing of a fish drifting downstream with the lure. Because of this, you'll hook more fish and fewer snags on upstream casts than would be possible with orthodox spinning gear.

You'd think you'd have to reel like mad to keep your lure moving at least as fast as the current in fast water, but the extra-fast gear ratio of an UL reel takes care of that. The ideal UL reel picks up more than 5 turns of line every time you crank the handle around, which permits you to keep the lure up and moving in almost any current.

Most spin-fishermen try to fish their lures deep, and most of the time they should. However, there are times when fish are "looking up," and if dredging doesn't produce, it's smart to work lures close to the surface or even on it. The very light weight of UL lures, and the control the short rod and fast reel provide, make it easy to keep lures high, even to make them cut the surface. "Riffling," they call it in Newfoundland, where salmon fishermen

make their flies swim across the surface of the water.

So when you fish trout with UL gear, turn your back on whatever's downstream and try fishing straight up, or up and across, and see what happens.

The tiny UL plugs are death on trout, particularly in the early season when the fish, still sluggish in the icy water, are feeding chiefly on dace, shiner, muddler, and other minnows. Trout do very little surface feeding in early spring, and while they'll take nymphs, streamers, and wet flies, it's difficult for trout to see these artificials because of the high, discolored water. They seem to spot little plugs quickly, though, and often take them even better than natural bait. Trout probably "feel" vibrations sent out by these darting, wobbling plugs.

Tiny spoons are also good in the early season. So are many spinners and spinner-fly combinations. Most of these lures are effective because they reflect light, and the sparkle makes it easy for trout to see them in murky water. Of course, all these lures are effective throughout the season. But I generally rely on jointed plugs when I think trout are working on minnows, whether in midsummer or in spring.

When the water is high and dingy, fish spinning lures deep and very slow. Later, when the streams drop and become clear, cast across and downstream, stopping the cast just before the lure hits the water by applying fingertip pressure to the spool. This way the lure moves the instant it strikes the water, and is kept moving as the current bows the line and the plug or spinner starts moving across current. Keep the rod high, occasionally dropping the tip, then raise it sharply to give the lure a quick, darting action. Stream minnows never swim a straight course; they dart, duck, dive and dip. And that's what the angler should make his spinning lures do.

The average clear-water trout stream is just right for working a baby plug this way. Short casts are best, and

Casting a deep-running "minispoon" to brushy edge of river nets a trout for UL fisherman.

lift the line so that the bait swims right at the surface, creating a tiny "V" wake. Often it is effective to skitter the plug over the top, then pause and allow it to wiggle just from the force of the current. You can lower the rod tip and let the plug settle, then make it struggle back to the top. All gamefish have a passion for minnows that they believe are in trouble, and so will strike such plugs even when they are not hungry.

One June on Manitoba's God's River my Cree Indian guide showed me a small 2-pound brook trout fanning over the gravel in 3 feet of water. In God's River a 2-pound brook trout is hardly worth fishing for, since 4 and 5-pounders are common and 7-pounders are not rare. However, this was the first trout I'd seen that offered me a reasonable chance to score with hairline tackle.

The guide held the freighter canoe above the fish, and I dropped a spoon so that it worked over the trout's head. He didn't even bat a fin as the little wobbler flashed by. I tried a different spoon, and a couple of spinners, and was about ready to concede that the trout was not for me when I remembered the trick of wiggling a baby plug across the top. I tied on a perch-finish plug, only 1½-inches long, and cast it into the current edge a yard above and to one side of the brookie. The little bait grabbed in the current and swung over the trout, settling in the flow 3 feet above the fish, where it wiggled furiously.

At first the trout ignored the plug, but when I began twitching it like an injured minnow struggling helplessly in the current, the fish began to stir. He darted left and then right, settled back, then started all over again. I thought he'd pop a scale! Following a drop-back, I lifted the plug to the surface, which it creased into a tiny "V." The trout suddenly detached himself from the gravel, bolted upward, and inhaled the plug. We beached him on a granite island 21 minutes later, and although I took much larger trout on flies from the river that same day,

the UL-caught squaretail is the one indelibly printed on my memory.

This method of fishing UL lures on the surface produces the same deadly results on the large, smooth pools of streams, in smallmouth bass water, and in ponds and lakes. The main difference between surface fishing the plugs in lakes, as compared to streams, is that there is no current by which you can activate the bait without actually moving it. But the "V" wake you can make the plug create is, in many ways, more effective in flat water. Probably lake or pond fish can detect a surface-struggling lure, because of its wake, even more readily than stream fish can.

One spring I made a 1300-mile tour of trout streams in Michigan and Wisconsin. I started in lower Michigan and fished the Pere Marquette River, the Platte, Manistee, Boardman and Ausable. Then I crossed the Straits of Mackinac to the upper peninsula's Fox, Manistique, and Big Indian rivers. From there I drove south to Wisconsin's Peshtigo, Oconto, and Wolf rivers. The hairline tackle caught trout all the way, but probably the fastest fishing came one day on a broad, deep stretch of the lower Manistee River, near High Bridge, Michigan.

Here the Manistee winds through long meadows, its current unbroken by logs or boulders. There are no ripples, no bumpy water. In the absence of rising fish, you have to cast "blind." I waded downstream, casting first to the left bank, then the right, using a small wobbling spoon. All I caught in that first half-hour was one 6-inch brownie. I switched to miniature plugs, and upped the score by another brown—a 1-pounder. Then I changed lures regularly, running through a field of hairline hardware. Finally I tried a "sonic" spinner to see if the vibrating blade would attract more fish.

I overshot the first cast and plunked it into weeds on the far bank. When I twitched the lure free it fell into the

Though fish is small, veteran UL angler plays fish carefully and stays alert to trout's last-minute surges.

Trout flops crazily at angler's feet but resiliency of rod and give-of-line prevents a break-off.

river, and by the time I lowered the rod and recovered slack it had settled in 8 feet of water. When I got the spinner moving, a rainbow that had been scratching his belly on gravel belted it. He weighed an ounce under 2 pounds!

Thereafter I made all casts directly shoreward, gave the spinner time to sink, and dredged up a couple more bullet-headed 'bows. But I discovered that the resistance of the blade caused the lure to rise when pulled against the current. So I about-faced, began wading upstream, and fished the water I'd covered previously. The current then washed the spinner deep, and while I had to reel a little faster to keep a tight line, the tiny lure hung rainbows that had just refused other offerings.

As a general rule, the major trick to fishing UL hardware is to get the lures *down* when it is necessary to scrape bottom for fish, which can be much of the time. Early in the season, for example, trout are likely to be deep, and again late in the season when the water is bright and warm, and still again when heavy stream traffic drives them to bedrock.

Another important trick, obvious as it may seem, is to work UL lures carefully in spots where trout are likely to be. Casting helter-skelter, and fishing only *water* instead of *trout-holding spots,* isn't likely to result in a heavy creel.

Once on Michigan's Ontonagan River, along the Middle Branch above Agate Falls, Bob Otto, Joe Grobarek, Ron Gentzen, and I started fishing with flies, using our ultralight spinning rods. (These midget spin-sticks throw a fly surprisingly well, once you get the feel of using them as fly rods. Most 54-inch spinning rods handle 50 feet of fly line (size HEH H-DT 5) easily, and with the double-haul can shoot even more.) Using streamers, the four of us caught three small trout while fishing downstream. Then working back upstream with UL gear, and fishing "sonic" spinners on hairline, we took 11 trout, including a 14-inch brown that was snaked from under a ledge. It was warm and sunny that day, the water low and clear, and the trout were sulking under rocks in shaded pockets. The trout never paid much attention to our flies, probably never even saw them half the time, but when we cast tiny spinners upstream and let them flutter and hum along the edges of the pockets, we took trout regularly.

That afternoon, Joe went down to the falls and had a picnic with small trout. He started at the head of the rapids and worked down, taking trout all the way by flipping a spinner into the foam and letting it wash naturally into the pockets. In that boiling current, even 7-inch trout felt like monsters, Joe said. He even lost several that size when they went rolling through white water and snapped his line.

Some of the techniques outlined here for trout are equally effective in fishing for bass in rivers or streams. However, in my opinion the lure still hasn't been made that demolished bass better than a piece of pork-chunk, and UL's hair-fine line is just the ticket for tossing a chunk up into the lilies—and bringing it back with a bigmouth bass attached. With UL gear you can cast a chunk—even a mere strip of porkrind—without adding a spinner, shot, or anything else for extra weight. A pork-chunk and hook, on hairline, doesn't leave a bass much

room for doubt; he thinks it's something good to eat because there's no telltale hardware, harness, or heavy line to arouse his suspicion.

Bubble fishing—the old method of using a plastic bubble partially filled with water to cast light poppers or flies—works very effectively with UL gear. What's needed, however, are some grape-size bubbles to replace the large bubbles now available. With such tiny bubbles it would be possible to fish dry flies, wet flies, and nymphs easily with UL tackle.

Of all the techniques open to the bubble-floating UL angler, perhaps the drifted nymph is most destructive to trout. I use the method often on large streams where extremely long casts are required and fly casting is impractical for one reason or another. Generally a size 10 or 12 weighted nymph is used (size 14 occasionally in late summer), and the bubble is attached to the line above the nymph. Reel the bubble close to the rod tip and reach up and out with the rod to start the cast. The casting movement must be in a long, slow, sweeping motion to prevent the dangling nymph from fouling. Casts are made up and across stream. The nymph settles close to the bottom and begins drifting naturally with the current. You have to reel in just enough line during the "float" to take up slack, and herein lies the "touch" that must be acquired for nymph fishing with a bubble. If you keep too taut a line during the bubble's float, you will impede the natural drift and upset the built-in effectiveness of the nymph. Reeling too slowly during the drift will give slack line, so that there may not be enough resistance to hook a striking fish. Ordinarily a trout coming to a bottombumping nymph will encounter just enough resistance from the floating bubble to prick himself. Thus hook points should be honed just as sharp as possible. Many trout will pick up drifting nymphs undetected, and the only hint of a strike is the slight pause, or tremor, of the floating bubble. At the instant the bubble appears to hesitate, tighten and raise the rod tip swiftly but smoothly to set the hook.

The distance between the bubble and nymph should vary, of course, according to water depth. Whenever possible a nymph should be fished so that it drifts close to bottom. On small streams the UL angler can work nymphs without a bubble by fastening a single splitshot to the line about 15 inches above the nymph. The problem here is to see the line and be able to detect a pause in the drift of the nymph, which denotes a strike. This is difficult even on short casts, unless you tie in a short piece of white thread at about the point where the line will enter the water on an average cast. Often you'll see a trout's side flash as he turns to take the lure. On some swift-water streams it is possible to fish nymphs with a split-shot and not be too concerned about detecting strikes, since many trout will hook themselves in fastmoving water.

A number of bubble-fishing variations can be worked out according to conditions. Many bubble fishermen use dry flies in conjunction with wet flies; the dry fly being hung from a dropper well up the line from the wet fly. Some Wisconsin fishermen use bubbles during the big annual mayfly hatch, but instead of fishing an artificial dry fly they bait up with a live mayfly. In the West, where

2½-inch long salmon flies hatch, these also are used—*alive*. These flies are so large they must be attached to the hook properly. When salmon flies are hooked behind the head, trout seem to take only the fleshy posterior, and miss the hook. Best way is to use a long-shank hook nearly as long as the fly, and attach the fly by inserting the hook point on an angle below the salmon fly's chin and run the hook back through the entire length of the body, letting the hook point protrude slightly at the tail.

In the weedy realm of the largemouth bass the UL angler must be extra cautious or go broke replacing his lost lures. There is a clearwater canal brushing the edge of the Overseas Highway on Key Largo, Florida. Once, while all the tourist world barreled by in hasty pursuit of salt water fish, I walked the road and stopped occasionally to fish through small openings in the wall of mangroves that shields the canal. I'd poke my 4½-foot UL rod through, make a bow-and-arrow or catapult cast, and drop my lure against the opposite bank which was only 15 or 20 feet away. I caught a number of bass in the ½ to 2-pound bracket, but better fish rushed up or downstream and the line went . . . *pop!*

Yellow perch, crappies, and white perch all feed mainly on small minnows, and there's no better way to take them than with small UL lures. As with most panfish, however, it's necessary to master the very slow retrieve to score consistently on yellow perch. Slightly faster retrieves can be used on white perch when they're schooling and on a feeding spree.

Spinner-fly combinations are good for river panfish, particularly rock bass, or "red-eye." The red-eye really sees red when you drift a spinner-fly to him and twitch it gently past his nose. For panfish in moving water, concentrate on the current edges, the holes, and sheltered pockets, remembering that panfish dislike strong currents.

Most panfish go hard for a mere sliver of white porkrind on a size 4 hook. Use inch-long, ¼-inch wide (at the base) porkrind strips tapered to a point, and fish them along the outside edge of lily pad beds. Cast the porkrind to the lilies, then allow it to settle slowly, wiggling and worming its way down. Gentle nudging with the rod tip activates the porkrind. In dingy water add a small chrome spinner and red bead just in front of the hookeye.

For crappies in 10 to 15 feet of water try the UL plugs and spoons first, and if these fail switch to a white or yellow weighted marabou streamer fly (size 8, 3X-long hook), and as second choice a red-and-white or red-and-yellow bucktail. The marabous seem to have the edge, and I always tie my weighted crappie flies on flat or ringed-eye hooks so that when I mount a spinner in front of the fly the little blade will wobble freely.

The trick to crappie fishing, of course, is to find 'em—then to sink your lures deep enough so the crappies will not have to go chasing around to find them. Once you locate a school of crappies, make a cast, allow the lure to sink, then keep it working in the fish-holding area until you get a strike. Crappies prefer a very slow-moving lure, animated by twitching the rod tip. In crappie fishing there's no need to keep a lure swimming rapidly in a horizontal line.

Some saltwater fish are structurally perfect for UL fishing. Gainey Maxwell of Key West used ultralight to take this little snapper.

Spinning lures have a tendency to spin faster, sometimes, than a swivel can operate. When this occurs the line picks up some twist, and a twisted line will not spool smoothly or come off the reel in neat spirals. Most of this trouble can be avoided by tying a small swivel into the line about 6 inches above the lure. The swivel seems to work more efficiently in that position than when it is attached directly to the end of the line. In addition, tiny UL lures need plenty of freedom to perform best, and they seem to act best when the soft monofilament is clinch-knotted directly to the eye of the lure. When fishing heavy water, and you find that its speed and resistance are making your lures spin drastically, you may need two swivels to take up the twist. Rather than hook them together at the end of the line, tie a barrel swivel into the line above the lure and a snap swivel at the lure.

Walleyes, pickerel, and northern pike—even lake trout—are fair game for ultralight when the fish average under 5 pounds and 2 or 3 pound test line is used. In Manitoba's Cranberry Portage country I caught lake trout up to 4 pounds and a northern of 8 pounds on a 1-pound line, but this is not practical. In each case the fish were literally nursed to the net, and that's not exactly legitimate angling.

If you locate walleyes, pickerel, northerns, or lake

trout in reasonably open water, and use 2-pound line, then there is nothing remarkable about scoring repeatedly on fish 5 pounds or better. But most walleyes and lakers haunt rocky areas; pickerel and pike live among snags and weeds, so the hairliner would do well to stick with the smaller stuff.

Although most walleyes, lake trout and northerns of average size move deep in hot weather, most small fish of these species remain in comparatively shallow water. Thus UL fishing can provide good sport with these cold water fish even in hot weather. As an example, Nokomis Lake in northwestern Manitoba has a year-round shoreline population of lake trout running up to 4 pounds but averaging from 1½ to 2 pounds. While these fish would provide little excitement on standard tackle, they're big stuff with ultralight. I fished Nokomis with Frank Gilbert and Earl Kennedy, both of Winnipeg, and for 3 hours we jigged and trolled the deep dropoffs trying to raise some of the lake's 20-to-40-pounders. Finally we went ashore for lunch, and while waiting for the beans to heat I cast a small jig from the rocks. I caught a baby lake of about 2 pounds, then a 3-pounder, then a few more, all small but a barrel of fun on ultralight. I found the fish cruising the shoreline, hovering over rocks 3 to 6 feet down. After lunch I excused myself from further deep-water work, stayed with my UL outfit, and had a ball catching those adolescent lakers. I beached 21 of them, and lost some, and though Earl and Frank finally put-putted in towing a 32-pounder, I felt that I'd had a better day!

Some salt water fish seem *structurally* perfect for ultralight fishing. One afternoon, for example, a gent with the magnificent name of Ygnacio Carbonell, his pal Albert Greene, and I, left the docks at Key West, Florida to fish the flats, mangrove channels and guts that border the lower Keys. Following the usual fracases with bonefish, barracuda, and bonnet sharks, we settled down to jig the bottom of a deep channel which Ygnacio said often produced "lookdowns," a fish considered by gourmets to be even more desirable for the platter than pompano. The first few casts proved the lookdowns were there, and while we caught a few, many more followed our jigs up out of the green depths, looked at 'em, then turned away waving their forked tails.

The lookdown, which is similar to the moonfish but has elongated dorsal and anal fins, is paper-thin and has a mouth to match. Beneath the lookdown's towering forehead is a mouth about the size of a large bean. It became obvious that the fish following our jigs wanted a smaller lure, so I fed them an inch-long jig with ultralight tackle. Each cast brought a lookdown, and Ygnacio and Albert became so fascinated over the productiveness of the midget spinning outfit that I was forced to take a seat while they borrowed it and caught lookdown after lookdown, giggling like kids each time a fish bowed the light rod.

Small mackerel, bluefish, sand perch, and many other salt water species are easy pickin's with ultralight. It may be necessary with some salt water fish to use a short, fine braided wire leader or a heavy nylon shock tippet since many salt water fish have serrated teeth that can sever fine mono like a razor. Salt water fish are, of course, much stronger than fresh water fish, but most of the salt water species will be hooked in comparatively open water, so they can be played out with the very lightest of UL tackle. There normally are no stumps, logs, lily stems or snags in the salt, only occasional coral or pier pilings that may break things up. And even these problems are seldom encountered by the salt-going UL angler, since most of the fish haunt mud or sand bottom channels and canals, or live around docks and boats in marinas.

IX—Bait Fishing With Ultralight

The story of ultralight spinning wouldn't be complete without mentioning its usefulness in fishing natural baits.

Take, for instance, the August day when my wife and I fished a nameless pond near Minong, Wisconsin. Phyllis used one of my ultralight outfits while I went off with a fly rod to see if I could find some rising trout. I didn't. But when I returned an hour later, Phyllis had two plump brook trout. She'd taken them on worms she'd rooted out of a bed of daisies. Phyllis used the worms on a No. 4 hook, and cast them 40 feet without added weight.

Hairline gear is perfect for bait fishing because you can cast a worm, crayfish, hellgrammite or minnow without a lead sinker. This is of tremendous value when fishing clear water where a heavy line or a hunk of lead might scare fish, or interfere with the natural movement of the bait.

Many trout fishermen plunk themselves down on the bank and leisurely dangle worms, small crayfish, or minnows, and wonder why fish don't come their way. Bank fishermen do catch the occasional trout, of course, but their catches are minor compared to the fish taken by the trouter who washes his worms naturally over the bottom.

More successful than the stillfisherman working from the bank is the fly-rodder or spinfisherman who wades upstream, casting his bait to the far bank and letting it wash down naturally with the current. But even this bait expert comes in second best to the ultralight fan fishing the same way. The difference is that the UL angler casts his bait without fish-scaring lead weight, with much finer line, and his baits drift more life-like in the current. The most important single factor in fishing natural bait is to present the bait in such a manner that the fish gets no hint that the bait is booby-trapped with a hook. The drag of line or a sinker alerts more trout to possible hanky-panky than any other mistake the bait fisherman can make.

Small worms are best for trout, and you should use a single worm on a size 4, short shank hook. The worm should be hooked in and out the middle just once so that it lies straight in the water, with both ends free to wiggle enticingly. Generally it is best to work upstream, for a number of reasons, but chiefly because it permits "floating" the worm naturally with the current.

A stream floor normally slopes from a shallow side to a deep side, and by casting from the shallow bank to the opposite, you can swing a worm over the spots most likely to hold trout. Cast up-and-across stream, or straight upstream, halting the cast with the finger tip just before the worm hits. Close the reel bail, and reel in the slack

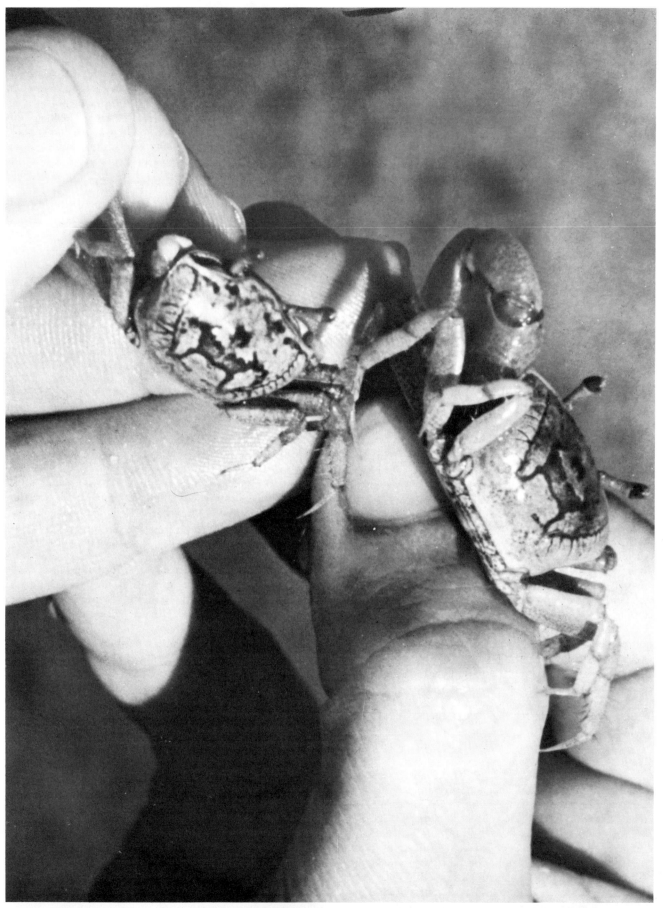

Tiny fiddler crabs like these are a perfect bait for UL fishing in saltwater. They have all the weight necessary for ultralight casting.

as the worm washes down. Follow the path of the bait with the rod tip so there'll be little drag and the drift will be as natural as possible.

The same basic system is used in all stream or river fishing, for both trout and bass, with any bait—worms, minnows, crayfish, hellgrammites, nymphs, crickets, grasshoppers, or grubs. The live mayfly nymph, incidentally, is a deadly bait for trout and smallmouth bass. Get them by turning over rocks in streams, catching them with a wire screen or burlap cloth as they drift down. Many fishermen get nymphs by digging them out of the mud banks of the larger streams, then they freeze them in cartons so they have a year-around supply. The 1½-inch long mayfly nymphs, called "wrigglers" in the Midwest, are hooked through the thorax, and while they are not the hardiest bait they hold up reasonably well. With a heavy wire No. 4 hook it's possible to cast a large wriggler on ½-pound test line without adding weight, but with a heavier line it will be necessary to add a split shot about a foot above the nymph. Since nymphs are most effective fished right on bottom, where they bounce along over the trout's natural feeding grounds, it's generally best to fish one with a single split shot sinker.

Late in the season, when trout so often resort to eating tiny midges to the exasperation of many fly fishermen, try getting a dozen or so large black ants. The ants that live along the banks of my favorite creek are ½-inch long, and always remind me of the *bala*, or bullet, ants of Costa Rica. Fish the ants by pushing a tiny size 18 or 20 dry fly hook into the ant's fanny, and add a split shot to the line a foot above to gain casting weight. Cast the ant upstream, and let it drift down "dead," with no movement at all imparted to the bait. Fishing ants this way calls for exceptional "touch" and skill, but in thin, clear water it sometimes will outfish other methods 10 to 1.

Ultralight even makes surface fishing with certain baits possible. You can use large grasshoppers and crickets, locusts (cicadas), beetles, praying mantis, dragon, stone and willow flies, and any other large insect having some substance, to take not only trout but also bass and panfish. Beetles are a secondary choice in the bait department, since most of them tend to sink anyway, as do caterpillars much of the time. But all these baits can be fished to genuine advantage by the ultralight angler. Use small, fine-wire hooks (ordinary bait hooks are too heavy and will pull a bug under), and as fine line as is practical. Anyone who has ever visited a hatchery and kicked up grasshoppers that blew into the holding pools knows of the lusty appetite trout have for surface-struggling insects.

I'm sure you have never walked along the shores of a meadow stream without seeing tiny, ½-inch frogs squirting through the grass. Until ultralight, it was virtually impossible to fish such tiny frogs with any semblance of naturalness. Now, however, by using UL, you can hook one of these midget kickers through the lips with a size 10 or 12 hook, and flip him 30 feet onto the slate-smooth surface of your favorite trout pool. Unhurt, the frog will kick his spots off trying to make the nearest grassy over-hang, but then the pool opens up in a shower of spray and the frog disappears as you tighten and feel the satisfying, throbbing jolts of a good fish.

Those baby crawfish that populate most slow-moving trout streams are another bait that should not be overlooked. They're equally good for smallmouth bass. Of all smallmouth baits, however, I suspect the hellgrammite (larvae of the dobson fly) is the most consistent producer. The bottom of most good smallmouth streams literally crawls with hellgrammites, so bronze-backs are accustomed to feeding on them heavily. Hook a hellgrammite under its "collar" with a short-shank hook. Many bait fishermen remove the hellgrammite's "pincers" to keep him from grabbing onto rocks. For this reason hellgrammites (and crayfish too) should be kept off bottom, but as close to it as possible.

Incidentally, Falcon grip type hooks—those with tiny bait-saver barbs along the shanks—are best for most kind of bait fishing since they help keep the bait on the hook.

The common house cockroach is a delicacy for sunfish, and in parts of the South they sell for as much as $1.25 a dozen. Corn-borers, catalpa worms, and pine-borers also are devasting panfish baits, and all of them can be presented better with UL gear than by any other means.

Minnow fishing for bass with ultralight tackle is practical only when the smaller shiner or chub minnows are used; those big 6 to 10-inch chubs used for pot-bellied bass in some areas certainly are too heavy to handle on UL.

There are a number of methods used for hooking live minnows, but I prefer the simple method of passing a small hook through both lips of a minnow. Attached this way the minnow casts best, doesn't turn over in the air or foul the line. When the minnow hits the water, close the reel bail immediately, and gradually swim the minnow back, slow enough so it can dart around and thus attract fish. A good stock of minnows is needed for this kind of hairlining, but the investment in bait will pay dividends in bass-in-the-pan.

One of the best methods I know for taking bass, walleyes and northern pike, as well as over-sized rainbow and brown trout, is UL dunking of minnows in deep holes. Remember that big fish are likely to be lying right on bottom, in the deepest part, so place yourself so that you'll be in a position to drift a minnow into the deepest part of a hole—and resign yourself to waiting that lunker out. Keep plenty of slack line ready, and leave the bail of your reel open. When your notice the line moving steadily away, signalling that a fish has picked up your minnow, pay out line smoothly and give the fish his head. When he's had time enough to mouth the minnow solidly, close the reel bail, take up the remaining slack, and hit the fish as hard as the strength of line will allow.

Many fishermen scale their minnows and fish them dead right on bottom. The theory is that the naked bait releases more scent, and fish can smell it from a greater distance. You might try this sometime when fishing is slow.

The possibilities of bait fishing with ultralight are unlimited, just as in fishing artificial lures with matchstick tackle. You'll find that during nearly every fishing trip ultralight will fit in some special way, just as hors d'oeuvres and cocktails brighten a dinner party.

11

Custom Rod Building

Skilled craftsmen still turn out quality rods.

Joe Bonadonna, one of America's finest custom rod-builders, uses sandpaper and lathe to shape a spinning rod's handle.

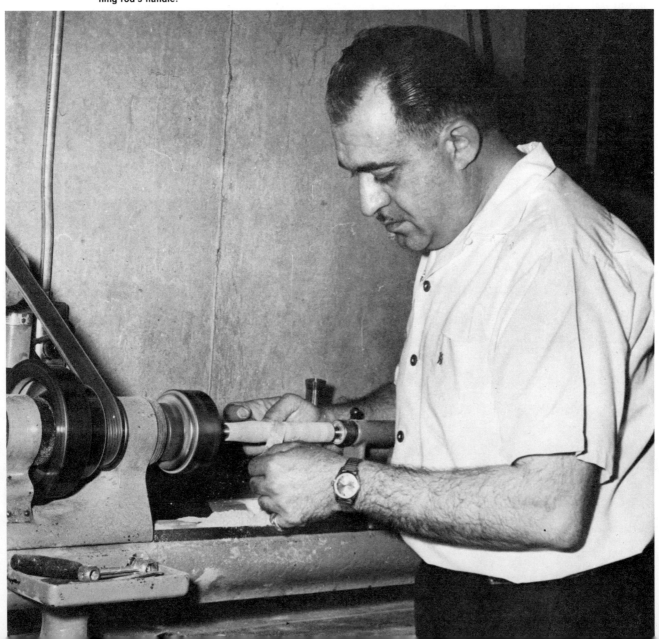

Some of the finest fishing rods produced in America come out of a tiny workshop in Mundelein, Illinois. They are the product of the craftsmanship, fishing, and casting skills of Joe Bonadonna, a serious and life-long angler.

A one-time tournament caster, Bonadonna started building rods in 1939. At first he constructed rods only for his own use. Then friends started demanding some. Finally, the business grew until today Joe has a deluxe shop in Mundelein and several aides, and produces custom rods all year long.

Bonadonna's rod building firm, called the Bon-A-Don Tackle Company, not only manufactures all sorts of custom glass rods, but also handles repairs of the "customizing" of any glass or bamboo rod. Bonadonna has a vast stock of glass blanks with which to build or repair any make rod. He also has a large inventory of bamboo sections, rare these days, for the repair or building of bamboo rods. Having tested all makes of glass rod blanks, Bonadonna now uses Conolon glass exclusively in his custom line of Bon-A-Don rods, believing it superior. His shop, incidentally, turns out about 200 custom-made rods yearly, ranging in price from $42.50 on up.

Why custom rods?

"There are many reasons for the custom-building of rods," says Bonadonna. "For one, the glue used in making rods takes a long time to dry. Many big manufacturers, who work on a production basis, can't allow rods they make to set around for months just for the glue to dry properly. As a result, one day the reel seat of such a rod turns right in the fisherman's hand, or one of the ferrules pulls off.

"Also, the majority of factory-made rods simply do not have enough guides. In turning out our custom rods, we never skimp on guides, and we place the guides properly so that a rod has just the right action. Then too, some factory-made rods have ferrules that are merely pinched on instead of being mounted with epoxy glue.

Any rod having a pinched-on ferrule eventually will break at the ferrule."

A Bon-A-Don custom rod will have a cork grip shaped to fit individual specifications and tastes. And the action of the rod will be designed to give the best performance with the kind of reel, size of line, and lure weights most often used by the fisherman for whom the rod is being made. Most factory rods nowadays are of excellent quality, but a lot are designed for use with a wide range of lures and reels. Some manufacturers, in fact, claim their rods will perform properly with a wider range of lure weights than is physically possible.

"No fisherman should ever test a rod he wants to buy with practice tournament casting weights," Bonadonna advises. "Instead, he should try the rod with the kind of plugs, spoons, spinners, jigs, and other lures that he actually fishes with to see how well the rod casts. Such lures cast a lot differently than ordinary tournament or practice plugs. When I build a custom rod for a fisherman I have him try it, actually cast with it, many times before the rod is completely finished. The fisherman will cast with the reel, line, and lures he normally uses when fishing. If the rod doesn't perform perfectly, or suit the fisherman exactly, alterations can be made before the rod is completed."

Bonadonna spends weeks upon weeks testing tackle and making design changes. Once, for example, he took, literally, a "truck load" of rods to Great Bear Lake in the Northwest Territories to try them out on monster lake trout. Not long ago he took another big batch of rods to the Colorado River in Costa Rica where he matched them against hard-fighting, bone-jawed, heavyweight tarpon.

Speaking of rod repair, Joe says that most of the rods brought to his shop for repair are broken through carelessness. "It's funny," he reports, "how few fishermen want to admit they broke a rod by stepping on it, or by

Lou Gnadt (left) and Al Hajduk at work building Bon-A-Don custom rods.

Hajduk mounts guides on a bait-casting rod.

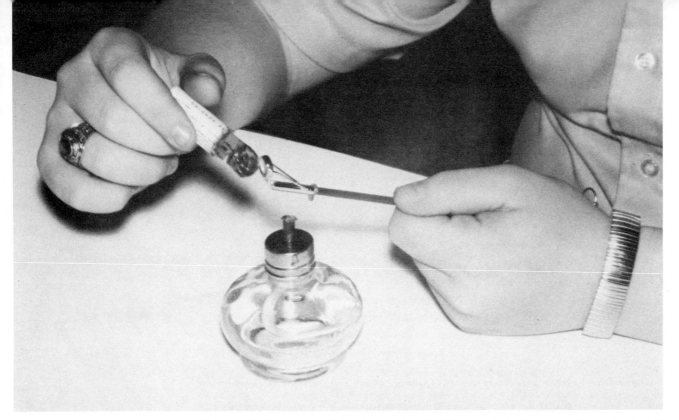

Tip-top is glued onto a rod with ferrule cement. Rod-builders use alcohol lamps to melt cement, but afield anglers can use cigarette lighters or a match to soften glue for emergency repairs. Metal tip-tops are fitted to rod tips to within $\frac{1}{64}$ of an inch, allowing sufficient space for the glue. Many tip-tops are fitted too tight, forcing out most of the glue. New tip-tops should be checked for cuts or abrasions before mounting on rods. Tip-tops are subjected to the most wear, and if nicked they will fray or cut lines.

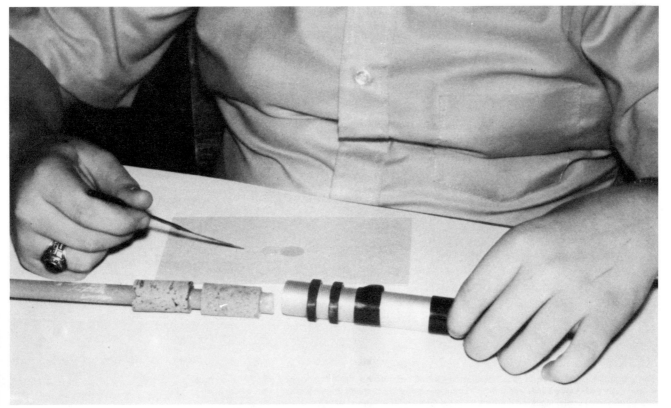

Gluing a reel seat over cork "bushings" provides air space, less weight, and a more perfect cementing bond. Double-locking reel seats should be used when possible.

Broken sections of a hollow glass rod are repaired by splicing. Splicing works, however, only when broken section of rod is ¼-inch in diameter or more. Broken part of rod is cut at an angle and filed smooth, so that both ends meet flush. A piece of fiberglass with outside diameter the same as the inside diameter of the broken piece is then inserted into the break and cemented with epoxy. After glue dries the excess is filed off, and the repair then wrapped over to conceal it. Rod's action can be almost as good as new.

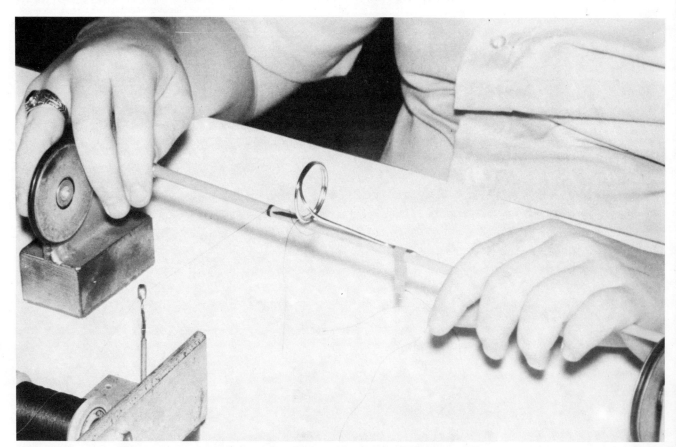

When wrapping new guide to rod, end of guide's "leg" should be stoned down and smoothed so that wrapping thread climbs easily and tightly. Taping down one leg of guide allows worker to have both hands free to turn rod evenly. Most rod builders use size A nylon for wrapping of fresh water rods, and size D for salt water rods. Wrapping "uphill" toward the guide, and keeping even tension on thread, is most important to mounting guide properly.

slamming a car door on it. They nearly always lie and say a fish they hooked snapped the rod."

Once a fisherman brought Bonadonna a glass rod that had been broken in four places. "I really don't know why it broke," the guy said to Bonadonna with a straight face. "It was just a little bass."

"What?" exclaimed Joe! "You mean to say a little bass busted this rod in *four* places?"

Joe reminds fishermen always to keep rods in their aluminum or fiber cases when not in use. A rod properly protected can't be broken. Remember, too, that rods should be put into their cases with the tips up, which will make it less likely for damage to occur to the tip than if placed into a case tip-down. When returning a rod to its case always be careful not to knock the rod's guides against the side of the case, since that will bend, loosen, or break off a guide.

A glass rod placed carelessly into a car trunk may get nicked or fractured, and it will later break cleanly right

Weighted rollers and heavy thread holders plus good lighting help Mark Bonadonna turn an otherwise difficult job into an enjoyable hobby.

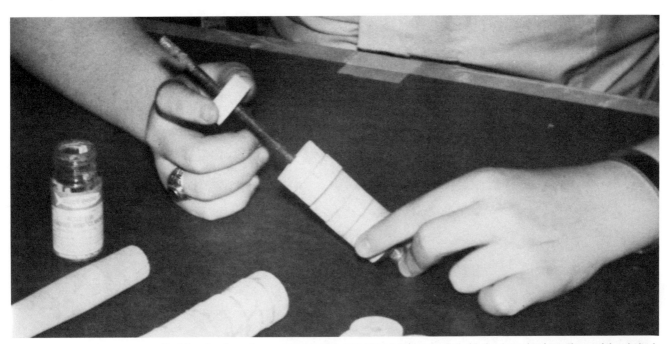

Cork handles for rods are made from "½-inch triple A Species cork," with the rings glued together and then bolted tight on a ¼-inch threaded steel rod, using a large washer and winged nut to force rings tightly together. When glue is dry and rings secured, they are removed and center hole is filed out to proper diameter for rod.

Parts and some of the equipment used in turning out custom glass rods includes rod blanks (butt section and tip section), guides, cement, nylon thread, varnish, color preservative, etc.

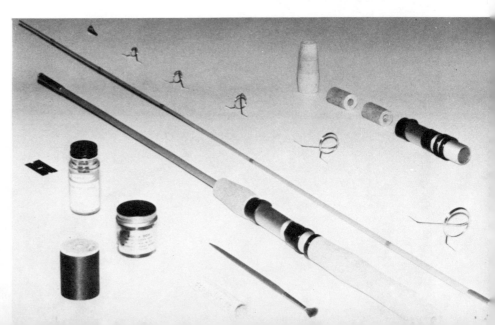

where it was nicked. A screwdriver sliding into a glass rod can nick it, and cause it to break the next time the rod is flexed or put under "load."

Bonadonna gives an interesting demonstration of how easily a glass rod can be broken, once a part of the glass is fractured. He takes a discarded glass rod section, and shows how it is almost impossible to break it by bending it between close-held thumbs. Then he takes a small knife and, using the dull side of the blade, taps the glass rod section very lightly. Just a hairline mark then shows

on the glass. But Joe now snaps the glass section between his thumbs with a minimum of pressure.

Joe Bonadonna—like other fine rod craftsmen around the country—takes fierce pride in his work. Unfortunately, there are too few fishermen around who care about quality tackle.

One evening, for example, a man arrived at the Bon-A-Don shop and asked Joe, "Do you make fishin' poles?" "No," Joe replied turning away. "Only God can make a pole. I make fishing rods!"

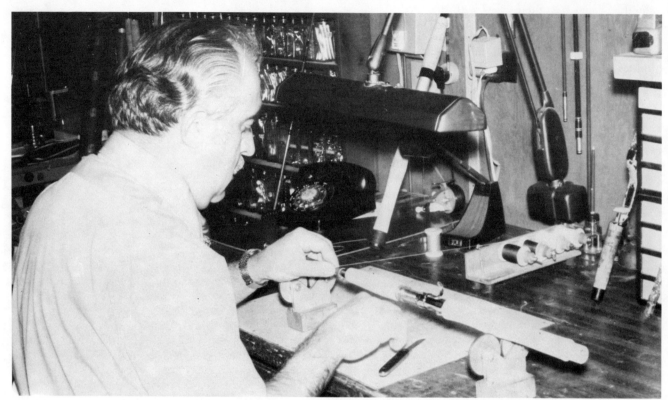

Bonadonna checks thread tension before beginning a wrap on one of his custom heavy-duty bait-casting rods.

Guide alignment is checked carefully on every Bon-A-Don rod before color preservative or varnish is applied to wrappings.

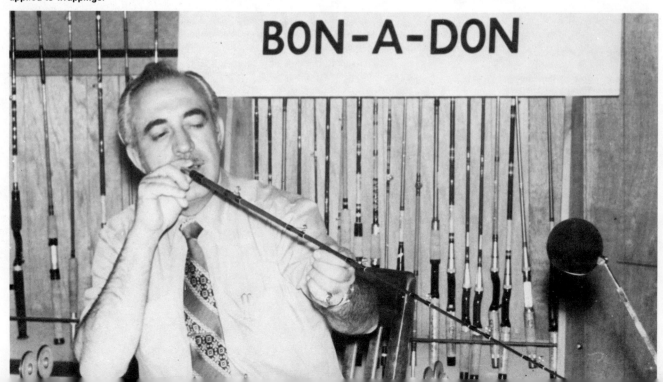

12

Glossary of Knots

A friend once wrote that a knot is "a means of fastening together the parts of one or more flexible materials such as rope, line, or leader, or of fastening such material to a stanchion, mast, or cleat. Knots include bends, hitches, and splices."

That is probably as good a definition of a knot as is possible, but it doesn't help the fisherman who wants to learn how to tie one.

The average angler under average fishing conditions need know only a few knots. For example, probably 90% of fishing situations can be taken care of by the fisherman who knows how to tie a "clinch knot," a "barrel knot," a "double surgeon's knot," and a "nail knot." However, there are many dozens of different kinds of knots, and under certain circumstances each is valuable. Thus a skilled fisherman can tie several kinds of knots.

All other factors being normal, the angler's knots are the weakest part of his equipment. More prize fish are lost because knots pull out, slip, or cut themselves than are lost because of a broken line, fractured rod, or jammed reel. In some kinds of fishing—say, still-fishing for bluegills—knot-tying may be relatively unimportant; but in other kinds of fishing, such as tarpon angling, billfishing, taking large northern pike on flies, etc., skillful knot-tying means the difference between boating fish and losing fish.

In learning to tie a new knot it is better to practice it with heavy cord or light rope rather than with monofilament or other fishing line. The heavier material will show more clearly how the knot is shaped and formed, and once the knot is quickly and easily tied with heavy material it then can be readily tied with fishing line.

After a knot is formed it must be slowly and carefully drawn up tight. Almost without exception, knots that are not properly tightened pull out. In some instances it is easier to tighten a knot in heavy monofilament nylon if the line is moistened with saliva prior to forming the knot.

Any knot will reduce the strength of fishing line to some extent, and this includes the so-called "100% Knot." But some knots, such as the "Double Surgeon's Knot," reduce line strength more than others. The average quality knot, however, when properly tied should reduce line strength to no more than 85% and the best knots will give around 95% of the line strength.

Tarpon fishing is a test of the angler's knot-tying skills.

SINGLE SHEET BEND   DOUBLE SHEET BEND

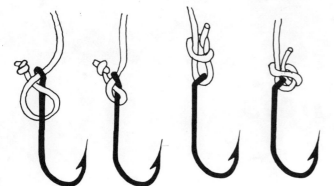

DOUBLE EYE KNOT

1. Tie a "Single Running" Knot (half-hitch) to end of leader and push thru eye of hook.

2. Pass loop over bend of hook and draw up to hook eye.

3. Take short end of "Single Running" Knot, push under loop, against the shank, and draw tight.

4. Finished knot.

SLIDING OVERHEAD KNOT   ROUND-TURN FISHHOOK TIE

RETURN KNOT   RETURN KNOT

This is used for tying a fly or lure to a leader, and it may also be used for tying the tippet end of your leader to your fly. It is a little more difficult than the Turle or Figure Eight Knots, but it is very strong and especially well adapted for nylon leaders. The easiest way is to tie it directly on the hook, as follows.

Figure 1

Thrust the end of the leader through the eye of the hook. Pass it down behind the hook and up the front, holding the loop open between your thumb and forefinger, as shown in Fig. 1.
Then make a second turn behind the first, holding the loop again open, as shown in Fig. 2.

Figure 2

Next pass the end under both loops, and pull on the standing part of the leader. As the coils draw up, be sure that the loops are pushed over the eye of the hook, as shown in Fig. 3.

TURLE KNOT

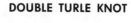

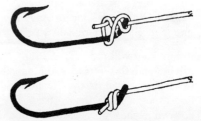

Figures 3 and 4

Finally, pull up the knot tightly and it will appear as in Fig. 4. This is the neatest and probably the most secure of all hook knots.

DOUBLE TURLE KNOT

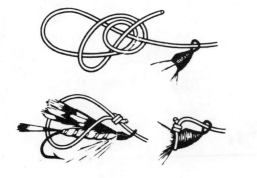

FIGURE EIGHT KNOT

CLINCH OR "HALF-BLOOD" KNOT

IMPROVED CLINCH OR PANDRE KNOT

JAM KNOT WITH AN EXTRA TUCK

CLINCH ON SHANK

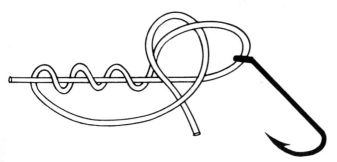

DOUBLE LOOP CLINCH KNOT

LOOP KNOT

JANSIK SPECIAL

HOMER RHODE LOOP

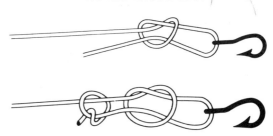

DAVE HAWK'S DROP LOOP KNOT

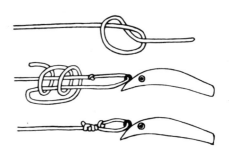

Tie a simple knot in leader about 5 inches from end and draw it tight. Pass end of leader thru eye of lure bringing it back parallel with running leader. Bend terminal down and around, forming a circle below parallel strands. Pass end around and thru circle in leader twice. Draw it tight, slowly. Pull on lure and the jam knot will slide down to the simple knot, leaving lure attached with a loose loop permitting it to vibrate or wiggle freely.

NAIL LOOP

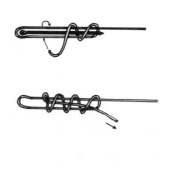

SALMON HOOK KNOT

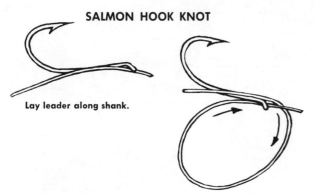

Lay leader along shank.

Bring Loop around and insert thru eye whole length of leader.

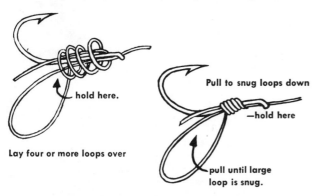

hold here.

Lay four or more loops over

Pull to snug loops down

—hold here

pull until large
loop is snug.

DOUBLE SALMON KNOTS

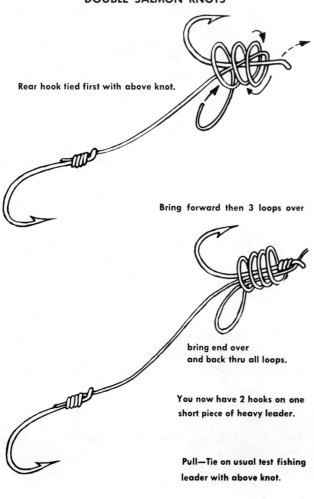

Rear hook tied first with above knot.

Bring forward then 3 loops over

bring end over
and back thru all loops.

You now have 2 hooks on one
short piece of heavy leader.

**Pull—Tie on usual test fishing
leader with above knot.**

BUMPER TIE

Run short end back thru eye—Remaining leader.

Bring over cut side of hook eye—Make loop.

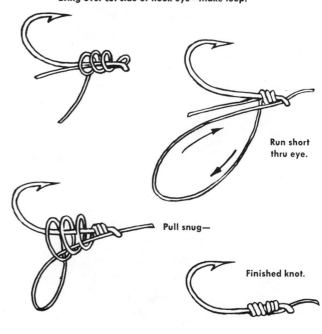

Run short
thru eye.

Pull snug—

Finished knot.

DROPPER SNELL KNOT

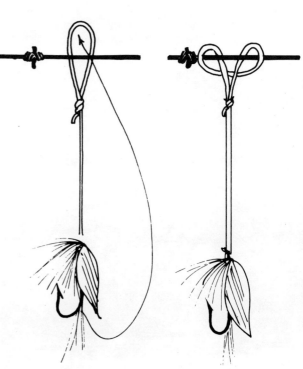

OVERHAND DROPPER TIE

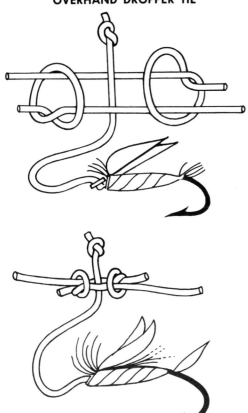

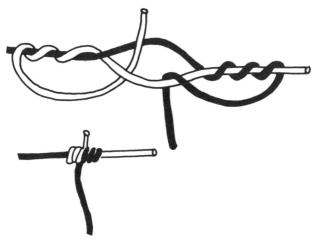

EXTENSION BLOOD KNOT

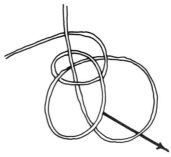

EMERGENCY DROPPER KNOT

This is also used for tying dropper snells to a leader. As shown below this knot is simple and strong, but is recommended only in cases where tying the Extension Blood Knot is impractical.

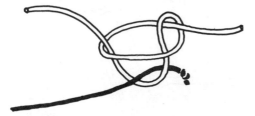

PERFECTION LOOP KNOT

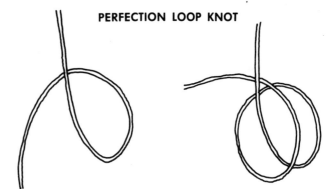

1. The Perfection Loop Knot is tied by first making a single loop (left) and then another loop over it as at right.

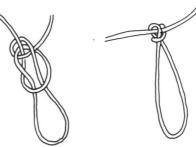

2. Holding the loop bases between a thumb and forefinger, a small wrap is made between the two loops. Then as the arrow shows, the top loop is passed through the lower.

3. The knot is completed by pulling all the slack leader into the dropper loop until the knot becomes hard as at right. The final loop should be 2½ to 3 inches long.

IMPROVED DROPPER LOOP

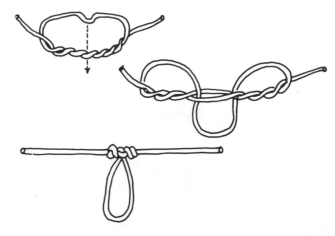

MULTIPLE CLINCH KNOT

This is used for joining a line to a leader. Many bait casters use nylon leaders of 6 or 8 feet in length, and consequently they need a knot which will join the line to leader with little or no bulk so that it will pass from the reel through the guides with a minimum of friction. Such a knot is subject to extreme wear, and for this purpose the Multiple Clinch Knot illustrated below is ideal.

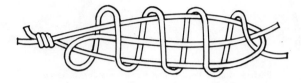

BLOOD KNOT

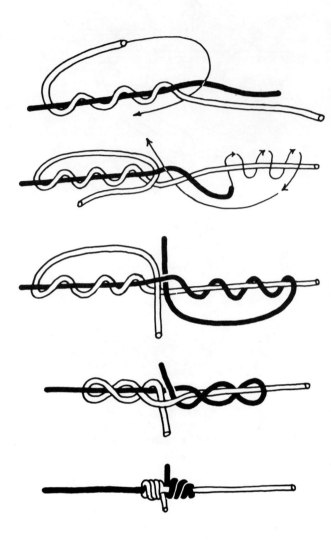

DOUBLE IMPROVED CLINCH KNOT

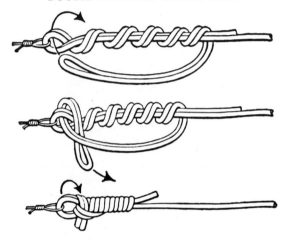

COMPOSITE KNOT

1. Six Turns—Tighten Heavy Knot First

2. Clip ends close

IMPROVED BLOOD KNOT

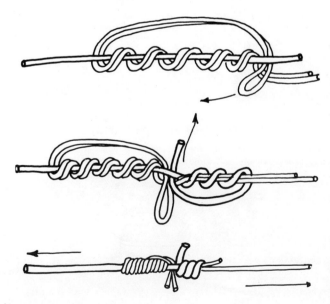

SURGEON'S KNOT

FISHERMAN'S BEND

VARIATION OF FISHERMAN'S BEND

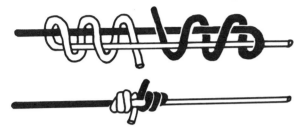

THIRD VARIATION OF FISHERMAN'S BEND

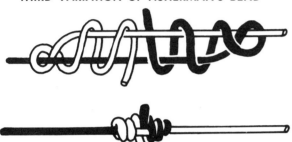

BARREL KNOT

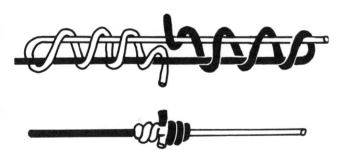

WATER KNOT

TUCKED SHEET BEND KNOT

For joining a line to leader, this is the safest and easiest knot to tie. In this knot the end of the line is brought back and "tucked" through the loop on the end of the leader. The four following illustrations show the method of tying this knot.

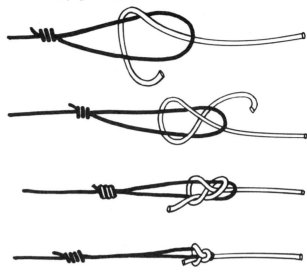

JAM KNOT

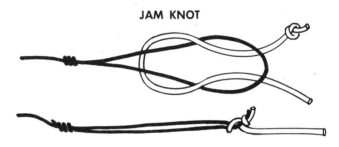

JAM KNOT—SECOND METHOD

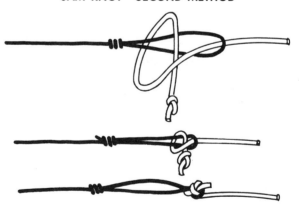

TILLER KNOT (or "SLIPPED HITCH")

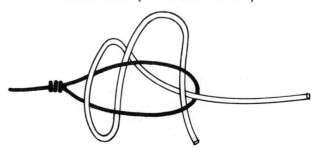

LEADER KNOT
(for tying nylon to nylon)

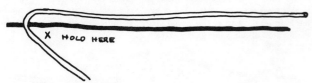

1. Lap the ends of the strands as shown, holding with thumb and forefinger where indicated.

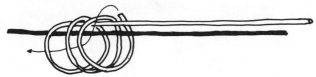

2. Loop end around both strands three times and pull end through all three loops as indicated by arrow. Then pull up slowly and evenly until this part of the knot takes the form of "A".

3. Now loop the other short end around the other strand similar to above.

4. When both sections of the knot have been pulled up to look like this, take the long ends and pull the two sections together slowly, then pull them up tight.

5. Appearance of the finished knot. All that remains to be done is to cut off the short ends close to the knot.

SHOCKER KNOT

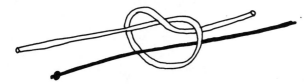

END LOOP

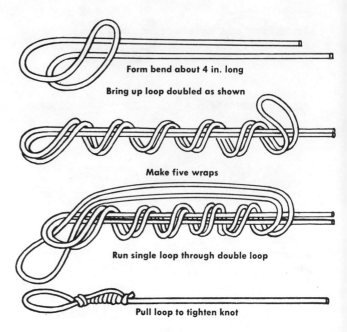

Form bend about 4 in. long

Bring up loop doubled as shown

Make five wraps

Run single loop through double loop

Pull loop to tighten knot

PERFECTION LEADER END LOOP

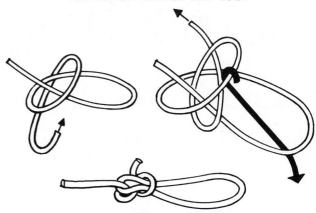

BUFFER LOOP

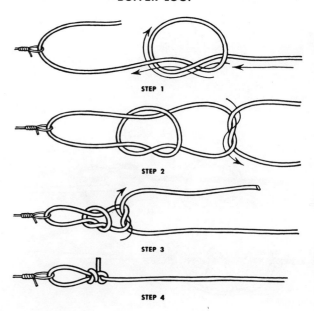

STEP 1

STEP 2

STEP 3

STEP 4

NAIL KNOT

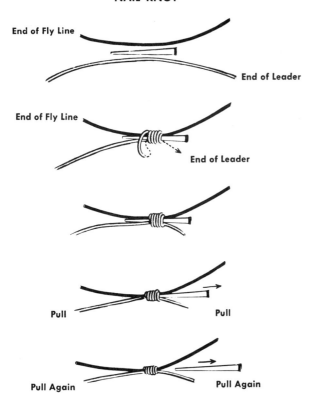

DOUBLE NAIL KNOT

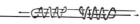

OFFSET NAIL KNOT

NAIL KNOT USING LINE LOOP INSTEAD OF NAIL

Make approx. 6 turns with end of leader, as illustrated. Bring end of leader out through loop in short section of monofilament.

While holding loops together with thumb and forefinger, grasp both ends of short section with other hand, and pull entire piece, along with end of leader, back through 6 loops as shown. Trim section of mono.

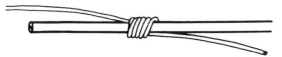

Pull leader from both ends to tighten around body of fly line.

Trim the end of fly line and leader at ⅛." Be sure knot is pulled up tight before trimming.

"KEY" KNOT SPLICE OR "KEY LOOP"
(Also called Albright Special)

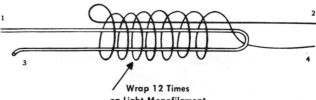

Wrap 12 Times
on Light Monofilament

Hold lines at position B and position A. Retaining position A firmly with thumb and forefinger, pull line 3 tight. Retaining position B, pull line 2. Holding lines 1 and 3, draw knot tight. Trim 3 and 4 close to knot. This knot ties nylon braid to monofilament or monofilament to monofilament. Flows thru guides for spinning, and makes a non-slipping, small splice for tying fly line to leader.

KNOT FOR FASTENING BACKING TO REEL

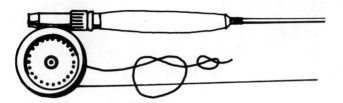

KNOTTING BACKING TO FLY LINE

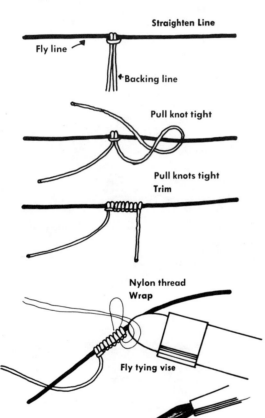

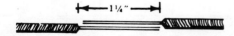

QUICK FLY LINE SPLICE

1. Clean 1¼ inch of each line end with acetone or nail-polish remover and place lines side-by-side.

2. Wrap ends together with tight turns of fine nylon thread. Give finished splice two or three coats of varnish.

NEEDLE KNOT

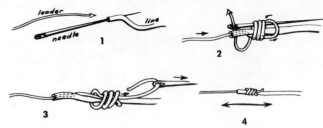

THE CROTCH SPLICE

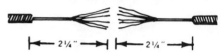

1. Fray out line ends for about an inch. A pin or needle does this job.

2. Spread the frayed ends as shown and push forked fibers together.

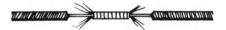

3. Wrap splice as shown, cut off protruding fibers.

4. Wrap over thread splice and lacquer.

MAKING A FLY LINE LOOP

1. Dip 3-in. length of line butt in acetone or nail-polish remover and scrape clean.

2. Fray end and cut.

3. Fold trimmed end to form loop.

4. Wrap tightly with nylon thread, leaving open loop. Varnish, or lacquer.

FORMING FLY LINE LOOP

1. Clean and scrape an inch of the fly line end.

2. Place ends of a piece of bait-casting line to fit as shown above.

3. Wrap with nylon thread and varnish.

SQUARE KNOT

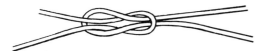

COMPOUND KNOT

ANCHOR HITCH

DOUBLE BECKET BEND

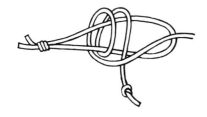

JAPANESE FISHERMAN'S KNOT

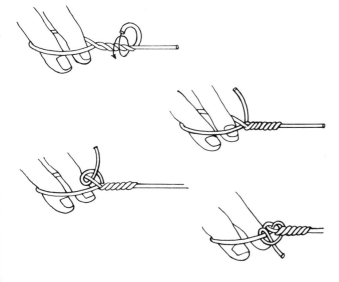

QUICK SNELL KNOT

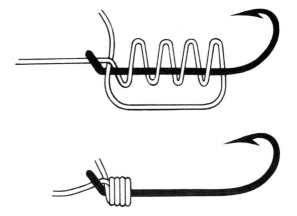

SNELLING A HOOK

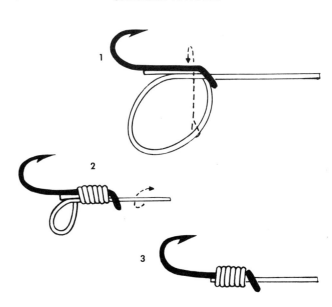

LARK'S HEAD KNOT

DOUBLE JAM KNOT

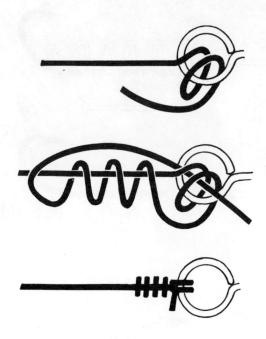

BIMINI TWIST

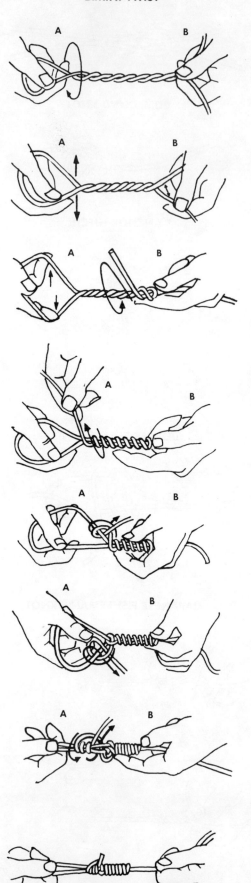

HAYWIRE TWIST

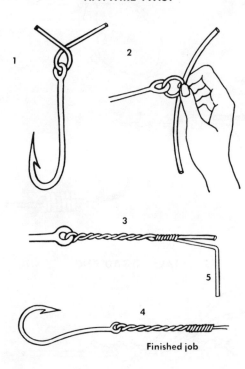

1

2

3

5

4

Finished job

ANOTHER NAIL KNOT

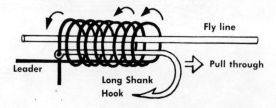

Fly line

Pull through

Leader

Long Shank
Hook

LEADER KNOT

1

X Hold here

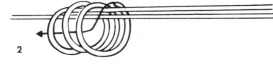

2

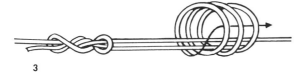

3

4

COMPOUND KNOT

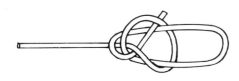

COMMON LOOP KNOT

SQUARE KNOT

BOWLINE

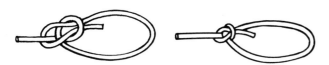

TAUTLINE HITCH

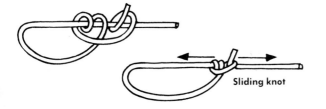

Sliding knot

METAL SLEEVE SECURING A LOOP OF WIRE

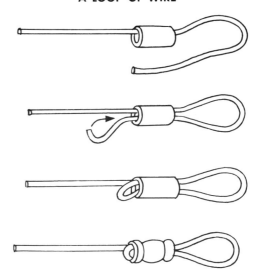

METAL SLEEVE AND KNOT

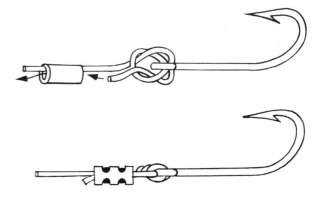

ATTACHING LEADER TO FLY LINE

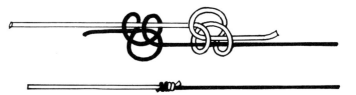

DOUBLE LINE LOOP

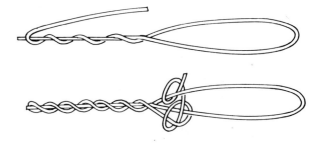

SPLICED LOOP

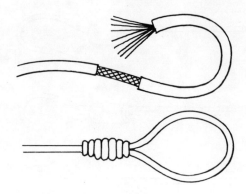

PALOMAR KNOT

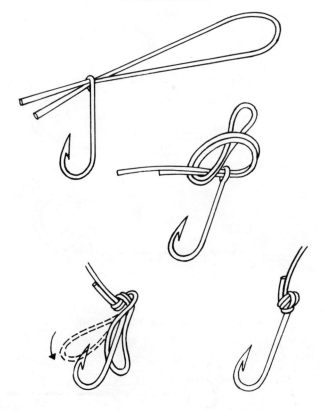

THE CRAWFORD KNOT

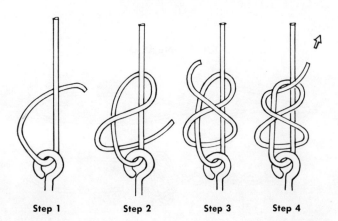

Step 1   Step 2   Step 3   Step 4

KNOT FOR ATTACHING HOOK TO WIRE WITH METAL SLEEVE

Step 1.
Thread nylon-coated wire thru sleeve and hook eye.

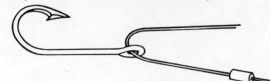

Step 2.
Make overhand knot.

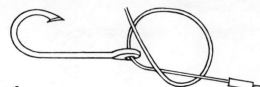

Step 3.
Go thru hook 2nd time.

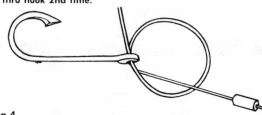

Step 4.
Make 2nd overhand knot thru sleeve, draw up loop and crimp twice.

KNOT FOR TYING NYLON-COATED WIRE TO MONOFILAMENT LINE

Note: All tying is done with mono. Do not attempt to tie wire.

1. Lay mono over wire in loops.
(Light line denotes wire.)

2. Wind mono around wire loop.

Wind short end of mono around loop of wire five or six times, putting short end of wire thru mono loop and short end of mono thru wire loop.

3. Form knot

While holding, slowly draw long ends to form knot.

4. Draw knot tight—dip ends.

Finished knot is small and compact.

13

Best Times, Places to Fish Florida

By Jim Hardie

The Miami Herald's Outdoor Editor explains when to go, and where, for the best of Florida's fishing.

The fast-running bonefish is among the angler's top prizes, and spring, summer fishing for them is best.

Florida fishing in spring and early summer is enough to delight even the most discriminating angler.

Some of the most exciting salt water gamefish are striking at their seasonal best in May and June—fish such as the tarpon, bonefish, snook, and dolphin.

And on the fresh water scene fly rod enthusiasts are virtually in heaven as they cast top-water poppers at bluegills that are almost large enough to cover a dinner plate.

The chamber of commerce stories about fish hitting year around in the Sunshine State are true. But often these accounts neglect to point out that the fishing is subject to seasonal ups and downs.

For example, there is an old saying in South Florida that goes, "May moon over Marco." It applies to snook

fishing and means that the peak of the season is the time when the moon is full over Marco Island.

To fully appreciate the significance of "May moon over Marco" there are a couple of things you should know.

First off, the snook is one of the most prized gamefish in Florida. It shows a distinct preference for fast-moving surface plugs such as the yellow Creek Chub Darter or Zara Spook.

Secondly, the two days before and the two days after the full moon are times when the tide swells to its fullest and times when you can expect the greatest current in the water due to tide change.

Snook are spawning in the spring and are at their aggressive best. And during the strong tides of May the

Big tarpon rolls up and out in attempt to throw mullet bait. Florida's tarpon fishing at proper season borders on the extraordinary.

Jean Crooks of Miami Springs, Fla. hoists a big spring-time snook he took fishing along the Tamiami Trail.

Billfishing, too, is frequently best in the warmer months. This angler has boated one sailfish and has another close.

snook seem most abundant and most willing to smash any plug you drop into the water.

For many years the snook carried the infamous nickname "soap fish." This was because people were cooking them with the skin of the fish intact, which caused a distinct taste—that of a bar of soap! But remove the skin and broil or pan fry the snook and it is one of the piscatorial delicacies.

In general terms, snook are found on both coasts and in the Florida Keys in the southern half of the state. Although the average size is under ten pounds, some in the twenty-pound class are taken each season and even a few in the thirty-pound range.

Many of the bridges in South Florida have catwalks for fishermen. And nighttime efforts for snook are often productive, especially if you use live bait (mullet, shrimp, or pinfish).

Besides the plugs mentioned for surface fishing, probably the single most productive snook lure is the bucktail jig. The idea behind the bucktail is to hop it through the water or along the bottom to stimulate a moving shrimp.

Captain Doug House, at Everglades City on the lower west coast of Florida is a snook fishing specialist. He fishes from a 19-foot skiff, furnishes the bait, tackle and know how for $75 per day. He prefers two anglers, but will take three.

Marco Island and Flamingo in Everglades National Park rank with Everglades City as top snook fishing areas.

To insure having a boat and guide during a visit to Florida, it is recommended that you make advanced reservations. Some of the guides book months in advance, so you risk being left at the dock if you wait until the day you want to go fishing to try and hire a guide.

There are any number of fishing centers where you can make reservations. The Rod and Gun Club in Everglades City, Captain's Landing at Marco Island, or Everglades Park Company in Miami (For Flamingo in Everglades National Park)—to name a few.

Tarpon rate as probably the No. 1 light tackle sports fish in Florida. Since its food value is poor, it is fished strictly for sport. Normally all those except the ones kept for mounting are released unharmed to fight another day.

Even largemouth bass fishing in Florida is best at certain times through May and June, even though the bigmouth hit baits willingly all year long.

Super tarpon jumps at boatside after socking fisherman's plug.

Captain Jim Brewer of Islamorada in the Florida Keys shows a bone-fish, one of the most highly prized gamefish and the choice of light-tackle anglers.

Spring tides bring spectacular snook fishing in Florida, particularly in Marco Island area.

The things which make tarpon so attractive to sports-men are their willingness to strike artificial lures and the spectacular jumping battles they stage when finally hooked.

You are lucky to hook one out of four tarpon that strike because the inside of their mouth is almost entirely bone and there are few spots for a hook to take hold. And you are lucky to land one out of ten that are hooked be-cause of the violence of their fight.

Already this year three tarpon over 190 pounds have been landed in Florida waters. The largest—a 196-pounder—was taken at Marco Island on a dead mullet for bait. At Key West, one weighing 195 pounds and 8 ounces was caught on an Atom plug. And at Marathon in the Florida Keys, a 195-pounder was caught on a live mullet.

Fly rod fishermen rate the big tarpon one of the su-preme tests. To take one in the 100-pound class is a milestone in a fly fisherman's career. The tarpon go for huge streamer flies of bright yellow or orange.

Tarpon have a characteristic of rolling at the surface much the way a porpoise does. It is commonplace and always exciting to see schools of tarpon surface around bridges in the Keys, often at night and at daylight and dusk.

George Hommell at Islamorada in the Keys was one of the most distinguished light tackle guides in Florida. A few years ago he opened a travel agency and tackle store named Worldwide Sportsman. It has become a hub of activity for guides and fishermen.

Hommel says the rates for a skiff and professional guide in his area are $75 per day and they can accommo-date two anglers. Again tackle is furnished. It is up to the angler to provide box lunches, drinks, and to pay for the ice (and sometimes the bait).

In the Upper Keys you can expect to pay about $18 a night for a motel room (double) and meals will cost about $8 to $10 per day per person.

It is in the Keys that you also find superb bonefish action in May and June. The bonefish is another supreme test for the light-tackle fisherman because it involves a combination of hunting and fishing.

The bonefish move out of the deep channels and onto the shallow flats to feed on shrimp, crabs, and other crustaceans. You need a sharp eye and an accurate cast to catch them.

Once hooked, the bonefish are famed for their bullet-like run. Like the tarpon, they are poor in food value, so you normally release them unharmed unless you plan to have them mounted.

Bud and Mary's Marina in Islamorada and Islamorada Yacht Basin are two spots where many skiff guides can be found. In Marathon, many of the guides gather for breakfast at Ted and Mary's Restaurant. Incidentally, Ted and Mary Bartz are open only for breakfast. Both are bonefishing enthusiasts and they close up their restaurant every day after breakfast and go fishing!

One fact that seems to surprise many visitors to Florida is that some of the best bonefishing is in Biscayne Bay practically within view of downtown Miami. Several

This husky bull dolphin was caught off Panama City in Gulf of Mexico. Dolphin in a variety of sizes are plentiful during May and June.

guides operate at Key Biscayne (Crandon Marina and Key Biscayne Yacht Club). They regularly catch some of the biggest bonefish in the state.

Turning to deep sea fishing, May and June are the months when giant bluefin tuna are migrating northward along the Bahamas Banks in the areas of Cat Cay and Bimini. You can try for these monsters that weight 500 pounds and more! A few of them migrate along the southeast Florida coast and are caught each season.

But a much more attractive and popular fish that is abundant offshore in May and June is the dolphin (not to be confused with the porpoise). The dolphin fish is a golden-greenish fish that travels in schools and is found all along the edge of the Gulf Stream.

The dolphin normally is caught from charterboats (or private boats) with trolled baits or lures.

Marinas all along the famed Florida Gold Coast have charterboats that go after the dolphin. Rates vary from a high of $200 per day for up to six people to $130 for four anglers in the Keys. As a rule of thumb, the higher rates are in the Miami area and as you get further away you will notice a decrease in charter costs.

One word of caution. Have a clear understanding about rates, who gets to keep the fish (some boat captains claim the catch, believe it or not!), and if you plan to have any of the catch mounted it's important to settle first about who keeps the fish.

There are many other fish that can be caught during May and June in Florida waters. Especially numerous are sea trout, mutton snapper, and (offshore) sailfish.

It's no wonder so many Florida anglers wear smiles in May and June; the time between strikes then is brief!

Florida fishermen head out at dawn to try for a variety of scrappy gamefish.

14

Bonanza Land for Bass and Pike

For smallmouth bass and northern pike, Ontario waters are hard to match.

One bright June afternoon my son, Bob, and I were bugging the clear waters of Joan Lake. Joan Lake is one of many hundreds of small lakes adjacent to big Lake-Of-The-Woods at Kenora, Ontario.

As our Indian guide paddled us slowly parallel to shore, Bob pointed to a fallen spruce tree that stretched 30 feet from the bank, its twisted limbs providing good bass cover in about 10 feet of water.

"See that tree?" said Bob. "I'm gonna' catch three or four bass right there!"

Bob tossed a small yellow popping bug up close to the tree. But instead of letting it rest momentarily as is usually the most productive way when fishing bugs, Bob started pumping the bug back across the surface, popping it along furiously. It seemed he was making enough racket with that bug to put down every bass in the lake. He fished the bug all the way back, working it as hard as he could, then cast again to the same spot. Once more he retrieved it immediately, popping it along hard and fast. He did the same thing a third time, and a fourth.

After the last cast he put his rod down. "Just hold the boat right here for a few minutes," Bob instructed our guide. "We'll relax a bit, then I'll clean up on small-mouths that are laying under that tree."

In about five minutes Bob stood up and made a cast close-in to the tree. This time, instead of raising a quick ruckus with the bug, he let it rest motionless on the surface. I watched intently as the bug floated almost life-lessly. For a long time nothing happened. Then Bob twitched the popper gently. KAAAPPOWWWWW! That quick a 3-pound smallmouth had it, and now, solidly hooked, the fish was leaping crazily.

Shortly Bob collared the bass, admired it briefly, then released it. He cast a second time, and the action was the same—short rest of the bug, a single twitch, another bass. Bob did that three times, taking three good small-mouths on three successive casts!

Another time at Peshu Lake, in southeastern Ontario, I stood on shore-line rocks with my wife, Phyllis. Peshu

is in the Algoma District, along the Chapleau Route, northeast of Sault Ste. Marie. Out from shore about 30 feet was a patch of lily pads. With her spinning outfit, Phyllis plunked a silver spoon with pork-rind-strip into the pads. She hadn't turned the reel handle three times when she had a strike, and line sizzled from the reel. Fifteen minutes later Phyllis had a 16-pound northern pike sprawled on the bank and panting out his last.

And still another time Casey Popielewski, of Glenview, Illinois, and I were fishing Eagle Lake at the town of Vermilion Bay, north of Fort Frances, Ontario. Us-

Fishermen with loads of gear prepare to take a Rusty Myers charter plane to a remote Ontario lake.

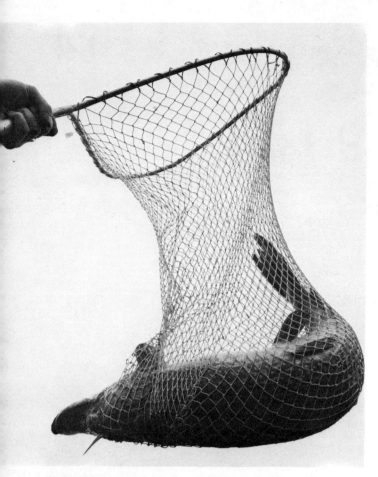

Big northern pike like this one, pictured punching its nose through a net, are one of angling's big attractions in Ontario.

there is a *lot of it* that would be hard to match anywhere.

I have fished all of the good smallmouth bass waters in North America. I grew up taking smallmouths out of Maryland's great Potomac River. I've caught smallmouths from Pennsylvania's Susquehanna, New York's Delaware, Kentucky's Lake Cumberland, Tennessee's Dale Hollow, Arkansas' Buffalo River, Missouri's Current, Wisconsin's Green Bay, Maine's Schoodic, Michigan's North Manitou, and Minnesota's Winnibigoshish. Those are some of the places where I've caught smallmouths. A couple others include New Brunswick's Skiff Lake, and Manitoba's superb Winnipeg River.

But of the places I've fished for bronzebacks, one of my all-time favorite spots is Rainy Lake at Fort Frances, in Ontario's Rainy River country. Rainy is just about as accessible as Chicago's Loop. You can drive to it from Chicago over excellent highways in less than 12 hours. Scheduled airliners drop in at International Falls (Minnesota), across Rainy River from Fort Frances, from points all over the country at every hour of the day. Fort Frances, which is right on the lake, is serviced by trains, buses, and charter planes. No place could be much more easily reached—yet I know of no place that provides more consistently good fishing, for *large* northern smallmouths, than Rainy Lake.

Houseboating is the best way to fish Rainy.

There are a couple of houseboating outfitters on the lake. One is based at International Falls. That's Lee Kulaver, who has several houseboats, ranging from little ones to big ones, for rent. The small houseboats are like a comfortable cabin on a sea-worthy raft; the large houseboats are like a sizable and deluxe apartment built on a catamaran type hull.

You and your friends, or you and the family, can take any of the small or medium size houseboats out for a trip on Rainy by yourselves, but with the larger boats a guide or "captain" goes along. Many fishermen take a small houseboat and go out by themselves, towing a couple of fishing skiffs, and roam all over Rainy, fishing wherever they like, for anywhere from a few days to a month or more. The ideal trip is for a week, figuring five days of fishing, and allowing a day to get to Rainy and a day to get home again.

Rainy is a huge lake straddling the Minnesota-Ontario border. It's waters are very clear but appear mahogany-hued from staining by tamarack roots. It is typical, and classical, smallmouth water. There are the heavily-wooded banks and rocky shores, shallow reefs and bars (ideal smallmouth spawning areas), scattered islands both big and small, cliffs and bluffs dropping straight to the waters edge, and sand-and-gravel shallows spotted with pencil reeds and lily pads.

Rainy has the best average-size smallmouths I've seen anywhere, that is, I'd guess that the lake's average bass weighs about two pounds—which is an extraordinary *average* for northern smallmouths. Three pounders are common at Rainy, and in a normal good day you should get quite a lot of 3½ pounds, and maybe a couple weighing an honest 4 pounds. You'll take an occasional 5-pounder, too, but if you get more than two of that size in a week or so of hard fishing you've done extremely well.

For fly fishing especially—and for plug and spin fisher-

ing a red-and-yellow, 6-inch long "McNally Magnum" streamer fly, I shot a cast toward a rocky point. I let the fly settle down 4 or 5 feet, then started it back in foot-long hauls. When the fly was only about 20 feet from the boat I saw a pike trailing it. He looked as round as a football and as long as a canoe paddle. He boiled into the fly, and I set the hook hard. He put up a good, long scrap out in the open water, but everything held and I eventually landed him. He weighed 21½ pounds.

That's how the bass and pike fishing can be—and usually is—at the wilderness lakes in Ontario.

Despite the fact that most Ontario lakes are wilderness waters (there is "wilderness" just outside the big cities of Port Arthur-Fort William and Fort Frances) some Ontario lakes have been fished hard for many years. There are a lot of lakes and rivers in the Province that are too easily reached, readily accessible by auto, and consequently they have been fished too much. Even some comparatively "inaccessible" fly-in lakes have been fished too much (or suffered too much commercial netting) to provide good fishing today. I recall once, for example, flying in via float plane to a lake I won't name that is 70 bush miles north of Fort Frances. George Strickler, of Chicago, a guide, and I camped on the lake and fished 4 days. In that time our total catch was one 4-pound lake trout, one 3-pound northern pike, and three 3-pound walleyes.

So *all* of Ontario's fishing isn't good—but nonetheless

Typical "shore lunch" scene at Ontario lake shows Indian guides, fishermen, enjoying fried fish, freshly caught, along with the usual "fixin's."

men, too—I'd recommend the first two weeks in June for either smallmouth bass or northern pike at Rainy lake or anywhere else in Ontario. The fishing can be very good in May, but the weather then can still be unsettled and rain likely much of the time, along with damaging winds. (Wind disrupts any fishing.) In June, though, the weather is usually stable, generally in the mid-70s on bright, sunny, spring-like days, down to the low 60s or 50s at night. That's when the bass leave the deep reefs and come to the shallow reefs and bars, and shallow rocky points, preparatory to spawning. You can pick them off then with fly-rod popping bugs or streamer flies, or by spinning, spin-casting, or bait-casting with small surface or underwater plugs, various spinners, plastic worms, spoons, etc. Natural bait takes fish too, with crayfish and hellgrammites (larvae of the Dobson fly) excellent, as well as nightcrawler worms and lake-shiner minnows.

Ontario has 68,282 square miles of water area—which means there is a lake here and another there every time you turn around. Thus it isn't easy to pin-point all of the Province's good bass and pike fishing, particularly in a single article.

However, I'd be remiss if I failed to mention the good fishing in Quetico Provincial Park, in the Lake-Of-The-Woods and Kenora section, the Dryden and Red Lakes area, the Sioux Lookout and English River section, and in the Nipigon country.

In my opinion there is only fair fishing (and sometimes not that good) for smallmouth bass and northern pike in Lake-Of-The-Woods. But smaller lakes virtually adjoining or connecting to Lake-Of-The-Woods provide some super bass fishing and some specific lakes give excellent northern pike fishing. Each camp operator in or near Lake-Of-The-Woods has his own special bass and pike waters. Joan Lake, mentioned earlier, and another close by and equally good called Bass Lake, are two smallmouth waters fished by guests of Crow Rock Muskie Camp (Kenora) on Lake-Of-The-Woods. Either of those lakes is a short boat run from the Crow Rock island camp, and a short portage from the big lake.

The English River and Separation Lake—north of Kenora and west of Ear Falls—offer some of the finest smallmouth fishing in Ontario. These are pure wilderness waters, but there are deluxe camps on both. English

Big smallmouth bass aren't unusual at Ontario's Rainy Lake.

Eagle Lake at Vermilion Bay, Ont. gave up this 20-pound northern for Norm Barry of Des Plaines, Ill.

River, incidentally, is more like a lake than a river, and you'll be fishing currentless water there all the time.

There are countless good bass and pike lakes reachable from the town of Red Lake, with fly-in camps scattered all through the bush up in that country. West of Dryden a short way is big Eagle Lake, and while it is easily accessible (you can drive there) and has been popular with anglers for many years, it still gives fine fishing for smallmouths, northern pike, walleyes, lake trout, and muskies. At Eagle I usually fish out of Norm Barry's Little Norway Camp, on the northern end of the lake at the town of Vermilion Bay. Early May through early June is the time for northerns there, and while the average pike from Eagle weighs well under 10 pounds, you are just as likely to belt out a 25-pounder there as anywhere else.

June is the best month for smallmouths at Eagle, and late September through to the end of the muskie season in November is the best time for muskies. Eagle's late fall muskie fishing can be exceptional, and like every northwoods resort owner, Barry swears there is a world's record muskellunge out there somewhere beyond his docks. Anyway, muskies well up in the 40-pound range are caught from Eagle every fall.

Immense and island-studded Lac Seul, at the town of Sioux Lookout, in recent years has produced some of Ontario's largest northern pike, giants ranging from 30 to 40 pounds. Many are taken in deep water by trolling with large spoons, but Seul also rewards the caster who fishes early or late in the season. Lake Nipigon also contains some very large northern pike.

Some very special smallmouth and northern pike fishing can be found in the Province's Quetico Provincial Park area, which abuts the U.S. border and this country's Superior National Park in Minnesota. This is the unique Borderland Canoe Area, officially designated as a no-resort, no fly-in, no outboard-boating, true-wilderness country. The only way to fish it is to go in via canoe and camp, and there are canoeing "trails" and arranged camp sites throughout the Borderland country. Many of the lakes there give really good smallmouth fishing, spots such as Basswood Lake, and many others have northern pike that hit as readily as bluegills in an overstocked farm pond. The Ely, Minnesota Chamber of Commerce can provide much information on camping-canoeing-fishing in Quetico-Superior because, even though Quetico is in Ontario, Ely is a "jumping-off" spot for fishermen going there.

A recent innovation in Ontario fishing is the "fly-out-and-do-it-yourself" deal. A few Ontario outfitters—such as Rusty Meyers, Meyers' Flying Service, Fort Frances —have established tent camps on wilderness lakes. The tents are boarded with plywood walls and floors, with only the roof being canvas. They are large and roomy, equipped with propane refrigerators, comfortable bunks, and reliable wood-burning stoves. Plenty of firewood is kept cut and on hand for in-coming fishing parties, and aluminum boats, with outboard motors and plenty of gas and oil, also are in these camps. The deal is that your outfitter will fly you and your family or friends out to one of these wilderness camps offering "virgin" fishing, and leave you there to enjoy yourself. Supplies are flown in with you. You handle the usual camp chores, although there aren't many, and do your own cooking and "guiding." Cooking, doing dishes, keeping fires going—these are the chief chores and they take little time and, for many men, are joyful work when out in the woods. The plane that brought you in will be back in camp on any appointed day to take you out again (weather permitting), and if there should be an emergency and someone has to get out before scheduled departure time, there is a dependable two-way camp radio by which you can call for assistance, send out messages, request supplies, etc.

These fly-out-and-camp-yourself trips are very inexpensive, and are a lot of fun for the family man or for a group of fellows who "want to get away" for a while and who want to do just as they please from day to day.

It's one of the good fishing things going on these days in Ontario—but then, Ontario is the kind of place where good things for fishermen have been the rule for many, many, years.

Frisky little pike whips around as fisherman holds on.

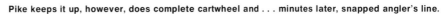

Pike keeps it up, however, does complete cartwheel and . . . minutes later, snapped angler's line.

15

A Practical First-Aid Kit for Fishermen

No angler should make lengthy field trips without a good medical kit.

Ordinary fisherman's tackle box serves as handy case for first-aid supplies.

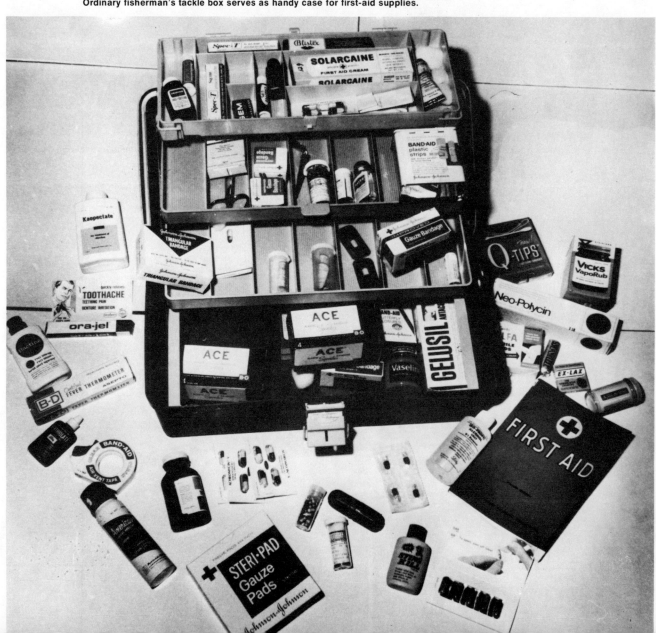

Fishermen travel these days as never before. Many anglers now fish in countless wilderness areas of Canada, even across the Artic Circle and beyond. Still others fish in Mexico, Costa Rica, British Honduras, the out islands of The Bahamas, South America, India—just about everywhere.

How many of these wide-ranging outdoorsmen are properly prepared when they make such trips? Imagine, for example, that you are fishing bonefish and tarpon on the Yucatan Peninsula in Mexico. What if a guide makes a bad move with a machete and accidentally slices someone's arm? Suppose while wading a flat you step on a sea urchin, and one of its needle-like spines drives through your sneaker and into your foot? Suppose you're walking the bank of a Wisconsin creek one day next spring, and an alder limb whips back and smacks you in the eye? If any of those accidents occurred, or some other health problem arose while on a fishing trip, would you be prepared to administer at least token first-aid?

Once at Nejanilini Lake in far northern Manitoba, my son, Bob, drove a dry fly hook into his finger. At the time we were "weathered in," and even if it had been desirable to fly out to a hospital, we would not have been able to do so for three days, not until the fog lifted. Supposing, in that time, someone had broken a leg, an arm, or suffered some other serious, painful injury? What could have been done? The hook incident, of course, was minor. Bob simply clenched his teeth and pushed the barb through and out.

Feeling that someone, sometime—on one or another of the many trips I make annually to remote fishing areas—may get hurt and be in need of reasonably effective and immediate first-aid, I met with my doctor to design a suitable fisherman's first-aid kit. Naturally such a kit will not be taken on one-day, near-to-home jaunts where doctors, hospitals, or medication are quickly and easily attainable, but it will go along on all other fishing and camping trips.

Every angler should see his personal physician if he is interested in making up a quality first-aid kit, since one's own doctor is familiar with any specific health problems one may have. For example, penicillin is okay for some people, no good for others who require a different antibiotic.

The medicines and medications suggested by my physican, Dr. Harold Wedell of Glenview, Illinois, cost about $75 and, along with some things I chose to add, packed easily into a medium-size plastic tackle box.

Some of the items Dr. Wedell recommended for the kit were: pain pills, sterile gauze pads and bandage, butterfly closures (to close open wounds), thermometer, snake bite kit, nasal spray, forceps, surgical scissors, triangular bandages, oral antibiotic, antihystamine, medication to fight skin infection, medication to counteract poison ivy-oak-sumac or some similar skin infection, alcohol, cotton wadding, and a Red Cross first-aid booklet.

Items I added included: cotton swabs, razor blades, first-aid cream (for severe sunburn, etc.), salt tablets, aspirin, inhaler, plastic-strip band-aids, medicine to treat diarrhea, antibacterial troches, petroleum jelly, anti-acid, medication for toothache, first-aid spray, methiolate, cold pills, an aerosal spray can of tropical anti-

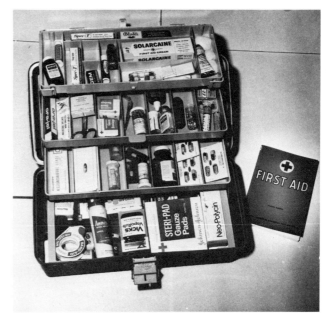

When packed carefully tackle box accommodates a large quantity of medical items.

septic insect repellent, and "Sting-Kill," a very effective oil that takes the itch or sting out of various insect bites. Naturally other items may be added in making up a sportsman's emergency first-aid kit. Fishermen who organize special fishing parties, incidentally, ought to particularly be sure that they have a quality first-aid kit on hand before heading for the woods. Where large groups are concerned, it's almost certain someone will have need for at least minor medical attention before the trip is over.

Cold-weather Foe: Frostbite

Like most injuries to the human body, frostbite can range from something so minor as to go virtually unnoticed to a tragedy leading to complete loss of fingers, toes, and entire limbs.

But unlike most injuries, frostbite can strike and cause grievous damage before its victim becomes aware of any threat. And the danger is not limited to the extremities or just to head and facial areas.

Ice fishermen and late season hunters after snowshoe hares are exposed often to frostbite conditions, as are campers, hikers, trappers, snowmobilers, skiiers, and others trying to enjoy the frigid outdoors.

Younger children are particularly susceptible to frostbite's insidious attack, and frozen ears and noses are common among tots. A youngster may not heed the "numbness warning" and he doesn't know about the chalk-white skin color that means frostbite has set in.

Though fingers and feet are exposed to a lesser extent than facial areas, they too can be frozen when a victim is working or playing without adequate shelter.

Wind is an important cause of frostbite. Any temperature below freezing coupled with winds of 10 to 20 mph can bring on rapid freezing of the skin's surface. The chilling effect of 20-degree air moving at 45 mph is the same as 40-below-zero air on a still day. In such weather, walking in the wind along an open area such as a lakefront is especially dangerous to the person dressed only for home, office, or factory conditions. An uncovered ear can be severely damaged in a two-block walk.

An intense "biting" discomfort followed by loss of sensation and an odd stiffness are the earliest symptoms of frostbite. The numbed parts may turn glossy white or grayish yellow, but at this point there's little pain and the victim may not be aware of trouble.

Frostbite is the freezing of tissue—such as skin, muscle, bone, and even nerves. Water that exists within and between various tissue cells is changed to crystals. These ice crystals tend to draw water out of the cells, thereby increasing the injury. Physicians advise that much of the injurious effect of frostbite is caused by damage to capillary blood vessels that bring necessary oxygen and nutrients to the tissues.

There are various degrees of frostbite damage, as there are degrees of tissue damage resulting from burns.

Frostbite injury may be first, second, third, or fourth degree. First and second degree injuries usually involve damage only to the surface layers of tissue, but when deeper layers are damaged third and fourth degree frostbite is suffered. In the more serious cases gangrene almost always results, followed by the permanent loss of tissue.

The sportsman outdoors in the dead of winter should be alert to "tingling" sensations in the skin. Fingers, ears, and toes that stop hurting from the cold may already be frostbitten.

Conditions that bring about frostbite are cold weather and bad circulation. An ice fisherman suffered first degree frostbite to his hands when snow drifted into his gloves.

Another man received second degree frostbite injuries to his ears after walking for 25 minutes in minus-3 degree weather with wind up to 25 mph. He was even wearing a cotton earband but some earbands are inadequate because they restrict the blood flow into the ears.

A young hunter suffered frostbite to his hands that was so severe he lost two fingers. He became frostbitten while trying to start a fire in a metal stove at temperatures below zero while wearing two pairs of gloves. The gloves were too tight and restricted circulation.

A Wisconsin trapper put on four pairs of socks and rubber boots, then walked his trap line. He felt no pain or numbness. When he removed his boots he found his toes were white, cold to the touch and hard. After 20 days of treatment for fourth degree frostbite, two of his toes were amputated.

If recognized quickly and given proper treatment, frostbite may do no serious damage.

Don Malmberg of Helena, Montana, a member of that state's conservation department and an expert on winter survival, suggests that outdoorsmen never fish or travel alone when temperatures drop to freezing and below.

"By not traveling alone, a sportsman and his partner can check each other periodically," said Malmberg. "They can examine one another's nose and ears to see if they are turning white.

Minor degrees of frost "nip" on the nose or ears can be warmed by body heat or by getting indoors. Real frostbite requires careful treatment.

Anyone who suspects frostbite should get to a hospital as quickly as possible. In the field, the frozen part should be protected against further injury by covering and warming.

The old-fashioned frostbite remedy called for cold water—or worse, snow or ice—to be applied to the affected area. Under no circumstances should you rub ice, snow, or even bare hands on frostbitten skin. Even light rubbing can do damage to frozen tissues.

Treatment and care of frozen tissue vary according to the injury. Modern treatment is just the opposite of the "old methods." Today it's rapid rewarming in lukewarm water that is advised. Water temperature should never exceed 112 degrees F., however.

Bring the victim indoors for treatment so he can be thoroughly warmed with blankets and a hot drink. Adults should have no alcohol and they shouldn't smoke. Minor cases of frostbite that occur during outdoor activity, such as hunting or ice fishing, should be treated by covering the affected parts with warm hands. Frostbitten hands can be warmed by holding them motionless in the armpits.

Malmberg offers a few simple rules to help avoid frostbite:

1. Clothing should be clean. Dirty, sweaty clothing does not conserve body heat well because air pockets which normally trap and retain warm air near the body become clogged.

2. Avoid overheating by removing outer clothing during heavy exercise or higher temperatures. Otherwise, clothes may become sweaty and the subsequent evaporation of water as they dry will lower the body temperature.

3. Clothing should be loose and dry. This prevents constriction of blood vessels and loss of body heat.

4. Avoid handling metal with bare hands in sub-zero weather. Because of moisture in the hands they may freeze on contact with the metal.

5. Avoid alcoholic beverages when the temperature is below zero. Alcohol can cause the loss of body heat.

Remember that severe frostbite is a medical emergency that calls for skilled treatment, particularly during the recovery period.

How to Remove Wayward Fish Hooks

To readily remove a fish hook imbedded in flesh, all that's needed is a short length of string of fishing line. The string should be looped around the curve of the hook and its ends held firmly around the index finger. Then, with the patient's hand on a firm surface, take the eye and shank of the hook between the thumb and forefinger of your free hand and depress the shank, thereby disengaging the barb. After that align the string, or monofilament or other fishing line, in the plane of the hook-shank's long axis and—*yank!* The entire procedure takes only seconds.

Emergency Medicine, a medical journal, recommends the method described, and suggests yet another simple method of hook removal. The second technique requires an 18 gauge "hypo" type needle. The needle should be introduced along the curvature of the hook with the bevel toward the inside of the curve so that the needle opening can engage the barb. Pressure along the hook shank is used to disengage the barb from the flesh. "When the needle engages the barb," says Dr. Warren Longmire of Hitchcock, Texas, who is credited with originating this system, "the needle has a positive locking action, and both needle and hook can then be withdrawn by rotating the hook and holding the needle tightly down over the barb."

Either technique—using string or a hypo needle—has been proved 100 percent effective.

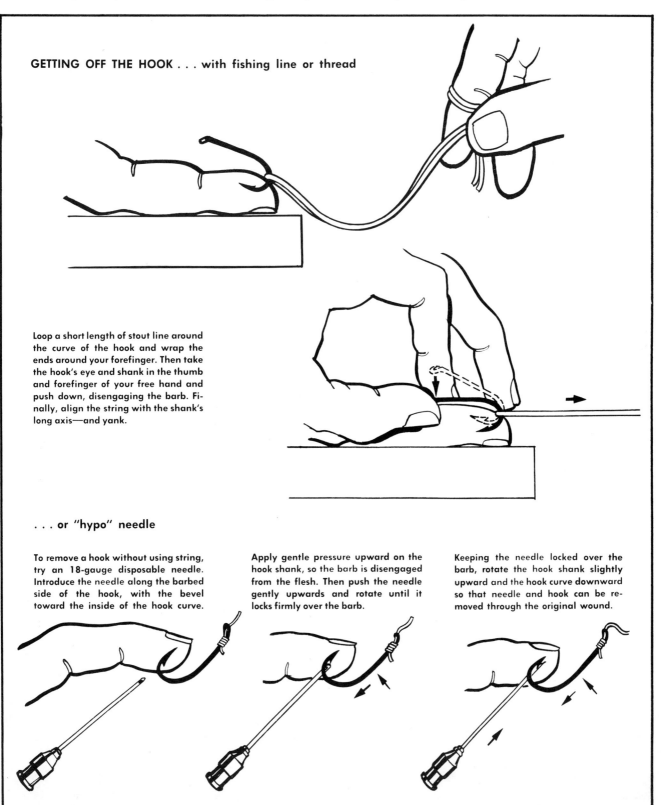

GETTING OFF THE HOOK . . . with fishing line or thread

Loop a short length of stout line around the curve of the hook and wrap the ends around your forefinger. Then take the hook's eye and shank in the thumb and forefinger of your free hand and push down, disengaging the barb. Finally, align the string with the shank's long axis—and yank.

. . . or "hypo" needle

To remove a hook without using string, try an 18-gauge disposable needle. Introduce the needle along the barbed side of the hook, with the bevel toward the inside of the hook curve.

Apply gentle pressure upward on the hook shank, so the barb is disengaged from the flesh. Then push the needle gently upwards and rotate until it locks firmly over the barb.

Keeping the needle locked over the barb, rotate the hook shank slightly upward and the hook curve downward so that needle and hook can be removed through the original wound.

16

Salmon Snagging! New Great Lakes Fishing Kick

Salmon snagging is a community affair. The woman with the net is trying to dip a salmon foul-hooked by the gent next to her with the rod, while all the neighborhood watches approvingly.

This angler, or rather snagger, has a big coho-size net stuffed into his waders. Big nets are the rule and a necessity.

If good old, sporty old Izaak Walton were alive today and could see what's going on in some Michigan rivers, he'd roll over in his grave.

Coho and Chinook salmon that fill many Michigan rivers by the tens-of-thousands in the fall as they return from Lake Michigan to inland waters to spawn and die are easily snagged by fishermen.

Because the state's fishery biologists get all the salmon eggs and milt they need for Michigan's hatcheries from fish trapped in weirs, it is lawful to deliberately snag salmon in certain parts of certain rivers. Also, salmon do not strike lures or bait as well when spawning time nears, and snagging is considered okay since the fish are going to die anyway.

Nonetheless, to a serious sports fisherman or an old angler like Izaak, it is somewhat shaking to observe dozens of fishermen utilizing heavy tackle, big hooks and lead weights to foul hook or snag, husky gamefish.

How successful is foul-hooking? One day at a dam on the Big Sable River, in Ludington State Park near the town of Ludington, Michigan, seventy-two fishermen snagged 276 coho salmon. Most of the fish ranged ten to twelve pounds, bug hook-jawed males and fat hen fish, but some weighed close to twenty pounds.

Tackle shop proprietors in the area love this snagging. How else is an average fisherman likely to hook into a dozen or so big husky salmon in a few hours of casting?

Each fisherman is legally allowed five salmon a day, but a man might foul a dozen or more before he successfully lands five. In the process of fighting so many fish of such size, lines frequently snap, terminal rigs break, expensive rods pop, and many quality reels simply fall apart. Every day fishermen trek to the tackle stores to buy new gear. "These salmon are making a sales bonanza for me," a Ludington tackle shop owner said happily, as he showed a surf-type, heavy-duty spinning reel that had been "coho demolished."

One fall day at the Big Sable Dam fishermen were lined up shoulder-to-shoulder on both sides of the river, wearing chest-high waders and standing in water about three feet deep. Almost to a man they had ultraheavy tackle, huge spinning rods and reels suitable for beating white marlin, lines testing to eighty pounds, and terminal gear comprised of one or two treble hooks, plus a heavy lead sinker.

They'd cast out—valiantly trying to prevent crossed lines—let their hooks sink to bottom, then begin yanking the rig across the bottom trying to connect with one of

Coho salmon swarm into Michigan's Sable River, and other Lake Michigan feeder rivers, to spawn in fall. Congestion like this makes snagging easy.

Shoulder-to-shoulder snagging isn't unusual when the salmon fill Michigan's rivers.

Fishermen below Big Sable River dam cast to snag cohos.

One caster hits a salmon and his buddy scoops it up in a big net . . .

. . . and goes lunging ashore with the prize . . .

. . . until, finally, the coho is held aloft for the camera by the proud fisherman.

the hundreds of salmon grouped in the river below the dam. Every few minutes one or more of the fishermen would foul-hook a salmon, then the cry would go up: "Fish On! Fish On!"

Other fishermen in the vicinity would reel in lines to prevent tangles, then grab huge nets and stand by waiting to help net the prize. Crowds of people, mostly curious nonfishermen, jammed the banks and a catwalk atop the dam. Whenever a salmon was netted there'd be loud, appreciative "ooohs and aaahs" and shouts like "that's a good one!" or "boy what a beauty!"

The salmon don't really fight very hard, considering

their weight. When they feel the hooks and the restraint from the line they bolt and splash heavily at the surface, do some twisting and turning, but then usually are drawn steadily shoreward and netted or beached. With heavy gear the average salmon is probably landed in five minutes or less. An occasional fish, however, makes a fairly good low, but clear, leap.

The salmon are, of course, in bad condition compared to fish caught earlier in the season in the open waters of Lake Michigan. The Sable River salmon, as with others in Michigan rivers, in the fall, are in the throes of atrophy —wasting and withering, and about to die—and cannot

Another Sable River fisherman hangs a coho, and his rod bends more than double under the strain.

A barefoot youngster comes to assist with net. Note here the bend to the fisherman's rod.

fight as they do in spring and summer.

The late fall salmon are dark fish, wearing their deep spawning colors, rather than the bright, silvery chrome they sport earlier in the fall.

Nonresidents visiting Ludington State Park to observe this salmon fiasco are required to purchase $2 park permits, and an additional permit also is required to participate in the fishing, or rather, snagging.

There's nothing wrong, of course, with this deliberate foul-hooking of salmon. While it is a type of fishing that will not appeal to many anglers, others who participate get a genuine kick out of it, and they utilize the fish they catch. The salmon are going to die anyway, and if they are not removed by snaggers the carcasses would befoul many a Michigan stream.

Voila! Success!

17

Way Out Fishin' Boat

A fisherman can loaf while he floats in this unique "boat."

Unique chair-type "boat" is light enough to carry easily with one hand.

Imagine drifting lazily down a creek or over a placid pond, leisurely casting for fish, yet still being as comfortable as though you were lounging in a favorite living room chair. Sounds wonderful—and it is!

An Indiana firm manufactures an item called the "Floater Loafer," which makes a lounge-chair kind of fishing possible. The Floater Loafer is molded of polystyrene foam, which has exceptional buoyancy, and has a built-in chair of aluminum tubing and plastic webbing. You sit back in a Loafer, relax, and go floating around just as though you were sitting in a deep lounge chair.

The manufacturer designed the Loafer primarily for use in swimming pools—something for the kids to play around with, and for older folks to loaf in while enjoying the sun and the water. But the gadget makes a terrific fisherman's item.

Wearing waders, angler launches "Floater Loafer." Paddle rests on arms of lounge chair boat.

For fishing small ponds and lakes, or trout streams, the Loafer has much to offer. To begin, it is more comfortable than the truck tire tube boats that have been on the market for years. You've got a regular chair to sit in, which supports your back. In addition, there's a special attachment on which to rest your legs, or you can use the same attachment or another like it as a head rest attached to the top of the seat.

A Loafer weighs only 10 pounds, and is light enough for a child to carry. It dismantles readily for storage in a car trunk, or even on the back seat of a car. A fisherman wanting to float some hidden pond, or drift a creek in an out-of-the-way area, can hike in to a spot toting his Loafer, then drift or paddle to where the fish are.

No paddles or other accessories for fishermen come with these unique boats. I use a single, watertight, floating aluminum paddle, lightweight and only four feet long. The paddle is tied to the Loafer on a short rope, and when not in use is simply dropped and allowed to float beside the Loafer. The paddle also can be placed across the Loafer's arms when the fisherman needs both hands for casting.

An anchor is a necessity, particularly when floating streams. A small boat anchor is tied to a 15 foot rope. When floating down a stream, the fisherman drops the anchor over anytime he wants to work out a spot carefully. When not in use, the anchor is placed behind the Loafer seat where it's out of the way.

In warm water a fisherman can use the Loafer without waders, but in spring and when floating cool streams, it's best to wear chest-high trout fisherman's waders. Wearing waders keeps you perfectly dry in the Loafer, since the water never comes higher than just under your armpits.

Two small holes in each arm of the Loafer will hold glasses—or a bottle of beer. A fisherman who uses his

Fisherman shoves off, makes a few casts . . .

. . . and promptly hooks three pound smallmouth bass in northern Illinois lake.

Subdued, bass is lifted out and admired. Angler in a "Loafer" can land fish simply by sliding them into his lap.

Loafer often would want to mount a waterproof box on one side for his lunch, and another box on the other side to hold lures. Of course, a fisherman's vest or jacket can be worn while fishing from the "arm-chair boat," and usually such garments hold all the gear a fellow needs.

Though a fisherman is sitting *in* the water when using a Loafer, casting is easy, even fly casting. However, beginning fly casters may have to concentrate on throwing higher back-casts than usual.

Fish are easy to hook, play, and land from a Loafer. To land a fish you merely slide him right into your lap, where you can take the hook out and release him or put him on a stringer tied to the Loafer.

A Floater Loafer handles easily with just one paddle,

but again, a fisherman using his Loafer often might want to mount small oar locks and use two lightweight paddles.

These floating chairs have no air chambers to leak, so accidental gouges or cuts do not impair their efficiency. I struck sharp rocks and countless snags while floating the Beaverhead River in Montana, but the jolts didn't mean a thing to the performance of the Loafer.

There are, however, a couple hazards to fishing from a Floater Loafer. One day I used the Loafer on Green Lake, west of McHenry, Illinois. I was so comfortable bugging for bass that I settled too far back in the Loafer, and water poured in over the top of my chest-high waders. And a little later I had a husky 3 pound smallmouth bass that towed me and the Loafer halfway around the lake!

18

Saga of Armstrong's Creek

Some far-sighted fishing tackle companies, a brewery, and individual sportsmen have preserved one of the world's finer trout streams for public fishing. A famed Montana creek that would have been leased for private fishing has, instead, been "reserved" by individual and business donations so that it remains open not for fishing by a favored few, but for fishing by all anglers.

The stream is Armstrong's Spring Creek, just a few miles west of Livingston, Montana. It is unique.

As trout streams go, Armstrong's is short, singing along for a distance of only two miles—from where it bubbles up in natural, water-cress fringed springs to where it melts into the Yellowstone River. It is gin-clear, and rich, producing an unbelievable wild trout population. It has brown, rainbow, and cutthroat trout, with the average fish weighing probably a pound while many exceed two to three pounds, and the occasional lunker goes to four to six pounds. Following a recent electrical fish-shocking survey by Montana Conservation Department biologists, it was determined that the stream supported a remarkable 5,700 "catchable size" trout per mile.

Having such characteristics, it is no surprise that not long ago the rancher who, literally, owns Spring Creek was approached by wealthy types and asked to lease the fishing rights for a reputed $12,000 annually. Armstrong figured he'd inform his old fishing friends—who for years had truly enjoyed the stream—about the offer before he made a commitment. Spring Creek habituals like Dan Bailey, proprietor of the famed fly and tackle shop in Livingston, couldn't stomach the idea of NO FISHING signs going up on Spring Creek. So they engineered a campaign that ultimately produced $6,000—enough to get the rancher to stay "public-minded" and to forego the offer of $12,000—and so, in effect, saved Spring Creek as a public fishing spot . . . at least for one year.

National Trout Unlimited, the nation-wide, nonprofit sportsmen's organization dedicated to maintaining and improving trout fishing generally, kicked-in with $1,000. Then four fishing tackle firms followed suit. They were *Scientific Anglers, Inc., Fenwick/Sevenstrand Co., The Shakespeare-Pflueger Corp.,* and *Dan Bailey's Fly and Tackle Shop.* Individual anglers scattered around the country contributed enough for another $1,000, so the $6,000 needed to lease the stream for one season was accumulated. Later, two other companies contributed funds so that the money needed to lease the stream in 1971 was obtained; they are the *Johnson Reels Co.* and *Lucky Breweries.*

Today an attractive rustic sign stands in a parking area beside the stream. The heading reads, ARMSTRONG SPRING CREEK, and below that are the words *"Fly Fishing Permitted on This Famous Stream Through the Generosity of Those Listed Below Who Have Leased The Fishing Rights Here For Your Enjoyment."* Below that are listed the names of each contributing company.

So one of the world's finest trout streams continues to be public fishing water, at least for a time. So long as some of America's businessmen feel content to contribute corporate funds to keep Spring Creek as public fishing water, so long as *Trout Unlimited* supports the project, and so long as some individual anglers contribute, Armstrong's Spring Creek will remain a magic stream where *all* anglers may fish in total contentment.

Large brown trout are not unusual catches at Armstrong's Creek. Tom McNally took this 22 inch, 3¾ pound Spring Creek brown on a size 18 Cahill Dry.

19

'Way Down on the Bottom

Deep fishing pays off on most gamefish species.

One bright August afternoon several years ago Willie Weaver and I were bugging the shoreline of a southern Wisconsin lake, which I'd prefer not to name. We came to a rocky point and saw a couple of skin-divers in rubber suits fooling with fishing tackle. One of them had rigged a short, stiff bait-casting rod, and as Willie and I rowed close he slipped into the water and disappeared—rod and all.

"How's it going?" I called to the remaining diver, by way of greeting.

"Okay," he replied. "We've found a big school of bass laying under a ledge down there at 65 feet."

"Bass!" Willie roared. "You ain't spearin' 'em, are you?"

"Hell no," said the diver. "We're gonna' get a couple to eat, using a rod and reel."

Under Wisconsin laws it is illegal, of course, to skin-dive and spear any gamefish. Generally speaking, the law stipulates that gamefish must be taken "on rod and reel." Nothing in the regulations state that the "rod and reel" must be held out of the water, or that the fisherman cannot take his "rod and reel" underwater.

Shortly the first diver surfaced and, splashing, kicked his way to the rocks. He handed the rod and reel to his partner, and the rod bowed under the weight of a big largemouth. It was a plump four-pounder!

"How the heck did you catch him?" Willie asked.

"Easy," grinned the returning diver. "I just swam up to that school and stuck this rod out at one of the big bass. I let my glob of worms hang in front of him, and for a while he didn't pay any attention. Then I started moving the bait around, back-and-forth, in a circle, then figure-eights—like that. Pretty quick this bass swam up and . . . *Cluuuuummmmmmppppp!* . . . I had 'im."

"How many bass you figure's down there?" Willie wanted to know.

"Must be 20 or 25," one diver stated. "There's almost always bass down there. In this lake fish are most always

deep. You're wasting your time fishing the shoreline."

Willie and I are fully aware that bass and most other gamefish spend the bulk of the time in deep water, usually near some kind of underwater structure such as a rock pile, depression, or ridge. But, because we prefer to take bass on popping bugs and fly rods, we always start out by fishing the shallows with poppers. When that fails we try shallow-running lures, using spinning, bait-casting, or spin-cast tackle. If no luck, we start fishing moderate depths with medium-running baits. If that fails too, we know the fish are not close-in but, rather, are somwhere down deep. So we start hunting them, and start trolling or jiggling the promising deep-water areas. Invariably the deep-down fishing pays off!

As a long-time SCUBA (self-contained underwater breathing apparatus) diver, I've personally observed bass and other important gamefish schooled at surprising depths, and have also had other divers report observing fish 'way down deep.

Once with Sal Savaglio of Lombard, Illinois I did some underwater exploring at clear, cold Lake Geneva in Wisconsin. Geneva's shallows are weed infested, and the long, thin weed stems fill the water like a forest from the shore all the way out to a depth of about 50 feet. Excepting the occasional panfish that poke around through the weeds, most of Geneva's fish haunt the bottoms somewhere beyond the weed line. This means, of course, that *most of the time* no one is going to catch much at Geneva unless he fishes at depths of 50 feet or more.

It's not possible in limited space to present an ichthyological discourse on why fish are so often down deep, but suffice it to say that black bass, for example, in most lakes and large, slow-moving rivers, will normally be found in deep-water "sanctuaries" except when actively feeding. Moreover, the fish will be in schools. At any time of day or night—and this includes the hot, middle part of a summer day—bass may move from their deep-water sanctuaries along specific migration routes to the

Almost simultaneously, these two fishermen land their northern pike. They hooked them in a shallow bay, but even northern pike frequently go deep.

shallows where they disperse to individually hunt forage fish. When feeding is completed they return to deep water. (All this, of course, excludes the early spring spawning season when most fish are in the shallows nesting.)

How deep fish may go depends on the individual lake. Clarity of the water, bottom formation, penetration of sunlight, to some extent temperature, the availability of oxygen at various depths—all those things and more determine how deep fish may be in a given lake. So each fisherman must "check out" the lakes he fishes, that is, work them thoroughly end to end, and at all depths, so that he comes to know a lake's bottom structure, the type of bottom, and habits of its fish.

Too many fishermen—including some veteran anglers

—feel certain species of fish—such as black bass and muskies—always are in shoreline shallows, while some other species—like walleye and lake trout—always are deep. The facts are that most species usually are down deep, only periodically moving into shallows to feed (or spawn). Species that are deep the bulk of the time include largemouth and smallmouth black bass, northern pike, walleyes, lake trout, lake whitefish, white bass, and crappies.

To give just a couple examples of fish being deep, one June day George Strickler, former Sports Editor of the *Chicago Tribune*, and I fished a very shallow weedy bay in Eagle Lake at Vermilion Bay, Ont. As nearly as we could figure we caught around 70 pike, weighing from a mere pound to about 10 pounds, in water *four feet deep*

How deep fish may go depends on the individual lake. This big laker was taken at a depth of 65 feet from Clearwater Lake, Man. by Kit Kitney of Winnipeg.

Contrary to the beliefs of many fishermen, largemouth bass most of the time are down deep.

Walleyes are notorious for spending most of the time in deep water. To take them consistently, deep fishing is necessary, particularly when fishing air-clear water under a bright sun.

or less. We returned to the bay the very next day, and found it *empty of pike.* I caught one tiny 15-incher! The fish had left that shallow bay and moved to a deep-water reef.

Muskies? Most fishermen figure muskies are the original shallow-water giant, but it isn't so. True, muskies haunt shallows frequently, hanging around food-filled, weedy bays, or around logs, stumps, and such other cover—but a lot of the time muskies, too, are down deep. I met a skin-diver once whose name I can't recall who told me of seeing a pod of some 30 muskies at a depth of 40 feet in Lac Court O'Reilles in northern Wisconsin. He said they were stretched out side-by-side like so many logs along the underwater face of a cliff.

How to fish deep is a story all its own, but a couple items the deep-water angler should have include a depth-sounder or electronic fish-finder, and contour maps of the lake or river being fished. Contour maps save a lot of chasing around, because they generally give depth as well as bottom type. And electronic sonar equipment does about the same things, as well as revealing the actual location of fish.

Deep trolling is about the best way to find fish that are scratching their bellies on bottom, but deep-jigging with lead-head jigs and even bait fishing on or near bottom also are top methods.

The important thing to remember is that, no matter where you're fishing or for what species, if you can't find fish in the shallows they are some place else—namely in deep water.

So the answer to "What's Down Deep?" is simple; nothing, probably, except fish!

20

Fishing Frontiers: Norway

One of the last great strongholds of Atlantic salmon, Scandinavia beckons to anglers around the world.

On Norway's Driva River, Tom McNally casts a fly to edge of fast water on far bank.

So great is the allure of salmon fishing in Norway that anglers from all over the world congregate on its crystalline rivers that spill out of the high mountains, wind through deep fjords, and tumble into the sea.

A two-mile stretch of the Driva River near Sunndalen, Norway is leased and operated for salmon fishing by MyTravel International, a Norwegian tourist agency. Fishermen are boarded at the 300-year-old Frederic Fale farmhouse overlooking the river.

Once, following a day's fishing, at the Fale dinner table could be found Norwegians, Germans, Austrians, a Pole, and this American peasant. A few days earlier the river, the farmhouse, and the dinner table had been host to a French general, an English lord and his lady, a Dane of royal ancestry, and an Italian industrialist.

When people of the world are thrown together in common pursuit of Atlantic salmon, nationalities and world politics are forgotten.

One afternoon at a Driva River pool I watched a German assisting a Frenchman trying for a large salmon resting in a chute of water between two boulders. The Frenchman stood in the river upstream and, on direction from the German atop one of the boulders, endeavored to cast and properly present a shrimp to the salmon.

Using a spinning rod, the Frenchman delivered several poor casts.

"Not far enough," said the German in English.

"I'm doing my best," replied the Frenchman in German.

"It's not good enough," said the German in French.

"Watch closely," answered the Frenchman in English, "I'll make a longer cast."

He did, and the shrimp swung in the current before the salmon. The fish moved forward, but at the crucial moment the impatient Frenchman reeled in his shrimp.

"No, no, no!" the German, irked, yelled in English. "You pulled it away from him. Now you must cast again."

The next cast was right, the salmon took the shrimp and was landed, the German assisting the Frenchman throughout the fight. When it was over the pair of them, gleeful as kids, triumphantly lugged the salmon home, walking slowly arm in arm, laughing all the way.

That evening at dinner the German gave a long dissertation, in English, on the problems of the world and a possible solution.

"The heads of all nations," he concluded, "should come together on a Norwegian salmon river. Here there is no politics, there are no wealthy and no poor. Everyone communes perfectly to discuss the ways of the salmon. On a river such as the Driva one thinks only of the peaceful pursuits."

Members of five nations quickly agreed.

Atlantic salmon are sheathed in silver and lined with gold.

While inexpensive salmon fishing—costing around $5 a day for a "card" giving permission to fish a specific "beat"—is available in places throughout Norway, the finest salmon angling requires the expenditure of many dollars.

Excluding rare stretches of government or public water, all salmon rivers are owned by someone. If the fishing is only so-so in a given stretch owned by a farmer or

A sea-run brown trout hits and is soon collared.

McNally removes fly from three-pounder . . .

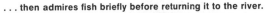

. . . then admires fish briefly before returning it to the river.

two, public fishing may be allowed for a small fee.

If the fishing is extraordinary, landowners will likely lease the fishing rights annually or under long-term contract for a sizable sum.

With more of the world's fishermen more willing than ever to travel and to pay for good salmon fishing, MyTravel International (19 Nedre Vollgt., Oslo), acquired fishing rights to several of the nation's—and the world's—best salmon waters. Their United States agent is Ernest Prossnitz, Special Tours and Travel, 8 North Michigan Avenue, Chicago, Illinois.

One spot is the famous Malangsfoss salmon pool on the internationally known Mals River near the town of Bardufoss, Norway. MyTravel built a superb fishermen's lodge close to the pool at a cost of about $50,000.

It accommodates ten persons and the food and service are excellent. The lodge is within yards of the Bardu River, where grayling and brown trout dimple the surface and go virtually unmolested by visiting anglers, who think only of salmon.

MyTravel or Special Tours will make all arrangements for fishing the Malangsfoss. Parties of four to six persons are normal, and the usual fishing period is six days, at a cost of around $136 per man per day.

Until some years ago, fishing in the Malangsfoss was controlled by eighteen Norwegian families. The annual salmon catch from the pool was their major means of support.

An incident occurred in the famed Malangsfoss pool that I'll long remember. It originated with a fleeting moment of anger, but it cost an Atlantic salmon its life.

Years ago the salmon—spawned and hatched and reared in the upper Mals—had grown from a fingerling to a parr, then to the smolt stage, at which time it descended to the sea.

For years the salmon roamed the North Atlantic, gaining poundage and waxing fat on the ocean's rich forage. Then this magnificent salmon, bright, strong, and laden with sea lice, returned to the Mals to spawn. It ascended the river and ultimately reached a barrier falls at the head of the Malangsfoss pool. Here the salmon rested and waited for the river to drop, which would enable it to pass the falls via a "fish ladder" blasted out of riverside rocks.

The salmon, restless and eager to reach natal gravel beds far upriver, mingled with hundreds of other salmon below the falls. It cruised impatiently, then turned away from the turbulence and swam out into the pool. The salmon set himself against the current and sulked. At that moment a four-inch-long object glittered and flashed before him, reflecting sun rays that illuminated the pool. Angered at this intrusion, primed by frustration and his restlessness, the salmon bulleted forward and struck.

Treble hooks stung his jaws. A strange force partially restrained him. To rid himself of the metal spoon, the salmon lurched to the surface and arched out in a showering leap. Falling back, he raced in looping circles through the Malangsfoss, then turned and ran for the sea. His first rush took him to the end of the pool and a shallow riffle breaking into the river proper. The salmon flashed through the riffle, leaped again and again, rested, then continued its run downriver.

Swimming swiftly with the current, it passed a large island, and fought relentlessly for a half mile downstream until, finally, its strength waned. After an hour, no longer able to resist the force pulling against its jaw, the salmon was led into shallows. In knee-deep water the fish gathered its remaining strength, churned and struggled briefly, then rolled on its side.

A gaff was slipped into the salmon and the fish slid onto the gravel beach. Bright as chrome, with iridescent blue and pink hues and black spots, the salmon's colors changed continually. The gaff was removed and the salmon was hoisted on a heavy scale by a Norwegian guide.

"Thirty-nine and one-half pounds!" he announced to the fisherman, who still held his rod. "The finest salmon taken so far this season in the Malangsfoss!"

The fisherman was American angler Leo Guthman.

Such drama occurs daily in the Malangsfoss, doubtless the world's best salmon pool.

With Guthman on that trip were fellow Americans Ed Robson, Derald Ruttenberg, and Pete Bensinger, all of whom had been fishing the Malangsfoss for several days. While Guthman's giant 39-pounder, trophy-size salmon

Twenty-two pound salmon, like this, aren't unusual in the Driva River.

Gillie wades in with 16-pounder he gaffed for McNally on the lower Reisa River.

Chicago sportsman Ted Bensinger photographs a 26-pound Atlantic taken from famed Malangsfoss salmon pool.

was the party's best, other salmon had been beached daily.

The first full day of fishing produced 16 salmon. One was 27¾ pounds, another 24 pounds. Several weighed 15 to 20 pounds. One day Guthman caught a 30¾ pound salmon, one of 29¾ pounds, a 27¾ pounder, and a "baby" of 16 pounds. The very first salmon taken by one of the group weighed 28 pounds. In several days of fishing the Malangsfoss, five fishermen took nearly 900 pounds of salmon.

The largest salmon ever caught on rod and reel from the pool weighed 74 pounds. One season, over a five-week period, the Malangsfoss produced 800 salmon, most of which weighed 22 to 25 pounds apiece. In addition to the salmon, 120 grilse were killed.

Fishing for six days here, the Guthman party caught 42 salmon, including a 30 and a 31¼-pounder.

Fishing from shore at the pool is possible, but not generally productive. Three boats are available to take three anglers into the pool, where fishing with long, heavy fly rods, monofilament line, lead sinkers, and spoons is customary, at least through most of the season. The pool is deep, and taking salmon on flies there is difficult when the water is high and cold. August is best time to try fly fishing.

I fly fished the Malangsfoss for long hours with no results. When time ran out and it was necessary to leave, I lowered a weighted spoon, promptly had a strike, and soon landed a 24-pounder.

Fishing with spoons or even shrimp bait is legal in the Malangsfoss and other MyTravel-leased waters, though only fly fishing for salmon is permitted most other places in Norway.

The Malangsfoss pool is more than 200 miles north of the Arctic Circle. In the summer there is no full darkness, so a fishing day can be 24 hours long beneath the "midnight sun."

Some snow is on mountain peaks thereabouts all year. Thus the winter sports enthusiast, who might possibly tire of catching salmon, can go skiing if he likes.

Though the Malangsfoss is well into the Arctic, the Gulf Stream swings close to the Norwegian coast, so summer days normally are pleasant.

Gillies (guides) on the Malangsfoss bleed salmon that are caught immediately by cutting their gills. It may only be an "old gillies' tale," but they believe prompt bleeding betters a salmon's meat.

This is how it is at the world's top salmon pool. In the Malangsfoss, even the most astute salmon angler can be quickly and lastingly spoiled.

One time MyTravel bid $25,000 for the fishing rights for one season on a short stretch of the Alta river. It wasn't enough. A New York sportsman, who previously had leased the beat for around $13,000 annually for a five-year period, offered $30,000. In addition to the initial leasing cost for the season's fishing rights, the New Yorker also had to pay for gillies, guards to prevent poaching, etc. It is estimated that total cost to him for Alta river fishing for the season approached $50,000. The "season" ran about one month!

MyTravel also acquired fishing rights to a "new" river, the Reisa.

The Reisa (pronounced Rayza) is owned by the Norwegian government but for years the salmon fishing rights have been in the hands of landowners along the river. Netting has been going on in the lower river and the fjord, and landowners have done some rod and reel salmon fishing.

It was felt it might be best if all netting were stopped and the Reisa turned into a "sport" river. But no angler, other than local farmers using shrimp baits and spoons, had ever fished the river. At the invitation of the Norwegian government, I went there to check the Reisa's sport fishing possibilities. They appeared to be unlimited.

As a result of the sport fishing study, netting was halted.

Despite the commercial netting that had been going on, the Reisa one season gave up nearly 1,000 salmon to rod-reel fishermen. Average weight was 18–22 pounds. A record for the river is 70½ pounds. One day, 30 salmon were caught in the river on regulation tackle.

The Reisa rises in Finmark and is about 225 miles north of the Arctic Circle. It winds for about 80 miles through indescribably beautiful mountains, alpine parks and meadows. Some 50 miles of it is fishable, chiefly by wading but also by boat fishing in the lower pools. It has many excellent runs, holes and pools, with countless salmon "holding" and "taking" areas.

Only controlled fee fishing is allowed now. The Reisa ranks as one of the world's outstanding salmon fly fishing rivers. It is said to have the best salmon spawning grounds in all of Norway.

The Reisa gets a big run of sea trout (sea-run browns) in early August. The main river, and numerous feeders, also provides superb fishing for resident brown trout. July is peak month for salmon, August is best for trout. Trout in the upper river and side streams average better than one pound apiece, with ones 12–15 pounds possible. A 36-pound brown trout was netted in the lower river. Arctic char, and grilse, come into the main river in August.

MyTravel operates it for "bargain" salmon fishing— at a cost of about $500 per person per week.

In addition to the ordinary salmon fishing fees, the salmon enthusiast suffers incidental costs. One is the travel expense, more than $800, for example, round-trip Chicago to Oslo, Norway, via SAS airways. A single salmon fly costs $2.50 or more. And, of course, there are other equipment costs.

The president of a large travel agency tells of a wealthy Italian who came to the Reisa to fish for salmon but hadn't brought chest-high waders. The Italian asked him to buy twelve pairs of waders.

"Twelve pairs?" exclaimed the president. "What size?"

"All different sizes," replied the Italian. "If I knew the correct size, I'd order only one pair."

Thinking about Norway's famed salmon fishing— there was a 90-year-old Russian who leased a mile of the Aaroy River. The guy was a salmon fishing nut. To him scrapping with a hooked salmon was sort of a man-to-man encounter. Once he hooked a huge salmon and, with 70-pound test line and a big rod, refused to let the salmon

Giant salmon are almost the rule in many Norwegian rivers. This one weighed 28 pounds.

budge an inch downstream. He locked himself up like a weightlifter, then somehow held that powerful salmon dead still in the current until it was dead. The fish weighed 68 pounds, was mounted, and is displayed in the Bergen museum.

The old Russian did that sort of thing all the time. Twice while fighting big salmon that way he fainted, and was carried to his cottage by his gillies. People who knew this ancient angler insisted he wanted to die while holding a salmon rod and fighting a hooked fish. Well, if one must go, I guess that's a pretty good way.

Float Fishing Fun

A lazy summer day, a curling Ozark stream, and bass or trout to be caught—what could be finer?

Float fishing the Ozark streams is leisurely, easy angling everyone can enjoy.

Visualize, if you can, a soft summer day deep in the Ozark hills in northern Arkansas. You are floating lazily down a clearwater stream, sitting comfortably in a camp-type chair which is fitted snugly into the flat-bottomed "John-boat." Your guide is behind you, in the stern, paddling slowly and quietly, saying little.

Occasionally you flip out a cast to a sunken boulder or to overhanging tree limbs. At first your fishing was done earnestly and excitedly, but then the magic of the surroundings caught you until, finally, you became almost content to just sit back and enjoy the river and the jade-colored hills.

Now the silence of the bordering woodlands, the complete absence of other people, the murmur of the river, the bright sun and clear skies—all this has given you a sense of tranquility that you had believed impossible to attain nowadays.

The boat drifts over deep pools, around sheltered bends, through canyons, and occasionally bumps and grinds past shallow riffles. No other fishermen are encountered. The only vestige of civilization has been a single bridge and a few cattle spied in distant meadows. At last lunch time is at hand, so your guide eases the boat onto a sandbar and, while you relax lying in the sun, he prepares a "shore lunch." He builds a wood fire, and before long you are feasting on browned, fresh-caught fish, baked beans, french-fries, homemade bread (Ozarks style), apple pie better than Gram'mom made, and coffee brewed of river water.

You eat more than you should, and discover that, after-

Ozark rivers and streams still provide some of the finest float fishing for smallmouths to be found anywhere.

wards, you seem only good for an hour's nap there on the sand, cap over your eyes, the sun beating down. At last you rouse, join your guide in the boat, and continue your journey downriver.

The afternoon passes swiftly. The sun is setting. And, as dusk nears, whippoorwills begin their evening's chorusing. The boat is beached once more, a fire built, the evening meal prepared and eaten. For a time you sit and smoke and look at the fire, and talk a bit to the guide, but mostly you listen to the frogs and the crickets and the melodious "whipppooooorwilll! . . . whipppooooorwilll! . . . whipppooooorwilll!"

It has been a full day. Wood smoke thickens in your nose now as the fire dies. You lift yourself wearily and contentedly, and stroll to the tent, which the guide has readied, noticing that the stars seem brighter than you've ever seen them before. You slip into your sleeping bag and stretch out. Then you slip into a deep, dreamless sleep.

The next day and the next night, and all that follow, are repetitions of the first. Eventually, with some of life's tranquility completely regained, your Ozark float trip is over and you return to "home and civilization."

Vacation, fishing, and plain "leisure" trips of this sort in the vast Ozark hills that bridge much of mid-America have fascinated millions of U.S. and even foreign citizens for centuries. Government dam builders have destroyed countless miles of Ozark float streams, but fortunately much excellent float water remains.

Five pound rainbow trout, like this, are not unusual catches.

Tim Sampson of Glenview, Ill. swings in a typical White River rainbow . . .

. . . then adds it to a well-filled stringer. Trout will be prepared for a tasty shore lunch.

One of the best known float streams today is the White River in Arkansas. Years ago, before construction of big Bull Shoals dam on the White River near the towns of Mountain Home and Flippin, the White River was world famous for its smallmouth bass fishing. Now the water that comes through the base of the dam, from the depths of Bull Shoals lake, is too cold to provide good habitat for smallmouth bass. But it is excellent for rainbow and brown trout. Thus, while the upper White River no longer is top smallmouth bass water, it has become a mecca for trout fishermen.

The White was stocked with trout years ago, and is replenished annually by trout reared at a nearby federal hatchery. Water temperature of the river for miles below the dam is constantly in the upper 50s year-around, so the trout feed and grow rapidly for 12 months each year. Some of the largest trout taken anywhere in the nation are now caught in the White River. Rainbow trout bettering 20 pounds have been landed there, and brown trout of over 30 pounds. Rainbows of 5 to 8 pounds are common.

Numerous float-trip and camping outfitters, and very capable guides, operate on the White River. Float trips for fishing, camping, photography—or merely to loaf and enjoy the scenery—can be arranged at Flippin, Mountain Home, Bull Shoals, Cotter and other points along the river. One of the most popular White River float guides is Forrest Wood of Flippin, Ark.

Float trips on the White River, as elsewhere, can be arranged for almost any distance or length of time. Half-day or one day trips are easy to do. Trips lasting three or four days are popular, but many people make floats lasting a week or two. Naturally, overnight trips involve camping.

Trips are handled by "putting in" with boats at a spot upriver, perhaps not far below Bull Shoals dam, then floating downriver to the "take out" spot. The flat-bottomed John-boats are usually trucked to the "put in" spot, and the guide arranges for the trucks to meet the boats at a pre-arranged time at some spot downriver. Just how far downriver the "take out" spot will be depends on the duration of the trip.

The guides provide all equipment except fishing tackle, but they'll also provide that if necessary. Although it isn't essential, persons wishing to camp should bring their own sleeping bags. Tents, cooking utensils, and other necessities will be provided by the guide or outfitter. On float trips requiring several days, extra boats holding only camping supplies and foods are taken along.

The costs of such trips vary somewhat, but as a rule you can figure about $20 per day per person for ordinary fishing floats. Fishing-camping trips will run around $35 a day per person, everything included.

Arkansas' Buffalo River is another superb float stream. It is extremely picturesque, in many places winding through towering limestone bluffs rising 150 feet above the river. This is a smallmouth bass stream, unfortunately one of the last remaining first class smallmouth

float waters in the United States. The government's Corps of Engineers is now pressing to construct a dam on the river, but sportsmen, conservationists, and others interested in preserving our outdoors are fighting to prevent construction of the dam which, incidentally, has been declared "totally unnecessary" by various authorities.

Crooked Creek is another Arkansas float stream, but compared to the White and the Buffalo it gives only fair fishing. Crooked Creek is smaller, and in times of drought floating it can be difficult, with too many shallow bars and riffles to work through.

The better known float streams in Missouri are the Gasconade River and Current River. There are others, but none of the Missouri streams provide the fishing available in the Arkansas rivers listed above.

The Current River lies in eastern Missouri and flows for more than 100 miles south where it crosses the Arkansas line. The Current is primed by a large number of springs, and therefore maintains a reasonably constant level. Points to start out from for Current River float trips are the towns of Doniphan, Van Buren, and Eminence. Best time to float the Missouri streams is in September and October.

Detailed information on Missouri float trips can be obtained free by writing Missouri State Conservation Commission, Farm Bureau Building, Jefferson City, Missouri. Details on Arkansas trips will be provided by Arkansas State Game and Fish Commission, Game and Fish Building, State Capitol Grounds, Little Rock, Arkansas.

One last word regarding float trips. Whether you are a seasoned fisherman and outdoorsman, or simply a nature-lover looking for a different kind of vacation adventure, don't think you can make a "one time" float trip. I doubt if anyone has ever made an Ozarks float trip and not returned, at his first opportunity, for another.

Float trips are like that. They grow on you.

Ozarks guide Forrest Wood loads "John boats" on the White River.

One day float trips, or lengthy fishing-camping trips, are easily arranged in the Missouri-Arkansas Ozarks.

Fish Florida the Easy, Inexpensive Way

Surf fishing, canal fishing, pier fishing, wading flats—
it's all available to anyone for little or no money.

Some of the good but inexpensive winter fishing in Florida is the sea trout fishing in the Cocoa area. Big trout like these are taken after dark by spinning with "Needlefish" plugs.

For the average tourist-type angler, much of the fishing available in Florida is expensive. A day's fishing aboard a charter cruiser, for example, can run to $150, figuring tips and other incidentals. A day on the bonefish flats, with a good guide, will run more than $50, everything included.

Yet some of the most interesting fishing for important gamefish in the Sunshine State often can be had for no more than the cost of a half-tank of gasoline, or the few bills it takes to rent a skiff.

One of the biggest tarpon I took in Florida in *winter,* a 102-pounder, I caught by the Bahia Honda bridge in the Keys, plug casting from a skiff-and-motor rig I'd rented for $12. In one day off West Palm Beach, in Lake Worth, I've caught Spanish mackerel, ladyfish, snook, jack crevalle and bluefish—all for no more than the cost of boat rental. One of the finest snook I've taken on a fly in Florida, twelve pounds, I got in the Tamiami Canal. All it cost me was gasoline.

One day years ago, while I was still a college student and a buck was a buck, I rented a rowboat for $1.25 at Lake Okeechobee—and came back with the biggest largemouth bass I ever caught, eleven pounds. Some of the fastest snook fishing I've had has been in the Loxahatchee and St. Lucie Rivers, and for a lot less than it costs me to take Mama out on the town one night. The first

bonefish I ever caught I got nearly twenty years ago while wading the flats at North Key Largo with Baltimorean Harry Rehmert. We had no guide and no boat. Harry and I had simply driven to the edge of the flat, and gone wading and hunting for bones' on our own.

The St. Lucie River, on the east coast at the town of Stuart, is famed for its snook, largemouth bass, and tarpon fishing. At times it also gives excellent ladyfish, bluefish, sea trout, pompano, and grouper angling. Occasionally, at the river's mouth, large king mackerel appear.

The St. Lucie River isn't very long. It probably is no more than twenty-five miles from where the river starts in the mangrove forests of St. Lucie County to its mouth at Stuart. The lower parts of the river range from salt water to brackish, and are affected by the tides. The upper reaches are fresh water, stained mahogany by mangrove roots.

The St. Lucie is the sort of river, offering the sort of fishing, that is beloved by light tackle anglers and fresh water fishing enthusiasts. The lower parts of the river are wide and open, and fishing there is like working a large inland lake. Farther upstream the river narrows and is lined with brooding mangroves. Here the water is so sheltered that fishing is possible almost anytime regardless of weather conditions. The upper, fresh water areas

Hard-fighting, good-eating snook are available in countless rivers and bays in south Florida. Skiffs can be rented inexpensively for Loxahatchee River fishing, which can bring snook, tarpon, bluefish, trout, etc.

A ladyfish leaps by the gunnel of a skiff in Florida's Lake Worth.

Florida fishing expert Vic Dunaway brings in a fine snook at Marco Island on the west coast. Hundreds of square miles of wadable water, "for free," is available to anyone who cares to wet a line.

offer fishing for largemouth bass and plate-size "bream" or bluegills. The brackish and salt water sections offer a smorgasbord kind of fishing, with the river actually sheltering more than 200 varieties of fish.

Tarpon are caught regularly in the St. Lucie, some being resident fish, others migratory. It is, however, rabalo, the snook, for which the river is best known. As elsewhere in Florida, the finest snook fishing in the St. Lucie is in May and June, although snook are present in the river year-around. On any day a fisherman casting plugs or flies, or using live mullet for bait, might hook a thirty-pounder, although he is not *likely* to. The average fair snook from the St. Lucie weighs six or seven pounds. Ones weighing ten to fifteen pounds are taken frequently, and lunkers of twenty to thirty pounds or more are not uncommon.

Many fishermen work the St. Lucie from large runabouts and small cruisers but an ordinary 12-foot skiff and 10 horsepower motor is more than adequate. Boats and motors can be rented at various liveries near Stuart, as well as at the Port St. Lucie Country Club and Marina, at Port St. Lucie, just upriver from Stuart. Just below the U. S. Route 1 bridge, near Stuart, there's a boat livery and fishing camp where a skiff and outboard can be rented for around $8 a day, and that includes a tank of gas.

Another great Florida river—just as easy to fish and just as inexpensive as the St. Lucie, and every bit as good—is the Loxahatchee. The Lox', fifteen miles north of West Palm Beach, is a finger of black mahogany water winding its way through mangroves to the sea. It's a highway for fish, a regular fish bowl. The Lox' has both resident and migratory fish, and when things are right

its dark water is nearly stiff with fish. Its lower reaches have bluefish, sea trout, occasional mackerel, ladyfish, snook, pompano, gaff-topsail catfish, crevalle, tarpon, lookdowns, sharks, snappers, even tripletails. Frequently porpoises sweep in from the sea to feed on the river's swarming mullet. There's a place upriver in the Loxahatchee that has tarpon which, on the average, range five to fifty pounds. Push your boat into a mangrove-lined cut behind an island I know, and chances are you'll see a dozen or more tarpon rolling. You'll see the water well up, a tarpon's slick back emerge, then his dorsal fin and its long, trailing, spiney ray.

LaMont Albertson of West Palm Beach is perhaps the best-known and most active Loxahatchee guide. He has an excellent skiff, and charges about $40 a day, one or two anglers, all included except lunch. Anglers trailing their own boats to Florida can fish the Lox' successfully. It's not a difficult river to navigate, and no alert boater could become lost even in the river's wild, upper reaches. There's a public launching facility where the river crosses U. S. Route 1. Also, boats and motors can be rented, for around $6 a day, at a boat livery downriver from the U. S. 1 bridge.

Lake Worth, the big tidal lagoon that extends for miles north and south of West Palm Beach, often offers spectacular fishing. Due to dredging and other conservation errors, Lake Worth doesn't have the fabulous snook fishing it once did, but good snook still are taken there, as well as Spanish mackerel, king mackerel, ladyfish, bluefish, crevalle, and so on. There are numerous causeways over Lake Worth, and fishing from most of them is permitted. From these bridges you can spin or bait cast with jigs or

Canal fishing in Florida is open to anyone, at no charge, and frequently can be fast, sporty fishing for baby tarpon, snook, or largemouth bass. This angler is working a section of the famed Tamiami Trail Canal.

other lures, or use bait, and the cost is nil.

A better way to fish Lake Worth, of course, is by skiff and outboard. There are many excellent marinas renting boats and motors in and around West Palm Beach, as well as at other towns bordering Lake Worth. In winter, Spanish mackerel swarm into the "lake," and when the mackerel are running you'll see a flotilla of hundreds of small boats out there, their occupants trolling, stillfishing or casting for the tough little, good-eating mackerel. Catches of forty or fifty mackerel in an afternoon are not unusual, per boat.

I especially enjoy taking ladyfish in Lake Worth. I've never caught a large ladyfish there, but then a ladyfish of any size is scrappy and fun on light tackle. And there are usually plenty of them, at various places all through Lake Worth. Various kinds of boats and motors can be rented at the marinas on Lake Worth. You can get a big runabout, for example, with a giant, powerful motor, or a

small rowboat with a 7½ or 10 h.p. motor. A small skiff and outboard is all you'll need.

Fishing the various canals in Florida certainly is some of the least expensive angling to be found anywhere. All you need do is rig your fly, spinning or bait casting outfit, then drive along a canal, stopping here and there to fish. Many expert canal fishermen drive the canal roads very slowly, all the while watching the water for "wakes" or "bulges" caused by moving fish such as snook, tarpon and largemouth bass. Less serious fishermen go to a canal, find a good looking "hole," then sit the day out right there stillfishing for bream, or anything else that might grab the bait.

The North New River Canal is a good one. It borders Route 84, going west out of Fort Lauderdale. The canal is alive with baby tarpon. It also has good largemouth bass and bluegills. Most of the tarpon range two to fifteen pounds, with the average four to eight pounds. But there are bigger ones too, like forty and fifty pounders, and ones of eighty pounds are seen occasionally. Tarpon in the Route 84 canal are landlocked, which means the fish are always there, even though it may take a while to find which part of the canal they are "using" on a particular day. And sometimes when you do get right on them, they may not hit. Tarpon are that way!

What may be Florida's most difficult, hazardous and hilarious fishing exists in a narrow canal bordering U. S. Route 1 a few miles south of Homestead. In winter streams of refugees from the north roar down the highway daily, all headed for sun, fun, frolic, and fishing farther on in the Florida Keys. Few of those motorists know that the tiny canal, only inches from their fenders, has largemouth bass and tarpon living in harmonious coexistence.

The canal averages twenty feet across. It's lined on both sides with dense mangroves. Here and there is a pool, perhaps thirty feet across. Part the mangroves nearly anywhere, peer into the water, and you'll likely see several small gar, a few bass (most under two pounds) and, if you keep looking in the right places, you'll see some baby tarpon, too. Two or three pound tarpon are average, but ones of six to eight pounds are there also.

The canal can be fished only from the roadside. The road's shoulder is about ten feet wide, narrower in places. You must squeeze your car off the road and onto the shoulder, then walk along the road edge and look for openings in the mangroves. Find an opening, then jockey around in the brush and try to cast. You can always use a bow-and-arrow or catapult cast with spinning and bait outfits, but with a fly rod the fishing's really tough. With any tackle it's no trick at all to hang your lure in a mangrove, either on your side of the canal or, worse, in mangroves behind you on the far side of the road.

The hazardous part of fishing this and most other Florida canals is that you are angling beside a road where cars pass at 65 m.p.h. You've got to watch the traffic, and, when fly casting, be sure no auto is barreling down just as you send your backcast out over the road. While fishing the Tamiami Canal once, I saw a fly fisherman's backcast snag the aerial of a passing car. The driver didn't know he'd caught a fisherman's line. The moving car stripped line off the man's reel, while the yelling fisherman went running off after the car. The backing line finally broke, and there went the car and the angler's $14 fly line trailing down the road. I've often wondered what that driver thought when he finally parked and saw that fly line snagged on his aerial.

The Tamiami Canal, paralleling U. S. Route 41 west out of Miami, is well known for its snook, although it also has largemouth bass, bream, gar and baby tarpon.

In places along the Tamiami fishermen have cut down brush and mangroves to make casting easier. One day on the Tamiami I saw a novice fisherman hook a good snook. He was so excited he didn't reel in, merely started back-

Outdoor writer and veteran angler Charley Waterman tussels with an Everglades snook he hooked by the "jiggerbobbing" method.

Even bonefishing can be done in Florida at no cost. All the visitor need do is go to the Keys, find a flat, wade out, and, with luck and skill, latch onto a couple of husky bones'. These were taken by a fly fisherman wading flats at North Key Largo.

ing up into the middle of the road. A car screeched to a stop, then others, until finally cars were piled up in two directions, horns blowing, drivers hollering, then at last the fisherman slid his snook out onto the road. Snook of around twenty pounds are taken with fair regularity in the Tamiami.

There are more canals, with baby tarpon but with no bass, along macadam backroads on North Key Largo. The Ocean Reel area has plenty of them. Good canals, with tarpon and snook, are near the West Coast, in the vicinity of Naples and Royal Palm Hammock along the Marco Road. I think baby tarpon are the most fun in these canals. Frequently a tarpon hooked in a narrow canal will leap and clear the water by several feet. He curves over in midair, falls back, and crashes smack into knotted mangrove limbs. It can be disconcerting to stand at water's edge holding your rod while helplessly watching your hooked fish flip-flopping down through tree limbs.

There are other minor problems to Florida canal fishing, namely snags, chiggers, and mosquitos. In winter mosquitos are usually scarce, moccasins occasional, and chiggers constant. Repellent handles mosquitos, caution takes care of the snakes, and fingernail polish helps sooth the chiggers, a little!

Lake Okeechobee, in south-central Florida, has long been famous for its largemouth bass. Bass are the big lake's primary gamefish, but it also has superb bluegill

Tarpon are available in numerous areas in Florida and can be reached easily via runabout or small skiff.

fishing, along with crappies and catfish. Okeechobee can be fished successfully from shore in a lot of places, though you're better off renting a boat at one of the many boat liveries.

From the latter part of February to about the middle of March is generally considered the best time for bass in Okeechobee. Usually in late February the bass leave the deep water and move into Okeechobee's shallow "hay-fields," where they spawn in the weed-filled water. Any-time at Okeechobee in late winter the bass fishing is likely to be excellent, although, naturally enough, it sometimes will die off for a few days.

Okeechobee is about thirty-five miles long and thirty miles wide. That's a lot of "living room" for bass. It has open canals and deep, clear areas, but the bays and pro-tected shores are thick with peppergrass and hyacinths. In places the peppergrass grows taller than a man's head and is thicker than Brazilian jungle. Water depth in these "hayfields" ranges from six feet to a few inches—and during the winter season, that's where the bass are. Fish-ermen poling skiffs through the shallows or wading often see weeds shaking as a cruising bass bores his way along. On days when the bass are really moving you'll see pep-pergrass waving everywhere, occasional splashes and swirls, and frequent long "V" wakes pushed up by a bass swimming in only inches of water. All this makes for an unusual kind of bass fishing.

At times I've had good sport at Okeechobee fly fishing with bass bugs in the open pockets, along the edges of peppergrass, and in the narrow, weed-free channels cleared by outboards. Other times weedless lures were best. It's possible to use weedless lures at Okeechobee with spinning gear, but the best equipment for this type of fishing is a bait-casting outfit with at least ten pound test line. Most Okeechobee regulars use twenty pound test line. Such heavy line is necessary to pull lures free of grass when they snag, and to hold bass which, when hooked, try to plow head-long through the reeds.

One of the most popular lures at Okeechobee is a black spoon with a black porkrind eel or plastic worm attached. In addition to plastic worms and porkrind eels, however, another popular lure at Okeechobee is a plastic snake. Some of the eel and snake lures used there are ten and twelve inches long, mounted with two or three tandem-type hooks. They take Okeechobee's lunkers, which, occasionally, weigh twelve to sixteen pounds spawn-filled.

Okeechobee fishing is done both from boats and by wading. Most fishermen boat out to the weedy bays, don chest-high waders, then work throuh the peppergrass casting around themselves in circles. Whenever wading fishermen hook bass they walk straight toward the fish, reeling fast, so they can get to the bass and fight it on a short line, thus getting a full scrap out of the fish and lessening the chance of the bass fouling in weeds.

Bass fishing at Okeechobee, as elsewhere in Florida, is year-around. The limit is ten bass daily. Guides, boats, motors, licenses—everything you need—can be obtained at various camps on the lake. Perhaps best of all, a day's fishing at Okeechobee can cost you from nothing—if you fish from shore or wade—to just a few dollars if you rent a boat.

Some of Florida's most touted fishing can be enjoyed at no cost whatever. That's bonefishing. All that's needed to catch bonefish is tackle and a bonefish flat with bone-fish on it. Remember, no one owns a bonefish flat. There is no law saying you *must* have a $50 a day guide, with skiff and motor, to go bonefishing. Certainly that is the best way to go about it, especially if you are a novice, but it is quite possible to park your car at a tidal flat, wade out, and find some bonefish. There are some great flats along North Key Largo, at Marthon, Islamorada, Big Pine Key, Upper and Lower Matecumbe Keys, and at various other places all the way down to Key West, where fishermen can go wading for bonefish entirely on their own. A bonus to this sort of fishing, depending on precisely where you are, the time of year, and weather conditions, are barra-cuda, red fish (channel bass), snappers, ladyfish and jack crevalle.

No special tackle is required for any of the fishing dis-cussed here. Bait-casting, spinning and fly tackle all will do the job and, in fact, having at least one outfit of each is the ideal set-up. Generally speaking, most of the ordi-nary fresh water gear you own will do for this fishing, al-though you should take your heavier outfits, too.

No matter where you go in Florida, the local tackle shop is the place to really learn what to do, how to do it, when to do it, and where. A tackle shop proprietor gen-erally knows what is hitting where, so the neighborhood tackle shop is the best possible place from which to start a Florida fishing junket.

Surf fishing opportunities are available on both coasts of Florida, year-around. Cobia, averaging 30 pounds, are common spring-time catches along Florida beaches.

23 *FEATURE STATES:*

Maryland

Fishing in ocean, bay, lake, or stream – it's all available in Maryland.

Taxidermist's aide prepares to skin white marlin on dock at Ocean City, Md. More white marlin are taken at Maryland port than anywhere else in North America.

Sportsmen living in or near the Free State of Maryland are fortunate indeed. They are blessed with unusual opportunities to enjoy a great variety of fishing.

Maryland has, for example, the finest white marlin fishing to be had anywhere in North America. Its huge Chesapeake Bay offers year-around fishing for striped bass, locally called "rockfish," as well as other salt water species. The brackish waters of the Chesapeake region provide extraordinary fishing for largemouth black bass, and many of the bay-country feeder rivers each spring get big runs of hard-fighting hickory shad and good-eating American or white shad. Inland, through the Piedmont Plateau, are beautiful lakes such as Loch Raven Reservoir and Pretty Boy Dam for largemouth and small-mouth bass and panfish, and rivers such as the Potomac and Monocacy to float and flip for smallmouths. And just about throughout the state, with the exception of the Eastern Shore, are numerous trout streams offering fair to excellent fishing.

Considering all of Maryland's fishing, possibly the most unique is its white marlin angling out of Ocean City. In any season, more white marlin are caught off this port than anywhere else in the country. Normally, from 600 to well over 1,000 white marlin are registered annually at Ocean City.

Ocean City, about 150 miles from Baltimore, is a summer resort town. It is located on a sand spit separating the Atlantic from Sinepuxent Bay, and has, therefore, exceptional harbor facilities for all types of sports fishing craft. Charter boats are readily available, and certainly some of Ocean City's white marlin skippers are among the most talented in the world. Paul Mumford, a highly skilled and experienced angler and host of Ocean City's best-known tackle shop, can arrange charters. Charters for white marlin angling also can be handled through the town's Chamber of Commerce, or through the Ocean City Charterboat Captains Association.

Rates for a day's charter on a marlin cruiser vary, of course, but figure somewhere around $100 to $135 a day for a party of four, slightly additional for a group of six. The best time for marlin fishing here—at the famed off-shore grounds such as the Jack Spot, Winter Quarter Lightship, and Tide Rips—is June and again in September. Most fishing is done, however, in the vacation months of July and August, and as a result the majority of the season's catch is brought in during those months. Very little fishing is done in September, but the ratio of marlin-catch to fisherman-effort that month is better than at any other time of the year. The difficulty with September offshore fishing in Maryland, however, is weather. Wind can build high seas at that time, and it frequently requires a good sailor to enjoy the angling possibilities. Also, many of the summertime charterboats by September have pulled anchor and headed south to Carolina or Florida waters. Despite that exodus, it's always possible to arrange an Ocean City charter for marlin in September.

There's a great deal of other fishing along Maryland's Sinepuxent and other coastal bays, and periodically those waters swell with small bluefish, called "tailers." Surf fishing is popular at Assateague Island, and good-size red drum or channel bass are taken from the beaches in the fall. Twenty years ago Assateague was wild and unsettled, a haven for waterfowl, shore birds, and small game, and was reachable only by a rustic little ferry. Today the island is bridged and developed, but nonetheless it periodically provides good fishing.

Moving inland from the Atlantic, and surveying Maryland's Eastern Shore, one must acclaim its great large-mouth bass fishing. Every county on the Eastern Shore is spotted with bass "ponds," big and small, and numerous rivers which provide unmatched largemouth fishing in either their upper fresh water reaches, or in their lower tidal, brackish water stretches.

The town of Salisbury is a good headquartering spot

Small bluefish frequently move into Chesapeake and are targets for light tackle anglers.

Fly fisherman casts for striped bass from grassy Chesapeake bank. Chesapeake's major fishing is for "rock," or striped bass.

Numerous Chesapeake estuaries provide spectacular fishing for shad, both hickory and American (white), in spring months. Jack Bunch of Baltimore took this white shad from the lower Wicomico River.

for fishermen who want to work the numerous bass lakes in that area. Some of the better-known rivers for bass fishing on the Eastern Shore include the Pocomoke—cypress-kneed and jungle-lined—the Nanticoke, and the upper Choptank. The brackish areas of those rivers, as well as the marshy bays abutting the Chesapeake, all provide exceptional opportunities for taking striped bass on light tackle.

Chesapeake Bay proper is world renown as a "nursery" for striped bass—one of our finest game and food fishes.

Fishing for "rock" is carried on throughout the bay—north to south, east to west—at all seasons, although late summer and early fall fishing is preferred by many Marylanders. Deep trolling is the rule, but chumming with ground or chopped fish, or crab, often results in large hauls of "pan rock," stripers of three pounds or less. Many Bay anglers drift-fish, or anchor at spots known for their productivity, and fish crab pieces or lower live eels over to float with the tide. Striped bass of 10, 15, 20 pounds or more are not particularly unusual.

Popular areas for Chesapeake fishing via charter or "party" boats are Solomon's Island, Tilghman's Island, Kent Island, Cambridge, Annapolis, Crisfield and Baltimore. In addition to the popular striped bass, Chesapeake fishermen can expect to catch great numbers of

Hickory shad are high-jumping, strong fish that are a delight to light tackle anglers throughout the Bay Country in early spring.

Shad fishermen line up on Deer Creek, a Susquehanna River feeder stream.

Small lakes like this one near Salisbury, Md., locally called ponds, provide exceptional largemouth bass fishing. Spring fishing is best.

Norfork spot, white perch, small bluefish at times, but few if any hardheads or "croakers," which once were abundant in the bay but apparently were over-fished by commercial netters.

Each spring, beginning in early March, hickory shad move into the Chesapeake from the sea and begin an up-bay, up-river spawning migration. They run rivers such as the Wicomico on the lower western side of the Chesapeake, the Potomac at Washington, D.C., the Severn, Patuxent, Patapsco, Gunpowder, Bush, and Susquehanna rivers.

The Susquehanna, at the head of Chesapeake Bay, receives a very heavy run of shad, although not as many fish arrive today as in the spring-time runs of years ago—thanks to pollution and over-fishing by commercials. The Susquehanna proper, and two feeder rivers below Conowingo Dam, Deer Creek, and Octoraro River, are popular hickory shad fishing spots. Usually the hickory runs reach a peak in this area by mid-April, and fishermen have great sport with these scrappy, wildly jumping acrobats, taking them on spinning and fly-tackle, using tiny spoons, small jigs, or shad flies.

Rivers on Maryland's Eastern Shore also receive hickory and white shad in the spring, and this includes most rivers all the way from the Northeast River at the head of the Cheasapeake to the Pocomoke, which is well down the bay. The hickory shad usually complete their runs by mid-May, and survivors return to sea, but the delectable and larger American or white shad run later—peaking in the Susquehanna sometime in May and frequently remaining through June.

In an all-around sense, Maryland's lower Susquehanna River—from Conowingo Dam downriver to where it empties into the Cheaspeake—is probably the state's best fishing hole. It would be next to impossible for even a mediocre angler to fish it on a summery day and leave without the makings for a fine fish dinner. The Susquehanna in this section holds striped bass that move in from the bay, shad, smallmouth and largemouth black bass, yellow and white perch, channel catfish, walleyes ("Susquehanna salmon"), eastern chain pickerel, and even occasional brown and rainbow trout that move into the big river following plantings in small feeder streams.

Tributary waters at the mouth of the Susquehanna, particularly Northeast River, in recent years have been providing very good winter ice fishing. Not only do fishermen there get pickerel and perch through the ice, but also some very nice largemouth bass.

Mayland has a number of fine lakes giving good black bass fishing, in addition to the ponds already mentioned that spot the Eastern Shore. Probably the most notable are Loch Raven, Pretty Boy, Liberty, and Tridelphia reservoirs, all in the Baltimore-Washington area. Lock Raven is a clear, picturesque lake only twelve miles from the City of Baltimore, yet it has produced smallmouth bass of more than seven pounds, and numbers of largemouths of eight pounds plus. Rental boats are available for fishermen at all four reservoirs.

Deep Creek Lake in far western Maryland is a cold, deep, very clear body of water that in recent years has been providing some good fishing for a variety of species,

Harvey Schemm displays a typical Maryland pond bass.

Chesapeake Bay's brackish estuaries offer many hundreds of miles of black bass water.

Bug fishermen swap notes on the Potomac River, the state's top smallmouth stream.

not the least of which is trout. Northern pike were introduced to the impoundment successfully.

Maryland has some fine float streams offering fair to good fishing for smallmouth bass. The best of these is the Potomac River, chiefly in the upper reaches around Harper's Ferry, Sheperdstown, and Brunswick. This is broad, open, rock-strewn, fast-moving water, and while most of the bass taken by anglers range small, some of three to five pounds are not uncommon.

Another float stream sometimes giving up good smallmouths is the Monocacy River, but it is silted heavily in reaches and frequently muddies so badly as to ruin the fishing for weeks on end.

Stream trout fishing in Maryland is mostly on a put-and-take basis, and for the inexperienced trout fisherman this angling is productive only for a few weeks after the streams are planted with hatchery-reared rainbows and brook trout. However, the knowledgeable fly fisherman can find much interesting and productive fishing in Maryland streams, and rarely pass a day on any one of the state's streams without enjoying considerable action.

Jones' Falls is a meadow stream almost within the Baltimore City limits that normally is well-stocked, but in addition it has some "native" brown trout, usually carry-overs that have wisened for a few seasons to the ways of anglers. The building of subdivisions, however, have done the watershed little good, so much better fishing is to be found elsewhere.

The upper Gunpowder River, below Pretty Boy Reservoir, is a popular spot with early-season trout fishermen who frequently get limits following spring-time releases. The Gunpowder flows for dozens of miles to the Chesapeake, but it provides trout fishing only in the areas immediately below Pretty Boy Dam.

Maryland's most popular trout stream is Big Hunting Creek in Frederick County, near the town of Thurmont, not so much because it is the best but because it is the best within an easy drive of the state's heavy population centers of Baltimore, Washington, and Annapolis. Big Hunting is well-stocked, as a rule, and it is a "natural" and very picturesque trout stream, spring fed, and while poor management and erosion of the watershed have changed the stream from what it was years ago, it remains one of Maryland's most attractive trout waters. Nearby is Fishing Creek—in many ways better than Big Hunting—and also nearby is Little Hunting Creek, a

Holes like this produce stocked trout in Big Hunting Creek near Thurmont, Md.

mountain stream coming out of the Catoctin Hills and the site, where, incidentally, presidents have been entertained at a private lodge. A presidential lodge, originally named Shangrila by President Franklin D. Roosevelt and changed to Camp David by President Dwight D. Eisenhower, is within a short cast of Big Hunting Creek, but it's hidden away in the woods.

Some of Maryland's finest trout streams, comparatively little-fished, are in the extreme western part of the state, in mountainous Garrett County. These include Big Savage River, Cherry Creek, and Bear Creek. The Youghiogheny River in this area—quite possibly one of the best-looking "trout" streams to be seen anywhere—is horribly

polluted by coal mine seepage and from an angler's viewpoint it is worthless.

All told, Maryland has about 50 trout streams in the northern and western portions of the state, totaling nearly 150 miles of "trout water."

But the trout fishing is, of course, only some of the rod-reel sport to be had year-round in "The Old Line State."

(Details on Maryland angling, and informative brochures, can be obtained by writing Department of Tourism, State Office Building, Annapolis, Maryland, or the Maryland Game and Inland Fish Commission, at the same address.)

John Daley cleans Big Hunting Creek catch of rainbows and bro trout.

Illinois

With the introduction of salmon in Lake Michigan, Illinois fishermen have more angling than ever.

Illinois sport fishing does not compare favorably with that of many other states because, generally speaking, Illinois has few suitable rivers and lakes and its winters are severe. Illinois is a prairie state—flat and open—and its topography isn't the sort that holds much water. As a consequence, many of its streams, rivers and lakes are badly silted from erosion, and others are badly polluted.

Which is not to say, however, that Illinois does not have any fishing. It assuredly does.

Since the introduction of coho and Chinook salmon into Lake Michigan, Illinois fishermen have been able to catch salmon from spring through fall. Moreover, lake trout are "coming back" in Lake Michigan, and the big lake now also provides good fishing for giant brown trout, for "steelhead," rainbows, and even brook trout.

WHAT EXCITEMENT: A GAL'S FIRST COHO!

Robin Beauchamp boats first coho off Waukegan . . .

. . . and squeals with glee as bloody fish struggles.

In addition, the Illinois Conservation Department has been building small lakes and developing warm-water fisheries over much of the state, particularly in the rural southern half.

Prior to 1968—the year when the first plantings of salmon in Lake Michigan simultaneously reached maturity and world-wide notoriety—about all a Chicago lake-front fisherman could hope to catch would be a 10-inch yellow perch. Perch fishing all along the Illinois portion of Lake Michigan is still good, but nowadays a Lake Michigan fisherman isn't surprised when he hooks into a big coho or Chinook salmon, or a plump brown trout.

In the spring of '72, for example, a fisherman was trolling a half mile off Chicago, from a small boat, and hooked and landed a coho or silver salmon that weighed 20 pounds, 9 ounces. Still another fisherman, angling from shore within the city limits of Chicago, tossed a hook baited with a nightcrawler worm into the waters of Montrose Harbor and hauled out a *24-pound Chinook salmon!* Such fishing would be remarkable anywhere, but when it occurs at the doorstep of one of the world's largest cities it is, well, extraordinary.

Most fishermen, and fishery biologists, are convinced that soon a world's record coho will be caught from Lake Michigan—quite possibly in the Illinois sector—and they believe, too, that the big, cold, deep lake might also soon produce a world's record Chinook. There is no doubt whatever that world record cohos are cruising Lake Michigan because a coho topping the existing world's record was trapped in a conservation department weir. It weighed 33 pounds, while the existing world record is a 31-pound coho from Cowichan Bay, British Columbia.

A heavy smelt population, along with hordes of alewifes, provide ample forage for all of the gamefishes of Lake Michigan. The alewifes, in particular, are what Lake Michigan's salmon and trout are waxing fat on. Brown trout of more than 10 pounds have been caught from the Illinois sector of Lake Michigan, and steelhead and rainbow trout of almost 20 pounds have been taken.

The Lake Michigan coho fishing begins in early spring, as soon as the weather breaks enough to permit sensible fishing. That's usually about mid-March, and then shore-bound fishermen casting from piers, docks, and breakwaters get coho weighing, on the average, 2-4 pounds, but the occasional lunker is caught then, too. As the weather improves sufficiently to allow boat fishing, generally about mid-April, salmon then are caught a mile or two offshore, as well as close in. From early spring to about the end of June there is salmon trolling all along the Illinois lake front, and particularly in the clear waters off Waukegan and Zion, in northern Illinois. Lake trout are taken in the same areas.

With the coming of coho and Chinook salmon to Lake Michigan, a new industry was founded for Illinois—the charterboat business. Charter cruisers can be hired right in Chicago, and at Waukegan as well. Rates for these Lake Michigan salmon fishing charters vary, of course, but they probably average about $225 for a day's fishing (eight hours), four anglers, all tackle, etc. provided, but not lunch or refreshments.

Throughout inland Illinois, the important gamefish is the largemouth black bass, followed by the smallmouth,

Still apprehensive that fish might flip free, anglerette tightens grip and strives to pose for camera.

Aaahh! Fish is securely collared, and there's time to smile for the camera.

Jay Johnson of Evanston, Ill. removes plug from a spring coho hooked in Illinois' portion of Lake Michigan. Much larger salmon also are taken.

Giant, alewife-stuffed brown trout was hooked along Lake Michigan shore.

Flooded strip-mine pits provide bass fishing in central part of Illinois.

Al Lopinot, Illinois' chief fishery biologist, measures a largemouth for study purposes while electro-fishing Lake Sara in central Illinois.

Bass fisherman releases four-pounder he hooked at a conservation department wildlife conservation area lake.

which is not so nearly well-distributed or abundant. The Kankakee River, in the northwestern part of the state, is certainly one of the better smallmouth rivers, but it has largemouths, too, as well as big channel catfish. The Kankakee, however, is best known for very large walleyes, taken not infrequently by skilled fishermen who know the river. Walleyes of 9-10 pounds are caught each spring, along with some 12-pounders. The state record walleye, 14 pounds, came from the Kankakee.

The Chain-of-Lakes in northern Illinois, some 35 miles from downtown Chicago, is a heavily fished, heavily boated, heavily swam–in, heavily polluted, heavily silted group of shallow glacial lakes. These lakes have a good population of stunted crappies, a small population of small bluegills, and some largemouth bass, walleyes and northern pike. Occasionally a good-sized northern is taken, or a largemouth of 6-7 pounds, but such catches are exceptional. The Chain-of-Lakes area is over-used, and nearly all of the lakes are developed, with year-round homes side-by-side on their shores.

Possibly the finest fishing in Illinois is in the Mississippi River and its sloughs and backwaters. A series of locks and dams convert the river into a chain of great pools. Top fishing normally is just below the dams, and in myriad sloughs and clear backwater "lakes." In these broad, sleepy waters are found largemouth bass, white

and yellow bass, other panfish, and walleyes. The best bass fishing normally is from about mid-June through October. There is no bass season in Illinois.

Generally, the Mississippi's best fishing in the Illinois part of the river is from the Wisconsin-Illinois line down-river to about Hamilton, Illinois. Locks, dams, and pools formed by the dams are numbered on the Mississippi, and according to the Illinois Conservation Department, the best fishing in spring is in Pools 12, 16, and 18; in summer in Pools 15, 17; and in fall Pools 14, 17.

Below the cities of Rock Island-Moline are the Analusia Islands, easily one of the better bass-producing sections of the Mississippi. The islands split the river, providing sheltered, weed-filled bays. Top-water bass fishing in this area can be exceptional, even in the "dog days" of mid-summer.

Well-known bass lakes in southern Illinois include Little Grassy Lake, Crab Orchard Lake, Devil's Kitchen Lake, new Carlyle Lake, Lake-of-Egypt, Horseshoe Lake, and Lake Murphysboro. Lakes especially managed for fishing are found in a couple dozen conservation department wildlife-recreation areas, each of which is described in detail in a special booklet entitled "Fishing In Illinois," and available at no charge from the Illinois Department of Conservation, State Office Building, Springfield, Illinois.

25 *FEATURE STATES:*

California

Far-roaming albacore schools arrive off the California coast in July.

Unlike most states, California offers some extraordinary variety in its fishing. There are, for example, the high mountain lakes and streams with their trout fishing, and the warm water rivers and lakes providing largemouth bass and panfish. The coastal rivers receive annual runs of shad, and striped bass are plentiful in coastal rivers and estuaries—with some of the best striper fishing right in San Francisco Bay in sight of the Golden Gate Bridge.

All that, and there's ocean fishing, too. Striped marlin and broadbill swordfish roam California's salty coast, and there are Pacific baracuda, albacore, bonito, sea bass, and many other species.

California's albacore fishing is a big thing. Come early summer, southern Cal anglers from Santa Monica Bay to San Diego head for the sea to enjoy the albacore runs. Albacore, or longfin tuna, along with schools of bluefin tuna, usually first appear about early July. These are fast-moving fish, always traveling, but when schools are located and brought to feeding frenzy by chumming, the sport can be hair-raising.

Most albacore fishing is done from party or head boats, out of ports like San Diego, Live sardines are a preferred bait, and tackle is on the heavy side. Long rods are popular and a necessity, and reels should have sturdy, dependable drags and contain at least 300 yards of 20-pound test line.

Little is known about albacore, the here-today, gone-tomorrow fish. Their growth rate, spawning grounds, and spawning season remain a mystery to marine biologists. They occur throughout the Pacific, and some authorities believe they may wander in an immense circle, swimming far beyond the Hawaiian Islands only to appear later off California. An albacore tagged off California one August was caught near Japan nine months later. If it had traveled a straight line, which is unlikely, it would have covered 4,724 miles.

Famed fly fisherman Myron Gregory wades San Franciso Bay for striped bass, using fly rod and shooting line with mono' backing held in clothespins fixed to waders.

Billfish, including swordfish, are available in the warm Pacific.

Striped bass imported from New Jersey's Navesink River in 1879 were introduced to California's coastal reaches, and they've prospered ever since. Stripers spawn successfully in many of California's brackish rivers, and today many anglers consider striped bass to be the state's number one salt water gamefish.

California striper fishing is done in the surf, in coastal bays, and in the lower reaches of brackish rivers. About mid-June smelt and anchovies swarm inshore, and with them come foraging stripers. On the average the bass running California's beaches range 15 to 25 pounds, with an occasional 30-pounder. The best of the surf striper fishing normally is in the early part of July.

Heavy runs of spawning stripers occur in San Francisco Bay, and adjoining San Pablo Bay. The Napa River receives spawning fish, but considerably more go to the Suisun Bay area, where they have the Sacramento and San Joaquin Rivers in which to spawn, and hundreds of miles of shallow, brackish sloughs. April, May, and June are top months, but in San Francisco Bay and similar areas there is interesting striped bass fishing from spring through fall.

In addition to the striped bass, California rivers get runs of other anadromous fish, including steelhead,

Popular outdoor writer and angler Larry Green shows what skillful fly fishing can produce in San Francisco Bay.

American (white) shad, and sea-run cutthroat trout. The state's most popular steelhead river is probably the Klamath, which gets both winter and summer runs of fish. The Klamath comes up in the mountains of Oregon, and in California developes into a huge, turbulent stream rolling over boulders and car-size rocks. It has salmon fishing, as well as its famed steelheadin'.

Other select California rivers for both steelhead and salmon are the Smith, famed for its large salmon, and the Eel, producer of record-size steelhead for the state. Other fine streams are the Trinity, Van Duzen, Scott, Salmon, Mattole, and the Mad.

In the Sierra Nevada, flowing out of Lake Tahoe, is the Truckee River which, if not one of California's most productive trout streams, is certainly one of the most accessible and popular. It is well stocked with rainbow and brown trout by the state's conservation department, and has produced very large browns.

The Carson and Walker Rivers are good high-altitude trout streams, but even better is the Owens River, according to conservation department fishery biologists.

Surf casting, particularly for striped bass that frequently approach 30 pounds, is popular along California beaches.

Pacific salmon about to be netted by charter skipper off northern Cal' coast.

Thousands of sea birds dip and dive off a California beach as striped bass begin a feeding orgy.

American or white shad—hard-fighting and good-eating—are common in spring to many coastal rivers. Fish were originally introduced to Pacific rivers, along with striped bass, from New Jersey.

Steelhead trout and big salmon are among important anadromous fishes that fill some California rivers.

California boasts some fine largemouth bass lakes. Dams constructed on countless rivers have at least partially destroyed much good stream fishing for trout and salmon, but in most cases the resultant lakes have provided exceptional largemouth bass angling. And California bass come big! In the northern part of the state Trinity Lake and Lake Shasta often give up 10 pound largemouths, a trophy-size bass anywhere.

Reservoirs outside Fresno, Los Angeles and San Diego have not only good bass fishing but also prime sport with panfish and catfish.

Clear Lake is undoubtedly one of California's most consistently productive largemouth lakes. Known as the "bass capital of the West," it is the state's largest natural lake. Scenically attractive, it's the spot where "tule-dipping" for bass originated. Tuledipping is the technique of paddling close to brush piles in winter and using a long glass pole to lower and "jig" lead-head jigs and jig-spinner combinations around the cover where bass lurk. The lake is filled with beds of reeds called "tules," and these also provide fine bass fishing areas.

(For additional information on California fishing write California Department of Fish and Game, 722 Capitol Ave., Sacramento, California).

Sierra Nevadas are lined with dozens of quality trout streams.

26

Camping Out (and Fishing) with a Travel Trailer

Having a camp on wheels is the only way to go, say many fishing-camping veterans.

This roadside rest area in South Dakota's Black Hills provided solitude amidst natural beauty.

As a professional newspaper-magazine writer-photographer, I spend twelve months of the year fishing and hunting and writing about these sports. I travel an average of 50,000 miles annually, by both plane and auto, in pursuit of fish and game—the only material normally recognized by my cameras and my typewriter.

Until a few years ago, I made most of my outdoor sorties alone, simply because they were too "rough" to bring the family along. Occasionally, however, my wife Phyllis and our two sons Bobby and Marc would come along. Sometimes there was considerable discomfort or expense—or both—to these family safaris. Often Phyllis and I discussed the possibilities in trailer travel, but I always ruled against trailering, believing it was impractical, if not impossible, to utilize a trailer in many of the out-of-the-way places I had to frequent.

Of course we saw hundreds of trailers in use during our family travels, but it wasn't until we made a camping-fishing trip into southern Ontario one August that I realized nothing beats a camp on wheels.

I'd had an assignment from a national magazine to "take your family on a wilderness fishing trip," so Phyllis, the boys and I loaded our station wagon with camping gear and drove north from our home near Chicago to Thessalon, Ontario. The magazine editor had stressed "wilderness fishing," meaning he wanted me to plunk the family down on some remote and comparatively inaccessible lake. So I checked the Ontario map, and noted that the unimproved dirt road north out of Thessalon terminated at the bush town of Chapleau.

It was 100 miles from Thessalon to Chapleau, over a corduroy, pock-marked road that jolted the station wagon. This was the Algoma District, with nothing but wide and wonderful wilderness stretching away for miles on either side of the road. It's a land where countless clear lakes speck the forest floor; where crystalline rivers wind over granite slopes to Lakes Superior and Huron; a land of moose and bear and deer, of trout and walleyes and muskies and pike.

At Chapleau we stocked up on groceries, then headed out over a deserted logger's road for Peshu Lake, which doesn't show on most maps of the area. The narrow, dirt road was rough—even grown-up in places—and there were moments when I wondered if I'd get the station wagon through. I had visions of having a wilderness world all my own once we reached the lake, because Peshu is a sparkling watery jewel tucked away in the barren wilderness some seventy miles from Chapleau, the nearest town. But I nearly collapsed when, finally, we bumped over a hill and got our first look at the lake.

Below, in a broad clearing at the edge of the lake, were half-a-dozen travel trailers and a couple tents. My respect for travel trailers soared, for I'd never dreamed it possible to haul a travel trailer into such a remote area and over such a road.

We had to cook and eat in the open, while the trailerites dined in comfort regardless of the weather. In good weather we slept in sleeping bags on army cots beside the station wagon, and in bad weather we all curled up, crowded and uncomfortable, on the deck of the wagon. The trailer folks, of course, had no sleeping problem.

Insects were a constant worry to us, as were our sanitary problems and need for privacy. There were so many obvious advantages to trailer living for the sportsman and his family that I determined to begin trailer travel. Most important, I had learned that a well-constructed travel trailer will go most anywhere your car will go.

Our next trip was from Chicago to Montana and back, a distance of more than 3,000 miles, and not only were Phyllis and the boys along but also our Miniature Schnauzer. This time we had a nineteen-foot Shasta trailer—and with it suddenly learned that even rugged outdoor life can be beautiful.

At one stage of the trip we parked the trailer right on the shoulder of the Big Hole River, in a secluded stand of cottonwoods. There wasn't a soul near. Nearest town was Twin Bridges, twenty miles away. It could as easily have been 100 miles away, the trailer made us so independent. The car was detached, so we could run up or down the river to fish different areas, and once every few days Phyllis would drive to town for groceries. The trailer was a "self-contained" unit—with gas range, heater, sink, shower, refrigerator and toilet. Each day after fishing I'd waddle out of the river, hot and sweaty, and enjoy a cooling shower. Then I'd curl up in a lawn chair on the river bank with a tall cool one, and watch the rising trout.

Since that first trailer trip, I've traveled many thou-

Many fishermen these days utilize pick-up coach-campers like this "Pathfinder," rather than house trailers.

sands of miles towing my camp behind me. I've made trailer trips after fish or game alone, with a couple of buddies or my family, and have toured many states—including Florida all the way to Key West—as well as parts of Canada. Now I wonder how I ever got along without a trailer.

On one trip we took our trailer through, or rather over, Wyoming's Big Horn Mountains. We had to travel a dirt road under construction, hooking around hair-pin turns, one moment climbing steeply up, the next dropping swiftly down, and did it without a qualm.

You cannot take a trailer over a grown-up logging road, even though you might beat your car through, but modern trailers are so well made you can take them nearly anywhere your car will go. We hauled ours for hundreds of miles over bumpy back roads. That time that we drove up to the shoulder of the Big Hole River, the nearest road was eight miles away. Another time we forded a stream with our trailer, and once we drove it across the prairie and into the foothills of the Bitterroot Mountains on an antelope hunt. I doubt if any sportsman ever hunted antelope in greater comfort.

I always remember that on our western trips, instead of being awakened by noisy tourists, our mornings sparkled with the cries of magpies, the tail-slapping of beavers, the murmur of the trout stream, and the bleats of antelope watching from the sweet grass plains.

Having a trailer in tow does not mean nights must be spent in trailer "camps" or "parks," as I've already indicated. Most trailer parks are entirely desirable to the average trailer traveler, but on fishing and hunting trips you'll want to go it alone. A sportsman wants privacy and seclusion. He can get both with his trailer.

For added seclusion, convenience, and, to some extent, to save a little money, I use roadside rest areas when possible. In most states these areas seem to be everywhere along the major roads. Some maps indicate rest areas, but normally we just drive until we decide it's time to pull over. When that time comes we start looking for a spot, and usually one comes along before much time passes. If you take your trailer to Florida for some fishing and hunting, chances are you'll have to stay in a trailer park most of the time. Someone (probably resort and hotel owners) slipped a law through in Florida making it illegal to camp or park a trailer overnight in roadside rest areas. Once you get off the beaten track in nearly any state, however, you'll find it's possible to pull over beside a lake or stream, or just into a nice grove of pine trees, and spend the night or longer without anyone interfering.

Nearly all state parks have facilities for trailers and general camping, as veteran trailer travelers already know. These state or national parks have varying facilities from mere parking spots to paved stalls where you

Fishermen using house trailers like this 19-footer have the advantage of auto mobility while leaving the trailer "parked" where they wish.

can hook up electricity, water and sewer line, and the charge per night may range from nothing to one dollar. Of special interest for those having trailers without showers or toilets, many public park areas have bathing quarters for men and women as well as toilets, and some even have laundering facilities. Normally, coin-operated laundry machines are available.

I'm told that about 40 percent of the trailer business today is in the manufacture of units that will be used, for the greater part, on fishing and hunting trips. The outdoors today is much different from what it was ten or twenty years ago, since hundreds of wilderness areas have been split wide open with roads or passable auto trails. Accessibility now is common nearly everywhere—even in Canada's bush, the western mountains, the deserts of the southwest. Today you can plan on taking your trailer in comfort and safety to many places you wouldn't have considered trying to horseback to a few years ago.

Of course you must use common sense once you leave the paved roads. Getting stuck is a possibility, but it never becomes a probability until you grow careless. Always watch ahead for signs of soft earth or slick mud, or anything else that might bog you down. Whenever towing on a back road, miles from nowhere, I always stop and walk ahead to check spots that look bad. And if ever I think some byway may offer trouble, I park the trailer and detach it from the car on the surfaced road, then I reconnoiter with just the car. This requires a little more time and mileage, but it's worth it when there's some doubt about trailer passage.

If you intend to stick your neck out and travel mere game trails or strike out across the prairie, include a shovel, ax, heavy rope or cable, and some burlap bags among your gear. The shovel may come in handy to free a bogged wheel. The ax will cut poles for leverage or logs to go under wheels. The rope or cable may be attached to a car to help haul out a difficult trailer. And burlap bags provide good traction under spinning wheels when there's mud, slick clay, loose sand, or snow.

Something else: remember, in traveling the byways, that it's hard to back a trailer any distance, so you must never head in to a place where you may not be able to turn around. Be particularly cautious about wooded areas.

A friend of mine once took off over a mountain road, and all was fine until he passed a lake where trout were jumping wildly. He wheeled his trailer into the first turn-off he saw. It was narrow and went in a circle. When he got part way around he discovered that the turn was so tight that trees would smash the side of his 26-footer if he went farther. It was quite a predicament, but gradually —inch by careful inch—he managed to back the trailer out.

In really rough country the smaller trailers (under twenty feet), are desirable. When necessary, many of them can be unhooked and turned around by hand. If the ground is too soft to let down the frontend jack and roll the trailer around on its jack wheel, the hitch weight is so light (usually less than 200 pounds) that a couple of men can take hold of the tongue and pull the trailer around.

In some ways trailer width is more important than

There's nothing like being parked beside a western trout stream and bringing home lunkers that fill a trailer's oven.

length when it comes to using a trailer in fishing and/or hunting. Most trailers are eight feet wide, and some are ten, but many sport models are only six and a half or seven feet wide. A wide trailer is okay out on the paved highways, and you'll get along with one most of the time in the out-of-the-way places too, but unless you're careful and able to anticipate difficulties you may find an extra foot or so in trailer width can be a liability.

The trailer or mobile home that is to serve occasionally as a sportsmen's camp on wheels must be sturdily built. The trailer that will take a hearty pounding over all kinds of roads is the best buy. It's smart to remember that a quality, well-built trailer—though more expensive initially—can be operated virtually trouble-free and will, when you're ready to sell, have a higher trade-in value.

Well-built trailers usually have an outer shell of stressed heavy grade aluminum riveted to ribs and roof bows of flexible aluminum channel at least an inch deep, and an identical interior shell. Insulation goes between the two shells. This is airplane-type construction, with the obvious advantages of extreme lightness and strength.

Trailers put together with rivets or screws are preferred, with screw-nail construction not so good. I think aluminum exterior is just about essential, and wheel wells should be metal and leakproof.

I learned about adequate tire size the hard way. One trailer we owned was a little job, only ten feet long, and we thought its small size would make it ideal for really rough overland, backwoods jaunts. But the wheels were undersized even for that small shell, so the trailer towed

One way to fish and camp is via the so-called "micro-bus." These are generally excellent units but lack storage space and will accomodate limited numbers of fishermen comfortably.

A travel trailer offers good living quarters and still provides auto mobility. Once camped at an appropriate site the car can be detached and then is available for side trips.

very hard, bounced like crazy, and it seemed I was forever repairing tires. That trailer was quickly retired from travel, and now sets beside the Oconto River, in Wisconsin's Menominee Indian Reservation, where I use it as a cabin during the trout season.

Be sure tire size is adequate to carry the load, and avoid tires of odd-sizes. They're hard to replace in remote areas. Truck-type wheels and tires are best for the larger trailers, and every experienced trailerite knows that trailer brakes, reliable ones, are essential.

Having a good "equalization" hitch between trailer and car is most important when running off the hard-top roads. It's necessary to minimize the load as much as possible. The main beam of the hitch should go under the gas tank, and be attached to the car's frame. An extra cross support should be installed inside the rear bumper.

Many trailer owners do not use helper or booster springs on their cars, and perhaps they are not needed with light trailers on good equalization hitches. But it may be well to relate here one experience I had. We were towing a twenty-four footer over an extremely bumpy road one blistering day in early September. Suddenly I hit the auto brake pedal, and it went clean to the floor. The auto brakes were dead. Fortunately this occurred on level terrain. I got out, went under the car, and discovered that the brake fluid hose to one rear wheel had been burned through by the hot exhaust pipe. Whenever we'd hit a hard bump, the trailer forced the rear of the car down so far that the fluid hose pressed against the exhaust pipe, eventually burning through.

Most trailerists tend to overload their rigs, and this seems especially true of families heading into primitive areas. You'll have to convince Mama that she'll have no need for a cosmetic kit out in the bush; that 75 percent of

A major problem facing today's fishermen-campers; overcrowded public camp grounds.

the clothing she'd like to take will be out-of-place; and that certain household items preferred at home or at trailer parks are useless when "roughing it."

All bulky articles should be omitted, and wherever possible items that can be folded or dismantled should be chosen. A good stock of stable canned or jarred foods is necessary, and include plenty of those new concentrated food packets. These concentrates (not to be confused with war-time dehydrates) are packed in small cartons, with the foods individually packaged in air-tight water-proof foil envelopes. Most of the foods can be cooked in their containers, and they're as tasty as food prepared in your own home and every bit as nutritional.

Several good water pails are additional "musts" for backwoods trailer travel and living. If you should be careless water might be scarce at times, but if you're carrying a full tank of water, plus a couple milk cans of water you'll make out okay. Such large cans also make it unnecessary to be lugging water constantly from some lake, stream or spring.

Pack your trailer more carefully than usual for back-road travel. Conserve space, and get a more stable packing, by not shelving or closeting single items unless necessary. In other words, use a carton to pack away

canned goods rather than placing cans singularly on shelves. A small suitcase will accommodate many clothes and take up little space, leaving closet room for other packaged items. Since I carry more than a dozen fishing rods on a trip, I've made special racks for them, on the ceiling.

Leaving a trailer unattended deep in some woodland glen, miles from a paved road, is not quite like parking overnight elsewhere. To not encourage breaking-in by any character who might happen along, we keep attractive items out-of-sight in the trailer and the curtains drawn. Also, a floater insurance policy covers the possibility of loss. However, someone usually is at the trailer or close by, since we've discovered it's so easy to place our camp on wheels on the exact spot where we want to be. There was one exception to that, though!

One summer we trailered out to a friend's dude ranch at Gallatin Gateway, Montana. We left the trailer at the ranch and made a week-long pack trip via horseback high into the Spanish Peaks wilderness. It was breath-taking country and fishing was excellent, but I'll always remember what Phyllis said one evening as we crawled stiffly into our sleeping bags:

"Wouldn't it be wonderful," she sighed, "if we had the trailer 'way up here!"

The fisherman-camper can live "back-in" and take trout that fill a fry pan.

27

The Future of Fly Fishing

Serious fly fishermen are a different breed, but there's a
lot going for them.

It is a fundamental truth of *this time,* or of any other, that most fly fishermen are gentle men living in a constant state of contained restlessness. Regardless of what a dedicated fly fisherman may be doing at a specific moment—laboring at his profession, dining, conversing, shopping—chances are his present activity is receiving no more than 60 percent of his mental acumen; the other 40 percent is, consciously or unconsciously, OUT THERE SOMEWHERE on a distant trout stream, bonefish flat, grayling river, or secluded bass pond.

The fly fisherman is, indeed, a very different breed of cat.

He is by nature restless, sensitive, inquisitive. His higher intellectual level is a cut above that of the average angler. He is adventurous and ever on the trail of angling excitement. He is demanding. His standards *for* and definition *of* "sport" are high, and mediocrity to him is a deadly bore. Usually the typical fly fisherman, if at all skillful and accomplished, is basically athletic and well-coordinated, and in his mind anything short of the perfect cast is a useless dud.

Thus the serious fly fisherman is nothing at all like the average man who "goes fishing." In this day of more and more fishermen, of more money to spend on fishing, of

Stream improvement to create more fishing areas, and a better distribution of hatchery-reared fish, will help to end scenes like this. These are trout fishermen at Bennett Springs, Missouri.

better transportation and more leisure time—all of which point to greater demands on our natural resource of "recreational water"—what, then, does the future hold for the addicted fly-rodder?

While it is true there remains much room for improvement of fly fishing conditions as they exist today, the distant future holds great promise for coming generations of fly fishermen.

One afternoon about four years ago famed fly fisherman Charles Ritz of Paris and I were testing and comparing various fly tackle at a Chicago park lagoon. In the course of several hours of casting we agreed that fly tackle was better than ever, that more top fishing places were catering specifically to fly fishermen, that conservation departments were greatly improving stream management techniques, and that modern transportation facilities now make it possible for a fly fisher to catch salmon in Norway's Mals River today, and brown trout in Argentina's Chimehuin tomorrow.

"Yes," M. Ritz concluded wistfully, "I only wish that, as a fly fisherman, I were being born today . . . now."

One thing fly fishermen have going for them these days is that there now are more fly fishermen than ever before. No longer is the fly angler an unimportant member of a minor minority group.

The advent of spinning following World Catastrophe II created additional millions of fishermen, as has spincasting. These nearly "fool-proof" casting methods encouraged more men, women and children to fish because they found it relatively easy to learn to cast. In a natural course of events many beginners advanced beyond spincasting and spinning to fly fishing—and the trend to "advance" to fly fishing continues among the millions of non-fly fishermen.

So there are enough fly-rodders around nowadays, and more coming, that state conservation departments as well as the federal Fish and Wildlife Service must pay heed to the fly fisher's needs.

The demands of organized fly fishermen no longer fall on deaf ears. Because there are more fly fishermen many conservation departments (at least the progressive ones) are establishing more "flies only" and "fish for fun" streams. In addition, special areas, frequently at hatchery locations, are being managed solely for trout fishing by fly fishermen. Bait and "hardware" are disallowed at such spots.

By dint of numbers alone, it seems certain that fly fishermen, at last, are coming into their own. Tackle manufacturers report the largest increase in tackle sales to be in fly fishing tackle—fly rods, reels, lines and accessories are selling as never before. More fly fishing opportunities will be established in all states, in the future, to meet the demand.

Already state conservation departments throughout the country appreciate the need for public fishing areas, and, realizing that the demand for public angling will increase as more landowners post their property, a lot of conservation departments are spending vast sums of money on land acquisition. With federal financial assistance, wild tracts properly timbered with clear streams and lakes are being purchased by various state conservation agencies and are being converted and managed as

Greater interest in salt water fly fishing also is bettering the fly fisherman's future.

public fishing-hunting grounds. Pennsylvania and Wisconsin are two examples of states having conservation departments that are pushing hard at land acquisition.

Pollution is finally getting the national public attention it has so long deserved. Newspapers, magazines, radio and television blast the dirty hand of industrial pollution, and public indifference and tolerance to pollution exist no more. Streams, lakes, and rivers are being cleaned—and while it will take years to renew waters already destroyed, progress is being made and already some formerly polluted areas have been restored and now provide good fishing. (New Jersey's Brandywine and Montana's Clark Fork River are good examples.) With further scientific advance, continued public disdain of pollution, and so on, there ultimately will be little if any polluted water. The advantage of *that* to fly fishermen of the future is obvious.

Many conservation departments also are learning that there is little advantage to short seasons, and in many states year-around fishing is coming into vogue. Trout streams having little or no natural reproduction of fish are in many instances left "open" to fishing year-around, and nearly every state now permits year-long fishing for panfish and black bass because studies have proved that fishermen in no way affect annual total fish populations. Not all states yet permit year-around fishing, but the no-closed seasons or short closed seasons are the coming

Public demand for pollution-free waters, and curtailment of unnecessary federal dam building, will help give future fly fishermen angling such as this.

thing, so ultimately fly fishermen everywhere will have much more "fishing time" annually than their grandfathers had.

Another factor pointing to a brighter future for fly fishermen is improved hatchery methods as well as better stream and lake management.

Conservation departments and the federal Fish and Wildlife Service now are able to raise brook, brown and rainbow trout quicker and better than ever, and at reduced costs in terms of the return for money expended. Science has taken over the fish-rearing business, and today because of better foods, better control of fish diseases, etc., hatcheries are able to stock more fish, and larger fish—as well as types better suited to the available environment. This means, naturally, that in most streams and ponds better and bigger fish are and will continue to be available to the fly fisherman. *Let's never forget that one cannot catch something that isn't there!*

Scientific management of streams, lakes, rivers and ponds also means more and better fish—not just for fly fishermen, but for all anglers. Some states are farther along in practical and productive fish management than others, but all states profit from what is learned by one through the exchange of scientific papers and accounts.

New horizons are being opened to the vast army of fly fishermen by those now pursuing the fly-rodder's art in salt water. For example Larry Green—a fine fly fisherman, outdoor writer, and California resident—has by his writing done a great deal to publicize, promote, and inform on Pacific Coast fly fishing opportunities. In the period B.G. (before Green) very few Pacific anglers were much aware of the salt water fly fishing opportunities that exist right in their own front yard.

South Atlantic and Caribbean salt water fly fishing has been more generally publicized, for a longer time, but even so, many thousands of fly fishermen each year take fresh water "sabbaticals" for the first time and go dunk their flies in the salt. Thus the salt water environment, of itself, is offering the world's fly fishermen of *today* and *tomorrow* some truly remarkable fishing.

Possibly a final indication of how good things are going to be for fly fishermen is the fact that—after all these many hundreds of years of fly fishing—fly rodders *today* have their own specific, nation-wide organizations. One is the Federation of Fly Fishermen, another is the Salt Water Fly Rodders of America. And Trout, Unlimited—dedicated to the preservation of trout fishing—is comprised chiefly of fly fishermen.

All of which again reminds me of what friend Charlie Ritz said the day we were casting at Lincoln Park Lagoon. I agree with Charlie. I too, wish that, as a fly fisherman, I were being born today!

Modern equipment properly matched by manufacturers is making fly fishing easier for beginners. This is a Scientific Anglers (Midland, Mich.) "System 9" outfit.

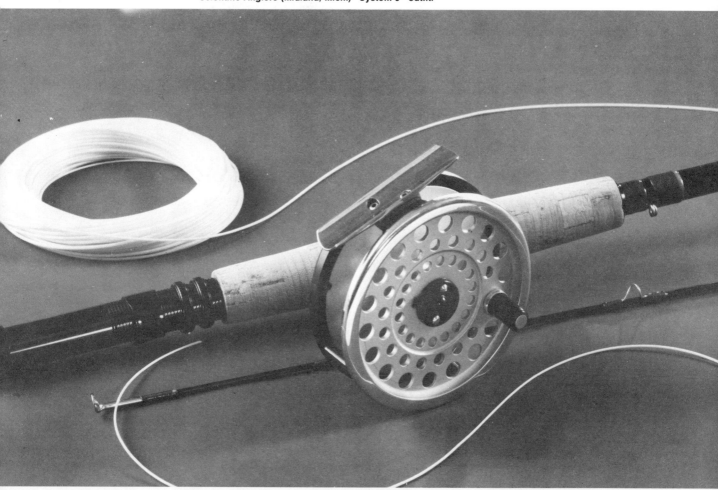

28

Bag of (New) Tricks for Everyday Angling

Some gulf coast fishermen have a good thing going for them. It's crickets!

While crickets are almost unheard of as fishing bait in many areas, a lot of Mississippi anglers would sooner stay at home than go fishing without a bunch of them.

"You put a nice fat, lively cricket on a hook, drop it anywhere near a bream, and man!—you got yourself a fish and the makings for some good eating," said the proprietor of a bait shop on Fort Bayou, near Ocean Springs, Mississsippi. Bream are, of course, what northern anglers call sunfish. The southern "bream" is the same as the northern "sunny," except that most sunfish in the Deep South are two or three times larger than the average northern sunfish. Some Mississippi bream are platter-size and an inch-and-a-half thick!

Crickets are so popular in the Mississippi bayou country that nearly every tackle and bait shop raises them. Each bait shop has its specially-designed, indoor "cricket farm."

A cricket farm is nothing more than a large box, usually open at the top, but with a wide band of paint around the top edge. The crickets can't jump out because they are unable to jump straight up. "Dunno why it is," said the bait shop owner mentioned earlier, "but them crickets always jump forward or backwards, never up. If they'd jump up, they'd get free. Plain dumb."

Crickets can walk up a wall, and so walk all over the sides of the box in which they are imprisoned. But they can't walk out of the bait box because there's a band of white paint around the top edges. Seems the crickets have good footing until they get on the paint, and then they slip and fall back.

A good box for crickets—also known as "leaping orthopterus insects with long antennae and three segments in each tarsus"—should have an electric light bulb which when lit, will provide enough heat to keep the bugs warm and alive should the temperature drop. Some water should be provided, and lettuce leaves or meal can be kept in the box to provide the potential fish-bait with food.

The crickets will multiply naturally, and if anything, a good cricket farm may become overpopulated. Then the long-legged, chirping bugs eat one another.

There's no denying the effectiveness of live crickets on pan-

Simple, homemade box houses thousands of crickets, the perfect pan-fish bait.

fish, and even largemouth bass take them with gusto. And, since they are so easy to raise, so easy to keep in a "farm," it's surprising more fishermen in more areas don't play the cricket game!

⊙

Big game fishermen after such trophy monsters as giant black marlin frequently have shark problems. That is, about every time they hook a good marlin and fight it near the boat, a shark arrives and wreaks havoc. But a still worse problem is to have big sharks take the baits meant for the marlin. There's no way you can get into marlin if, everytime you slide a bait back, it is taken by a shark that you are forced to fight for hours.

One way of solving the shark problem is to rig up with three strands of 150-pound test nylon, braided. Big sharks quickly bite through these and free themselves (and the angler)whereas marlin and other billfish will not. Wherever fishermen have a "shark problem" several such leaders should be tied up in advance of the actual fishing.

Fishermen can make very handy car-top canoe or boat carriers with lengths of 2 X 4's, some foam rubber, (or foam plastic), screw eyes, straps, and car-top clasps.

To make a first grade boat carrier, cut two lengths of 2 X 4's to the proper lengths, that is, a few inches short of the width of your car top. Fix to the 2 X 4's with strong glue padding sections, which may be of foam plastic or rubber. A screw-eye in each end of the 2 X 4's will hold straps that can be fixed to the car's roof edges (see photos).

Such boat carriers are very inexpensive, long-lasting, and they do the job required. They're as good as any you can buy.

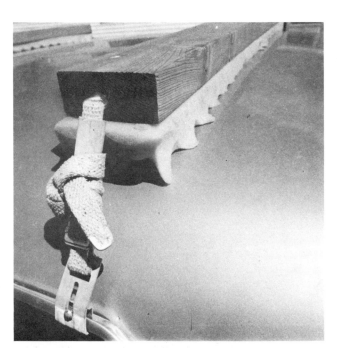

Close-up of homemade boat carrier shows straps knotted to hook-eye in 2 x 4 and car roof-top holder.

Two-by-four carriers are spaced according to auto's roof space, and size of canoe or boat to be transported.

Fishermen hoist aluminum canoe to auto top with ease, and homemade carriers easily hold and support canoe. Canoe is tied down with fore and aft ropes and straps over sides.

Fishermen owning lake-front cottages, or fishing camps or resorts—anyone having a need to provide a decent storage place for rods—might consider a rod-rack built along the New Brunswick (Canada) rivers by local guides.

Guides in the northern maritime province know the value of "salmon rods," and they know that a rod laid carelessly down against a streamside rock, or leaned against a tree along a river's edge, could be easily knocked down and broken.

To avoid a chance of broken rods, the guides build simple stream-side racks so that when an angler wants to take a break he puts his rod in the "rack" where it will be safe from possible damage. Such rod racks ought to be at boat docks, fishing camps, and wherever fishermen come in and go to lodgings or rooms and then, the next morning, head out fishing again.

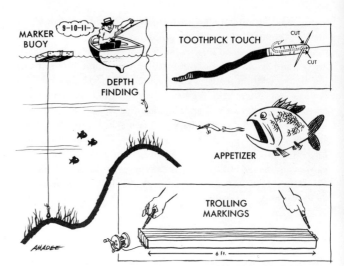

A quality marker buoy can be made from foam plastic. Trolling fishermen should mark lines so they know how much line is out, a strip of porkrind or other material on a lure will induce strikes, and an ordinary toothpick can be used to keep a plastic worm on the hook.

New Brunswick guides built this handy rod rack along the Miramichi River at "The Channels" Pool. Such racks could be constructed in camps, etc. to eliminate much needless rod breakage.

⊙

Experienced fishermen know that it is worthwhile to have marker buoys to toss out when they hook into school fish such as walleyes, yellow perch, white bass, and others. A good marker can be made of monofilament line, a bell sinker, and a section of foam plastic. One end of the line is tied to the sinker and the other end to the plastic floater, and the line then is wound around the plastic. When the fisherman wants to make a spot, he simply tosses one of his foam-plastic "buoys" over and the sinker goes down, unwinding the line, and marks the spot.

Something else: good trollers know that it is important to know how much line they have out. With too little line a lure may not run deep enough; too much and it may run too deep or strikes may be missed. Smart fishermen mark their lines so they will know *exactly* how much line they have trailing behind.

One good way to mark your lines is to get a 6-foot length of board, and wind your fishing line on the board lengthwise. Then mark the line on each end of the board with a suitable dye, marking pencil, or India ink. Afterward the line is reeled onto

the reel and, with it being marked every 6 feet, the fisherman will know precisely how much line he has out at any time.

On those days when fish seem to be striking short, not really hitting your lure, try attaching a short strip of porkrind or rubber or plastic material to the lure. This is an appealing way to spice up a lure, and it stops those short strikes.

The problem of keeping a soft plastic worm on a hook can be solved with a toothpick. Thread the worm as usual on a long-shank hook, but be sure to push the worm over the hook-eye. Push the toothpick through the worm and through the eye of the hook, then clip the excess ends of the toothpick as they protrude through the plastic worm.

⊙

A small sponge rubber ball makes an ideal fishing float. All you need do is punch a hole through the ball with a heavy needle and it will accept your fishing line. It will then be easy, because of friction, to adjust the line to fish at whatever depth you desire.

You can freeze a half-gallon plastic jug of water, and have ice water all day while fishing.

If you'd like to alter the action of your top-water plugs—give the fish something they haven't seen before—try clamping a split-shot lead sinker to a surface plug's trailing hook. This will give the lure a dipping, darting action it wouldn't have had otherwise, and it just might make the difference between fish in the boat and no fish.

⊙

There are better ways to transport a couple of canoes, but if you've got an emergency situation where you want to move two canoes from one spot to another quickly, and you have a station-wagon handy, you can load both canoes into the wagon and make out reasonably well.

Most fishermen wouldn't believe it, but two full-length (16-

Two canoes can be loaded into and transported reasonably well for short distances in an ordinary station wagon.

foot canoes) can be transported in a 'wagon. The canoes stick out, of course, and should be well-tied and "red-flagged," but you can move 'em in a wagon. Just drive slowly, not too far, and be careful.

⊙

Many fly fishermen have little imagination or creativeness when it comes to attaching lead split-shot or other sinkers to their leaders. Invariably a fisherman wanting some weight to get a fly down deep simply pinches a split shot onto his leader several inches up from the fly.

That method frequently is okay, but there are other ways to try. For example, some anglers pinch shot onto the bend of a fly's hook, instead of on the leader. This makes casting easier and doesn't interfere with hooking fish. Another way to attach a split-shot is pinching it onto the head of a streamer or wet fly. And many fishermen prefer to attach a split-shot sinker to the leader right at the hook-eye, while some others leave a short strand of nylon hanging down after tying a fly to the leader, and then pinch the shot to it.

⊙

A ballpoint pen with its "innards" removed makes an ideal container for small hooks or split-shot. It can be easily carried and kept handy in a shirt pocket.

Don't throw old casting reels away. Instead, attach them to a discarded rod handle or to a broomstick. Such a reel makes the frequent job of transferring line from one reel to another easy.

Empty half-gallon plastic bleach jugs with dropper cords and weights attached to the handles make excellent buoys for marking hot fishing spots.

⊙

Salt water fishermen are wise to the deadliness of a lead-head jig that is tipped on the hook with a small piece of crab, conch, shrimp or fish, but few fresh water anglers ever "dress up" their jigs.

A jig used in fresh water fishing for bass, walleyes, northern pike or crappies will have a lot more fish-getting appeal if its hook is tipped with a small minnow, piece of worm, soft-shell crawfish, or strip of fish flesh. A small strip of porkrind on a jig also can add to its effectiveness.

⊙

Cover can hardly become too thick to attract largemouth black bass, or to limit their feeding. Even in areas where moss, grass, and lily pads cover the water surface so thickly it looks like dry land, bass can be coaxed into hitting a lure.

This fishing is often nerve-wracking because striking fish are sometimes missed and hooked fish frequently lost, but it's fishing that can be rewarding too, for anglers who have the patience to stay with it.

Weedless lures such as a weedless spoon with pork-chunk, pork frog, or strip of porkrind attached, should be used. Casts should be kept short for better control of the lure. Hold the rod high following a cast, and reel the lure or "stroke" it back as slowly as possible. Remember, in thick stuff bass need time to get to a lure and to wallop it.

Whenever your lure reaches an opening in the pads or weeds, quit reeling and allow it to flutter down tantalizingly. And, if a bass should strike but miss, take another rod quickly that is ready to go and loaded with a plastic worm, and toss the worm to the bass. Chances are he'll hit it solidly.

⊙

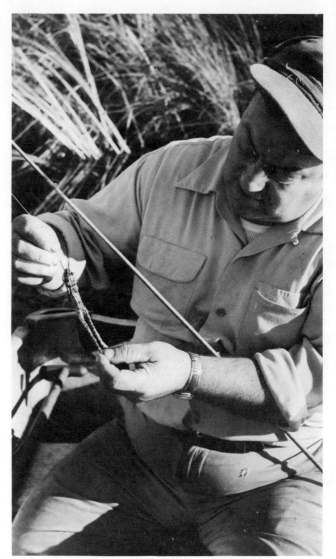
Charley Haling checks frog he has rigged for bass.

Fisherman reads water temperature on scale of Ray Jefferson Model 90 "Fish Probe."

Experienced fishermen know that no fish, gamefish or other, will remain in water that is too cold or too hot for its liking. All species of fish have decided water temperature preferences (see "Preferred Feeding Temperatures For Fresh And Salt Water Gamefish" elsewhere in this book), and they will seek out areas and depths having temperatures that make them most comfortable.

Thus part of the trick to catching fish is finding the exact depth and area where water temperature matches the preference of the fish you are after. A handy gadget for aiding fishermen in determining water temperatures at various depths is the Ray Jefferson Model 90 "Fish Probe" Fishing Thermometer. The Fish Probe reads water temperature down to 125 feet, and from 30 to 90 degrees Fahrenheit. The thermometer's cable is calibrated in 10-foot lengths so that the fisherman knows just how deep to go to catch fish.

⊙

Want a change of pace in your bass fishing, and maybe a lot more bass in the boat?

Try fishing with a very light outfit, using 4 to 6-pound line, and small green frogs for bait. Rig with a live frog if that is permitted by the conservation laws of your state (some states prohibit using live frogs for bait).

Hook the frog through both lips, toss him onto weedy banks or lily pads, pull him off, and work him slowly along. If there are any bass around they'll hit in a hurry.

⊙

Good fly casters extend their casting arm, reaching out as far as possible, when they "shoot" line on long casts.

The line should be released on the forward part of a long cast when the rod reaches the 10 o'clock position, and then the rod is gradually lowered in an extended position to about 9 o'clock as the line shoots through the rod guides.

Reaching out and holding the rod in proper position reduces

Casting to distant tarpon, fly-rodder "reaches out" and holds rod in proper position for maximum "shoot" of line.

Heavy-jawed, chunky northern pike couldn't resist fly fisherman's 6-inch long "Magnum" streamer fly. Fish is an 18 pounder.

friction on the line as it fires through the guides, and aids considerably in lengthening casts.

⊙

Veteran trout fishermen know that the "creep and crawl" technique of trout fishing is vital to catching wary trout in clear streams. The trout that sees a fisherman is the trout the fisherman won't catch.

Much the same is true in bass fishing, whether after largemouths in a clear lake or smallmouths in a clear stream. If you can avoid it, don't let bass see you. Don't stand in boats when casting; you can be too easily seen. And when fishing from shore, pussyfoot along and keep low, using available cover so that the bass do not see you and become spooked.

Spinning from shore for bass, wise fisherman uses cover to stay hidden, and casts from low position. Like trout, bass that spot fishermen rarely strike.

Many species of fish have bone-hard mouths and it takes some doing to sink hooks into their jaws. Notable among such fish are tarpon, muskellunge, bonefish, and the bill fishes.

The way to get a hook into hard-mouthed fish is to keep a tight line at all times, to hold the rod very low during retrieves, and to "strike" back with the rod hard and several times when a fish hits.

The proper method of hooking bonefish is an exception to that technique. Best way to hook a bonefish is to wait momentarily after the fish has mouthed the lure, fly, or bait, and then to raise the rod slowly but firmly as the fish turns and starts to run. Handled this way, a bonefish normally will hook himself right in the side of the jaw, where it is easiest to get a hook into the fish.

⊙

Even though thousands of words have been printed in newspapers, magazines, and books about the effectiveness of fly fishing for large northern pike, many fishermen still are skeptical, believing that flies and fly rods just aren't the gear for pike. Pure nonsense!

Popping bugs (particularly large ones with big hooks and designed for salt water fishing) and large streamer flies are absolute death on pike. Pike hanging out in shallow water cannot resist big streamers in particular. The trick is to retrieve very slowly. Pike will, in fact, more frequently hit a streamer that is merely idling in the water than one that is darting along. Something about a slowly wiggling, pulsating streamer 5 to 7 inches in length totally unhinges big pike.

⊙

"Keep it clean" is the name of the game in caring for fishing tackle as well as for our scenic outdoors.

It is impossible to cast well with dirty reels clogged with grit and dried grease. Not even in the hands of an expert will such tackle perform properly.

It is not only wise to keep reels clean and lubricated correctly so that they will cast well, but such proper care lengthens the working life of any reel.

Use a toothbrush and gasoline or kerosene to clean dirt from reels. Then oil the moving parts, according to the manufacturer's instruction sheet, with a high grade of lightweight oil, such as Hoppe's gun oil. Next, apply thin layers of gear grease to gears and other areas that should be greased rather than oiled.

Proper reel maintenance pays off in many ways.

⊙

Bait-casting, fly and spinning reels all require periodic cleaning, oil, and greasing to perform satisfactorily.

29

Top Trout Streams of Southern Wisconsin

by Bob McNally

Put the odds in your favor by knowing where to go for southern Wisconsin trout.

Willow Creek is a typical southern Wisconsin trout stream, with brush-lined banks and slick, deep runs.

Anglers who want good trout fishing in the midst of pastoral splendor will find southern Wisconsin their promised land.

Southern Wisconsin has hundreds of air-clear, spring-fed creeks that are full of plump, hard fighting brook, brown, and rainbow trout. Many of these streams are stocked by the state's Conservation Department, yet some of the creeks are stable enough to sustain at least a moderate number of native browns, brookies, and rainbows.

Although the trout fishing pressure is heavy during the first week or two of the season, which normally opens on the second Saturday in May, it eases off after most of the stocked trout have either been caught, or educated enough so the average worm dunker has difficulty in catching them. This is when the "die hard" trout fisherman can have the most fun and catch the most southern Wisconsin trout.

A few of the hundreds of trout streams in the southern part of the state deserve special mention because of their consistently good trout fishing. One such stream is Bluff Creek, in Walworth County, south of the town of Whitewater. This creek is a slow-moving meadow stream, surrounded by lush green flora, with watercress abounding in its pure waters. It is easily accessible and offers some of the finest brown trout fishing in that area.

Bluff Creek is over-run by weekend anglers for several weeks after the trout season opens, but soon few fishermen waste their time fishing the creek because they think that most of the trout have been taken out by the heavy fishing pressure it receives. To some extent this is true. The stocked rainbows the Conservation Department puts in the creek are normally fished out within a few weeks, but the smart and elusive brown trout are usually barely touched during this time. Being well educated, the browns are frequently difficult to catch, and consequently provide a challenge to the serious fisherman.

One morning, about three weeks after the opening weekend, Mike Ooston of Skokie, Illinois, and I were fishing Bluff Creek. After several hours we caught 8 plump browns and rainbows, some measuring 12 inches. Just as we called it a day we met another fisherman heading back to his car. We exchanged greetings and asked how he had done that morning. He responded by opening his creel to show us a nice rainbow of about eleven inches, and then, one at a time, he lifted out three brown trout of about a pound each. Finally, grinning like a father with his first born son, he brought out a brown that was easily three pounds!

Bluff Creek is formed by a dozen or so small springs that flow out of the surrounding hills of the glaciated area around Whitewater. Most of the larger trout are taken at the headwaters, although good sized browns are caught all along its two-mile course.

About 100 miles north of Bluff Creek, in Marquette and

A stogey-puffing Al Miller of Oshkosh, Wis. admires an upper Tomorrow River brook trout. Brookies and browns are native to this stream.

Fast, broken runs like this one on the lower Tomorrow River are not commonplace to southern Wisconsin streams. Most stretches of lower Wisconsin streams are smooth, deep, but strong-running.

Waushara counties north of the town of Montello, is one of the famous trout streams in the state, the Mecan River. This slow-moving, sand and mud bottom stream holds a good population of brown trout. Some browns and rainbows are stocked here, but stocking is moderate and native fish remain in the majority. Most important, large browns can be taken here with regularity.

The Mecan has deep holes, large pools, and many under-cut banks. The Mecan is also lined by trees and brush and contains a lot of fallen timber, which makes fishing from the bank almost impossible. Wading is a must to fish this river properly. One of the best stretches of the Mecan is above the town of Richford. In this part of the river there are many native brookies and browns and some large rainbows. One beautiful aspect of the Mecan is that it's in the heartland of Wisconsin's fine whitetail deer country, and many times fishermen can see deer grazing along the bank or drinking from the cool waters.

In addition to the Mecan, there are a few smaller streams feeding the river that get very little fishing pressure. One such feeder stream is Chaffee Creek, which flows into the Mecan south of the town of Dakota, in Marquette County.

Chaffee Creek is smaller than the Mecan River and the

fishing pressure here is very light, and many times an average fisherman can do much better here than on the river. The Chaffee is also slow-moving and it has a mud and sand bottom and many deep under-cut banks with overhanging limbs that hold some fine browns. Often a fly rodder can drift a weighted nymph or wet fly through these deep pockets, or under tree limbs, and do very well, even during the brightest part of the day.

The brown trout in Chaffee Creek are on the average smaller than the fish in the Mecan, averaging around 11 inches, but some two and three-pounders have been taken on the lower part of the creek where it flows into the Mecan.

The Wisconsin Conservation Department has recently improved Chaffee Creek considerably, reinforcing the the banks to stop erosion and cutting away a lot of the brush that made it difficult to walk along the creek well. Yet there remains plenty of the stream cover that brooks, browns, and rainbows need.

These two crystalline streams, the Mecan and the Chaffee, are especially productive after a good rainstorm. Then, many insects, larva, and various types of worms are washed down stream, and the trout frequently go into a "feeding frenzy" that both the fly fisherman and the bait fisherman can cash in on.

There are two other good trout streams in Waushara County worth mentioning. These are Willow Creek and the Pine River.

The Pine River, winding its way back and forth above the town of Wild Rose for about fifteen miles, has some of the best brook and brown trout fishing in the state. Both upper and lower parts of the river have a large population of native brookies and browns. Both parts have sand, gravel, and mud bottoms and some deep holes, brushy banks, and large trees that harbor nice trout, making for some very exciting and interesting fishing. And there are places where the Pine runs through some fairly open and accessible areas, which makes fishing easier. The lower Pine, from just above the town of Wild Rose to the town of Poy Sippi, is bordered by large areas of public land. Fishing here is open to anyone. The upper Pine, northwest of the town of Wild Rose, shorter than the lower, flowing only for about five miles, is bordered mainly by private lands. Here anglers should get permission before fishing.

Willow Creek is located below the town of Wild Rose, east of the upper Pine River. This is also a clear, slow-moving stream, with large populations of native brown and brook trout. It flows for about 17 miles through both dense wood thickets and open, pasture-like areas, offering the fisherman a variety of trout waters.

The first time I fished the Willow I floated it in a canoe. I had been told by a "reliable source" that it was perfect for a float trip that would take me to the lower stretches that are seldom fished. Tim Sampson of Glenview, Illinois, had the misfortune of undertaking this insane venture with me. We spent an entire morning portaging over one fallen tree after another, growing more and more tired and angry, and not catching a single trout because of all the noise we made. The lesson here is easy to state: don't trust "reliable sources." Wade both Willow Creek and the Pine River. There is so much brush and tree−lined banks along these streams that wading is the *only* way to fish them.

The Tomorrow River, another good trout stream, lies farther north in Portage County. This picturesque stream, particularly in its upper sections, offers some fine brook and brown trout fishing. Recently the lower section of the Tomorrow, below the town of Amherst, was poisoned by the Conservation Department to kill suckers, chubs, and carp that had somehow got into the river. Of course, along with these trash fish, many large brown trout in the 4, 5, and 6−pound class were also killed. It will be several years until this lower part of the river will again produce excellent brown trout fishing, although the upper and middle sections of the Tomorrow, above the town of Amherst, still has some extraordinary brook and brown trout fishing.

The Tomorrow is an amazingly clear, gravel bottom river with numerous deep runs, sharp drop-offs, under-cut banks, and fast glides where large boulders make eddies that occasionally hold some nice trout. Large areas of public land border the upper Tomorrow, making it easily accessible for the average fisherman.

The Tomorrow River also has several tributary streams worth exploring. One is Leary Creek, also called Bear Creek, southeast of Amherst. Leary is much smaller than

Eddie Lachmann, a professional fly-tyer at Amherst, Wis., slips the hook from a Tomorrow River rainbow.

the Tomorrow and not as deep, but its native brookies and browns are scrappy. Leary Creek twists and winds through several miles of lush woodland, colored by hundreds of wild flowers of every imaginable hue, which makes for some of the prettiest scenery one can find along any trout water.

Another good stream emptying into the Tomorrow is the Crystall River, flowing south of the town of Waupaca in Waupaca County. This is an air-clear river with a good gravel and sand bottom. It has many stocked browns and some natives. The river is very brushy and difficult to fish from its banks, but it is well-known for the spectacular canoe trips its 12-mile course offers. And the river is ideal for a trout fishing canoe trip that can be arranged with local outfitters in the town of Waupaca.

Most southern Wisconsin streams are narrow, and for this reason tackle should be "scaled down" proportionally. For the fly rod fisherman, a small 6 or 6½-foot fly rod with a quality DT5 (HEH) flyline is all that's needed on any of the streams mentioned. Almost any of the standard flies will take southern Wisconsin trout. Some of the outstanding dry flies include the Wulffs (Gray, White, and Grizzly), Light Hendrickson, Black Spider, Red Variant, Blue Dun, and Light Cahill. When the mayflies and the green drakeflies begin their hatches, around the first of June, most of the trout streams in southern Wisconsin come alive with rising fish. The last hour and a half before dark is normally best, and a good high-floating fly such as those listed above or a well-tied Deer Hair, Irresistible, or Goofus Bug should spell trouble for gourmet-minded trout. Best streamers and bucktails

Creep-crawl method pays off in fishing clear, slow-moving Mecan River.

include the White Muddler, White Marabou Muddler, Muddler Minnow, Joe's Hopper, Michigan Hopper, Black-Nosed Dace, Mickey Finn, Yellow Tiger, Black Ghost, and Gray Ghost, all on long shank hooks in sizes 6 to 12. Nymphs are also good at times, and a fly rodder should be sure to include Mossbacks (light and dark), May Fly Nymph, in sizes 10 and 12, and also black, gray, and orange nymphs, in sizes 14 and 16.

Ultralight spinning tackle is best equipment for the artificial or bait fisherman. Small single-spin lures or spoons are perfect for the artificial spin-fisherman, and they should be cast upstream or quartering across and fished back along under-cut banks, over-hanging tree limbs, or around breaks in the flow of the stream. Worms or corn are the best baits for the bait fisherman to use, and they should be fished similar to a spinner or a spoon.

The streams discussed here represent just a sampling of the fine trout waters found throughout southern Wisconsin. There are many others.

Recently all Wisconsin trout streams have been clas-

sified into three groups. Class 1 streams are high-grade trout waters with conditions favorable to the production of a native population of trout, requiring little or no stocking. Class 2 streams have some native trout but moderate to heavy stocking of trout is necessary to maintain good fishing. Class 3 streams are marginal trout habitats, and stocking is necessary to provide fishing.

By referring to this classification of trout streams a fisherman can select the type he wants to fish. A detailed booklet explaining the different types of streams and indicating their location, along with regional maps of the state, can be obtained by writing the Department of Natural Resources, Madison, Wisconsin. County highway maps may also benefit fishermen, and these can be purchased for 5¢ each. Specify the county you're interested in to the Wisconsin Department of Transportation, 699 Hill Farms State Office Building, Madison, Wisconsin.

A state license is required to fish all Wisconsin trout waters. A resident license is $3.25, a non-resident license $6.50.

30

Seventy-five "Quickie" Fishing Tips

Fly fishermen can buy single-action reels with interchange-able spools. Two similar lines can be mounted on each spool. When one line starts to sink it can be quickly removed from the reel and the second spool with the dry line can be snapped in. Or two different kinds of lines, such as a floating line and a sinking line, or a torpedo-tapered line and a double-tapered line, can be mounted on the reel spools.

⊙

Monofilament lines, used on bait casting, spinning, or spin-cast reels should occasionally be trailed behind a moving boat to remove kinks and twists.

⊙

Wire snaps and wire snap-swivels sometimes open when a hooked fish is being played. Always be sure snaps and snap-

swivels are closed properly, and sometimes it pays to close them tightly with pliers.

⊙

As with most other things, it's practice that makes for perfect casting. Excellent casting practice can be had indoors or out—in gyms, halls, at the nearest park, or in your own back yard.

Certain portable "props" can be used when practicing casting that will help you to improve rapidly, particularly in accuracy. Accuracy is the expert fisherman's ace-in-the-hole—it's one of the things that consistently helps him to put fish in the pan.

A fisherman who constantly fights with his equipment can't concentrate on working a lure, and he'll probably spend as much time recovering plugs from trees as he will actually fishing. The skilled angler, however, deftly drops his lure near this log or that stump, effortlessly and continuously, and thus spends most of his time tantalizingly working his lures where fish can get at them. Remember that it's the lure that plunks naturally into that tiny pocket in the weeds that takes fish—not the plug that is cast to the other side of the pond.

⊙

Drags on spinning reels should be set only strong enough so that there is sufficient resistance that hooks will be set when fish strike. The farther and faster a hooked fish runs, the more the drag should be decreased—*not* increased.

⊙

Most fishermen when walking from cars or from one spot to another carry their rods tip-first. If they stumble, the rod tip often digs into the ground and . . . "snaaapppp!" A rod carried tip-first also tends to catch in limbs and brush, or the line or attached lure will snag.

⊙

Some fishermen say tadpoles are poor bass bait. Don't you believe it!

A friend of mine has seven largemouths, five to six inches long, in a large home aquarium. Drop a "taddy" in there and even though the bass are well fed (they get live shiner minnows daily) it's like . . . *Pow!* . . . as the little bass strike with blinding speed and the tadpole simply disappears.

Those baby bass are capable of eating a tadpole fully half their size.

⊙

The ferrules or "joints" of a quality fishing rod always fit snugly. Trouble is, the ferrules of a good rod sometimes join so tightly it's difficult to separate them.

Before joining a rod's ferrules lubricate the male ferrule so that disassembling the rod later will be simpler. Running the male ferrule through the hair or beside the nose usually will apply sufficient "natural oils" to properly lubricate it.

Keep rod ferrules clean, free of rust and dirt, and occasionally apply high-quality, lightweight lubricating oil to the male ferrule, then wipe it dry.

For most fishing, it is necessary to know how to tie only a few good knots. Important ones include the "clinch" or "improved-clinch" knots; "barrel" or "blood" knots; "dropper loop" knot; "nail" knot; and "double surgeon's" knot.

⊙

Few fishermen clean and oil bait casting reels as often as they should. A bait casting reel is a minature winch, and operates smoothly only if clean and properly lubricated. Use only a little oil on these reels, but oil them at least a couple times in the course of a day's fishing.

⊙

The proper tempo in fly casting is a slow one. The basic cast consists of three parts: the backcast, the pause, and the forward cast. It helps, when learning to fly cast, to say to yourself as the backcast is started: "One . . . and wait . . . and two." "One" is the backcast; "and wait" is the necessary pause; and "two" is the start of the forward cast.

⊙

Much successful fishing depends simply on hard work.

Fishermen who angle for a couple hours and then quit rarely make consistently good catches. Good fishermen often start early and fish without let-up until dark. Only the lure or the bait that is in the water catches fish.

⊙

Contrary to popular belief, largemouth black bass do not always strike best in early morning and late afternoon. Best fishing often is from 10 A.M. to 2 P.M.

⊙

When using monofilament line on a bait casting reel, it is wise to first put a cork arbor on the reel's spool before winding on the line. If no cork arbor is used, then first wind on several yards of soft braided line. An arbor or braided line serves as a cushion for the monofilament line which, when wound onto a reel under pressure, tends to expand. If the mono has no "cushion" it can spread and jam a reel's spool flanges.

⊙

Casting accuracy is much more important than distance. And the way a lure is "worked" through the water is often more important than selection of the lure.

⊙

The best all-around bait is the common earthworm. Don't "ball up" worms when putting them on hooks. They'll usually take more fish when they look "long and natural" in the water.

⊙

Bait fishermen frequently spend too much time in one place. When fishing a lake from shore, or a river from its banks, don't stay too long in one spot if it doesn't produce fish. Move around from place to place, trying by this rock pile, by that submerged tree and so on, until fish are caught. When you're after school fish such as yellow perch, walleyes, or crappies, a spot giving up one fish usually has several others.

⊙

A small, ordinary, chrome-plated spinner used with a short, fine strip of porkrind is an excellent lure for bass, northern pike, and various panfish. Toss it out near weeds or lily pads and as it settles, give it gentle twitches.

⊙

Proper way to net a fish is to first put the net in the water, hold it still, then lead the fish into it head-first.

⊙

When worn out, chest-high waders can be converted into useful boat shoes. Usually the uppers go first on waders. Cut the uppers off from the boot-foot section, and use the boot-foots as slip-on boat shoes.

⊙

If there's no pond nearby where you can practice casting, an open area in your back yard will do. For targets, get a couple of chairs and a board, and an old inner tube or tire.

The inner tube or tire can be placed on the ground and used as a target for spin-casting, fly, bait, or spinning tackle. Practice or "tournament" plugs of rubber or plastic can be used with plug cast, spinning, and spincasting gear, or you can use a regular spoon or plug with the hooks removed for a casting weight. Practice plugs of plastic are best for outdoor use because they won't bounce; rubber ones are for indoor casting.

Start casting about fifty feet from your target, using the overhead cast, until you're able to drop the plug into the target area consistently. When you've mastered that, try the side cast, underhand cast, and bow-and-arrow and catapult casts.

Walk around the target and cast from different directions, and as you improve, increase the range. You'll find this sort of accuracy casting practice every bit as much fun as smacking golf balls down a driving range.

The two chairs and board mentioned earlier are used to make an opening to cast to—simulating the casting problem facing

the fisherman who wants to put his lure under or between the drooping limbs of a tree.

Start with the chairs well apart and the board as high as possible. With casting tackle, try to shoot a flat trajectory overhead cast into the "hole," then try to shoot other casts right under the board and between the chairs. See if you can put the practice plug in there using a sidearm cast and bow-and-arrow and catapult casts.

The bow-and-arrow cast is accomplished by grasping the practice plug in the fingers of the left hand and, with only a few feet of line hanging from the rod tip, drawing the line back to put a good bend in the rod. The rod is arched back and up, then the plug is released. The resulting bow-like action of the rod will fire the plug straight out, and you'll learn quickly to keep the trajectory of the cast low so that the plug will sail under the board and between the chairs. The catapult cast is identical to the bow-and-arrow except that the rod is bent the other way, toward the ground, rather than up. It is simply an inverted bow-and-arrow cast.

In casting with bait casting, spinning, or spincasting tackle be sure in these practice sessions that you hold the rod right so that proper wrist action results. Always turn your wrist sideways, so the palm of the hand faces down, when aiming and starting a cast. This is the only way you can get correct wrist action.

⊙

Too many anglers lose prize fish they hook because they do not "play" or fight the fish properly.

Recently Lien Tvedt of Mankato, Minnesota was fishing a Canadian lake for muskies. Using a spin-cast outfit and chucking a spoon around in a weedy bay, he hooked a fifteen-pounder. The muskie exploded out of the water, cut this way and that, and nearly tore that bay apart. Once—just when the muskie was almost ready for boating—it leaped right at the boat and nearly

fell into Tvedt's lap. But Tvedt did everything right, and seven minutes after he'd hooked the muskie he had it safe in the boat.

Tvedt is a veteran and skillful angler, and passes on these tips on how to play fish:

1. Be sure your tackle is right. Check the line and leader, adjust the reel's drag carefully, and keep hooks needle-sharp.
2. Set the hooks as hard as possible when a fish strikes.
3. Work the fish in by pumping and reeling. "Pump" the rod by raising it and pulling it back toward you, then spool line by lowering the rod tip and reeling. Repeat this "pump 'n reel" routine until the fish is ready to land.
4. Keep the rod high as you play your fish so that the fish fights the bend or flexing of the rod.
5. When a hooked fish leaps, lower the rod quickly. Put the rod tip right down to the water. This puts slack into the line immediately and makes it nearly impossible for the fish to throw the lure or break the line.
6. Except when a fish leaps, keep a tight line. Put a constant pressure on the fish but don't "horse" him in.
7. If the fish makes a strong run, let him go. Trying to stop a determined run can pull hooks out or break the line.
8. Be especially careful when the fish is near the boat and ready to be landed. Most fish will make one last lunge, or leap, when close to the boat.
9. If using a net, lower the net into the water and draw the fish to it head-first. Never allow a companion or guide to chase your fish around with a net.
10. Don't try to land a "green" fish. This is one that's still got a lot of fight in him. Always wear a fish down before trying to land it.

After presenting those ten tips, expert angler Tvedt was asked if anything might be added that would help fishermen land more fish.

"Yes," he said. "Just add a little luck!"

⊙

Every fisherman knows what it's like to have a kinky fly fishing leader, or a twisted monofilament line.

A quick and easy way to get the kinks out of a nylon leader is to draw the taut leader back-and-forth for its full length several times across a rubber shoe sole. If you wear sneakers when fishing, they're perfect for the job. Bad kinks near the front end of a monofilament spinning, spin-casting or bait casting line can be removed the same way.

If too much of a casting line has been twisted or kinked to straighten it by drawing across a shoe sole, then troll the loose line behind a boat without a lure attached, or tie the end of the line to something stable and stretch it.

⊙

Fish are nearsighted, which means they have good vision at close range. Fish can see color, too, but only in shades and not as sharply as by humans. Scientists have proven that fish can distinguish shades of red, green, yellow, and blue.

The depth and clarity of the water have a lot to do with how well fish can distinguish colors. In turbid or cloudy water color intensity is altered. And since light is required for colors to be distinguished, the deeper a lure is fished the less important its color. Water absorbs light rapidly, so while a red lure may be brilliant at five or ten feet it likely will appear colorless to a fish at thirty-five feet or more. The deeper a fish is, the duller the colors it sees.

No one knows why, but white, orange, red, and yellow seem to excite fish. They appear to show up the best in the water, and gamefish certainly have a preference for lures of those colors.

Most fish have remarkable eyesight.

Thus it's not smart to stand in a boat when casting clear shallows for bass, nor to walk boldly upright to the bank of a gin-like trout stream.

Fish can smell, too.

The sense of smell, however, is better developed in some species than in others. Carp, catfish, and bullheads have keenly developed sensory organs and use them to root out food from muddy bottoms. Salt water fishermen often attract sharks to their boats by chumming with bits of fish or by pouring blood (usually from cattle) into the water.

Fish can hear, but not as humans do.

Sounds fish hear are not sounds as we understand them, but simply vibrations. There's a series of minute organs along the center line of a fish's body called the "lateral sense line," and through these organs fish are able to pick up vibrations in the water.

Fish can't hear talking, a radio playing, or any other "surface" noise, but scuff a foot in a boat, or walk heavily along a stream bank, and your presence will be no surprise to any gamefish around. They'll detect vibrations your actions impart to the water.

⊙

The salt water boys were doing it years ago—deep jigging, that is. The common lead-head jig, with bucktail or nylon winging, has been around for a long, long time but it's been only in recent years (comparatively speaking) that they've been used in fresh water fishing. Today just about every fresh water angler knows about, and uses, a variety of lead-head jigs.

Every species of fresh water gamefish will hit a jig, but the lead-heads are at their best in deep fishing, particularly for walleyes. Fish the deep reefs, rock points, and islands—using jigs of various sizes and colors. Let 'em sink right to the bottom, then twitch 'em along slowly by raising and lowering the rod tip. Remember to set the hook fast and hard when "Old Marble-eyes," the walleye, latches on.

⊙

When casting lures in the surf, don't cast in front of an incoming wave. Wait until it breaks and then cast *behind* it. If you cast in front of a wave, the onrushing water will kill the action of your lure and create slack line. Casting behind the wave, however, will give the lure better action and keep the line taut.

⊙

When using a surface popping plug, add a porkrind skirt to the tail hook to catch striped bass, bluefish, weakfish, and sea trout, snook, tarpon, and other salt water species.

⊙

Generally speaking, if you fail to catch largemouth and smallmouth black bass, walleyes, perch, crappies, and pike when fishing lakes, you are fishing where the fish are not. Fish deeper, and try to locate bottom "structures"—deep-down reefs, underwater peninsulas, bottom humps, ridges, and rock piles. Even muskies, thought by most fishermen to always be in weedy shallows, frequently go to depths of fifty, sixty feet and more.

⊙

When bass fishing in deep reservoirs, try the "slow-roll"

technique. Using a lead-head jig-and-spinner type of lure (such as the "Single-Spin" or "Twin-Spin"), attach a black porkrind eel or plastic worm to the hook, cast close-in to shore, then retrieve the lure very slowly. If you barely turn the reel handle, the lure will sink along the bank and then rise toward the boat, executing a U-shaped path through the water. Thus the lure is fished at several depths. Bass most often strike a lure fished the "slow-roll" way just as the lure starts up from the bottom of the U.

⊙

Spin-casting reels, as well as open-face spinning reels, perform best if the line is re-spooled tightly on the reels following each cast. Line that is re-wound firmly onto a reel's spool comes off the reel evenly and smoothly on the next cast; conversely, line re-wound loosely may billow off the spool, cause unnecessary friction, shorten the cast, and otherwise foul things up.

To get monofilament line re-wound firmly on the reel's spool, just wind the line in as you hold it between the thumb and forefinger, applying enough pressure to get the line back on the spool properly. You'll find that line firmly re-wound minimizes a whole bunch of casting problems!

⊙

⊙

Spinning and spin-cast fishermen most often miss hooking fish that strike because of slack line or because the reel's drag is set too light. Conversely, large fish can pop a line if drags are set too tight.

⊙

To fish light lures deep when fishing a stream or river, cast upstream and let the lure settle and wash deep with the current, reeling in just enough to keep the line reasonably taut. This is an especially good way to fish spinners, small spoons, plastic worms, or live bait. Be alert for strikes, and set the hook hard and fast anytime the lure or bait's downstream progress is halted.

⊙

Take your time when battling hooked fish, and "play" them carefully. "Horsing" a fish, or getting too excited and anxiously trying to boat it while the fish is still "green," invariably results in a lost fish.

⊙

Keep slack out of your line at all times, and yank the rod briskly upward to drive hooks home when a fish strikes. Check knots carefully after tying, and periodically cut back a few feet from the end of your line—it may have become frayed or weakened.

⊙

Fish migrate and move around a lot. Some species, such as black bass, may migrate once or twice a day (or not at all), moving from one well-defined area to another.

⊙

Ever try dog food on catfish or carp? Mix ordinary canned dog food with some cotton batting, kneading together so that the dog food won't wash off the hook. Use a small treble hook.

When settling down to fish an area with your dog-food bait, first try "chumming" catfish or carp by tossing out some dried oatmeal.

⊙

Learn to "hunt" fish. Work various areas thoroughly until you find fish. Remember, it's possible to locate fish but not catch them; but it's impossible to catch fish without locating them.

⊙

It's surprising how many anglers fish with reels only partially filled with line. This is poor policy, since it cuts down your casting distance and speed of retrieve—and there's the danger that a big fish will run off the remaining line on your spool. Also, a reel that is filled with the correct amount of line casts more efficiently and smoothly.

⊙

Few fish properly hooked ever "throw" the hooks. Usually the fish that gets away is the one that never was hooked to begin with.

If you want to land more of the fish that strike, follow these steps:

1. Keep all hooks needle-sharp. Use a small file or whetstone to hone them.
2. Keep slack out of your line, and the line taut at all times.
3. Keep alert for a possible strike. Don't be caught napping!
4. Keep your rod tip low to the water, then strike sharply up-

wards with it when a fish hits. Holding the rod tip low during retrieves gives you "striking room."
5. Keep hitting fish fast and hard. Your tackle will take it, and the hooks will be driven home!

⊙

Fishermen who are not careful about replacing rods in aluminum, plastic, or fiberglass cases are going to suffer some rod damage. Frequently when rods are shoved carelessly back in cases the guides nick the edge of the case and become bent or broken. Many fishermen who see twisted or busted rod guides wonder how the damage occurred, not knowing it's the result of replacing the rod too roughly in its case.

The proper way to slip a rod into its case is to circle the case opening with the fingers, thus providing a soft "cushion" should the rod wobble around on its descent into the case. Rod guides can't be damaged this way and, after all, it's small effort to assure longer life to rod guides.

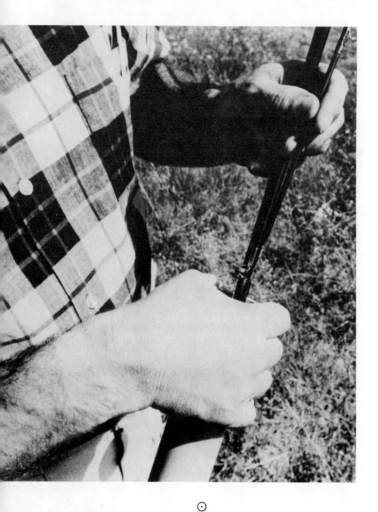

⊙

When using preserved or dead minnows for bait in fresh water they should be given some movement. In streams or rivers, cast them upstream and let them drift and tumble in the current. In quiet pools, retrieve them slowly with a stop-and-go action.

⊙

The Uncle Josh "Weed Runner" weedless hook is a revolutionary departure from the conventional wire guard type you've

been using for years. When a fish strikes, the guard band—which has a soft, fleshy resilience—"gives," exposing the hook point and the barb. It is an ideal hook for pork rind, plastic worms, and various forms of live and cut bait.

⊙

Lake trout come into the shallows in the spring soon after the ice is out and it's great sport to cast for them. Cloudy days are usually best for fishing. If the day is bright and sunny, fish for lake trout early in the morning and in the evening.

⊙

When using lures for striped bass, retrieve them fairly fast if the water is clear and calm. If the water is rough and white or a bit dirty, reel more slowly. Retrieve faster in the daytime than at night.

⊙

Strong tides, currents, and rips—especially around the full moon and new moon—create favorable fishing periods for salt water gamefish. At such times striped bass, bluefish, weakfish, tarpon, snook, and other fish chase smaller baitfish or forage for shrimp, crabs, and other food being tossed and swept about by the strong currents.

⊙

Especially in dark or murky water the addition of a strip of porkrind to your favorite plug will make your lure more visible to the fish. Be certain the porkrind strip isn't too large or it may hinder the action of your plug. If this happens, switch to a smaller size strip or use a knife and trim to the size desired.

⊙

Use big streamer and bucktail flies for trout when the water is high and roily, early in the morning, in the evening, and at night. They're also good on dark, rainy or stormy days. Use small bucktails or streamers when the water is clear and on bright days.

⊙

One of the best spots for landlocked salmon in the spring is the mouth of a stream where smelt are spawning. The smelt usually run up stream at dusk and return at daybreak. So, two good fishing periods are the hours just before dark and the first hour or two after daybreak.

⊙

If you are using small whole mullet for channel bass, slash the baitfish with a knife in several places before putting it on the hook. The blood and body juices oozing out will attract channel bass more quickly.

⊙

To keep the free end of a fishing line or leader material on a spool from slipping off, simply tie a rubber band to the end of the line and snap it over the spool.

⊙

Cobia fishermen take the first fish caught and tie it on a strong line under the boat to act as a decoy. This often attracts other cobia.

⊙

Chumming is the best way to bring mackerel to your boat where they can be hooked on lures or bait. Bunker or menhaden, finely ground, work best and should be ladled overboard at regular intervals. A small dipperful every minute or two will spread, and will then hold fish near the boat.

⊙

The quickest and easiest way to thread a fly line and leader through fly rod guides is by doubling the fly line before passing it through the guides. The doubled line is easier to see than a thin, transparent leader and it is easier to handle.

⊙

Always "pump" in fish you hook when using spin-cast tackle, rather than simply reeling them in. If you just reel a fish in you'll put twist in the line.

⊙

Fish hooks should be honed to needle sharpness. The proper way to hone a hook is to stroke *toward* the point, never backwards toward the barb.

⊙

Safest place for fishing rods during a lunch break is on the top of an auto roof, where the rods lay flat and cannot be knocked down, stepped on, or caught in a slamming car door.

⊙

Never adjust drag tension on a spin-cast or other drag-equipped reel by simply pulling line from the reel to check the tension. Best way is to thread line through the rod guides, tie the end to something sturdy, then apply pressure and bend the rod. Adjust the drag according to the pressure you'll want to exert with the rod and line.

⊙

Do you use a lot of tiny lead split-shot sinkers? The pellets from shotgun shells are just as good. Get a variety of shot sizes, from BB and Buck No. 4 and 6, and just split the pellets halfway through with a sharp knife.

⊙

One of the best ways to catch early-season trout from streams is to rig a spin-cast outfit with a single worm on a small hook and three or four split-shot sinkers to give casting weight and to take the bait down. Cast upstream, and let the current wash the worm down, bouncing it naturally along the bottom.

⊙

To catch nightcrawler worms, cover the lens of a flashlight with red or yellow cellophane and hunt the worms at night after a warming rain. Red fingernail polish also can be painted on a flashlight lens, then cleaned off with fingernail polish remover. Nightcrawlers won't spook from colored light.

⊙

Wrap part of a flexible wire pipe cleaner around the lower shaft of a fishing rod and it can serve to hold the fishing line, a hook, or a lure when not in use.

⊙

Print your name, address, and phone number on gummed labels and stick them on your tackle boxes, rod cases, and other valued pieces of equipment. If the gear is lost, the labels *might* get it back to you.

⊙

To help reduce fish-scaring boat noises, some fishermen glue strips of foam rubber to the bottoms of tackle boxes.

⊙

One of the best and easiest ways to clean the inside of a female ferrule on a fishing rod is with a wire rifle-cleaning brush, .22 caliber.

⊙

One of the best ways to present lures to fish when spin-casting, particularly in shallow water, is to depress the reel's "thumb-trigger" just as the lure passes over and slightly beyond the target. This stops the flight of the lure immediately, and brings

it down into the water at an angle. Raising the rod tip backwards as the lure hits will give the lure fish-getting action immediately.

⊙

If you have trouble "shooting" a fly line, it may be due to improper guides on the fly rod. The guides may be too small or too far apart. Large guides are best and should be spaced rather close to reduce line friction of the casts.

⊙

Hold your rod tip low, close to the water, when retrieving lures or fishing bait. From this position it will be easy to whip the rod up and back, *hard*, to set the hooks into a striking fish.

⊙

Important fishing tools are a barometer, fisherman's thermometer, and depth-finder or electronic fish-finder.

⊙

A circular pad of sponge rubber or thick, soft felt glued in the top cap of plastic and metal rod cases will protect the rod tip from damage and keep rod sections from rattling. A wad of cotton batting forced to the bottom of a case protects the other ends of the rod.

⊙

Best way to grease or clean a fly line is to stretch it between two trees or two other objects, such as a car and a fence. Once the line is stretched it's an easy matter to walk up and down its length, drawing the line between fingers holding the felt greasing pad.

⊙

When a hooked fish dives under your boat don't hesitate to push your rod down into the water, even so deep that the reel is submerged too, if necessary. Dunking won't hurt a rod and reel, but such a quick maneuver on your part may save you from losing a good fish.

⊙

Do you need to teach someone how to fish? Wife? Girlfriend? Son or daughter? The easiest and simplest way to teach casting to any beginner is with a quality spin-cast outfit. No other casting method is easier to learn.

31

Preferred Feeding Temperatures For Fresh And Salt Water Gamefish

Water Temperature One Clue To Fishing Success

Determining water temperature is one way of locating fish, and therefore, of enjoying fishing success. All fish have "preferred" temperatures—that is, those water temps at which the fish are most active and probably feeding. Knowledgeable anglers check their fishing conditions not only for depth and bottom structure but also for "preferred temperature." Find the conditions of water temperature that the fish you are seeking prefer, and chances are good you'll locate fish. The accompanying chart shows the temperatures at which most fresh water and marine gamefish are actively feeding.

Albacore	64	Chinook	54	Northern Pike	63	Sockeye (Wash.)	52
Amberjack	65	Cod	45	Panfish	65	Steelhead	47
Barracuda	67	Coho (Mich.)	54	Permit	72	Striped Bass	55
Big Eye Tuna	58	Crappie	65	Pollack	45	Sturgeon (River)	66
Billfish	57-81	Cutthroats	47	Rainbow Trout	47	Sunfish	65
Bluefish	68	Dolphin	75	Red Snapper	57	Tuna	73
Bluegill	69	Flounder	67	Salmon	52	Walleye	58
Blue Marlin	74	Kelp	65	Sauger	58	White Bass	70
Bonito	64	Kokanee	50	Shark	70+	White Marlin	68
Brook Trout	50	Lake Trout	47	Skipjack	73	White Sea Bass	67
Brown Trout	50	Largemouth Bass	68	Smallmouth Bass	62	Yellow Fin Tuna	72
Chain Pickerel	63	Mackinaw	47	Smelt	50	Yellow Perch	68
Channel Catfish	72	Muskie	63	Splake	49	Yellowtail	65

SOURCES:

Natural Resources Institute, University of Maryland.

Chesapeake Biological Laboratory, Solomons, Md.

Fisheries Research Board of Canada, Biological Station, Nanaimo, B.C.

Annual Report, International Pacific Salmon Fisheries Comm.

Conservation Departments of Iowa, Missouri, Ohio, Wisconsin, Michigan, New York and Washington.

Savannah River Ecology Laboratory (AEC).

Department of Oceanography, Texas A/M University.

Division of Fishery Research, U. S. Bureau of Sports Fisheries and Wildlife (Washington, D.C.).

Tiburon Marine Laboratory, California, U. S. Dept. of Sport Fisheries and Wildlife.

Sandy Hook Marine Laboratory, U. S. Department of Sport Fisheries and Wildlife.

National Marine Fisheries Services, Gulf Coast Fisheries Center, Panama City, Fla.

John G. Shedd Aquarium, Chicago.

Maine Department of Sea and Shore Fisheries.

Fish Ecosystem Research, Division of Fishery Research, Washington, D.C.

U. S. Department of Commerce, National Oceanic and Atmospheric Administration, La Jolla, Calif.

32 Coho Deep Trolling Rigs

During most of the fishing season, coho and Chinook salmon in the Great Lakes are taken by deep trolling. A wide variety of down-riggers and deep fishing devices, many home-made, are used. However, among the more popular and effective deep fishing rigs are those produced by Big Jon, Inc., in Traverse City, Michigan. The various methods of trolling with Big Jon rigs are presented here.

STANDARD DOWN-RIGGER LINE RELEASE

Big Jon's standard down-rigger line release (Model LR-800) is designed as a down-rigger or out-rigger line release. The release holds line fast to the fishing weight until a strike is had. The line is then released from the weight so that the fish may be properly played with the rod and reel. The release pressure is varied by using different shaft sizes from light to stiff. Line is released at any angle.

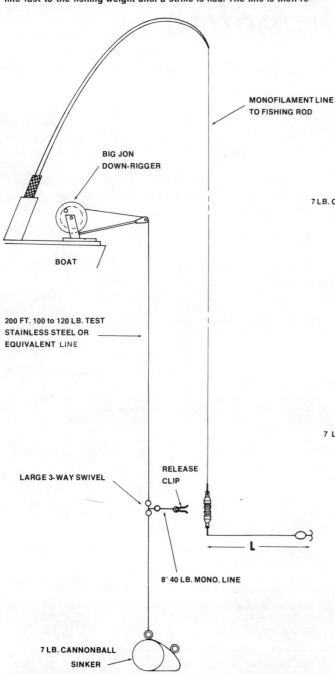

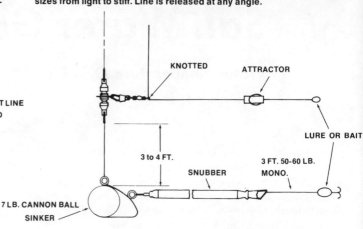

Down-rigger line attached to BIG JON LR-800 release ends, with standard release.
Note optional snubber (RS-700) attached to cannonball.

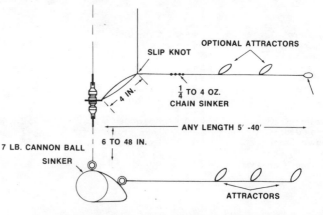

When fish strikes, slip knot slips & pulls release clip from release body. Fish then can be played in normal fashion.
Release clip is lost in this method and must be replaced.

L (length of this monofilament line) is determined by the length of the rod when the barrel is reeled to the tip of the rod. This leader should be about two feet shorter than the rod.

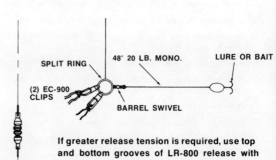

If greater release tension is required, use top and bottom grooves of LR-800 release with (2) BIG JON EC-900 clips on large split ring.

FREE-LOADER DOWN-RIGGER LINE RELEASE

Big Jon's "Free-Loader" down-rigger line release (Model LR-651) permits fishing as many rods as desired without pulling up the down-rigger line. Free-Loader slides down the down-rigger line to any pre-determined depth regulated by the fishing line. Subsequent fishing lines can be added at progressively higher intervals. When a strike is had, another Free-Loader is lid down the line and set at the desired depth. First Free-Loader is retrieved when down-rigger line is pulled up. Free-Loaders can be used outside the line with clips, as shown in accompanying illustrations, or can be rigged through Loader's center bore.

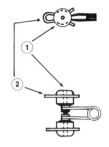

To assemble free-loader release, place spring ② against free-loader body ① and squeeze with pliers.

Free-loader release is also supplied with standard release clip. The standard release clip may be used in place of the spring, when longer leaders behind the free-loader are not required

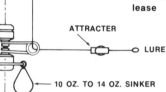

DOWN-RIGGER
DOWN-RIGGER LINE
FREE LINE
ATTRACTER
LURE
10 OZ. TO 14 OZ. SINKER
CANNON-BALL SINKER

APPLICATION NO. 1: Line through free-loader body, with spring release

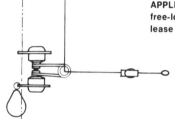

APPLICATION NO. 2: Line through free-loader clip, with spring release

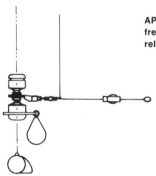

APPLICATION NO. 3: Line through free-loader body, with standard release

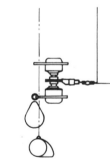

APPLICATION NO. 4: Line through free-loader clip, with standard release

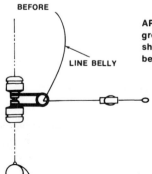

BEFORE
LINE BELLY

APPLICATION NO. 5: At depths greater than 30 feet, added weight should be used to prevent line belly

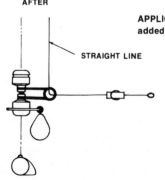

AFTER
STRAIGHT LINE

APPLICATION NO. 6: Result of added weight to free-loader

33

150 Trout Fishing Tips

by Bob McNally

1. Make sure hook points are needle sharp. Check them periodically to be sure they haven't been dulled by rocks, logs, gravel on the bottom, or other obstructions.

2. Sinker size and weight is important in all trout fishing. Be sure you always carry a variety of split shot and sinkers; there's nothing worse than being unprepared after you've begun to fish.

3. In river fishing look for small coves, back eddies, or places where the stream has flooded an edge of a field. The water here is usually a little warmer, and often trout move into these places during the spring to escape the cold, heavy currents of the faster water.

4. On the opening weekend of trout season it is often shoulder to shoulder fishing. Fish the smaller creeks and brooks. Fishing pressure will be much lighter, and often the trout will be more numerous, and larger than you'd think.

5. In fishing the smaller streams and creeks, "make like an Indian." Sneak along the edges of the stream, use available cover to your advantage, and don't let your shadow move along the water's edge.

6. When fishing is slow go to a lighter line or leader tippet. The fish may be spooky, and see your line before your fly or bait has a chance to entice them.

7. Trout lie under a bank of a stream or river. Look for such places when you're fishing. Drift a nymph, worm, or other bait along such places and you should take trout.

8. When baiting a nightcrawler, hook him once and only once, in about the middle. This will cause him to wiggle and twitch as the current carries him, and the worm will be more readily noticed by trout.

9. In the early spring when trout are sluggish feeders, change lures, flies, and bait often. Eventually you should find what the fish want.

10. When walking through heavy under-brush that surrounds most trout water, be mindful of your rod-tip. It's always easiest to carry your rod with tip facing behind. This way you can move brush out of the way before your rod passes through, thus avoiding a broken rod.

11. Sinkers and split-shot scare wary trout. But if you tie a sinker or afix a split-shot a foot or foot-and-a-half above the bait or lure, you may get better results.

12. If fishing is slow and you're using a weighted worm or nymph, take off your weight, no matter how light it is. Let the bait drift naturally without added weight.

13. When fishing a worm, hellgrammite, or other bait, use a small, light wire hook, with barbs also on the shank. This will help keep your bait firmly on the hook, under all water conditions.

14. When the large mayflies begin to hatch, most bait fishermen can score as easily as the fly-rodders by catching these insects and hooking them on very small number 18 or 20 hooks and using ultra-light spinning tackle, with a light bobber tied on well above the bait to improve casting ability.

15. A tight line and proper reel drag, are necessary in most trout fishing. This prevents missed strikes, and allows you to strike faster.

16. Excessive handling of small trout will sometimes kill them. If you twist the hook or fly back and forth a few times, the trout may come free without any handling at all.

17. If you're plagued with small trout and you're gunning for only the big ones, change to a larger fly, lure, or bait. This should keep the little ones away.

18. When you have a long walk through brush and woods, it's often easier not to "string" your rod until you have reached the area you want to fish.

19. On many of the smaller streams of the East and Midwest the trout are numerous, but small. If you want to reduce the amount of injured fish you hook, just take a pair of pliers and pinch the hook's barb down to the shank. You may lose more fish, but your chances of hurting the small ones is greatly reduced.

20. When wading a stream always walk very slowly. Walking fast will muddy the water you are going to be fishing next, if you're working downstream.

21. When tying on a fly, lure, or hook, be sure your knots are tied as tightly as possible. Most fish that are lost are lost because of poorly tied knots.

22. When wading fast water with a friend it's much safer and easier to wade and hold hands with one another. This will make each of you more sturdy while wading.

23. During a hatch of flies match your patterns as closely as possible to the flies on the water. Color is important— flies of gray, brown, and mixed hackles being best—but most important is the size of the fly the trout are feeding on. A wise fisherman carries patterns in sizes 8, 10, 12, 14, 16, 18, 20, and 22. Which he uses depends on the water being fished and the time of year.

24. It's best to clean trout as soon as possible after fishing. Be sure to remove the dark blood along the backbone. A thumb-nail or pocket-knife is all that's needed.

25. A bait fisherman should take advantage of a heavy rain storm. After a rain many insects, larva, and worms are washed into the stream, river, or lake, and trout often begin feeding.

26. Large trout prefer slow-moving, deep pools. Try fishing

Spinning with ultralight tackle frequently produces trout when all other methods fail. Fisherman here is wearing a head net for protection against mosquitoes and black flies.

them with extra care, and use flies and lures larger than normal.

27. If you have a choice of fishing upstream or downstream, always fish against the current. This way the lures, flies, and bait you're fishing will drift more naturally.

28. Never release a deeply hooked trout or one that's hooked in the gills. It's not worth the risk that he may die afterwards.

29. When wading difficult water, slow deliberate movements help. Also, if you keep your feet wide apart you're more stable, and there's less chance of a spill.

30. When fishing rainbow water never pass up fishing a fast-water riffle. Rainbows especially like fast water, and nymphs or worms drifted through these areas are very productive.

31. Fishing in the early morning or late evening will often result in more trout. Trout feed more at these times, because like most fish, they dislike the sun during the heat of the day.

32. When fishing dry flies always make sure your fly line has been cleaned with a quality fly dressing; it will help the line and fly stay afloat.

33. On a long hike up or down river it's often tiresome to walk in waders or hip boots. Carry your boots over your shoulder, and wear light sneakers. When you reach the area you want to fish, take them off, slip them in your fishing jacket or vest, and put on your boots.

Dave Duffey, well-known sportsman and Dog Editor of *Outdoor Life Magazine,* holds rod properly high as he fights a husky trout in heavy water of Wisconsin's Wolf River.

34. Be careful when tying on a hook of any type. One slip and you're hooked in the finger or hand. The best way is to tie your knot, hold the hook by the bend behind the barb, and pull the knot tight. Even if the knot slips, chances are you won't get hooked.

35. Quality dry fly oil is a must for any fly fisherman. Use it on all of your dry flies, and occasionally on streamers or bucktails you want to skim across the surface.

36. It's important to have your leader lay out flat and not to "curl" when presenting a fly to a trout. To help straighten your leader, hold it by the ends and run it quickly under your wader boot, or on a *clean* tennis shoe sole. The friction will take out the kinks.

37. Release an exhausted trout very carefully. Hold him upright, and ease him into the water, otherwise he may not survive the current.

38. Learn to "read" trout water. Fish above, below, and on the sides of all obstacles in a stream, river, or lake. Overhanging tree limbs, and under-cut banks are also prime trout habitat.

39. Watch the birds. When the night hawks and swallows begin to skim the surface, that's the time to tie on a dry fly. The trout should soon be coming up.

40. A rule of thumb for trout fly fishermen is "as long and fine as you dare." This normally means 12 to 14-foot tapered leaders with a 2X or 3X tippet for broken water and on larger streams, and 7 to 9-foot leaders tapered to 4X or 5X tippets for clear small streams or for flat water.

41. When trout fishing in the evening it helps to have a small pencil flashlight. It will come in handy for tying on flies, and when walking back to the car.

42. While fishing a dry fly with a "natural" float, mend your line so as to prevent line drag and drowning your fly. Sometimes a trout will refuse a drowned dry fly.

43. Trout almost always begin to feed when the water temperature begins to warm after a long cold spell. When the weather warms hatches of flies begin, and fishing normally improves.

44. When fishing with nymphs always watch your fly line where the leader and fly line are joined. If you see the line stop in the slightest, strike quickly, yet firmly. Often a trout won't strike with force, but will merely "mouth" the fly.

45. Sometimes a dry fly that is activated by twitching the fly rod and making the fly skip or hop will do much better than a fly that is allowed to drift normally with the current.

46. During the late evening it is often difficult for a trout to see a fly or lure well. Help him out by slowing down the retrieve.

47. Fishing with waders can be uncomfortable. A belt worn on the outside of the waders around the waist makes it a bit more bearable, and safer in case you should fall, because the belt traps air in the boots, which will cause you to float.

48. A newly built beaver dam often produces some fine trout fishing. Never pass up the pools above without making a few "serious" casts.

49. When casting to a rising trout, never cast directly to the spot where he came up. Instead cast just above the dimple where he was. In this way you won't spook him.

50. Occasionally a greased fly will stay afloat much better than one that has been dipped in dry fly oil. This technique is very effective with streamers, bucktails, and various types of hoppers, such as the Michigan Hopper, Joe's Hopper, and the Muddler Minnow.

51. When fishing a weighted nymph through a "run," twitch it on the tail end of the drift as the fly comes to the surface. Trout often think it's a nymph about to hatch into a fly at the surface.

52. Late summer and early fall is the best time for the fly rodder, because the water is low and it's much easier for trout to see a fly in shallow water.

53. Brown trout fishermen should take advantage of the late fall run of these fish when they begin to spawn. They sometimes hit almost anything, and the big ones are easier to catch when they come up the smaller streams from the lakes.

54. Big, deep holes should be "scraped" thoroughly on the bottom with flies, lures, or bait. Work the area over and over again. Many times a big trout will be lying on the bottom and it may take a few passes of your fly, lure, or bait to get him mad enough to strike.

55. Be selective in choosing dry flies. Pick only ones with good stiff hackles, light wire hooks, and those tied well enough so that the materials won't pull out after a few fish are caught on it.

56. To avoid line drag in fly casting, throw an "S" cast by twitching the rod tip back and forth just before the fly touches the water.

57. Sometimes when fishing is slow during the heat of the afternoon, a big, bushy, deer hair fly or bug twitched across the surface will wake trout up.

58. Trout can be kept cool in your fishing vest or in your creel by lining it with wet moss, damp towel, or moist sponge. This will keep your catch fresh and preserve the flavor.

59. Trout often ignore a fly more because of its size than its color or design. Try a smaller version of the same fly before changing patterns.

60. When fly casting, always check to see if you have any knots in your leader. Knots are common to all fly fishermen, even the expert, and if not corrected may cost you a fish.

61. Fish the spring holes and the smaller brooks that feed your trout water. During the summer months trout congregate at the coolest places in both rivers and lakes.

62. Adding glitter to a fly, or lure is sometimes helpful in getting a trout to strike. Take a strip of tin foil about one inch

Trout to be released should be handled gently. Firm lip-grip on fish holds trout securely without injury.

long and ¼ inch wide, and pinch it just above your fly, lure, or bait.

63. Don't miss out on trout fishing in the early fall. The fish are very active and fishing pressure is normally light.

64. When you see trout swirling at the surface, and yet they refuse to take a dry fly, try a nymph. Often the trout are feeding on nymphs coming up to the surface to hatch.

65. Trout like a lure that flops and flutters more than one that just "spins." When retrieving a spinner "stroke it" through the water in sweeps, then reel up the slack. This way the spinner's blades will flutter and flop. Be sure to use a snap swivel on all of these types of lures to prevent line twist.

66. If you tie your own streamers and bucktails, tie a few on ringed eye hooks. Flies tied on these hooks are good to use with spinners. Flies tied on hooks with other eyes don't ride well behind a spinner blade.

67. Casting a large streamer fly is difficult on a windy day. It will help if you cut your leader back to a larger diameter. This way the fly will fight air resistance, and lay out better on a cast.

68. During cold weather trout fishing is normally better during the brighter, warmer parts of the day. This is when the hatches are on, and the fish begin to feed.

69. When wading in fast or deep trout water, the smart fisherman uses a collapsible wading staff, or a stiff alder branch,

to add support in crossing streams and rivers, and possibly avoiding an accident.

70. Waders should always be hung upside down to dry after being used, or when you are storing them for the winter. This prevents dry-rotting and mildew.

71. Never cast just for the sake of casting. Always pick a target like a rock, log, or under-cut bank. Trout lie around such obstructions in the water.

72. Learn the habits of the trout in your favorite stream or river. Study their movements, and learn where to look for them. Know where they go during hot and cold weather, and where they spawn.

73. After you catch one trout from around a rock or under some brush, try several more casts to the same area. You may come up with another one or two.

74. When using minnows for trout always hook them in the lips. The minnows will stay livelier longer and they will face naturally into the current.

75. As a general rule smaller dry flies such as ones around size 14 are more effective on quiet pools than are larger dries.

76. Sometimes a small minnow-shaped piece of porkrind with a number 8 or 10 hook is the ticket for trout.

77. In fly fishing, a left or right curve cast can be helpful in keeping the fly line from going over a trout before the fly does, and it can help prevent line drag.

78. The way you work a lure, bait, or fly is very important. Vary the retrieve and action of it until you find the method that is productive for that particular day.

79. When fishing for trout, especially in shallow water or on small streams, keep noise to a minimum. Noises travel far in water and can spook fish.

80. Always "play out" a trout before trying to bring him in. More trout are lost by "horsing" them in than in any other way.

81. Trout can be fussy about the color and shades of lures and flies. It's wise to carry an assortment.

82. When fishing a new stream, river, or lake for the first time, try to get a map of the area. And also learn what kind of bottom it has: mud, sand, gravel, or a combination. The bottom composition can give clues as to what kinds of lures, baits, and flies to use.

Heavy hatch of flies like this is sure to bring great dry fly fishing.

83. Weather is a factor in trout fishing. Good fishing can coincide with either rain or sunshine. It's always wise to check with the weather-man before going fishing.

84. Keep a trout fishing journal. It comes in handy when you're trying to recall the types of flies, lures, or bait you used, the places you fished, and the time of year and day you were on a particular stream, river, or lake.

85. Tiny stream-side leopard frogs sometimes make excellent trout bait.

86. If you put a hole in a pair of waders and don't have a repair kit along, go to an auto service station. Most will be happy to put a tire patch on your boots, and it's inexpensive.

87. When you want a deep-running wet fly or a deep-going nymph, and the fly is not getting down far enough, try using a sinking line.

88. An experienced fisherman often carries several interchangable spools for his fly reel. One spool will have a sinking line for fishing wet flies and nymphs, and the other a floating line for fishing dry flies.

89. Check the bite of the hook on flies before purchasing them. Often a heavily-tied fly won't have enough space between body and hook point, and consequently hooking a trout with it will be difficult.

90. Occasionally a dry fly will become "water-logged". A good way to dry off a dry fly is to squeeze it in a shirt sleeve, or a fold in a handkerchief.

91. When fishing is slow, try using a nymph, with a dry fly tied on a dropper line about a foot-and-a-half above the nymph.

92. The riffling hitch is the perfect knot to use with a streamer, bucktail, Muddler Minnow, or some hopper that you want to skim across the surface.

93. It's wise to always have Polaroid sunglasses and a good cap with a brim to cut down glare while trout fishing.

94. Big trout often make tiny dimples on the surface while feeding. Don't overlook the slightest disturbance in the water.

95. Nail clippers are a great deal of help to a trout fisherman. They can be used to cut excess line from knots and for trimming down flies. They're small and light and can be attached to a fishing jacket or vest with heavy monofilament fishing line.

96. Try wading "wet" with just sneakers and shorts during the summer months. The water is warmer, and you won't sweat as when wearing heavy, hot waders or hip boots.

97. Two or three red-colored beads threaded on the leader above your fly or lure will help in attracting trout, and make the fly or lure sink better.

98. Carry a small plastic bag with you while trout fishing. It's perfect for carrying your catch home in, and your fishing jacket or vest will be cleaner.

99. Try baiting with a grasshopper, or using a fly imitation of a 'hopper, during the summer months. Fish it over deep pools and under brush and trees along stream, river, and lake banks.

100. A small chunk of pork rind, worm, or minnow attached to the hook of a lure is a good method of catching trout.

101. To help keep longer life in your fly line for trout fishing, reverse the line three or four times during the fishing season. Don't wind the line too tight onto the reel, as this will form kinks and ruin the finish of the line.

102. It's easier to take a rod apart if the ferrules are first "oiled" by running the male end of the ferrule through your hair or against your nose. Graphite is also a good lubricant.

103. Over-dressing a fly line with fly cleaner can make casting difficult because it "gums" up the rod guides. Be sure to wipe off excess fly line cleaner with a cloth.

104. Be sure to use "stiff" monofilament for leader material. Leader mono that is too soft will not permit a fly to "turn over" as it should, and the fly will not lay out correctly.

105. When fly fishing it's much easier to play a fish "off the reel." After hooking a fish, wind up the slack as soon as possible.

106. Follow your lure, fly, or bait in the water with your eyes. Never look away when fishing for trout. Not being ready to strike can cost you fish.

Trout this small needn't be handled at all prior to releasing. By holding the hook and giving a quick shake the fish usually will flip free.

107. The tail end of a "drift" of almost any fly or lure is often the "honey spot" of the entire cast. When the line "bows" and the fly or lure turns up against the current, be especially alert for a trout to strike.

108. Remember that a trout's mouth is small. When fishing a stream or river *start* with small lures, flies, or bait hooks. Size 10 or smaller hooks are best.

109. Vary the retrieve of your bucktails and streamers while fly fishing. Quick 3 and 4 inch sweeps of the fly are good, then slow 5 and 6 inch sweeps, then barely twitch the fly and let the current take it.

110. The pour-over at the lip of a pool is sometimes a good place for trout. Trout often station themselves here to catch insects that "funnel" through the head of the pool.

111. It's often more effective to place a spinner up above bait—about 8 or 10 inches is the best length—rather than right against the bait.

112. Remember to lower the rod tip when a trout jumps. This will put slack in the line and prevent the fish from pulling the hook out of his mouth or falling on a tight line and breaking it.

113. Don't forget to wiggle the rod tip occasionally when working lures, live bait, or flies. This added action helps to entice trout.

114. Buy good equipment. It doesn't have to be the most expensive made, but it should have practical qualities that will last.

115. One of the finest trout baits available is the sculpin minnow. Catching some for bait may be difficult, but they're well worth the effort.

116. Keep your tackle in excellent condition. A rod or reel that needs repair will hinder fishing in any trout water.

117. When fishing big trout water for large fish, sometimes a small "bass bug" twitched across the surface will produce trout.

118. A worm with a spinner attachment and a piece of split shot is a deadly lure for trout.

119. Never give up. The successful trout fisherman is the one who fishes from morning until night without being discouraged.

120. When a trout strikes near a snag or an over-hanging tree, move the fish into deeper water as quickly as possible. Many trout are lost when they "hang up" the line on obstructions.

121. Knowing how to hook a trout is one of the most important aspects of trout fishing. Learn when to strike hard, easy, or to delay the strike—as in bait fishing.

122. The wise trout fisherman is always prepared. He knows he must have equipment with him so he can fish on the surface, on the bottom, or at a middle depth.

123. Always stop the lure or bait just before it touches down on the water. This will help line control and stop backlashes,

and it will give you a tight line immediately after the lure or bait hits the water so you'll be prepared for a sudden strike.

124. When fishing a creek or river for the first time try to go out with a local guide or experienced fisherman who knows the area.

125. When approaching a trout stream or river always fish the near bank first. Chances are there may be a fish lying there, and a long cast made over him will make him spook.

126. Bridge supports and old dams usually have a lot of forage fish around them. For this reason there are normally trout lurking nearby. Fish these areas carefully and well.

127. Get a trout away from the area you hooked him in as quickly as possible. There may be other trout in the area, and his struggling may spook them.

128. Always carry a small hook hone in your fishing vest or jacket. It comes in handy when hooks become dull while fishing.

129. When casting to a rising trout make the first cast the best possible. If the fish refuses to strike on the first cast, chances are he won't hit because he has probably been spooked by the line.

130. Make sure the leader sinks when fishing dry flies. Be sure not to get any fly line dressing on the leader, and fish slime will help the leader to sink if rubbed into the nylon.

131. Learn the "trick" types of casts—they do come in handy. The bow-and-arrow cast, the catapult cast, the flick cast, the tight bow cast, and the roll cast will save many flies and lures, and will allow presentation of flies, baits, and lures under difficult situations.

132. When fishing a large deep pool, go directly to the tail of it. It is here that most trout will be feeding.

133. Big brown trout are almost always nocturnal. Use this to your advantage by not fishing until early evening, and fishing until well after dark.

134. Carrying a spare rod on your jacket or vest can sometimes save a day's fishing on an unknown river or stream. Many times you'll wish you had a fly rod, at other times a spinning rod.

135. When it's dark and impossible to see rising trout, try casting to sounds or surface disturbances. Chances are your cast will be close enough for a strike.

136. At dusk pick a dry fly that is easy to see and rides high on the water. A fly with large wings is good, like the Royal Coachman, or any of the deer hairs, like the Goofus Bug.

137. Invest in a fly box with a magnetic bottom. They're invaluable when fishing in the wind, and one may save your finest dry flies from blowing away.

138. Buy hooks or flies of the finest quality. Hooks that are too brittle or too soft will break or bend; either way you will lose fish.

139. Tie wet flies and nymphs with materials that absorb water well. Use wool bodies and heavy wire hooks so they sink quickly.

140. Often a fisherman "over-shoots" a likely place for trout and hangs up his fly or lure on a log or in brush. Throw a roll cast over the fly or lure. Sometimes this will free it without you having to wade over to retrieve it or break the line.

141. Always buy boots with felt bottoms. Most trout streams have slippery bottoms, and felted boots are best. The extra expense is well worth it.

142. Practice casting pays off when fishing a trout stream that is full of snags and cover. The accurate caster often produces more fish because he can fish the difficult areas that trout inhabit.

143. When fishing 'hoppers, it's often smart to cast your fly or live 'hopper right onto a grassy bank, then twitch it off. Trout will often see it "hop" off the weeds, and then strike.

144. When you pick a streamer to fish, try a marabou type first. The slightest twitch or current will make the marabou flutter and fan, so it looks very "alive" to trout.

145. Big trout frequent the same water. If you get a nice one from a pool or riffle, try it again in a day or two; you may hook up with another.

146. Tapered leaders are a must for the trout fly fisherman. The best leaders taper down from a butt section of 30-pound test to sections of mono testing 25, 20, 15, 10, 8, 6, 4, 2, and then a leader tippet—size depending on time of day and water conditions.

147. When fishing clear trout waters wear clothing with drab color. Light colored clothing is easily seen by trout, and may spook them.

148. Learn to select the right flies, lures, and bait. Types used should be based on the color of water being fished, depth of fish, kind of cover, and the types of food natural to the water.

149. When playing a trout always keep your rod high, and have the fish fighting the bend in the rod.

150. Go to the local tackle store or shop and talk to the owner for information when fishing in a new area. This can pay off, and it can save you a lot of time in locating a good trout area.

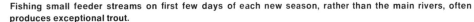

Fishing small feeder streams on first few days of each new season, rather than the main rivers, often produces exceptional trout.

34

Sizing Fly Lines To '72-'73 Model Fly Rods

Most beginning fishermen, and many an experienced angler, too, has difficulty casting well because he uses the wrong size fly line on his rod. If a rod is too heavy or "stiff" for the line used with it, the line will not "work" or properly flex the rod, and therefore correct casting will be impossible. The same is true when a line is too heavy for a rod's action.

Scientific Anglers, Inc., the Midland Mich. fly line manufacturer, has compiled the accompanying charts to aid fishermen in selecting lines that are suitable for their rods. All the fisherman need do to determine what size line will work best on his fly rods is to locate the rods he owns on the chart, then check the adjoining column for the AFTMA (American Fishing Tackle Manufacturer's Association) recommended fly line size.

Manufacturer and Model Number	Rod Length	AFTMA Line Weight
ALGONQUIN		
T11-731	8'	7
T11-742	8'	7
T11-784	8'3"	7
T10-710	8'6"	9
T10-720	8'6"	9
T10-725	8'6"	8
T10-726	8'6"	9
T11-773	8'6"	8
T11-795	8'6"	9
T10-716	9'	9
T10-755	9'	10
ANGLER		
UL 36	6'	5
UL 37	6'6"	5
880	8'	7
8 Special	8'	7
1880	8'	8
890	9'	9
1890	9'	8-9
BERKLEY		
PG 40	6'3"	5-6
F 40	7'	6
PG 40	7'	5
C 40	7'6"	7
F 40	7'6"	7
PG 40	7'6"	6
PC 40	7'6"	6
B 40	8'	7
C 40	8'	7

Manufacturer and Model Number	Rod Length	AFTMA Line Weight
F 40	8'	7
PG 40	8'	6
PC 40	8'	6
T 40	8'	8
B 40	8'6"	8
C 40	8'6"	8
F 40	8'6"	7
PG 40	8'6"	7-8
PC 40	8'6"	7
T 40	8'6"	8
F 40	9'	7
PG 45	9'3"	9
BROWNING		
322960	6'	5
322970	7'	6
322975	7'6"	6
322980	8'	6-7
322985	8'6"	7
322986	8'6"	8-9
322990	9'	8
322991	9'	9-10
CORTLAND		
*444 Ltd.	6'6"	5
Crown	6'6"	5-6
ProCrest	6'6"	5-6
*444 Ltd.	7'	6
Crown	7'	6-7
ProCrest	7'	5-6
*444 Ltd.	8'	7

Manufacturer and Model Number	Rod Length	AFTMA Line Weight
Crown	8'	7-8
ProCrest	8'	6-7
*444 Ltd.	7'6"	7
Crown	7'6"	6-7
ProCrest	7'6"	6-7
*444 Ltd.	8'6"	7-8
Crown	8'6"	7-8
ProCrest	8'6"	7-8
Crown	9'	8-9
DAIWA		
3043	7'	6
3044	7'6"	7
6044	7'6"	5
8044	7'6"	7
8344	7'6"	6
9344	7'6"	7
2045	8'	7
3045	8'	8
6045	8'	7
8045	8'	7
8345	8'	7
9345	8'	7
3046	8'6"	8
6046	8'6"	7
8046	8'6"	8
8346	8'6"	8
9346	8'6"	7
3047	9'	9
9347	9'	9

Manufacturer and Model Number	Rod Length	AFTMA Line Weight
FARLOW		
*Ultimate	5'10"	6
*Midge	6'	6
Gold Band	8'	6
Gold Band	8'6"	6-7
Gold Band	9'	6-7
Gold Band	9'3"	8
Gold Band	9'6"	7-8
FENWICK		
FF 60	6'	5
FF 70	7'	6
FF 70-4	7'	6
SF 74-4	7'	6
FF 75	7'6"	6
FF 75-4	7'6"	6
SF 75-5	7'6"	6
FF 77-7	7'10"	5
FF 79	8'	6
FF 80	8'	7
FF 80-4	8'	6
FF 83	8'6"	4
FF 84	8'6"	5
FF 85	8'6"	8
FF 85-5	8'6"	8
FF 86	8'6"	6
FF 86-5	8'6"	6
FF 107-5	8'10"	9
FF 90	9'	8
FF 92	9'	9
FF 98	9'	11

Manufacturer and Model Number	Rod Length	AFTMA Line Weight	Manufacturer and Model Number	Rod Length	AFTMA Line Weight	Manufacturer and Model Number	Rod Length	AFTMA Line Weight	Manufacturer and Model Number	Rod Length	AFTMA Line Weight
FF 107	9'	9	8-55385	8'6"	7	RF82	8'	8	42	9'	8
FF 108	9'	10	8-55885	8'6"	7	RB6Y2F	8'	7	42H	9'	9
FF 109S	9'	11-12	**HARDY**			RB6YPB4F	8'6"	8	52	9'	8
FF 117	9'	11-12	*Palakona	6'	5	RB6Y4F	8'6"	8	52H	9'	9
DFT 111	9'3"	7-8	*Palakona	6'8"	5	RB6Y1J	8'6"	8	62	9'	9
FF 112S	9'3"	10	Jet 4 2 pc.	7'	4	105-HE	8'6"	8	72	9'	10
FF 112-5	9'3"	10	Riccardi	7'	6	RB6Y7F	9'	10	63	9'6"	10
FF 114	9'3"	11	*Palakona	7'2"	5	RF92	9'	9	73	9'6"	10
FF 120	10'	7-8-9	*Palakona	7'6"	6	*RH8D	9'	7	74	10'	8
FF 126	10'6"	8-9	Jet 5 2 pc.	7'6"	5	RB6Y6F	9'	9	75	10'6"	9
FF 1200-3	12'	11-12	*Palakona	8'	7	**HORROCKS-IBBOTSON**			91	11'	10
GARCIA			Jet 6 2 pc.	8'	6	1306½	6'6"	6	92	12'	12
2070	6'	5	Jet 6 3 pc.	8'	6	1406½	6'6"	5	93	13'	13
2060	6'6"	7	Smuggler	8'	6	1307½	7'6"	8	94	14'	14
2072	7'	6-7	Smuggler 4 pc.	8'	8	1347½	7'6"	7			
2402	7'	5	*Palakona	8'6"	8	1350	7'6"	7	**L. L. BEAN**		
2914-D	7'	6	Jet 6 2 pc.	8'6"	6	1407½	7'6"	7	Double L	6'	6
2061	7'1"	7	Jet 6 3 pc.	8'6"	6	1457½	7'6"	7	Double L	6'6"	6
2636	7'3"	6	Jet 7 2 pc.	8'6"	7	1308	8'	7	Double L	7'	6
B542	7'6"	7	*J.J.H.	8'9"	6	1348	8'	7	Double L	7'6"	6
2073	7'6"	6	Jet 8 2 pc.	8'9"	8	1408	8'	7	Pack Rod	7'6"	7
2062	7'10"	7	Jet 6 2 pc.	9'	6	1458	8'	7	Double L	8'	6
2536C	7'10"	7	Jet 6 3 pc.	9'	6	1308½	8'6"	8	Double L	9'	8
2074	8'	6-7	Jet 7 2 pc.	9'	7	1348½	8'6"	8	**OLD PAL**		
2404	8'	6	Jet 9 2 pc.	9'	9	1349	8'6"	8	TBR600	6'6"	7
B541	8'	6	Jet 10 2 pc.	9'3"	10	1408½	8'6"	8	R676	7'6"	7
2637	8'	6	Walker Reservoir	9'3"	8	1458½	8'6"	8	**ORVIS**		
8237-D	8'	7	ESK	10'	7	1489	9'	9	*M9501	5'	5
2063	8'2"	7	Jet Salmon	12'6"	10	**KODIAK**			*M9502	5'	5
2064	8'5"	9	Jet Salmon	14'3"	10	2301	8'	7	*M9500	5'9"	4
2065	8'5"	10				3300	8'	7	*M9505	5'9"	4
2075	8'6"	7	**HEDDON**			3301	8'	7	*M9600	6'	6
2405	8'6"	7	8540	6'6"	6	4300	8'	7	*M9650	6'6"	6
2537	8'6"	9	8452	7'	6	5301	8'	7	*M9652	6'6"	6
2638	8'6"	7	8542	7'	6	2301	8'6"	8	*M9653	6'6"	6
2916-D	8'6"	7	8303	7'6"	6	3300	8'6"	8	*M9654	6'6"	6
2066	8'10"	11	8453	7'6"	6	3301	8'6"	8	*M9656	6'6"	4
2076	9'	9-10	8546	7'6"	6	3301M	8'6"	9	*M9657	6'6"	4
2639	9'	8	976	8'	7	4300	8'6"	8	*M9659	6'6"	6
GLADDING-SOUTH BEND			4885	8'	7	5301	8'6"	8	*M9660	6'6"	6
1-432-270	7'	6	8245	8'	7	2301	9'	9	R9993	6'6"	6
1-446-270	7'	6	8305	8'	6	3300	9'	9	R9994	6'6"	6
1-632-270	7'	7	8355	8'	6				*M9701	7'	6
1-428-276	7'6"	6-7	8455	8'	7	**LEONARD**			*M9703	7'	6
1-432-276	7'6"	6-7	8465	8'	7	**(All bamboo)**			*M9704	7'	6
1-436-276	7'6"	6	8545	8'	7	36	6'	4	R9068	7'	5
1-438-276	7'6"	6-7	8548	8'	7	36H	6'	4	R9076	7'	7
1-446-276	7'6"	6	8299	8'3"	9	37	6'6"	4	R9990	7'	6
1-450-276	7'6"	6	978	8'6"	8	37H	6'6"	4	R9991	7'	7
1-428-280	8'	6-7	4887	8'6"	8	47	6'6"	4	*M9707	7'3"	6
1-432-280	8'	6-7	8247	8'6"	8	47H	6'6"	4	*M9750	7'6"	6
1-436-280	8'	6-7	8307	8'6"	8	38	7'	4	*M9751	7'6"	6
1-438-280	8'	6	8357	8'6"	8	38H	7'	4	*M9753	7'6"	6
1-442-280	8'	7	8407	8'6"	8	48	7'	4	*M9754	7'6"	6
1-446-280	8'	6-7	8457	8'6"	8	48H	7'	4	*M9755	7'6"	7
1-450-280	8'	6-7	8467	8'6"	8	39	7'6"	5	*M9757	7'6"	7
1-428-286	8'6"	6	8547	8'6"	8	39H	7'6"	6	*M9758	7'6"	5
1-432-286	8'6"	7	2506	9'	10	49	7'6"	5	*M9759	7'6"	5
1-436-286	8'6"	8	8309	9'	8	49H	7'6"	6	*M9762	7'6"	6
1-438-286	8'6"	7	8409	9'	8	40	8'	6	R9077	7'6"	6
1-442-286	8'6"	8	8459	9'	8	40H	8'	7	R9986	7'6"	7
1-446-286	8'6"	7	8469	9'	9	50	8'	6	R9987	7'6"	5
1-450-286	8'6"	7-8	8549	9'	9	50H	8'	7	R9988	7'6"	7
1-428-290	9'	7-8	**HERTER'S**			60	8'	7	*M9765	7'9"	5
1-432-390	9'	8-9	RFSC6	6'	6	70	8'	7	*M9800	8'	8
1-450-390	9'	9	RFSC7	6'8"	6	41	8'6"	7	*M9801	8'	8
1-446-393	9'3"	9	RPFS	7'	7	41H	8'6"	8	*M9803	8'	8
GREAT LAKES			RB6YPF	7'1"	7	51	8'6"	7	*M9804	8'	4
8-5518	8'	7	RB6Y1F	7'6"	7	51H	8'6"	8	*M9806	8'	9
8-55185	8'6"	7	*RH8C	8'	6	61	8'6"	8	*M9808	8'	7
			RB6YPB2F	8'	7	71	8'6"	8	*M9809	8'	6

Manufacturer and Model Number	Rod Length	AFTMA Line Weight
R9078	8'	7
R9980	8'	8
R9981	8'	5
R9982	8'	8
*M9850	8'6"	9
*M9851	8'6"	9
*M9853	8'6"	9
*M9854	8'6"	9
*M9855	8'6"	8
*M9857	8'6"	8
*M9858	8'6"	9
*M9859	8'6"	7
R9079	8'6"	9
R9976	8'6"	8
R9978	8'6"	9
*M9815	8'9"	10
R9081	8'9"	11
*M9900	9'	9
R9080	9'	10
R9975	9'	9
*M9951	9'6"	9
*M9970	12'	10-11
PAUL H. YOUNG (All bamboo)		
Midge	6'3"	4
Driggs	7'2"	5
Perfectionist	7'6"	4
Martha Marie	7'6"	5
Para	8'	5
Boat	8'	6
Texan	8'6"	6
Texas General	8'6"	7
Para	8'6"	8
Bob Doerr	9'	8
Florida Special	9'	8
Power House	9'6"	9
PEZON et MICHEL (All bamboo)		
CS 260-S	6'	4
CS 261-S	6'6"	5
CS 221-N	7'2"	5
CS 223-C	7'2"	6
CS 230-N	7'2"	5
CS 232-C	7'2"	6
CS 262	7'3"	6
CS 263	7'7"	6
CS 221-N	8'	5
CS 223-C	8'	6-7
CS 230-N	8'	5
CS 232-C	8'	6-7
CS 266	8'5"	5-6
CS 221-N	8'6"	5
CS 223-C	8'6"	6-7
CS 230-N	8'6"	5
CS 232-C	8'6"	6-7
CS 221-N	9'	6
CS 223-C	9'	6-7
CS 230-N	9'	6
CS 232-C	9'	7
PFLUEGER		
501F7-0	7'	7
101F7-6	7'6"	7
201F7-6	7'6"	7
101F8-0	8'	9
201F8-0	8'	9
362F	8'	7
101F8-6	8'6"	9
201F8-6	8'6"	9
362F	8'6"	8
101SWF9-6	9'6"	11
PHILLIPSON		
RWF60C	6'	6
MF60C	6'	6
RWF66C	6'6"	6
MF66	6'6"	6
EF70	7'	6
RWF70C	7'	6
MF70	7'	6
DFS470	7'	6
*Peerless	7'	5
EF76	7'6"	6
RWF76	7'6"	6
DF76	7'6"	6
DF76B	7'6"	8
MF76L	7'6"	5
MF76	7'6"	6
DFS476	7'6"	6
*Peerless	7'6"	5
EF80	8'	6
RWF80	8'	6
DF80	8'	7
MF80L	8'	5
MF80	8'	7
*Peerless	8'	6
RWF86	8'6"	7
DF86	8'6"	7
DF86B	8'6"	8
MF86	8'6"	7
*Peerless	8'6"	6
DF90B	9'	8
EF96	9'6"	5
RUSS PEAK		
662SL	5'	3
662SL	5'6"	3
66RL	5'6"	4
442L	5'6"	4
TOLE-OXL	5'6"	4-5
662SL	6'	3
66RL	6'	4
442L	6'	4
TOLE-OXL	6'	4-5
442	6'	5-6
662SL	6'6"	3
66RL	6'6"	4
442L	6'6"	4
TOLE-OXL	6'6"	4-5
442	6'6"	5-6
66R5	7'	4-5
442L	7'	4-5
TOLE-OXL	7'	4
TOLD-OXL	7'	5
TOLD-105L	7'	5-6
442	7'	5-6
TOLE-105XL	7'6"	4-5
TOLD-105XL	7'6"	5
TOLD-BZ2	7'6"	5-6
P604C	7'6"	6
P606D	7'6"	6
P605C	7'6"	7
P606D	7'9"	6
TOLD-105L	8'	5
T1B-105	8'	6
T1B-BZ2	8'	6
P606D	8'	6
P605C	8'	6-7
P603C	8'	7
24Z-BZ4	8'	8
20Z-108L	8'3"	9
T1B-105L	8'6"	6
T1B-BZ3	8'6"	6-7
P747	8'6"	7-8
24Z-BZ5	8'6"	8
33Z-BZ810	8'6"	8-9
34Z-BZ810	9'	9
22Z-108L	9'	9-10
34Z-804L	9'	10
34Z-804	9'	11
22Z-804L	9'5"	9-10
SCIENTIFIC ANGLERS		
System 4	7'2"	4
System 5	7'7"	5
System 6	8'1"	6
System 7	8'5"	7
System 8	8'8"	8
System 9	8'11"	9
System 10	9'1"	10
System 11	9'3"	11
System 12	9'	12
SEARS		
30482	7'6"	6
30483	8'	7
30464	8'6"	7
30484	8'6"	8
30466	9'	8
30485	9'	9
30487	9'	11
SHAKESPEARE		
FY-A910UL	6'6"	5
FY-A910UL	7'	5
FY600UL	7'	5
FY-B310	7'6"	6
FY-A250	7'9"	6
FY-C215	7'9"	7
FY-A250	8'	7
FY-B310	8'	7
FY-B510	8'	7
FY-C110	8'	8
FY-C500	8'	8
FY-D120	8'	8
FY600	8'6"	8
FY940	8'6"	11
FY-A250	8'6"	8
FY-B310	8'6"	8
FY-B510	8'6"	8
FY-C110	8'6"	9
FY-C215	8'6"	8
FY-C500	8'6"	8
FY-D120	8'6"	8
SP860	8'6"	8
FY940	9'	11
FY-C215	9'	8
FY-C500	9'	8
FY940	9'6"	11
SHARPE (All bamboo)		
Featherweight	7'	5
Featherweight	7'6"	5
Seventy-Nine	7'9"	6
Featherweight	8'	6
Eighty-Three	8'3"	6
Featherweight	8'6"	6
Eighty-Eight	8'8"	6
Scottie	9'	7
Salmon	9'	8
Spliced	9'	7
Aberdeen	9'	6
Scottie	9'6"	7
Scottie #2	9'6"	8
Aberdeen	9'6"	7
Scottie	10'	7
Spliced	10'	7
Aberdeen	10'	7
Salmon	12'	8-9
Salmon	13'	9
Salmon	14'	10-11
Salmon	15'	11
ST. CROIX		
7090XXL	6'8"	5
7785MF	7'	7
92	7'6"	7-8
8009	7'6"	7
9000	7'8"	7-8
7090XL	8'	6
9000	8'	6
9100	8'	6
900	8'3"	7
983	8'3"	7
4000	8'3"	7
7090XL	8'6"	8
9000	8'6"	8
9065	8'6"	9
9100	8'6"	8
7090XLM	9'	9-10
9000	9'	8
9100	9'	8
9100	10'	9
TRIMARC		
747-8F	8'4"	8
TRUE TEMPER		
250T	7'	7
1255B	7'6"	7
1255A	8'	7
805	8'6"	8
1005	8'6"	8
1255	8'6"	7
1505	8'6"	7
1755	8'6"	8
5005	8'6"	9
1255C	9'	7
WINSTON		
*1¾ oz.	5'6"	3
*2 oz.	5'6"	4
1⅝ oz.	5'6"	5
*2 oz.	6'	3
*2¼ oz.	6'	4
*2½ oz.	6'	5
1¾ oz.	6'6"	3
*2⅛ oz.	6'6"	3
*2½ oz.	6'6"	5
*2¾ oz.	6'6"	5
2 oz.	6'6"	5
*2½ oz.	7'	3
*2⅝ oz.	7'	4
*2⅞ oz.	7'	5
*3 oz.	7'	5
2⅛ oz.	7'	5
*3⅛ oz.	7'6"	4
*3¼ oz.	7'6"	5
*3½ oz.	7'6"	5
2¼ oz.	7'6"	5
2¾ oz.	7'6"	6
*3⅝ oz.	8'	4
*3¾ oz.	8'	5
*4 oz.	8'	5
3⅛ oz.	8'	5
3½ oz.	8'	5
*4⅛ oz.	8'6"	5
*4¼ oz.	8'6"	6
*4½ oz.	8'6"	7
*4¾ oz.	8'6"	8

Manufacturer and Model Number	Rod Length	AFTMA Line Weight	Manufacturer and Model Number	Rod Length	AFTMA Line Weight	Manufacturer and Model Number	Rod Length	AFTMA Line Weight	Manufacturer and Model Number	Rod Length	AFTMA Line Weight
3½ oz.	8'6"	5	4¾ oz.	9'	10	M6TMU6'9"	6'9"	9	M2A8	8'	7
3⅞ oz.	8'6"	6	5¼ oz.	9'	11	MLWFF	7'	6	M4A8	8'	7
4 oz.	8'6"	7	5⅝ oz.	9'	11	M2A7	7'	6	3A8	8'	7
*4⅝ oz.	8'9"	7	*5½ oz.	9'3"	10	B8A7	7'	6	B-2585	8'6"	7
*4¾ oz.	8'9"	8	*5¾ oz.	9'3"	11	M2A7½	7'6"	7	B-8A8½	8'6"	7
*5 oz.	8'9"	9	5⅜ oz.	9'3"	11	M4TM57½	7'6"	7	M2A8½	8'6"	7
4⅛ oz.	8'9"	7	*6 oz.	9'6"	11	M4TMU7½	7'6"	7	M4A8½	8'6"	7
4¼ oz.	8'9"	8	5½ oz.	9'6"	11	4FRF	7'6"	7	M4MF8½	8'6"	7
*4⅞ oz.	9'	7	**WRIGHT & McGILL**			4FRU7½	7'6"	7	3A8½	8'6"	7
*5 oz.	9'	8	MLWFF	6'	6	4PLP7½	7'6"	7	M8599	9'	10
*5¼ oz.	9'	9	MLWF	6'6"	6-7	B-8A7½	7'6"	7	B-8A9	9'	8
*5½ oz.	9'	10	MLWFF	6'6"	6	3A7½	7'6"	7	M2A9	9'	8
4¼ oz.	9'	7	M4TMUL6½	6'6"	7	B-2580	8'	7	MPLF-9	9'	10
4½ oz.	9'	9	M6TMF6'9"	6'9"	7	B-8A8	8'	7	3A-9	9'	8

*Split Bamboo Rod

LINE RECOMMENDATIONS—Line recommendations are given in the AFTMA designations. Where two sizes are recommended, the rod balances equally well with either size. To insure proper balance between your rod and line, simply use any Scientific Anglers fly line with the same number as the recommended AFTMA line weight. For example, if a No. 8 line is recommended, use any of the following floating lines: level, L-8-F; double taper, DT-8-F; weight forward, WF-8-F. In a sinking line, use a level L-8-S; double taper DT-8-S; weight forward, WF-8-S; Shooting Taper ST-8-S. A separate bulletin describing the AFTMA numbering system for fly line weights (Bulletin LS-1) is available upon request. Please send stamped, self-addressed envelope.

For specific information on fly rods contact any of these manufacturers.

Algonquin Mfg., Ltd., 6 Bartlett Ave., Toronto 4, Ontario, Canada
Angler Rod Co., 1426 Oakland Ave., St. Clair, Mich. 48079
Berkley and Co., Inc., Highways 9 & 71, Spirit Lake, Iowa 51360
Browning Arms Co., Route #1, Morgan, Utah 84050
Cortland Line Co., 67 East Court St., Cortland, New York 13045
Daiwa Corp., 1526 West 166th St., Gardena, Calif. 90247
C. Farlow & Co., Ltd., 3-11 Skene Square, Aberdeen, AB9 1 FE, Scotland
Fenwick Products, Inc., P.O. Box 696, Bainbridge Island, Wash. 98110
Garcia Corp., 329 Alfred Ave., Teaneck, N.J. 07666
Gladding-South Bend Tackle Co., P.O. Box 260, Syracuse, New York 13201
Great Lakes Products, Inc., 312 Huron Blvd., Marysville, Mich. 48040
The House of Hardy, P.O. Box 3, Willowburn, Alnwick, England
Daisy/Heddon, Dowagiac, Mich. 49047
Herter's, Incorporated, R.R. #1, Waseca, Minn. 56093
Horrocks-Ibbotson Co.' Utica, N.Y. 13502
Kodiak Corp., P.O. Box 467, Ironwood, Mich. 49938
H.L. Leonard Rod Co., P.O. Box 393, Central Valley, New York 10917

L. L. Bean. Inc., Freeport, Maine 04032
Woodstream Corp., Lititz, Penna. 17543
Orvis Co., Inc., Manchester, Vt. 05254
Paul H. Young Co., 14039 Peninsula Dr., Traverse City, Mich. 49684
George N. Vitt, Sugarloaf Dr., Wilton, Conn. 06897
Pflueger Sporting Goods Division, P.O. Box 310, Hallandale, Fla. 33009
Phillipson Rod Co., 2705 High St., Denver. Col. 80205
Russ Peak, 21 N. Allen Ave., Pasadena, Calif. 91106
Scientific Anglers, Inc., P.O. Box 2007, Midland, Mich. 48640
Sears, Roebuck and Co., 925 S. Homan Ave., Chicago, Ill. 60607
Shakespeare Co., Kalamazoo, Mich. 49001
C. Farlow & Co., Ltd., 3-11 Skene Square, Aberdeen, AB9 1 FE, Scotland
St. Croix Corp., Park Falls, Wis. 54552
Trimarc Corporation, 228 North LaSalle, Chicago, Illinois 60601
True Temper Corp., 1623 Euclid Ave., Cleveland, Ohio 44115
R. L. Winston Rods, 475 Third St., San Francisco, Calif. 94107
Wright and McGill Co., 1400 Yosemite St., Denver, Colo. 80220

35

How to Improve Your Casting

Balanced equipment and consistent practice can make you an expert at fly casting, plug-casting and spinning.

Fly Casting

One of the popular fallacies in fishing is the notion that fly casting is easy. Fly casting is the most graceful and picturesque form of casting. It is also the most difficult.

Nearly anyone can pick up a fly rod and, by merely waving it back-and-forth and sawing line through the air, cast thirty or forty feet. But a good fly caster is one who can cast a GAF(WF-9) line 100 feet and *do it effortlessly* with no more than two false casts; he can handle eighty feet of HDH line with an eight-foot rod and do it easily and gracefully; he has mastered the "double haul"; he can shoot line on both the backcast and the forward cast; he can roll cast, throw curves left and right, cast a "tight bow," knows how to "mend" line, do backcasts and side casts and execute numerous other fly fishing manuevers. Moreover, he is capable of casting large streamers and bulky bass bugs from dawn to dark without fatigue.

None of these things, all of which are in the repertoire of the *skilled* fly caster, are easily learned. Becoming a *good* fly caster takes practice and experience. Moreover, no fly caster ever completely masters the game. There are fishermen who'd have the world believe they've mastered fly casting, but it isn't so. A skilled fly caster knows what his tackle is capable of, and knows how little of that capability he ever achieves. As in golf or billiards, absolute perfection in fly casting is not only elusive but unattainable. But it's fun trying to improve, year after year.

Having properly "balanced" tackle is vital in fly casting. A skilled caster always can get out at least *some* line with a poor fly fishing outfit, but not even a champion can cast *well* with a bad rod-line combination.

In other forms of casting—bait casting, spinning, and others—the weight of the lure pulls the line after it. But in fly casting the weight of the line furnishes the momentum to carry out the lure, or fly. The fly, attached

Quick tug on line with left hand along with backward movement of rod gets fly line underway for full backcast.

to a nylon leader tied to the end of the fly line, merely rides along during the cast. In fly casting it's the *line* that's cast. The heavy line "works" the rod as the caster moves the rod back-and-forth. On the backcast the line extends straight behind the caster, bending the rod. When the rod straightens and flexes forward, with an assist from the caster, it furnishes the propulsion that drives the line forward. The fly follows along, and lights on the water. None of this can be properly accomplished if the line does not "match" or "balance" the rod.

The fly line must be of the correct size (weight) to flex the fly rod. If the line is too light for the rod, it will not bend the rod and proper casts cannot be made. If the line is too heavy for the rod, it will "overwork" the rod and the rod could easily be broken.

The fly rod's "action" (that is, its type and amount of resistance to bend) must be right. A rod that has "soupy" action, one that is very willowy and "soft," will not cast well in anybody's hands. Nor will a fly rod that is too stiff. A good fly rod has an action that is somewhere between "soft" and "stiff." When waggled back-and-forth, it should flex from its tip to its butt, but with this "action"

gradually diminishing from the rod's tip-top to its handle.

Most tackle manufacturers today print on rods the sizes of fly lines that "match" the rod. For the most part these manufacturer's line recommendations are accurate, but not always. Experienced fly casters have no difficulty matching lines to rods, but novices should ask tackle salesmen (if they are qualified) to recommend fly lines. An alternative is to try two or three different size fly lines on a rod, and see which casts best.

The fly reel contributes nothing to the cast. It merely furnishes storage space for the line. Thus the reel is, comparatively speaking, unimportant. Nonetheless it pays to get a good reel. Fly reels come in various sizes, and you should get one that fits your rod well both as to its weight and size. Moreover, the reel must have adequate line capacity. If your rod calls for a large line, GAF for example, you won't get all the line on a very small, featherweight-type, fly reel.

Most experienced fly fishermen prefer single-action reels to automatic reels. They feel automatics are unnecessarily heavy, that automatic line retrieval isn't needed, that they do not balance a rod well, that their

Left hand slides upward with line as backcast unfolds behind.

Forward cast begins with forward movement of rod as line hand slowly starts downward tug.

line capacity is too little, and that a fast fish cannot run line out against an automatic reel's drag without breaking the leader.

For heavy fly fishing, particularly in salt water, the reel should have great line capacity and a strong, reliable drag. A good drag is difficult to find in inexpensive fly reels. It is needed not only to prevent overruns when a fast fish scoots off, but also to prevent an overrun when the caster tries to quickly strip line from the reel.

Fundamentally, fly casting is a simple back-and-forth motion of the fly rod, with the line moving in cadence in front of and in back of the caster. This is enough to throw the line and carry the fly seventy feet *when the caster's timing is correct*. The simple physics of fly casting is the application of power from pivot points (the wrist and elbow) with haltering but smoothly coordinated movements. There are pauses; points where power is expended; and drifts; but all are combined into one smooth, graceful motion. Almost all casts begin with "starting" power in originating the backcast, advance to "speed up" power, then to a pause and a drift, and finally a return to the "starting" and "speed up" powers on the forward cast.

The idea that good fly casting is achieved by using only one's wrist, learning by holding a handkerchief at the side with the elbow of the rod arm, is incorrect. Skilled fly casters use their wrists and all of their rod arms to power their casts. In distance casting in particular, it is necessary to use the *whole* arm, even adding some shoulder and body weight. On short casts with light fly fishing outfits, wrist and forearm action is adequate. As casts are lengthened, however, more and more of the arm and rod side of the body come into play.

Some fly fishermen also have the false notion that a fly rod should always be halted at the 12 o'clock position on the backcast. This may be true when delivering short casts, but not when casting a long line. In distance casting the rod must go back, often well beyond the 2 o'clock position. On long casts the rod *pauses* at around the 12 o'clock position, but it is allowed to *drift* much farther back. This is necessary because there is more line in the air, taking more time to unfold, and the backcast must unfold completely before the forward cast may begin. The longer a cast, the farther back the rod must go, and the longer the caster must wait before commencing the forward cast. On an extremely long cast,

Wrist and arm apply forward pressure to rod as caster's left hand tugs heavily on line in executing "forward haul."

Rod comes forward smoothly and strong as left hand completes full "haul."

the caster must gradually begin nudging the rod forward *before* the backcast unfolds completely. Otherwise the fly line will touch down behind the caster, and the rod will not have a sufficient bending area to bring the long backcast forward.

Except when making very short casts, reach up and back with your rod arm. This gives added height, greater leverage, and properly brings all of the arm and not just the wrist into the cast. And use the thumb-on-top grip on the rod handle, not the thumb-on-side grip. The best fly casters—such as the late Johnny Dieckmann and Jon Tarantino—all used the thumb-on-top grip. With the thumb-on-top, it's natural to stop the rod at about 1 o'clock on the backcast, yet this grip allows continued "drift" of the rod. This grip also gives a better application of power on the forward cast, because the thumb and the heel of the thumb push against the rod handle.

To execute a normal forward cast, hold the rod firmly but comfortably with the thumb of the casting hand *on top* of the rod handle. Strip twenty or thirty feet of line from the reel, and extend it out on the water by waving the rod back-and-forth, almost with a whiplike movement. Now, with the line out in front of you, lift the rod tip

Electronic flash camera shows all stages of fly caster's "double haul."

slowly to 10 o'clock, taking all slack out of the line and raising most of it from the water. Next snap the rod tip back sharply, stopping between 12 and 1 o'clock, then allowing the rod to drift back a bit farther. *Turn your head* and watch the line unroll and straighten behind you, and note how the rod tip bends under the weight of the line. Slowly start the rod tip moving forward, then speed up and add power as the full weight of the line bends the rod. Stop the rod at about 9 o'clock, and let the line straighten and drop to the water.

To make a longer cast, strip more line off the fly reel and let it fall in loose coils on the ground. Then lift the rod sharply, just as before, to raise the extended fly line off the water and into the air. Make the usual backcast and then a forward cast, only don't finish this cast; keep the line in the air, "false casting," until you can properly deliver all the line on a final cast. Always strive to keep false casting at a minimum. Good casters, in fact, rarely false cast more than twice.

The above are the rudiments of fly casting. With the basic movements described, the caster eventually learns to "shoot" line, that is, power the forward cast so that yards of additional line are shot through the rod guides. Also to be learned is the "double haul," a technique of tugging on the line at proper moments with the left hand to increase line speed and thus deliver a longer cast. All fly casters must use the left hand (the right hand for left-handed casters) in order to properly control the line. Without at least some use of the other hand, it is not possible for the average caster to cast much beyond forty feet; and without use of the "double haul," he will not cast beyond eighty feet.

Any fly caster is at his best after several days of casting, when his arm muscles have tuned and his timing sharpened, but brute strength contributes little to fly casting. Many fishermen, in striving for distance, attempt to "power" a cast and thus lose all semblance of timing, muscular coordination, and the proper application of rod power. Failing to develop timing, they attempt to make up for this by strength—little of which is transmitted correctly to the rod. The short road to good fly casting is the slow and easy one, letting the rod and the line do the work.

To become a skilled fly caster, and thereby get additional pleasure from fly fishing, takes practice. You must "stay with it" and use your fly tackle—if not all of the time, at least most of your fishing time. You can't get good at it any other way.

Bait-casting, Spinning

Anyone having normal coordination and eyesight can learn to cast well. And nearly every fisherman can learn to cast better. Striving for perfection is part of the fun of spinning and bait-casting.

In using a bait or plug-casting outfit, hold the rod so the reel handles are up during most casts. This permits free wrist movement and easy, smooth thumb-control on the revolving reel spool. Most of the power used in plug-casting is generated by the wrist, with only slight assistance from the forearm. Most forearm movement comes during the "follow through."

The overhead cast is most important. It is the one cast

Proper way to hold a bait-casting outfit is with the reel handles up.

Correct grip allows full wrist movement, proper thumb control, and application of power through fingers of casting hand.

Start of overhead cast sees angler with arm extended, rod pointed to target.

Angler concentrates on target as forward cast is delivered. Note wrist action.

that permits maximum accuracy, and it's the safest cast when fishing from a boat with a companion.

An overhead cast is started by extending the rod in front of you, pointing it at the target. Look directly at the target, using peripheral vision to line up the rod. Keep your forearm relaxed, pointing upward and forward, with the rod at an angle above the horizontal. The plug should hang three to twelve inches from the rod tip, depending on the weight of the plug and the rod's action. With the elbow serving as a fixed pivot, raise your forearm and activate the wrist to swing the rod tip up and back until the rod handle is vertical. Now stop backward movement of your forearm and wrist. The plug will continue back as its weight bends the rod. When maximum rod bend is reached, start the forward cast—increasing speed and power by wrist movement. Generally speaking, the forward cast should be twice as fast and strong as the backcast. The rod should bend smoothly under

the weight of the plug, and act as a spring that shoots the plug forward once the caster's thumb releases the reel spool.

The spool should be released gradually as the rod passes the vertical on the forward cast, but slight thumb pressure on the spool is maintained as the rod nears a horizontal position. This prevents "over-run" of the reel spool and tangling of the line.

As the plug nears the water more thumb pressure is applied to the spool to slow the flight of the plug. Just before the plug hits the water the thumb is applied firmly to stop the revolving spool.

The physics of plug-casting involves momentum (centrifugal force) furnished the reel spool by the moving plug swinging pendulum-like from the rod tip. The plug pulls line from the reel, with the reel acting as a tiny winch.

When the overhead cast is mastered, other useful

throws such as the side cast, backhand, and flipcast can be learned. The forces involved are precisely the same as those in the overhead cast.

Choice of tackle is vitually important to the bait-caster. Buy the best reel you can afford; fill it with fine diameter line, and select a rod with the right action and length for the kind of lures and fish you will handle. As a general guide, rods six to six and one-half-feet long, with "fast" tips, handle light lures best. Shorter, stiffer rods usually are preferred for casting heavy lures.

"Spinning" is an American name for bait or plug-casting with a stationary spool reel, and specifically one with an "open" face. "Spin-casting" is an American derivation of spinning, using a "closed face" spinning reel. Spinning has been popular in France for years, where it's called *lancer leger.*

During its acceptance by American anglers some twenty-five years ago, spinning was thought to be a

Reel is "palmed" in fisherman's left hand as reel handles are turned to retrieve lure.

First step to casting with open-face spinning reel is opening of reel's bail and securing mono line on finger tip.

Line should be held only on tip of finger so that cast can be released smoothly.

Thumb-on-top is proper grip on spinning rod.

Thumb and three lower fingers power the rod on forward cast as index finger releases the line.

"Feathering" a cast with spinning reel is accomplished by dropping tip of index finger to reel's spool.

method for casting only light lures. But today, U. S. fishermen consider spinning to be just about a perfect system for casting lures of almost any weight, from the very lightest to the heaviest.

The manual control of a spinning reel and line during casting is different from that with a conventional baitcasting reel, but the mechanics of executing a cast are the same.

The flexing and power of a spinning rod drives the lure out, and the lure's momentum pulls line from the reel. The flexibility or "springiness" of the rod does the work, with the rod storing energy at the end of the backcast, then imparting this energy to the lure during the forward cast.

To make an overhead cast, open the bail of the spinning reel and secure the line on the *tip* of the second finger. Then swing the rod up-and-back, smoothly, in one steady motion. Stop the rod at about 12 o'clock, while the momentum of the backswing continues to flex the rod. As the backcast attains its maximum bend, start the forward cast without hesitation, allowing the line to slip off the forefinger when the rod reaches a 10 o'clock position in coming forward. Now "follow through" by lowering the rod as the lure flies out to the target. You can "feather" or stop the flight of the lure by placing the forefinger on the reel spool to contact the line.

For right or left hand side casts use little or no backcast. Just a snap of the wrist will do. By holding the rod tip at the side and close to the ground, you can execute an underhand cast that is useful for putting lures under overhanging brush, or when casting is confined quarters.

The "catapult" or "inverted bow-and-arrow" cast also is useful when you're surrounded by brush. To execute this cast, let out line about one-half the rod's length. Grasp the tail hooks of the plug in the left hand, pull it back towards your beltline to bend the rod—then release the plug. The rod tip will snap forward, pulling the plug out, and jerking the line from your finger-tip and the reel spool. Always let the momentum of the lure pull the line from your finger-tip.

Spinning is one of the simpler casting methods, but it has an important place in the world of angling.

Rod flexes smoothly in 1 o'clock position as caster drives lure towards target.

36

Feed Bluegills for "Instant Fishing"

By Barbara Helmle

Leo Pachner of Kankakee, Illinois, publisher of *Farm Pond Harvest Magazine,* says there's an easy, sure-fire method of providing consistently good fishing for bluegills.

"All you have to do," Pachner insists, "is feed the fish." "By feeding, you'll get continuous, sure-fire catches of the heftiest bluegill you ever hooked into!" Pachner says. He's designed an easy way to do it and he's come up with data to show that the method works. Leo Pachner has made "instant fishing" a reality. "Along lakeshores and in ponds," according to Pachner, "bluegill and even bass and other freshwater game fish can be fed, fattened and caught where you want 'em!"

Discovering how to produce better crops of fish and telling others about what he's learned is Leo Pachner's business. His *Farm Pond Harvest* is a unique magazine for pond owners and those who fish in ponds. A veteran *Chicago Tribune* Fishing School instructor, Pachner teaches fishing classes at annual sessions for Kankakee Community College in Illinois, and at occasional seminars. He is well-known in the fishing tackle trade as a designer and former manufacturer.

Feeding program produced these prime, extra-chunky bluegills from undersized fish. Weight more than doubled in short time.

"Just reporting is not in my purpose," Pachner says. "Our magazine staff is constantly in the field testing the information that comes to us from biologists, conservationists, and other technicians. And we work out our own methods of getting more and better fish."

Pachner's quest for bigger and better bluegill started in a pond, and led to the development of a management tool he believes could change the fishing habits of a nation. Prospects for good pond fishing dwindle when the fishing-out doesn't match the hatching-out; the result is stunted fish. The reason? Simply not enough food to go around. The solution? Pachner found it.

One solution would be to draw down the whole works, or seine out or poison the stunted fish—which would destroy all normal-sized fish too—and restock with fingerlings. This, of course, would mean no fishing at all for a couple of years. Pachner had a better idea.

"Stunted fish have a grocery problem," he reasoned. "Why not increase the victuals instead of decreasing the fish?" So he and his co-workers gathered some 300 stunted bluegill into a floating cage and fed them commercial pellets, the kind used in some catfish and trout ponds to produce thousands of pounds of fish per acre. The bluegill were mostly three and four inches long and well below average weight.

The scheme worked. By the end of a five-month feeding period, the fish had grown beyond expectations. Most were now from five to seven inches long, showing a gain in length that normally takes two years! Weight increase had more than kept pace with growth. According to Illinois Department of Conservation charts, five-inch bluegill could be expected to weigh 2¾ ounces, but the once-skinny fish that had reached that length weighed 4¼ ounces. Seven-inch bluegill in Illinois usually weigh about 5 ounces; Pachner's seven-inch fish weighed 6¼ ounces. Some were 7½ to 8 inches long and weighed as much as 8¼ ounces.

"These formerly stunted fish were the chunkiest bluegill you ever laid eyes on!" Pachner reported. We knew

Tiered trays of Farm Pond Harvest Stand-up Feeder make it easy for fish to feed in water 3 to 5 feet deep.

we were on to something good for maximum pond production."

Free-swimmers congregated daily to scrounge food drifting out of the cage. A feeder was quickly designed to accommodate them, and the fish made immediate and vigorous use of it. If fish could be counted on to take up residence around a feeding station as these had, that spot would offer excellent fishing.

Bill McLarney of the New Alchemy Institute East, Woodshole, Massachusetts has produced scientific data to show that bluegills in one Michigan lake ranged no further than 65 yards. A third of them hadn't moved at all from where they were originally captured and tagged. Sunfish, and rock and black bass display similar characteristics. Some sunfish and rock bass studied in an Indiana stream over a four-year period—virtually the entire adult life span of some of the fish—did not travel more than 200 feet, even under severe flood conditions. Black bass kept within a 400-foot range.

More evidence of the bluegill's homebody tendencies comes from a survey of the fish in a ten-acre quarry in the middle of a Kankakee, Illinois city park. It was stocked fifty years ago. Park regulations prevent fishermen from removing many of the busily reproducing fish. Consequently, the severely overpopulated body of water might be expected to harbor no normal-sized fish. Where limestone cliffs tower at the water's edge, it does produce only stunted fish. But there are plenty of good-sized fish in the water along the level shores where park visitors toss in a generous supply of bread and other food. Fish receiving the extra food apparently aren't wandering off to other parts of the quarry. Sportfishing along those shores where fish have been fed would produce fish worth catching.

Pond owners, if they want to repeat Pachner's success, now have their choice of two Farm Pond Harvest Feeders. One is a stand-up, tiered-tray device designed to make the best use of inexpensive pellets in water three to five feet deep. Fish nose right into the trays to feed. The other is a floating feeder for use in deep water. A combination of wire mesh and floats, it attaches conveniently to a dock or pier.

"Pond owners, sportsmen's clubs, conservation departments, individual anglers, or people who have cottages on lakeshores, can use these feeders to maintain top populations of large, close-to-home bluegills," Pachner has pointed out. "Neighboring bass will soon be involved, too, because they seem to learn from the bluegills how to use feeders." Consistently good fishing that isn't left to chance and that doesn't depend on going all over the lake—that's what I call instant fishing!"

Aquaculture—or "pond farming"—is a growing enterprise. Sportsmen's clubs, market-fish farmers, individuals who love to fish, fee-fishing enterprises, hatcheries, and a wide variety of governmental, commercial, or private owners utilize natural and artificial ponds and lakes to plant fingerlings and harvest crops of fish. They use converted quarries, strip mines, or gravel pits. They use the thousands of waterfilled excavations called "borrow pits" left by interstate highway construction gangs that remove dirt to build raised roadway approaches. The number of all ponds available is growing daily.

Carefully stocked and nurtured, these bodies of water offer some of the finest sportfishing found anywhere. And businesses based on well-managed ponds are thriving.

As a recreational resource the pond is unsurpassed. Americans are travelling farther and searching harder to find uncrowded recreation areas. The close-to-home pond on one's own or a friend's land, on private club land, or on public club land used for a moderate fee, to many people wishing to fish is a welcome alternate to a far-distant lake. An angler can get out any day the "signs" are right, even for just an hour or two before or after work. In Illinois, a state that shares the Lake Michigan shoreline and is criss-crossed with streams, nearly half the licensed fishermen now make all their catches in ponds.

For many thousands of families, the pond is as reliable a family food source as the backyard garden, and just as money-saving. For the owner of a fee-fishing pond, the pond can produce instant money as well as instant fishing. And a pond can produce many varieties of fish in commercially harvestable volume as well.

Japan has long made excellent use of closed water fish farming. Fertilization procedures were pioneered there. Pond-raised carp—for gefilte fish—is an important Israeli export. In the United States, channel catfish and rainbow trout are often raised to "butchering" size. In 1971, more than a hundred tons of such fish, raised mostly in ponds, were marketed in the U.S. and Canada to restaurants or for over-the-counter sale. Bass and bluegill could conceivably be raised in the same volume with new feeding methods.

The increasing popularity of pond fishing naturally expands the demand for fingerlings for restocking. The demand for baitfish also goes up, and existing government and private sources can no longer supply sufficient numbers of many species of fingerlings to meet it. Alert pond owners are learning how to turn a profit from their own private hatcheries.

But good ponds don't just happen. Ten years ago, Roger Harms, Illinoisian who owned some rural land, decided to construct a pond in conjunction with a small stream that meandered through his land. He hired a bulldozer and dug out about a half-acre of earth to form his basin. Spring rains helped fill the excavation. Picturing the beauties that would soon be jumping there, Harms jubilantly planned orders to bluegill and bass hatcheries. He proposed to put the fish in as soon as the mud settled. The mud didn't settle—the water did! By mid-summer Harms had a little stream trickling into a wide muddy hole where the water seeped into the ooze and disappeared. Inadequate watershed coupled with underground drainage had robbed Harms of his dream.

Jim Gordon, another Illinois resident, runs a successful fee-fishing business at the pond he originally built for his own fun. He opens it to fee-fishing, however, only when he thinks he's getting an over-supply of fish. Gordon knows that if a part of the fish are removed regularly, the remaining fish will grow larger. Young fish will have a better chance to grow up. Besides earning him a good supplemental income—fishermen pay him $5 per day plus 10¢ per inch for any trout they take over the limit of five—fee-fishing insures Gordon's own continued

good fishing. With respect to ponds, the more one is fished the better the fishing is likely to get.

"Know-how makes the big difference," Leo Pachner says. "You have to do more than dig a hole and fill it with water. And when you have a holeful of water and fish, you can waste the whole works or you can manage it the same way a modern farmer manages his land, and with the same highly productive results."

Pachner's *Farm Pond Harvest* is a pioneer in the field. He created the magazine in 1967 to narrow a communications gap between technicians and fishermen, between biologists and commercial producers, "between people and fish," as he has put it. Circulation has increased tenfold in five years. "I've always loved to fish," Pachner says, "and I got into this thing because I couldn't stand to see the waste going on for lack of a few simple facts."

As Pachner has pointed out, engineering and even financial help are available from the government to avoid construction disasters like the Roger Harms mudhole. "And you can't toss in any old fish you take a fancy to. The ecology of a pond is a delicate thing. 'Hit or miss' stocking guarantees a 'miss'—an out-of-balance pond that can take years to reclaim. We tell how to avoid that, but, if it's already happened, in the magazine we tell what to do about it."

Weeds can be as much of a problem in a pond as they are in a cornfield. But, Pachner says, "Aggravation is giving way to information. "We're getting rid of weeds, we're finding better ways of harvesting—sportfishing included—and we're growing bigger fish."

The results of Pachner's bluegill feeding experiment convinced him that supplemental feeding is here to stay as a pond-management tool. It leads to maximum pond production. To the businessman, this means money; to the sportsman, it means superb fishing—a bonanza any way you look at it.

If you own or are planning a pond, if you have a home on a lake, or if you just like to fish, you can learn more about "instant fishing" and feeding and management programs from *Farm Pond Harvest*, Box 884FB, Kankakee, Illinois, 60901.

Farm Pond Harvest Floating Feeder serves the fish at dock or pier, with no limit on depth of water.

37

Salt Water Tips

These 25 tips will aid Atlantic, Gulf, and Pacific anglers in getting more fish.

1. Brightly-colored nylon monofilament line is a boon to the blue-water, deep-sea angler trolling baits far astern. Lines of brilliant orange or yellow show up clearly, whereas ordinary mono far out is virtually invisible.

   When you can see your line readily regardless of how much line is out, line tangles become rare. Even more important, good line visibility makes it simpler to "drop back" properly when billfish strike baits.

2. As in fresh water fishing, the salt water angler must be careful to see that hooks are always needle-sharp. Whether fishing for tarpon, Atlantic blue marlin, or Pacific yellow-tails, always be certain that hooks are as sharp as possible.

   Stones or very small files will do to sharpen the smaller hooks, but the bigger salt water hooks will require filing with a good-size file. Sharpen hooks with firm strokes of the file *away from the barb*.

3. The condition of the tide, not time-of-day, has the greater effect on salt water fishing. Some salt water species strike best on incoming or rising tide; others on a falling or outgoing tide.

   Generally speaking, many salt water fish will move shoreward on an incoming or flooding tide to feed in close, while some salt water species will feed heavily at river mouths and in estuaries as a falling or ebb tide brings down baitfish, crustaceans, and other food.

   The condition of the tide, and the movement of offshore currents, even have an effect on fishing for billfish many miles out in the ocean.

4. In heavy salt water fishing, as in tarpon angling or taking sailfish and marlin, it is desirable to "set" the hook in a striking fish not once but several times. Some species, notably tarpon and billfish, are particularly difficult to hook so hooks must be driven home several times.

5. When arranging an offshore charter fishing trip, be sure you fully understand the deal. In some areas, for example, it is the rule that the charterboat captain gets the fish that are caught. And some skippers might charge a rental fee if they provide the tackle, though in most areas tackle is provided at no additional cost—unless the tackle is lost or damaged.

6. Some salt water big game fishermen are proud that they do not use a gaff. They claim that no gaff is needed if a fish is properly played out. The question is, who is going to determine with authority when a really big salt water gamefish, say a Pacific blue marlin, is "properly played out."

Live broadbill swordfish have been known to put their swords through 20 inches of oak, and the thrashing tail of a broadbill can make a shambles of a small boat.

When there are such fish involved, big billfish or giant sharks, it is wise to use a gaff, and a gaff of 8 feet or so isn't too short.

7. Most big-game fishermen prefer a shoulder harness rather than a kidney harness as an aid in fighting giant blue-water fish.

Kidney harnesses, such as the Dixon "saddle back" for example, keep all of the pressure of fighting a giant salt water fish on the angler's extreme lower back. Shoulder harnesses, on the other hand, put the pressure on the angler's shoulders and back, where he has the most strength and resistance to the pull of the fish.

8. Most fishermen who want flounders use live minnows, which they fish right on bottom, knowing that flounders have a habit of burying themselves in the sand bottom and hiding in wait for minnows.

However, few fishermen know that flounders will readily strike a streamer fly if presented to them correctly. Try fly fishing for flounders with a fast-sinking fly line and a lively streamer fly pattern, such as a white marabou or silver body, letting the sinking line take the fly down, then creeping the fly slowly over the bottom. If there are flounders around, they'll be sure to take.

9. Most salt water anglers using spinning tackle prefer monofilament line. For the light salt water outfit, lines testing from 8 to 10 pounds are best. For the medium-weight spinning outfit, lines of about 12 pounds may be used, while the heaviest spinning outfits call for lines of 15 to 20 pounds.

To withstand the shock of casting and the wear-and-tear on a line that comes from fishing around reefs, rocks, piers, etc., most fishermen tie heavier nylon "leaders" to their lines. Such leaders may be 5 or 10 feet long, depend-

ing upon tackle and fishing conditions, and they will test 5 or 10 pounds, or more, heavier than the fishing line.

10. It is a common error among many salt water anglers to increase the drag on their reels as a hooked fish runs out line. A fish is hooked and goes running off, streaking out yards and yards of line. The normal reaction to this by the average angler is to increase drag tension in hopes of slowing the fish. Nothing could be more wrong. In fact, increasing the drag tension as a fish runs out a great quantity of line will almost surely result in losing the fish. The reason for this is that the drag tension increases *automatically* as a fish runs out great lengths of line.

As line feeds out of a reel with a pre-set drag tension, the drag increases. For example, a 6-inch reel spool, with the drag set at 30 pounds, will provide a 30-pound drag so long as there is sufficient line on the spool to fill the 6-inch diameter. However, when a fish takes enough line to decrease the diameter of the line on the spool to 5 inches, then the drag resistance will increase to 36 pounds. At 4-inch diameter the drag will be 45 pounds, at 3-inch, 60 pounds, and at 2-inch, 90 pounds—probably more than enough, several times over, to snap the line—and another prize fish is lost.

11. Even in this day of countless electronic fishing devices, a great many charterboat skippers and non-professional big game fishermen after sailfish, marlin, and other billfish spend their time relentlessly trolling over the surface. Yet studies have proved that sailfish, as well as other billfish, are down deep as frequently as they are anywhere near the surface.

White marlin and Atlantic sailfish, for example, have been observed frequently by deep-going divers at depths of 100 feet and more. So . . . when surface trolling doesn't bring billfish, try going deep.

12. The "End Loop Knot" (see knots section) is one of the best for tying jigs and other salt water lures to heavy monofilament line.

This knot forms a large loop around the lure's "eye" so that the lure will have a natural, free action when worked through the water. Much of a lure's natural, built-in action is destroyed when tying very heavy nylon tight up against a lure's eye.

13. Generally speaking, there are three basic hook positions when baiting with live baitfish. You can hook a fish through both lips, through the eye sockets, or through the top of the back.

When hooking through the back, the hook can be passed through the baitfish in front or behind the dorsal fin, or at the dorsal by pushing the hook through the center of the fish's body, below the dorsal fin, entering one side of the fish and exiting at the opposite side.

When baiting through the eye-sockets, insert the point of the hook carefully through the fish's eye-sockets between the eyes and the bony structure around the eys. With the lip hook-up, the hook should be passed through the bottom lip first and then on through the upper lip. This will cause the hook to ride point up, and also keep the baitfish riding properly in the water.

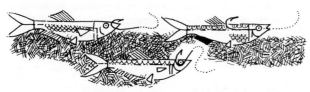

14. Salt water anglers with "know-how" take full advantage of the various conditions that result from tide change. For example, if fishing in an area where geography permits them to be in position before or after the tide change, they are able to successfully fish several choice spots in the course of the day. Since a tide change occurs at a specific time at a specific place every day, the change can be forecast either earlier or later at some other location. Smart bridge fishermen, learned in tide prediction, will drive from bridge to bridge to fish each spot at the exactly best time, according to the tide.

The same technique can be employed equally well by skiff fishermen. Estuarian areas, with typical tidal creeks and winding march channels, often are sufficiently broken to create a great variation in tide conditions. In such places, a tide change can vary as much as three hours spot-to-spot, even though only a few miles separate the areas.

15. A "leaded" mullet is the perfect trolling bait for bluefin tuna, and it also is used frequently by anglers after billfish or when fishing in heavy seas that otherwise would keep tossing an ordinary bait high into the air.

To rig a mullet with lead slide an egg sinker (one to two ounces), onto the leader wire before inserting the wire

through the head of the mullet and the hook. After the wire is inserted in the bait and is ready to be wrapped, slide the sinker down to beneath the mullet's lower jaw and hold it there as you make a tight wrap with the wire.

Rigged as described, a mullet will troll beautifully, staying trim and "natural," yet it will stay down well below the surface.

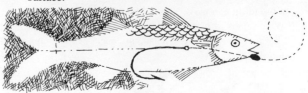

16. Striped bass can be tough to catch. They're temperamental, move a lot, and frequently change feeding habits from day-to-day.

It's most important to first locate stripers, striving always never to fish "empty" water but only places where the fish are.

Small school stripers generally frequent inlets, small bays, and river mouths. Fish for them around piers, bridges, and breakwaters. Surf casters try for the big stripers around the inside of sandbars, rocks, deep holes, and tidal breaks.

Boatmen after striped bass watch the birds, moving to areas where gulls or terns are seen diving on baitfish driven to the surface by schools of heavy-feeding bass. The same bird-watching tactic also works when fishing for bluefish.

17. There never will be one "all-purpose" rod for salt water fishing. But for the beginning salt water angler who will not be doing any deep-sea trolling for billfish or crowded party-boat fishing, the ideal starting outfit would be a spinning rod of 8 to 9 feet, with medium "heavy" action.

The reel to match naturally would be an open-face spinning reel, with a good strong drag, and a line capacity of at least 300 yards of 15-pound test monofilament line.

18. Eels are slippery, strong, squirmy—tough to get onto a hook. An old towel or burlap bag will help in holding them for hooking, or when removing one that you've caught. Another way is to keep a bucket of sand handy, and to wet your hand then dip it into the sand before grasping an eel.

19. Many varieties of important gamefish relish live eels. They are superb baits, in fact, for striped bass and large bluefish.

When using a live eel for bait, hook it through both lips, first passing the hook point through the eel's lower jaw, then through the top lip. Some fishermen hook eels through the top of the back, still others hook them through the tail.

When an eel has been hooked to use for bait, it should be tossed overboard immediately. If there is any delay, the eel will squirm and twist the line or leader into a horrible mess. But when tossed into the water, a hooked eel will swim and not twist and foul your line.

20. Too many salt water anglers become lure collectors.

There is no need to be a walking tackle shop, with every imaginable lure, regardless of the species of fish sought. Instead of procuring a great variety of spoons, jigs, and plugs, try to stick to the best known, popular, and time-tested lures. Get these known "killers" in different sizes and colors, and you'll be well-equipped for any salt water fishing situation.

21. "Do-it-yourself" billfishing is growing in popularity. Used to be that the only sailfish, marlin, and other billfish caught were those taken off the sterns of expensive ocean-going cruisers, but today outboard motors and small boats are so well built, so dependable that countless salt water anglers are going out to sea with them, at least far enough to tangle with bluewater billfish.

Timing is important to the small boat billfisherman. Since small boat anglers naturally cannot go running all over the ocean, they must keep close tabs on billfish migrations, and know where the schools are *now,* and where they will show *next.* The small boat angler must be ready to move out at a moment's notice, the instant that sailfish, marlin or swordfish are in close enough for him to get action.

A tip for these "mosquito fleet" billfish anglers: troll a large tandem rig of sewn natural baits, with keel and flashy spinners. This looks like a baitfish chasing a school of smaller fish. A flashy salt water spoon on a second rod, trolled by the tandem rig, also will get fish.

22. The versatile lead-head jig is probably the most effective, all-around salt water lure.

Rig a lead-head with porkrind strip, or nylon or rubber skirting for added effectiveness. A jig tipped with a piece of shrimp is a fantastic lure for bonefish, permit, and many other species. A strip of fish flesh or skin on the hook of a jig is a real fish-getter, too, and a jig with a whole ballyhoo (balao) is often just the ticket for big jewfish, etc.

23. Good marlin rigs are made from whole, dead bonito—mostly 3, 4, or 5 pounds, although 10 pound bonito are used, too. The common bonito is preferred over the white bonito because the common has a very hard head and can be fished all day.

The larger bonito are best when the angler is really out for marlin and wants little interference from sailfish. Sailfish will strike the larger baits but generally all they do is mess them up: there's seldom a hookup between angler and sail' and so no lost time.

24. Veteran surf anglers of Assateague Island, in Maryland, believe that channel bass, or redfish, come in closest to the beaches on the flood tide, and drop back out with the outgoing tide.

Moreover, when fishing at night—certainly one of the best times—they keep auto lights down dim and off the water for fear of spooking fish.

25. Night is really the prime time to fish for many salt water species. This includes striped bass, flounders, sea trout, tarpon, and snook, to name just a few of the fish that really "work" at night.

Most of these fish seem to have preferred feeding times, according to the tide, when they are on the cruise, and if you hit a place just right one night, and get fish, go back the next night an hour later (allowing for the change in tide time) and chances are you'll get the same good fishing enjoyed the night before.

38

Muskie Secrets: Fish Long, Hard

Keeping a lure in the water, hour-after-hour, is more than half the secret to catching muskies.

One reason why so many fishermen have a mania for muskies; they fight with abandon.

There are two kinds of fresh water fishermen: those who fish for muskies, and those who don't.

The muskellunge has been cussed and discussed from Canada to the Mississippi Valley. Arguments for and against "Old Needlenose" rise in executive suites and over back yard fences. Nothing is ever resolved by such debates except possibly all agree that "once a muskie fisherman, always a muskie fisherman!"

One day following some great bass fishing on Lac Court O'Reilles near Hayward, Wis., Willie Weaver and I strolled down to the dock. A lone fisherman was just pulling in. He had the most elaborate tackle I ever saw, as well as the longest face I ever saw on a fisherman.

"Any luck?" Willie asked.

"Naw!" snarled the incoming angler. "Fished all day. Started before sun-up. Not one lousy strike!"

"That's funny," I said, "Willie and I got a couple dozen smallmouths apiece."

"*Smallmouths!*" roared the unhappy fisherman. "Who the hell wants bass? I'm a *muskie* fisherman!"

We learned later that the guy damn well *was* a "muskie fisherman." The camp owner told us that the man had started fishing exclusively for muskies ten years ago. Each season he fished for muskies at every opportunity from the day the season opened in May until it closed in November. The guy fished for muskies on weekends, on holidays, and throughout his three-weeks annual vacation. In those ten years, our wild-eyed "muskie fisherman" had caught a total of three muskies. They weighed eight and a quarter pounds, eleven pounds, and thirteen and a half pounds. That's a total of thirty-two and three-quarters pounds of muskie meat in ten years of angling!

That's how addicted muskie fishermen are. They figure the sun rises and sets in the muskie bays and nowhere else. They are convinced that in all the world there is only one fish—*Esox Masquinongy*—The Great One, Himself, the Mighty Muskellunge!

What is the great attraction of muskie fishing? What causes "muskie mania," that burning desire to catch muskies and more muskies?

Possibly the major appeal of muskie fishing is that the muskie is the largest fresh water gamefish the angler may hope to catch. Some catfish and sturgeon exceed maximum muskie weights, but they are not generally rated as gamefish. The world's record muskie, taken in New York's St. Lawrence River in 1957 by Arthur Lawton, weighed sixty-nine pounds, fifteen ounces— but muskies of fifty to fifty-five pounds are caught annually. Muskies in the forty pound class are taken with considerable regularity and, looking at the nation's muskie records as a whole, thirty pound fish are common.

Something else that probably adds to the appeal of muskie fishing is that most muskie angling is done in shallow inland lakes and rivers—places that usually produce modest-size fish such as bass, walleyes, and pike. The fisherman normally works from a small boat with light, fresh water tackle. All that adds up to explosive excitement when a muskie wallops a lure.

Considering availability and distribution alone, a good-size muskie *has* to be fresh water's biggest prize. Compared to other fresh water species—including lake trout—muskies simply are not plentiful, . . . *anywhere.*

Fishery biologists have estimated it takes four to five acres of productive water to support one mature muskie. Some fishermen cast away a lifetime and never catch a decent muskie. This fishing might be likened to deer hunting. No one gets very excited over shooting a rabbit, yet all the neighbors come for a look when Uncle Joe shoots a buck.

Because muskies are anything but numerous, many sportsmen refer to muskie fishing as muskie "hunting." A lot of time is passed just trying to locate a muskie. Much of the time muskie fishing comes down to routine casting (or trolling where permitted), casting, casting, casting— to that stump, to this log, over that reef, along those weeds. The best muskie fisherman I know estimates he executes an average of 5,000 casts for each muskie caught. That's a lot of casting for *one* fish!

Where is the best muskie fishing? Wisconsin? Ontario?

Giant muskies like this are not everyday occurances, not anywhere.

The St. Lawrence? Where?

It isn't easy to pin-point the world's best muskie waters, no more than it is easy to state—on the basis of ordinary catch reports—when is the best time to go muskie fishing. How good muskie fishing is at a given place or given time can not be determined solely on the total number of fish caught. What is important is the "man hours" of fishing, and the quantity of fish caught. In simpler form, if 100 anglers fish Big Stuff Lake one day and catch ten muskies, that's not as good as ten anglers fishing Small Fry Lake and taking five muskies. If your arithmetic is a little rusty, the Big Stuff Lake catch comes down to one muskie caught for each ten fishermen, while the Small Fry Lake statistics amount to one muskie boated for each *two* fishermen. Thus at Small Fry the angler had a 50-50 chance, or 2-to-1, that he'd catch a muskie, while anglers at Big Stuff faced 10-to-1 odds. Obviously Small Fry Lake has the better fishing.

Ratio of effort-to-catch is the thing.

The same sort of science applies to *when* to go muskie fishing. The Wisconsin Conservation Department has interesting data on muskie catches. They've shown, season-after-season, that more muskies are caught from Wisconsin lakes and rivers in August than during all other open-season periods combined. Many fishermen therefore assume that the time to go for muskies in Wisconsin is August. Nothing could be more wrong. The August catches are high because this is the peak vacation month—and Dad and Mom and the kids have rolled out of cities such as Chicago, Milwaukee, Des Moines, and Detroit, and come to loaf and fish and swim at good old Lake Winnibigoshamitty. And so a pile of muskies are caught that month. But there's a pile of people fishin' for them.

The same Wisconsin statistics show that a small core of dyed-in-the-wool, *smart* and *experienced* muskie fishermen go in October and early November—and catch quite a few muskies. The ratio of catch to man-hours of fishing is far, far higher in October and the first-half of November than at any other time through the season. Thus catch statistics, when properly analyzed, prove that late fall is the best time to fish for muskies.

It's a little more difficult to pin-point the best muskie waters because catch statistics and fishermen-efforts are not maintained throughout this country's muskie states and Canada. But certainly Wisconsin has more lakes and rivers containing good populations of muskellunge than any other state. Close behind Wisconsin—in total number of muskie waters—are Michigan and Minnesota. Southern Canada offers some superb muskie fishing. Other states whose muskie fishing occasionally gets attention include Pennsylvania, Ohio, West Virginia, Tennessee, and Kentucky.

One of the very best muskie lakes in Wisconsin is Big Arbor Vitae near the town of Woodruff. Other exceptional muskie lakes include Chippewa Flowage, Flambeau Flowage, Spider Lake, Lac Court O'Reilles, Lake Tomahawk, the Eagle River Chain of Lakes, and Big St. Germain Lake—which is naming just a few. In general Wisconsin's muskie waters are all in the northern third of the state, from the north-central part to the northwestern counties. Good towns to headquarter for muskie fishing in Wisconsin's north country include Hayward (self-proclaimed "muskie capital"), Woodruff, Rhinelander, and Eagle River.

Wisconsin's north-central Vilas County conducts a "Muskie Marathon" promotion each year, and perhaps some of those figures will be of interest. In the '69 season the best muskie entered was a fish weighing forty-three and a half pounds, taken from Plum Lake near the town of Sayner. The second-place fish, thirty-seven pounds, thirteen ounces, came out of Twin Lake near Phelps, and

This big muskie was taken on a stout rod and salt water type reel at a lake in Sawyer County, Wisconsin.

the third, thirty-six and a half pounds, was caught at Lac Vieux Desert. I should have pointed out Vieux Desert earlier as one of the state's very best muskie lakes. All told, 1,257 muskies were entered in the Vilas County muskie marathon in 1969. Their combined weights reached 15,012 pounds!

In Michigan the St. Clair River has good muskie fishing, and Lake St. Clair, at Detroit, is a very popular and very productive muskie trolling area. Homer LeBlanc, a guide operating out of the suburban town of St. Clair Shores, scores repeatedly on large fish in Lake St. Clair.

Minnesota's best-known muskie lake is Leech Lake, where in one short period one season dozens of very large muskies were taken. Cass Lake is very good, too, as in Lake Winnibigoshish, and Moose and Spider Lakes.

Ontario's best-known muskie lake is probably Lake-of-the-Woods at Kenora. This isn't to say it remains *the* best muskie lake in the province, but it has been longest fished and most publicized, and therefore is best-known. And it's good, too. A friend of mine, Ray Ostrom of Minneapolis, maintains a huge and expensive houseboat on Lake-of-the-Woods solely to capitalize on its muskies—many of which go well over forty pounds.

Eagle Lake, at the town of Vermilion Bay, Ontario (due north of Fort Frances-International Falls), has some remarkable muskie fishing and, suprisingly, few fishermen take advantage of it. There are many camps on Eagle Lake, but I'd like to recommend one in particular: it is Norm Berry's Little Norway Camp, close to the town of Vermilion Bay. First of all, this camp is all you'd want it to be for overall accommodations and food; secondly, Norm is a skilled and addicted muskie fisherman. The only time, that is the *best* time, to fish Eagle's muskies is in the fall, September and October. The weather may be rough—cold for sure and snow probable—but if you *go at it* and fish you are almost certain to have quite a lot of muskie action in the course of a few days of serious fishing.

Another good Ontario muskie lake is Lower Manitou, a fly-in lake not far north of Fort Frances. Since it's stiff with smallmouth bass, walleyes, and some lake trout, it is underfished in the muskie department.

Pennsylvania has muskies in Pymatuning Reservoir, Lake Erie, Shenango and Allegheny rivers, Conneaut Lake, and Lake LeBoeuf. Ohio has muskies in Rocky Fork Lake, the Muskingum River and other waters; in West Virginia, Elk River has a muskie population, and other muskies can be found in Little Kanawha River, Hughes and Pocatalico rivers; Obed River and Crab Orchard Creek in Tennessee are among that state's most popular muskie areas; while in Kentucky top muskie spots seem to be the Ohio, Barren, and Green rivers.

Finding a promising spot to fish for muskies is only one of the problems involved in catching one. Among other things that must be "just right" if you're to score on old "Hard Head" is your tackle.

The best all-around outfit for muskies is a baitcasting or plug casting outfit. Few other rigs will satisfy the addicted muskie hunter as much as a good plug casting outfit. A quality level-wind reel such as the Garcia Ambassadeur 5,000, filled with 15 to 25 lb. test line (depending on area fished), and a medium to heavy action rod mea-

suring five to six feet, is probably the most popular muskie rig.

Medium to heavy spinning and spin-cast outfits will do, too, and so will a heavy fly fishing outfit. If you're going to use those giant-size plugs and spoons that so many fishermen throw at muskies—lures weighing several ounces and measuring up to a foot in length—you'll need a heavy-duty, stout-action rod. This is necessary not because the muskie is a particularly tough fighter, but because it takes a fairly stiff rod to handle ultra-large lures.

Muskies are fair game for fly fishermen and, in fact, they'll take a big streamer fly about as greedily as will a northern pike—who likes nothing better than a five to six inch-long, red-and-yellow streamer.

Very few muskies have been taken on flies but this is not because the fly outfit is inadequate. Rather, it's because so few fishermen *try* for muskies with fly fishing tackle. I've had more muskie strikes on McNally Magnum streamers, actually, than on any other tackle.

My preferred fly outfit for muskies is a nine-foot, heavy-action glass rod, two-piece, weighing five to six ounces (depending on make). It takes a WF-9 (GAF) line, and I use a quality single-action reel. The leader is no less than nine feet long, more commonly twelve to fourteen feet, and tapered down to twelve pounds with a twelve-inch "shock" tippet of forty to sixty pound test nylon monofilament.

Muskellunge will take either popping bugs or streamer flies. If using poppers, don't fish ordinary fresh water type bass bugs; rather, use salt water type popping and skipping bugs, ones that are strongly-made with large, tough hooks. You'd have a bad time trying to sink the hook into the rock-hard jaw of a muskie if you used an ordinary bass-type popper, and if you did manage to get

Many fishermen disdain the use of bait on muskies, even dead suckers like this, but some fishermen insist "Old Needlenose" can be taken only with "meat."

the hook into him he'd probably lose no time straightening it out for you.

My favorite streamers for muskies are ones of my own design. It is neither my intention nor need to become commercial here, but I haven't yet found better flies for muskellunge than the "McNally Magnum" and "McNally Smelt." Both of these streamer patterns range in length from five to seven inches, and therefore they more nearly approach forage-fish size than do ordinary commercially-made streamers. If you're interested in these flies they are made to order by pro-tyer Jim Poulos, 411 Stone, Wheeling, Illinois. Other flies that also work well on muskies are the salt water varieties, particularly patterns intended for tarpon fishing. Phillip's Fly and Tackle Company, Alexandria, Pennsylvania, makes some good streamers for muskies—including their "blonde" series of bucktails (1/0 to 5/0 hooks), and their "bead-head" multi-wing streamers.

Regardless of the *kind* of tackle (bait casting, spinning, etc.) you elect to pursue muskies with, be sure to use a "shock" tippet or leader. The fly-rodder needs a heavy tippet, as indicated, but the caster or troller also should attach a length of heavy nylon to the business end of his line, or a wire leader. I personally abhor wire; I think it shies fish away, destroys lure action, and is lousy to cast. But this is a matter of preference; certainly the majority of muskie fishermen use six to twelve-inch wire leaders, with snaps and swivels attached.

A heavy nylon or light wire leader is needed in muskie fishing because Himself, The Great One, has a maw full of needles and spikes that can easily cut and fray a line. There are many thousands of tiny teeth on a muskie's tongue and palate, and these too will wear a line through quickly.

Muskies will hit a variety of lures.

The majority of muskies are taken on large surface plugs, but I don't know if that attests to the appeal a surface lure has to muskies, or merely that the bulk of muskie fishermen use top-water baits. Certainly the well-equipped angler will arm his tackle box with a good assortment of surface poppers, wobblers, creepers and sputtelers, but he should also have a variety of spoons, shallow and deep-running plugs, and ultra-deep lures such as lead-head jigs.

Porkrind baits are especially good, and don't fail to try a black porkrind "eel" attached to a weedless lead-head jig, casting it far back into weeds and snaking it slowly through across the shallow bottom. If there's a muskie around he'll have a tough time resisting it.

One of the top muskie producers—season after season—is a giant size spinner-and-bucktail combination. Large numbers of these lures are being made, and there's about as much variety in them as there is in ladies' hair-styles, but—as with the gals—all of them seem to make out, at least some places some of the time.

Most veteran muskie fishermen prefer a very fast retrieve when working lures, almost regardless of the type of lure. I've seen some muskie addicts work a top-water plug across the surface of a lake so fast a king mackerel would have trouble catching it. Apparently the results would indicate that muskies do, indeed, prefer a fast-moving lure, but when that fails the thinking angler will switch to halting, jerking, stop-and-go retrieves. Repeated casts to one spot often pay off, too.

While more muskies are taken on giant plugs and spoons than on smaller, bass-size lures, this is due as much to the fact that most fishermen use large baits as it may be to any preference on the part of the fish. So don't use big "muskie" plugs exclusively; when they fail, go to smaller baits. Remember that large lures take large fish, but small lures take small fish *and* large fish. Lures in the ⅜ to ⅝ range seem to be especially productive in hard-fished muskie lakes.

Keep hooks of lures needle-sharp, honing them frequently. A muskie's mouth is bone-hard and not easy to

Homer LeBlanc, well-known guide at Lake St. Claire at Detroit, Mich., shows what muskie fishing is all about. The fisherman who gets a brace like these comes back again and again.

drive a hook into. Always keep a taut line when retrieving, and the instant a fish hits rear back hard and fast with the rod to drive the hooks home. Set the hooks repeatedly, four, five, six times.

A muskie often will grab a plug sideways, just as it frequently strikes a sucker or a walleye. Holding the plug in its jaws this way makes it difficult, if not impossible, for the angler to move the plug to set the hooks. This is a common occurrence with muskies, and there isn't much one can do about it.

Many years ago E. L. "Buck" Rogers of Columbia, Missouri and I were fishing Long Lake near Phillips, Wisconsin. I was fishing from the bow, using a fly rod and yellow popping bug. I'd put a cast into a pocket in some lily pads, allowed the bug to rest motionless for a moment, then gave it a good *pop. Blam!* Water sprayed for yards around as a muskie hit. I reared back with the rod four or five times, hard as I could, to drive the hook home. Convinced the fish was solidly hooked, I settled down to play him. He jumped a couple times, then soon was at the boat, apparently played out. The water in Long Lake is as clear as air, and both Buck and I could see the muskie lying "dead" in the water ten feet down to one side of the boat. I put pressure on to bring the fish up, and I'll never forget what I saw then: the muskie simply opened his mouth, out floated the yellow bug, and it then came bobbing all the way up to the surface.

That muskie *never had been hooked,* but I was able to play him and to keep him on—even through some great *jumps*—because he never opened his mouth during the fight. The fish wasn't big, probably no more than eight or nine pounds, but he gave us a perfect exhibition of how a muskie will hit and hold a lure.

At its best muskie fishing is unpredictable, but they seem to be solitary by nature, so the angler who "covers" a lot of water and keeps his baits working is most likely to boat fish. Some fish remain in one small area throughout a season, or longer, unless they are too often disturbed, or driven out for some other reason, or caught. Often a fisherman will locate a muskie, that is, discover that a specific bay or point or log jam is "home" to a particular muskie, and ultimately catch the fish through repeated efforts.

Like most other fish, muskies migrate or roam to some extent, but as indicated they usually are solitary and do little traveling—generally preferring to haunt a weed bed, lily-filled bay, rocky reef, log-strewn shore, near a point or around the mouth of a feeder stream or river.

The majority of muskies caught are taken at depths of five to fifteen feet. But they do go deeper, particularly on bright, mid-summer days. A friend of mine once saw what he estimated to be thirty or forty muskies hanging under a ledge fifty-five feet down in Wisconsin's Lake Minocqua one August afternoon. He was skin-diving with a Dacor lung, so was able to observe the fish for some time.

A muskellunge may strike a lure at any time during the retrieve, or he may hit the instant the lure falls to the water, or not until it is almost back to the rod tip. A muskie fisherman *must* stay alert and be prepared to set the hooks instantly at any moment.

Muskies have an affinity for following or trailing a

A particularly handsome specimen of "tiger muskie," 44 pounds, 4 oz., courtesy of Orvil Klein, of West Bend, Wis. Orvil took his prize "tiger" from Pioneer Lake near the town of Eagle River, Wis.

moving lure. Every experienced muskie fisherman has seen, probably many times, the lurking bulk of a long, gray muskie detach itself from a stump, log or other cover, and come rolling up behind his lure—not to hit it but only to trail it all the way to the boat. The water humps up into a large "V" wake as the muskie closes in on the lure, his eyes fixed on it, and it is masterful understatement to say that at this moment the suspense to the fisherman is indescribable.

I prefer to speed up my retrieve when a muskie is seen following, moving the lure as fast as I can for several feet. If no strike, I halt the lure momentarily, then start moving it swiftly again in leaps and jerks. If a muskie follows all the way to the boat, baleful eyes glaring, there is nothing much to do except to swish the rod back-and-forth and make the lure continue to travel, in a figure "8", at boatside. Occasionally this continued action with the lure will trigger a strike. If the muskie doesn't hit and returns to cover, "rest" the area for a half-hour or so, then

One good way to lose a muskie; reel it up too close to the rod tip.

fish it again but with a completely different lure. If the fish earlier trailed a surface plug, offer him an underwater lure the next time around. If you fail to get the muskie after "resting" him, leave the area and don't try again for several hours. If the muskie still doesn't hit, don't try for him again for at least a couple of days.

The bulk of muskie veterans prefer cloudy, rainy, cold, wind-swept, dark days for their fishing. A couple of Milwaukee fishermen I know eagerly await the first snow storm of the year, and when it comes they drop all professional and domestic duties and rush to the northern "muskie country."

Catch statistics seem to support the good-fishing-in-bad-weather theory, and one reason for this could be that under such conditions muskies are not so well alerted to the presence of fishermen. Most muskie lakes are clear, a fish can see a boat a long way, and he also can spot a fisherman standing in a boat at fifty yards when weather is clear. Bright, warm days shouldn't be avoided, though, because some giant muskies have been caught during excellent weather conditions.

Sport fishing (and writing about it) is my business. It has made me a top living for twenty-five professional years. In the course of my work it has been my duty to fish around the world for all of the major gamefish species. But the hardest fish of all to catch, in my opinion, is that old Hardhead, the muskie.

I've known muskie addicts who lost their jobs over muskie fishing. One discovered a muskie he believed to be a new world's record. He kept trying for the fish day-after-day long after he was due back to work. Consequently, he lost a fine job.

Saddest of all, though, was the friend who lost a wife over muskie fishing. His wife used to call my wife and complain that "all he does is run up to lake so-and-so and fish muskies. We never see him because he's always off after muskies. One of these days I'm going to tell him that he'll have to make a choice, either it will be muskies or me."

She did.

And he did.

And, . . . that's right. He chose muskies!

39

Angler's Showcase

1. Recreonics, Inc., Stinson Beach, California recently announced "the development of a revolutionary new fishhook it has named The Grabber."

Because of mini-barbs and an extremely sharp point, this hook doesn't have to be set in the "traditional way," so says the manufacturer. In baiting The Grabber, there aren't any large barbs to gash or tear the bait and in order for the fish to take the bait it must also take the hook.

For the angler who wants to return his catch to the water, just spread the flesh around the hook with your fingers. This causes little damage to the fish.

It is available in a wide variety of sizes.

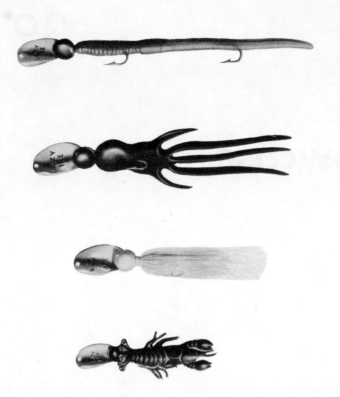

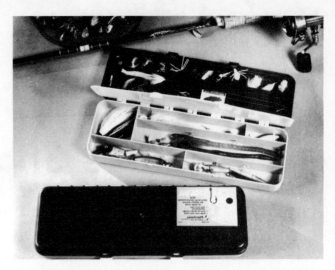

4. Flambeau Plastics Corporation, Baraboo, Wisconsin offers a Pocket Tackle Box that can be divided into two compartments. A separate cover, with lock tab, for the lid compartment will hold small items such as flies, hooks and sinkers. The bottom compartment has sections that are long enough to hold plastic worms and other large fishing lures. This box is $12 \times 4\frac{1}{2} \times 1\frac{3}{4}$ inches. Should it slip into the water, it will float even when fully loaded.

2. Lazy Ike Corporation, Fort Dodge, Iowa has added four new lures to their already famous line. Called Lazy Ike Wigly Series, the lures all have the "exclusive" jig head with built-in spoon.

The Wigly Squid, originally designed for saltwater, is equally effective now on fresh water fish. It measures 6½ inches of soft plastic and comes in six colors. The Wigly Crawler, also made of soft plastic, has the look of a nightcrawler. Five colors and four different sizes are available. The Wigly Crawfish, looking like its namesake and the Wigly Jig Ike, complete this fish-getting series.

3. Creek Chub Bait Company, Garrett, Indiana is now making its popular plastic Creek Chub Mouse available in wood.

This lure is a top water floater that "wiggles furiously" on surface or under water—depending on retrieving speed. There are five finishes to select from and it has two rust-resistant treble hooks. This particular lure is recommended by the manufacturer for fresh water gamefish.

5. Vlchek Plastics Company, Middlefield, Ohio is manufacturing two new tackle boxes—for the beginner and the advanced angler.

AdVenturer 1099 for the novice fisherman has a single, six-compartment tray and measures, overall, $12^3/_8 \times 7 \times 4^5/_8$ inches. It's priced at $2.98 and would be ideal for short trips and/or storing extra tackle.

AdVenturer 1987 sells for $26.95. It has extra large compartments, fifty-six in all. Designed to hold items that are needed by fresh and saltwater fishermen.

Both boxes, along with other features, are crushproof.

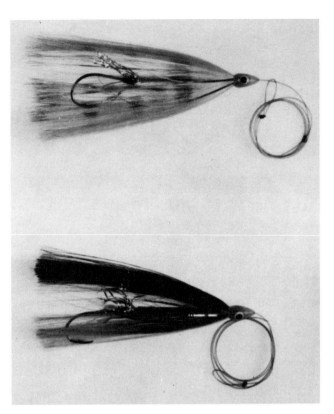

6. The Fenwick House, Miami, Oklahoma offers comfort for the fisherman who likes to sit 'n fish. This tackle box has a 3 inch foam rubber vinyl-covered cushion that tops the box. Doors open downward on either side, showing four cantilever style trays for small tackle and a large tray for the larger items. "Sit 'n Fish Tackle Box" uses basket-type handles for easy carrying. The box is made of strong metal and has a brown, wrinkle paint finish. Dimensions are $10 \times 12^1/_2 \times 19$ inches and the shipping weight is 16 pounds. Cost is $39.95 postpaid.

fluorescent fire-bead head. The body is of mylar, protected by clear tubing. There are additional mylar strips in the wings that add glitter and increase effectiveness. All four trolling flies have snelled long-shank hooks with 40-pound test leaders.

7. Bing McClellan of Burke Fishing Lures at Traverse City, Michigan has introduced four new salmon trolling flies called hotheds. The new lures are fashioned after the alewife, yellow perch, rainbow, and emerald shiner minnows.

These hotheds use Pola-Hair fibres that are locked into a

8. Woodstream Corporation, Lititz, Pennsylvania has added a new big lure, Flash Raposa, to the well-known "Old Pal" line. Designed with the big fish in mind, the $10^1/_2$ inch body is sure to catch bluefish, king salmon, muskies, and others.

Flash Raposa runs deep, depending on the retrieve speed, with a side-to-side glide and roll action and will float at rest. It is metallic-scaled and is available with black, blue or mackerel backs. Having been vacuum metallized, it is bright and shiny and best of all, it "sparkles" at any depth. A wire through the body locks head eye to trebles, thus helping to prevent the loss of fish or lost hooks.

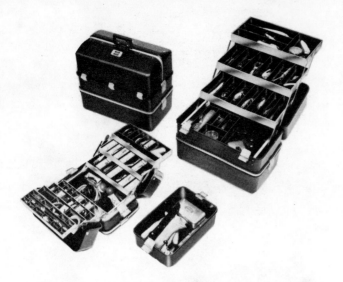

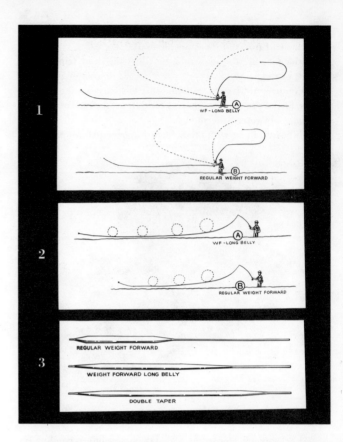

9. Umco Corporation, Cape Girardeau, Missouri has an outstanding array of tackle boxes. With the success of their Umco Possum Belly last year, they have added 27 new models giving them a total of over 50 different "possums."

New this year are the double possum bellies. They feature almost 2000 cubic inches additional storage space, leaving plenty of room for extra gear, food, and clothing.

Also of interest are the new single and double possum models that will have insulated inserts—making them "refrigerated" tackle boxes.

Umco backs all models with a 10-year guarantee. Suggested retail prices are from $31.00 to $68.00.

11. The Garcia Corporation of Teaneck, New Jersey introduces the Weight Forward-Long Belly Fly Line. This new line reportedly will let the angler make cast corrections throughout the cast. It also makes it possible to roll cast longer lengths of fly line—as all of the "belly" can be rolled for its full length, because of the forward tapers.

Retailing for less than $15, it is packaged in 30-yard coils.

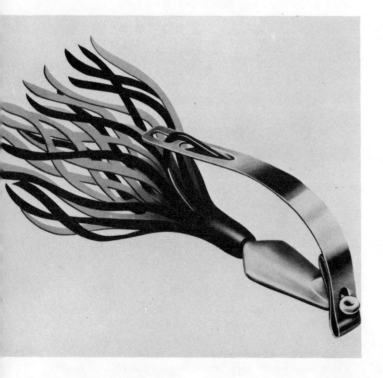

10. Subria Corporation, Montclair, New Jersey has a new lure called Ded-I-Wiggle that is sure to attract bass and other gamefish. Wearing a rubber skirt that comes in nine color combinations of solids and two toned—this lure can be interchanged with the Ded-I Jig and E-Z Bite weed guard. The Ded-I Wiggle is a bargain at the retail price of 85¢.

12. Tycoon Fin-Nor Corporation, Miami, Florida introduces its new Master Series. This series is a Fin-Nor reel with hand engraving. The fisherman can also have his name engraved on the reel during its manufacture. Price variations depending on the type reel selected.

13. Tycoon Fin-Nor Corporation, Miami, Florida now has available for the first time a brand new anti-reverse fly reel. This new Fin-Nor incorporates all the features of the firm's world famous fly reels, plus offering a new anti-reverse feature in which the handle does not turn while a hooked fish is running.

The reel uses the Fin-Nor "full circle" drag which is easily adjustable with a preset knob that is located on the right-hand side of the reel. The crank has a double handle and is inset into the reel housing to eliminate tangling line in the handle. The frame of the reel is from one-piece aluminum bar stock. There are no screws, no seams. This is truly an outstanding reel and would satisfy the most critical angler.

15. Sears, Roebuck and Company, Chicago, Illinois has a portable electronic Fish Finder that features an alarm signal that goes "beep." This unit can measure depths to 240 feet and has a "fish finding" range of 120 feet. The retail price is $169.

14. Shakespeare Company, Kalamazoo, Michigan is making a tackle outfit called "A Kit For A King."

There is a "money-back guarantee" on both rod and reel. The kit contains a push button reel with 12-pound test line and a matched six-foot, two-piece Wonderod. This outfit can be fished with either live bait or artificial lures.

16. United Binocular Company, Chicago, Illinois is offering a deluxe assortment of 15 quality flies at 20¢ each. These "economy priced" flies come in all sizes and colors with Streamers in both Feather and Bucktail designs.

Packaged in a plastic fly box with dividers and hinged cover with snap fastener—they include Muddlers, Streamers and Dry Flies.

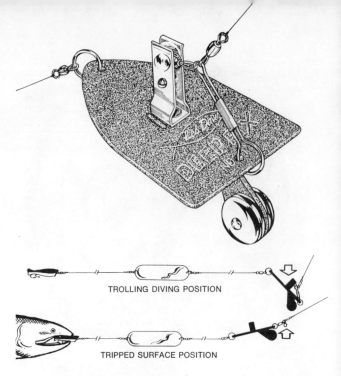

TROLLING DIVING POSITION

TRIPPED SURFACE POSITION

17.   Berkley and Company, Spirit Lake, Iowa offers a compact rod and reel travel case with the PRR-30 Spinning Outfit enclosed. The case is made of durable wood-grain and measures $3\frac{1}{2} \times 5\frac{1}{2} \times 22$ inches, making it a perfect fit for the suitcase of the travelling angler. It also features double locking latches and a carrying handle. ·

The fishing equipment consists of Berkley's Para/Metric Standard five-piece, seven-foot spinning rod with glass ferrules and curved taper design. Also the 4200A Adapter Spinning Reel that can be used in fresh and salt water. On the reel is 100 yards of 6-pound test Berkley Trilene monofilament, plus an extra 100 yard spool of 10-pound test and 125 yards of 17-pound test. Extra storage space and foam lining for "impact protection" are the remaining features.

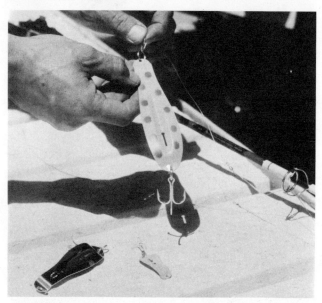

18.   From Reb Manufacturing Company, Pontiac, Michigan comes the Bayou-Special. This lure is effective on both salt and fresh water fish. It can be used for jigging, spin-casting or trolling and is especially effective during a slow retieve, so says the manufacturer.

Twenty different finishes that include eight in chrome with nickel, color striping, brass, copper and eight different color combinations. Capable of hooking most species of game fish, it comes in three different sizes.

19.   Les Davis Fishing Tackle Company, Tacoma, Washington offers the Deep Six diving sinker. Weighing less than four ounces, it is supposed to go to great depths while trolling without using heavy sinkers. The tension on the sinker is controlled by a small screw. Larger and heavier lures won't upset the tripping clip.

Davis explained that "the unique feature of the Deep Six diving sinker is a controlled tripping device which will trip when the fish hits. When this occurs the Deep Six is immediately planed to the surface."

20.   Burke Flexo-Products Company, Division of McClellan Industries, Inc., Traverse City, Michigan recently announced a new product called "Miracle Patch." This pocket-sized repair kit is an adhesive patch that is easily applied to almost any item

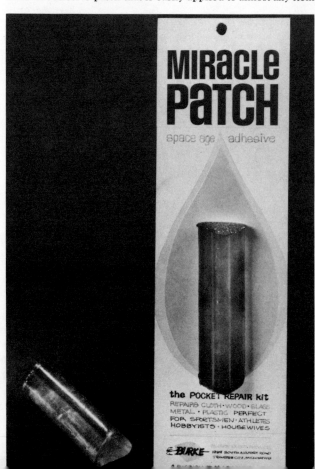

that is in need of repair—while out in the field or in the home.

It is flexible, waterproof, resilient and sold in one ounce sticks and works equally well on cloth, wood, glass, or metal.

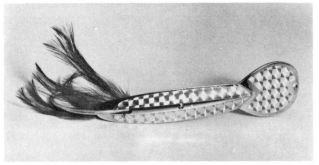

21. Glen L. Evans, Inc., Division of Gladding Corporation, Caldwell, Idaho introduces the Flectolite finish, a new fishing lure finish.

Its purpose is to break down the light rays in any water conditions, and to duplicate the colors of bait fish.

The loco lure and the Gad-about both have the new Flectolite finish.

22. Reel-Assist Corporation, Casper, Wyoming offers the fisherman an item called Reel-Assist, which clips onto the reel shank and holds the line in place, thus preventing any line tangles.

Merely unclip the line and run through the guides—and you're ready to fish. When finished, pull the line back through the guides and clip on the reel shank.

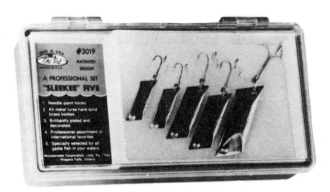

23. Woodstream Corporation, Lititz, Pennsylvania offers some new Old Pal selections. Five selected plugs and a matched set of six "Ultra-Lite" spoons—also the "Sleekee" assortment of five spoons in three sizes and made of solid brass.

The Master Lure set is a variety of six of the best Old Pal spoons. Finished in brilliant colors, this outfit can fit in the pocket of any fisherman.

24. Brandle Corporation, Morristown, New Jersey introduces the "Trig-Matic" Model S-410, an "almost automatic" spinning reel. It no longer is necessary to cock the bail with the left hand. There is a trigger geared to the bail and all the angler needs to do is take the line and trigger together with the tip of the index finger on the right hand. "Squeezing the trigger cocks the bail in the casting or open position and leaves the line under the tip of the finger ready for casting," so says the manufacturer.

When the handle is turned to bring back the line, the bail closes for level winding and returns the trigger to the upright position.

Along with a five-year warranty and a spare spool and spool case, the retail price is $29.95.

This reel has been designed for light salt water use and/or fresh water. Having been field tested for fifteen years the reel's other features include tungsten carbide line guide, machine cut gears, pinion ball bearings, multiple disc drag spools and positive anti-reverse.

25. Vyking Tackle Company, Palatine, Illinois offers just the lure for the fisherman who wants to make his own. A kit for the angler who likes fishing with worms is now available. These

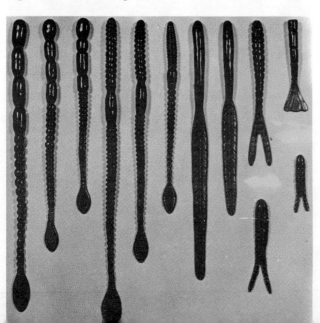

floating worms can be made as soft as wanted and in any color. A special feature—"worms used during trips may be melted and made over again and again," the manufacturer reports. Complete instructions for "worm making" come with the kit.

26. Daiwa Corporation, Gardena, California introduces the Mono-Dex—a new limp but smooth monofilament. It's big on strength but low on stretch, making it easier for the fisherman to haul in his catch. It's easy to knot and one of its main features is that it's invisible to fish.

Also from Daiwa comes the Danish-made sinking lures, Ertner. With heavy lead construction and "deceptive" wiggling motion, they are ideal for the fisherman after the "elusive" bottom fish. Offering a variety of sizes and color combinations, they can also be fished in salt and fresh water.

27. Creek Chub Bait Company, Garrett, Indiana offers a variety of new baits to please the fisherman. Mackerel Pikies are available in hard plastic and wood finishes. The deep diver chrome Pikies come with deep diver mouthpiece, heavy hardware, and three large, rust-resistant treble hooks in both straight and jointed lures. For striped bass and bluefish surf casting is the Striper series, available in fluorescent red. The manufacturer says that these poppers are "generally retrieved in a series of vigorous jerks of the rod to produce maximum popping action on the surface."

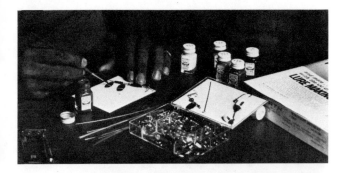

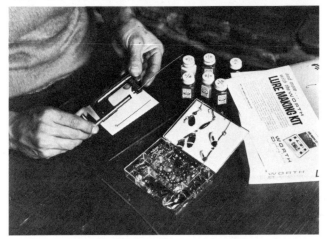

28. The Worth Company, Stevens Point, Wisconsin introduces for the fisherman who likes to make his own lures the LM-1 Lure Making Kit. All the material needed for 25 lures is included.

You can create your own "lures" or follow the instructions on how to make jig spinners, French and Reflex style spinning lures and even wire leaders.

The suggested retail price is $12.25 and some of the other items in this kit are—beads, spinner blades, hooks, split rings, lure bodies, swivels, snaps, wire shafts, and six colors of fast-drying paint with brush.

From the same company comes a Split Ring Pliers that should be helpful to both anglers and hobbyists. The item can be used to open split shot and as a crimping tool for making fishing leaders. Instructions for its use come packaged with an assortment of rings.

29. Berkley and Company, Spirit Lake, Iowa is offering two new "types" of fishing line—Hi-Dac is a braided line of high

density polyester, and the Silver Glide series are floating fly lines.

Hi-Dac resists stretching and has greater strength at smaller diameters than other braided lines. It comes in tests of 10 to 40 pounds. For the beginner, it is suggested by the manufacturer that the silver grey color line of the Silver Glide series would be ideal.

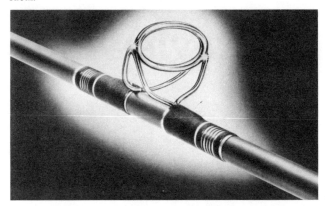

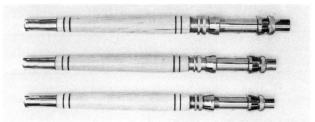

30. New from Allan Manufacturing Company, Hicksville, L. I., New York comes Big Game Trolling Handles and Light Weight Ovallan Guides.

The guides, according to the manufacturer, have been "tested and proved to reduce line wear up to 500%."

The handles are "a matched combination of heavy duty reel seat and handle of chrome plated brass with heavy machined hoods, a chrome plated brass double slotted dimbal—all mounted on an ultra smooth polyurethane coated hickory handle."

31. Vlchek Plastics Company, Middlefield, Ohio has on the market a new series of "pocket-sized" tackle boxes. Called AdVenturer 400 Series Velure Boxes, they measure 8⅜ × 4½ × 1¹¹/₁₆ inches and are olive green polypropylene, crush-proof.

Four different styles are offered. A single compartment for accessories or tackle is Model V-401. Twin compartment box, Model V-402 is for large spoons, plastic worms, etc., and by using a removable divider in Model V-410 you get a box that converts from ten compartments to five. A single compartment with top and bottom sections Velfoam-lined to protect and hold jigs, and flies is Model V-401F.

Reviewing New Tackle

Rods

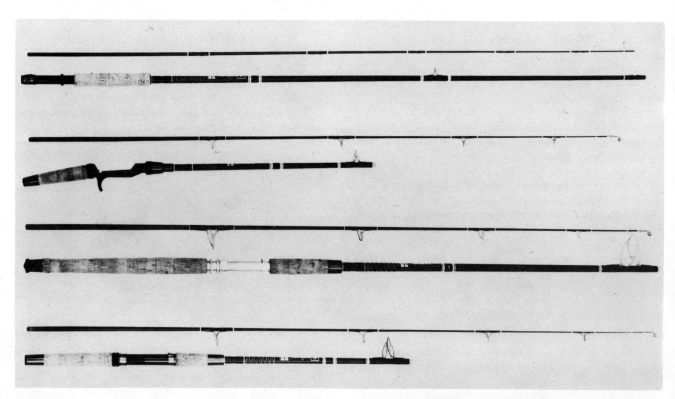

1. New from the Daiwa Corporation is their 8300 series of "Super Power" rods. These two-piece rods are of excellent quality and feature glass-to-glass ferrules for extra lightness and strength. They have a one-piece look and one-piece action. Some anglers believe glass joints instead of metal ferrules give rods "continuous action" and "resilient strength."

Some bonus features on Daiwa's "Super Power" rods are chromeplated, stainless steel bridged guides, carbide tip tops, specie cork grips, and aluminum anodized reel seats. Daiwa's 8300 series includes 6, 6½, and 7-foot fresh water spinning rods; 8 and 9-foot salt water spinning rods; 6 and 6½-foot fresh water spin-casting rods; and 7½, 8, and 8-foot fly rods.

The rods are richly finished in burgundy color, with gold wraps.

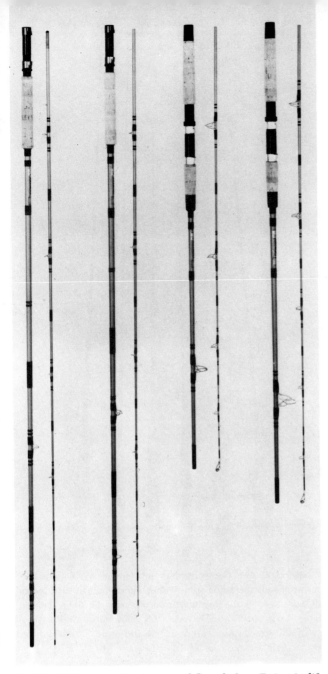

big game fishing rods offering extra strength in the butt section (where so much breakage occurs), while still providing "sporty tip action."

2.   The 9000 series of spinning and fly rods from Daiwa is different from anything on the market today, according to the manufacturer. These rods feature a new kind of super-hard finish, applied by hand, which gives a high-gloss surface that has "a depth and hardness which become more durable with age." Despite the special finish, these rods have the same famous Daiwa action as other rods made by this firm, and they have the glass-to-glass ferrules and similar features of Daiwa rods.

3.   True Temper Corporation has introduced a "100 series" of

4.   True Temper also has a new line of extra heavy boat and big game rods. These rods combine added strength with extra heavy action for ocean and what the firm calls "deep lake fishing." The "7500 series" of True Temper rods are made of solid glass. They have much-wanted roller guides and tip-tops, and detachable locking reel seats. Lengths are 6½ feet.

5.   Uni-Spin by True Temper, which the company says means "universal spinning," combines some of the features of both spinning and spin-casting. It offers push-button type of spin-casting ease in the reel, but it also has much of the dependable control typical of open-face spinning reels. The Uni-Spin outfit consists of a special rod butt section, which can be used with any of three interchangeable tips, and a built-in push button reel

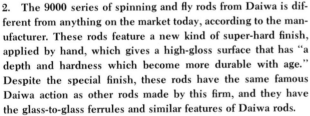

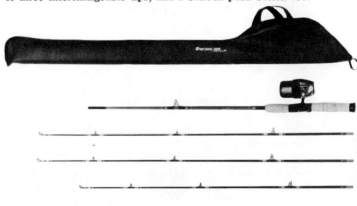

with its button conveniently located in the rod's handle. The rod's interchangeable tips are "fast taper" (for light lines and lures); "intermediate taper" (for intermediate weight line and lures); and "magnum taper" (for heavy lines and lures or trolling).

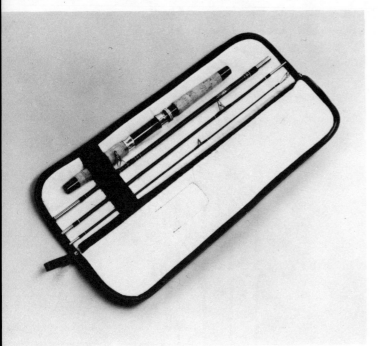

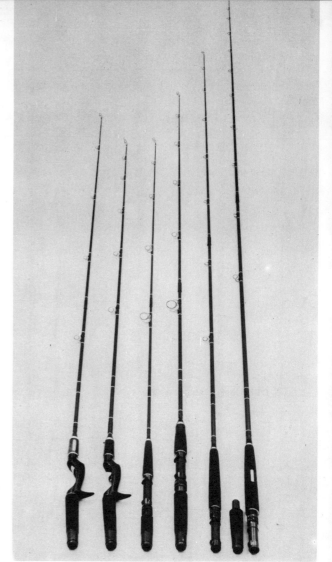

7. Berkley and Company has introduced a "Para/metric" series of rods including spin-casting, spinning, bait-casting, and fly rods, which the manufacturer says are the only "curved-taper" rods on the market today. All salesmanship aside, these are quality glass rods, well designed, with good action, and well worth their prices.

Spin-Cast Reels

---

8. Zebco/444, under-the-rod spin-cast reel: body and covers are of non-corrosive, impact-resistant, super-tough Kralastic plastic material. Power drag. Instant line retrieve. Filled with 75 yards, 10-pound test, Zebco monofilament line.

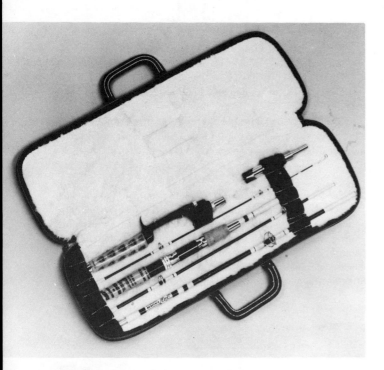

6. The St. Croix Corporation of Park Falls, Wisconsin is making two superb "rod packs" for traveling sportsmen, executives, and fishermen who need light, easily-carried fishing outfits. One pack consists of a 7-foot spinning rod that converts to a fly rod, while the other unusual and attractive pack has five sections that can be combined in different ways to form a spinning rod, fly rod, or spincast rod.

9. A new spinnerhead, super-strong gears, and a new fiber-filled Lexan body are some of the features of Zebco's Model 600 spincast reel. Reel comes spooled with 105 yards of 8-pound mono line. Extra interchangeable spools available with 4, 6, 10, and 12-pound line.

11. Lightest of the new spin-cast reels is Daiwa's 6400 reel. Designed for light to medium fresh water fishing, it features an exclusive positive roller pin pickup and a unique twist-free star drag. Automatic push-button line release. Filled with 100 yards, 8-pound line and comes with a practice casting plug.

12. The 9900 spin-cast reel by Daiwa has right or left hand retrieve, and is a deluxe, heavy-duty reel. Gear ratio is 4:1 and bronze bushings and bronze spool bearings give smooth-as-silk operation. Dial drag easily adjusts to desired setting. Converts to right, left retrieve in seconds. Royal blue finish. Comes spooled with 100 yards, 10-pound line.

10. The 6700 heavy duty salt water spin-cast reel by Daiwa is one of the few closed-face reels made today that is genuinely adequate for salt water fishing. A big, tough reel. Strong, dependable, star drag. Gear ratio, 4.2:1, for good, fast retrieve. Comes with 120 yards, 15-pound mono.

13. True Temper's new Model 885 spin-cast reel has unique double handle, and easily-reached push-button. Quick, convenient take-down, reel is smooth, dependable, inexpensive.

Spinning Reels

14. The Garcia Mitchell 508 has a "rear-swept" reel stem. It offers big line capacity (150 yards, 8-pound mono), and total weight of 8 ounces. Completing this unique lightweight offering by Garcia is a selection of four, 2 piece Conolon Brown Three Star rods with special locking mechanisms to secure the 508 reel in place more readily and solidly than conventional reel seats.

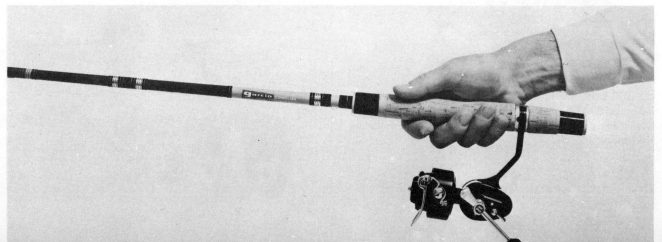

15. Penn 712 "Spinfisher" reel is light, faster version of firm's popular Model 710. For heavy fresh or light salt water fishing. Ball bearing retrieve brings in two feet of line with each turn of handle, a 4.1:1 ratio. Capacity: 200 yards, 8-pound mono.

18. Berkley Tackle Company's new Model 405 spinning reel is a "budget" model designed to compete with low-priced spinning reels by other manufacturers. Ideal for the novice angler. All-aluminum frame and rotor. Selective anti-reverse. Adjustable drag. Weight, 6 ounces.

16. New from Penn, and designed for light fresh water spinning with 4, 6, 8-pound line is the "722." Weight, 9¾ ounces. Fast, 5:1 gear ratio; Teflon drag system; two spools; stainless bail and line roller. Holds 200 yards, 6-pound mono.

19. Daiwa Model 1500 open-face spinning reel is lightweight with gear ratio of 3.8:1. Meant for bass and other light fresh water fishing. Convertible for right, left-hand retrieve. Unique feature is a line distance meter clip. Corrosion resistant, silver-grey finish. Holds 200 yards, 10-pound line.

20. The Model 2500 Daiwa spinning reel features a "skirted spool" that covers and protects internal parts of the reel from sand, dirt, salt water, etc. Stainless steel ball bearings. Suited to either fresh or salt water fishing. Holds 200 yards, 12-pound line. Gear ratio, 4.1:1.

17. Ball-bearing construction, anodized spool, chrome line-roller, collapsible bail, and multi-disc drag system are features of Eagle Claw's new line of spinning reels. A total of 15 models are available.

21. Daiwa Tackle Company's Model 7000 heavy-duty salt water spinning reel features "skirted, exposed" reel spool that allows direct, easy finger braking of the line as it leaves the reel spool. Skirted feature prevents line from working behind spool. Stainless steel ball-bearings.

aluminum. Corrosion-resistant finish. Stainless steel rust-proof line guides. Colors: gray and black.

22. Designed for either right or left-hand fishing, the Daiwa 7850RL spinning reel is heavy-duty, has sealed ball-bearings, machine-cut helical gears, and 3.5:1 retrive ratio. Takes 300 yards of 20-pound line. Weight, 23 ounces.

24. The Daiwa corporation's new Model 111 automatic fly reel handles up to a 9 weight fly line. Light, just over 9 ounces. A vertical reel, it has fold-away trigger that takes up slack at a touch. Retrieves 50 percent more line without winding than most automatics.

25. Silent, quick, easy winding is one feature of Daiwa's new automatic fly reels. Durable, stainless steel line protectors are another feature.

23. The Shakespeare Company, Kalamazoo, Michigan probably America's oldest tackle manufacturing firm operating today, has introduced a new series of four sturdy, smooth and dependable "Purist" single-action fly reels. These reels feature quick take-apart, making line change or cleaning easy. Extra spools are available. Reels have a constant drag accompanied by a light click. Easily converted for left-hand use. Frames are of

26. Garcia also has introduced four "totally" new single-action Mitchell fly reels with "push button" release for rapid changing of spools and, therefore, lines. They have adjustable chromed line guards and simple conversion from right to left hand retrieve. Machined from lightweight aluminum alloy. Long, full-grip handles. Drag can be adjusted while fish runs out line without rapping of knuckles.

27. True Temper's new Model 85 "Visa-Matic" is an attractive, well-made automatic fly reel with easy-to-reach "trigger" and quick-winding feature. Compact. Competitively priced.

Salt Water Reels

28. Unsurpassed for deep sea fishing, Daiwa Corp. offers "precision" ocean trolling reels. Packaged in "custom" wood boxes. The Daiwa "60" is 6/0 size with a capacity of about 600 yards of 50-pound test Dacron line, or 400 yards of 80-pound Dacron. Gear ratio 3:1. Plate diameter is 4½ inches; spool width, 2¹⁄₁₆ inches.

29. The "Ventura" series of tourney deep-sea reels by Daiwa provide ultimate line capacity, plus reel-frame and spool of one-piece aluminum construction, machine-cut. Four stainless steel ball-bearing in each reel. One-piece machine-cut main shaft and master gear made of special black chrome-plated steel. Large disc drag.

30. The new Garcia-Mitchell 1090 (⁹⁄₀) big game salt water trolling reel (left) with a capacity of 650 yards of 80-pound Dacron line joins Garcia's 1040 (⁴⁄₀) (center) and 1060 (⁶⁄₀) (right) in Garcia's big-game reels. Machined from stainless steel and duraluminum for added strength and corrosion resistance, the firm's new salt water reel is handcrafted to exacting tolerances. Self-aligning "Ferodo" disk drag, and big capacity spool. Extra-wide, precision-crafted stainless steel ball-bearings give the reel's spool smooth support. Retrieve ratio is 3:1.

Tackle Boxes

31. The Vlchek Plastics Company offers the "Adventurer Select-O-Matic" tackle box, a unique box that has six spillproof trays with 40 different compartments. Over-all measurements: 18½ × 10¼ × 10⅜ inches.

32. New "Tip-Proof" AdVenturer tackle boxes by Vlchek Plastics Company achieve box balance by employing two stabilizing outriggers. Attached to the base of the lower tray, they rest upon molded supports in the box sides. Because of this design, it is almost impossible to tip boxes through overloading.

41 DEPARTMENTS:

World Fishing Records

Field & Stream Magazine

FRESH WATER RECORDS

Field & Stream annual fishing contest entry blanks may be obtained by writing Mike Ball, Fishing Contest Editor, Field & Stream, 383 Madison Ave., New York, N. Y. 10017.

SPECIES		CAUGHT BY ROD AND REEL						CAUGHT BY ANY METHOD	
Common Name	**Scientific Name**	**Wt.**	**Length**	**Girth**	**Where**	**When**	**Angler**	**Lb. Oz.**	**Where**
BASS, Largemouth	*Micropterus salmoides*	22 lbs. 4 oz.	32½″	28½″	Montgomery Lake, Ga.	June 2 1932	George W. Perry	Same	
BASS, Redeye	*Micropterus coosae*	6½ lbs.	20½″	15⅘″	Hallawakee Cr., Ala.	Mar. 24 1967	Thomas L. Sharpe	Same	
BASS, Smallmouth	*Micropterus dolomieui*	11 lbs. 15 oz.	27″	21⅔″	Dale Hollow Lake, Ky.	July 9 1955	David L. Hayes	Same	
BASS, Spotted	*Micropterus punctulatus spp*	8 lbs. 8 oz.	25″	17¾″	Smith Lake, Ala.	May 23 1968	Wreford James	Same	
BASS, White	*Roccus chrysops*	5 lbs. 4 oz.	17″		Toronto, Kans.	May 4, 1966	Henry A. Baker	Same	
BLUEGILL	*Lepomis macrochirus*	4 lbs. 12 oz.	15″	18¼″	Ketona Lake, Ala.	Apr. 9 1950	T. S. Hudson	Same	
BULLHEAD, Black	*Ictalurus melas*	8 lbs.	24″	17¾″	Lake Waccabuc, N.Y.	Aug. 1 1951	Kani Evans	Same	
CARP	*Cyprinus carpio*	55 lbs. 5 oz.	42″	31″	Clearwater Lake, Minn.	July 10 1952	Frank J. Ledwein	83-8	Pretoria, So. Africa
CATFISH, Blue	*Ictalurus furcatus*	97 lbs.	57″	37″	Missouri River, S.D.	Sept. 16 1959	Edward B. Elliott	117	Osage R., Mo.
CATFISH, Channel	*Ictalurus punctatus*	58 lbs.	47¼″	29⅛″	Santee-Cooper Res., S.C.	July 7 1964	W. Whaley		
CATFISH, Flathead	*Pylodictis olivaris*	66 lbs.	48½″	—	Spavinow, L., Okla.	July 25 1970	Norman N. Freling	Same	
CHAR, Arctic	*Salvelinus alpinus*	29 lbs. 11 oz.	39¾″	26″	Arctic River N.W.T.	Aug. 21 1968	Jeanne P. Branson	Same	
CRAPPIE, Black	*Pomoxis nigromaculatus*	5 lbs.	19¼″	18⅝″	Santee-Cooper Res., S.C.	Mar. 15 1957	Paul E. Foust	Same	
CRAPPIE, White	*Pomoxis annularis*	5 lbs. 3 oz.	21″	19″	Enid Dam, Miss.	July 31 1957	Fred L. Bright	Same	
DOLLY VARDEN	*Salvelinus malma*	32 lbs.	40½″	29¾″	L. Pend Oreille, Idaho	Oct. 27 1949	N. L. Higgins	Same	
GAR, Alligator	*Lepisosteus spatula*	279 lbs.	93″		Rio Grande, Texas	Dec. 2 1951	Bill Valverde	Same	
GAR, Longnose	*Lepisosteus osseus*	50 lbs. 5 oz.	72¼″	22¼″	Trinity River, Texas	July 30 1954	Townsend Miller	Same	
GRAYLING, Arctic	*Thymallus arcticus*	5 lbs. 15 oz.	29⅞″	15⅛″	Katseyedie R., N.W.T.	Aug. 16 1967	Jeanne P. Branson	Same	
MUSKELLUNGE	*Esox masquinongy*	69 lbs. 15 oz.	64½″	31¾″	St. Lawrence R., N.Y.	Sept. 22 1957	Arthur Lawton	102	Minocqua Lake, Wisconsin
PERCH, White	*Roccus americanus*	4 lbs. 12 oz.	19½″	13″	Messalonskee Lake, Me.	June 4 1949	Mrs. Earl Small	Same	
PERCH, Yellow	*Perca flavescens*	4 lbs. 3½ oz.			Bordentown, N.J.	May 1865	Dr. C. C. Abbot	Same	

SPECIES		CAUGHT BY ROD AND REEL						CAUGHT BY ANY METHOD	
Common Name	Scientific Name	Wt.	Length	Girth	Where	When	Angler	Lb. Oz.	Where
PICKEREL, Chain	*Esox niger*	9 lbs. 6 oz.	31"	14"	Homerville, Ga.	Feb. 17 1961	Baxley McQuaig, Jr.	Same	
PIKE, Northern	*Esox lucius*	46 lbs. 2 oz.	52½"	25"	Sacandaga Res., N.Y.	Sept. 15 1940	Peter Dubuc	Same	
SALMON, Atlantic	*Salmo salar*	79 lbs. 2 oz.			Tana River, Norway	1928	Henrik Henriksen	103-2	River Devon, Scotland
SALMON, Chinook	*Oncorhynchus tshawytscha*	92 lbs.	58½"	36"	Skeena River, B.C.	July 19 1959	Heinz Wichmann	126-3	Petersburg, Alaska
SALMON, Landlocked	*Salmo salar*	22 lbs. 8 oz.	36"		Sebago Lake, Maine	Aug. 1 1907	Edward Blakely	35	Crooked River, Maine
SALMON, Coho or Silver	*Oncorhynchus kisutch*	31 lbs.			Cowichan Bay, B.C.	Oct. 11 1947	Mrs. Lee Hallberg	Same	
SAUGER	*Stizostedion canadense*	8 lbs. 5 oz.	28"		Niobara, Nebr.	Oct. 22 1961	Mrs. Betty Tepner	Same	
STURGEON, White	*Acipenser transmontanus*	360 lbs.	111"	86"	Snake River, Idaho	Apr. 24 1956	Willard Cravens	Same	
SUNFISH, Redear	*Lepomis microlophus*	4 lbs. 4 oz.	15"	16¼"	Lee County, N.C.	Feb. 3 1968	Wm. M. Arnold	4-4	Gordon, Alabama
TROUT, Brook	*Salvelinus fontinalis*	14 lbs. 8 oz.	31½"	11½"	Nipigon River, Ontario	July 1916	Dr. W. J. Cook	Same	
TROUT, Brown	*Salmo trutta*	39 lbs. 8 oz.			Loch Awe, Scotland	1866	W. Muir	40	Great Lake, Tasmania
TROUT, Cutthroat	*Salmo clarki*	41 lbs.	39"		Pyramid Lake, Nev.	Dec. 1925	John Skimmerhorn	Same	
TROUT, Golden	*Salmo aguabonita*	11 lbs.	28"	16"	Cook's Lake, Wyo.	Aug. 5 1948	Chas. S. Reed	Same	
TROUT, Lake	*Salvelinus namaycush*	65 lbs.	52"	38" "	Great Bear L., N.W.T.	Aug. 8 1970	Larry Daunis	102	Lake Athabaska, Sask.
TROUT, Rainbow, Stlhd. or Kamloops	*Salmo gairdneri*	37 lbs.	40½"	28"	L. Pend Oreille, Idaho	Nov. 25 1947	Wes Hamlet	42	Corbett, Oreg.
TROUT, Sunapee	*Salvelinus alpinus*	11 lbs. 8 oz.	33"	17¼"	Lake Sunapee, N.H.	Aug. 1 1954	Ernest Theoharis	Same	
WALLEYE	*Stizostedion vitreum*	25 lbs.	41"	29"	Old Hickory L., Tenn.	Aug. 1 1960	Mabry Harper	Same	
WARMOUTH	*Chaenobryttus gulosus*	1 lb. 2 oz.	10"	10"	Cooper River, S.C.	May 18 1968	Robert L. Joyner	1-9	Black R., S. C.
WHITEFISH, Mountain	*Prosopium williamsoni*	5 lbs.	19"	14"	Athabasca R., Alberta	June 3 1963	Orville Welch	Same	

International Game Fish Association

MARINE FISHES

ALL TACKLE RECORDS FOR BOTH MEN AND WOMEN

International Game Fish Association, world record entry forms may be obtained by writing: I.G.F.A., 2190 S.E. 17th St., Ft. Lauderdale, Fla., 33316.

FISH	Scientific Name	Weight	Length	Girth	Place	Date	Angler	Line Lbs.
ALBACORE	*Thunnus germo*	69 lbs. 2 oz.	3' 10"	32"	Montauk, New York	Aug. 21 1964	Larry R. Kranz	80
(3-Way Tie)		69 lbs. 1 oz.	4' ½"	33¼"	Hudson Canyon, N.J.	Oct. 8 1961	Walter C. Timm	50
		69 lbs.	3' 6"	32½"	St. Helena, Atlantic Ocean	Apr. 7 1956	P. Allen	130
AMBERJACK	*Seriola lalandi*	149 lbs.	5' 11"	41¾"	Bermuda	June 21 1964	Peter Simons	30

		Weight	Length	Girth	Location	Date	Angler	
BARRACUDA	*Sphyraena barracuda*	83 lbs.	6' ¼"	29"	Lagos, Nigeria	Jan. 13 1952	K. J. W. Hackett	50
BASS, Calif. Black Sea	*Stereolepis gigas*	563 lbs. 8 oz.	7' 5"	72"	Anacapa Island California	Aug. 20 1968	James D. McAdam, Jr.	80
BASS, Calif. White Sea	*Cynoscion nobilis*	83 lbs. 12 oz.	5' 5½"	34"	San Felipe, Mexico	Mar. 31 1953	L. C. Baumgardner	30
BASS, Channel	*Sciaenops ocellatus*	83 lbs.	4' 4"	29"	Cape Charles, Va.	Aug. 5 1949	Zack Waters, Jr.	50
BASS, Giant Sea	*Promicrops itaiara*	680 lbs.	7' 1½"	66"	Fernandina Beach, Fla.	May 20 1961	Lynn Joyner	80
BASS, Sea	*Centropristes striatus*	8 lbs.	1' 10"	19"	Nantucket Sound, Mass.	May 13 1951	H. R. Rider	50
BASS, Striped	*Roccus saxatilis*	72 lbs.	4' 6½"	31"	Cuttyhunk, Mass.	Oct. 10 1969	Edward Kirker	50
BLACKFISH or TAUTOG	*Tautoga onitis*	21 lbs. 6 oz.	2' 7½"	23½"	Cape May, N. J.	June 12 1954	R. N. Sheafer	30
BLUEFISH	*Pomatomus saltatrix*	24 lbs. 3 oz.	3' 5"	22"	San Miguel, Azores	Aug. 27 1953	M. A. da Silva Veloso	12
BONEFISH	*Albula vulpes*	19 lbs.	3' 3⅝"	17"	Zululand, South Africa	May 26 1962	Brian W. Batchelor	30
BONITO, Oceanic	*Katsuwonus pelamis*	39 lbs. 15 oz.	3' 3"	28"	Walker Cay, Bahamas	Jan. 21, 1952	F. Drowley	50
(Tie)		40 lbs.	3' 2¾"	27½"	Baie du Tambeau, Mauritius	April 19, 1971	Joseph R. P. Caboche, Jr.	50
COBIA	*Rachycentron canadus*	110 lbs. 5 oz.	5' 3"	34"	Mombasa, Kenya	Sept. 8 1964	Eric Tinworth	50
COD	*Gadus callarias*	98 lbs. 12 oz.	5' 3"	41"	Isle of Shoals, Mass.	June 8 1969	Alphonse J. Bielevich	20
DOLPHIN	*Coryphaena hippurus*	85 lbs.	5' 9"	37½"	Spanish Wells, Bahamas	May 29 1968	Richard Seymour	50
DRUM, Black	*Pogonias cromis*	98 lbs. 8 oz.	4' 5"	40"	Willis Wharf, Virginia	June 12 1967	Gary Hilton Kelley	50
FLOUNDER	*Paralichthys*	22 lbs. 1 oz.	3' 1"	35"	Caleta Horcon, Chile	Dec. 8 1965	F. I. Aguirrezabal	30
KINGFISH	*S. Cavalla*	78 lbs.	5' 6½"	28½"	Guayanilla, Puerto Rico	May 25 1963	Ruth M. Coon	50
MARLIN, Black	*Makaira indica*	1560 lbs.	14' 6"	81"	Cabo Blanco, Peru	Aug. 4 1953	Alfred C. Glassell, Jr.	130
MARLIN, Blue	*Makaira ampla*	845 lbs.	13' 1"	71"	St. Thomas, Virgin Islands	July 4 1968	Elliot Fishman	80
MARLIN, Pacific Blue	*Makaira Nigricans*	1153 lbs.	14' 8"	73"	Ritidian Point, Guam	Aug. 21 1969	Greg Perez	180
MARLIN, Striped	*Makaira mitsukurii*	415 lbs.	11'	52"	Cape Brett, New Zealand	Mar. 31 1964	B. C. Bain	80
MARLIN, White	*Makaira albida*	159 lbs. 8 oz.	9'	36"	Pompano Beach, Florida	Apr. 25 1953	W. E. Johnson	50
PERMIT	*Trachinotus goodei*	50 lbs. 8 oz.	3' 8¾"	33¾"	Key West, Florida	Mar. 15 1971	Marshal Earnest	20
POLLACK	*Pollachius virens*	43 lbs.	4'	29"	Brielle, New Jersey	Oct. 21 1964	Philip Barlow	50
RUNNER, Rainbow	*Elagatis bipinnulatus*	30 lbs. 15 oz.	3' 11"	22"	Kauai, Hawaii	Apr. 27 1963	Holbrook Goodale	130
ROOSTERFISH	*Nematistius pectoralis*	114 lbs.	5' 4"	33"	La Paz, Mexico	June 1 1960	Abe Sackheim	30
SAILFISH, Atlantic	*Istiophorus americanus*	141 lbs. 1 oz.	8' 5"		Ivory Coast, Africa	Jan. 26 1961	Tony Burnand	130
SAILFISH, Pacific	*Istiophorus greyi*	221 lbs.	10' 9"		Santa Cruz, Is., Galapagos Is.	Feb. 12 1947	C. W. Stewart	130
SHARK, Blue	*Prionace glauca*	410 lbs.	11' 6"	52"	Rockport, Mass.	Sept. 1 1960	Richard C. Webster	80
(Tie)		410 lbs.	11' 2"	52½"	Rockport, Mass.	Aug. 17 1967	Martha C. Webster	80
SHARK, Mako	*Isurus oxyrhynchus I. glaucus*	1061 lbs.	12' 2"	79½"	Mayor Island, New Zealand	Feb. 17 1970	James Penwarden	130
SHARK, Man-Eater or White	*Carcharodon carcharias*	2664 lbs.	16' 10"	9' 6"	Ceduna, So. Australia	Apr. 21 1959	Alfred Dean	130
SHARK, Porbeagle	*Lamna nasus*	430 lbs.	8'	63"	Channel Islands, England	June 29 1969	Desmond Bougourd	80
SHARK, Thresher	*Alopias vulpinus*	729 lbs.	8' 5"	61"	Mayor Island, New Zealand	June 3 1959	Mrs. V. Brown	130
SHARK, Tiger	*Galeocerdo cuvier*	1780 lbs.	13' 10½"	103"	Cherry Grove, South Carolina	June 14 1964	Walter Maxwell	130
SNOOK or ROBALO	*Centropomus undecimalis*	52 lbs. 6 oz.	4' 1½"	26"	La Paz, Mexico	Jan. 9 1963	Jose Haywood	30

SWORDFISH	Xiphias aladius	1182 lbs.	14' 11¼"	78"	Iquique, Chile	May 7 1953	L. Marron	130
TANGUIGUE	Scomberomorus commerson	81 lbs.	5' 11½"	29¼"	Karachi, Pakistan	Aug. 27 1960	George E. Rusinak	80
TARPON	Tarpon atlanticus	283 lbs.	7' 2 3/5"		Lake Maracaibo, Venezuela	Mar. 19 1956	M. Salazar	30
TUNA, Allison or Yellowfin	Thunnus albacares	296 lbs.	6' 9"	56"	San Benedicto Island, Mexico	Mar. 7 1971	Edward Malnar	80
TUNA, Atlantic Bia-Eyed	Thunnus obesus	295 lbs.	6' 6½"	40"	San Miguel, Azores, Portugal	July 8 1960	Dr. Arsenio Cordeiro	130
TUNA, Pacific Big-Eyed	Parathunnus sibi	435 lbs.	7' 9"	63½"	Cabo Blanco, Peru	Apr. 17 1957	Dr. Russel V. A. Lee	130
TUNA, Blackfin	Thunnus atlanticus	38 lbs.	3' 3¼"	28¾"	Bermuda	June 26 1970	Archie Dickens	30
TUNA, Bluefin	Thunnus thynnus	1065 lbs.	10' 3"	96"	Cape Breton, Nova Scotia	Nov. 19 1970	Robert Glen Gibson	130
WAHOO	Acanthocybium solandri	149 lbs.	6' 7¾"	37½"	Cat Cay, Bahamas	June 15 1962	John Pirovano	130
WEAKFISH	Cynoscion reaalis	19 lbs. 8 oz.	3' 1"	23¾"	Trinidad, West Indies	Apr. 13 1962	Dennis B. Hall	80
WEAKFISH, Spotted	Cynoscion nebulosus	15 lbs. 3 oz.	2' 10½"	20½"	Ft. Pierce, Florida	Jan. 13 1949	C. W. Hubbard	50
(Tie)		15 lbs. 6 oz.	2' 9"	23¾"	St. Lucie River, Florida	May 4 1969	Michael J. Foremny	30
YELLOWTAIL	Seriola lalandi	111 lbs.	5' 2"	38"	Bay of Islands, New Zealand	June 11 1961	A. F. Plim	50

International Game Fish Association

RECORD CATCHES FOR MEN
From 130 lb. line test down to 12 lb. line test.

RECORD CATCHES FOR MEN

130 LB. LINE TEST RECORDS (over 80 lbs., up to and including 130 lbs.)

FISH	Scientific Name	Weight	Length	Girth	Place	Date	Angler	
ALBACORE	Thunnus germo	69 lbs.	3' 6"	32½"	St. Helena, Atlantic Ocean	April 7 1956	P. Allen	
AMBERJACK	Seriola lalandi	133 lbs.	5' 6"	37"	Islamorada, Florida	Apr. 6 1968	Louis E. Woster	
BARRACUDA	Sphyraena barracuda							
BASS, Calif. Black Sea (Tie)	Stereolepis gigas	514 lbs.	7' 2"	82"	San Clemente, California	Aug. 29 1955	J. Patterson	
		514 lbs	7' 6"	80"	Box Canyon California	Nov. 15 1961	Joe M. Arve	
BASS, Calif. White Sea	Cynoscion nobilis							

FISH	Scientific Name	Weight	Length	Girth	Place	Date	Angler
BASS, Channel	Sciaenops ocellatus						
BASS, Giant Sea	Promicrops itaiara	396 lbs.	7' 10"	67"	Islamorada, Florida	Mar. 22 1968	Frank J. Posluszny
BASS, Sea	Centropristes striatus						
BASS, Striped	Roccus sa atilis						
BLACKFISH or TAUTOG	Tautoga onitis						
BLUEFISH	Pomatomus salatrix						
BONEFISH	Albula vulpes						
BONITO, Oceanic	Katsuwonus pelamis	38 lbs.			Black River, Mauritius	Mar. 15 1961	Frank Masson
COBIA	Rachycentron canadus						
COD	Gadus callarias						
DOLPHIN	Coryphaena hippurus	72 lbs. 8 oz.	4' 10½"	35¼"	Honolulu, Hawaii	Mar. 13 1956	G. Perry
DRUM, Black	Pogonias cromis						
FLOUNDER	Paralichthys						
KINGFISH	S. Cavalla	76 lbs. 8 oz.	5' 3"	31"	Bimini, Bahamas	May 22 1952	R. E. Maytag
MARLIN, Black	Makaira indica	1560 lbs.	14' 6"	81"	Cabo Blanco, Peru	Aug. 4 1953	Alfred C. Glassell, Jr.
MARLIN, Blue	Makaira ampla	810 lbs.	13' 1"	68"	Hatteras, N. Carolina	June 11 1962	Gary Stukes
MARLIN, Pacific Blue	Makaira Nigricans	1100 lbs.	13' 9½"	79½"	Le Morne, Mauritius	Feb. 20 1966	Andre D'Hotman DeVilliers
MARLIN, Striped	Makaira mitsukurii						
MARLIN, White	Makaira albida						
PERMIT	Trachinotus goodei	38 lbs. 8 oz.	3' 4½"	31¼"	Boca Grande, Florida	Sept. 9 1953	R. H. Martin
POLLACK	Pollachius virens						
RUNNER, Rainbow	Elagatis bipinnulatus	30 lbs. 15 oz.	3' 11"	22"	Kanai, Hawaii	April 27 1963	Holbrook Goodale
ROOSTERFISH	Nematistius pectoralis	100 lbs.	4' 6"	32"	Cabo Blanco, Peru	Jan. 12 1954	Miguel Barrenechea
SAILFISH, Atlantic	Istiophorus americanus	141 lbs. 1 oz.	8' 5"		Ivory Coast, Africa	Jan. 26 1961	Tony Burnand
SAILFISH, Pacific	Istiophorus areyi	221 lbs.	10' 9"		Santa Cruz Is., Galapagos Is.	Feb. 12 1947	C. W. Stewart
SHARK, Blue	Prionace glauca	341 lbs. 8 oz.	10' 1"	45½"	Las Palmas, Canary Island	Oct. 31 1966	John D. Nixon
SHARK, Mako	Isurus oxyrhynchus I. glaucus	1061 lbs.	12' 2"	79½"	Mayor Island, New Zealand	Feb. 17 1970	James B. Penwarden
SHARK, Man-Eater or White	Carcharodon carcharias	2664 lbs.	16' 10"	9' 6"	Ceduna, S. Australia	April 21 1959	Alfred Dean
SHARK, Porbeagle	Lamna nasus						
SHARK, Thresher	Alopias vulpinus						
SHARK, Tiger	Galeocerdo cuvier	1780 lbs.	13' 10½"	103"	Cherry Grove, South Carolina	June 1964	Walter Maxwell
SNOOK or ROBALO	Centropomus undecimalis						
SWORDFISH	Xiphias gladius	1182 lbs.	14' 11¼"	78"	Iquique, Chile	May 7 1953	L. Marron
TANGUIGUE	Scomberomorus commerson	Vacant—Minimum Acceptance Weight—81 lbs.					
TARPON	Tarpon atlanticus						
TUNA, Allison or Yellowfin	Thunnus albacares	291 lbs.	5' 11"	60"	San Benedicto Island, Mexico	Jan. 18 1971	Gilbert Gardner

FISH	Scientific Name	Weight	Length	Girth	Place	Date	Angler
TUNA, Atlantic Big-Eyed	*Thunnus obesus*	295 lbs.	6' 6½"	40"	San Miguel, Azores, Portugal	July 8 1960	Dr. Arsenio Cordeiro
TUNA, Pacific Big-Eyed	*Parathunnus sibi*	435 lbs.	7' 9"	63½"	Cabo Blanco, Peru	April 17 1957	Dr. Russel V. A. Lee
TUNA, Blackfin	*Thunnus atlanticus*						
TUNA, Bluefin	*Thunnus thynnus*	1065 lbs.	10' 3"	96"	Cape Breton, Nova Scotia	Nov. 19 1970	Robert Glen Gibson
WAHOO	*Acanthocybium solandri*	149 lbs.	6' 7¾"	37½"	Cat Cay, Bahamas	June 15 1962	John Pirovano
WEAKFISH	*Cynoscion regalis*						
WEAKFISH, Spotted	*Cynoscion nebulosus*						
YELLOWTAIL	*Seriola lalandi*	89 lbs.	4' 9"	34"	Mayor Island, New Zealand	Jan. 29 1968	L. R. Hooper

International Game Fish Association

RECORD CATCHES FOR MEN

80 LB. LINE TEST RECORDS (over 50 lbs., up to and including 80 lbs.)

FISH	Scientific Name	Weight	Length	Girth	Place	Date	Angler
ALBACORE	*Thunnus germo*	69 lbs. 2 oz.	3' 10"	32"	Montauk, New York	Aug. 21 1964	Larry R. Kranz
AMBERJACK	*Seriola lalandi*	142 lbs. 14 oz.	5' 11¾"	42¼"	Bermuda	Aug. 7 1969	Nelson Simons
BARRACUDA	*Sphyraena barracuda*	67 lbs.	5' 5"	29¾"	Islamorada, Florida	Jan. 29 1949	Harold Goodstone
BASS, Calif. Black Sea	*Stereolepis gigas*	563 lbs. 8 oz.	7' 5"	72"	Anacapa Island California	Aug. 20 1968	James D. McAdams, Jr.
BASS, Calif. White Sea	*Cynoscion nobilis*	74 lbs.	5' 3"	33"	Catalina Island	May 11 1968	Allan D. Tromblay
BASS, Channel	*Sciaenops ocellatus*						
BASS, Giant Sea	*Promicrops itaiara*	680 lbs.	7' 1½"	66"	Fernandina Beach, Florida	May 20 1961	Lynn Joyner
BASS, Sea	*Centropristes striatus*						
BASS, Striped	*Roccus saxatilis*						
BLACKFISH or TAUTOG	*Tautoga onitis*						
BLUEFISH	*Pomatomus saltatrix*	22 lbs. 12 oz.	3' 2"	21⅞"	Arguineguin, Gran Canaria	July 19 1971	Kenneth V. Oulton
BONEFISH	*Albula vulpes*	18 lbs. 2 oz.	3' 5½"	17¹⁵⁄₁₆"	Mana, Kauai, Hawaii	Oct. 14 1954	Wm. Badua
BONITO, Oceanic	*Katsuwonus pelamis*	38 lbs. 8 oz.	2' 10½"	29"	Waianae, Hawaii	June 13 1964	Sneo Okimoto
COBIA	*Rachycentron canadus*	90 lbs.	5' 5½"	31"	Ocean City, Maryland	Aug. 31 1949	Charles J. Stine
COD	*Gadus callarias*						
DOLPHIN	*Coryphaena hippourus*	75 lbs. 8 oz.	4' 2"		Mafia Channel, East Africa	Dec. 10 1950	A. Conan-Doyle
DRUM, Black	*Pogonias cromis*						
FLOUNDER	*Paralichthys*						
KINGFISH	*S. Cavalla*						

FISH	Scientific Name	Weight	Length	Girth	Place	Date	Angler
MARLIN, Black	Makaira indica	1077 lbs. 8 oz.	14'	76"	Cairns, Australia	Oct. 22 1970	William Wilkie
MARLIN, Blue	Makaira ampla	845 lbs.	13' 1"	71"	St. Thomas, Virgin Is.	July 4 1968	Elliot J. Fishman
MARLIN, Pacific Blue	Makaira Nigricans	652 lbs.	10' 3½"	64"	Bay of Islands, New Zealand	Jan. 30 1965	George Wooller
MARLIN, Striped	Makaira mitsukurii	415 lbs.	11'	52"	Cape Brett, New Zealand	Mar. 31 1964	B. C. Bain
MARLIN, White	Makaira albida						
PERMIT	Trachinotus goodei	34 lbs. 8 oz.	3' ¼"	28"	Naples, Florida	Feb. 1 1951	R. R. Channel
POLLACK	Pollachius virens						
RUNNER, Rainbow	Elagatis bipinnulatus	28 lbs. 6 oz.	4' 1½"	21½"	Pulmo Reef, Gulf of Calif.	Nov. 11 1967	Joe C. Stuard
ROOSTERFISH	Nematistius pectoralis	90 lbs.	4' 11½"	32"	Loreto, California	Dec. 22 1960	Clement Caditz
SAILFISH, Atlantic	Istiophorus americanus						
SAILFISH, Pacific	Istiophorus greyi	198 lbs.	10' 6"	33"	Mazatlan, Mexico	Nov. 10 1954	G. N. Anglen
SHARK, Blue	Prionace glauca	410 lbs.	11' 6"	52"	Rockport, Mass.	Sept. 1 1960	Richard C. Webster
SHARK, Mako	Isurus oxyrhynchus I. glaucus	820 lbs.	10' 5"	68"	Cavalli Islands, New Zealand	Mar. 28 1964	T. Culshaw
SHARK, Man-Eater or White	Carcharodon carcharias	2344 lbs.	15' 1"	108"	Streaky Bay, Australia	Nov. 6 1960	Alfred Dean
SHARK, Porbeagle	Lamna nasus	430 lbs.	8'	63"	Channel Islands, England	June 29 1969	Desmond Boubourd
SHARK, Thresher	Alopias vulpinus	501 lbs.	13' 7"	58"	Port Stephens, Australia	Mar. 27 1967	Barry Caldwell
SHARK, Tiger	Galeocerdo cuvier	1305 lbs.	13' 7½"	86½"	Coogee Wide, Sydney, Aust.	May 17 1959	Samuel Jamieson
SNOOK or ROBALO	Centropomus undecimalis	37 lbs.	3' 9½"	26"	Lake Worth, Florida	July 28 1959	James P. Nora
SWORDFISH	Xiphias gladius	530 lbs.	12' 5"	59"	Shinnecock, L. I., N.Y.	Aug. 26 1960	Walter Margulies
TARPON	Tarpon atlanticus	214 lbs. 12 oz.	7' 4½"	44"	Lagos, Nigeria	Jan. 26 1953	J. N. Zarpas
TUNA, Allison or Yellowfin	Thunnus albacares	296 lbs.	6' 9"	56"	San Benedicto Island, Mexico	Mar. 7 1971	Edward Malnar
TUNA, Atlantic Big-Eyed	Thunnus obesus	198 lbs.	5' 7"	51"	St. Helena, Atlantic Ocean	April 13 1960	Donald J. Taylor
TUNA, Pacific Big-Eyed	Parathunnus sibi	332 lbs.	7' 3½"	58"	Cabo Blanco, Peru	Jan. 26 1953	Emil Wm. Steffens
TUNA, Blackfin	Thunnus atlanticus						
TUNA, Bluefin	Thunnus thynnus	881 lbs.	9' 11½"	80¾"	Newburyport, Mass.	Sept. 20 1970	Wilbur E. Tobey
WAHOO	Acanthocybium solandri	139 lbs.	6' 9"	33¾"	Marathon, Florida	May 18 1960	George Von Hoffman
WEAKFISH	Cynoscion regalis	19 lbs. 8 oz.	3' 1"	23¾"	Trinidad, West Indies	April 13 1962	Dennis B. Hall
WEAKFISH, Spotted	Cynoscion nebulosus						
YELLOWTAIL	Seriola lalandi	108 lbs.			Cape Brett, New Zealand	Jan. 15 1962	Robin O'Connor

International Game Fish Association

RECORD CATCHES FOR MEN

50 LB. LINE TEST RECORDS (over 30 lbs., up to and including 50 lbs.)

FISH	Scientific Name	Weight	Length	Girth	Place	Date	Angler
ALBACORE	Thunnus germo	69 lbs. 1 oz.	4' 1/4"	33 1/4"	Hudson Canyon, N. J.	Oct. 8 1961	Walter C. Timm
AMBERJACK	Seriola lalandi	132 lbs.	5' 3"	39 1/4"	La Paz, Mexico	July 21 1964	Howard H. Hahn
BARRACUDA	Sphyraena barracuda	83 lbs.	6' 1/4"	29"	Lagos, Nigeria	Jan. 13 1952	K. J. W. Hackett
BASS, Calif. Black Sea	Stereolepis gigas	557 lbs. 3 oz.	7' 4 1/4"	78"	Catalina Island, Calif.	July 1 1962	Richard M. Lane
BASS, Calif. White Sea	Cynoscion nobilis	77 lbs. 4 oz.	5' 1"	33"	San Diego, Calif.	April 8 1950	H. P. Bledsoe
BASS, Channel	Sciaenops ocellatus	83 lbs.	4' 4"	29"	Cape Charles, Va.	Aug. 5 1949	Zack Waters, Jr.
BASS, Giant Sea	Promicrops itaiara	369 lbs.	6' 5"	65"	Marathon, Florida	April 25 1956	C. F. Mann
BASS, Sea	Centropristes striatus	8 lbs.	1' 10"	19"	Nantucket Sound, Mass.	May 13 1951	H. R. Rider
BASS, Striped	Roccus saxatilis	72 lbs.	4' 6 1/2"	31"	Cuttyhunk, Mass.	Oct. 10 1969	Edward J. Kirker
BLACKFISH or TAUTOG	Tautoga onitis	20 lbs. 14 oz.	2' 8"	30"	Newport, R. I.	Oct. 20 1955	W. R. Peckham
BLUEFISH	Pomatomus salatrix	21 lbs.	3' 5 1/4"	19"	Virginia Beach, Virginia	July 18 1971	Walter L. Ansell, Jr.
BONEFISH	Albula vulpes	17 lbs. 8 oz.	3' 4"	18"	Oahu, Hawaii	Aug. 23 1952	Jack Yoshida
BONITO, Oceanic	Katsuwonus pelamis	39 lbs. 15 oz.	3' 3"	28"	Walker Cay, Bahamas	Jan. 21 1952	F. Drowley
(Tie)		40 lbs.	3' 2 3/4"	27 1/2"	Baie du Tambeau, Mauritius	April 19 1971	Joseph R. P. Caboche, Jr.
COBIA	Rachycentron canadus	110 lbs. 5 oz.	5' 3"	34"	Mombasa, Kenya	Sept. 8 1964	Eric Tinworth
COD	Gadus callarias	78 lbs. 4 oz.	4' 9"	37"	Mass. Bay, Mass.	Oct. 8 1966	John M. Michna
DOLPHIN	Coryphaena hippurus	85 lbs.	5' 9"	37 1/2"	Spanish Wells, Bahamas	May 29 1968	Richard Seymour
DRUM, Black	Pogonias cromis	98 lbs. 8 oz.	4' 5"	40"	Willis Wharf, Virginia	June 12 1967	Gary Hilton Kelley
FLOUNDER	Paralichthys	21 lbs. 4 oz.	3' 1/2"	35"	Maitencillo, Chile	Dec. 8 1959	Daniel Veras Serano
KINGFISH	S. Cavalla	72 lbs.	5' 1"	29"	Bimini, Bahamas	June 27 1963	Joseph J. Janulis, Jr.
MARLIN, Black	Makaira indica	1124 lbs.	14'	75"	Cairns, Australia	Oct. 31 1969	Edward Seay
MARLIN, Blue	Makaira ampla	620 lbs.	13' 8"	66"	Atlantic City, New Jersey	Aug. 5 1964	Joseph A. Teti, Jr.
MARLIN, Pacific Blue	Makaira Nigricans	475 lbs.	9' 3"	54 1/2"	Cavalli Islands, New Zealand	Feb. 25 1966	William Sherman
MARLIN, Striped	Makaira mitsukurii						
MARLIN, White	Makaira albida	159 lbs. 8 oz.	9'	36"	Pompano Beach, Florida	April 25 1953	W. E. Johnson
PERMIT	Trachinotus goodei	47 lbs. 12 oz.	3' 9"	32"	Boca Grande Pass, Florida	May 5 1960	Frank G. Burke, Jr.
POLLACK	Pollachius virens	43 lbs.	4'	29"	Brielle, New Jersey	Oct. 21 1964	Philip Barlow
RUNNER, Rainbow	Elagatis bipinnulatus	28 lbs.	4' 1"	21 1/2"	Pinas Bay, Panama	Jan. 15 1967	Thomas C. Dickinson
ROOSTERFISH	Nematistius pectoralis	80 lbs.	3' 10"	27 1/4"	Cabo Blanco, Peru	June 13 1954	Clyoce J. Tippett
SAILFISH, Atlantic	Istiophorus americanus	123 lbs.	10' 4"	32 3/4"	Walker Cay, Bahamas	April 25 1950	H. Teetor
SAILFISH, Pacific	Istiophorus greyi	192 lbs.	10' 5"	40 1/2"	La Paz, Mexico	Sept. 6 1950	Gay Thomas
(Tie)		192 lbs. 7 oz.	10' 3"	42"	Acapulco, Mexico	Oct. 4 1961	W. W. Rowland

FISH	Scientific Name	Weight	Length	Girth	Place	Date	Angler
SHARK, Blue	Prionace glauca	371 lbs. 8 oz.	11' 3"	47"	Montauk, N. Y.	Sept. 27 1969	Jack Bellock
SHARK, Mako	Isurus oxyrhynchus I. glaucus	690 lbs.	10' 6"	61"	Cavalli Islands, New Zealand	Nov. 7 1970	Noel R. Brady
SHARK, Man-Eater or White	Carcharodon carcharias	1876 lbs.	15' 6"	101½"	Cape Moreton, Australia	Aug. 6 1955	Bob Dyer
SHARK, Porbeagle	Lamna nasus	388 lbs.	8' 5½"	62"	Montauk Point, N.Y.	Oct. 28 1961	John S. Walton
SHARK, Thresher	Alopias vulpinus	380 lbs.	7' 1¼"	54"	San Pedro Channel, Calif.	Nov. 1 1970	Henry P. Galle, Jr.
SHARK, Tiger	Galeocerdo cuvier	1018 lbs.	13' 3"	68"	Cape Moreton, Australia	June 12 1957	Bob Dyer
SNOOK or ROBALO	Centropomus undecimalis						
SWORDFISH	Xiphias gladius	444 lbs.	12' 1"	57"	Pompano Beach, Florida	Apr. 27 1951	Fred J. Fleming
TANGUIGUE	Scomberomorus commerson	78 lbs.	5' 6"	29"	Cape Moreton, Australia	April 8 1967	Ronald G. Jenyns
TARPON	Tarpon atlanticus	242 lbs. 4 oz.	7' 4⅝"	43⅖"	Cienaga Ayopel, Colombia	Jan. 7 1955	A. Salazar
TUNA, Allison or Yellowfin	Thunnus albacares	240 lbs.	6' 1¾"	51"	Kona, Hawaii	July 20 1966	Rufus P. Spalding, Jr.
TUNA, Atlantic Big-Eyed	Thunnus obesus	167 lbs.	6' 3"	47"	Miami Beach, Florida	Jan. 18 1957	Jerry Mills
TUNA, Pacific Big-Eyed	Parathunnus sibi	280 lbs.	6' 11"	52½"	Salinas, Ecuador	Jan. 21 1967	Luis Alberto Flores A.
TUNA, Blackfin	Thunnus atlanticus	36 lbs.	3' ¼"	28⅞"	Bermuda	July 14 1963	Joseph Baptiste, Jr.
TUNA, Bluefin	Thunnus thynnus	640 lbs.	9' 2"	72"	Mass. Bay, Mass.	Sept. 5 1971	Joseph M. DiCarlo
WAHOO	Acanthocybium solandri	124 lbs.	6' 4"	36"	St. Thomas, Virgin Islands	Mar. 29 1967	Joseph H. C. Wenk
WEAKFISH	Cynoscion regalis						
WEAKFISH, Spotted	Cynoscion nebulosus	15 lbs. 3 oz.	2' 10½"	20½"	Ft. Pierce, Florida	Jan. 13 1949	C. W. Hubbard
YELLOWTAIL	Seriola lalandi	111 lbs.	5' 2"	38"	Bay of Islands, New Zealand	June 11 1961	A. F. Plim

International Game Fish Association

RECORD CATCHES FOR MEN

30 LB. LINE TEST RECORDS (over 20 lbs., up to and including 30 lbs.)

FISH	Scientific Name	Weight	Length	Girth	Place	Date	Angler
ALBACORE	Thunnus germo						
AMBERJACK	Seriola lalandi	149 lbs.	5' 11"	41¾"	Bermuda	June 21 1964	Peter Simons
BARRACUDA	Sphyraena barracuda	68 lbs. 8 oz.	5' 7½"	28⅞"	Queensland, Australia	Sept. 4 1971	Bradley D. Beath
BASS, Calif. Black Sea	Stereolepis gigas	388 lbs. 8 oz.	6' 6"	72"	Catalina Island Calif.	Sept. 29 1962	John W. Scott, Jr.
BASS, Calif. White Sea	Cynoscion nobilis	83 lbs. 12 oz.	5' 5½"	34"	San Felipe, Mexico	March 31 1953	L. C. Baumgardner
BASS, Channel	Sciaenops ocellatus	76 lbs.	4' 5¾"	34¼"	Wreck Island Virginia	May 16 1968	J. Thomas Savage
BASS, Giant Sea	Promicrops itaiara	430 lbs.	8'	67"	Ft. Lauderdale Florida	Apr. 25 1967	Curt Johnson

FISH	Scientific Name	Weight	Length	Girth	Place	Date	Angler
BASS, Sea	*Centropristes striatus*	4 lbs. 15 ¾ oz.	1′ 10½″	15½″	Virginia Beach, Virginia	Sept. 14 1970	George F. Moore
BASS, Striped	*Roccus saxatilis*	45 lbs.	4′ 1″	26¾″	Cuttyhunk, Mass.	June 26 1954	Luis de Hoyos
BLACKFISH or TAUTOG	*Tautoga onitis*	21 lbs. 6 oz.	2′ 7½″	23½″	Cape May, N. J.	June 12 1954	R. N. Sheafer
BLUEFISH	*Pomatomus saltatrix*	22 lbs.	3′ 3″	22″	Avon, N. Carolina	Nov. 27 1969	Michael E. Hayes
BONEFISH	*Albula vulpes*	19 lbs.	3′ 3⅝″	17″	Zululand, South Africa	May 26 1962	Brian W. Batchelor
BONITO, Oceanic	*Katsuwonus pelamis*	33 lbs. 4 oz.	3′ 1″	27″	San Juan, Puerto Rico	July 14 1966	Jose L. Campos
COBIA	*Rachycentron canadus*	100 lbs.	5′ 11½″	36″	Point Lookout, Queensland	Oct. 4 1962	Peter R. Bristow
COD	*Gadus callarias*	81 lbs.	4′ 6⅞″	35½″	Brielle, N.J.	March 15 1967	Joseph Chesla
DOLPHIN	*Coryphaena hippurus*	59 lbs. 8 oz.	5′ 8″	34″	Bimini, Bahamas	Mar. 21 1957	Irving Devine
DRUM, Black	*Pogonias cromis*	92 lbs.	4′ 3½″		Cambridge, Maryland	Aug. 27 1955	James Aaron
FLOUNDER	*Paralichthys*	22 lbs. 1 oz.	3′ 1″	35″	Caleto Horcon, Chile	Dec. 8 1965	F. I. Aguirrezabal
KINGFISH	*S. Cavalla*	75 lbs.	4′ 9″	32″	Walker Cay, Bahamas	May 22 1966	Thomas J. Sims, Jr.
MARLIN, Black	*Makaira indica*	816 lbs.	12′ 8″	69″	Cairns, Australia	Sept. 19 1971	Patrick Gay
MARLIN, Blue	*Makaira ampla*	480 lbs.	11′ 11″	54″	Bimini, Bahamas	July 23 1949	G. A. Lyon, Sr.
MARLIN, Pacific Blue	*Makaira Nigricans*	403 lbs.	10′ 6½″	54″	Keahole, Hawaii	Aug. 17 1971	Stephen Zuckerman
MARLIN, Striped	*Makaira mitsukurii*						
MARLIN, White	*Makaira albida*	130 lbs. 4 oz.	8′ 3″	33″	Bimini, Bahamas	April 18 1959	Leonard Hendrix
PERMIT	*Trachinotus goodei*	41 lbs. 2 oz.	3′ 8″	31¼″	Key West, Florida	April 11 1963	Webster Robinson
POLLACK	*Pollachius virens*	36 lbs.	3′ 10½″	26″	Montauk, N. Y.	May 28 1957	William E. Davis
RUNNER, Rainbow	*Elagatis bipinnulatus*	25 lbs. 12 oz.	3′ 8¾″	21″	Oahu, Hawaii	Nov. 26 1967	Richard Y. Sakimoto, M.D.
ROOSTERFISH	*Nematistius pectoralis*	114 lbs.	5′ 4″	33″	La Paz, Mexico	June 1 1960	Abe Sackheim
SAILFISH, Atlantic	*Istiophorus americanus*	108 lbs. 12 oz.	8′ 5½″	31½″	Placer de la Guaira, Venezuela	Sept. 12 1970	Gildo Bellini Rangel
SAILFISH, Pacific	*Istiophorus greyi*	198 lbs.	11′ 2″	41″	La Paz, Mexico	Aug. 23 1957	Charles Kelly
SHARK, Blue	*Prionace glauca*	350 lbs.	11′ 5″	43″	Sydney Heads, Australia	Oct. 29 1961	John C. Kellion
SHARK, Mako	*Isurus oxyrhynchus I. glaucus*	854 lbs.	11′ 8½″	73½″	Port Stephens, N.S.W., Australia	May 9 1971	John Howard Barclay
SHARK, Man-Eater or White	*Carcharodon carcharias*	1053 lbs.	12′ 8″	68″	Cape Moreton, Australia	June 13 1957	Bob Dyer
SHARK, Porbeagle	*Lamna nasus*	191 lbs. 8 oz.	6′ 4″	42″	Montauk, N. Y.	May 28 1964	Carl Monaco
SHARK, Thresher	*Alopias vulpinus*	227 lbs.	11′ 9″	40″	Cavalli Islands, New Zealand	July 6 1971	Douglas Rooke
SHARK, Tiger	*Galeocerdo cuvier*	362 lbs.	11′ 2″	52½″	Cape Moreton, Australia	July 6 1957	Bob Dyer
SNOOK or ROBALO	*Centropomus undecimalis*	43 lbs.	3′ 11″	26½″	Lake Worth, Florida	May 18 1952	Lee K. Spencer
SWORDFISH	*Xiphias gladius*						
TANGUIGUE	*Scomberomorus commerson*	73 lbs. 8 oz.	5′ 5″	28″	Queensland, Australia	May 9 1971	Edward J. French
TARPON	*Tarpon atlanticus*	283 lbs.	7′ 2⅗″		Lake Maracaibo, Venezuela	March 19 1956	M. Salazar
TUNA, Allison or Yellowfin	*Thunnus albacares*	187 lbs. 12 oz.	6′ 2½″	47″	Sydney, N.S.W., Australia	July 15 1965	Frank Pfeiffer
TUNA, Atlantic Big-Eyed	*Thunnus obesus*						
TUNA, Pacific Big-Eyed	*Parathunnus sibi*	163 lbs.	5′ 1″	50½″	San Diego, California	Aug. 15 1970	Forrest N. Shumway
TUNA, Blackfin	*Thunnus atlanticus*	38 lbs.	3′ 3¼″	28¾″	Bermuda	June 26 1970	Archie L. Dickens

FISH	Scientific Name	Weight	Length	Girth	Place	Date	Angler
TUNA, Bluefin	*Thunnus thynnus*	172 lbs.	5' 5"	45"	Cape Pillar, Tasmania	May 8 1959	C. I. Cutler
WAHOO	*Acanthocybium solandri*	98 lbs. 10 oz.	6' 1½"	33"	Bermuda	Sept. 5 1963	William P. Imhauser
WEAKFISH	*Cynoscion regalis*	10 lbs. 10 oz.	3'		Fire Is. Light, N. Y.	Sept. 20 1951	J. E. Bailey
WEAKFISH, Spotted	*Cynoscion nebulosus*	15 lbs. 6 oz.	2' 9"	23¾"	St. Lucie River, Jensen Beach, Fla.	May 4 1969	Michael J. Foremny
YELLOWTAIL	*Seriola lalandi*	88 lbs.	4' 7½"	33"	Cape Brett, New Zealand	June 25 1963	J. R. Chibrall

International Game Fish Association

RECORD CATCHES FOR MEN

20 LB. LINE TEST RECORDS (over 12 lbs., up to and including 20 lbs.)

FISH	Scientific Name	Weight	Length	Girth	Place	Date	Angler
ALBACORE	*Thunnus germo*						
AMBERJACK	*Seriola lalandi*	101 lbs. 8 oz.	5' 1"	39"	Palm Beach, Florida	Feb. 26 1964	Robert R. Boomhower
BARRACUDA	*Sphyraena barracuda*	60 lbs. 10 oz.	5' 4½"	26½"	Cairns, Australia	Nov. 5 1968	Desmond R. Schumann
BASS, Calif. Black Sea	*Stereolepis gigas*	425 lbs.	7' 1"	76"	Point Mugu, California	Oct. 1 1960	C. C. Joiner
BASS, Calif. White Sea	*Cynoscion nobilis*	72 lbs.	4' 11¾"	30½"	Catalina, Calif.	Aug. 13 1958	Dr. Charles Dorshkind
BASS, Channel (Tie)	*Sciaenops ocellatus*	62 lbs.	4' 4"	30½"	Cape Hatteras, N. C.	Nov. 3 1958	John Twachtman
		62 lbs.	4' 7"	30"	Ship Shoal Is., Virginia	Oct. 4 1966	Rudy S. Kuhnel
BASS, Giant Sea	*Promicrops itaiara*	343 lbs.	6' 10"	61"	Flamingo, Florida	Jan. 6 1968	Ralph Delph
BASS, Sea	*Centropristes striatus*	6 lbs. 1 oz.	2' ⅛"	17"	Seabright, N. J.	July 13 1958	William Young
BASS, Striped (Tie)	*Roccus saxatilis*	67 lbs.	4' 7"	29½"	Block Island, R. I.	May 31 1963	Jack Ryan
		67 lbs.	4' 6⅛"	32½"	Greenhill, Rhode Island	Oct. 3 1965	Wilfred Fontaine
BLACKFISH or TAUTOG	*Tautoga onitis*	21 lbs.	2' 6"		Jamestown Island, R. I.	Nov. 6 1954	C. W. Sundquist
BLUEFISH	*Pomatomus saltatrix*	22 lbs. 12 oz.	3' 3"	23"	Rodanthe, N. C.	Nov. 22 1969	Joseph J. Menzaco
BONEFISH	*Albula vulpes*	14 lbs.	2' 10¼"	17½"	Bermuda	Dec. 29 1950	Dr. H. R. Becker
BONITO, Oceanic	*Katsuwonus pelamis*	32 lbs. 8 oz.	3' 0"	26"	San Juan, P. R.	May 23 1959	Juan Carellas, Jr.
COBIA	*Racrycentron canadus*	91 lbs.	4' 8"	30"	Crystal Beach, Florida	April 25 1962	Roy English
COD	*Gadus callarias*	98 lbs. 12 oz.	5' 3"	41"	Isle of Shoals, Mass.	June 8 1969	Alphonse J. Biglevich
DOLPHIN	*Coryphaena hippurus*	64 lbs. 12 oz.	5' 9"	32¾"	Islamorada, Florida	June 7 1970	Donald H. Jackson
DRUM, Black	*Pogonias cromis*	72 lbs. 6 oz.	4' 4½"	38"	Tuckerton, N. J.	July 12 1970	Michael J. Sandone
FLOUNDER	*Paralichthys*	20 lbs.	3' 1"	32"	Long Island, N. Y.	Sept. 7 1948	P. H. Kessell
KINGFISH	*S. Cavalla*	77 lbs.	5' 5"	29"	Bimini, Bahamas	May 12 1957	Clinton Olney Potts
MARLIN, Black	*Makaira indica*	381 lbs.	10' 4"	56¼"	Pinas Bay Reef, Panama	Mar. 6 1970	Russell M. Anderson

FISH	Scientific Name	Weight	Length	Girth	Place	Date	Angler
MARLIN, Blue	Makaira ampla	430 lbs.	11' 6"	54"	St. Thomas, Virgin Islands	Aug. 31 1970	Charles R. Senf
MARLIN, Pacific Blue	Makaira nigricans	220 lbs.	9' 6"	42"	B.C., Mexico	Nov. 25 1967	W. Matt Parr
MARLIN, Striped	Makaira mitsukurii	338 lbs.	10' 5"	47½"	Sydney, Australia	Mar. 9 1960	James F. Baldwin
MARLIN, White	Makaira albida	128 lbs. 8 oz.	8' 6"	36"	Bimini, Bahamas	April 11 1963	Mrs. J. W. Walters
PERMIT	Trachinotus goodei	50 lbs. 8 oz.	3' 8¾"	33¾"	Key West, Florida	Mar. 15 1971	Marshall E. Earnest
POLLACK	Pollachius virens	33 lbs.	3' 3"	26"	Wedgeport, Nova Scotia	Aug. 30 1966	Dr. Duncan Sinclair
RUNNER, Rainbow	Elagatis bipinnulatus	25 lbs.	4'	23"	Pinas Bay, Panama	May 9 1965	Donald J. S. Merten
ROOSTERFISH	Nematistius pectoralis	85 lbs. 13 oz.	4' 10½"	42¾"	LaPaz, BC, Mexico	June 15 1966	Willard E. Hanson
SAILFISH, Atlantic	Istiophorus americanus	108 lbs. 8 oz.	8'	34"	Miami, Florida	Apr. 17 1969	James L. Clayman
SAILFISH, Pacific	Istiophorus greyi	158 lbs.	9' 1"	35½"	Santa Cruz Island, Galapagos	Mar. 4 1954	A. Hall
SHARK, Blue	Prionace glauca	218 lbs. 2 oz.	9' 9"	42"	Montauk, New York	July 22 1955	M. B. Mittleman
SHARK, Mako	Isurus oxyrhynchus I. glaucus	242 lbs. 12 oz.	8' 1"	44"	Montauk, New York	July 12 1958	M. B. Mittleman
SHARK, Man-Eater or White	Carcharodon carcharias	1068 lbs.	12' 6"	77"	Cape Moreton, Australia	June 18 1957	Bob Dyer
SHARK, Porbeagle	Lamna nasus	180 lbs.	8' 7½"	37"	Block Island, R. I.	Aug. 9 1960	Frank K. Smith
SHARK, Thresher	Alopias vulpinus	81 lbs. 8 oz.	6'7"	30"	Santa Cruz, Calif.	Aug. 2 1958	E. G. Volpe
SHARK, Tiger	Galeocerdo cuvier	341 lbs.	10'	55½"	Cape Moreton, Australia	July 6 1957	Bob Dyer
SNOOK or ROBALO	Centropomus undecimalis	41 lbs. 8 oz.	3' 6"	29"	Palm Beach, Florida	June 30 1968	H. Wilder Clapp
SWORDFISH	Xiphias gladius	183 lbs. 8 oz.	10'	41"	Cabo San Lucas, Baja California	May 4 1971	Charles C. Yamamoto
TANGUIGUE	Scomberomorus commerson	78 lbs.	5' 7½"	33½"			
TARPON	Tarpon atlanticus	158 lbs. 8 oz.	6' 8½"	39¼"	New Orleans, La.	Aug. 23 1958	J. J. Lincoln
TUNA, Allison or Yellowfin	Thunnus albacares	148 lbs.	5' 7"	40"	Jupiter, Florida	May 16 1971	Rudolph Steinhauser, Jr.
TUNA, Atlantic Big-Eyed	Thunnus obesus						
TUNA, Pacific Big-Eyed	Parathunnus sibi	108 lbs.	4' 3½"	37½"	San Diego, California	Aug. 10 1968	John E. Muckenthaler
TUNA, Blackfin	Thunnus atlanticus	31 lbs. 2 oz.	3' 3"	26"	Bermuda	Oct. 17 1968	Vincent F. Schiumo
TUNA, Bluefin	Thunnus thynnus	114 lbs. 8 oz.	5' 1"	42"	Montauk, New York	July 25 1959	Mundy I. Peale
WAHOO	Acanthocybium solandri	115 lbs.	6' 3½"	32"	Bermuda	July 2 1961	Leo Barboza
WEAKFISH	Cynoscion regalis	8 lbs. 12 oz.	2' 6½"	16"	Ocean City, Md.	June 2 1951	P. V. Mumford
WEAKFISH, Spotted	Cynoscion nebulosus	13 lbs. 12 oz.	3'	19"	Vero Beach, Florida	Mar. 11 1957	W. Miller Shaw, Jr.
YELLOWTAIL	Seriola lalandi	74 lbs.	4' 11"	31¼"	Cavalli Islands, New Zealand	May 29 1969	William Pocklington

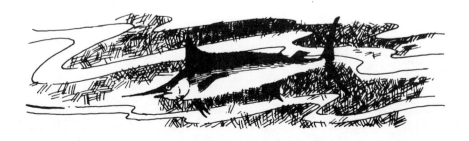

International Game Fish Association

RECORD CATCHES FOR MEN

12 LB. LINE TEST RECORDS (up to and including 12 lbs.)

FISH	Scientific Name	Weight	Length	Girth	Place	Date	Angler
ALBACORE	Thunnus germo	39 lbs. 8 oz.	3' 7½"	32½"	Balboa, Calif.	July 23 1958	Dr. R. S. Rubaum
AMBERJACK	Seriola lalandi	76 lbs. 10 oz.	4' 9"	32"	Bermuda	Sept. 8 1963	Joseph Henry Stubbs
BARRACUDA	Sphyraena barracuda	49 lbs. 4 oz.	4' 8"	21½"	Margarita, Venezuela	Jan. 9 1960	Gerardo Sanson
BASS, Calif. Black Sea	Stereolepis gigas	112 lbs. 8 oz.	4' 9"	44"	San Francisco Is., Mexico	June 12 1957	D. B. Rosenthal
BASS, Calif. White Sea	Cynoscion nobilis	65 lbs.	4' 10"	28"	Ensenada, Mexico	July 8 1955	C. J. Aronis
BASS, Channel	Sciaenops ocellatus	60 lbs. 8 oz.	4' 2¾"	29¾"	Kill Devil Hills, N. C.	Oct. 24 1954	A. Clark Jr.
BASS, Giant Sea	Promicrops itaiara	349 lbs.	6' 10"	62"	Florida Bay, Florida	May 25 1969	Ralph Delph
BASS, Sea	Centropristes striatus	5 lbs. 6 oz.	1' 9½"	16"	Virginia Beach, Virginia	May 16 1970	J. David Wright
BASS, Striped	Roccus saxatilis	61 lbs. 10 oz.	4' 5"	30"	Block Island, R. I.	July 5 1956	L. A. Garceau
BLACKFISH or TAUTOG	Tautoga onitis	12 lbs.	2' 1½"	20½"	Block Island, R. I.	Oct. 18 1952	D. V. Marshall
BLUEFISH	Pomatomus saltatrix	24 lbs. 3 oz.	3' 5"	22"	San Miguel, Azores	Aug. 27 1953	M. A. da Silva Veloso
BONEFISH	Albula vulpes	16 lbs.	2' 9½"	18½"	Bimini, Bahamas	Feb. 25 1971	Jerry Lavenstein
BONITO, Oceanic	Katsuwonus pelamis	23 lbs. 7 oz.	2' 9"	23"	Oahu, Hawaii	Aug. 10 1958	Raymond Y. Kaaihara
COBIA	Rachycentron canadus	70 lbs.	5'	31½"	Gulf of Mexico, Texas	May 13 1955	H. A. Norris, Jr.
COD	Gadus callarias	55 lbs.	5' 6"	38"	Plum Island, Mass.	July 6 1958	W. C. Dunn
DOLPHIN	Coryphaena hippurus	59 lbs. 8 oz.	5' 4"	33"	Pinas Bay, Panama	Jan. 28 1971	Russell M. Anderson
DRUM, Black	Pogonias cromis	89 lbs.	4' 3"	40½"	Delaware Bay, New Jersey	May 14 1971	John K. Osborne, Jr.
FLOUNDER	Paralichthys	16 lbs. 8 oz.	2' 7"	34"	Ft. George, Florida	Oct. 18 1967	J. R. Wohanka
KINGFISH	S. Cavalla	52 lbs. 4 oz.	4' 11½"	25½"	Miami, Florida	Apr. 13 1958	H. Marin
MARLIN, Black	Makaira indica	309 lbs.	10' 4"	49"	Pinas Bay, Panama	Jan. 24 1971	Russell M. Anderson
MARLIN, Blue	Makaira ampla	448 lbs.	11' 6½"	55"	St. Thomas, Virgin Islands	Sept. 6 1971	Frank L. Miller
MARLIN, Pacific Blue	Makaira nigricans	112 lbs.	7' 5"	32½"	The Peak, Australia	Mar. 20 1966	Kevin Alfred Brennan
MARLIN, Striped	Makaira mitsukurii	103 lbs. 8 oz.	8' ½"	31½"	Bimini, Bahamas	Apr. 8 1952	G. A. Bass
MARLIN, White	Makaira albida	122 lbs.	8' 3"	44"	Bimini, Bahamas	Mar. 30 1953	Dorothy A. Curtice
PERMIT	Trachinotus goodei	50 lbs.	3' 7"	34½"	Miami, Florida	Mar. 27 1965	Robert F. Miller
POLLACK	Pollachius virens	36 lbs.	3' 11"	32"	Hunts Point, Nova Scotia	Aug. 10 1965	Perry MacNeal
RUNNER, Rainbow	Elagatis bipinnulatus	18 lbs. 12 oz.	3' 2⅞"	20½"	Las Cruces, Baja California	May 31 1961	Bing Crosby
ROOSTERFISH	Nematistius pectoralis	50 lbs. 11 oz.	4' 8"	32"	Guerro, Mexico	Jan. 15 1961	Joseph Krieger, Jr.
SAILFISH, Atlantic	Istiophorus americanus	85 lbs.	7' ½"	31"	Carayaca, Venezuela	July 15 1962	Guillermo Yanes Pares
SAILFISH, Pacific	Istiophorus greyi	159 lbs.	9' 11"	36"	Pinas Bay, Panama	July 23 1957	J. Frank Baxter
SHARK, Blue	Prionace glauca	312 lbs.	10' 7"	47"	Montauk Point, New York	Oct. 28 1963	John S. Walton
SHARK, Mako	Isurus oxyrhynchus I. glaucus	261 lbs. 11 oz.	7' 4"	44½"	Montauk, N. Y.	Oct. 1 1953	C. R. Meyer

FISH	Scientific Name	Weight	Length	Girth	Place	Date	Angler
SHARK, Man-Eater or White	Carcharodon carcharias	96 lbs. 10 oz.	5' 7"	27½"	Mazatlan, Mexico	April 30 1964	Ray O. Acord
SHARK, Porbeagle	Lamna nasus	66 lbs.	4' 10"	30"	Montauk, N. Y.	June 8 1958	M. H. Merrill
SHARK, Thresher	Alopias vulpinus	92 lbs. 8 oz.	4' 9"	31"	Long Beach, California	Dec. 12 1959	D. F. Marsh
SHARK, Tiger	Galeocerdo cuvier						
SNOOK or ROBALO	Centropomus undecimalis	37 lbs.	3' 11"	24½"	Boynton Beach, Florida	June 18 1959	Durling Drake
SWORDFISH	Xiphias gladius	120 lbs.	8' 7"	33"	Palmilla, Baja California	June 1 1968	Russell M. Anderson
TANGUIGUE	Scomberomorus commerson	52 lbs. 4 oz.	5' 2"	29½"	Hayman Island, Australia	July 27 1968	Clive H. Michael
TARPON	Tarpon atlanticus	170 lbs. 8 oz.	7'	40"	Big Pine Key, Florida	Mar. 10 1963	Russell C. Ball
TUNA, Allison or Yellowfin	Thunnus albacares	145 lbs.	5' 5½"	40½"	Port Stephens, NSW Australia	Aug. 23 1970	Don McElwaine
TUNA, Atlantic Big-Eyed	Thunnus obesus						
TUNA, Pacific Big-Eyed	Parathunnus sibi	32 lbs.	3' 2½"	25"	Salinas, Ecuador	May 18 1968	Cesar Baquerizo
TUNA, Blackfin	Thunnus atlanticus	29 lbs. 12 oz.	3' ¼"	27"	Bermuda	Aug. 24 1968	Jay William Rewalt
TUNA, Bluefin	Thunnus thynnus	56 lbs.	3' 11½"	32"	S. Neptune Is., Australia	Apr. 12 1965	Eldred H. V. Riggs
WAHOO	Acanthocybium solandri	66 lbs.	5' 5"	26½"	St. Thomas Virgin Islands	Apr. 7 1967	Dr. Lyman J. Spire
WEAKFISH	Cynoscion regalis	9 lbs. 2 oz.	2' 7½"	17"	Tuckerton, N.J.	May 15 1963	Melvin Parker
(3 Way Tie)		9 lbs. 2 oz.	2' 7½"	15¼"	Oak Beach, N. Y.	Oct. 16 1953	B. L. DeClue
		9 lbs. 3½ oz.	2' 5"	16½"	Ocean City, Md.	May 26 1954	Bob Gilbert
WEAKFISH, Spotted (Tie)	Cynoscion nebulosus	13 lbs.	2' 10½"	18"	Jupiter, Fla.	July 19, 1956	L. B. Dukes
		13 lbs. 4 oz.	2' 9"	18½"	Cocoa, Fla.	Mar. 13, 1957	R. L. Fink
YELLOWTAIL	Seriola lalandi	54 lbs. 8 oz.	4' 2½"	28"	Cavalli Islands, New Zealand		B. V. Nathan

International Game Fish Association

ALL TACKLE RECORD CATCHES FOR WOMEN
From 130 lb. line test down to 12 lb. line test.

International Game Fish Association, world record entry forms may be obtained by writing: I.G.F.A., 2190 S.E. 17th St., Ft. Lauderdale, Fla., 33316.

MARINE FISHES
ALL TACKLE RECORDS FOR WOMEN

FISH	Scientific Name	Weight	Length	Girth	Place	Date	Angler	Line lbs.
ALBACORE	Thunnus germo	55 lbs. 4 oz.			Catalina, Calif.	Sept. 1927	Mrs. L. M. Doxie*	30
AMBERJACK	Seriola lalandi	106 lbs. 8 oz.	5' 5"	39"	Pinas Bay Panama	July 9 1960	Helen Robinson	80
BARRACUDA	Sphyraena barracuda	66 lbs. 4 oz.	5' 10"	25-1/5"	Cape Lopez, Gabon, Africa	July 17 1955	Mme. M. Halley	80

FISH	Scientific Name	Weight	Length	Girth	Place	Date	Angler	Line lbs.
BASS, Calif. Black Sea	Stereolepis gigas	452 lbs.	7' 2¼"	64¼"	Coronado Is., California	Oct. 8 1960	Lorene Wheeler	80
BASS, Calif. White Sea	Cynoscion nobilis	62 lbs.	4' 9"	28"	Malibu, Calif.	Dec. 6 1951	Mrs. D. W. Jackson	20
BASS, Channel	Sciaenops ocellatus	69 lbs. 8 oz. (30-lb. record for men & women)	4' 3½"	33¼"	Cape Hatteras, N. C.	Nov. 16 1958	Jean Browning	30
BASS, Giant Sea	Promicrops itaiara	204 lbs.	5' 11"	51"	Bahia Honda, Fla.	Mar. 1 1958	Mrs. Phyllis Carson	80
BASS, Sea	Centropristes striatus	5 lbs. 1 oz.	1' 8½"	16"	Panama City Beach, Fla.	July 21 1956	Mrs. R. H. Martin	50
BASS, Striped	Roccus saxatilis	64 lbs. 8 oz. (30-lb. record for men & women)	4' 6"	30"	North Truo, Mass.	Aug. 14 1960	Rosa O. Webb	30
BLACKFISH or TAUTOG	Tautoga onitis	16 lbs. 8 oz.	2' 6"	22"	Seventeen Fathoms, N. Y.	Nov. 1 1953	Edna De Fina	50
BLUEFISH	Pomatomus saltatrix	19 lbs. 4 oz.			Long Island Sound, N. Y.	Oct. 19 1958	Elanor Plasko	30
BONEFISH	Albula vulpes	15 lbs.	2' 8½"	18½"	Bimini, Bahamas	Mar. 20 1961	Andrea Tose	12
BONITO, Oceanic (Tie)	Katsuwonus pelamis	31 lbs.	2' 11"	24"	Kona, Hawaii	June 16, 1963	Anne H. Bosworth	130
		31 lbs.	2' 10½"	24½"	San Juan, P. Rico	Dec. 26, 1954	Gloria G. de Marques	50
		31 lbs.	2' 11"	24¾"	Nassau, Bahamas	Jan. 25, 1956	Mrs. Barbara Wallach	80
COBIA	Rachycentron canadus	97 lbs. (80-lb. record for men & women)	5' 6½"	33"	Oregon Inlet, N. C.	June 4 1952	Mary W. Black	80
COD	Gadus callarias	71 lbs. 8 oz. (20-lb. record for men & women)	4' 10"	31"	Cape Cod, Massachusetts	Aug. 2 1964	Muriel Betts	20
DOLPHIN	Coryphaena hippurus	73 lbs. 11 oz. (30-lb. record for men & women)	4' 11½"	43½"	Baja Calif., Mexico	July 12 1962	Barbara Kibbee Jayne	30
DRUM, Black	Pogonias cromis	93 lbs.	4' 2½"	42"	Fernandina Beach, Fla.	Mar. 28 1957	Mrs. Stella Moore	50
FLOUNDER	Paralichthys	20 lbs. 7 oz.	3' 1"	29½"	Long Island, N. Y.	July 8 1957	Mrs. M. Fredriksen	50
KINGFISH or TANGUIGUE	C. Commersonii S. Cavalla	78 lbs. (50-lb. record for men & women)	5' 6½"	28½"	Guayanilla, Puerto Rico	May 25 1963	Ruth M. Coon	50
MARLIN, Black	Name being revised	1,525 lbs.	14' 4"	80"	Cabo Blanco, Peru	Apr. 22 1954	Kimberley Wiss	130
MARLIN, Blue	Makaira ampla	730 lbs.		60¾"	Cat Cay, Bahamas	June 6 1939	Mrs. Henry Sears*	80
MARLIN, Pacific Blue	Name being revised	583 lbs. 8 oz.	12' 3"	60"	Kailua Kona, Hawaii	Jan. 26 1969	Sally H. Rice	130
MARLIN, Striped	Makaira mitsukurii	430 lbs.	10' 8½"	54½"	Mayor Island, New Zealand	Apr. 9 1955	Mrs. H. J. Carkeek	80
MARLIN, White	Makaira albida	152 lbs. (130-lb. record for men & women)	8' 3"	40"	Bimini, Bahamas	Mar. 14 1936	Mrs. Marion Stevens*	130
PERMIT (Tie)	Trachinotus goodei	38 lbs.	3' 7"	31"	Key West, Fla.	Apr. 9, 1963	Helen Robinson	30
		38 lbs.	3' 7"	33"	Islamorada, Fla.	June 11, 1961	L. Meulenberg	20
		38 lbs.	3' 4"	30½"	Islamorada, Fla.	Mar. 21, 1954	Mrs. W. Edmunds	20
POLLACK	Pollachius virens	29 lbs.	3' 6"	24¼"	Manasquan, N. J.	Nov. 3 1958	Ann Durik	50
RUNNER, Rainbow	Elagatis bipinnulatus	23 lbs. (50-lb. record for men & women)	3' 6"	19½"	Oahu, Hawaii	May 9 1961	Lila M. Neuenfelt	50
ROOSTERFISH	Nematistius pectoralis	85 lbs. 2 oz. (50-lb. record for men & women)	4' 6"	36"	La Paz, Mexico	Nov. 24 1956	Mrs. Esther Carle	50
SAILFISH, Atlantic	Istiophorus americanus	104 lbs. 8 oz.	7' 11"	31"	Miami Beach, Fla.	Mar. 22 1939	Ruth Edmands Pope*	80
SAILFISH, Pacific	Istiophorus greyi	196 lbs.	10' 7"	40"	Acapulco, Mexico	Feb. 9 1951	Mrs. F. Bart	80
SAWFISH	Pristis pectinatus	134 lbs. (120-lb. record for men & women)	8' 10"	32"	Long Key Florida	Mar. 27 1963	Olive M. Senn	20
SHARK, Blue	Prionace glauca	334 lbs. (130-lb. record for men & women)	10' 8"	47½"	Rockport, Massachusetts	Sept. 4 1964	Cassandra Webster	130
SHARK, Mako	Isurus oxyrhynchus I. glaucus	911 lbs. 12 oz.	11' 2"	70"	Palm Beaches, Florida	April 9 1962	Audrey Cohen	130

FISH	Scientific Name	Weight	Length	Girth	Place	Date	Angler	
SHARK, Man-Eater or White	Carcharodon carcharias	1,052 lbs.	13' 10"	72½"	Cape Moreton, Australia	June 27 1954	Mrs. Bob Dyer	130
SHARK, Porbeagle	Lamna nasus	271 lbs. (130-lb. record for men & women)	8' 2"	49"	Looe, Cornwall, England	Aug. 18 1957	Mrs. Hetty Eathorne	130
SHARK, Thresher	Alopias vulpinus	729 lbs.	8' 5"	61"	Mayor Is., New Zealand	June 3 1959	Mrs. V. Brown	130
SHARK, Tiger	Galeocerdo cuvier	1,314 lbs.	13' 9"	89"	Cape Moreton, Australia	July 27 1953	Mrs. Bob Dyer	130
SNOOK or ROBALO	Centropomus undecimalis	52 lbs. 6 oz. (30-lb. record for men & women)	4' 1½"	26"	La Paz, Mexico	Jan. 9 1963	Jane Haywood	30
SWORDFISH	Xiphias gladius	772 lbs. (80-lb. record for men & women)	12' 10"	70"	Iquique, Chile	June 7 1954	Mrs. L. Marron	80
TARPON	Tarpon atlanticus	203 lbs.	7' 11"	44"	Marathon Florida	May 19 1961	June Jordan	80
TUNA, Allison or Yellowfin	Thunnus albacares	254 lbs.	6' 3"	52"	Kona, Hawaii	Aug. 19 1954	Jane Carlisle	130
TUNA, Atlantic Big-Eyed	Thunnus obesus	182 lbs.	5' 8"	56"	Cat Cay, Bahamas	June 2 1958	Mrs. Pablo Bardin	130
TUNA, Pacific Big-Eyed	Parathunnus sibi	336 lbs.	7' 3"	56½"	Cabo Blanco, Peru	Jan. 16 1957	Mrs. Seymour Knox III	130
TUNA, Blackfin	Thunnus atlanticus	32 lbs. 2 oz. (20-lb. record for men & women)	3' 2"	26¾"	Bermuda	Oct. 23 1968	Mrs. Herbert N. Arnold	20
TUNA, Bluefin	Thunnus thynnus	882 lbs.	9' 2"	83½"	Wedgeport, N. S.	Sept. 6 1947	Mrs. A. D. Crowinnshield*	130
WAHOO (Tie)	Acanthocybium solandri	110 lbs. 110 lbs.	6' 1½" 6'	36½" 29"	Port Eades, Louisiana Walker Cay, Bahamas	June 22 1964 Apr. 1 1941	Mrs. Homer J. Moore, Jr. Mrs. A. D. Crowninshield*	130 130
WEAKFISH	Cynoscion regalis	11 lbs. 12 oz.	2'7¾"	18"	Newport R., N. C.	Oct. 29 1950	Mrs. L. A. Denning	50
WEAKFISH, Spotted (Tie)	Cynoscion nebulosus	10 lbs. 9 oz. 10 lbs. 4 oz.	2' 7½" 2' 6½"	15" 16"	Jupiter, Florida Jupiter, Florida	May 30, 1964 June 1, 1958	Jane H. Cole Nancy Dukes	30 12
YELLOWTAIL	Seriola dorsalis or S. grandis	81 lbs.	4' 9½"	32½"	Cape Brett, New Zealand	May 18 1960	Kura Beale	80

International Game Fish Association

RECORD CATCHES FOR WOMEN

130 LB. LINE TEST RECORDS (over 80 lbs., up to and including 130 lbs.)

FISH	Scientific Name	Weight	Length	Girth	Place	Date	Angler
ALBACORE	Thunnus germo						
AMBERJACK	Seriola lalandi	81 lbs.	5' 2"	31"	Pinas Bay, Panama	Feb. 13 1960	Mildred Warden
BARRACUDA	Sphyraena barracuda						
BASS, Calif. Black Sea	Stereolepis gigas						
BASS, Calif. White Sea	Cynoscion nobilis						
BASS, Channel	Sciaenops ocellatus						
BASS, Giant Sea	Promicrops itaiara	161 lbs.	5' 4½"	44"	Marathon, Fla.	Feb. 20 1957	Mrs. Patricia Demaret

FISH	Scientific Name	Weight	Length	Girth	Place	Date	Angler
BASS, Sea	Centropristes striatus						
BASS, Striped	Roccus saxatilis						
BLACKFISH or TAUTOG	Tautoga onitis						
BLUEFISH	Pomatomus saltatrix						
BONEFISH	Albula vulpes						
BONITO, Oceanic	Katsuwonus pelamis	31 lbs.	2' 11"	24"	Kona, Hawaii	June 16 1963	Anne H. Bosworth
COBIA	Rachycentron canadus						
COD	Gadus callarias						
DOLPHIN	Coryphaena hippurus						
DRUM, Black	Pogonias cromis						
FLOUNDER	Paralichthys						
KINGFISH	S. Cavalla						
MARLIN, Black	Name being revised	1,525 lbs.	14' 4"	80"	Cabo Blanco, Peru	Apr. 22 1954	Kimberley Wiss
MARLIN, Blue	Makaira ampla	606 lbs.	12' 2¾"	63"	Bimini, Bahamas	July 29 1949	Mrs. Harley Earl
MARLIN, Pacific Blue	Name being revised	583 lbs. 8 oz.	12' 3"	60"	Kailua Kona, Hawaii	Jan. 26 1969	Sally H. Rice
MARLIN, Striped	Makaira mitsukurii	403 lbs.	10'	52¼"	Tocopilla, Chile	June 21 1940	Mrs. Michael Lerner
MARLIN, White	Makaira albida	152 lbs. (130-lb. record for men & women)	8' 3"	40"	Bimini, Bahamas	Mar. 14 1936	Mrs. Marion Stevens*
PERMIT	Trachinotus goodei						
POLLACK	Pollachius virens						
RUNNER, Rainbow	Elagatis bipinnulatus						
ROOSTERFISH	Nematistius pectoralis						
SAILFISH, Atlantic	Istiophorus americanus						
SAILFISH, Pacific	Istiophorus greyi	163 lbs.	10'	44"	Pinas Bay, Panama	Aug. 14 1964	Nancy Smith
SHARK, Blue	Prionace glauca	334 lbs. (130-lb. record for men & women)	10' 8"	47½"	Rockport, Massachusetts	Sept. 4 1964	Cassandra Webster
SHARK, Mako	Isurus oxyrhynchus I. glaucus	911 lbs. 12 oz.	11' 2"	70"	Palm Beach, Florida	Apr. 9 1962	Audrey Cohen
SHARK, Man-Eater or White	Carcharodon carcharias	1,052 lbs.	13' 10"	72½"	Cape Moreton, Australia	June 27 1954	Mrs. Bob Dyer
SHARK, Porbeagle	Lamna nasus	271 lbs. (130-lb. record for men & women)	8' 2"	49"	Looe, Cornwall, England	Aug. 18 1957	Mrs. Hetty Eathorne
SHARK, Thresher	Alopias vulpinus	729 lbs.	8' 5"	61"	Mayor Is., New Zealand	June 3 1959	Mrs. V. Brown
SHARK, Tiger	Galeocerdo cuvier	1,314 lbs.	13' 9"	89"	Cape Moreton, Australia	July 27 1953	Mrs. Bob Dyer
SNOOK or ROBALO	Centropomus undecimalis						
SWORDFISH	Xiphias gladius	759 lbs.	13' 11"	73"	Iquique, Chile	June 30 1952	Mrs. D. A. Allison
TARPON	Tarpon atlanticus						
TUNA, Allison or Yellowfin	Thunnus albacares	254 lbs.	6' 3"	52"	Kona, Hawaii	Aug. 19 1954	Jean Carlisle

TUNA, Atlantic Big-Eyed	*Thunnus obesus*	182 lbs.	5' 8"	56"	Cat Cay, Bahamas	June 2 1958	Mrs. Pablo Bardin
TUNA, Pacific Big-Eyed	*Parathunnus sibi*	336 lbs.	7' 3"	56½"	Cabo Blanco, Peru	Jan. 16 1957	Mrs. Seymour Knox III
TUNA, Blackfin	*Thunnus atlanticus*						
TUNA, Bluefin	*Thunnus thynnus*	882 lbs.	9' 2"	83½"	Wedgeport, N. S.	Sept. 6 1947	Mrs. A. D. Crowninshield*
WAHOO	*Acanthocybium solandri*	110 lbs.	6' 1½"	36½"	Port Eades, Louisiana	June 22 1964	Mrs. Homer J. Moore, Jr.
		110 lbs.	6'	29"	Walker Cay, Bahamas	April 1 1941	Mrs. A. D. Crowninshield* Tie
WEAKFISH	*Cynoscion regalis*						
WEAKFISH, Spotted	*Cynoscion nebulosus*						
YELLOWTAIL	*Seriola dorsalis or S. grandis*	73 lbs.	4' 9"	31"	Mayor Is., New Zealand	Jan. 5 1959	Marie C. Wilson

International Game Fish Association

RECORD CATCHES FOR WOMEN

80 LB. LINE TEST RECORDS (over 50 lbs., up to and including 80 lbs.)

FISH	Scientific Name	Weight	Length	Girth	Place	Date	Angler
ALBACORE	*Thunnus germo*	29 lbs.	3' 1"	23"	Morro Bay, Cayifornia	Sept. 24 1967	Theresa Bullard
AMBERJACK	*Seriola lalandi*	106 lbs. 8 oz.	5' 5"	39"	Pinas Bay, Panama	July 9 1960	Helen Robinson
BARRACUDA	*Sphyraena barracuda*	66 lbs. 4 oz.	5' 10"	25⅕"	Cape Lopez, Gabon, Africa	July 17 1955	Mme. M. Halley
BASS, Calif. Black Sea	*Stereolepis gigas*	452 lbs.	7' 2¼"	64¼"	Coronado Is., California	Oct. 8 1960	Lorene Wheeler
BASS, Calif. White Sea	*Cynoscion nobilis*						
BASS, Channel	*Sciaenops ocellatus*						
BASS, Giant Sea	*Promicrops itaiara*	366 lbs.	7' 4½"	68"	Guayabo, Panama	Feb. 8 1965	Betsy B. Walker
BASS, Sea	*Centropristes striatus*						
BASS, Striped	*Roccus saxatilis*	56 lbs. (80-lb. record for men & women)	4' 5½"	33½"	Sandy Hook, N. J.	June 7 1955	Mrs. H. J. Sarnoski
BLACKFISH or TAUTOG	*Tautoga onitis*						
BLUEFISH	*Pomatomus saltatrix*	21 lbs. 8 oz.	3' 3¾"	21½"	Virginia Beach, Virginia	Aug. 8 1971	Katherine K. Ayers
BONEFISH	*Albula vulpes*						
BONITO, Oceanic	*Katsuwonus pelamis*	31 lbs.	2' 11"	24¾"	Nassau, Bahamas	Jan. 25 1956	Mrs. Barbara Wallach
COBIA	*Rachycentron canadus*	97 lbs. (80-lb. record for men & women)	5' 6½"	33"	Oregon Inlet, N. C.	June 4 1952	Mary W. Black
COD	*Gadus callarias*	81 lbs. 12 oz.	4' 11¾"	39"	Middlebank, Massachusetts	Sept. 24 1970	Mrs. Sophie Karwa
DOLPHIN	*Coryphaena hippurus*	67 lbs.	5' 5"	32"	Chub Cay, Bahamas	Mar. 13 1966	Ruth Stanley
DRUM, Black	*Pogonias cromis*						

FISH	Scientific Name	Weight	Length	Girth	Place	Date	Angler
FLOUNDER	*Paralichthys*						
KINGFISH	*S. Cavalla*	65 lbs.	5'	28''	N. Eleuthera, Bahamas	Dec. 20 1969	Mrs. Elizabeth W. A. Lapey
MARLIN, Black	*Makaira indica*	1028 lbs. 8 oz.	13' 1''	75½''	Cairns, Australia	Oct. 29 1970	Mrs. Colleen Seay
MARLIN, Blue	*Makaira ampla*						
MARLIN, Pacific Blue	*Makaira nigricans*	555 lbs.	11' 11''	58½''	Kailua-Kona, Hawaii	Aug. 9 1964	Mrs. R. H. Baldwin
MARLIN, Striped	*Makaira mitsukurii*	333 lbs.	10' 2''	48''	Ruahine Reef, New Zealand	Apr. 20 1971	Jennifer Amos
MARLIN, White	*Makaira albida*	142 lbs.	8' 2''	34''	Ft. Lauderdale, Florida	Mar. 14 1959	Marie Beneventi
PERMIT	*Trachinotus goodei*						
POLLACK	*Pollachius virens*						
RUNNER, Rainbow	*Elagatis bipinnulatus*						
ROOSTERFISH	*Nematistius pectoralis*	66 lbs.	4' 8''	29½''	La Paz, Mexico	Dec. 1 1964	Lily Call
SAILFISH, Atlantic	*Istiophorus americanus*						
SAILFISH, Pacific	*Istiophorus greyi*	199 lbs.	10'	42''	Pinas Bay, Panama	Jan. 17 1968	Carolyn B. Brinkman
SHARK, Blue	*Prionace glauca*	410 lbs.	11' 2''	52½	Rockport, Massachusetts	Aug. 17 1967	Martha C. Webster
SHARK, Mako	*Isurus oxyrhynchus I. glaucus*	880 lbs. (80-lb. record for men & women)	10' 11''	75¾''	Bimini, Bahamas	Aug. 3 1964	Florence Lotierzo
SHARK, Man-Eater or White	*Carcharodon carcharias*	912 lbs.	11' 11''	71½''	Cape Moreton, Australia	Aug. 29 1954	Mrs. Bob Dyer
SHARK, Porbeagle	*Lamna nasus*	230 lbs.	7' 3½''	43''	Montauk, New York	May 17 1965	Bea Harry
SHARK, Thresher	*Alopias vulpinus*	413 lbs. (80-lb. record for men & women)	15'	49½''	Bay of Islands, New Zealand	June 28 1960	Mrs. E. R. Simons
SHARK, Tiger	*Galeocerdo cuvier*	1173 lbs.	12' 4''	84''	Cronulla, N. S. W.	Mar. 24 1963	June Irene Butcher
SNOOK or ROBALO	*Centropomus undecimalis*						
SWORDFISH	*Xiphias gladius*	772 lbs. (80-lb. record for men & women)	12' 10''	70''	Iquique, Chile	June 7 1954	Mrs. L. Marron
TANGUIGUE	*Scomberomorus commerson*	64 lbs.	5' 7''	26''	Mozambique, East Africa	Sept. 12 1959	Mrs. A. C. Lee
TARPON	*Tarpon atlanticus*	203 lbs.	7' 11''	44''	Marathon, Florida	May 19 1961	June Jordan
TUNA, Allison or Yellowfin	*Thunnus albacares*	193 lbs. 12 oz.	5' 10''	48''	Pompano Beach, Florida	Nov. 7 1957	Mrs. D. W. Miller
TUNA, Atlantic Big-Eyed	*Thunnus obesus*	62 lbs.	3' 7''	31''	St. Helena, Atlantic Ocean	Oct. 30 1957	Mrs. Brenda Dunlop
TUNA, Pacific Big-Eyed	*Parathunnus sibi*	335 lbs. (80-lb. record for men & women)	7' 1''	59½''	Cabo Blanco, Peru	Mar. 25 1953	Mrs. Wendell Anderson, Jr.
TUNA, Blackfin	*Thunnus atlanticus*	29 lbs. 4 oz.	3' ½''	25½''	Bermuda	Nov. 13 1965	Theresa Mary Phillips
TUNA, Bluefin	*Thunnus thynnus*	717 lbs.	9'	74''	Prince Edward Island, Canada	Sept. 1 1969	Doris R. Watts
WAHOO	*Acanthocybium solandri*	104 lbs.	6' 6''	30¼''	Walker Cay, Bahamas	May 2 1965	Mrs. Lloyd Dalzell
WEAKFISH	*Cynoscion regalis*						
WEAKFISH, Spotted	*Cynoscion nebulosus*						
YELLOWTAIL	*Seriola lalandi*	81 lbs.	4' 9½''	32½''	Cape Brett, New Zealand	May 18 1960	Kura Beale

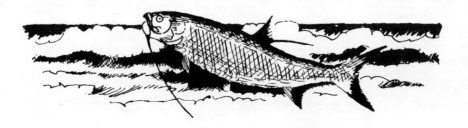

International Game Fish Association

RECORD CATCHES FOR WOMEN

50 LB. LINE TEST RECORDS (over 30 lbs., up to and including 50 lbs.)

FISH	Scientific Name	Weight	Length	Girth	Place	Date	Angler
ALBACORE	Thunnus germo	41 lbs.	3' 6"	27"	Morro Bay, California	Sept. 17 1967	Theresa Bullard
AMBERJACK	Seriola lalandi	108 lbs.	5' 9"	36"	Palm Beach, Florida	Dec. 30 1967	Peggy Kester Luke
BARRACUDA	Sphyraena barracuda						
BASS, alif. Black Sea	Stereolepis gigas	419 lbs. (50-lb. record for men & women)	7' 3¾"	63½"	Coronado Is., California	Oct. 8 1960	Bettie Sears
BASS, Calif. White Sea	Cynoscion nobilis	44 lbs. 3 oz.	4' 5"	25"	Catalina Island	May 2 1968	Gail Cruz
BASS, Channel	Sciaenops ocellatus	55 lbs.	4' 2"	29"	Smith Island, Virginia	Oct. 19 1966	Margaret M. Hutson
BASS, Giant Sea	Promicrops itaiara	290 lbs.	6' 7½"	60"	Marathon, Florida	May 5 1967	Mrs. Leslie Lear
BASS, Sea	Centropristes striatus	5 lbs. 1 oz.	1' 8½"	16"	Panama City Beach, Florida	July 21 1956	Mrs. R. H. Martin
BASS, Striped	Roccus saxatilis	64 lbs.	4' 2"	31"	Sea Bright, New Jersey	June 27 1971	Mrs. Asie Espenak
BLACKFISH or TAUTOG	Tautoga onitis	17 lbs. 6 oz.	2' 3½"	23¼"	Virginia Beach, Virginia	May 5 1971	Lillian T. Barrett
BLUEFISH	Pomatomus saltatrix	23 lbs. 15 oz.	3' 4½"	23½"	Nags Head, North Carolina	Nov. 19 1970	Mrs. Joyce Payne Bell
BONEFISH	Albula vulpes						
BONITO, Oceanic	Katsuwonus pelamis	31 lbs.	2' 10½"	24½"	San Juan, P. R.	Dec. 26 1954	Gloria G. de Marques
COBIA	Rachycentron canadus	85 lbs.	5' 7"	30½"	Queensland, Australia	Aug. 15 1964	Margaret Keid
COD	Gadus callarias	54 lbs. 2 oz.	4' 7¼"	33"	Nantucket Isl., Massachusetts	Sept. 28 1970	Gail A. Mosher
DOLPHIN	Coryphaena hippurus	67 lbs.	5' 8"	31¾"	Miami Beach, Florida	Jan. 2 1968	Janet Shepro
DRUM, Black	Pogonias cromis	93 lbs.	4' 2½"	42"	Fernandina Beach, Florida	March 28 1957	Mrs. Stella Moore
FLOUNDER	Paralichthys	20 lbs. 7 oz.	3' 1"	29½"	Long Island, N. Y.	July 8 1957	Mrs. M. Fredriksen
KINGFISH	S. Cavalla	78 lbs. (50-lb. record for men & women)	5' 6½"	28½"	Guayanilla, Puerto Rico	May 25 1963	Ruth M. Coon
MARLIN, Black	Makaira indica	584 lbs. (50-lb. record for men & women)	12' 6"	68"	Pinas Bay, Panama	Jan. 14 1962	Helen Robinson
MARLIN, Blue	Makaira ampla	633 lbs. 8 oz.	13'	50"	Bimini, Bahamas	Mar. 27 1970	Mrs. Audrey Grady
MARLIN, Pacific Blue	Makaira nigricans	428 lbs. (50-lb. record for men & women)	11' 2"	52½"	Kailua-Kona, Hawaii	Nov. 2 1965	Jeannette Alford
MARLIN, Striped	Makaira mitsukurii	401 lbs.	9' 2"	50½"	Cavalli Islands, New Zealand	Feb. 24 1970	Mrs. Margaret Williams
MARLIN, White	Makaira albida	130 lbs.	7' 11"	34"	Montauk, L.I., N.Y.	Aug. 13 1951	Mrs. P. Dater
PERMIT	Trachinotus goodei	39 lbs.	3' 5"	30"	Islamorada, Florida	Apr. 2 1966	Shelagh B. Richards
POLLACK	Pollachius virens	29 lbs.	3' 6"	24¼"	Manasquan, N. J.	Nov. 3 1958	Ann Durik
RUNNER, Rainbow	Elagatis bipinnulatus	23 lbs. (50-lb. record for men & women)	3' 6"	19½"	Oahu, Hawaii	May 9 1961	Lila M. Neuenfelt
ROOSTERFISH	Nematistius pectoralis	85 lbs. 2 oz. (50-lb. record for men & women)	4' 6"	36"	La Paz, Mexico	Nov. 24 1956	Mrs. Esther Carle
SAILFISH, Atlantic	Istiophorus americanus	108 lbs. 4 oz.	8' 9½"	34"	Luanda, Angola	Mar. 30 1971	Mrs. Ellen Botha
SAILFISH, Pacific	Istiophorus greyi	192 lbs. (50-lb. record for men & women)	10' 5"	40½"	La Paz, Mexico	Sept. 6 1950	Gay Thomas
SHARK, Blue	Prionace glauca	298 lbs.	11' 6"	40"	Montauk, N. Y.	Oct. 5 1959	Valerie Wuestefeld
SHARK, Mako	Isurus oxyrhynchus I. glaucus	478 lbs.	11'	46"	Broughton Island, Australia	May 17 1957	Mrs. Ron Duncan

FISH	Scientific Name	Weight	Length	Girth	Place	Date	Angler
SHARK, Man-Eater or White	Carcharodon carcharias	801 lbs.	11' 3"	75"	Cape Moreton, Australia	June 11 1957	Mrs. Bob Dyer
SHARK, Porbeagle	Lamna nasus	238 lbs. 8 oz.	7' 8"	41"	Montauk, New York	May 17 1966	Bea Harry
SHARK, Thresher	Alopias vulphinus	248 lbs	12" 1"	40"	Broughton Island, Australia	Aug. 16 1956	Mrs. Ron Duncan
SHARK, Tiger	Galeocerdo cuvier	458 lbs.	10' 7"	57"	Cape Moreton, Australia	July 3 1957	Mrs. Bob Dyer
SNOOK or ROBALO	Centropomus undecimalis	31 lbs. 8 oz.	3' 5½"	23"	Stuart, Florida	July 17 1951	Mrs. B. N. Fox
SWORDFISH	Xiphias gladius	492 lbs. 4 oz.	11' 9"	54"	Montauk Pt., N.Y.	July 4 1959	Dorothea Cassullo
		(50-lb. record for men & women)					
TANGUIGUE	Scomberomorus commerson	63 lbs.	5' 7"	25½"	Hayman Island, Australia	Apr. 26 1970	Marie Gloria Maestracci
TARPON	Tarpon atlanticus	190 lbs. 8 oz.	7'	45"	Boca Grande, Florida	May 27 1970	Patricia J. Mang
TUNA, Allison or Yellowfin	Thunnus albacares	204 lbs. 4 oz.	6' 2"	48"	Kona, Hawaii	July 22 1971	Michelle Spalding
TUNA, Atlantic Big-Eyed	Thunnus obesus						
TUNA, Pacific Big-Eyed	Parathunnus sibi	240 lbs.	6' 3¼"	52¾"	Salinas, Ecuador	Jan. 11 1969	Helen C. King
TUNA, Blackfin	Thunnus atlanticus	31 lbs.	3'	26⁵⁄₁₆"	Bermuda	Aug. 30 1967	Mrs. Glenn Sipe
TUNA, Bluefin	Thunnus thynnus	518 lbs.	9' 1"	69"	Bimini, Bahamas	May 13 1950	Mrs. G. A. Bass
		(50-lb. record for men & women)					
WAHOO	Acanthocybium solandri	113 lbs.	6' 2"	33¼"	Yanuca, Fiji	June 30 1967	Jan K. Bates
WEAKFISH	Cynoscion regalis	11 lbs. 12 oz.	2' 7¾"	18"	Newport R., N. C.	Oct. 29 1950	Mrs. L. A. Denning
WEAKFISH, Spotted	Cynoscion nebulosus						
YELLOWTAIL	Seriola lalandi	72 lbs.	4' 2½"	32"	Cape Brett, New Zealand	May 22 1964	Kura Beale

International Game Fish Association

RECORD CATCHES FOR WOMEN

30 LB. LINE TEST RECORDS (over 20 lbs., up to and including 30 lbs.)

FISH	Scientific Name	Weight	Length	Girth	Place	Date	Angler
ALBACORE	Thunnus germo	59 lbs. 8 oz.	3' 9½"	29½"	Montauk, New York	Aug. 14 1971	Eileen B. Merten
AMBERJACK	Seriola lalandi	101 lbs.	5' 7"	45"	Palm Beach, Florida	Mar. 31 1970	Cynthia Boomhower
BARRACUDA	Sphyraena barracuda	43 lbs.	5'	26"	Key Largo, Florida	Dec. 9 1956	Mrs. Robert M. Scully
BASS, Calif. Black Sea	Stereolepis gigas	108 lbs. 8 oz.	4' 7"	42½"	San Pablo, Mexico	Dec. 29 1963	Frances Enfinger
BASS, Calif. White Sea	Cynoscion nobilis	59 lbs. 8 oz.	4' 7¼"	30"	Catalina Island	May 2 1968	Janice Jackson
BASS, Channel	Sciaenops ocellatus	69 lbs. 8 oz.	4' 3½"	33¼"	Cape Hatteras, N. C.	Nov. 16 1958	Jean Browning
		(30-lb. record for men & women)					
BASS, Giant Sea	Promicrops itaiara	318 lbs.	7' 3"	65"	Dry Tortugas, Florida	Mar. 14 1966	Dottie Hall
BASS, SEA	Centropristes striatus						

FISH	Scientific Name	Weight	Length	Girth	Place	Date	Angler	Line Lbs.
BASS, Striped	Roccus saxatilis	64 lbs. 8 oz. (30-lb. record for men & women)	4' 6"	30"	North Truo, Massachusetts	Aug. 14 1960	Rosa O. Webb	
BLACKFISH or TAUTOG	Tautoga onitis	11 lbs. 3 oz.	2' 2"	19½"	Virginia Beach, Virginia	May 17 1971	Mrs. Charlotte Wright	
BLUEFISH	Pomatomus saltatrix	21 lbs. 8 oz.	3' 1"	23"	Truro, Mass.	Oct. 10 1970	Ruth M. Anderson	
BONEFISH	Albula vulpes							
BONITO, Oceanic	Katsuwonus pelamis	28 lbs. 8 oz.	2' 8¼"	23"	Walanae, Hawaii	June 8 1954	Mrs. C. T. Nottage	
COBIA	Rachycentron canadus	68 lbs. 8 oz.	5'	28½"	Onancock, Virginia	June 6 1968	Mrs. Frances Roberts	
COD	Gadus callarias	26 lbs.	3' 5"	25"	Wedgeport Nova Scotia	July 19 1964	Catherine Bauer	
DOLPHIN	Coryphaena hippurus	73 lbs. 11 oz. (30-lbs. record for men & women)	4' 11½"	43½"	Baja Calif., Mexico	July 12 1962	Barbara Kibbee Jayne	
DRUM, Black	Pogonias cromis	74 lbs.	3' 11½"	37"	Island Beach, N. J.	July 12 1956	Mrs. E. H. Conlon	
FLOUNDER	Paralichthys	13 lbs. 11 oz.	2' 9"	27½"	Long Branch, N. J.	Aug. 20 1953	Mrs. Leslie H. Taylor	
KINGFISH	S. Cavalla							
MARLIN, Black	Makaira indica	552 lbs. (30-lb. record for men & women)	12' 3"	62"	La Plata Is., Ecuador	July 3 1953	Mrs. W. G. Krieger	
MARLIN, Blue	Makaira ampla	364 lbs.	10' 8"	52"	Walker Cay, Bahamas	May 14 1965	Patricia E. Church	
MARLIN, Pacific Blue	Makaira nigricans	264 lbs. (30-lb. record for men & women)	10' ½"	45"	Kailua-Kona, Hawaii	Nov. 9 1965	Jeannette Alford	
MARLIN, Striped	Makaira mitsukurii	289 lbs.	10' 1"	45"	Iquique, Chile	May 18 1954	Mrs. L. Marron	
MARLIN, White	Makaira albida	120 lbs. 10 oz.	7' 5¾"	32¼"	Bimini, Bahamas	Mar. 29 1956	Mrs. M. Meyer, Jr.	
PERMIT	Trachinotus goodei	38 lbs.	3' 7"	31"	Key West, Florida	Apr. 9 1963	Helen Robinson	
POLLACK	Pollachius virens	30 lbs. 12 oz.	3' 7"	26"	Brielle, N. J.	Apr. 17 1968	Ruth Gifford	
RUNNER, Rainbow	Elagatis bipinnulatus	12 lbs. 2 oz.	3' 4"	16¼"	Guerro, Mexico	Jan. 21 1963	Mrs. Joseph Krieger, Jr.	
ROOSTERFISH	Nematistius pectoralis	99 lbs.	4' 11½"	34½"	La Paz, Mexico	Nov. 30 1964	Lily Call	
SAILFISH Atlantic	Istiophorus americanus	84 lbs.	8' 2"	29"	Jupiter, Florida	May 3 1971	Jeanne C. Chatham	
SAILFISH, Pacific	Istiophorus greyi	178 lbs.	9' 11½"	37"	Santa Cruz Is., Galapagos Is.	Feb. 27 1955	Mrs. A. Hall	
SHARK, Blue	Prionace glauca	284 lbs. 8 oz.	10' 8"	42"	Montauk, N. Y.	Aug. 11 1959	Jacqueline Mittleman	
SHARK, Mako	Isurus oxyrhynchus I. glaucus	376 lbs.	10'	46"	Sydney, Australia	Sept. 7 1969	Helen Gillis	
SHARK, Man-Eater or White	Carcharodon carcharias	803 lbs.	12' 5"	70"	Cape Moreton, Australia	July 5 1957	Mrs. Bob Dyer	
SHARK, Porbeagle	Lamna nasus	222 lbs. 8 oz.	6' 3"	44"	Isle of Wight, England	Aug. 14 1969	Mrs. Paula Everinaton	
SHARK, Thresher	Alopias vulpinus							
SHARK, Tiger	Galeocerdo cuvier							
SNOOK or ROBALO	Centropomus undecimalis	52 lbs. 6 oz. (30-lb. record for men & women)	4' 1½"	26"	La Paz, Mexico	Jan. 9 1963	Jane Haywood	
SWORDFISH	Xiphias gladius							
TANGUIGUE	Scomberomorus commerson	68 lbs.	5' 8"	26"	Hayman Island, Australia	May 14 1969	Lady Joan Ansett	
TARPON	Tarpon atlanticus	171 lbs.	6' 11"	42¾"	Marathon, Florida	May 21 1968	Mrs. Henry Sage	
TUNA, Allison or Yellowfin	Thunnus albacares	137 lbs.	5' 3½"	41¾"	Challenger Bank, Bermuda	Sept. 12 1965	Jan T. Helsel	
TUNA, Atlantic Big-Eyed	Thunnus obesus							
TUNA, Pacific Big-Eyed	Parathunnus sibi	133 lbs.	5' 2½"	41¾"	Coronado Isl., California	Oct. 7 1970	Mrs. Sally Johnson	

FISH	Scientific Name	Weight	Length	Girth	Place	Date	Angler
TUNA, Blackfin	Thunnus atlanticus	31 lbs. 4 oz.	3' 1⅞"	26¼"	Bermuda	June 23 1963	Mary Anne Eve
TUNA, Bluefin	Thunnus thynnus	117 lbs. 8 oz.	5' 1³⁄₁₆"	42"	San Diego, California	Sept. 10 1968	Gladys A. Chambers
WAHOO	Acanthocybium solandri	107 lbs. 4 oz.	6' ½"	33"	Eleuthera, Bahamas	Apr. 4 1965	Mrs. S. F. Briggs II
WEAKFISH	Cynoscion regalis						
WEAKFISH, Spotted	Cynoscion nebulosus	14 lbs.	2' 9"	18"	Stuart, Florida	Apr. 25 1970	Marilyn C. Albright
YELLOWTAIL	Seriola lalandi	68 lbs.	4' 6½"	32"	Mayor Island, New Zealand	Apr. 17 1969	Mrs. Marjorie West

International Game Fish Association

RECORD CATCHES FOR WOMEN

20 LB. LINE TEST RECORDS (over 12 lbs., up to and including 20 lbs.)

FISH	Scientific Name	Weight	Length	Girth	Place	Date	Angler
ALBACORE	Thunnus germo	50 lbs.	3' 9½"	29"	Ocean City, Maryland	Sept. 3 1970	Mrs. Carol R. Moss
AMBERJACK	Seriola lalandi	83 lbs. 14 oz.	4' 9¼"	36"	Challenger Bank, Bermuda	July 28 1966	L. Edna Perinchief
BARRACUDA	Sphyraena barracuda	48 lbs.	5' 4½"	26"	Heron Island, Australia	Aug. 21 1970	Mrs. Glenn MacTaggart
BASS, Calif. Black Sea	Stereolepis gigas	120 lbs.	4' 7"	40"	Malibu, California	Jan. 6 1957	Jane D. Hill
BASS, Calif. White Sea	Cynoscion nobilis	62 lbs.	4' 9"	28"	Malibu, Calif.	Dec. 6 1951	Mrs. D. W. Jackson
BASS, Channel	Sciaenops ocellatus	51 lbs. 8 oz.	4' 3"	28"	Avon, N. C.	Nov. 15 1970	Mrs. Michael E. Hayes
BASS, Giant Sea	Promicrops itaiara	42 lbs. 8 oz.	3' 7"	29"	Florida Bay, Florida	Nov. 7 1969	Helen Robinson
BASS, Sea	Centropristes striatus	5 lbs. 2 oz.	1' 11"	15"	Virginia Beach, Virginia	May 17 1971	Charlotte J. Wright
BASS, Striped	Roccus saxatilis	57 lbs. 8 oz.	4' 2"	30"	Block Is. Sound, N. Y.	Aug. 28 1959	Mary R. Aubry
BLACKFISH or TAUTOG	Tautoga onitis	10 lbs. 12 oz.	2' ⅝"	18¾"	Asharoken Beach, Long Island	May 7 1962	Trudy H. King
BLUEFISH	Pomatomus saltatrix	18 lbs. 6 oz.	3' 2¼"	20½"	Oregon Inlet, N. Carolina	Nov. 23 1969	Sammie Jill Everhart
(Tie)		18 lbs. 13 oz.	3' ¼"	21¾"	Port Canaveral Inlet, Florida	Mar. 24 1970	Inez Martines
BONEFISH	Albula vulpes	13 lbs. 12 oz.	2' 6¾"	17½"	Exuma, Bahamas	Jan. 3 1956	Mrs. B. A. Garson
BONITO, Oceanic	Katsuwonus pelamis	25 lbs.	2' 9"	22½"	San Juan, P. R.	Oct. 2 1900	Carmen Perez Agudo
COBIA	Rachycentron canadus	67 lbs.	5'	29"	Cape Charles, Virginia	July 5 1968	Judith Anne Gingell
COD	Gadus callarias	71 lbs. 8 oz. (20-lb. record for men & women)	4' 10"	31"	Cape Cod, Massachusetts	Aug. 2 1964	Muriel Betts
DOLPHIN	Coryphaena hippurus	69 lbs.	4' 10"	31¼"	Islamorada, Florida	Dec. 12 1966	Mrs. Frank K. Smith
DRUM, Black	Pogonias cromis	76 lbs.	4'	36"	Titusville, Florida	Jan. 25 1966	Theresa Becht
FLOUNDER	Paralichthys	16 lbs. 15½ oz.	2' 10½"	28½"	Cap Tree, New York	July 4 1971	Florence Eidman
KINGFISH	S. Cavalla	65 lbs. 8 oz.	5' 4"	25½"	Palm Beach, Florida	Feb. 14 1965	Patricia E. Church

FISH	Scientific Name	Weight	Length	Girth	Place	Date	Angler
MARLIN, Black	Makaira indica	418 lbs.	10' 10''	59''	Pinas Bay, Panama	Jan. 11 1968	Mrs. Carl Dann III
MARLIN, Blue	Makaira ampla	243 lbs.	9' 11½''	47¼''	Walker Cay, Bahamas	April 19 1965	Patricia E. Church
MARLIN, Pacific Blue	Makaira nigricans	252 lbs. 4 oz.	10' 4½''	47''	Mazatlan, Mexico	May 28 1969	Marguerite H. Barry
MARLIN, Striped	Makaira mitsukurii	321 lbs.	10' 7¼''	47''	Iquique, Chile	June 8 1954	Mrs. L. Marron
MARLIN, White	Makaira albida	129 lbs. 4 oz.	8' 7''	33½''	Bimini, Bahamas	April 11 1963	Mrs. J. M. Watters
		(Tie 20-lb. record for men & women)					
PERMIT		38 lbs.	3' 7''	33''	Islamorada, Florida	June 11 1961	Louise Meulenberg
(Tie)	Trachinotus goodei	38 lbs.	3' 4''	30½''	Islamorada, Florida	March 21 1954	Mrs. W. K. Edmunds
POLLACK	Pollachius virens	18 lbs. 8 oz.	2' 11¼''	22''	Wedgeport, Nova Scotia	July 31 1962	Mrs. Alfred Bridgford, Jr.
RUNNER, Rainbow	Elagatis bipinnulatus	12 lbs. 13 oz.	3' 2¼''	17''	Challenger Bank, Bermuda	Aug. 16 1969	Mrs. Harriet Moss
ROOSTERFISH	Nematistius pectoralis	50 lbs. 9 oz.	4' 6½''	30''	Baja Calif., Mexico	Nov. 20 1959	Lily Call
SAILFISH, Atlantic	Istiophorus americanus	78 lbs.	7' 7''		Guanta, Venezuela	Oct. 23 1949	Mrs. F. J. Woodsmalll
SAILFISH, Pacific	Istiophorus greyi	157 lbs.	10' 2''	37''	La Plata Is., Ecuador	Sept. 14 1961	Jeannette Alford
SHARK, Blue	Prionace glauca	293 lbs.	10' 6½''	44''	Montauk, New York	July 21 1963	Lucette Rinfret
		(20-lb. record for men & women)					
SHARK, Mako	Isurus oxyrhynchus I. glaucus	316 lbs.	8' 2½''	48½''	Bimini, Bahamas	May 25 1961	Dorothea L. Dean
		(20-lb. record for men & women)					
SHARK, Man-Eater or White	Carcharodon carcharias	369 lbs.	9' 3''	57''	Cape Moreton, Australia	July 6 1957	Mrs. Bob Dyer
SHARK, Porbeagle	Lamna nasus						
SHARK, Thresher	Alopias vulpinus						
SHARK, Tiger	Galeocerdo cuvier						
SNOOK or ROBALO	Centropomus undecimalis	35 lbs.	3' 7''	25½''	Fort Myers, Florida	Feb. 16 1962	Mrs. Wade Miller
SWORDFISH	Xiphias gladius	141 lbs.	8' ¾''	42''	Pamilla, Baja California	Apr. 1 1970	Jeanne Godshall
TANGUIGUE	Scomberomorus commerson	Vacant—Minimum Acceptance Weight—50 lbs.					
TARPON	Tarpon atlanticus	145 lbs.	6' 6''	39½''	Marathon, Florida	May 24 1959	Florence G. Clady
TUNA, Allison or Yellowfin	Thunnus albacares	98 lbs.	4' 9''	38''	Sydney, N.S.W., Australia	Sept. 4 1965	Signa Paton
TUNA, Atlantic Big-Eyed	Thunnus obesus	46 lbs.	3' 7''	2'7''	No. Key Largo, Fla.	Jan. 17 1959	Dorothea L. Dean
		(20-lb. record for men & women)					
TUNA, Pacific Big-Eyed	Parathunnus sibi	27 lbs.	2' 10''	24''	Cabo Blanco, Peru	Aug. 13 1955	Mrs. O. Owings
		(20-lb. record for men & women)					
TUNA, Blackfin	Thunnus atlanticus	32 lbs. 2 oz.	3' 2''	26¾''	Bermuda	Oct. 23 1968	Mrs. Herbert N. Arnold
		(20-lb. record for men & women)					
TUNA, Bluefin	Thunnus thynnus	93 lbs.	4' 5⅛''	37½''	Provincetown, Mass.	Sept. 14 1958	Willia H. Mather
WAHOO	Acanthocybium solandri	83 lbs.	5' 11''	30''	St. Thomas, Virgin Islands	Mar. 5 1968	Gloria J. Appleaate
WEAKFISH	Cynoscion regalis						
WEAKFISH, Spotted	Cynoscion nebulosus	10 lbs.	2' 6''	18''	Pellicer Creek, Fla.	Feb. 25 1950	Mrs. Bertram Lee
YELLOWTAIL	Seriola lalandi	66 lbs. 8 oz.	4' 5''	32½''	Cape Brett, New Zealand	July 12 1970	Margaret Niven

International Game Fish Association

RECORD CATCHES FOR WOMEN

12 LB. LINE TEST RECORDS (up to and including 12 lbs.)

FISH	Scientific Name	Weight	Length	Girth	Place	Date	Angler
ALBACORE	*Thunnus germo*	29 lbs. 8 oz.	3' 1"	24½"	San Diego, California	Oct. 5 1963	Jane Holland
AMBERJACK	*Seriola lalandi*	78 lbs. 4 oz.	5' ¼"	34½"	Key Largo, Florida	Mar. 23 1969	Pamela J. Habicht
		(12-lb. record for men & women)					
BARRACUDA	*Sphyraena barracuda*	41 lbs.	4' 11"	21"	Jupiter, Florida	Nov. 20 1967	Mrs. Cynthia Boomhower
BASS, Calif. Black Sea	*Stereolepis gigas*						
BASS, Calif. White Sea	*Cynoscion nobilis*	52 lbs. 6 oz.	4' 6"	27¾"	Newport Harbor, Calif.	June 3 1959	Ruth Jayred
BASS, Channel	*Sciaenops ocellatus*	51 lbs. 8 oz.	4' 2¼"	29"	Cape Hatteras, N. C.	Nov. 19 1958	Joan S. Dull
BASS, Giant Sea	*Promicrops itaiara*	110 lbs.	4' 10½"	39½"	Islamorada Florida	Aug. 2 1961	Mrs. Gar Wood, Jr.
		(12-lb. record for men & women)					
BASS, Sea	*Centropristes striatus*	2 lbs. 8 oz.	1' 5½"	12½"	Block Island, R. I.	July 12 1957	Mrs. C. Shanks
BASS, Striped	*Roccus saxatilis*	47 lbs.	4' 1½"		Umpqua R., Oregon	Aug. 21 1958	Mrs. Margaret Hulen
BLACKFISH or TAUTOG	*Tautoga onitis*	6 lbs. 7¾ oz.	1' 8"	13½"	Virginia Beach, Virginia	Apr. 4 1971	Mrs. Michael E. Hayes
BLUEFISH	*Pomatomus saltatrix*	16 lbs. 10 oz.	3'	19"	Montauk, L. I., N. Y.	June 24 1961	Gloria Better
BONEFISH	*Albula vulpes*	15 lbs.	2' 8½"	18½"	Bimini, Bahamas	Mar. 20 1961	Andrea Tose
		(12-lb. record for men & women)					
BONITO, Oceanic	*Katsuwonus pelamis*	24 lbs. 6 oz.	2' 6½"	21"	Walker Cay, Bahamas	Mar. 26 1965	Patricia E. Church
COBIA	*Racrycentron canadus*	55 lbs.	5' 5⁄16"	29⅜"	Islamorada, Florida	Feb. 14 1971	Marcia Maizler
COD	*Gadus callarias*	14 lbs. 7½ oz.	2' 11"	17½"	Nova Scotia, Canada	July 9 1963	Janet D. Wallach
DOLPHIN	*Coryphaena hippurus*	55 lbs. 2 oz.	4' 11¾"	32½"	Mazatlan, Mexico	Oct. 18 1964	Marguerite H. Barry
		(12-lb. record for men & women)					
DRUM, Black	*Pogonias cromis*	58 lbs. 12 oz.	3' 9⅜"	36"	Atlantic Beach, N. C.	May 8 1959	Juel W. Duke
FLOUNDER	*Paralichthys*	12 lbs. 2 oz.	2' 7¼"	25¼"	Avalon, N. J.	Sept. 8 1957	Mrs. Alfred J. Bernstein
KINGFISH	*S. Cavalla*	44 lbs. 2 oz.	4' 4"	24½"	St. Thomas, Virgin Islands	May 7 1969	Gloria J. Appleqate
MARLIN, Black	*Makaira indica*	353 lbs.	10' 6½"	55"	Pinas Bay, Panama	Mar. 6 1968	Evelyn M. Anderson
MARLIN, Blue	*Makaira ampla*	223 lbs. 1 oz.	10' 2½"	42"	Bimini, Bahamas	April 9 1960	Suzanne H. Hiaas
MARLIN, Pacific Blue	*Makaira nigricans*						
MARLIN, Striped	*Makaira mitsukurii*	210 lbs.	9' 6"	40"	Las Cruces, Mexico	June 20 1959	Lynn F. Lee
MARLIN, White	*Makaira albida*	122 lbs.	8' 3"	44"	Bimini, Bahamas	Mar. 30 1953	Dorothy A. Curtice
		(12-lb. record for men & women)					
PERMIT	*Trachinotus goodei*	36 lbs.	3' 6"	29"	Content Key, Florida	Mar. 16 1964	Lynette G. Siman
POLLACK	*Pollachius virens*	15 lbs. 7 oz.	2' 9¾"	19"	Nova Scotia, Canada	July 9 1963	Janet D. Wallach
RUNNER, Rainbow	*Elagatis bipinnulatus*	10 lbs. 14 oz.	3' 2¼"	15"	Key Largo, Florida	Aug. 10 1969	Pamela J. Habicht
ROOSTERFISH	*Nematistius pectoralis*	45 lbs.	4' 4½"	30"	San Jose del Cabo, Mex.	June 11 1951	Mrs. W. G. Krieger
SAILFISH, Atlantic	*Istiophorus americanus*	83 lbs.	6' 11¾"	32¼"	Key Largo, Florida	Apr. 4 1965	Harriet K. Grant
SAILFISH, Pacific	*Istiophorus greyi*	146 lbs. 8 oz.	9' ½"	35½"	Palmilla, Mexico	Nov. 14 1962	Evelyn M. Anderson
SHARK, Blue	*Prionace glauca*	150 lbs.	8' 0"	32"	Montauk, New York	July 22 1962	Dorothea L. Dean

FISH	Scientific Name	Weight	Length	Girth	Place	Date	Angler
SHARK, Mako	Isurus oxyrhynchus I. glaucus	148 lbs.	6' 6"	39"	Chub Cay, Bahamas	Apr. 29 1970	Mrs. Richard H. Grant
SHARK, Man-Eater or White	Carcharodon carcharias						
SHARK, Porbeagle	Lamna nasus						
SHARK, Thresher	Alopias vulpinus						
SHARK, Tiger	Galeocerdo cuvier						
SNOOK or ROBALO (Tie)	Centropomus undecimalis	32 lbs. 8 oz. 32 lbs. 8 oz.	3' 10" 3' 9"	23¼" 24"	Ft. Lauderdale, Florida Jupiter, Florida	July 24 1966 Aug. 2 1957	Rosemary Schafer Mrs. Nancy Neville
SWORDFISH	Xiphias gladius						
TANGUIGUE	Scomberomorus commerson	Vacant—Minimum Acceptance Weight—40 lbs.					
TARPON	Tarpon atlanticus	111 lbs.	6' 4"	37½"	Homosassa, Florida	June 7 1971	Betty Parlasca
TUNA, Allison or Yellowfin	Thunnus albacares	76 lbs.	4' 11"	33"	St. Thomas, Virgin Islands	May 10 1969	Gloria J. Applegate
TUNA, Atlantic Big-Eyed	Thunnus obesus						
TUNA, Pacific Big-Eyed	Parathunnus sibi	27 lbs. 1 oz.	3' ¼"	24"	Salinas, Ecuador	Jan. 29 1970	Mrs. Marilyn Schamroth
TUNA, Blackfin	Thunnus atlanticus	26 lbs. 12 oz.	2' 11"	23½"	Bermuda	Oct. 18 1957	Mrs. L. Edna Perinchief
TUNA, Bluefin	Thunnus thynnus	39 lbs. 8 oz.	3' 8½"	28"	Tasmania, Australia	May 27 1963	Mrs. Bob Dyer
WAHOO	Acanthocybium solandri	66 lbs. (Tie 12-lb. record for men & women)	5' 8"	25"	St. Thomas, Virgin Islands	Feb. 27 1969	Gloria J. Applegate
WEAKFISH	Cynoscion regalis	8 lbs. 14 oz. (Tie 12-lb. record for men & women)	2' 8"	15"	Fire Island, N. Y.	June 19 1954	Mrs. M. S. Hirsch
WEAKFISH, Spotted	Cynoscion nebulosus	10 lbs. 4 oz. (12-lb. record for men & women)	2' 6½"	16"	Jupiter, Florida	June 1 1958	Nancy Dukes
YELLOWTAIL	Seriola lalandi						

Following are the spin fishing world records certified
by the International Spin-Fishing Assoc. through 1970.

FRESH WATER RECORDS

International Spin Fishing Association, world record entry forms may be
obtained by writing: I.S.F.A., P.O. Box 81, Downey, California, 90241.

Line Test	Weight	Date Caught	Angler	Waters Caught
BASS (Largemouth)				
2 lb.	9 lbs. 1 oz.	Jan. 1 1961	Leonard Hartman, Florida	Lake Okeechobee, Florida
4 lb.	9 lbs. 8 oz.	May 4 1970	Ron Whiteley	Long Pond, Connecticut
6 lb.	12 lbs. 12 oz.	Feb. 21 1960	Charles D. Jacobs, Florida	Lake Tarpon, Florida
8 lb.	19 lbs. 0 oz.	June 26 1961	W. A. Witt, Florida	Lake Tarpon, Florida
10 lb.	14 lbs. 13 oz.	Nov. 27 1960	Mrs. Walter Wall, Florida	Lake Tsala Apopka, Florida
12 lb.	10 lbs. 6 oz.	Oct. 8 1969	Ken Asper, Pennsylvania	Letterkerry Res., Pennsylvania
BASS (Smallmouth)				
2 lb.	5 lbs. 11 oz.	June 20 1966	Art Micklei, New York	Honeoye Lake, New York
4 lb.	6 lbs. 1 oz.	Sept. 30 1955	Gene M. Schwietering, Wisconsin	Lac Du Flambeau, Wisconsin
6 lb.	6 lbs. 11 oz.	Apr. 5 1970	H. L. Miller, Tennessee	So. Holiston Lake, Tennessee
8 lb.	5 lbs. 8 oz.	Dec. 14 1968	A. Douglas Yelton Tennessee	Watauga Lake, Tennessee
10 lb.	6 lbs. 4 oz.	Feb. 5 1968	Wm. Kinch, Tennessee	Watauga Lake, Tennessee
12 lb.	6 lbs. 1 oz.	Sept. 10 1970	Clyde E. Rickard	Lake Manitou, Michigan
CATFISH				
2 lb.	3 lbs. 5 oz.	July 10 1970	Tom Miller, California	Lake Irvine, California
4 lb.	10 lbs. 8 oz.	Apr. 15 1969	Karl Fogerland, California	Alondra Park Lake, California
6 lb.	21 lbs. 1 oz.	Oct. 14 1969	Al White, California	Lake Casitas, California
8 lb.	Open			
10 lb.	Open			
12 lb.	Open			
CRAPPIE				
2 lb.	2 lbs. 9 oz.	Aug. 3 1963	Gene Newman, California	Lake Mead, Arizona
4 lb.	3 lbs. 4 oz.	Feb. 26 1963	Floyd Randolph California	Puddington Dam California
6 lb.	2 lbs. 4 oz.	July 27 1963	Ray Caliman, Pennsylvania	Alloway, New Jersey
8 lb.	1 lb. 4 oz.	July 21 1967	Neil Krey, Illinois	Castle Rock Flow, Wisconsin
GRAYLING (Arctic)				
2 lb.	4 lbs. 9 oz.	June 28 1968	John Case, Illinois	Great Slave Lake, Canada
4 lb.	3 lbs. 8 oz.	July 10 1968	Craig Nelsen, Kansas	Great Slave Lake, Canada
6 lb.	4 lbs. 0 oz.		Dale Slocum, Arizona	Great Bear Lake, Canada
8 lb.	3 lbs. 0 oz.	July 24 1962	Mrs. R. B. Brown, Illinois	Camsell River, N. W. T. Canada
10 lb.	2 lbs. 4 oz.	July 10 1967	Richard Renz, California	Great Bear Lake, Canada
12 lb.	OPEN			

Test Line	Weight	Date Caught	Angler	Waters Caught
MUSKELLUNGE				
2 lb.	18 lbs. 7 oz.	July 15 1959	Leonard Hartman, New York	St. Lawrence River, New York
4 lb.	42 lbs. 3 oz.	Sept. 7 1963	Leonard Hartman, New York	St. Lawrence River, New York
6 lb.	47 lbs. 1 oz.	Sept. 2 1962	Leonard Hartman, New York	St. Lawrence River, New York
8 lb.	59 lbs. 13 oz.	Aug. 6 1960	Leonard Hartman, New York	St. Lawrence River, New York
10 lb.	67 lbs. 15 oz.	Aug. 10 1961	Leonard Hartman, New York	St. Lawrence River, New York
12 lb.	61 lbs. 0 oz.	Nov. 8 1964	Leonard Hartman, New York	St. Lawrence River, New York
PICKEREL (Chain)				
2 lb.	7 lbs. 1 oz.	July 18 1968	Wm. Spaulding, Sr., Massachusetts	Assawamsett Pond, Massachusetts
4 lb.	6 lbs. 14 oz.	May 1 1968	Wm. Spaulding, Sr. Massachusetts	Pocksha Pond, Massachusetts
6 lb.	6 lbs. 15 oz.	July 15 1968	Wm. Spaulding, Sr., Massachusetts	Pocksha Pond, Massachusetts
8 lb.	6 lbs. 0 oz.	April 19 1965	Ralph Campitello, New Jersey	Upper Erskin Lake, New Jersey
10 lb.	7 lbs. 4 oz.	July 28 1968	Wm. Spaulding, Sr., Massachusetts	Pocksha Pond, Massachusetts
12 lb.	7 lbs. 1 oz.	July 18 1968	Wm. Spaulding, Sr., Massachusetts	Assawampsett Pond, Massachusetts
PIKE (Northern)				
2 lb.	17 lbs. 5 oz.	May 8 1961	Leonard Hartman, New York	St. Lawrence River, New York
4 lb.	18 lbs. 14 oz.	June 7 1962	Leonard Hartman, New York	St. Lawrence River, New York
6 lb.	30 lbs. 9 oz.	Aug. 15 1963	Ed Zaleski, Canada	Lake Abitibi, Canada
8 lb.	31 lbs. 0 oz.	Nov. 12 1955	Capt. R. J. Oostdyke, USAF	Nortdeich, Wolfersheim, Germany
10 lb.	40 lbs. 0 oz.	June 11 1969	Ken D. Asper	Delay Lake, Canada
12 lb.	Open			
SHAD (American)				
2 lb.	3 lbs. 15 oz.	May 23 1964	Henry Drew, Massachusetts	Conn. River, Massachusetts
4 lb.	6 lbs. 8 oz.	May 9 1968	Wm. Spaulding, Sr., Massachusetts	Indian River, Massachusetts
6 lb.	5 lbs. 10 oz.	May 31 1968	R. N. Schliesmayer	Feather River, California
8 lb.	6 lbs. 4 oz.	May 9 1968	Wm. Spaulding, Sr., Massachusetts	Indian River, Massachusetts
10 lb.	5 lbs. 3 oz.	June 6 1967	Henry Drew, Massachusetts	Connecticut River, Massachusetts
12 lb.	7 lbs. 10 oz.	May 17 1968	Wm. Spaulding, Sr., Massachusetts	Indian River, Massachusetts

SHEE

Test Line	Weight	Date Caught	Angler	Waters Caught
2 lb.	OPEN			
4 lb.	22 lbs. 12 oz.	June 28 1957	Mrs. Lily Call, California	Kobuk R., Alaska
6 lb.	14 lbs. 4 oz.	June 28 1957	Mrs. Lily Call, California	Kobuk R., Alaska
8 lb.	13 lbs. 4 oz.	June 28 1957	Mrs. Lily Call, California	Kobuk R., Alaska
10 lb.	17 lbs. 8 oz.	June 28 1957	Raymond F. Call, California	Kobuk R., Alaska
12 lb.	21 lbs. 8 oz.	June 29 1957	Raymond F. Call, California	Kobuk R., Alaska

TROUT (Brook)

Test Line	Weight	Date Caught	Angler	Waters Caught
2 lb.	4 lbs. 2 oz.	July 4 1965	Edwin D. Kennedy, New Jersey	Kepimits River, Canada
4 lb.	4 lbs. 2 oz.	June 13 1970	David Bonser, Pennsylvania	Aquashilcoa, Pennsylvania
6 lb.	8 lbs. 8 oz.	June 25 1954	Donnell Culpepper, California	Canada
8 lb.	Open			
10 lb.	3 lbs. 9 oz.	Aug. 17 1969	Ivan (Gerry) Grimshaw	So. Knife River, Manitoba
12 lb.	Open			

TROUT (Cutthroat)

Test Line	Weight	Date Caught	Angler	Waters Caught
2 lb.	4 lbs. 8 oz.	April 26 1960	Irene Umberham, California	Topaz Lake, Nevada
4 lb.	8 lbs. 15 oz.	April 27 1955	Lee Baun, California	Walker Lake, Nevada
6 lb.	12 lbs. 0 oz.	Mar. 4 1957	Clem DeRocco, California	Walker Lake, Nevada
8 lb.	14 lbs. 7 oz.	Mar. 18 1956	Leonard Hyduke, California	Walker Lake, Nevada
10 lb.	8 lbs. 5 oz.	April 6 1956	Alan C. Zeller, California	Walker Lake, Nevada
12 lb.	7 lbs. 7 oz.	Mar. 14 1958	Ed Baun, California	Walker Lake, Nevada

TROUT (Dolly Varden)

Test Line	Weight	Date Caught	Angler	Waters Caught
2 lb.	5 lbs. 0 oz.	July 30 1960	Art Hamill, Oregon	Metolius River, Oregon
4 lb.	17 lbs. 0 oz.	Nov. 27 1961	Yvonne Donaldson, Washington	Lake Pend Oreille, Idaho
6 lb.	18 lbs. 8 oz.	June 8 1962	Y. Donaldson, Washington	Lake Pend Oreille, Idaho
8 lb.	20 lbs. 0 oz.	May 8 1963	Yvonne Donaldson, Nevada	Lake Pend Oreille, Idaho
10 lb.	OPEN			
12 lb.	OPEN			

TROUT (Brown)

Test Line	Weight	Date Caught	Angler	Waters Caught
2 lb.	9 lbs. 0 oz.	Oct. 16 1959	Ralph Munsen, Oregon	Wickiup Reservoir, Oregon
4 lb.	21 lbs. 1 oz.	June 5 1970	James W. Hatcher, California	Robinson Creek, California
6 lb.	18 lbs. 1 oz.	July 9 1967	Julie Stedman, California	Fallen Leaf Lake, California
8 lb.	28 lbs. 3 oz.	Sept. 11 1970	Lewis R. MacFarland, M.D.	White River, Arkansas
10 lb.	6 lbs. 8 oz.	May 13 1967	Kim MacDonald, California	Birchum Canyon, California
12 lb.	16 lbs. 4 oz.	Nov. 7 1970	Andy Lipjanel, California	Rush Creek, California

TROUT (Kamloops)

Test Line	Weight	Date Caught	Angler	Waters Caught
2 lb.	24 lbs. 14 oz.	Oct. 17 1962	Ralph Munsen, Oregon	Lake Pend Oreille, Idaho
4 lb.	25 lbs. 13 oz.	May 19 1962	Yvonne Donaldson, Nevada	Lake Pend Oreille, Idaho
6 lb.	29 lbs. 12 oz.	Nov. 24 1961	Jim Parsons, Idaho	Lake Pend Oreille, Idaho
8 lb.	25 lbs. 4 oz.	Nov. 17 1960	Lester H. Lundblad, Oregon	Lake Pend Oreille, Idaho
10 lb.	23 lbs. 0 oz.	Oct. 27 1953	Frank P. Natta, Washington	Lake Pend Oreille, Idaho
12 lb.	OPEN			

TROUT (Lake or Mackinaw)

Test Line	Weight	Date Caught	Angler	Waters Caught
2 lb.	19 lbs. 0 oz.	July 27 1965	Edwin D. Kennedy, New Jersey	Great Slave Lake, Canada
4 lb.	37 lbs. 12 oz.	July 26 1966	James Thurston, Canada	Tazin Lake, Canada
6 lb.	32 lbs. 9 oz.	Aug. 6 1969	Herbert Prentice, California	Great Beak Lake, Canada
8 lb.	37 lbs. 8 oz.	June 21 1959	Richard Newland, South Dakota	Lac La Ronge, Canada
10 lb.	36 lbs. 0 oz.	July 5 1968	Bob Aurand, California	Great Bear Lake, Canada
12 lb.	46 lbs. 4 oz.	July 16 1968	Dale L. Slocum, Arizona	Great Bear Lake, Canada

TROUT (Rainbow)

Test Line	Weight	Date Caught	Angler	Waters Caught
2 lb.	11 lbs. 0 oz.	May 28 1967	A. C. Anderson, N. Z.	Lake Tarawera, N. Z.
4 lb.	8 lbs. 7 oz.	May 8 1964	John D. Miner, Florida	Antisana, Ecuador, S. A.
6 lb.	17 lbs. 2 oz.	June 29 1958	Keith Davidson, Washington	Pend Oreille River, Washington
8 lb.	25 lbs. 1 oz.	Nov. 5 1954	Jim Parsons, Idaho	Lake Pend Oreille, Idaho
10 lb.	5 lbs. 4 oz.	Apr. 25 1970	Dick Graves, California	Lake Mohave, Arizona
12 lb.	8 lbs. 8 oz.	July 11 1970	B. A. Bixler, California	Upper Lake Klamath, Oregon

TROUT (Steelhead)

Test Line	Weight	Date Caught	Angler	Waters Caught
2 lb.	12 lbs. 1 oz.	May 2 1954	Frank Natta, Washington	Washougal R., Washington
4 lb.	22 lbs. 0 oz.	Feb. 22 1959	Carlyle Brown, Washington	E. Fk. Lewis R., Washington
6 lb.	23 lbs. 10 oz.	Oct. 20 1955	Norman LaFleur, Washington	E. Fk. Lewis R., Washington
8 lb.	24 lbs. 6 oz.	Feb. 21 1959	W. H. Winseman, Jr., Washington	Skykomish R., Washington
10 lb.	28 lbs. 11 oz.	July 5 1952	Rex S. York, California	Klamath R., California
12 lb.	23 lbs. 6 oz.	Oct. 15 1968	Riley Compton	Kispox River, B. C.

TROUT (Golden)

Test Line	Weight	Date Caught	Angler	Waters Caught
2 lb.	4 lbs. 4 oz.	Oct. 14 1961	Michael Mansfield, California	Horton Lake 3, California
4 lb.	3 lbs. 5 oz.	July 12 1960	Dick More, Colorado	Valentine Lake, Wyoming
6 lb.	2 lbs. 2 oz.	July 22 1959	E. L. Sharp, California	Cook Lake, Wyoming
8 lb.	1 lb. 5 oz.	Aug. 2 1970	Gene Newman, California	Skyblue Lake, California
10 lb.	Open			
12 lb.	Open			

WALLEYE

Test Line	Weight	Date Caught	Angler	Waters Caught
2 lb.	8 lbs. 11 oz.	Aug. 31 1960	Leonard Hartman, New York	St. Lawrence River, New York
4 lb.	13 lbs. 3 oz.	June 5 1962	Leonard Hartman, New York	St. Lawrence River, New York
6 lb.	13 lbs. 2 oz.	July 5 1963	Floyd Randolph, California	Curren River, Missouri
8 lb.	14 lbs. 8 oz.	Oct. 19 1966	Fred Golden, Michigan	Otter Lake, Michigan
10 lb.	12 lbs. 2 oz.	June 1 1961	Leonard Hartman, New York	St. Lawrence River, New York
12 lb.	9 lbs. 2 oz.	Oct. 19 1962	Leonard Hartman, New York	St. Lawrence River, New York

SALT WATER RECORDS

Line Test	Weight	Date Caught	Angler	Waters Caught
ALBACORE				
2 lb.	OPEN			
4 lb.	25 lbs. 10 oz.	Aug. 10 1960	Wm. Hill, Jr., California	San Diego, California
6 lb.	25 lbs. 2 oz.	Aug. 25 1960	H. S. Bonner, California	San Diego, California
8 lb.	25 lbs. 11 oz.	July 31 1957	Dr. E. Z. Hershman, California	Coronados Isl., California
10 lb.	28 lbs. 8 oz.	Aug. 11 1954	H. E. Levitt, California	San Clemente Isl., California
12 lb.	39 lbs. 8 oz.	July 23 1958	Dr. R. S. Rubaum, California	San Clemente Isl., California
AMBERJACK				
2 lb.	6 lbs. 2 oz.	May 29 1961	Roy H. Martin, Florida	Gulf of Mexico, Florida
4 lb.	9 lbs. 6 oz.	May 19 1963	Louis D. Tesar, Florida	Gulf of Mexico, Florida
6 lb.	14 lbs. 12 oz.	May 6 1962	Louis D. Tesar, Florida	Gulf of Mexico, Florida
8 lb.	56 lbs. 0 oz.	June 12 1966	Mrs. Carl Dann, III, Florida	Vero Beach, Florida
10 lb.	42 lbs. 0 oz.	Oct. 13 1960	Karl Osborne, Florida	Vero Beach, Florida
12 lb.	78 lbs. 4 oz.	Mar. 23 1969	Pamela Habicht	Key Largo, Florida
BARRACUDA (Great)				
2 lb.	15 lbs. 4 oz.	Sept. 11 1963	Dr. R. B. Hehenberger, Florida	Gulf of Mexico, Florida
4 lb.	30 lbs. 0 oz.	Mar. 6 1969	Ray O. Acord, California	Palau Islands
6 lb.	25 lbs. 0 oz.	June 18 1966	Skip Mackey, Florida	Big Pine Key, Florida
8 lb.	37 lbs. 4 oz.	June 7 1960	Al Zapanta, California	St. George Cay, Br. Honduras
10 lb.	32 lbs. 0 oz.	June 7 1960	Al Zapanta, California	St. George Cay, Br. Honduras
12 lb.	42 lbs. 10 oz.	Oct. 19 1959	Bill Moeser, Florida	Key Largo, Florida
BARRACUDA (Pacific)				
2 lb.	10 lbs. 9 oz.	Aug. 13 1958	Dr. E. A. Hershman, California	San Diego, California
4 lb.	10 lbs. 9 oz.	Apr. 17 1960	Bob Dragoo, California	Paradise Cove, California
6 lb.	12 lbs. 4 oz.	May 18 1953	H. W. Craine, California	Catalina Island, California
8 lb.	13 lbs. 8 oz.	Sept. 15 1969	Ken Matheson, Nicaragua	San Juan del Sor, Nicaragua
10 lb.	13 lbs. 8 oz.	Nov. 9 1969	Alfredo Bequillard, Jr., Nicaragua	San Juan del Sor, Nicaragua
12 lb.	12 lbs. 7 oz.	May 20 1960	Ernest Blumenthal, California	Redondo Beach, California
BASS (Black sea)				
2 lb.	OPEN			
4 lb.	OPEN			
6 lb.	8 lbs. 1 oz.	Feb. 24 1963	James Haun, California	Seal Beach, California
8 lb.	23 lbs. 4 oz.	Aug. 24 1958	Geo. Al Teachout, California	Dana Point, California
10 lb.	112 lbs. 8 oz.	June 12 1957	David B. Rosenthal, California	San Francisco Isl., BC, Mexico
12 lb.	83 lbs. 4 oz.	Feb. 23 1958	J. N. Bertolino, California	Box Canyon, California

Line Test	Weight	Date Caught	Angler	Waters Caught
BASS (Channel)				
2 lb.	9 lbs. 0 oz.	Jan. 18 1961	James G. Mastry, Florida	St. Petersburg, Florida
4 lb.	37 lbs. 4 oz.	July 6 1961	W. H. Watters, N. Carolina	North Inlet, S. Carolina
6 lb.	53 lbs. 8 oz.	July 24 1960	C. M. Vellines, N. Carolina	Portsmouth Island, N. Carolina
8 lb.	44 lbs. 4 oz.	April 18 1968	Dave Elliott	Cape Hatteras
10 lb.	44 lbs. 4 oz.	Jan. 22 1961	R. E. Robinson, Texas	Galveston, Texas
12 lb.	60 lbs. 8 oz.	Oct. 24 1954	Arthur Clark, Jr., Pennsylvania	Nags Head, N. Carolina
BASS (Kelp)				
2 lb.	8 lbs. 3 oz.	May 17 1961	William Hill, Jr., California	San Diego, California
4 lb.	10 lbs. 7 oz.	July 17 1954	Art Parra, California	Horseshoe Kelp off Long Beach, Calif.
6 lb.	8 lbs. 12 oz.	June 2 1955	Jack L. Rous, California	San Clemente Isl., California
8 lb.	9 lbs. 12 oz.	Oct. 7 1955	Fred Anderson, California	Santa Barbara, California
10 lb.	9 lbs. 8 oz.	June 12 1967	Jack O. Hinshaw, California	Oceanside, California
12 lb.	10 lbs. 2 oz.	June 29 1959	Bob Dragoo, California	Malibu, California
BASS (Sand)				
2 lb.	5 lbs. 2 oz.	June 27 1960	Willis C. Carr, California	Long Beach California
4 lb.	5 lbs. 0 oz.	June 9 1963	Bob Dragoo, California	Newport Bay, California
6 lb.	8 lbs. 4 oz.	Jan. 26 1965	Bob Bennett, California	Newport Bay, California
8 lb.	8 lbs. 14 oz.	May 10 1958	Maj. E. T. Nobles, USMC	Box Canyon, California
10 lb.	7 lbs. 4 oz.	May 14 1964	Roland R. Boyer, California	Newport Bay, California
12 lb.	4 lbs. 15 oz.	June 30 1962	Carlton Bishop, California	San Onofre, California
BASS (Striped)				
2 lb.	14 lbs. 13 oz.	July 18 1969	Mrs. Frances Pasche, Massachusetts	Plum Isle, Massachusetts
4 lb.	40 lbs. 8 oz.	May 28 1969	Doug Crawford, Oregon	No. Fork Coos River, Oregon
6 lb.	48 lbs. 0 oz.	Apr. 20 1961	John H. Froehlich, Maryland	Susquehanna River, Maryland
8 lb.	52 lbs. 8 oz.	Aug. 18 1969	John O'Neil, Massachusetts	Merrimac River
10 lb.	57 lbs. 1 oz.	July 8 1963	Jon Kodwyck, New Hampshire	Plum Island, Massachusetts
12 lb.	53 lbs. 8 oz.	May 2 1962	Jack Stewart, Oregon	Coos River, Oregon
BLUEFISH				
2 lb.	11 lbs. 3 oz.	Mar. 21 1970	Wm. Leffingwell, Florida	Port Canaveral, Florida
4 lb.	10 lbs. 8 oz.	July 20 1968	John Fernandez, New York	Long Island, New York
6 lb.	17 lbs. 4 oz.	Mar. 27 1970	Skip Mackey, Florida	Port Canaveral, Florida
8 lb.	19 lbs. 8 oz.	Nov. 19 1970	D. M. Tatem, Jr.	Nags Head, N. Carolina
10 lb.	15 lbs. 1 oz.	Feb. 2 1959	W. E. Green, Illinois	Lake Worth, Florida

Test Line	Weight	Date Caught	Angler	Waters Caught
12 lb.	16 lbs. 13 oz.	Oct. 8 1970	Howard Reynolds, Connecticut	Long Island Sound, Connecticut

BONEFISH

Test Line	Weight	Date Caught	Angler	Waters Caught
2 lb.	7 lbs. 10 oz.	Mar. 17 1968	Fred Johnson, Alabama	Bahia Honda Key, Florida
4 lb.	11 lbs. 0 oz.	Mar. 29 1968	J. Hilton Parsons, Jr., S. Carolina	Islamorada, Florida
6 lb.	14 lbs. 8 oz.	Apr. 18 1963	Patricia Ross, Wisconsin	Bimini, Bahama Islands
8 lb.	14 lbs. 2 oz.	Oct. 6 1956	Jack Yamanaka, Hawaii	Honolulu, Hawaii
10 lb.	13 lbs. 14 oz.	Apr. 15 1969	N. J. Brown, Jr., Illinois	Islamorada, Florida
12 lb.	15 lbs. 0 oz.	Feb. 28 1961	Nat Carlin, New York	Islamorada, Florida

BONITO (Atlantic)

Test Line	Weight	Date Caught	Angler	Waters Caught
2 lb.	2 lbs. 7 oz.	Nov. 15 1960	G. O. Thorne, Florida	Panama City Beach, Florida
4 lb.	11 lbs. 5 oz.	June 23 1967	John Holcomb, Jr., Florida	Marathon, Florida
6 lb.	7 lbs. 0 oz.	Aug. 19 1968	Jeanette Alford	Haulover Beach, Florida
8 lb.	18 lbs. 0 oz.	July 6 1970	Bill Kieldsen, Florida	Key Biscayne, Florida
10 lb.	15 lbs. 8 oz.	June 14 1970	Mike Liverone, Florida	Key West, Florida
12 lb.	20 lbs. 0 oz.	May 29 1970	Marshal Ernst, Florida	Miami, Florida

BONITO (Oceanic)

Test Line	Weight	Date Caught	Angler	Waters Caught
2 lb.	OPEN			
4 lb.	6 lbs. 2 oz.	April 8 1960	Dr. E. A. Hershman, California	Bay of Palms, BC, Mexico
6 lb.	12 lbs. 8 oz.	June 15 1966	John Irvin, Florida	Vero Beach, Florida
8 lb.	9 lbs. 10 oz.	July 26 1963	Wm. S. Rosenthal, Pennsylvania	Barnegat, New Jersey
10 lb.	23 lbs. 7 oz.	Aug. 10 1958	Raymond Kagihara, Hawaii	Oahu, Hawaii
12 lb.	17 lbs. 8 oz.	May 24 1963	Alton Rowland, Florida	Boynton Beach, Florida

BONITO (Pacific)

Test Line	Weight	Date Caught	Angler	Waters Caught
2 lb.	8 lbs. 10 oz.	Jan. 12 1961	Wm. R. Hill, Jr., California	San Diego, California
4 lb.	11 lbs. 2 oz.	Aug. 24 1959	Bob Dragoo, California	Ensenada, BC, Mexico
TIE				
4 lb.	11 lbs. 2 oz.	Nov. 4 1970	Gordon Prentice, California	Loreto, BC, Mexico
6 lb.	13 lbs. 8 oz.	Aug. 8 1963	John A. Miner III, Florida	Antofagasta, Chile
8 lb.	14 lbs. 6 oz.	June 24 1959	George Ramsey, California	Bahia de Palmas, BC, Mexico
10 lb.	12 lbs. 2 oz.	June 26 1959	Clifford M. Getz, California	Bahia de Palmas, BC, Mexico
12 lb.	17 lbs. 1 oz.	Apr. 3 1953	Dan Alan Felger, California	Coronados Isls., California

CABRILLA

Test Line	Weight	Date Caught	Angler	Waters Caught
2 lb.	2 lbs. 1 oz.	Jan. 11 1970	Gordon Prentice, California	Loreto, BC, Mexico
4 lb.	4 lbs. 4 oz.	Jan. 11 1970	Gordon Prentice, California	Loreto, BC, Mexico
6 lb.	16 lbs. 0 oz.	Jan. 14 1966	Bernard Zwilling, California	Rancho Buena Vista, Mexico
8 lb.	28 lbs. 0 oz.	Nov. 8 1960	Russell M. Anderson, California	San Jose del Cabo, BC, Mexico
10 lb.	13 lbs. 0 oz.	Feb. 27 1959	Paul Braslow, California	Loreto, BC, Mexico
12 lb.	22 lbs. 0 oz.	May 8 1970	Denton Hill, California	Rancho Buena Vista, BC, Mexico

COBIA

Test Line	Weight	Date Caught	Angler	Waters Caught
2 lb.	3 lbs. 9 oz.	Aug. 24 1961	John D. Miner III, Florida	Destin, Florida
4 lb.	28 lbs. 0 oz.	Sept. 2 1961	Phil Francis, Florida	Pine Isl. Sound, Florida
6 lb.	47 lbs. 0 oz.	June 18 1966	Mrs. Carl Dann, III, Florida	Vero Beach, Florida
8 lb.	52 lbs. 8 oz.	April 17 1968	James Masters	St. Petersburg, Florida
10 lb.	50 lbs. 0 oz.	Sept. 28 1961	Richard Delvalle, Florida	Tampa Bay, Florida
12 lb.	64 lbs. 8 oz.	April 3 1965	Tommy Norred, Florida	Destin, Florida

CORBINA

Test Line	Weight	Date Caught	Angler	Waters Caught
2 lb.	4 lbs. 14 oz.	July 10 1969	Karl Fogerlund, California	Venice, California
4 lb.	7 lbs. 4 oz.	June 18 1967	Tom W. Miller, California	Ventura, California
6 lb.	7 lbs. 6 oz.	July 10 1966	Butch McCullough, California	Newport Bay, California
8 lb.	5 lbs. 3 oz.	Sept. 9 1962	George Stickler, California	Newport Bay, California
10 lb.	12 lbs. 0 oz.	July 12 1963	Jack Smith, Florida	Club de Pesca, Panama, C.Z.
12 lb.	5 lbs. 8 oz.	Dec. 12 1959	Arthur R. Baca, California	Newport Bay, California

CORVINA

Test Line	Weight	Date Caught	Angler	Waters Caught
2 lb.	11 lbs. 4 oz.	Oct. 5 1961	Willis C. Carr, California	Salton Sea, California
4 lb.	11 lbs. 1 oz.	May 23 1970	Ken Hadden, California	Salton Sea, California
6 lb.	12 lbs. 4 oz.	May 2 1962	Ira E. Shoemaker, California	Salton Sea, California
TIE				
6 lb.	12 lbs. 4 oz.	May 16 1964	H. J. Ray, California	Salton Sea, California
8 lb.	34 lbs. 0 oz.	May 25 1961	Maurine Cloe, California	San Felipe, BC, Mexico
10 lb.	25 lbs. 8 oz.	May 15 1962	Willis C. Carr, California	Salton Sea, California
12 lb.	23 lbs. 4 oz.	Apr. 7 1968	Ed Hammerschmidt, California	Salton Sea, California

CROAKER (Spotfin)

Test Line	Weight	Date Caught	Angler	Waters Caught
2 lb.	8 lbs. 2 oz.	Feb. 3 1963	Milton S. Miller, California	Newport Bay, California
4 lb.	8 lbs. 0 oz.	Mar. 12 1961	Ben D. Martin, California	Newport Bay, California
6 lb.	11 lbs. 13 oz.	July 9 1963	Robert M. Austin, California	Agua Hedionda Lagoon, California
8 lb.	10 lbs. 11 oz.	Apr. 18 1970	H. J. Ray, California	Newport Bay, California
10 lb.	7 lbs. 12 oz.	Mar. 25 1959	Jim Cunningham, California	Newport Bay, California
12 lb.	9 lbs. 8 oz.	Apr. 24 1962	R. M. Harrison, California	Newport Bay, California

DOLPHIN

Test Line	Weight	Date Caught	Angler	Waters Caught
2 lb.	5 lbs. 4 oz.	June 8 1970	Fred Johnson, Alabama	Marathon, Florida
4 lb.	18 lbs. 9 oz.	May 24 1967	John C. Fernandez, New York	Bahia Honda Key, Florida
6 lb.	31 lbs. 0 oz.	Aug. 5 1952	Myron J. Glauber, California	Las Cruces, BC, Mexico
8 lb.	36 lbs. 4 oz.	July 17 1965	Mrs. Carl Dann III, Florida	Pinos Bay, Panama, C.Z.
10 lb.	35 lbs. 3 oz.	May 24 1957	Robert Bruchez, California	Rancho Buena Vista, BC, Mexico
12 lb.	33 lbs. 0 oz.	Apr. 5 1953	Myron J. Glauber, California	Mazatlan, Mexico

DRUM (Black)

Test Line	Weight	Date Caught	Angler	Waters Caught
2 lb.	1 lb. 14 oz.	Dec. 3 1960	G. O. Thorne, Florida	Panama City Beach, Florida
4 lb.	30 lbs. 8 oz.	Jan. 25 1969	James Masters, Florida	St. Petersburg, Florida

Test Line	Weight	Date Caught	Angler	Waters Caught
6 lb.	45 lbs. 0 oz.	Jan. 14 1958	Gus Getner, Texas	S. Padre Island, Texas
8 lb.	64 lbs. 0 oz.	July 20 1960	Joseph Bucciarelli, New Jersey	Manahawkin, New Jersey
10 lb.	53 lbs. 0 oz.	May 20 1966	Joseph D. Dove, Maryland	Cape Charles, Virginia
12 lb.	55 lbs. 0 oz.	May 16 1970	Joseph D. Dove, Maryland	Cape Charles, Virginia

HALIBUT

Test Line	Weight	Date Caught	Angler	Waters Caught
2 lb.	15 lbs. 8 oz.	Aug. 13 1969	John Smart, Washington	Fort Casey, Washington
4 lb.	35 lbs. 11 oz.	Aug. 10 1969	John Smart, Washington	Fort Casey, Washington
6 lb.	38 lbs. 8 oz.	July 4 1965	Eugene L. Duke, California	Newport Bay, California
8 lb.	57 lbs. 2 oz.	June 1 1958	Merlin Wilson, Oregon	Coos Bay, Oregon
10 lb.	74 lbs. 1 oz.	June 3 1957	Paul McDonald, Oregon	Coos Bay, Oregon
12 lb.	35 lbs. 8 oz.	Sept. 6 1964	Al Binder, California	Santa Barbara Isl., California

JACK CREVALLE

Test Line	Weight	Date Caught	Angler	Waters Caught
2 lb.	7 lbs. 4 oz.	Dec. 6 1966	Ted C. Eggers, Florida	Lake Worth, Florida
4 lb.	17 lbs. 8 oz.	Jan. 3 1966	G. S. Braden, Florida	Dry Tortugas, Gulf of Mexico
6 lb.	14 lbs. 8 oz.	Mar. 18 1955	Dr. Earl Hershman, California	Mazatlan, Mexico
8 lb.	25 lbs. 8 oz.	April 19 1957	Harry Y. Okamura, Hawaii	Oahu, Hawaii
10 lb.	39 lbs. 8 oz.	May 16 1961	P. A. Lund, Florida	Hobe Sound, Florida
12 lb.	32 lbs. 2 oz.	Aug. 1 1965	Mrs. Carl Dann, Florida	Vero Beach, Florida

LADYFISH

Test Line	Weight	Date Caught	Angler	Waters Caught
2 lb.	3 lbs. 0 oz.	Dec. 22 1960	Allen Dix, New York	Lake Worth, Florida
4 lb.	6 lbs. 0 oz.	June 28 1959	Jackson Morisawa, Hawaii	Pearl Harbor, Hawaii
6 lb.	5 lbs. 9 oz.	Mar. 26 1954	Dr. Alexis A. Burso, Hawaii	Oahu, Hawaii
8 lb.	12 lbs. 5 oz.	Jan. 26 1956	Dr. Alexis A. Burso, Hawaii	Pearl Harbor, Hawaii
10 lb.	8 lbs. 0 oz.	Mar. 3 1957	Ralph Ohtani, Hawaii	Oahu, Hawaii
12 lb.	4 lbs. 1 oz.	Oct. 6 1960	Wm. L. Smith, Florida	Panama City Beach, Florida

MACKEREL (King)

Test Line	Weight	Date Caught	Angler	Waters Caught
2 lb.	12 lbs. 0 oz.	June 17 1962	Douglas Carl, Florida	Panama City Beach, Florida
4 lb.	12 lbs. 12 oz.	April 29 1962	Nancy Tobias, Florida	St. Petersburg, Florida
6 lb.	40 lbs. 0 oz.	April 19 1964	James L. Gerling, Florida	Anna Maria Island, Florida
8 lb.	36 lbs. 6 oz.	May 30 1966	John H. Irvin, Florida	Vero Beach, Florida
10 lb.	43 lbs. 1 oz.	April 28 1959	Eugene Wilhite, Florida	St. Petersburg, Florida
12 lb.	44 lbs. 0 oz.	May 20 1963	Clyde Fore, Florida	Anna Marie Island, Florida

MACKEREL (Spanish)

Test Line	Weight	Date Caught	Angler	Waters Caught
2 lb.	8 lbs. 0 oz.	Feb. 15 1964	Dr. R. B. Hehenberger, Florida	Miami Beach, Florida
4 lb.	11 lbs. 1 oz.	Dec. 20 1970	Gordon Prentice, California	Loreto, BC, Mexico
6 lb.	9 lbs. 1 oz.	Nov. 6 1970	Gordon Prentice, California	Loreto, BC, Mexico
8 lb.	10 lbs. 4 oz.	Dec. 29 1969	Ed Macaulay, New York	Islamorada, Florida
10 lb.	8 lbs. 8 oz.	Nov. 2 1958	Richard E. Gregory, Florida	Palm Beach, Florida

Test Line	Weight	Date Caught	Angler	Waters Caught
12 lb.	13 lbs. 0 oz.	Mar. 8 1958	Lily Call, California	Loreto, BC, Mexico

MARLIN (Black)

Test Line	Weight	Date Caught	Angler	Waters Caught
2 lb.	OPEN			
4 lb.	OPEN			
6 lb.	OPEN			
8 lb.	176 lbs. 6 oz.	Aug. 2 1962	B. Zwilling, California	Rancho Buena Vista, B. C. Mexico
10 lb.	247 lbs. 0 oz.	Jan. 2 1967	Dr. Carl Dann, III, Florida	Pinas Bay, Panama
12 lb.	312 lbs. 3 oz.	July 17 1958	Robert Gaxiola, California	Guaymas, Mexico

MARLIN (Striped)

Test Line	Weight	Date Caught	Angler	Waters Caught
2 lb.	OPEN			
4 lb.	129 lbs. 0 oz.	June 8 1962	Dr. R. Rubaum, California	Palmilla, B. C. Mexico
6 lb.	OPEN			
8 lb.	126 lbs. 7 oz.	Mar. 14 1958	Al Zapanta, California	Mazatlan, Mexico
10 lb.	183 lbs. 7 oz.	July 15 1958	Robert Gaxiola, California	Guaymas, Mexico
12 lb.	165 lbs. 0 oz.	Mar. 15 1955	Harry V. Goza, Jr., California	Mazatlan, Mexico

MARLIN (White)

Test Line	Weight	Date Caught	Angler	Waters Caught
2 lb.	Open			
4 lb.	Open			
6 lb.	Open			
8 lb.	Open			
10 lb.	Open			
12 lb.	41 lbs. 0 oz.	June 25 1970	Billy Crawford, New Jersey	Caysol Bank, Bahama Isle

MILK FISH

Test Line	Weight	Date Caught	Angler	Waters Caught
2 lb.	OPEN			
4 lb.	12 lbs. 13 oz.	Dec. 9 1956	Thomas Shintani, Hawaii	Pearl Harbor, Hawaii
6 lb.	11 lbs. 6 oz.	Aug. 20 1955	James Nakai, Hawaii	Hilo, Hawaii
8 lb.	17 lbs. 9 oz.	Aug. 30 1964	Curtis Ohama, Hawaii	Honolulu, Hawaii
10 lb.	18 lbs. 2 oz.	Aug. 20 1958	Hank Uechi, Hawaii	Oahu, Hawaii
12 lb.	21 lbs. 3 oz.	Dec. 4 1957	Robert E. Becht, Hawaii	Honolulu, Hawaii

OPALEYE

Test Line	Weight	Date Caught	Angler	Waters Caught
2 lb.	4 lbs. 3 oz.	Mar. 17 1962	Jim Phelan, California	Laguna Beach, California
4 lb.	6 lbs. 4 oz.	Oct. 27 1968	Roger J. Lawrence, California	Long Beach, California
6 lb.	5 lbs. 8 oz.	June 4 1967	Roger J. Lawrence, California	Long Beach, California
8 lb. TIE	4 lbs. 8 oz.	April 28 1957	Wallace Crook, California	Long Beach, California
8 lb.	4 lbs. 8 oz.	Sept. 8 1968	Charles Brain, California	Laguna Beach, California
10 lb.	4 lbs. 10 oz.	Mar. 6 1966	Jessie Harmon, California	Laguna Beach, California
12 lb.	4 lbs. 5 oz.	Oct. 3 1958	Carl N. Wood, California	Laguna Beach, California

PERCH (Salt Water)

Test Line	Weight	Date Caught	Angler	Waters Caught
2 lb.	4 lbs. 4 oz.	May 24 1969	John W. Smart, Washington	Dungeness, Washington
4 lb.	4 lbs. 10 oz.	May 16 1966	John W. Smart, Washington	Dungeness, Washington
6 lb.	5 lbs. 3 oz.	June 4 1967	Roger Lawrence, California	Long Beach, California
8 lb.	3 lbs. 10 oz.	Mar. 31 1956	Tom Payne, California	BC, Mexico

Test Line	Weight	Date Caught	Angler	Waters Caught
10 lb.	4 lbs. 1 oz.	Apr. 12 1957	P. T. Peterson, California	Santa Monica, California
12 lb.	3 lbs. 12 oz.	Apr. 7 1956	James F. Johnson, California	Hermosa Beach, California

PERMIT

Test Line	Weight	Date Caught	Angler	Waters Caught
2 lb.	18 lbs. 12 oz.	Oct. 11 1962	B. A. Knauth, Florida	Big Pine Key, Florida
4 lb.	24 lbs. 0 oz.	Sept. 23 1968	Stanley Fried, Florida	Biscayne Bay, Florida
6 lb.	28 lbs. 8 oz.	July 27 1959	Mrs. Frances E. Fitts, Florida	Grand Cay, Bahamas
8 lb.	32 lbs. 4 oz.	Sept. 3 1963	Rex Cole, Florida	Boca Grande, Florida
10 lb.	41 lbs. 4 oz.	Mar. 19 1968	Walt Reed, New York	Marathon, Florida
12 lb.	40 lbs. 8 oz.	May 18 1967	A. Martin Mondl, Florida	Bahia Honda Key, Florida

POMPANO

Test Line	Weight	Date Caught	Angler	Waters Caught
2 lb.	2 lbs. 13 oz.	May 28 1961	G. O. Thorne, Florida	Panama City Beach, Florida
4 lb.	5 lbs. 3 oz.	June 4 1963	Roy H. Martin, Florida	Panama City Beach, Florida
6 lb.	6 lbs. 0 oz.	Nov. 9 1970	Chip Laudone, Florida	Lake Worth, Florida
8 lb.	6 lbs. 3 oz.	Feb. 15 1959	Myrtis Shrives, Florida	Vero Beach, Florida
10 lb.	12 lbs. 8 oz.	June 14 1960	Harry R. Gearhart, Jr.	Guantanamo Bay, Cuba
12 lb.	5 lbs. 12 oz.	Dec. 13 1958	Myrtis Shrives, Florida	Vero Beach, Florida

POMPANO (African)

Test Line	Weight	Date Caught	Angler	Waters Caught
2 lb.	Open			
4 lb.	7 lbs. 12 oz.	Mar. 6 1969	Ray O. Acord, California	Palau Islands
6 lb.	13 lbs. 7 oz.	Jan. 14 1966	Bernard Zwilling, California	Rancho Buena Vista, BC, Mexico
8 lb.	24 lbs. 8 oz.	Feb. 1 1969	Bob Kilgore, Florida	Triumph Reef, Florida
10 lb.	11 lbs. 0 oz.	June 15 1964	Joyce Perkins, California	Rancho Buena Vista, BC, Mexico
12 lb.	23 lbs. 2 oz.	Dec. 14 1969	William Kieldsen, Florida	

ROOSTERFISH

Test Line	Weight	Date Caught	Angler	Waters Caught
2 lb.	10 lbs. 2 oz.	Apr. 4 1960	Dr. E. A. Hershman, California	Bahia de Palmas, BC, Mexico
4 lb.	2 lbs. 9 oz.	July 11 1970	Jack Ridenoure, California	Rancho Buena Vista, BC, Mexico
6 lb.	27 lbs. 8 oz.	July 15 1967	Bernard Zwilling, California	Rancho Buena Vista, BC, Mexico
8 lb.	26 lbs. 7 oz.	Dec. 19 1970	Gordon Prentice, California	Loreto, BC, Mexico
10 lb.	50 lbs. 0 oz.	Sept. 6 1954	Maurice Levy, Jr., California	Loreto, BC, Mexico
12 lb.	50 lbs. 11 oz.	July 15 1967	Ron Zollinger, California	Rancho Bueno Vista, BC, Mexico

SAILFISH (Atlantic)

Test Line	Weight	Date Caught	Angler	Waters Caught
2 lb.	Open			
4 lb.	Open			
6 lb.	39 lbs. 8 oz.	Dec. 21 1969	Dr. Wm. Tarlton, Florida	N. Key Largo, Florida
8 lb.	57 lbs. 8 oz.	Nov. 24 1968	Stu Apte, Florida	Marathon, Florida
10 lb.	73 lbs. 0 oz.	June 25 1970	Jeffery Cicero, Florida	Miami, Florida
12 lb.	72 lbs. 0 oz.	Mar. 16 1970	Bill Kanipe, Indiana	Marathon, Florida

SAILFISH (Pacific)

Test Line	Weight	Date Caught	Angler	Waters Caught
2 lb.	OPEN			
4 lb.	95 lbs. 0 oz.	April 10 1968	Stu Apte, Florida	Pinas Bay, Panama
6 lb.	123 lbs. 1 oz.	April 24 1959	Ben Rodkin, California	Mazatlan, Mexico
8 lb.	128 lbs. 0 oz.	May 24 1960	Evelyn Fuller, California	Mazatlan, Mexico
10 lb.	132 lbs. 0 oz.	Dec. 11 1958	George Ramsey, California	Mazatlan, Mexico
12 lb.	145 lbs. 0 oz.	Mar. 14 1955	Dr. Earl Hershman, California	Mazatlan, Mexico

SALMON (Chinook)

Test Line	Weight	Date Caught	Angler	Waters Caught
2 lb.	25 lbs. 8 oz.	Sept. 2 1966	John W. Smart, Washington	Double Bluff, Washington
4 lb.	45 lbs. 0 oz.	Sept. 22 1969	John W. Smart, Washington	Marrowstone Isl., Washington
6 lb.	53 lbs. 6 oz.	July 30 1955	Buzz Fiorini, Washington	Rivers Inlet, BC, Canada
8 lb.	55 lbs. 4 oz.	Sept. 21 1963	J. A. Bell, Sr., Canada	Alberni Inlet, BC, Canada
10 lb.	42 lbs. 8 oz.	July 10 1955	Herman Hudson, Oregon	Coos Bay, Oregon
12 lb.	56 lbs. 0 oz.	Oct. 16 1965	Al Weismeyer, California	Smith River, Oregon

SALMON (Silver)

Test Line	Weight	Date Caught	Angler	Waters Caught
2 lb.	18 lbs. 5 oz.	Oct. 29 1966	John Smart, Washington	Whidbey Island, Washington
4 lb.	22 lbs. 12 oz.	Oct. 27 1968	John Smart, Washington	Whidbey Island, Washington
6 lb.	23 lbs. 10 oz.	Sept. 25 1966	John Smart, Washington	Quillayuter, Washington
8 lb.	19 lbs. 15 oz.	Sept. 27 1964	John W. Smart, Washington	Whidbey Isl., Washington
10 lb.	20 lbs. 0 oz.	July 25 1967	Oscar Hagen, California	Shelter Cove, California
12 lb.	22 lbs. 8 oz.	July 27 1953	Henry B. Helmuth, California	Trinidad, California

SHARK (Mako)

Test Line	Weight	Date Caught	Angler	Waters Caught
2 lb.	21 lbs. 12 oz.	Feb. 7 1967	A. C. Andreson, N. Z.	Tl Point N. I., N. Z.
4 lb.	OPEN			
6 lb.	31 lbs. 4 oz.	Aug. 29 1960	Bob Dragoo, California	Paradise Cove California
8 lb.	OPEN			
10 lb.	OPEN			
12 lb.	261 lbs. 11 oz.	Oct. 1 1953	Chuck Meyer, New York	Montauk Pt., L. I., New York

SHARK (Thresher)

Test Line	Weight	Date Caught	Angler	Waters Caught
2 lb.	Open			
4 lb.	20 lbs. 1 oz.	June 19 1960	Clifford D. Garver, California	San Pedro, California
6 lb.	89 lbs. 0 oz.	June 4 1969	Tom Miller, California	Hermosa Beach, California
8 lb.	40 lbs. 0 oz.	May 29 1969	Henry Galle, California	Hermosa Beach, California
10 lb.	Open			
12 lb.	Open			

SNAPPER (Mutton)

Test Line	Weight	Date Caught	Angler	Waters Caught
2 lb.	Open			
4 lb.	6 lbs. 9 oz.	Mar. 21 1967	Fred Johnson, Alabama	Big Pine Key, Florida,
6 lb.	9 lbs. 4 oz.	July 24 1970	Stanley Fried, Florida	Biscayne Bay, Florida
8 lb.	14 lbs. 9 oz.	Apr. 30 1968	Dave Chambers, Jr., Florida	Biscayne Bay, Florida
10 lb.	20 lbs. 6 oz.	Dec. 18 1970	Bill Kieldsen, Florida	Key Biscayne, Florida
12 lb.	9 lbs. 13 oz.	Mar. 21 1967	Fred Johnson, Alabama	Big Pine Key, Florida

SNAPPER (Yellowtail)

Test Line	Weight	Date Caught	Angler	Waters Caught
2 lb.	1 lb. 6 oz.	May 6 1970	C. W. Adams, M.D., Tennessee	Big Pine Key, Florida

Test Line	Weight	Date Caught	Angler	Waters Caught
4 lb.	2 lbs. 8 oz.	Sept. 2 1969	Dr. James Robertson, Florida	Bimini, Bahamas
6 lb.	Open			
8 lb.	4 lbs. 12 oz.	Jan. 5 1963	John W. Shiel, Florida	Boynton Beach, Florida
10 lb.	2 lbs. 6 oz.	Oct. 28 1967	Fred Johnson, Alabama	Marathon, Florida
12 lb.	1 lb. 4 oz.	Mar. 21 1967	Nancy Johnson, Alabama	Big Pine Key, Florida

SNOOK

Test Line	Weight	Date Caught	Angler	Waters Caught
2 lb.	11 lbs. 9 oz.	Feb. 11 1961	Leonard Hartman, Florida	Caloosahatchee River, Florida
4 lb.	25 lbs. 8 oz.	July 12 1963	Theodore C. Eggers, Florida	Lake Worth, Florida
6 lb.	26 lbs. 12 oz.	June 6 1964	Theodore C. Eggers, Florida	Lake Worth, Florida
8 lb.	32 lbs. 8 oz.	Mar. 2 1959	Roy S. Patten, Florida	Boca Raton Lake, Florida
TIE				
8 lb.	32 lbs. 8 oz.	July 9 1960	John H. Klinck, Florida	Palm Beach Canal, Florida
10 lb.	30 lbs. 0 oz.	July 29 1959	Chas. Warwick, III, Florida	Lake Worth, Florida
12 lb.	36 lbs. 0 oz.	Sept. 26 1969	Donald Dobbins, Florida	Costa Rica

TARPON

Test Line	Weight	Date Caught	Angler	Waters Caught
2 lb.	17 lbs. 5 oz.	Mar. 14 1966	Fred Johnson, Alabama	Bahia Honda Key, Florida
4 lb.	18 lbs. 12 oz.	Mar. 12 1966	Fred Johnson, Alabama	Bahia Honda Key, Florida
6 lb.	88 lbs. 0 oz.	May 17 1955	Chuck Meyer, New York	Summerland Key, Florida
8 lb.	53 lbs. 4 oz.	June 9 1960	Al Zapanta, California	Booth's River, British Honduras
10 lb.	115 lbs. 0 oz.	Aug. 18 1958	Gus Getner, Texas	Port Isabel, Texas
12 lb.	103 lbs. 4 oz.	Apr. 4 1970	Franz Johansen, Utah	Marathon, Florida

TOTUAVA

Test Line	Weight	Date Caught	Angler	Waters Caught
2 lb.	Open			
4 lb.	Open			
6 lb.	Open			
8 lb.	16 lbs. 2 oz.	May 27 1969	Chuck Berto, California	Puertecitos, BC, Mexico
10 lb.	20 lbs. 6 oz.	Mar. 11 1958	Harold Lane, California	San Felipe, BC, Mexico
12 lb.	28 lbs. 14 oz.	Feb. 24 1962	Bob Dragoo, Califorina	Puertecitos, BC, Mexico

TRIPLETAIL

Test Line	Weight	Date Caught	Angler	Waters Caught
2 lb.	7 lbs. 2 oz.	June 25 1966	Gerald Braden, Florida	St. James, Florida
4 lb.	14 lbs. 0 oz.	Oct. 1 1965	Gerald Braden, Florida	San Carlos Bay, Florida
6 lb.	24 lbs. 4 oz.	May 20 1965	Gerald S. Braden, Florida	Caloosahatchee R., Florida
8 lb.	20 lbs. 14 oz.	Aug. 9 1967	Brownie Hayes, Florida	Pine Island, Florida
10 lb.	18 lbs. 8 oz.	July 28 1968	Loretta Rollins, Florida	Pine Island, Florida
12 lb.	32 lbs. 0 oz.	Sept. 28 1960	Clarence Wieder-echt, Louisiana	Venice, Louisiana

TUNA (Blackfin)

Test Line	Weight	Date Caught	Angler	Waters Caught
2 lb.	Open			
4 lb.	Open			
6 lb.	Open			
8 lb.	15 lbs. 2 oz.	Nov. 22 1968	Stu Apte, Florida	Marathon, Florida
10 lb.	Open			
12 lb.	15 lbs. 0 oz.	Apr. 20 1970	Bill Kieldsen	Key Biscayne, Florida

TUNA (Bluefin)

Line Test	Weight	Date Caught	Angler	Waters Caught
2 lb	Open			
4 lb.	16 lbs. 0 oz.	Sept. 20 1953	A. E. Moore, California	Guadalupe Island, Mexico
6 lb.	15 lbs. 6 oz.	Aug. 26 1962	Harry D. Vickers, California	San Diego, California
8 lb.	22 lbs. 3 oz.	July 15 1970	Dan Bartfield, California	Coronado Isle, Mexico
10 lb.	28 lbs. 0 oz.	July 17 1957	Ralph Chevalier, California	Long Beach, California
12 lb.	30 lbs. 4 oz.	Oct. 7 1956	Glenn R. Bracken, California	Catalina Island, California

TUNA (Little)

Line Test	Weight	Date Caught	Angler	Waters Caught
2 lb.	5 lbs. 7 oz.	Nov. 5 1960	G. O. Thorne, Florida	Panama City Beach, Florida
4 lb.	13 lbs. 6 oz.	June 25 1960	G. O. Thorne, Florida	Panama City Beach, Florida
6 lb.	15 lbs. 2 oz.	Sept. 18 1965	Wm. Rosenthal, Pennsylvania	Barneget, New Jersey
8 lb.	19 lbs. 0 oz.	May 27 1960	Dick Craik, California	Panama City, Florida
10 lb.	18 lbs. 9 oz.	July 18 1959	Robert G. Ryder, Florida	Palm Beach, Florida
12 lb.	19 lbs. 0 oz.	Feb. 8 1959	William Yamashita, Hawaii	Oahu, Hawaii

TUNA (Yellowfin)

Line Test	Weight	Date Caught	Angler	Waters Caught
2 lb.	Open			
4 lb.	5 lbs. 6 oz.	Sept. 7 1970	Ray O. Acord, California	Koror, Palau, Trust Terr.
6 lb.	23 lbs. 11 oz.	July 16 1967	Bernard Zwilling, California	Rancho Buena Vista, BC, Mexico
8 lb.	18 lbs. 3 oz.	Sept. 25 1960	Chet Umberham, California	Newport Beach, California
10 lb.	26 lbs. 6 oz.	Dec. 21 1960	N. R. Rehm, California	Cabo San Lucas, BC, Mexico
12 lb.	27 lbs. 3 oz.	July 16 1967	Ron Zollinger, California	Rancho Buena Vista, BC, Mexico

WAHOO

Line Test	Weight	Date Caught	Angler	Waters Caught
2 lb.	Open			
4 lb.	Open			
6 lb.	Open			
8 lb.	17 lbs. 0 oz.	Oct. 28 1969	Alfredo Bequillard, Jr., Nicaragua	San Juan del Sur, Nicaragua
10 lb.	38 lbs. 8 oz.	Mar. 18 1970	Ray O. Acord, California	Koror, Palau
12 lb.	50 lbs. 0 oz.	Mar. 24 1969	Lyman Spire, M.D., New York	Virgin Islands

WEAKFISH

Line Test	Weight	Date Caught	Angler	Waters Caught
2 lb.	8 lbs. 5 oz.	April 30 1959	S. F. Still, Florida	Banana Riv., Florida
4 lb.	10 lbs. 7 oz.	April 6 1969	J. C. Yokel, Florida	Port Canaveral, Florida
6 lb.	9 lbs. 12 oz.	Feb. 17 1962	John Zeman, Florida	Cocoa Beach, Florida
TIE				
6 lb.	9 lbs. 12 oz.	Feb. 8 1969	David Brown, Florida	Port Canaveral, Florida
8 lb.	11 lbs. 1 oz.	Jan. 25 1959	Harry Evans, Florida	Sebastian Inlet, Florida
10 lb.	10 lbs. 4 oz.	April 2 1966	Jack Smith, Florida	Jensen, Florida
12 lb.	12 lbs. 9 oz.	May 11 1957	Gus Getner, Texas	Arroyo Colorado, Texas

Test Line	Weight	Date Caught	Angler	Waters Caught
WHITE SEA BASS				
2 lb.	3 lbs. 12 oz.	April 14 1957	Robert Salamon, California	Dana Pt., California
4 lb.	12 lbs. 5 oz.	Aug. 20 1958	Dr. Earl Hershman, California	San Onofre, California
6 lb.	38 lbs. 14 oz.	May 20 1952	Rex S. York, California	Coronodos Isls., California
8 lb.	35 lbs. 8 oz.	July 19 1953	Wilfred Sargent, California	San Clemente, California
10 lb.	45 lbs. 8 oz.	July 15 1959	John Mullen California	Point Mugu, California
12 lb.	65 lbs. 0 oz.	July 8 1955	C. J. Aronis, California	Ensenada, BC, Mexico

Test Line	Weight	Date Caught	Angler	Waters Caught
YELLOWTAIL				
2 lb.	12 lbs. 6 oz.	Aug. 23 1959	Bob Dragoo, California	Ensenada, BC, Mexico
4 lb.	26 lbs. 4 oz.	April 27 1957	Floyd Randolph, California	Torrey Pines, California
6 lb.	26 lbs. 6 oz.	Oct. 11 1962	Willis Carr, California	La Jolla, California
8 lb.	22 lbs. 8 oz.	Feb. 25 1958	Dr. Earl Hershman, California	Rancho Buena Vista, BC, Mexico
10 lb.	42 lbs. 0 oz.	April 7 1955	Albert M. Zapanta, California	Rancho Buena Vista, BC, Mexico
12 lb.	36 lbs. 13 oz.	April 4 1951	D. Tomlinson, California	Coronado Isle, California

State Fishing Records

The state fishing records listed here are based on information provided by the various state conservation departments. There are considerable differences in record-keeping by the various states: some states do not maintain big-fish records, some states having both fresh and salt water fishing list records for only fresh water species, some states list only certain species of fish in their records, and some states recognize for record purposes large fish taken from private waters, while some other states do not.

ALABAMA

Species	Wt.	Where	When	Angler
BASS, Redeye	6 lbs. ½ oz.	Hallawakee Creek	Mar. 24 1967	Thomas L. Sharpe
BASS, Smallmouth	10 lbs. 8 oz.	Tennessee River	Oct. 8 1950	Owen F. Smith
BASS, Spotted	8 lbs. 8 oz.	Lewis Smith Lake	May 23 1968	James Wreford
BLUEGILL	4 lbs. 12 oz.	Ketona Lake	Mar. 9 1950	T. S. Hudson
DRUM, Freshwater	26 lbs.	Lake Jordan	Feb. 22 1970	Larry L. Roberts
SUNFISH, Redear	4 lbs. 4 oz.	Chattahoochee State Park	May 5 1962	Jeff Lashley

ALASKA

Freshwater Species	Wt.	Where	When	Angler
BURBOT	22 lbs. 8 oz.	Lake Louise	May 3 1968	Robert Bronson
CHAR, Arctic	17 lbs. 8 oz.	Wulik River	Sept. 26 1968	Peter Winslow
GRAYLING, Arctic	4 lbs.	Ugashik Lake	July 30 1967	Joseph Carlone
PIKE, Northern	28 lbs. 2 oz.	Wilson Lake	June 26 1971	Elmer Kurrus
SHEEFISH	52 lbs. ½ oz.	Kobuk River	Aug. 10 1968	Jim Keeline
TROUT, Lake	47 lbs.	Clarence Lake	June 28 1970	Daniel Thorsness
TROUT, Rainbow	42 lbs. 2 oz.	Bell Island	June 22 1970	David White
WHITEFISH	4 lbs. 12 oz.	Lake Creek	Aug. 3 1968	Curtis Duhon

Saltwater Species	Wt.	Where	When	Angler
HALIBUT	340 lbs.	Thomas Bay	Aug. 30 1971	George Rice

Saltwater Species	Wt.	Where	When	Angler
SALMON, King	87 lbs.	Favorite Bay	May 22 1971	Orville Carter
SALMON, Pink	11 lbs. 6 oz.	Biorka Island	June 22 1969	Phillip James
SALMON, Silver	22 lbs.	Vallenar Rock	June 30 1971	Edna Rogers

ARIZONA

Species	Wt.	Where	When	Angler
BASS, Largemouth	14 lbs. 10 oz.	Roosevelt Lake	Apr. 1966	
BASS, Smallmouth	4 lbs. 1½ oz.	Bartlett Lake	Nov. 1969	Carl Lewis
BASS, Striped	39 lbs. 11½ oz.	Colorado River	Aug. 1971	Ed Higgins
BASS, White	4 lbs. 10½ oz.	Upper Lake Pleasant	Dec. 1966	John Hoffman
BASS, Yellow	1 lb. 2½ oz.	Saguaro Lake	June 1971	Jeff Senn
BLUEGILL	3 lbs. 5 oz.	San Carlos Reservation	1965	Ernest Garcia
CATFISH, Blue	31 lbs.	Randolph Park	July 1970	Richard Lujan
CATFISH, Channel	35 lbs. 4 oz.	Topock Swamp	1952	Wando Tull
CATFISH, Flathead	65 lbs.	San Carlos Lake	1951	Pat Coleman
CRAPPIE, Black	4 lbs. 10 oz.	San Carlos Lake	1959	John Shadrick
CRAPPIE, White	1 lb. 11 oz.	Upper Lake Pleasant	Apr. 1971	Bill Blunck
PIKE, Northern	18 lbs. 6 oz.	Upper Lake Mary	May 1971	Joe Killeen
TROUT, Brook	8 lbs. 3 oz.	Big Lake	1943	
TROUT, Brown	17 lbs.	Lake Powell	May 1971	Chuck Holland
TROUT, Cutthroat	6 lbs. 9 oz.	Big Lake	1943	

Species	Wt.	Where	When	Angler
TROUT, Grayling	1 lb. 7 oz.	Big Lake	1942	
TROUT, Rainbow	21 lbs. 5½ oz.	Colorado River	Sept. 1966	John Reid
WALLEYE	5 lbs. 3 oz.	Lake Powell	July 1970	Forrest Turner

ARKANSAS

Species	Wt.	Where	When	Angler
BASS, Largemouth	12 lbs. 6½ oz.	Long Lake	Nov. 13 1971	Henry Self
BASS, Rock	1 lb. 6½ oz.	Lake Norfolk	May 5 1963	Randy Screws
BASS, Smallmouth	7 lbs. 5 oz.	Lake Bull Shoals	Apr. 1 1969	Acie Dickerson
BASS, Spotted	6 lbs. 9 oz.	Lake Bull Shoals	Apr. 1 1971	Joe Huff
BASS, Striped	40 lbs.	Lake Ouachita	Apr. 25 1971	Bill Bars
BASS, Warmouth	1 lb. 7 oz.	Spring River	Sept. 25 1965	Jay Kaffka
BASS, White	4 lbs. 15 oz.	Upper White River	May 8 1969	Bud Stopple
BLUEGILL	1 lb. 14 oz.	Lake Overcup	July 17 1966	Forrest Fields
CATFISH, Blue	47 lbs. 8 oz.	Arkansas River	Mar. 28 1970	Richard Been
CATFISH, Channel	18 lbs.	Lake Fayetteville	Mar. 27 1963	Elmer Powers
CATFISH, Flathead	33 lbs. 8 oz.	Little Red River	May 12 1966	Grover Hawkins
CRAPPIE, Black	3 lbs. 14 oz.	Rice Reservoir	Mar. 16 1966	Junior Berryman
CRAPPIE, White	4 lbs.	Private Pond	Mar. 21 1969	Charlie Jones
GAR, Alligator	215 lbs.	Arkansas River	June 31 1964	Alvin Bonds
PICKEREL, Chain	5 lbs.	Little Red River	Mar. 23 1971	Harvey Darnell
PIKE, Northern	8 lbs. 1 oz.	Lake Beaver	June 15 1969	Harold Webb
SAUGER	3 lbs. 15 oz.	Lake Norfolk	Mar. 23 1967	Lucille Cantwell
SUNFISH, Green	1 lb. 6 oz.	Private Pond	Apr. 25 1966	Bill Jones
SUNFISH, Longear	0 lb. 7 oz.	Mellwood Old River Lake	May 15 1971	Bill McCaughan
SUNFISH, Redear	2 lbs. 8 oz.	Lake Boswell	Oct. 30 1961	Charlie Henderson
TROUT, Brown	31 lbs. 8 oz.	White River	1972	Troy Lackey
TROUT, Rainbow	16 lbs. 2 oz.	North Fork River	June 14 1970	Frank Mandernach
WALLEYE	19 lbs. 12 oz.	White River	Feb. 12 1963	Mrs. L. E. Garrison

CALIFORNIA

Freshwater Species	Wt.	Where	When	Angler
BASS, Largemouth	16 lbs. 11 oz.	Miramar Lake	Jan. 17 1971	Randall Danio
BASS, Smallmouth	7 lbs. 11 oz.	Trapper Slough	Nov. 16 1951	C. H. Richey
BASS, White	3 lbs. 11 oz.	Nacimiento Lake	Mar. 11 1971	Nick Marazzo
BLUEGILL	2 lbs. 9 oz.	Middle Legg Lake	July 4 1971	Willie Mae McKinney
CARP	52 lbs.	Nacimiento Lake	Apr. 1968	Lee Bryant
CATFISH, Channel	40 lbs. 8 oz.	Lake Casitas	May 29 1971	Monte Monfore
CATFISH, Flathead	41 lbs.	Colorado River	Sept. 18 1971	Robert Jennings
CATFISH, White	15 lbs. 1 oz.	Snodgrass Slough	June 1 1951	O. J. McArdie
CRAPPIE, Black	4 lbs.	Mendota Pool	Mar. 16 1956	Alex Berg
CRAPPIE, White	4 lbs. 8 oz.	Clear Lake	Apr. 26 1971	Carol Carlton
SALMON, Kokanee	4 lbs. 6 oz.	Lake Tahoe	July 31 1968	Lisa Brumfield
SHAD, American	6 lbs. 15 oz.	Yuba River	June 7 1970	Hal Janssen
STURGEON	293 lbs.	San Pablo Bay	Apr. 15 1970	Glen Claypool, Jr.
TROUT, Brook	9 lbs. 12 oz.	Silver Lake	Sept. 9 1932	Texas Haynes
TROUT, Brown	25 lbs. 11 oz.	Crowley Lake	July 1 1971	Richard Reinwald
TROUT, Cutthroat	31 lbs. 8 oz.	Lake Tahoe	1911	William Pomin
TROUT, Dolly Varden	9 lbs. 1 oz.	McCloud Reservoir	May 1968	James Scott
TROUT, Golden	9 lbs. 8 oz.	Virginia Lake	Aug. 18 1952	O. A. Benefield
TROUT, Lake	35 lbs. 8 oz.	Lake Tahoe	June 1 1970	Sam Sigwart
TROUT, Steelhead	23 lbs. 4 oz.	Smith River	Jan. 7 1971	Lionel Borough

Saltwater Species	Wt.	Where	When	Angler
BASS, Striped	65 lbs.	San Joaquin River	May 16 1951	Wendell Olson
BASS, White Sea	77 lbs. 4 oz.	San Diego	Apr. 8 1950	H. P. Bledsoe
CORVINA	32 lbs. 8 oz.	Salton Sea	May 11 1960	Dick Paul
MARLIN, Blue	672 lbs.	Balboa	Aug. 18 1931	A. Hamann
SALMON, King	85 lbs.	Feather River	Oct. 1935	Manford Cochran
SALMON, Silver	22 lbs.	Paper Mill Creek	Jan. 3 1959	Milton Hain
YELLOWTAIL	62 lbs.	La Jolla	June 6 1953	George Willett

COLORADO

Species	Wt.	Where	When	Angler
BASS, Largemouth	9 lbs. 6 oz.	Cherry Creek Reservoir	1970	Richard Gasaway
BASS, Smallmouth	3 lbs.	N. Sterling Reservoir	1971	Jerry Acre
BASS, White	4 lbs. 7 oz.	Adobe Creek Reservoir	1963	Pedro Martinez

Freshwater Species	Wt.	Where	When	Angler
BLUEGILL	1 lb. 5 oz.		1972	Melvin Hanners
CATFISH, Channel	25 lbs. 9 oz.	Smith Lake	1969	Ron Pasley
CRAPPIE	3 lbs.	Kendrick Reservoir	1971	Dave Wood
PIKE, Northern	30 lbs. 1 oz.	Vallecito Reservoir	1971	Earl Walden
SALMON, Kokanee	3 lbs 11 oz.		1971	William Rhodes
SHEEPSHEAD	8 lbs. 12 oz.	Two Buttes Reservoir	1971	Gene Gold
TROUT, Brook	7 lbs. 10 oz.		1940s	George Knorr
TROUT, Brown	23 lbs.		1961	Jesse Brown
TROUT, Cutthroat	16 lbs.	Twin Lakes	1964	George Hranchek
TROUT, Lake	36 lbs.	Deep Lake	1949	R. H. Wisley
TROUT, Splake	12 lbs. 7 oz.	Island Lake	1971	C. E. Rose
WALLEYE	13 lbs.	Cherry Creek Reservoir	1971	George Uyeno

CONNECTICUT

Species	Wt.	Where	When	Angler
BASS, Largemouth	12 lbs. 14 oz.	Mashapaug Lake	1961	Frank Domurat
BASS, Smallmouth	7 lbs. 10 oz.	Mashapaug Lake	1954	Frank Domurat
BLUEGILL	1 lb. 12 oz.	Wheeler Pond	1970	Michael Brycki, Jr.
BULLHEAD, Brown	2 lbs. 14 oz.	Prichard Pond	1968	Albert E. Podzunes, Jr.
CATFISH, White	8 lbs. 8 oz.	Candlewood Lake	1958	Thomas Molloy
CRAPPIE	3 lbs. 13 oz.	Lake Saltonstall	1955	Raymond Stopka
PERCH, White	2 lbs. 8 oz.	Connecticut River	1961	Barney Walden
PERCH, Yellow	2 lbs. 2 oz.	Amos Lake	1967	Stanley Warykas
PICKEREL, Chain	7 lbs. 14 oz.	Wauregan Reservoir	1969	Charles Loman
PIKE, Northern	16 lbs. 11 oz.	Connecticut River	1960	Frank Domurat
SHAD, American	8 lbs. 9½ oz.	Connecticut River	1971	Robert Benson
TROUT, Brook	4 lbs. 6 oz.	Housatonic River	1950	Fred Mazzafemo
TROUT, Brown	16 lbs. 4 oz.	Mashapaug Lake	1968	Albert Jarish
TROUT, Lake	29 lbs. 13 oz.	Wononscopomuc Lake	1918	Dr. Thompson
TROUT, Rainbow	9 lbs. 7 oz.	Saugatuck Reservoir	1962	Ed Mayo
WALLEYE	14 lbs. 8 oz.	Candlewood Lake	1941	George Britto

DELAWARE

Freshwater Species	Wt.	Where	When	Angler
BASS, Largemouth	9 lbs. 8 oz.	Noxontown Pond	Apr. 25 1969	John Moore
BLUEGILL	1 lb. 4 oz.	Hearns Pond	Oct. 15 1971	Venus Harrison
CRAPPIE	3 lbs. 3 oz.	Noxontown Pond	May 13 1967	Harry Nicholson III
PERCH, White	1 lb. 13 oz.	Reynolds Pond	Oct. 17 1970	Helma Ranka
PERCH, Yellow	1 lb. 12 oz.	Nanticoke River	May 23 1969	Alexander Rybicki
PICKEREL, Chain	6 lbs. 12 oz.	Noxontown Pond	Apr. 27 1969	Michael Bienicewicz

Saltwater Species	Wt.	Where	When	Angler
ALBACORE	17 lbs.	Atlantic Ocean	Oct. 9 1971	John Mentzer
BASS, Channel	68 lbs. ¾ oz.	Slaughters Beach	May 21 1971	William Sollars
BASS, Sea	3 lbs. 12 oz.	Atlantic Ocean	Aug. 7 1971	Peter Smulski
BASS, Striped	39 lbs.	Indian River Inlet	Aug. 7 1971	Donald O'Day
BLUEFISH	18 lbs. 10 oz.	Cape Henlopen	Nov. 13 1971	Joe Christiansen
DOLPHIN	34 lbs.	S.E. Indian River	Sept. 6 1971	Tim Good
DRUM, Black	76 lbs.	Mispillion	June 1 1968	Carson Stoneman
FLOUNDER	17 lbs. 1 oz.	Massey's Landing	July 7 1968	Albert Leager
KINGFISH	2 lbs. 12 oz.	Bower Beach	May 28 1971	John Lynch
MARLIN, White	87 lbs.	S.E. Delaware Lightship	July 29 1969	Frank Saich
SHARK	390 lbs.	Bowers Beach	July 29 1967	Richard Muschamp
TAUTOG	14 lbs. 6½ oz.	East End Light	Oct. 29 1971	Don Daisey Sr.
TUNA	45 lbs.	S.E. "A" Buoy	Sept. 10 1966	Charles Lewis
WEAKFISH	8 lbs. 8 oz.	Harbor of Refuge	June 22 1970	Anthony Schmidt

FLORIDA
(No Records Maintained)

GEORGIA

Freshwater Species	Wt.	Where	When	Angler
BASS, Largemouth (World Record)	22 lbs. 4 oz.	Montgomery Lake	June 2 1932	George Perry
BASS, Rock	2 lbs. 10 oz.	Jacks River	July 4 1967	John R. Cockburn, Jr
BASS, Smallmouth	6 lbs. 5 oz.	Lake Blue Ridge	Dec. 11 1969	Jackie Suits
BASS, Spotted	7 lbs. 8 oz.	Little Tesnatee River	May 20 1969	Donald Palmer
BASS, White	5 lbs. 1 oz.	Lake Lanier	June 16 1971	J. M. Hobbins

Freshwater Species	Wt.	Where	When	Angler
BLUEGILL	2 lbs. 15 oz.	Okefenokee Swamp	Aug. 1965	Terry Cantrell
BOWFIN	15 lbs.	Lake Joy	Aug. 9 1970	Amos Hardy Jr.
CARP	35 lbs. 6 oz.	Sweetwater Creek	Apr. 17 1967	Albert B. Hicks, Sr.
CATFISH, Flathead	51 lbs. 15 oz.	Lake Nottely	June 2 1969	Hoyt McDaniel
CRAPPIE, Black	4 lbs. 4 oz.	Acrees Lake	June 1 1971	Shirley Lavender
CRAPPIE, White	4 lbs. 4 oz.	Lake Hartwell	Apr. 27 1968	Charles McCullough
MUSKELLUNGE	38 lbs.	Blue Ridge Lake	June 1957	Rube Golden
PICKEREL, Chain (World Record)	9 lbs. 6 oz.	Homerville Georgia	Feb. 1961	Baxley McQuaig, Jr.
SUNFISH, Redear	3 lbs. 1 oz.	McKenzie's Lake	Aug. 8 1971	John Reid
TROUT, Brook	3 lbs. 12 oz.	Moccasin Creek	Apr. 12 1969	Barry Lowe
TROUT, Brown	18 lbs. 3 oz.	Rock Creek	May 6 1967	William Lowery
TROUT, Rainbow	12 lbs. 4 oz.	Coosawatte River	May 31 1966	John Whitaker
WALLEYE	11 lbs.	Lake Burton	Apr. 13 1963	Steven Kenny

Saltwater Species	Wt.	Where	When	Angler
BASS, Striped	63 lbs.	Oconee River	May 30 1967	Kelly Ward

HAWAII
(No Records Maintained)

IDAHO

Species	Wt.	Where	When	Angler
BASS, Largemouth	10 lbs. 15 oz.	Anderson Lake		Mrs. M. W. Taylor
BASS, Smallmouth	5 lbs. 14 oz.	Snake River	May 1962	B. B. Bacharach
BLUEGILL	3 lbs. 8 oz.	C.J. Strike Reservoir	May 1966	Darrell Grim
BULLHEAD	2 lbs. 9 oz.	Private Pond	May 13 1967	Charles Carpenter
CATFISH, Channel	21 lbs. 8 oz.	Snake River	Mar. 27 1970	Gary Kluksdal
CATFISH, Flathead	25 lbs.	Snake River	May 17 1970	Bill Branstrom
CRAPPIE	2 lbs. 8 oz.	Shepherd Lake	1954	Mrs. Carl Tifft
LING	14 lbs.	Kootenai River	1954	P. A. Dayton
PERCH	2 lbs. 8 oz.	Murtaugh Reservoir		Dewey Julian
SALMON, Chinook	45 lbs.	Salmon River	Sept. 5 1964	Hurbert Staggie
SALMON, Kokanee	3 lbs. 10 oz.	Moose Creek	Sept. 1958	Ted Miller
SALMON, Sockeye	5 lbs.	Redfish Lake	Aug. 6 1970	Mrs. June McCray

Species	Wt.	Where	When	Angler
STURGEON	394 lbs.	Snake River	1956	Glen Howard
TROUT, Brook	6 lbs. 10 oz.	Deep Creek Reservoir	1958	Donald Kotschevar
TROUT, Brown	25 lbs. 12 oz.	Palisades Reservoir	Mar. 23 1969	Jim McMurtrey
TROUT, Cutthroat	18 lbs. 15 oz.	Bear Lake	Apr. 30 1970	Roger Grunig
TROUT, Cutthroat-Rainbow (hybrid)	23 lbs. 4 oz.	Blackfoot Reservoir	1957	Phil Adderly
TROUT, Dolly Varden	32 lbs.	Pend Oreille Lake	1949	Nelson Higgins
TROUT, Golden	5 lbs. 2 oz.	White Sands Lake	1958	George Wolverton
TROUT, Kamloops	37 lbs.	Pend Oreille Lake	1947	Wes Hamlet
TROUT, Lake	57 lbs. 8 oz.	Priest Lake	Nov. 14 1971	Lyle McClure
TROUT, Rainbow	19 lbs.	Hayden Lake	Nov. 1947	R. M. Williams
TROUT, Steelhead	29 lbs. 8 oz.	North Fork Clearwater River	Dec. 1966	Leonard Profitt
WHITEFISH, Mountain	5 lbs. 4 oz.	South Fork Payette River	1941	

ILLINOIS

Species	Wt.	Where	When	Angler
BASS, Largemouth	12 lbs. 8 oz.	Carlinville City Lake	1969	James Crandall
BASS, Rock	1 lb. 9 oz.	Strip Mine	1968	Eugene Matsko
BASS, Smallmouth	5 lbs. 13 oz.	Lake Bloomington	1970	Terry Gibson
BASS, Spotted	1 lb. 13 oz.	Hutchins Creek	1971	Steve Wunderle
BASS, White	4 lbs. 1 oz.	Crab Orchard Lake	1970	James Burgess
BLUEGILL	2 lbs. 10 oz.	Strip Mine	1963	Rip Sullivan
BUFFALO	48 lbs.	Mississippi River	1936	C. B. Merritt
BULLHEAD, Black	3 lbs. 7 oz.	Sutton Lake	1970	John Cearlock
BULLHEAD, Yellow	5 lbs. 4 oz.	Fox River	1955	Bill Snow
CARP	42 lbs.	Kankakee River	1928	Clarence Heinze
CATFISH, Blue (Tie)	65 lbs.	Alton Lake	1956	Ernest Webb
	65 lbs.	Alton Lake	1956	Andrew Coats, Jr.
CATFISH, Channel	28 lbs.	Strip Mine	1963	Tom Giles
CATFISH, Flathead	51 lbs.	Hennepin Canal	1950	Les Beyer
CRAPPIE, Black	4 lbs. 4 oz.	Craig Lake	1967	Gilbert Parker
CRAPPIE, White	4 lbs. 5 oz.	Farm Pond	1967	Alice Edwards
GAR	157 lbs.	Mississippi River	1944	Clarence Cousins

Species	Wt.	Where	When	Angler
PADDLEFISH	46 lbs. 8 oz.	Mississippi River	1968	Dick Vant
PERCH, Yellow	2 lbs. 5 oz.	Strip Mine	1951	William Hodgson
PIKE, Northern	20 lbs. 2 oz.	Strip Mine	1952	Raymond Kindlespire
SALMON, Chinook	29 lbs. 5 oz.	Lake Michigan	1972	Ronald Johnson
SALMON, Coho	20 lbs. 9 oz.	Lake Michigan	1972	Garry Vande Vusse
SAUGER	5 lbs. 12½ oz.	Mississippi River	1967	Bill Rolando
SHEEPSHEAD	35 lbs.	DuQuoin City Lake	1960	Joe Rinella
STURGEON, Lake	57 lbs. 2 oz.	Mississippi River	1971	John Hicks
SUNFISH, Green	1 lb. 4 oz.	Strip Mine	1971	Edward Smith
SUNFISH, Hybrid	2 lbs. 1 oz.	Farm Pond	1968	Dan Fisher
SUNFISH, Redear	2 lbs.	Farm Pond	1971	Donna Furlow
TROUT, Brook	4 lbs. 1 oz.	Lake Michigan	1970	August Bulleri
TROUT, Brown	13 lbs. 5 oz.	Lake Michigan	1971	Walter Bieszczat
TROUT, Lake	14 lbs. 11 oz.	Lake Michigan	1972	David Martinek
TROUT, Rainbow	16 lbs. 7 oz.	Lake Michigan	1971	Ross Roberts
WALLEYE	14 lbs.	Kankakee River	1961	Fred Goselin
WARMOUTH (World Record)	1 lb. 13 oz.	Farm Pond	1971	Wesley Mills

INDIANA

Species	Wt.	Where	When	Angler
BASS, Largemouth	11 lbs. 11 oz.	Ferdinand Reservoir	1968	Curt Reynolds
BASS, Rock	3 lbs.	Sugar Creek	1969	David Thomas
BASS, Smallmouth	6 lbs. 8 oz.	Stream	1970	Jim Connerly
BASS, Spotted	4 lbs. 9 oz.	Marriott Lake	1970	Charles Underhill
BASS, White	4 lbs. 3 oz.	Lake Freeman	1965	James Wagner
BLUEGILL	3 lbs.	Lake	1971	Raymond McClellan
BOWFIN	13 lbs. 8 oz.	Stream	1971	Jim Spice & J. Holtsclaw
BULLHEAD	3 lbs. 13 oz.	Pond	1970	Fred Stewart
CARP	38 lbs. 1 oz.	Lake	1967	Frank Drost
CATFISH, Blue	50 lbs.	White River	1970	Dick Teising
CATFISH, Channel	27 lbs.	Tippecanoe River	1970	Chester Keith
CATFISH, Flathead	79 lbs. 8 oz.	White River	1966	Glen Simpson
CRAPPIE	4 lbs. 7 oz.	Pond	1965	Mary Ann Leigh
MUSKELLUNGE	12 lbs.	Little Blue River	1965	Jim Vinyard

Species	Wt.	Where	When	Angler
PERCH, Yellow	1 lb. 11 oz.	Pond	1966	Jim Harper
PIKE, Northern	20 lbs. 12 oz.	Bass Lake	1964	George Byer
SALMON, Chinook	19 lbs. 14 oz.	Lake Michigan	1971	Donald Daugherty
SALMON, Coho (Tie)	19 lbs. 2 oz.	Lake Michigan	1969	Robert Scheerer
SALMON, Coho	19 lbs. 2 oz.	Lake Michigan	1972	Harold Gehrke
SAUGER	5 lbs.	Wabash River	1964	N. L. Merrifeld
SHEEPSHEAD	30 lbs.	White River	1963	Garland Fellers
SUNFISH, Redear	2 lbs. 11 oz.	Pond	1964	Joan Janeway
TROUT, Brook	1 lb. 13 oz.	Beaver Dam	1966	Tim Arney
TROUT, Brown	12 lbs. 4 oz.	Lake Michigan	1971	Ezell Smith, Jr.
TROUT, Lake	14 lbs. 1 oz.	Lake Michigan	1971	William Bond
TROUT, Rainbow	8 lbs. 5 oz.	Pretty Lake	1963	Francis Layson
TROUT, Steelhead	20 lbs. 10 oz.	Lake Michigan	1972	Dan Bowen
WALLEYE	13 lbs.	Kankakee River	1969	John McEwan

IOWA

Species	Wt.	Where	When	Angler
BASS, Largemouth	10 lbs. 5 oz.	Farm Pond	Aug. 1970	Paul Burgund
BASS, Smallmouth	6 lbs. 3 oz.	West Okoboji	June 1966	Marvin Singer
BASS, White	3 lbs. 7 oz.	West Okoboji	Sept. 1970	Tom Hamilton
BLUEGILL	2 lbs. 3 oz.	Farm Pond	Apr. 1971	Bob Adam
BULLHEAD (Tie)	4 lbs. 8 oz.	Farm Pond	Apr. 1966	Dennie Karas
	4 lbs. 8 oz.	Boyer River	Aug. 1971	Ralph Cooney
CARP	50 lbs.	Glenwood Lake	May 1969	Fred Hougland
CATFISH, Channel	30 lbs.	Viking Lake	Aug. 1971	Glen Harms
CATFISH, Flathead	62 lbs.	Iowa River	July 1965	Roger Fairchild
CRAPPIE	4 lbs. 1 oz.	Farm Pond	May 1969	John Lenhart
MUSKELLUNGE	23 lbs. 2 oz.	Clear Lake	June 1971	Brian Buehler
PADDLEFISH	81 lbs.	De Soto Bend	Apr. 1971	Duane Fisher
PERCH, Yellow	1 lb. 13 oz.	Mississippi River	Sept. 1963	Neal Palmer
PIKE, Northern	23 lbs. 8 oz.	Cedar River	Aug. 1970	Fred Stifter
SAUGER	5 lbs. 2 oz.	Mississippi River	Nov. 1963	Art Hurlburt
SHEEPSHEAD	46 lbs.	Spirit Lake	Oct. 1962	R. F. Farran
TROUT, Brown	12 lbs. 14¼ oz.	Elk Creek	Nov. 1966	Billy Lee

Species	Wt.	Where	When	Angler
TROUT, Rainbow	13 lbs. 8 oz.	Richmond Springs	Nov. 1968	C. Melvin Vaughn
WALLEYE	14 lbs. 2 oz.	Spirit Lake	Oct. 1968	Herbert Aldridge

KANSAS

Species	Wt.	Where	When	Angler
BASS, Largemouth Black	11 lbs. 3 oz.	Private Lake	Jan. 6 1965	Charles Prewett
BASS, Smallmouth	2 lbs. 7 oz.	Norton Reservoir	June 30 1971	Tom Williams
BASS, Spotted (Kentucky)	3 lbs. 15¼ oz.	Council Grove City Lake	Apr. 21 1970	Newell Julian
BASS, Striped	9 lbs. 9 oz.	Cheney Reservoir	Apr. 21 1971	Paul Person
BASS, White	5 lbs. 4 oz.	Toronto Reservoir	May 4 1966	Henry Baker
BLUEGILL	2 lbs. 5 oz.	Farm Pond	May 26 1962	Robert Jefferies
BUFFALO	54 lbs. 4 oz.	Farm Pond	May 24 1971	Randy Lee
BULLHEAD	4 lbs. 3½ oz.	Farm Pond	June 18 1961	Frank Miller
CARP	35 lbs. 4 oz.	Sand Pit	May 2 1970	W. Amos Henry
CATFISH, Channel	32 lbs.	Gardner City Lake	Aug. 14 1962	Edward Dailey
CATFISH, Flathead	86 lbs. 3 oz.	Neosho River	Aug. 24 1966	Ray Wiechert
CRAPPIE, Black	4 lbs. 10 oz.	Woodson Cty. State Lake	Oct. 21 1957	Hazel Fey
CRAPPIE, White	4 lbs. ¼ oz.	Farm Pond	Mar. 30 1964	Frank Miller
GAR	28 lbs.	Neosho River	June 17 1966	Mike Carter
PADDLEFISH	26 lbs.	Kaw River	Sept. 19 1962	John Huston
PIKE, Northern	24 lbs. 12 oz.	Council Grove Reservoir	Aug. 28 1971	Mr. and Mrs. H.A. Bowman
SHEEPSHEAD	27 lbs.	Howard City Lake	June 27 1953	Louis Hebb
STURGEON	4 lbs.	Kaw River	Nov. 17 1962	J. W. Keeton
SUNFISH, Green	2 lbs. 2 oz.	Strip Pit	May 28 1961	Louis Ferlo
WALLEYE	12 lbs. 3½ oz.	Kanopolis Reservoir	Mar. 8 1971	Glen Sherwood

KENTUCKY

Species	Wt.	Where	When	Angler
BASS, Kentucky	7 lbs. 10 oz.	Nelson Co.	June 1970	A. E. Sellers
BASS, Largemouth	13 lbs. 8 oz.	Greenbo Lake	Aug. 3 1966	Delbert Grizzle
BASS, Rock	1 lb.	Elkhorn Creek	Oct. 3 1971	Richard Haas
BASS, Smallmouth (World Record)	11 lbs. 15 oz.	Dale Hollow Lake	July 11 1955	David Hayes
BASS, Striped	44 lbs. 4 oz.	Herrington Lake	July 19 1970	James Fugate
BASS, White (Tie)	5 lbs.	Kentucky Lake	July 11 1943	Lorne Eli
	5 lbs.	Herrington Lake	June 3 1957	B. B. Hardin
BLUEGILL	3 lbs. 6 oz.	Buchanan Pond	May 30 1971	Wm. S. Wooley
BUFFALO	32 lbs.	Kentucky River	July 1969	P. Childers
BOWFIN	3 lbs. 4 oz.	Kentucky River	June 15 1971	Gladys Horton
CARP	54 lbs. 14 oz.	South Fork, Licking River	Mar. 13 1971	Ricky Vance
CATFISH, Blue	100 lbs.	Tennessee River	Aug. 21 1970	J. E. Copeland
CATFISH, Channel	9 lbs.	Lake Ellerslie	July 23 1969	Miller Welch, Jr.
CATFISH, Flathead	97 lbs.	Green River	June 6 1956	
CRAPPIE	4 lbs.	Harrods Creek	June 19 1951	Darrell Whitner
GAR	40 lbs.	Ohio River	Aug. 8 1956	Kelsie Travis, Jr.
MUSKELLUNGE	39 lbs. 14 oz.	Green River	Jan. 1969	Willard Parnell
SAUGER	4 lbs. 1 oz.	Tennessee River	Sept. 9 1968	Jim Boone
SHEEPSHEAD	31 lbs.	Kentucky Lake	June 2 1956	Jack Row
SPOONBILL	72 lbs.	Lake Cumberland	Mar. 6 1957	Ralph Pierce
STURGEON	36 lbs. 8 oz.	Lake Cumberland	Oct. 3 1954	Barney Frazier
SUNFISH, Redear	2 lbs. 5 oz.		May 30 1964	R. C. Masters
TROUT, Rainbow	13 lbs. 12 oz.	Cumberland River	Mar. 13 1971	Danny Antle
WALLEYE	21 lbs. 8 oz.	Lake Cumberland	Oct. 1 1958	Abe Black

LOUISIANA

Freshwater Species	Wt.	Where	When	Angler
BASS, Largemouth	11 lbs. 11 oz.		Nov. 1958	Elwin Husser
BASS, Spotted (Kentucky)	4 lbs. 3 oz.			Carroll Perkins
BREAM	2 lbs. 8 oz.		1959	Grant Kelly
CATFISH	62 lbs.		Mar. 1970	James Hibben
CRAPPIE	6 lbs.		Nov. 1969	Lettie Robertson
WARMOUTH	1 lb. 6 oz.		June 1971	Glenn Battle

Saltwater Species	Wt.	Where	When	Angler
AMBERJACK	86 lbs. 4 oz.		July 1969	Frank Ecker
BARRACUDA	50 lbs.		Aug. 1970	A. C. Mills
BLUEFISH	16 lbs. 4 oz.		Mar. 1971	Joseph Steverson

Saltwater Species	Wt.	Where	When	Angler
BONITO	24 lbs. 12 oz.		June 1970	Joseph Gex
COBIA	149 lbs. 12 oz.		May 1965	Garnett Caudell
CROAKER, Atlantic	5 lbs. 5 oz.		Aug. 1970	Eugene Lefort, Jr.
DOLPHIN	59 lbs. 12 oz.		June 1969	Stuart Wilson
FLOUNDER	12 lbs. 2 oz.		Feb. 1969	Clarence Craig
JACK CREVALLE	40 lbs.		July 1953	Edwin F. Stacy, Jr.
MACKEREL, King	67 lbs. 12 oz.		Dec. 1971	Monte Thrailkill
MACKEREL, Spanish	9 lbs. 1 oz.		Aug. 1971	James Antill
MARLIN, Blue	686 lbs.		Aug. 1969	Alvin E. DuVernay Jr.
MARLIN, White	134 lbs.		July 1967	Dennis Good
POMPANO	8 lbs. 8 oz.		Dec. 1969	Buddy Pons
REDFISH	56 lbs. 8 oz.		Sept. 1963	O. L. Comish
SAILFISH	96 lbs.		Oct. 1953	John Lauricella
SHARK, Mako	280 lbs.		Aug. 1967	Leander H. Perez Jr.
SHEEPSHEAD	14 lbs. 12 oz.		May 1970	John Bourg
SNAPPER	74 lbs.		Oct. 1963	Jim Meriweather
SPADEFISH	9 lbs. 4 oz.		Dec. 1969	Benny Avera
TARPON	198 lbs. 8 oz.		Sept. 1951	Oswald Frey
TRIPLETAIL	39 lbs. 8 oz.		July 1959	Mrs. Jimmy Toups
TROUT, Speckled	12 lbs. 6 oz.		May 1950	Leon Mattes
TUNA, Blackfin	24 lbs. 12 oz.		Nov. 1971	Mrs. Adelea Robichaux
TUNA, Bluefin	859 lbs.		June 1971	Jack Brown
TUNA, Yellowfin	201 lbs. 8 oz.		June 1971	Alvin DuVernay
WAHOO	110 lbs.		1964	Mrs. Homer J. Moore Jr.

MAINE

Species	Wt.	Where	When	Angler
BASS, Largemouth	11 lbs. 10 oz.	Moose Pond	1968	Robert Kamp
BASS, Smallmouth	8 lbs.	Thompson Lake	1970	George Dyer
PERCH, White	4 lbs. 10 oz.	Messalonskee Lake	1949	Mrs. E. Small
PICKEREL, Chain	6 lbs. 8 oz.	Sebago Lake	1969	Eugene Laughlin
SALMON, Atlantic	26 lbs. 2 oz.	Narraguagus River	1959	Harry Smith
SALMON, Landlocked	22 lbs. 8 oz.	Sebago Lake	1907	Edward Blakeley

Species	Wt.	Where	When	Angler
TROUT, Brook	8 lbs. 5 oz.	Pierce Pond	1958	Dixon Griffin
TROUT, Brown	19 lbs. 7 oz.	Sebago Lake	1958	Norman Stacy
TROUT, Lake	31 lbs. 8 oz.	Beech Hill Pond	1958	Hollis Grindle
WHITEFISH	7 lbs. 8 oz.	Sebago Lake	1958	Neil Sullivan

MARYLAND

Freshwater Species	Wt.	Where	When	Angler
BASS, Largemouth	10 lbs. 1 oz.	Loch Raven Reservoir	May 1966	Jerry Sauter
BASS, Smallmouth	8 lbs.	Loch Raven Reservoir	May 1968	Gene Carter
BLUEGILL	1 lb. 14 oz.	Wicomico River	Feb. 1970	Pete Tippett
CARP	44 lbs.	Patuxent River	May 1970	Jean Ward
CATFISH	24 lbs.	Potomac River	Oct. 1964	James Turner
CRAPPIE	3 lbs. 4 oz.	Rocky Gorge	Apr. 1968	Tyrone Fennell
GAR	16 lbs. 8 oz.	Pocomoke River	Aug. 1970	Thad Feetham
MUSKELLUNGE	31 lbs. 8 oz.	Susquehanna River	June 1966	Don Wise
PERCH, Yellow	2 lbs. 5 oz.	Allens Fresh	Mar. 1971	Anthony Aloi
PICKEREL, Chain	7 lbs. 9 oz.	Choptank River	Feb. 1970	Frank Shoemaker
PIKE, Northern	19 lbs. 4 oz.	Loch Raven Reservoir	Apr. 1970	Roger Bowen
TROUT, Brown	13 lbs. 8 oz.	Deep Creek Lake	Aug. 1968	Simon Cogley
TROUT, Rainbow	8 lbs. 2 oz.	Beaver Creek	Apr. 1971	Jack Willy
WALLEYE	8 lbs. 12 oz.	Deep Creek Lake	June 1970	Fred McGee

Saltwater Species	Wt.	Where	When	Angler
ALBACORE	18 lbs. 8 oz.	Ocean City	July 1971	Richard Roberts, Jr.
BASS, Channel	65 lbs.	Tangier Sound	May 1970	Lake Scott
BASS, Sea	7 lbs.	Ocean City	Nov. 1970	Ralph Walsh
BASS, Striped	50 lbs. 1 oz.	Dumping Grounds	July 22 1965	Carol Rothwell
BLUEFISH	20 lbs. 1 oz.	Ocean City	Oct. 1970	Joe Clarkson, Jr.
COBIA	99 lbs.	Chesapeake Bay	July 1948	R. B. Frost, Jr.
CROAKER	5 lbs. 11 oz.	Sharps Island	Aug. 1962	Jim Shupe
DOLPHIN	40 lbs.	Ocean City	Sept. 1965	Joseph Rogers
DRUM, Black	92 lbs.	Choptank River	Aug. 1955	James Aaron
FLOUNDER	16 lbs.	Sinepuxent Bay	July 1970	Jacob Fry

Saltwater Species	Wt.	Where	When	Angler
MACKEREL, King	21 lbs.	Ocean City	July 1970	Walter Pike
MARLIN, Blue	554 lbs.	Ocean City	July 1969	Francis Day
MARLIN, White	130 lbs. 8 oz.	Ocean City	Aug. 1956	H. Howard
PERCH, White	1 lb. 12 oz.	Susquehanna River	Apr. 1970	Philip Rizzo, Sr.
PORGY	6 lbs. 3 oz.	Ocean City	July 1966	Pearl Hopple
SHAD, Hickory	4 lbs. 4 oz.	Susquehanna River	May 1968	Pietro Matastasio
SHAD, White	8 lbs. 1 oz.	Wicomico River	Apr. 1971	Jim Revelle
SHARK	284 lbs. 8 oz.	Ocean City	Sept. 1970	Margaret Coleman
SPOT	1 lb. 4 oz.	Chesapeake Bay	June 1969	David Miles
TAUTOG	15 lbs. 8 oz.	Ocean City	May 1970	Robert Miller
TUNA	253 lbs.	Ocean City	Aug. 1970	Francis Day
WAHOO	90 lbs.	Ocean City'	Sept. 1970	Harper Smith
WEAKFISH	9 lbs.	Sharps Island	Sept. 1971	Gayle Mitchell
WHITING	2 lbs. 12 oz.	Ocean City	Oct. 1970	Gary Beckner

MASSACHUSETTS

Species	Wt.	Where	When	Angler
BASS, Largemouth	12 lbs. 1 oz.	Palmer River	May 9 1963	George Pastick
BASS, Smallmouth	6 lbs. 12 oz.	Pleasant Lake	May 14 1967	Thomas Paradise
BLUEGILL	1 lb.	Bog Pond	Oct. 17 1965	Robert Barrett
BULLHEAD	5 lbs. 9 oz.	Conn. River	June 8 1963	Mrs. Erna Storie
CATFISH, Channel	13 lbs. 14 oz.	Metacomet Pond	Sept. 15 1971	Wayne Briggs
PERCH, White	2 lbs. 4 oz.	Halfway Pond	June 9 1965	Richard Rock
PERCH, Yellow	2 lbs. 5 oz.	Wachusett Reservoir	Apr. 23 1970	Arnold Korenblum
PICKEREL	9 lbs. 5 oz.	Pontoosuc Lake	1954	Mrs. James Martin
PIKE, Northern	24 lbs. 8 oz.	Onota Lake	Jan. 13 1967	Kris Ginthwain
SALMON	9 lbs. 5 oz.	Quabbin Reservoir	1971	John Courtney
SHAD	8 lbs. 8 oz.	North River	May 6 1971	Richard Brown, Jr.
TROUT, Brook	6 lbs. 4 oz.	Otis Reservoir	June 24 1968	Thomas Laptew
TROUT, Brown	19 lbs. 10 oz.	Wachusett Reservoir	Sept. 13 1963	LeeRoy DeHoff
TROUT, Lake	13 lbs. 6 oz.	Quabbin Reservoir	Apr. 17 1971	Ronald Jatriuski
TROUT, Rainbow	8lbs. 4 oz.	Deep Pond	Oct. 15 1966	Roger Walker
WALLEYE	13 lbs. 8 oz.	Connecticut River	May 1971	John Lyons

MICHIGAN

Species	Wt.	Where	When	Angler
BASS, Largemouth	11 lbs. 15 oz.	Big Pine Island Lake	June 25 1934	William Maloney
BASS, Rock	3 lbs. 10 oz.	Lenawee Cty. Lake	June 26 1965	Edward Arnold
BASS, Smallmouth	9 lbs. 4 oz.	Long Lake	1906	W. F. Shoemaker
BLUEGILL	2 lbs. 10 oz.	Silver Lake	Aug. 5 1945	F. M. Broock
CATFISH, Channel	47 lbs. 8 oz.	Maple River	Aug. 6 1937	Elmer Rayner
CRAPPIE, Black	4 lbs. 2 oz.	Lincoln Lake	June 1947	E. Frank Lee
MUSKELLUNGE	62 lbs. 8 oz.	Lake St. Clair	June 23 1940	Percy Haver
PERCH, Yellow	3 lbs. 12 oz.	Lake Independence	1947	Eugene Jezinski
PIKE, Northern	33 lbs. 8 oz.	Bond Falls Basin	1969	Ed Bresmahan
SALMON, Chinook	42 lbs.	Manistee Lake	1970	Frank Evans, Jr.
SALMON, Coho	30 lbs. 8 oz.	E. Arm G. T. Bay	1971	George Adema
SHEEPSHEAD	17 lbs. 4 oz.	Muskegon Lake	June 26 1954	Mike Thomas
TROUT, Brook	6 lbs. 1 oz.	Whitefish Bay	1934	George Shipman
TROUT, Brown	21 lbs. 8 oz.	Crystal Lake	June 14 1969	Arthur Huls
TROUT, Lake	53 lbs.	Lake Superior	1944	K. Boyer, E. C. Watson
TROUT, Rainbow	22 lbs. 6 oz.	Lake Michigan, Manistee	1971	Harvey Huttas
TROUT, Splake	7 lbs. 8 oz.	Big Blue Lake	1968	Raymond Dukarski
WALLEYE	17 lbs. 3 oz.	Pine River	Nov. 8 1951	Ray Fedely

MINNESOTA

Species	Wt.	Where	When	Angler
BASS, Largemouth	10 lbs. 2 oz.	Prairie Lake	1961	Harold Lehn
BASS, Smallmouth	8 lbs.	West Battle Lake	1948	John Creighton
BLUEGILL	2 lbs. 13 oz.	Lake Alice	1948	Bob Parker
CARP	86 lbs.	Minnesota River	1906	C. A. Cameron
CATFISH, Channel	37 lbs.	White Bear Lake	1962	Larry Peterson
CATFISH, Mud	157 lbs.	Minnesota River	1930	
CRAPPIE	5 lbs.	Vermillion River	1940	Tom Christenson
DOGFISH	10 lbs.	Lake Minnetonka	1941	Roger Lehman
MUSKELLUNGE	56 lbs. 8 oz.	Lake-of-the Woods	July 24 1931	J. W. Collins
PERCH, Yellow	3 lbs. 4 oz.	Lake Plantaganette	1945	Merle Johnson
PIKE, Northern	45 lbs. 12 oz.	Basswood Lake	May 16 1929	J. V. Schanken
SALMON, Chinook	8 lbs. 5 oz.	Lake Superior	Sept. 1 1970	
SALMON, Coho	10 lbs. 6½ oz.	Lake Superior	Nov. 7 1970	Louis Rhode
SALMON, Kokanee	2 lbs. 15 oz.	Caribou Lake	Aug. 6 1971	Lars Kindem
SAUGER	6 lbs. 2½ oz.	Mississippi River	1964	Mrs. Marilyn Larson

Species	Wt.	Where	When	Angler
SHEEPSHEAD	30 lbs.	Mississippi River	1960	Dick Campbell
SPLAKE	9 lbs. 6 oz.	Beaver Lake	May 23 1971	Gerald Quade
STURGEON, Lake	236 lbs.	Lake-of-the Woods	1911	
SUCKER, White	8 lbs. 9 oz.	Mississippi River	Apr. 24 1971	Leonard Krueger
TROUT, Brook	9 lbs.	Ash River	1958	Frank Hause
TROUT, Brown	16 lbs. 8 oz.	Grindstone Lake	1961	Mr. Lovgren
TROUT, Lake	43 lbs. 8 oz.	Lake Superior	May 30 1955	G. H. Nelson
TROUT, Rainbow	15 lbs. 7 oz.	Lake Superior	Sept. 11 1970	Cliff Lovold
WALLEYE	16 lbs. 11 oz.	Basswood Lake	1955	

MISSISSIPPI

Species	Wt.	Where	When	Angler
BASS, Largemouth	13 lbs. 2 oz.	Theo Costas Lake	May 2 1963	Noel L. Mills
BASS, Striped	11 lbs. ¾ oz.	Ross Barnett Reservoir	Nov. 15 1971	J. T. Matthews
BASS, White	5 lbs. 2 oz.	Grenada Spillway	July 9 1969	Eddy Vaughn
BLUEGILL	2 lbs. 5 oz.	Mississippi River	May 20 1963	Leonard Busby
BOWFIN	16 lbs. 4 oz.	Ross Barnett Reservoir	Nov. 25 1967	Don R. Bush
CARP	74 lbs.	Pelahatchie Lake	June 13 1963	Curtis Wade
CRAPPIE, White	5 lbs. 3 oz.	Enid Reservoir	July 31 1957	Fred Bright
PADDLEFISH	23 lbs. 12 oz.	Ross Barnett Reservoir	Dec. 19 1968	Bob G. Ponds
PICKEREL, Chain	4 lbs. 4 oz.	Ross Barnett Reservoir	Apr. 25 1966	Mrs. Robert W. King
SUNFISH, Redear	2 lbs. 2 oz.	Lake Tiak O'Khata	July 2 1963	Ben Smythe

MISSOURI

Species	Wt.	Where	When	Angler
BASS, Kentucky	7 lbs. 8 oz.	Table Rock	Apr. 6 1966	Gene Arnaud
BASS, Largemouth	13 lbs. 14 oz.	Bull Shoals Lake	Apr. 1961	Marvin Bushong
BASS, Rock	2 lbs. 12 oz.	Big Piney River	June 15 1968	William Rod
BASS, Smallmouth	6 lbs. 7 oz.	Valley Dolomite Pond	1952	Burt Koester
BASS, Striped	5 lbs. 12 oz.	Lake Norfork	Apr. 1 1970	T. J. Robbins, Jr.
BASS, White (Tie)	4 lbs. 8 oz.	Lake Norfork	1952	Robert Ketchum
	4 lbs. 8 oz.	Bull Shoals Lake	Oct. 27 1962	Mrs. A. G. Morris
	4 lbs. 8 oz.	Bull Shoals Lake		Herbert Biest
BLUEGILL	3 lbs.	Pond at Bevier		Mike Giovanni
BOWFIN	19 lbs.	Duck Creek	Mar. 1963	Clois Coomer
BUFFALO	35 lbs.	Osage Osceola	May 1964	Bill Bradley
BULLHEAD, Black	2 lbs. 14½ oz.	Pond Jefferson City	July 29 1971	Leon Backes

Species	Wt.	Where	When	Angler
CARP	41 lbs.	Lake Taneycomo	Dec. 26 1969	Henry Hurla
CATFISH, Blue	56 lbs.	Osage River	June 5 1961	Melvin Smith
CATFISH, Channel	29 lbs. 12 oz.	Lake Jacomo	May 5 1969	Ricky Rodenbaugh
CRAPPIE, Black	4 lbs. 8 oz.	Fish Pond	May 28 1967	Ray Babcock
CRAPPIE, White	3 lbs. 12 oz.	Sugar Creek Lake	May 1964	Dee Embree
MUSKELLUNGE	14 lbs.	Pomme de Terre	May 15 1969	Dale Bland
PIKE, Northern	13 lbs. 10 oz.	Thomas Hill Reservoir	Feb. 29 1972	Morris Palmer
SHEEPSHEAD	34 lbs.	Warsaw	Apr. 19 1959	Gene Davis
SUNFISH, Green	2 lbs.	Stockton Lake	June 20 1971	Paul Dilley
SUNFISH, Longear	1 lb. 5 oz.	Kenney Pond	June 30 1966	Tom Nelson
SUNFISH, Redear	1 lb.	Pony Express	Sept. 23 1971	Paul Rogers
TROUT, Brown	14 lbs. 1 oz.	Current River	Aug. 15 1970	Michael Whiteker
TROUT, Rainbow	13 lbs. 14¾ oz.	Lake Tanevcomo	Jan. 26 1970	Charles Gott
WALLEYE	20 lbs.	St. Frances River	1961	John Vacholek

MONTANA

Species	Wt.	Where	When	Angler
BLUEGILL	2 lbs. 8 oz.	Dengel Reservoir	1967	George Schlosser
BURBOT	11 lbs. 12 oz.	Fort Peck Reservoir	1967	Jim Cooper
CATFISH, Channel	21 lbs. 5 oz.	Missouri River	1964	Gary Eppers
PADDLEFISH	131 lbs.	Missouri River	1968	Paul Frazee
PERCH, Yellow	1 lb. 4 oz.	Nelson Reservoir	1970	Kevin Bright
PIKE, Northern	27 lbs. 8 oz.	Fresno Reservoir	1969	Ivan Dibblee
SALMON, Coho	3 lbs. 12 oz.	Fort Peck Reservoir	1971	Unknown
SALMON, Kokanee	5 lbs. 4 oz.	Helena Valley Reservoir	1969	Unknown
SAUGER	4 lbs.	Fort Peck Reservoir	1971	Kevin Long
TROUT, Brook	9 lbs. 1 oz.	Lower Two Medicine Lake	1940	John Cook
TROUT, Brown	29 lbs.	Wade Lake	1966	E. H. Bacon
TROUT, Cutthroat	16 lbs.	Red Eagle Lake	1955	Wm. Sands
TROUT, Rainbow	20 lbs.	Cliff Lake	1952	C. J. Brohaugh
WALLEYE	12 lbs. 13 oz.	Nelson Reservoir	1969	James Crants

NEBRASKA

Species	Wt.	Where	When	Angler
BASS, Kentucky Spotted	3 lbs. 11 oz.	Sand Pit	Mar. 24 1968	Tom Pappas
BASS, Largemouth	10 lbs. 11 oz.	Sand Pit	Oct. 2 1965	Paul Abegglen, Sr.

Species	Wt.	Where	When	Angler
BASS, Rock	2 lbs.	Frenchman River	May 28 1966	Violet Kelly
BASS, Smallmouth	5 lbs. 2½ oz.	Red Willow Reservoir	Oct. 24 1971	Leo Weigel
BASS, Striped	10 lbs. 1 oz.	Lake McConaughy	Sept. 29 1970	Dixie Akers
BASS, White	4 lbs. 15 oz.	Sand Pit	1962	Frederick Baldwin
BLUEGILL	2 lbs. 8 oz.	Farm Pond	Aug. 27 1968	Charles Randolph
BUFFALO	33 lbs. 8 oz.	Seirs Lake	Sept. 4 1966	Mrs. Lyle Clemens
BULLHEAD	3 lbs. 8 oz.	Smith Lake	July 28 1963	Alfred Porter
CARP	28 lbs. 2 oz.	Hall County Lake	May 18 1967	Harry Lassen
CATFISH, Blue	100 lbs. 8 oz.	Missouri River	Nov. 29 1970	Raymond Promes
CATFISH, Channel	31 lbs. 12 oz.	Ericson	1944	Bob Nuquist
CATFISH, Flathead	76 lbs.	Missouri River	Mar. 10 1971	Orville Sudbeck
CRAPPIE	3 lbs. 15 oz.	Lake McConaughy	Apr. 29 1962	Delmer Butler
MUSKELLUNGE	18 lbs. 4 oz.	Merritt Reservoir	Apr. 20 1969	Kenneth Cook
PADDLEFISH	87 lbs.	DeSoto Bend Lake	Apr. 25 1971	Patrick Fox
PERCH, Sacramento	2 lbs. 8 oz.	Clear Lake	June 20 1971	John Bush
PERCH, Yellow	2 lbs.	Conway Lake	Jan. 16 1966	Joe Adams
PIKE, Northern	27 lbs. 8 oz.	Lake McConaughy	July 14 1962	Cletus Jacobsen
SALMON, Coho	5 lbs. 12 oz.	Lake McConaughy	July 3 1971	Lyle Fry
SALMON, Kokanee	4 lbs. 2 oz.	Lake McConaughy	July 11 1971	Neal Dunbar
SAUGER	8 lbs. 5 oz.	Missouri River	Oct. 22 1961	Mrs. Betty Tepner
SHEEPSHEAD	28 lbs. 4 oz.	Missouri River	Oct. 1 1971	Vincent Prazak
STURGEON	33 lbs.	Missouri River	May 22 1970	Melvin Bourn
SUCKER	4 lbs.	Lake Minatare	Apr. 29 1968	Jack Keller
SUNFISH, Green	1 lb. 1¼ oz.	Farm Pond	May 23 1968	William Fattig
SUNFISH, Redear	1 lb. 6 oz.	Conestoga Lake	May 4 1970	Gary Reagan
TROUT, Brook	5 lbs. 1 oz.	Pawnee Springs	Nov. 3 1965	Joe Gray
TROUT, Brown	12 lbs. 3 oz.	Snake River	July 4 1971	Richard Miller
TROUT, Rainbow	12 lbs. 8 oz.	Lake McConaughy	Aug. 4 1968	Wayne Rath
WALLEYE	16 lbs. 2 oz.	Lake McConaughy	July 5 1971	Herbert Cutshall

NEVADA

Species	Wt.	Where	When	Angler
BASS, Largemouth	10 lbs. 1 oz.	Lake Mohave	1970	Mrs. Ada Bradford
BASS, Striped	24 lbs.	Colorado River	1969	Rebel Brothers
BASS, White	3 lbs. 1 oz.	Lahontan Reservoir	1969	Al Cartwright
CRAPPIE, Black	2 lbs. 8 oz.	Lake Mead	1970	Dennis Garmann
CRAPPIE, White	2 lbs. 8 oz.	Lahontan Reservoir	1968	Charles Grant

Species	Wt.	Where	When	Angler
PERCH, Sacramento	4 lbs.	Pyramid Lake	1970	David Nojima
PIKE, Northern	10 lbs.	Bassett Lake	1970	Tilton Zumwalt
CARP	18 lbs.	Virginia Lake	1970	Kristi Adkisson
CATFISH, Channel	23 lbs. 8 oz.	Lake Mohave	1970	L. D. Moddy
CATFISH, White	11 lbs.	Lahontan Reservoir	1969	Stan Havens
SALMON, Kokanee	3 lbs. 6 oz.	Lake Tahoe	1970	George Watt
TROUT, Brook	5 lbs.	Lake Tahoe	1969	Fran Oppio
TROUT, Brown	12 lbs.	Topaz Lake	1968	Greg Melton
TROUT, Cut-Bow	9 lbs. 1 oz.	Pyramid Lake	1970	Don Pride
TROUT, Cutthroat	17 lbs. 14 oz.	Pyramid Lake	1970	Leo Longobardo
TROUT, Mackinaw	35 lbs. 8 oz.	Lake Tahoe	1970	Sam Sigwart
TROUT, Rainbow	13 lbs. 4 oz.	Lake Mohave	1968	Bruce Ingram

NEW HAMPSHIRE

Species	Wt.	Where	When	Angler
BASS, Largemouth	10 lbs. 5 oz.	Lake Potanipo	May 1967	G. Bullpit
BASS, Smallmouth	7 lbs. 14½ oz.	Goose Pond	Aug. 1970	F. H. Loud
PERCH, White	3 lbs.	Winnipesaukee Lake	May 1965	A. Santos
PERCH, Yellow	2 lbs. 6 oz.	Heads Pond	Mar. 1969	R. Hebert
PICKEREL, Chain	8 lbs.	Plummer Pond	Apr. 26 1966	C. R. Akerly
PIKE, Northern	16 lbs. 1 oz.	Spofford Lake	May 1967	D. Graves
SALMON, Landlocked	18 lbs. 8 oz.	Pleasant Lake	Aug. 31 1942	Mrs. E. D. Clark
SPLAKE	8 lbs. 8 oz.	White Lake	May 9 1963	R. Walker
TROUT, Brook	9 lbs.	Pleasant Lake	1911	A. V. Woodruff
TROUT, Brown	15 lbs 6 oz.	Connecticut River	May 30 1953	Calvin Hall
TROUT, Lake	28 lbs. 8 oz.	Newfound Lake	Apr. 24 1958	Albert Staples
TROUT, Rainbow	13 lbs.	Dublin Lake	1953	
TROUT, Sunapee	11 lbs. 8 oz.	Sunapee Lake	Aug. 1 1954	E. Theoharris
WALLEYE	9 lbs.	Merrimack River	Apr. 12 1971	Mrs. L. Herbert

NEW JERSEY

Freshwater Species	Wt.	Where	When	Angler
BASS, Largemouth	10 lbs. 12 oz.	Mt. Kimble Lake	1960	Logan Whitesell
BASS, Rock	1 lb. 2¼ oz.	Lake Hopatcong	1968	Harold Webb
BASS, Smallmouth	6 lbs. 4 oz.	Delaware River	1957	Earl Trumpore
BASS, Striped Landlocked	23 lbs. 8 oz.	Union Lake	1952	Mrs. Albert Beebe

Freshwater Species	Wt.	Where	When	Angler
BLUEGILL	2 lbs.	Farm Pond	1956	Silas Matthews, Jr.
BULLHEAD, Brown	22 lbs. 15 oz.	Spring Lake	1966	Robert Dorf
CATFISH, Channel	28 lbs.	Greenwood Lake	1918	William Otten
CRAPPIE	3 lbs. 5½ oz.	Alloway Lake	1961	William Hanna
MUSKELLUNGE	19 lbs.	Delaware River	1970	John Fleming
PERCH, White	2 lbs. 8 oz.	Lake Hopatcong	1950	Robert Huber
PERCH, Yellow	4 lbs. 3½ oz.	Bordentown	1865	Dr. C. C. Abbot
PICKEREL, Chain	9 lbs. 3 oz.	Lower Aetna Lake	1957	Frank McGovern
PIKE, Northern	21 lbs.	Lake Wawayanda	1971	Edward Kistner
SALMON, Landlocked	8 lbs.	New Wawayanda Lake	1951	John Mount
TROUT, Brook	6 lbs. 8 oz.	Lake Hopatcong	1956	George Hornung
TROUT, Brown	16 lbs. 11 oz.	Greenwood Lake	1964	Howard Devore
TROUT, Rainbow	8 lbs. 5½ oz.	Round Valley Reservoir	1970	Richard Ruis, Sr.
WALLEYE	12 lbs. 12¾ oz.	Delaware River	1934	Stanley Norman

Saltwater Species	Wt.	Where	When	Angler
ALBACORE	69 lbs. 1 oz.	Hudson Canyon	1961	Walter C. Timm
BASS, Channel	46 lbs.	Sandy Hook	1953	Dr. R. D. Alexander
BASS, Sea	6 lbs. 2 oz.		1958	Nick Ferrante
BASS, Striped	68 lbs.	Sandy Hook	1970	Donald Zboyan
BLACKFISH	21 lbs. 6 oz.	Cape May	1954	R. N. Sheafer
BLUEFISH	22 lbs. 11 oz.	17 Fathom	1968	Sigmund Gruszkowski
BONITO	13 lbs. 8 oz.	Sandy Hook	1945	Frank Lykes, Jr.
COD	81 lbs.	Brielle	1967	Joseph Chesla
DOLPHIN	48 lbs. 15 oz.	Cape May	1969	Yvonne DiSanto
DRUM, Black	92 lbs.	Delaware Bay	1944	Herschel Layton
FLOUNDER, Winter	3 lbs. 2 oz.	Great Egg Harbor River	1968	Frank Coleman
FLUKE	19 lbs. 12 oz.	Cape May	1953	Walter Lubin
MARLIN, Blue	620 lbs.	Atlantic City	1964	Joseph Teti, Jr.
MARLIN, White	123 lbs.	Ambrose Light	1968	Merrill Arden
POLLACK	43 lbs.	Brielle	1964	Philip Barlow
SHARK, Mako	322 lbs	Elberon	1952	W. J. Mahan
SWORDFISH, Broadbill	530 lbs.	Wilmington Canyon	1964	Edmund Levitt
TUNA	787 lbs.	Brielle	1950	Ray Fromm
WAHOO	93 lbs. 10 oz.	Cape May	1969	Dr. Wm. E. DiSanto
WEAKFISH	17 lbs. 8 oz.	Mullica River	1952	Weisbecker, A., Jr.

NEW MEXICO

Species	Wt.	Where	When	Angler
BASS	9 lbs. 8 oz.	Stubblefield Lake	May 8 1971	Bill Ford
BASS, Smallmouth	3 lbs. 4 oz.	Gila River	Oct. 9 1970	Bob Vaughn
BASS, White	3¼ lbs.	Elephant Butte Lake	June 20 1971	Frank Fisher
BLUEGILL	1 lb. 1 oz.	Reserve New Mexico	May 31 1971	Ida Mathews
CATFISH, Channel	17 lbs. 12 oz.	Ute Lake	June 30 1971	Hugh Jones
CATFISH, Flathead	62 lbs.	Elephant Butte Dam	Oct. 20 1970	Virgil Garrison
TROUT, Brook	4 lbs. 13 oz.	Willow Creek	June 3 1971	Derral Thomas
TROUT, Brown	20 lbs. 4 oz.	El Vado Ranch	July 31 1946	G. T. Calgrove
TROUT, Cutthroat	6 lbs. 12 oz.	Brazos Box	July 14 1929	Charles Draggett
TROUT, Rainbow	10 lbs.	Chama River	Nov. 4 1945	Charles DeWitt
WALLEYE	8 lbs. 10 oz.	Alamogordo Dam	June 11 1971	Earl O'Neal

NEW YORK

Species	Wt.	Where	When	Angler
BASS, Largemouth (Tie)	10 lbs. 6 oz.	Rensselaer County Pond	1931	J. L. Reed
	10 lbs. 6 oz.	Sacandaga Reservoir	1942	Peter Dubuc
BASS, Smallmouth	9 lbs.	Friends Lake Outlet	1925	George Tennyson
MUSKELLUNGE	69 lbs. 15 oz.	St. Lawrence River	1957	Arthur Lawton
PIKE, Northern	46 lbs. 2 oz.	Sacandaga Reservoir	1940	Peter Dubuc
SALMON	16 lbs. 14 oz.	Lake George	1958	Neil Hughes
TROUT, Brook	8 lbs. 8 oz.	Punchbowl Pond	1908	William Keener
TROUT, Brown	21 lbs. 5 oz.	Owasco Lake	1954	Thomas Klink
TROUT, Lake	31 lbs.	Follensby Pond	1922	Malcolm Hain
TROUT, Rainbow	21 lbs.	Keuka Lake	1946	Earl G. Crane
WALLEYE	15 lbs. 3 oz.	Chemung River	1952	Blanche Baker

NORTH CAROLINA

Freshwater Species	Wt.	Where	When	Angler
BASS, Largemouth	14 lbs. 15 oz.	Santeetlah Reservoir	Apr. 26 1963	Leonard Williams
BASS, Smallmouth	10 lbs. 2 oz.	Hiwassee Reservoir	June 1953	Archie Lampkin
BASS, Striped Landlocked	39 lbs. 4 oz.	Lake Hickory	May 10 1969	Bill Dula
BASS, White	4 lbs. 15 oz.	Fontana Reservoir	July 27 1966	Leonard Williams
BLUEGILL	4 lbs. 5 oz.	Edneyville Pond	July 27 1967	Danny Case
CATFISH, Channel	40 lbs. 8 oz.	Fontana Reservoir	Apr. 15 1971	P. P. Paine
CRAPPIE	4 lbs. 8 oz.	Tillery Lake	1960	Henry Griffin

Freshwater Species	Wt.	Where	When	Angler
PICKEREL, Chain	8 lbs.	Gaston Reservoir	Feb. 13 1968	John Leonard
SAUGER	5 lbs. 15 oz.	Lake Norman	July 25 1971	David Shook
SHAD, American	5 lbs. 4 oz.	Cape Fear River	Apr. 6 1968	Randall Neal
SHELLCRACKER	4 lbs. 4 oz.	Lee County Pond	Feb. 3 1968	Bill Arnold
TROUT, Brook	2 lbs. 12 oz.	Ravens Fork Creek	Sept. 25 1971	James Crews
TROUT, Rainbow	14 lbs. 1 oz.	Glenville Reservoir	Mar. 6 1949	Max Rogers
WALLEYE	13 lbs. 4 oz.	Santeetlah Reservoir	May 1966	Leonard Williams
WARMOUTH	1 lb. 8 oz.	Ellis Creek	Aug. 10 1971	William Butler

Saltwater Species	Wt.	Where	When	Angler
ALBACORE	57 lbs.	Off Oregon Inlet	Oct. 9 1971	Harry Lee Wray, Jr.
AMBERJACK	123 lbs.	Wrightsville Beach	Nov. 28 1964	Merrill Lockfaw
BARRACUDA	47 lbs.	Off Cape Lookout	Sept. 7 1969	David Meyers
BASS, Channel	82 lbs.	Avon N. C.	Nov. 9 1970	Jack Scott
BASS, Striped	57 lbs. 8 oz.	Surf, North of Rodanthe	Dec. 13 1970	Joseph Menzaco
BLUEFISH	24 lbs. 8 oz.	Nags Head	Nov. 19 1971	Mrs. Rita Mizelle
BONITO	22 lbs. 3 oz.	Wrightsville Beach	July 6 1968	J. W. Johnson, Jr.
COBIA	97 lbs.	Oregon Inlet	June 4 1952	Mrs. Mary Black
CROAKER	3 lbs. 12 oz.	Gloucester Straits	Oct. 11 1969	James Murphy
DOLPHIN	63 lbs.	Cape Hatteras	June 1934	Tom Eaton
DRUM, Black	83 lbs. 8 oz.	Surf, Topsail Island	Oct. 27 1959	George Sherrell
FLOUNDER	16 lbs.	Hatteras Inlet	Oct. 25 1969	Donald Geer
MACKEREL, King	57 lbs.	Cape Lookout	Oct. 10 1966	Russell Dement
MACKEREL, Spanish	10 lbs. 6 oz.	Topsail Island	Sept. 22 1970	Larry Lee
MARLIN, Blue	810 lbs.	Cape Hatteras	June 11 1962	Gary Stukes
MARLIN, White	108 lbs. 8 oz.	Oregon Inlet	Oct. 12 1968	Robert Luckwitz
POMPANO	6 lbs. 8 oz.	Wrightsville Beach	Oct. 19 1970	John Cain
SAILFISH, Atlantic	76 lbs.	Cape Hatteras	Aug. 6 1970	Judith Huff
SHEEPSHEAD	17 lbs. 8 oz.	Oregon Inlet	Sept. 18 1971	Larry Laws
TARPON	152 lbs.	Wrightsville Beach	June 1 1961	Bobby Kentrolis
TUNA, Atlantic Big-Eyed	211 lbs.	Oregon Inlet	Sept. 17 1970	Joe Dove
TUNA, Blackfin	29 lbs. 8 oz.	Oregon Inlet	May 21 1970	J. D. Thomas
TUNA, Bluefin	491 lbs.	Cape Hatteras	May 29 1963	Dick Derbyshire
TUNA, Yellowfin	203 lbs.	Oregon Inlet	July 30 1960	John Asburn
WAHOO	91 lbs. 8 oz.	Off Hatteras N. C.	Oct. 25 1970	Wm. Hurley

Saltwater Species	Wt.	Where	When	Angler
WEAKFISH	12 lbs. 4 oz.	Wrightsville Beach	Dec. 29 1961	John Kenyon, Jr.
WEAKFISH, Spotted	11 lbs. 6 oz.	Sneads Ferry	Sept. 19 1967	Elmer Rivenbark
WHITING (Tie)	3 lbs. 4 oz.	Kure Beach	Oct. 27 1931	Mrs. A. L. Freeman
	3 lbs. 4 oz.	Onslow Beach	Nov. 5 1970	Mrs. Sylvia Edwards

NORTH DAKOTA

Species	Wt.	Where	When	Angler
BASS, Largemouth	7 lbs. 12 oz.	Welk Dam	1951	George Marquardt
BASS, White	4 lbs. 4 oz.	Lake Sakakawea	1969	T. Porter
BLUEGILL	2 lbs. 12 oz.	Strawberry Lake	1963	Bud Hystad
CARP	21 lbs. 12 oz.	Red River	1958	Don J. Pasco
CATFISH, Channel	26 lbs. 8 oz.	Lake Sakakawea	1968	Clyde Coe
CRAPPIE	3 lbs.	James River	1958	John Kinney
PERCH, Yellow	2 lbs. 2 oz.	Lake Audubon	1966	Norman Hanson
PIKE, Northern	37 lbs. 8 oz.	Lake Sakakawea	1968	Melvin Slind
SAUGER	5 lbs. 12 oz.	Lake Sakakawea	1971	Mike Fischer
SHEEPSHEAD	8 lbs. 8 oz.	Sheyenne River	1964	Eliam Kuchera
TROUT, Brown	5 lbs. 15½ oz.	North Lemon Lake	1969	L. Shortridge
TROUT, Rainbow	9 lbs. 11 oz.	Garrison Tailrace	1960	Michael Stoick
WALLEYE	15 lbs. 12 oz.	Wood Lake	1959	Blair Chapman

OHIO

Species	Wt.	Where	When	Angler
BASS, Largemouth	9 lbs. 9 oz.	Lake Logan	May 1 1970	Terry Pierce
BASS, Rock	1 lb. 15½ oz.	Deer Creek	Sept. 3 1962	George Keller
BASS, Smallmouth	7 lbs. 8 oz.	Mad River	June 17 1941	James Bayless
BASS, Spotted	5 lbs. 4 oz.	Lake White	May 2 1967	Roger Trainer
BASS, White	3 lbs. 6 oz.	Lake Erie	Aug. 24 1954	Julia Morrison
BOWFIN	6 lbs. 9 oz.	Sandusky Bay	July 10 1970	Raymond Hobbs
BULLHEAD	3 lbs. 14¾ oz.	Glandorf Lake	May 9 1966	Roy Kuhlman
CARP	50 lbs.	Paint Creek	May 24 1967	Judson Holton
CATFISH, Channel	25 lbs.	Piedmont Lake	May 10 1964	Charles McGrath
CATFISH, Flathead	75 lbs. 8 oz.	Piedmont Lake	June 9 1970	Dale Yoho
CRAPPIE, Black	3½ lbs.	Scioto Lakes	Apr. 10 1968	M. W. Grover
CRAPPIE, White	3 lbs. 3 oz.	Muzzy Lake	July 27 1968	Christy Buckeye
GAR	25 lbs.	Ohio River	Aug. 31 1966	Flora Irvin
MUSKELLUNGE	44 lbs.	Piedmont Lake	June 2 1971	Richard Yares

Species	Wt.	Where	When	Angler
PADDLEFISH	16 lbs. 5 oz.	Brush Creek	June 4 1969	Buford Ricks
PERCH, Yellow	2 lbs. 8 oz.	Lake Erie	Nov. 14 1954	J. H. Olasky
PICKEREL, Chain	6 lbs. 4 oz.	Long Lake	Mar. 25 1961	Ronald Kotch
PIKE, Northern	14 lbs. 6 oz.	Lake Erie	Mar. 18 1961	Gary Beatty
SALMON, Coho	16 lbs. 4 oz.	Chagrin River	Oct. 17 1970	Phillip Focarelli
SHEEPSHEAD	20 lbs. 12 oz.	Muskingum River	Apr. 16 1969	Brennie Lynch
SUCKER	9 lbs. 10¾ oz.	Rocky River	Apr. 10 1954	Milan Kutner
SUNFISH	2 lbs. 4 oz.	Chagrin River	June 15 1970	Michael Moritoz
TROUT, Brook	2 lbs. 11 oz.	East Branch Chagrin River	June 30 1955	S. Graboshek
TROUT, Brown	13 lbs. 8 oz.	Cold Creek	Sept. 10 1942	J. S. Harris
TROUT, Rainbow	10 lbs. 8 oz.	Pickerel Creek	July 5 1951	John Fedlam
WALLEYE	15 lbs.	Pymatuning Reservoir	Nov. 13 1951	William Heathman

OKLAHOMA

Species	Wt.	Where	When	Angler
BASS, Largemouth	11 lbs. 15 oz.	Kiamichi River	June 5 1941	Herbert Rodgers
BASS, Smallmouth	4 lbs. 12 oz.	Mountain Fork River	Mar. 30 1968	Dan Moseley
BASS, Spotted	8 lbs. 2 oz.	Pittsburgh Co. Pond	June 27 1958	O. J. Stone
BASS, Striped	20 lbs. 2 oz.	Grand River	Aug. 1971	Paul Beeler
BASS, White	4 lbs. 14 oz.	Lake Eucha	Apr. 9 1969	Danny Feemster
BLUEGILL	1 lb. 7 oz.	Osage Co. Pond	Sept. 8 1968	David Noss
BUFFALO, Bigmouth	33 lbs. 8 oz.	Lake Tenkiller	Aug. 31 1968	Deborah Fanning
CARP	32 lbs. 12 oz.	Lake Rush	May 13 1968	Bob Penick
CATFISH, Blue	37 lbs.	Lake Draper	Sept. 6 1969	Glenn Meade
CATFISH, Channel	20 lbs. 2 oz.	Mayes Co. Pond	July 2 1968	Nicholas Boyko
CATFISH, Flathead	66 lbs.	Spavinaw	May 25 1970	Nick Freling
CRAPPIE, White	4 lbs. 13 oz.	Tillman Co. Pond	Mar. 4 1967	Buddy Mealor
PIKE, Northern	15 lbs. 12 oz.	Lake Carl Etling	Apr. 1971	Leroy Bass
SHEEPSHEAD	35 lbs. 4 oz.	Lake Texoma	Nov. 5 1967	R. J. Loilar
SUNFISH, Redear	1 lb. 13 oz.	Lake Niles	May 14 1966	Bobby Webb
TROUT, Rainbow	10 lbs. 4 oz.	Illinois River	July 3 1966	Billy Payne
WALLEYE	11 lbs. 4 oz.	Lake Hefner	Mar. 31 1967	Garret Knol

OREGON
(No Records Maintained)

PENNSYLVANIA

Species	Wt.	Where	When	Angler
BASS, Largemouth	8 lbs. 8 oz.	Stillwater Lake	1936	Stanley Pastula
BASS, Rock	3 lbs.	Swatara Creek	1966	John H. Rhodes
BASS, Smallmouth	6 lbs. 2 oz.	Conodoguinet Creek	1937	Ed Meadows
BLUEGILL		Hills Creek Lake	1965	Donald W. Correll, Jr.
BULLHEAD	11 lbs. 8 oz.	Allegheny River	1966	John Moore, Jr.
CARP	52 lbs.	Juniata River	1962	George Brown
CATFISH, Channel	35 lbs.	Allegheny River	1970	Jim Rogers
CRAPPIE	3 lbs. 8 oz.	Lake Ontelaunee	1967	Allen L. Roen
MUSKELLUNGE	54 lbs. 3 oz.	Conneaut Lake	1924	Lewis Walker, Jr.
PERCH		Oneida Dam	1936	Herman Rausch
PICKEREL, Chain	8 lbs.	Shohola Falls	1937	Frank Streznetcky
PIKE, Northern	15 lbs. 10 oz.	Mahoning Creek	1971	John Fulton
SHAD, American White	7 lbs. 4 oz.	Delamare River	1965	Vincent Graziano
SHEEPSHEAD	14 lbs.	Virgin Run Lake	1964	Gregory Parella
SUCKER	9 lbs. 12 oz.	French Creek	1938	George Kemper
TROUT, Brook	4 lbs. 4 oz.	Swago Lake	1966	Beth Ann Riker
TROUT, Brown	24 lbs.	Lake Wallenpaupack	1967	Frank Kociolek
TROUT, Lake	24 lbs.	Crystal Lake	1952	Mrs. Arthur Cramer
TROUT, Rainbow	9 lbs. 8 oz.	Logan Branch	1961	Paul Roberts
WALLEYE	12 lbs.	Allegheny River	1951	Firman Shoff

RHODE ISLAND

Species	Wt.	Where	When	Angler
BASS, Largemouth (Tie)	9 lbs. 12 oz.	Johnson Pond	June 1936	Daniel Hill
	9 lbs. 12 oz.	Barber Pond	1963	Edward Ahern
BASS, Striped (Tie)	67 lbs.	Block Island	1963	Jack Ryan
	67 lbs.	Green Hill	1965	Wilfred Fontaine

SOUTH CAROLINA

Species	Wt.	Where	When	Angler
BASS, Largemouth Black	16 lbs. 2 oz.	Santee-Cooper	1949	
BASS, Striped	55 lbs.	Lake Moultrie	Jan. 29 1963	Tiny Lund
CATFISH, Channel	58 lbs.	Lake Moultrie	July 7 1964	W. H. Whaley
CRAPPIE, Black	5 lbs.	Lake Moultrie	1957	
CRAPPIE, White	5 lbs. 1 oz.	Lake Murray	Mar. 6 1949	Mrs. H. F. Owen
PICKEREL, Chain	6 lbs.	Lake Marion	Jan. 10 1962	H. F. Avinger
TROUT, Brown	13 lbs. 4 oz.	Chauga River	July 27 1961	Julian Addis
WARMOUTH	1 lb. 2 oz.	Cooper River	May 18 1968	Robert L. Joyner

SOUTH DAKOTA

Species	Wt.	Where	When	Angler
BASS, Largemouth	8 lbs. 12 oz.	Hayes Lake	1957	Verne Page
BASS, Rock	1 lb. 4 oz.	Enemy Swim Lake	Jan. 30 1972	Jeff Nelson
BASS, Smallmouth	2 lbs. 15 oz.	Ft. Randall Tailwaters	1971	Darrel Schachumeyer
BASS, White (Tie)	4 lbs.	Enemy Swim Lake	1970	Todd Lohman
	4 lbs.	Enemy Swim Lake	1971	Clark Newman
BLUEGILL	2 lbs. 4¼ oz.	Leola Lake	1971	William Lapka
BUFFALO, Bigmouth	37 lbs. 8 oz.	Lake Mitchell	1970	Harry Durst
BUFFALO, Smallmouth	8 lbs. 2 oz.	Oahe Tailwaters	1969	Marvin Stratton
BULLHEAD, Black	3 lbs.	North Waubay Lake	1971	Jim Ewalt
BULLHEAD, Brown	2 lbs. 7 oz.	Crystal Lake	1963	Norman Clark
BURBOT	10 lbs. 2 oz.	Oahe Reservoir	1968	Edmund Arndt
CATFISH, Blue	100 lbs. 8 oz.	Missouri River	1964	Bob Millage
CATFISH, Channel	55 lbs.	James River	1949	Roy Groves
CATFISH, Flathead	36 lbs.	Missouri River	1969	Duane Mount
CRAPPIE, Black	3 lbs. 2 oz.	Ft. Randall Reservoir	1964	Richard Hermanek
CRAPPIE, White	2 lbs. 11 oz.	Oahe Reservoir	1967	Al Pfeifle
GAR, Longnose	13 lbs. 9½ oz.	Missouri River	1965	Terry Coulson
GAR, Shortnose	2 lbs. 3 oz.	Oahe Tailwaters	1970	Raymond Merchant
PADDLEFISH	110 lbs.	Big Bend Tailwaters	1969	Leland Nedved
PERCH, Yellow	2 lbs. 4 oz.	Cottonwood Lake	Feb. 20 1972	Martin Hartze
PIKE, Northern	35 lbs	Lake Sharpe	1972	Donald Matson
SAUGER	7 lbs. 7 oz.	Oahe Tailwaters	1960	Harvey Holzworth
SHEEPSHEAD	13 lbs. 12 oz.	Lake Mitchell	1970	Bob Wieland
STURGEON, Lake	25 lbs.	Missouri River	1968	Delbert Henn
STURGEON, Shovelnose	2 lbs.	Oahe Reservoir	1971	Joe Gruenstein
SUCKER	11 lbs. 11 oz.	James River	1967	Vernon Sarha
SUNFISH, Green	1 lb. 2 oz.	Hayes Lake	1971	Mike Pellerzi
TROUT, Brook	5 lbs. 6 oz.	Deerfield Reservoir	1966	Tom Sawyer
TROUT, Brown	18 lbs. 3 oz.	Rapid Creek	1928	Jess Wickersham
TROUT, Rainbow	11 lbs. 8 oz.	Pactola Reservoir	1967	Fred Wolfe
WALLEYE	15 lbs.	Lake Kampeska	1960	Carl Wiese

TENNESSEE

Species	Wt.	Where	When	Angler
BASS, Largemouth	14 lbs. 8 oz.	Sugar Creek	Oct. 17 1954	Louge Barnett
BASS, Rock	2 lbs 8 oz.	Stones River	1958	Billl Sanford
BASS, Smallmouth	11 lbs. 15 oz.	Dale Hollow Reservoir	July 13 1955	D. L. Hayes
BASS, Spotted	5 lbs. 2 oz.	Kentucky Lake	Mar. 21 1971	Ted Carpenter
BASS, Striped	20 lbs. 9 oz.	Watts Bar Dam	Mar. 3 1970	Christine Kyle
BASS, White	4 lbs. 10 oz.	Pickwick Tailwaters	1949	Jack Allen
BASS, White (Striped Bass Hybrid)	14 lbs. 8 oz.	Kentucky Lake	Mar. 1967	Robert Wofford
BLUEGILL (Tie)	2 lbs. 8 oz.	Linger Lake	Sept. 13 1956	Forest Kidwell
	2 lbs. 8 oz.	Cheatham Lake	Feb. 22 1961	Walter McFarland
BOWFIN	10 lbs.	Kentucky Reservoir	Sept. 10 1967	Lela Chaffee
BUFFALO	23 lbs.	French Broad River	May 20 1957	Bill Archer
BULLHEAD, Brown	1 lb. 15 oz.	Forked Deer River	Aug. 6 1968	Jerald Ledbetter
CARP	42 lbs. 8 oz.	Boone Lake	Aug. 12 1956	Al Moore
CATFISH, Blue	115 lbs.	Kentucky Lake	Oct. 9 1971	Joe Potts
CATFISH, Channel	24 lbs.	Laurel Hill Lake	Aug. 26 1967	Carl Spencer
CATFISH, Spoonbill	65 lbs.	Center Hill Lake	June 24 1969	David Buttram
CRAPPIE, Black	2 lbs. 12 oz.	Center Hill Lake	Apr. 4 1969	Tom Graham
CRAPPIE, White	5 lbs. 1 oz.	Garner Brown's Pond	Apr. 20 1968	Bill Allen
GAR, Longnose	23 lbs.	Pickwick Tailwaters	1963	Jimmy Gauvitts
MUSKELLUNGE	33 lbs.	Norris Reservoir	Feb. 5 1971	Joe Rogers
PICKEREL, Chain	5 lbs. 12 oz.	Kentucky Lake	1951	Donald Orgain
SAUGER	6 lbs. 10 oz.	Old Hickory Lake	Dec. 4 1965	Jack Goodman
SHEEPSHEAD	47 lbs.	Watts Bar Dam	Jan. 2 1955	Grover Parriman
SUNFISH, Redear	2 lbs. 5 oz.	Ft. Loudon Lake	June 8 1970	Carson Galyon
TROUT, Brown	26 lbs. 2 oz.	Dale Hollow Tailwater	May 1958	George Langston
TROUT, Rainbow	12 lbs. 10 oz.	Doe Creek	Apr. 1958	Jack Wilson
WALLEYE	25 lbs.	Old Hickory Lake	Aug. 3 1960	Mabry Harper
WARMOUTH	1 lb. 4½ oz.	Pipkins Pond	June 1961	Dave Bishop

TEXAS

Species	Wt.	Where	When	Angler
BASS, Largemouth	13 lbs. 8 oz.	Medina Lake	1943	H. R. Magee
BASS, Spotted	5 lbs. 9 oz.	Lake 'O the Pines	Mar. 1966	Turner Keith
BASS, White	5 lbs. 4 oz.	Colorado River	Mar. 1968	Raymond Rivers
CATFISH, Channel	36 lbs. 8 oz.	Pedernales River	1965	Mrs. Joe Cockrell
CATFISH, Flathead	58 lbs.	Dam B	1958	Floyd Hooks
CRAPPIE	4 lbs. 9 oz.	Navarro Mills Reservoir	Feb. 1968	G. G. Wooderson
GAR, Alligator	279 lbs.	Rio Grande River	1951	Bill Valverde
REDFISH	26 lbs.	Chub Lake	May 1971	Jack Kimbrough

Species	Wt.	Where	When	Angler
SHEEPSHEAD	55 lbs.	White Rock Lake	1924	Asa Short
TROUT, Rainbow	4 lbs. 12 oz.	Guadalupe River	1968	Ron Sharp

UTAH

Species	Wt.	Where	When	Angler
BASS, Largemouth	8 lbs. 8 oz.	Lake Powell	1968	Dale Brown
BASS, White	3 lbs. 14 oz.	Utah Lake	1970	Floyd Jensen
CARP	30 lbs.	Great Salt Lake Marshes	1960	Ralph Merrill
CATFISH, Channel	23 lbs.	Utah Lake	1970	LeRoy Mortensen
SALMON, Kokanee	4 lbs.	Utah Lake	1967	Park Leo
SQUAW FISH	14 lbs. 12 oz.	Green River	1961	Phil Dotson
TROUT, Brook	6 lbs. 4 oz.	Uintahs	1944	George Walkup
TROUT, Brown	25 lbs. 5¼ oz.	Logan Reservoir	1924	Wilford W. Smart
TROUT, Cutthroat	26 lbs. 12 oz.	Strawberry Reservoir	1930	Mrs. E. Smith
TROUT, Lake	36 lbs.	Fish Lake	1960	Katherine White
TROUT, Rainbow	21 lbs. 8 oz.	Mill Creek Reservoir	1947	LaMar Westra
WALLEYE	10 lbs. 2 oz.	Borham Reservoir	1969	Wayne Perank

VERMONT

Species	Wt.	Where	When	Angler
BASS, Largemouth	7 lbs. 6 oz.	Lake St. Catherine	Sept. 29 1971	Cecil Brown
BASS, Smallmouth	6 lbs. 7 oz.	Harriman Lake	Aug. 30 1969	Chester Burgess
BOWFIN	9 lbs. 15 oz.	Winooski River	Aug. 21 1971	John Shaw
BULLHEAD	1 lb. 8 oz.	Lake Hortonia	May 19 1969	John Finnessy
CATFISH, Channel	21 lbs. 4 oz.	Lamoille River	May 23 1969	Lloyd Hier
CRAPPIE, Black	1 lb. 2 oz.	Lake Bomoseen	Sept. 14 1971	Julian Sbardella
MUSKELLUNGE	23 lbs. 8 oz.	Highgate Falls	May 24 1970	Richard Gross
PICKEREL, Chain	4 lbs. 4 oz.	Lake Morey	Sept. 17 1971	Joseph O'Neill
PIKE, Northern	26 lbs.	Kellogg's Bay	Mar. 11 1970	Robert Bearor
SALMON	5 lbs. 8 oz.	Seymour Lake	Mar. 7 1969	Edward Ashman
SHEEPSHEAD	13 lbs. 2 oz.	Mallett's Bay	Aug. 19 1971	Ray Lavalley
TROUT, Brook	4 lbs.	Cole Springs	July 2 1971	Smith Stratton III
TROUT, Brown	10 lbs.	Sherman Dam	July 7 1969	Lewis A. Micou, Jr.
TROUT, Lake	27 lbs. 8 oz.	Little Averill	June 18 1971	Percy Mason
TROUT, Rainbow	10 lbs. 1 oz.	Lake Bomoseen	May 19 1969	Thomas Beauregard
WALLEYE	10 lbs. 7 oz.		Apr. 30 1970	Ronnie Wright

VIRGINIA

Species	Wt.	Where	When	Angler
BASS, Largemouth	13 lbs. 4 oz.	Gaston Lake	Aug. 1971	Charles Hamm
BASS, Rock	2 lbs. 2 oz.	Pigg River	Mar. 29 1964	J. Monaghan
BASS, Smallmouth	8 lbs.	Claytor Lake	May 22 1964	C. A. Garay
BASS, Striped Landlocked	32 lbs. 3 oz.	Gaston Lake	May 23 1969	Bryon Simmons
BASS, White	3 lbs. 6 oz.	Smith Mt. Lake	May 6 1971	Mrs. Joan Fisher
BLUEGILL	4 lbs. 8 oz.	Alberta Pvt. Pond	Feb. 7 1970	Thomas Jones
CATFISH, Channel	26 lbs.	Lake Brittle	July 9 1966	James Wilson
CATFISH, Flathead	45 lbs.	Claytor Lake	Aug. 6 1967	Howard Shelton
CRAPPIE	4 lbs. 13½ oz.	Lake Connor	Apr. 8 1967	E. L. Blackstock
GAR	20 lbs.	Western Branch	Aug. 8 1971	Robert Whitehead
MUSKELLUNGE	29 lbs.	Smith Mt. Lake	Apr. 21 1971	W. R. Pugh
PERCH, White	2 lbs.	Back Bay	Sept. 12 1969	W. R. Dilday
PERCH, Yellow	1 lb. 12 oz.	Aquia Creek	Mar. 14 1971	Billy Collins
PICKEREL, Chain	7 lbs. 11 oz.	Woodbridge Creek	Apr. 27 1971	Steve DeZulovich
PIKE, Northern	17 lbs.	Beaver Creek Lake	Oct. 7 1971	Hansford Vest
SALMON, Coho	8 lbs. 1 oz.	Philpott Dam	Sept. 2 1971	Rev. Elbert Hall
SUNFISH, Redear	4 lbs. 8 oz.	Chase City Private Pond	June 19 1970	Gene Ball
TROUT, Brook	3 lbs. 2 oz.	Quantico	Apr. 8 1964	W. F. Donovan
TROUT, Brown	11 lbs. 9 oz.	Marshall Draft	Oct. 31 1971	Nelson Creasy
TROUT, Lake	5 lbs. 6 oz.	Philpott Dam	July 6 1966	Arthur Conner
TROUT, Rainbow	9 lbs. 14 oz.	Pond Monterey	May 5 1967	D. L. Talbott
WALLEYE	17 lbs.	New River	Jan. 15 1965	W. C. Bradbury

WASHINGTON

Species	Wt.	Where	When	Angler
BASS, Largemouth	11 lbs. 8 oz.	Newman Lake	July 1966	Don Milleten
BASS, Smallmouth	8 lbs. 12 oz.	Snake River	Apr. 1967	Ray Wanacutt
CATFISH, Blue	14 lbs. 10 oz.	Yakima River	July 14 1970	DeVerne Dunnum
CATFISH, Channel	12 lbs. 8 oz.	Snake River		
CRAPPIE, Black	4 lbs. 8 oz.	Lake Washington		John Smart
TROUT, Brook	7 lbs.	Lake Cavanaugh		Vincent Fox
TROUT, Brown	22 lbs.	Sullivan Lake	May 1965	R. L. Henry
TROUT, Cutthroat	8 lbs. 12 oz.	Coffee Pot Lake	1956	Al Thomas
TROUT, Cutthroat (sea-run)	6 lbs.	Puget Sound	May 1943	B. Johnson
TROUT, Dolly Varden	22 lbs. 8 oz.	Tieton River	Apr. 1961	Louis Schott
TROUT, Lake	30 lbs. 4 oz.	Loon Lake	June 1966	Ken Janke
TROUT, Rainbow	22 lbs. 8 oz.	Waitts Lake	1957	Bill Dittner
TROUT, Steelhead	33 lbs.	Snake River	Jan. 1962	Homer Scott
WALLEYE	10 lbs.	Banks Lake		Oscar Carlson

WEST VIRGINIA

Species	Wt.	Where	When	Angler
BASS, Largemouth	9 lbs. 2 oz.	Bull Creek	1966	Allen Quimby
BASS, Rock	1 lb. 7 oz.	Big Sandy Creek	1964	Warren Ryan
BASS, Smallmouth	9 lbs. 5 oz.	South Branch	1971	David Lindsay
BASS, Spotted	3 lbs. 2 oz.	So. Fork Hughes River	1966	Henry Fenney
BASS, White	4 lbs.	Kanawha Falls	1964	Robert Peyton
BLUEGILL	2 lbs. 2 oz.	Farm Pond	1964	Dennis Criss
BOWFIN	3 lbs. 2 oz.	Shenandoah River	1971	Lloyd Smith
BUFFALO	30 lbs.	Tygart Creek	1970	Kenneth Casto
CARP	40 lbs. 1 oz.	New River	1970	Jerry Spicer
CATFISH, Bullhead	3 lbs.	Ohio River	1964	Robert McCord
CATFISH, Channel	19 lbs.	Coal River	1963	Donald Forman
CRAPPIE	4 lbs. 1 oz.	Meathouse Fork	1971	Leonard Edgell
GAR	17 lbs.	Little Kanawha	1952	A. J. Keith
MUSKELLUNGE	43 lbs.	Elk River	1955	Lester Hayes
PADDLEFISH	70 lbs.	Little Kanawha	1965	Charles Morgan
PICKEREL, Chain	4 lbs. 1 oz.	Back Creek	1970	Kenny Noll
PIKE, Northern	8 lbs.	Sutton Reservoir	1971	Carl Coulter
SAUGER	1 lb. 5 oz.	Kanawha Falls	1971	Frank Tasker
SHEEPSHEAD	25 lbs.	Kanawha Station	1954	Bill Dawkins
STURGEON	12 lbs. 5 oz.	Ohio River	1949	Emett Wheeler
TROUT, Brook	3 lbs. 7 oz.	Rich Creek	1969	Stephen Meadows
TROUT, Brown	16 lbs.	South Branch River	1968	Paul Barker
TROUT, Golden	2 lbs. 15 oz.	Spruce Knob Lake	1968	Ted Thomas, Jr.
TROUT, Rainbow	10 lbs.	Spruce Knob Lake	1956	John Manley
WALLEYE	16 lbs. 2 oz.	New River	1967	E. C. Cox

WISCONSIN

Species	Wt.	Where	When	Angler
BASS, Largemouth	11 lbs. 3 oz.	Lake Ripley	Oct. 12 1940	Robert Milkowski
BASS, Rock	1 lb. 12 oz.	Big Green Lake	Feb. 14 1971	Mrs. Celia Walker
BASS, Smallmouth	9 lbs. 1 oz.	Indian Lake	June 21 1950	Leon Stefoneck
BASS, White	3 lbs. 9 oz.	Wisconsin River	1962	J. L. Griffith
BLUEGILL	2 lbs. 4 oz.	Squash Lake	June 25 1971	Lee Ann & Lynn Marie Ferries
BULLHEAD, Black	2 lbs. 9 oz.	Trappe	May 24 1967	Richard Kincaid
BULLHEAD, Brown	3 lbs.	Nelson Lake	Aug. 11 1971	Mrs. Charles Barta
BULLHEAD, Yellow	2 lbs. 3 oz.	Blue Spring Lake	May 15 1971	Richard Hobson
CARP	57 lbs. 2 oz.	Lake Wisconsin	Aug. 28 1966	Mike Prorok
CATFISH, Channel	44 lbs.	Wisconsin River	1962	Larry Volenec
CATFISH, Flathead	61 lbs.	Fox River	June 28 1966	Mike Tanner
CRAPPIE, Black	4 lbs. 8 oz.	Gile Flowage	Aug. 12 1967	Allen Dollar
MUSKELLUNGE	69 lbs. 11 oz.	Lake Chippewa Flowage	Oct. 20 1949	Louis Spray
PERCH, Yellow	3 lbs. 4 oz.	Lake Winnebago	1954	Mike Lamont
PIKE, Northern	38 lbs.	Lake Puckaway	Aug. 6 1952	J. A. Rahn
SALMON, Chinook	35 lbs. 2 oz.	Lake Michigan	Aug. 25 1971	Roger Perry
SALMON, Coho	19 lbs. 12½ oz.	Lake Michigan	July 2 1969	Lyle Budnick
SAUGER (Tie)	4 lbs. 5 oz.	Mississippi River	Apr. 10 1970	Mrs. James Carlson
	4 lbs. 5 oz.	Mississippi River	June 4 1971	Lee Paul
SHEEPSHEAD	26 lbs.	Fox River	May 12 1971	Nolan Rothenbach
SPLAKE	14 lbs. 4 oz.	Ada Lake	June 7 1967	Bill Keeler
STURGEON	94 lbs. 3 oz.	Menominee River	Sept. 20 1968	Thomas Winter
SUNFISH, Green	1 lb. 9 oz.	Wind Lake	Aug. 23 1967	Thomas Tart
TROUT, Brook	9 lbs. 15 oz.	Prairie River	Sept. 2 1944	John Mixis
TROUT, Brown	29 lbs. 9 oz.	Lake Superior	May 24 1971	Michael Brasic
TROUT, Lake	47 lbs.	Lake Superior	Sept. 9 1946	Waino Roose
TROUT, Rainbow	19 lbs. 11 oz.	Lake Michigan	Aug. 31 1971	Delbert Stegemeyer
WALLEYE	18 lbs.	High Lake	Sept. 26 1933	Tony Brothers

WYOMING

Species	Wt.	Where	When	Angler
BASS, Largemouth	7 lbs. 2 oz.	Stove Lake	1942	John Teeters
CATFISH, Channel	18 lbs.	Powder River	1946	R. D. Matson
CRAPPIE, Black	1 lb. 7 oz.	Boyen Reservoir	1968	Jim Jacobsen
LING	19 lbs. 4 oz.	Pilot Butte Reservoir	1965	K. E. Moreland
SAUGER	6 lbs. 8 oz.	Wind River	1942	Unknown
TROUT, Brook	10 lbs.	Torrey Lake	1933	Unknown
TROUT, Brown	18 lbs. 2 oz.	Good Reservoir	1971	James Boyce
TROUT, Cutthroat	15 lbs.	Native Lake	1959	Alan Dow
TROUT, Golden	11 lbs. 4 oz.	Cook's Lake	1948	C. S. Read
TROUT, Grayling	4 lbs.		1936	Unknown
TROUT, Lake	44 lbs.	Jackson Lake	1967	Pat Christensen
TROUT, Rainbow	23 lbs.	Burnt Lake	1969	Frank Favazzo
WALLEYE	12 lbs. 3 oz.	Wind River	1968	Ralph Hedstrom
WHITEFISH	4 lbs.	Wind River		Unknown

DISTRICT OF COLUMBIA
(No Records Maintained)

43 DEPARTMENTS:

State Conservation Departments

ALABAMA
Department of Conservation and Natural Resources, 64 N. Union Street, Montgomery, Alabama 36104

ALASKA
Department of Fish and Game, Subport Bldg., Juneau, Alaska 99801

ARIZONA
Game and Fish Department, Arizona State Bldg., Phoenix, Ariz., 85001

ARKANSAS
State Game and Fish Commission, Game and Fish Building, State Capitol Grounds, Little Rock, Arkansas 72201

CALIFORNIA
Department of Fish and Game, 1416 Ninth Street, Sacramento, California 95814

COLORADO
Game and Fish Department 6060 Broadway, Denver, Colo. 80216

CONNECTICUT
State of Connecticut, Department of Environmental Protection, Fish and Water Life, State Office Building, Hartford, Conn. 06115

DELAWARE
Department of Natural Resources and Environmental Control, Division of Fish and Wildlife, Dover, Delaware 19901

FLORIDA
Game and Fresh Water Fish Commission, Farris Bryant Building,
620 S. Meridian Street, Tallahassee, Florida 32304

GEORGIA
Game and Fish Commission, Trinity-Washington Street Building,
270 Washington Street, S. W., Atlanta, Georgia 30334

HAWAII
Department of Land and Natural Resources, Division of Fish
and Game, 1179 Punchbowl Street, Honolulu, Hawaii 96813

IDAHO
Idaho Fish and Game Department, 600 S. Walnut Street,
Boise, Idaho 83706

ILLINOIS
Department of Conservation, Division of Fisheries, 102 State Office
Building, 400 S. Spring Street, Springfield, Illinois 62706

INDIANA
Department of Conservation, Division of Fish and Game,
311 W. Washington St., Indianapolis, Indiana 46204

IOWA
State Conservation Commission, E. 7th & Court Avenue,
Des Moines, Iowa 50309

KANSAS
Forestry, Fish and Game Commission, Box 591, Pratt, Kansas 67124

KENTUCKY
Department of Fish and Wildlife, State Office Building Annex,
Frankfort, Kentucky 40601

LOUISIANA
Wild Life and Fisheries Commission, Wild Life and Fisheries Building,
400 Royal Street, New Orleans, Louisiana 70130

MAINE
Department of Inland Fisheries and Game, State House,
Augusta, Maine 04330

MARYLAND
Department of Natural Resources, Fish and Wildlife Administration,
Annapolis, Maryland 21401

MASSACHUSETTS
Department of Natural Resources, Division of Fish and Game,
Boston, Massachusetts 02201

MICHIGAN
Department of Natural Resources, Lansing, Michigan 48926

MINNESOTA
Department of Conservation, Division of Game and Fish,
St. Paul, Minnesota 55101

MISSISSIPPI
State Game and Fish Commission, Woolfolk State Office Building,
Jackson, Mississippi 39201

MISSOURI
Missouri Department of Conservation, 2901 North Ten Mile Drive,
Jefferson City, Missouri 65101

MONTANA
Department of Fish and Game, Fisheries Division,
Helena, Montana 59601

NEBRASKA
Game and Parks Commission, State Capitol, Lincoln, Nebraska 68509

NEVADA
Department of Fish and Game, P. O. Box 10678, Reno, Nevada 89510

NEW HAMPSHIRE
Fish and Game Department, 34 Bridge Street, Concord,
New Hampshire 03301

NEW JERSEY
Information and Education Section, Division of Fish, Game and Shell
Fisheries, Box 1809, Trenton, New Jersey 08625

NEW MEXICO
Department of Game and Fish, State Capitol, Santa Fe,
New Mexico 87501

NEW YORK
State of New York, Department of Environmental Conservation,
Albany, New York 12201

NORTH CAROLINA
Freshwater records—Department of Natural and Economic Resources,
Travel and Promotion Division, Box 27687, Raleigh, North
Carolina 27611. Saltwater records—Sport Fisheries Studies,
P.O. Box 769, Morehead City, North Carolina 28557

NORTH DAKOTA
State Game and Fish Department, Bismarck, North Dakota 58501

OHIO
Outdoor Writers of Ohio, Inc., Record Fish Committee, c/o The
Fremont News-Messenger, 107 S. Arch Street, Fremont, Ohio 43420

OKLAHOMA
Department of Wildlife Conservation Information Education Division,
1801 N. Lincoln Blvd., Oklahoma City, Oklahoma 73105

OREGON
Game Commission, P. O. Box 3503, 1634 S. W. Alder Street,
Portland, Oregon 97208

PENNSYLVANIA
Fish Commission, Harrisburg, Pennsylvania 17120

RHODE ISLAND
Department of Natural Resources, Division of Fish and Wildlife,
Veterans' Memorial Building, Providence, Rhode Island 02903

SOUTH CAROLINA
Wildlife Resources Department, Information and Education,
P. O. Box 167, Columbia, South Carolina 29202

SOUTH DAKOTA
Department of Game, Fish and Parks, Pierre, South Dakota 57501

TENNESSEE
Game and Fish Commission, Ellington Agricultural Center,
P. O. Box 40747, Nashville, Tennessee 37220

TEXAS
Parks and Wildlife Department, Information and Education,
John H. Reagan Building, Austin, Texas 78701

UTAH
Department of Fish and Game, 1596 W. N. Temple,
Salt Lake City, Utah

VERMONT
State Fish and Game Commission, Montpelier, Vermont 05602

VIRGINIA
Commission of Game and Inland Fisheries, P.O. Box 11104,
Richmond, Virginia 23230

WASHINGTON
Department of Game, Fishery Management Division, 600 N.
Capitol Way, Olympia, Washington 98501

WEST VIRGINIA
Division of Wildlife Resources, Department of Natural Resources,
Charleston, West Virginia 25305

WISCONSIN
Conservation Department, Division of Fisheries,
Madison, Wisconsin 53702

WYOMING
Game and Fish Commission, Information and Education Division,
Cheyenne, Wyoming 82001

FEDERAL
United States Fish & Wildlife Service, Department of the Interior,
Washington, D. C. 20242

44 DEPARTMENTS:

Canada and the Bahamas Fishing Information Departments

ALBERTA
Department of Lands and Forests, Edmonton, Alta.

BRITISH COLUMBIA
Fish and Game Branch, Department of Recreation and Conservation, 567 Burrard St., Vancouver 1, B.C.

MANITOBA
Department of Mines and Natural Resources, Winnipeg, Man.

NEWFOUNDLAND
Department of Mines and Resources, St. John's, Newfoundland

NORTHWEST TERRITORIES
Northern Administration Branch, Department of Northern Affairs and National Resources, Ottawa, Ontario, Canada

NOVA SCOTIA
Department of Lands and Forests, Halifax, N.S.

ONTARIO
Department of Lands and Forests, Parliament Bldgs., Toronto, Ontario

PRINCE EDWARD ISLAND
Department of Industry and Natural Resources, Charlottetown, P.E.I.

QUEBEC
Department of Game and Fisheries, Quebec, Que.

SASKATCHEWAN
Department of Natural Resources, Government Administration Bldg., Regina, Sask.

YUKON TERRITORY
Game Department, Yukon Territorial Government, Box 2029, Whitehorse, Y.T., Canada

Bahamas Fishing Information Bureau
The Development Board, Nassau, The Bahamas

45 DEPARTMENTS:

Conservation, Professional and Sportmen's Organizations

AMERICAN CASTING ASSOCIATION: P.O. Box 51, Nashville 2, Tenn.

AMERICAN FISHING TACKLE MANUFACTURER'S ASSOCIATION: 20 North Wacker Drive, Chicago, Illinois 60606

AMERICAN INSTITUTE OF BIOLOGICAL SCIENCES: Box 9173, Roslyn Station, Arlington 9, Virginia

AMERICAN FISHERIES SOCIETY: 1404 New York Ave., N.W., Washington 5, D.C.

AMERICAN LITTORAL SOCIETY: Sandy Hook Marine Laboratory, Box 117, Highlands, New Jersey

ATLANTIC SEA RUN SALMON COMMISSION: University of Maine, Orono, Maine

ATLANTIC STATES MARINE FISHERIES COMMISSION: 336 E. College Ave., Tallahassee, Florida

FRIENDS OF THE WILDERNESS: 3515 E. 4th Street, Duluth 4, Minnesota

GULF AND CARIBBEAN FISHERIES INSTITUTE: Institute of Marine Science, University of Miami, 1 Rickenbacker Causeway, Virginia Key, Miami 49, Florida

GULF STATES MARINE FISHERIES COMMISSION: 312 Audubon Bldg., New Orleans 16, Louisiana

GREAT LAKES FISHERY COMMISSION: 106 Natural Resources Bldg., University of Michigan, Ann Arbor, Michigan

INTERNATIONAL ASSOCIATION OF GAME, FISH AND CONSERVATION COMM.: 16413 Canterbury Drive, Hopkins, Minnesota

INTERNATIONAL CASTING FEDERATION: 1400 South Peters Street, New Orleans 13, Louisiana

INTERNATIONAL COMM. FOR THE NORTHWEST ATLANTIC FISHERIES: Education Bldg., Dalhousie University, Halifax, North Carolina

INTERNATIONAL GAME FISH ASSOCIATION: Alfred 1, DuPont Bldg., Miami 32, Florida

INTERNATIONAL OCEANOGRAPHIC FOUNDATION: 1 Rickenbacker Causeway, Virginia Key, Miami 49, Florida

INTERNATIONAL PACIFIC SALMON FISHERIES COMM.: Box 30, New Westminster, B.C., Canada

INTERNATIONAL SPIN FISHING ASSOCIATION: P.O. Box 81, Downey, California

IZAAK WALTON LEAGUE OF AMERICA: Arlington, Virginia

NATIONAL ASSOCIATION OF MARINE ANGLER'S CLUBS: Box 117, Highlands, New Jersey

NATIONAL FISHERIES INSTITUTE, INC.: 1614 20th St., N.W., Washington 9, D.C.

NATIONAL PARTY BOAT OWNER'S ASSOCIATION: Box 117, Highlands, New Jersey

NATIONAL WILDLIFE FEDERATION: 1412 16th St., N.W., Washington, D.C.

NEW ENGLAND ADVISORY BOARD FOR FISH & GAME PROBLEMS: 319 Linwood St., West Lynn, Mass.

NEW ENGLAND OUTDOOR WRITER'S ASSOCIATION: 1003 N. Westfield St., Feeding Hills, Mass.

OUTBOARD BOATING CLUB OF AMERICA: 307 N. Michigan Blvd., Chicago, Ill.

OUTDOOR RECREATION INSTITUTE: 5003 Wapakoneta, Washington 16, D.C.

OUTDOOR WRITER'S ASSOCIATION OF AMERICA: 105 Guitar Bldg., Columbia, Missouri

PACIFIC MARINE FISHERIES COMM.: 741 State Office Bldg., 1400 S. W. Fifth Ave., Portland 1, Oregon

SPORT FISHERY RESEARCH FOUNDATION: 1404 New York Avenue, Washington 5, D.C.

SPORT FISHING INSTITUTE: Bond Bldg., Washington 5, D.C.

THE BROTHERHOOD OF THE JUNGLE COCK: 10 E. Fayette St., Baltimore, Md.

THE CAMP FIRE CLUB OF AMERICA: 19 Rector Street, New York 6, New York

TROUT, UNLIMITED: 900 Lapeer Avenue, Saginaw, Michigan

U.S. FOREST SERVICE, U.S. SOIL CONSERVATION SERVICE, U.S. BUREAU OF OUTDOOR RECREATION, U.S. FISH AND WILDLIFE SERVICE, U.S. NATIONAL PARK SERVICE: Washington 25, D.C.

U.S. TROUT FARMERS ASSOCIATION: 110 Social Hall Avenue, Salt Lake City 11, Utah

WILDLIFE MANAGEMENT INSTITUTE: 709 Wire Bldg., Washington 5, D.C.

DEPARTMENTS: 46

Directory of Fishing Tackle Manufacturers and Importers

Acme Tackle Company, 350 Dexter St., Providence, Rhode Island (Lures)

Actionrod, Inc., 912 W. State St., Hastings, Michigan (Rods)

Airlite Plastics Co., 2915 N. 16th St., Omaha, Neb. (Bobbers, Decoys, Minnow Buckets)

Aladdin Laboratories, Inc., 620 S. 8th St., Minneapolis, Minn. (Perrine Fly Reels)

Allan Manufacturing Co., 325 Duffy Ave., Hicksville, N.Y. (Fishing Rod Hardware)

Alliance Manufacturing, 3121 Milwaukee Ave., Chicago 18, Ill. (Landing Nets, Fish Bags, Tackle)

Al's Goldfish Lure Co., 516 Main St., Indian Orchard, Mass. (Lures)

American Foreign Ind., 640 Sacramento St., San Francisco, Cal. (Importers)

The American Pad and Textile Co., 6230 Bienvenue St., New Orleans 17, La. (Fishing Clothing, Life Vests, Cushions)

Anglers' Mfg. Corp., 1345 W. Thorndale Ave., Chicago, Ill. (Fishing tool)

Fred Arbogast Co., Inc., 313 W. North St., Akron, Ohio (Lures)

Arndt & Sons, Inc., 1000 Fairview Ave., Hamilton, Ohio (Baits)

The Arnold Tackle Corp., Box 87, Paw Paw, Mich. (Ice Fishing Tackle)

Art Wire and Stamping Co., 227 High St., Newark 2, N.J. (Tackle)

Atlantic Lures, Inc., 85 South St., Providence, R.I. (Lures, Terminal Tackle)

Bait Boy Products, 708 60th St. NW, Bradenton, Fla. (Bait Bucket Aerator)

Baker Mfg. Co., Box 60, Columbia, Pa. (Hookout)

Bay De Noc Lure Co., Box 71-2, Gladstone, Mich. (Swedish Pimple Lure)

The Bead Chain Mfg. Co., 110 Mountain Grove St., Bridgeport, Conn.

Berkley & Co., Inc., Highway 71 & 9, Spirit Lake, Iowa ("Trilene" Line leaders)

Betts Manufacturing Company, Park Falls, Wisconsin (Rods)

Black Panther Tool Co., 4051 S. Iowa Ave., Milwaukee, Wis. (Bob-er-Lite)

Bomber Bait Co., Gainesville, Texas

Boone Bait Co., Inc., Forsyth Road, Winter Park, Florida (Lures)

Bornemann Products Co., 2117 Rockwell Rd., Aurora, Ill. (Depth O Plug)

Bradlow, Inc., 3923 W. Jefferson, Los Angeles 16, Cal. (Quick Finessa Reel)

Brainerd Bait Co., 1564 Englewood Ave., St. Paul 45, Minn. (Dr. Spoon)

Bronson Reel Co., Bronson, Mich. (Fishing Reels, Rods)

Vernon Brown Co., 20 N. Wacker Dr., Chicago 6, Ill. (Spot Marker)

Browning-Silaflex Co., 1706 Washington Ave., St. Louis 3, Mo. (Rods)

L. Brust Mfg. Co., 1301 N. 14th Ave., Melrose Pk., Ill. (Saf-t-Grip)

Buckeye Bait Corp., 120 Liberty St., Council Grove, Kansas (Fishing Floats)

H.C. Buicke & Sons, 3431 Falls Blvd., N. Tonawanda, N.Y. (Fish Hook Holder)

Paul Bunyan Co., 1030 Marshall St. NE, Minneapolis, Minn. (Lures)

Burke Flexo-Products Co., 3249 Barlow Rd., Traverse City, Mich. (Lures)

Tony Burmek, 4173 N. 17th St., Milwaukee, Wis. (Burmek's Secret Bait)

Buss Mfg. Co., E. Lanark Ave., Lanark, Ill. (Buss Bedding)

Carron Net Company, 1623 17th St., Two Rivers, Wisconsin

Central Molding & Mfg. Co., 1509 Central Ave., Kansas City, Mo. (Tackle Boxes)

Champion Products Co., 2525 Park Ave., Muskegon Hts., Mich. (Handle Rod)

John Chatillon & Sons, 85 Cliff St., New York 38, N.Y. (Fish Scales)

Cisco Kid Tackle Co., Boca Raton, Fla. (Cisco Kid Lures & Rods)

Conolon Corp. (Garcia), 636 W. 17th St., Costa Mesa, Cal. (Rods)

Continental Arms Corp., 697 Fifth Ave., New York, N.Y. (Micron and Alcedo Reels)

Cortland Industries, Inc., Fishing Line Division, 67 E. Court St., Cortland, New York (Fishing Lines)

Cosom Corp., 6030 Wayzata Blvd., Minneapolis, Minn. (Bait Bucket)

Cover Guard Mfg. Co., 1414 S. Michigan, Chicago 5, Ill. (Rods & Reel Cases)

Creme Lure Co., Post Office Box 87, Tyler, Texas (Plastic Lures)

Ed Cumings, Inc., 2305 Branch Rd., Flint, Mich. (Nets, Rod Cases)

Davis Mills, Inc., Lake City, Tennessee (Nets)

Day Bait Co., 1824 Howard St., Pt. Huron, Mich. (Preserved Baits)

Dayton Bait & Marine Prod., Inc., 2701 S. Dixie Dr., Dayton 9, Ohio (Floats, Rod Holders)

De Long Lures, 18118 Syracuse Ave., Cleveland 10, Ohio (Plastic Lures)

Detty's Fish Gripper, 132 Atkins Ave., Lancaster, Pa. (Fish Gripper)

De Witt Plastics, 26 Aurelius Ave., Auburn, N.Y. (Boxes, Stringers, Buckets)

Dura-Pak Corp., 611 Pearl St., Sioux City, Iowa (Terminal Tackle)

Dynamic Sales, Inc., (Roddy Recreation Products, Inc.), 1526 W. 166th St., P.O. Box 431, Gardena, Cal. (Rods, Reels, Line)

Enterprise Mfg. Co., (Pflueger), 110 N. Union St., Akron, Ohio (Reels, rods)

Lou J. Eppinger Mfg. Co., 6340 Schaefer Highway, Dearborn, Mich. (Dardevle Lures)

Ero Mfg. Co., 714 W. Monroe St., Chicago, Ill. (Life Vest and Boat Cushions)

Glen L. Evans, Inc., Caldwell, Texas (Lures)

Ever-Wear Seal Co., 850 Main St., Lake Geneva, Wis. (Worm Lure)

Fabrico Mfg. Corp., 1300 W. Exchange Ave., Chicago 9, Ill. (Stocking Foot Wader, Parkas)

Falls Bait Co., Chippewa Falls, Wisconsin (Lures)

Famous Keystone Kits Corp., 1344 W. 37th St., Chicago 9, Ill. (Fishing Kits)

Feurer Bros. Inc., 77 Lafayette Ave., North White Plains, N.Y. (Reels)

The Fish Net and Twine Co., Menominee, Michigan

Florida Fish Tackle Mfg. Co., 2100 First Ave. S., St. Petersburg, Fla. (Lures)

Frabill Mfg. Co., 234 W. Florida St., Milwaukee, Wis. (Minnow Buckets, Boat Seats)

Isaac Franklin & Son, 1218 Warner St., Baltimore 30, Md. (Nets, Crab Traps)

Gapen Fly Co., Onoka, Minnesota

The Garcia Corp., 329 Alfred Ave., Teaneck, N.J. (Rods, reels, line and lures)

B.F. Gladding & Co., Inc., South Otselic, N.Y. (Line, Tackle Boxes)

Gliebe Co., 1154 Myrtle Ave., Brooklyn 21, N.Y. (Terminal Tackle)

B.F. Goodrich Footwear Co., 36 Nichols Ave., Watertown 72, Mass. (Fishing Footwear)

Great Lakes Products, Inc., 312 Huron Blvd., Marysville, Mich. (Rods, Reels)

Gudebrod Bros. Silk Co., Inc., 12 S. 12th St., Philadelphia, Pa. (Line)

The Hamilton-Skotch Corp., 295 Fifth Ave., New York 16, N.Y. (Tackle Boxes)

Harben Mfg. Co., 2328 Olive St., Racine, Wis. (Fish Scaler)

Harnell, Inc., 4094 Glencoe Ave., Venice, Cal. (Fishing Rods)

Harrison Industries, Inc., 250 Passaic St., Newark, N.J. (Centaure & Cargem Reels, Lures)

James Heddon's Sons, Dowagiac, Mich. (Rods, reels, line, lures)

Helin Tackle Co., 4099 Beaufait, Detroit 7, Mich. (Flatfish Lures)

Hettrick Mfg. Co., Taylorsville Rd., Statesville, N.C. (Fishing Clothing)

Hodgman Rubber Co., Tripp St., Framingham, Mass. (Waders, Fishing Clothing)

The Hofschneider Corp., 848 Jay St., Rochester 11, N.Y. ("Red Eye" Lures)

Holliday Reel Co., 1025 N. Main St., Akron 10, Ohio

Horrocks-Ibbotson Co., 20 Whitesboro St., Utica 2, N.Y. (Rods, reels, lures)

Hurricane Import Co., 70 Tenth St., San Francisco, Cal.

Ideal Fishing Float Co., Inc., 20th & Franklin St., Richmond 3, Va.

International Seaway Trading Corp., 1387 W. 9 St., Cleveland 13, Ohio

Irving Raincoat Co., 657 Broadway, New York 12, N.Y.

Jamison Tackle Co., 3654 Montrose, Chicago 8, Ill. (Lures)

Jet Aer Corp., 165 Third Ave., Paterson, N.J. (Insect Repellent)

Albert J. John Mfg. Co., 118 W. 69th St., Chicago, Ill. (Lead Sinkers)

Louis Johnson Co., 1547 Old Deerfield Rd., Highland Park, Ill. (Johnson Lures)

Johnson Reels, Inc., Johnson Park, Mankota, Minnesota

Kar-Gard Co., 2201 Grand Ave., Kansas City, Mo. (Lure Retriever)

Kennedy Mfg. Co., P.O. Box 151, Van Wert, Ohio (Tackle Boxes)

Kinfolks Inc., Main St., Perry, N.Y. (Hunting Knives)

Klamerus & Co., 4557 W. 59th St., Chicago 29, Ill. (Rod Holders)

Kolpin Bros. Inc., 119 S. Pearl, Berlin, Wis. (Fishing Accessories)

L & S Bait Co., Inc., 148 S. Vasseur Ave., Bradley, Ill. (L & S Mirrolures)

Land-O-Tackle, Inc., 4650 N. Ronald St., Chicago, Ill. (Lure Bodies, Components)

Lazy Ike Corp., 512 Central Ave., Fort Dodge, Iowa

Lectromatic Sports, Inc., 11405 E. 7th Ave., Aurora 8, Colo. (Battery Powered Reel, Rods)

Leisure Lures, 7315 Atoll Ave. (Box 353 Station 1) North Hollywood, Cal. (Plastic Lures)

Le Trappeur, Inc., Southwest Industrial Park, Westwood, Mass. (Luxor Reels)

Liberty Mfg. Co., 4026 N. 20th St., St. Louis 21, Mo. (Terminal Tackle)

Liberty Steel Chest Corp., 16 Dowling Place, Rochester 5, N.Y.

Lisk Fly Mfg. Co., 659 S. Spring St., Greensboro, N.C. (Lures, Rods)

Little Atom Lures, 1415 N. California, Chicago, Ill. (Orig. Pinkie Lures)

Longfellow Corp., 31795 Groesbeck Highway, Fraser, Mich. (Rods)

Lutz Pork Bait Co., 1234 Jefferson, Kansas City 5, Mo. (Pork Baits)

Magic Snell Tackle Co., Inc., 45 Niagara St., Canandaigua, N.Y.

Marathon Bait Co., Box 298, Wausau, Wisconsin

Martin Reel Co., Martin St., Mohawk, N.Y.

Mason Tackle, Otisville, Michigan (Line)

Maybrun Mfg. Co., 2250 Clybourn Ave., Chicago, Ill. (Pinchers, Pliers, Knives)

Meinzinger & Rade Co., 19000 Doris, Livonia, Mich. (Hooks, Scalers)

W. W. Mildrum Jewel Co., 230 Berlin St., East Berlin, Conn. (Rod Guides & Ferrules)

Mile Hi Tackle Co., P. O. Box 7022, Capitol Hill Station, Denver 6, Colo. (Snelled Hooks, Swivels)

Mill Run Products Co., 1360 W. Ninth St., Cleveland, Ohio (Lures, Stringers)

Mills Products Co., Mills Industrial Pk., Safety Harbor, Fla. (Lures)

Millsite Tackle Co., Howell, Michigan (Box/Stringers)

Minneapolis-Honeywell Co., 2753 4th Ave. S., Minneapolis, Minn. (Fish-o-therm)

Mit-Shel Co., 209 N. Third, Quincy, Ill. (Minnow Buckets)

Molded Carry-Lite Products, 3000 W. Clarke St., Milwaukee 45, Wis. (Bait Buckets)

National Expert Bait Co., Inc., 2928 Stevens Ave., Minneapolis 8, Minn. (Lures)

Nature Faker Lures, Inc., Windsor, Missouri

Newton Line Co., Inc., So. Main St., Homer N.Y. (Line)

O.A. Norlund Co., Div. Mann Edge Tool Co., Lewiston, Pa. (Gaffs)

Norton Mfg. Corp., 2700 N. Pulaski Rd., Chicago, Ill. (Bamboo Fishing Poles)

Oberlin Canteen Co., 212 Summer St., P. O. Box 208, Oberlin, Ohio

Old Pal, Inc., Lititz, Pa. (Minnow Buckets, Tackle Boxes)

Lee E. Olsen Knife Co., 7-11 Joy St., Howard City, Mich. (Filet Knives)

Charles F. Orvis Co., Manchester, Vermont (Orvis Reels, etc.)

Padre Island Co., Inc., 616 S. Staples St., Corpus Christi, Texas (Lures)

Palsa Sales, Box 55, Hales Corners, Wis. (Palsa Lure)

Paw Paw Bait Co., 400 S. Kalamazoo St., Paw Paw, Mich. (Lures)

Penn Fishing Tackle Mfg. Co., 3028 W. Hunting Park Ave., Philadelphia 32, Pa. (Reels)

Perfection Tip Co., 3020 E. 43rd Ave., Denver 16, Colo.

Phantom Products, Inc., 1800 Central, Kansas City, Mo. (Rods, Reels)

Phillips Fly & Tackle Co., Alexandria, Pa.

Plano Molding Co., 113 S. Center Ave., Plano, Ill. (Plastic Tackle Boxes)

Plas-Steel Products, Inc., Walkerton, Indiana (Rods)

J.R. Plasters Co., 111 N. Denver Ave., Kansas City 23, Mo. (Trot Lines, Floats, Leaders)

Plastics Research Corp., 3601 Jenny Lind, Fort Smith, Arkansas (Lures)

Plastilite Corp., P.O. Box 35, Ames Station, Omaha, Neb. (Floats, Minnow Buckets)

Prescott Spinner Co., P.O. Box 239, Mankato, Minnesota

Rapala, P.O. Box 5027, Minneapolis 6, Minn.

Rettinger Importing Co., 380 Lafayette St., N.Y. 3, N.Y. (Fishing Rainwear)

C. C. Roberts Bait Co., Mosinee, Wis. (Mud Puppy Lures)

St. Croix Sales Corp., Park Falls, Wis. (Fishing Tackle)

Scientific Anglers, Inc., 1012 Jefferson, Midland, Mich. (Fly Lines)

Seneca Tackle Co., Inc., 56 Cooper Square, N.Y. 3, N.Y. (Lures)

The Servus Rubber Co., 1100 Block Second St., Rock Island, Ill. (Fishing Footwear)

Sevenstrand Tackle Mfg. Co., 1207 Euclid Ave., Long Beach, Cal. (Leaders & Rods)

Shakespeare Co., 241 E. Kalamazoo Ave., Kalamazoo, Mich. (Rods, reels, line)

Sheldons, Inc., Hwy. 45 N, Antigo, Wis. (Mepps Spinners, etc.)

Shurkatch Fishing Tackle Co., Inc., S. Elm St., Richfield Springs, N.Y. (Gaffs, Floats, Terminal Tackle)

Simonsen Industries Inc., 1414 S. Michigan Ave., Chicago 5, Ill. (Tackle Boxes)

Skirt Minnow Seine Mfg. Co., P.O. Box 144, East Liverpool, Ohio

Snagproof Mfg. Co., 4153 E. Galbraith, Cincinnati 36, Ohio (Lures)

South Bend Tackle Co., Inc., Miami, Fla.

Sportsmen, Inc., 131 Saw Mill River Rd., Yonkers, N.Y. (Rods)

Staz-On Bait Co., Inc., Golden Pond, Kentucky

Steppe Importing Co., P.O. Box 32, RR #6, Guelph, Ontario (Fish Baskets)

Stratton & Terstegge Co., 1520 Rowan St., Louisville, Ky. (Tackle Boxes, Minnow Buckets)

Style-Cast Tackle Corp., 29866 John R., Madison Hts., Mich. (Rods)

Suick Lure Mfg. Co., Antigo, Wis. (Lures)

Sunset Line & Twine Co., Petaluma, Cal., Florence, Ala.

Sutton Co., Naples, New York (Lures)

Tack-L-Tyers, 939 Chicago Ave., Evanston, Ill. (Fly Tying Kits)

Taylor Instrument Co., Rochester 1, N.Y. (Fishermans Barometer)

Thompson Fishing Tackle Co., P.O. Box 275, Knoxville, Tenn. (Lures)

Townsend Engineering Co., P.O. Box 1433, Des Moines 5, Iowa (Fish Skinners)

True Life Minnow Harness, 29251 Grandview, Mount Clements, Mich.

True Temper Corp., 1623 Euclid Ave., Cleveland 15, Ohio

Tycoon/Fin-Nor Corp., 4027 N.W. 24th St., Miami 48, Florida

Umco Corp., Spring Park, Minnesota (Tackle Boxes)

Uncle Josh Bait Co., 524 Clarence St., P.O. Box 386, Fort Atkinson, Wis.

Union Steel Chest Corp., 54 Church St., LeRoy, N.Y.

U.S. Rubber Co., 1230 Ave. of Americas, N.Y. 20, N.Y. (Fishing Footwear)

Vlchek Plastic Co., P.O. Box 97, Valplast Rd., Middlefield, Ohio (Tackle Boxes)

Walker International, 2101 W. Lafayette, Detroit 16, Mich. (Tackle Importers)

Water Gremlin Co., 4370 Otter Lake Rd., White Bear Lake, Minn. (Lead Sinkers)

Water King Sales, P.O. Box 10, Pearl Beach, Michigan (Rods)

Weber Dot Line Mfg. Co., 4601 W. 47th St., Chicago 32, Ill. (Nets, Fish Bags, Rod Cases)

Weber Tackle Co., 133 W. Ellis St., Stevens Point, Wisconsin

West Indies Ocean Products Corp., Port Everglades (P.O. Box 13114 Sta.), Ft. Lauderdale, Florida (Shrimp Bait)

H.A. Whittemore & Co., Inc., 32 Kearney Rd., Needham Hts., Mass. (Lures)

Whopper-Stopper, Inc., P.O. Box 793, Sherman, Texas (Lures)

Williams Gold Refining Co., Inc., 2978 Main St., Buffalo 14, N.Y. (Lures)

Woodstock Line Co., 83 Canal St., Putnam, Conn. (Line)

World Famous Sales, Inc., 1601 S. Michigan Ave., Chicago 16, Ill. (Rain Suits, Tackle)

The Worth Co., P.O. Box 88, Stevens Point, Wis. (Terminal Tackle)

Wright & McGill Co., 1400 Yosemite, Denver 8, Colo.

York-Eger Mfg. Co., Inc., P.O. Box 1210, Sanford, Fla. (Nets, Lures)

Zebco Corp., 1131 E. Easton, Tulsa, Oklahoma

47 DEPARTMENTS:

Professional Fly Tyers

DAN BAILEY, Dan's Fly & Tackle Shop, Livingston, Mont.

PAT BARNES, Barnes' Fly Shop, West Yellowstone, Mont.

WAYNE BUSZEK, Visalia, Calif.

GEORGE CORNISH, Driftwood Marina, Box 296, Avalon, N.J. 08202.

RUBE CROSS, 606 Public St., Providence, R.I.

HARRY DARBEE, Livingston Manor, N.Y.

JIM DEREN, Angler's Roost, Chrysler Bldg., New York 17, N.Y.

ART FLICK, Westkill, N.Y.

BILL GALLASCH, 8705 Weldon Drive, Richmond, Va. 23229.

DON GAPEN, Gapen Fly Co., Anoka 8, Minn.

H. J. GREB, 2188 N.W. 24th Ave., Miami, Fla.

BILL KEANE, Box 371, Bronxville, N.Y. 10708.

ED KOCH, Koch's Tackle Shop, 936 Franklin St., Carlisle, Pa.

EDDIE LACHMANN, Amherst, Wis.

MERTON PARKS, Parks' Fly Shop, Gardiner, Mont.

PHIL PATTERSON, Phillip's Fly & Tackle Co., Alexandria, Pa.

JIM POULOS, 411 Stone Place, Wheeling, Ill.

HANK ROBERTS, 1033 Walnut St., Boulder, Colo.

HELEN SHAW, 246 E. 46th St., New York 17, N.Y.

NORM THOMPSON, Angler's Guide, 1805 N.W. Thurman, Portland 9, Ore.

DICK RIDEOUT, 78 Katahdin Ave., Millinocket, Me.

*Professional fly tyers not named here and wishing to be included in the fly tyers listing, 1973 Tom McNally's Fishermen's Bible, are urged to write Tom McNally, c/o Follett Publishing Co., 1010 W. Washington Blvd., Chicago, Ill. 60607.

48 DEPARTMENTS:

Fly Tying Materials Supply Houses

Each firm listed does not carry complete lines of fly tying materials. Write for catalogs or merchandise sheets.

ALL-LURE TACKLE CO., 47-10 48th St., Woodside 77, N.Y.

ANDY'S QUALITY FLY TYING MATERIALS, P.O. Box 269, Peabody, Mass.

R. S. CHASE CO., P.O. Box 208, South Duxbury, Mass.

DANIELSON FLY MFG. CO., P.O. Box 94, Mercer Island, Wash.

DERSH FEATHER AND TRADING CORP., 494 Broadway, N.Y. 12, N.Y.

F & S PRODUCTS CO., R-250, W. Sixth St., Mansfield, Ohio.

FINNY SPORTS (DD), Toledo 14, Ohio

GENE'S TACKLE SHOP, Box 162, Newark, N.Y.

HACKLE HOUSE, P.O. Box 1001, San Mateo, Calif.

D. E. HECHT, 80 University Place, New York 3, N.Y.

HERTER'S CO., Waseca, Minn.

E. HILLE ANGLER'S SUPPLY HOUSE, P.O. Box 269, Williamsport, Pa.

M. J. HOFFMAN CO., 989 Gates Ave., Brooklyn 21, N.Y.

J. J. KLEIN, LTD., 2077 E. Gouin Blvd., Montreal 12, Quebec, Canada

MANGROVE FEATHER CO., 42 West 38th St., New York 18, N.Y.

MARTIN TACKLE & MFG. CO., 431 Eastlake Ave. E., Seattle 9, Wash.

NETCRAFT CO., Box 5510, Toledo 13, Ohio

PASSLOFF, INC., 19 West 36th St., New York 18, N.Y.

PRIEST RIVER TACKLE CO., Landfall, Coolin, Idaho

REED TACKLE CO., Box 390, Caldwell, N.J.

HANK ROBERTS, INC., 1033-37 Walnut, Boulder, Colo.

M. SCHWARTZ & SONS, INC., 321 E. 3rd St., New York 9, N.Y.

SHOFF FISHING TACKLE CO., 407 W. Gowe St., Kent, Wash.

SONNIES, P.O. Box 126, Wilmot, Wis.

TACK-L-TYERS, 939 Chicago Ave., Evanston, Ill.

D. H. THOMPSON, 335 Walnut Ave., Elgin, Ill.

THOMPSON FISHING TACKLE CO., 2308 N. Broadway, Knoxville, Tenn.

UNIVERSAL VISE CO., P.O. Box 335, Holyoke, Mass.

E. VENIARD, LTD., 138 Northwood Road, Thorton Heath, Surrey, England

WOODSLORE PRODUCTS, Box 821, Costa Mesa, Calif.

WORTH CO., P.O. Box 88, Stevens Point, Wis.

PAUL H. YOUNG CO., 23800 W. Eight Mile Road, Southfield, Michigan

Rod Building Kits and Supplies

DUNTON & SON, INC., 4 Fiske Ave., Greenfield, Mass.

FINNY SPORTS, 462 Sports Bldg., Toledo 14, Ohio.

GLIEBE CO., 1154 Myrtle Ave., Brooklyn 21, N.Y.

HERTER'S CO., Waseca, Minn.

E. HILLE ANGLER'S SUPPLY HOUSE, P.O. Box 269, Williamsport, Pa.

IOWA ROYAL RODS, Perry, Iowa.

MAKIT FISHING ROD MFG. CO., 113 Adolph St., Fort Worth 7, Texas.

E. MILTENBERG, INC., 43 Great Jones St., New York 12, N.Y.

NETCRAFT CO., Toledo 13, Ohio.

CHARLES F. ORVIS CO., INC., Manchester, Vermont.

PASTOR & CO., 11423 Vanowen St., North Hollywood 3, Calif.

PRIEST RIVER TACKLE CO., Landfall, Coolin, Idaho.

REED TACKLE CO., Box 390, Caldwell, N.J.

REEDER MFG. CO., Box 346, Vancouver, Wash.

SHOFF FISHING TACKLE CO., 407 W. Gowe St., Kent, Wash.

PAUL H. YOUNG CO., 23800 W. Eight Mile Road, Southfield, Mich.

Roster of American Casting Association

CALIFORNIA

DOUGLAS SM ROD & GUN CLUB: Lloyd Van Shaw, Sec., 1609 Bentley, Los Angeles 25, Calif.

GASCO ROD & GUN CLUB: Frank Messersmith, 1440 Emory Drive, Whittier, Calif.

GOLDEN GATE ANGLING & CASTING CLUB: C. W. Bird, Sec., 111 Sutter St., San Francisco, Calif.

LONG BEACH CASTING CLUB: Don McGavin, Sec., P. O. Box 4063, Long Beach, Calif. 90804

OAKLAND CASTING CLUB: Sam Neely, Sec., 1100 Jefferson St., Oakland 7, Calif.

PASADENA CASTING CLUB: Earl E. Martin, Sec., 1440 Casa Grande, Pasadena, Calif.

RANCHO ROD & GUN CLUB: Henry Webster, Sec., 354 McCadden Place, Los Angeles 5, Calif.

CONNECTICUT

HARTFORD COUNTY CASTING CLUB: Miss Elsie Seiffert, Sec., 97 Roxbury St., Hartford 6, Conn.

FLORIDA

LUTZ CASTING CLUB: Dr. Karl K. Eychaner, Sec., Box 306, Lutz, Florida

ST. PETERSBURG ROD & GUN CLUB: Mrs. May V. Hunt, Sec., 770 32nd Ave. South, St. Petersburg, Florida

ILLINOIS

CATERPILLAR ROD CLUB: W. Les Matthey, Sec., 1712 N. Eighth St., Pekin, Ill.

JACKSON PARK CASTING CLUB: John Crewdson, Sec., 5756 Blackstone Ave., Chicago 37, Illinois

LINCOLN PARK CASTING CLUB: Herbert Schulz, Sec., 4550 N. Ashland Ave., Chicago 40, Illinois

ROXANA FLY & BAIT CASTING CLUB: Arthur H. Mikkelson, Sec., 403 N. Maple, Roxana, Illinois

INDIANA

GARY ANGLERS CLUB: Bill Chadwick, Sec., 1221 Garfield St., Hobart, Indiana

HAMMOND CASTING CLUB: Mrs. Rosemary Rainford, Sec., 7039 Monroe St., Hammond, Indiana

KENTUCKY

BLUE GRASS ANGLERS: Jack Perry, Sec., 625 Cecil Way, Lexington, Ky.

LOUISVILLE CASTING CLUB: Robert Budd, Sec., 1216 Akers Ave., Jeffersonville, Indiana

LOUISIANA

CRESCENT CITY CASTING CLUB: Ben Fontaine, Sec., P.O. Box 50638, New Orleans, La.

MICHIGAN

DETROIT BAIT & FLY CASTING CLUB: C. W. Wilcox, Sec., 16210 Roselawn, Detroit 21, Michigan

MINNESOTA

IWLA CASTING CLUB: Mrs. Lee Cumberland, Sec., 6629 Park Ave. So., Minneapolis 23, Minn.

MISSOURI

CARONDELET FLY & BAIT CASTING CLUB: Louis Meyer, Sec., 5454 Finkman St., St. Louis 9, Missouri

FERGUSON CASTING CLUB: Mrs. Mildred Deck, Sec., 401 Warfield Ave., Ferguson 35, Missouri

KANSAS CITY BAIT & FLY CASTING CLUB: Fritz R. White, Sec., 5609 Virginia, Kansas City 10, Missouri

NORTHEAST CASTING CLUB: Floyd W. Dessenberger, Sec., 107 N. Lawndale, Kansas City 23, Missouri

ST. LOUIS FLY & BAIT CASTING CLUB: Ed R. Lanser, Sec., 214 Hernan Drive, St. Louis 23, Missouri

NEW HAMPSHIRE

MANCHESTER FLY & BAIT CASTING CLUB: Michael Lang, Sec., 193 Ste. Marie St., Manchester, New Hampshire

NEW JERSEY

PATERSON CASTING CLUB: Frances Caillie, Sec., 212 Gordon Ave., Totowa Boro 2, New Jersey

NEW YORK STATE

BUFFALO ANGLER'S CLUB: Alfred W. Holland, Sec., 17 Briggs St., Buffalo 7, New York

BUFFALO BAIT & FLY CASTING CLUB: Mrs. Edna M. Templin, Sec., 78 Briggs Ave., Buffalo 7, New York

CAMPFIRE CLUB OF AMERICA INC.: Dr. R. A. Clinchy Jr., Sec., 19 Rector St., New York 6, New York

ONONDAGA CASTING CLUB: Mrs. Edna Stafford, Sec., Tully, New York

OHIO

BARBERTON CASTING CLUB: Joseph D. Mullins, Sec., 33 West Long St., Akron, Ohio

CINCINNATI CASTING CLUB: Ray Abrams, Sec., 994 North Bend Road, Cincinnati 24, Ohio

CLINTONVILLE CASTING CLUB: Arthur S. Kiefer, Sec., 86 Erie Road, Columbus 14, Ohio

COLUMBUS CASTING CLUB: Dr. W. T. Behnen, Sec., 148 E. State St., Columbus, Ohio

DAYTON CASTING ASSOCIATION: Herman Stauffer, Sec., 2591 Crestwell Place, Dayton 20, Ohio

DAYTON GYM CASTING CLUB: Mrs. Alma Kettering, Sec., 229 Cushing Ave., Dayton 29, Ohio

DELCO PRODUCTS CASTING CLUB: Joe Dalrymple, Sec., 3609 Fairbanks Ave., Dayton 7, Ohio

E. CLEVELAND ROD & GUN CLUB: Richard J. Siciliana, Sec., 1150 Worton Blvd., Cleveland 24, Ohio

SPRINGFIELD CASTING CLUB: Mrs. William Keener, Sec., 637 S. Clairmont Ave., Springfield, Ohio

TOLEDO CASTING CLUB: Elston Hubbard, Sec., 2305 Scottswood, Toledo 10, Ohio

WHETSTONE CASTING CLUB: Mrs. Barbara Weaver, Sec., 582 Melrose Ave., Columbus 2, Ohio

OKLAHOMA

TULSA ANGLERS CLUB: Tom DeVore, Sec., 1113 South Guthrie, Tulsa 19, Oklahoma

PENNSYLVANIA

LOWER MERION ROD & GUN CLUB: Mrs. Theresa A. LaRue, 606 Georges Lane, Ardmore, Pennsylvania

PHILADELPHIA CASTING CLUB: Sam Weitz, Sec., 517 Spruce St., Philadelphia, Penna.

PITTSBURGH CASTING CLUB: Dorothy Whitesell, Sec., 4609 Butler St., Pittsburgh 1, Penna.

SUBURBAN PHILADELPHIA CONSV. CLUB: Mrs. Ellen A. Dietrich, Sec., 1141 Roosevelt Drive, Upper Darby, Penna.

TENNESSEE

MEMPHIS ANGLERS CLUB: Albert Brandi, Sec., 191 Madison Ave., Memphis 3, Tenn.

NASHVILLE FLY & BAIT CASTING CLUB: John C. Adkins, Sec., 299 Wallace Road, Nashville, Tenn.

TEXAS

COWTOWN CASTING CLUB: Mrs. Irene Tuck, Sec., 5108 Barbara Road, Fort Worth, Texas

DALLAS FLY & BAIT CASTING CLUB: Juanita Leatherman, Sec., 1451 Autumn Leaves Trail, Dallas 16, Texas

HOUSTON ANGLERS CLUB: F. L. Gilbert, Sec., 3123 Plumb St., Houston 5, Texas

LUBBOCK CASTING CLUB: Sam Sayers, Sec., 3211—30th St., Lubbock, Texas

VIRGINIA & WASHINGTON, D.C.

NATIONAL CAPITAL CASTING CLUB: Fred A. Brady Sr., Sec., 5105 Tyburn St. S.E., Washington 22, D.C.

TIDEWATERS ANGLERS CLUB: Marion E. Hutson, Sec., 6785 Norlina Ave., Norfolk, Virginia

WISCONSIN

MILWAUKEE CASTING CLUB: Robert A. Brockman, Sec., 4817 West Villard Ave., Milwaukee 18, Wisconsin

PABST CASTING CLUB: Otto Johnson, Sec., 2139 N. 29th St., Milwaukee 8, Wisconsin

WAUKESHA CASTING CLUB: Clarence Anthes, Sec., 707 N. Moreland Blvd., Waukesha, Wisconsin

CANADA

TORONTO ANGLERS' & HUNTERS ASSN.: R. J. Mitchele, Sec., 85 King St. East, Toronto 1, Ontario

EDUCATIONAL INSTITUTIONS

UNIVERSITY OF ILLINOIS: Thomas Krizan, 201 Men's Old Gym, University of Illinois, Urbana, Ill.

UNIVERSITY OF NEW HAMPSHIRE: Miss Evelyn Browne, Dept. Phys. Ed for Women, Durham, New Hampshire

LADIES CLUBS

CARONDELET WOMEN'S CASTING CLUB: Mrs. Vera Ousley, Sec., 6730 Scanlan Ave., St. Louis 39, Missouri

HEART OF AMERICA ROD & REEL CLUB: Veronica A. Miller, Sec., 2750 Charlotte St., Kansas City 9, Missouri

KANSAS CITY WOMEN'S B & F CASTING CLUB: Mrs. Zelma Stevenson, Sec., 4123 Walnut St., Kansas City, Mo.

LONG BEACH WOMEN'S CASTING CLUB: Oletha Ward, Sec., 4718 Adenmoor Ave., Lakewood, Calif.

WRENTHAM SOCIETY OF SPORTSWOMEN: Mrs Marion E. Cafferky, Sec., 349 East St., Wrentham, Massachusetts

STATE & DISTRICT ASSOCIATIONS

DIXIE AMATEUR FLY & BAIT CASTING ASSN.: H. M. Weenick, Sec., P.O. Box 1347, St. Petersburg, Florida

EASTERN ASSN. OF AMATEUR CASTING CLUBS: Miss Elsie Seiffert, Sec., 97 Roxbury St., Hartford 6, Conn.

GREATLAKES AMATEUR CASTING ASSN.: Mrs. Mollie Schneider, Sec., RR 19—76 Willow Drive, Jeffersonville, Indiana

ILLINOIS AMATEUR CASTING ASSN.: Herbert Schulz, Sec., 4550 N. Ashland, Chicago, Illinois

MICHIGAN AMATEUR CASTING ASSN.: Charles W. Wilcox, Sec., 16210 Roselawn, Detroit 21, Michigan

MIDDLE ATLANTIC ASSN. OF CASTING CLUBS: Mrs. Ellen Deitrich, Sec., 1141 Roosevelt Drive, Upper Darby, Pennsylvania

MISSOURI VALLEY AMATEUR CASTING ASSN.: Mrs. Mildred Deck, Sec., 401 Warfield Drive, Ferguson 35, Missouri

OHIO STATE CASTING ASSN.: Zack Wilson Sr., Sec., 414 E. Beechwold, Columbus, Ohio

SOUTHWESTERN AMATEUR CASTING ASSN.: Mrs. Rilla Hickerson, Sec., 915 South Canton, Tulsa 12, Oklahoma

WESTERN ASSN. ANGLING & CASTING CLUBS: Mrs. Leslie Guggenheim, Sec., 1340 Lombard St., San Francisco, Calif.

(*) AMERICAN CASTING ASSOCIATION: P.O. Box 51, Nashville, Tenn., Phone Cypress 2-9427
Ben Fontaine, Pres., P.O. Box 50638, New Orleans, La.
Paul N. Jones, Exec. Secretary, P.O. Box 50638, Nashville, Tenn.

Federation of Fly Fishermen,

MEMBERSHIP SERVICE OFFICE
15513 Haas Ave., Gardena, Calif. 90249

MEMBER CLUBS

ANDOVER FLY FISHERS, Massachusetts
ANGLERS' CLUB OF CHICAGO, Illinois
ANGLERS' CLUB OF PORTLAND, Oregon
ARIZONA FLY CASTERS, Phoenix
BEA-MOC ROD & GUN CLUB, Roscoe, NY
BEAVERKILL FLY FISHERS, Roscoe, NY
BLUE DUN ANGLERS, Medford, Mass.
BOISE VALLEY FLY FISHERMEN, Idaho
BRODHEADS FOREST & STREAM ASSOC., Pa.
CALIFORNIA FLY FISHERMEN, Sacramento
CASCADE FLY FISHING CLUB, Washington
CASTLE CREEK FISHING CLUB, Corning, NY
CLEARWATER FLY CASTERS, Washington
CONNECTICUT FLY FISHERMEN'S ASSOC.
DESERT FLY CASTERS, Mesa, Arizona
DIABLO VALLEY FLY FISHERMEN, Calif.
EAST JERSEY CHAPTER—TROUT UNLIMITED
EVERGREEN FLY FISHING CLUB, Wash.
FLY CASTERS OF BOULDER, Colorado
FLYCASTERS, INC., Campbell, Calif.
FLY FISHERMEN FOR CONSERVATION, Calif.
FLY FISHERS CLUB OF ORANGE CO., Calif.
FONTINALIS FLY FISHERMEN, New York
FRONT RANGE FLY FISHERS, Denver, Colo.
GOLDEN GATE ANGLING & CASTING CLUB
GREEN COUNTRY FLY FISHERS, Oklahoma
HENRYVILLE CONSERVATION CLUB, NY
INDIANAPOLIS FLY CASTERS, Indiana
INGLEWOOD FLY FISHERMEN, Calif.
INLAND EMPIRE FLY FISHING CLUB, Wash.
INTERNATIONAL FARIO CLUB, Paris, France
JOE JEFFERSON CLUB, INC., New Jersey
KITTITAS VALLEY FLY CASTERS, Wash.
KLAMATH COUNTRY FLYCASTERS, Oregon
LIVERMORE FLY FISHERMEN, Calif.
LONG BEACH CASTING CLUB, Calif.
LONG BEACH WOMEN'S CASTING CLUB, Calif.

LOWER COLUMBIA FLY FISHERS, Washington
McKENZIE FLY FISHERS, Oregon
MONTREAL ANGLERS & HUNTERS INC., Canada
NAPA VALLEY FLY FISHERMEN, Calif.
NORTH COAST FLY FISHERMEN, Calif.
NORTHERN ILLINOIS FLY TYERS, Arlington
OAKLAND CASTING CLUB, Calif.
OLYMPIC FLY FISHERS, Edmonds, Wash.
PALM SPRINGS ROD & GUN CLUB, Calif.
PALO ALTO FLY FISHERS, Calif.
PASADENA CASTING CLUB, California
POTOMAC VALLEY FLY FISHERMEN, Maryland
PRAIRIE FLY FISHERS, Oklahoma
PUGET SOUND FLY FISHING CLUB, Wash.
PUTNAM TROUT ASSOCIATION, Carmel, NY
RHODY FLY RODDERS, Providence, R. I.
ROGUE FLY FISHERS, Central Point, Ore.
SALINAS VALLEY FLY FISHERMEN, Calif.
"SALTY" FLY RODDERS OF NEW YORK
SAN DIEGO FLY FISHERMEN, California
SOUTHWESTERN MONTANA FLY FISHERMEN
SUN VALLEY FLY FISHERS, Idaho
STANISLAUS FLY FISHERMEN, Calif.
SUSQUEHANNOCK FLY FISHERS, Lebanon, Pa.
THE STEAMBOATERS, Oregon
THEODORE GORDON FLY FISHERS, New York
TOTEM FLY FISHERS, Van., B.C., Canada
TWIN HARBORS FLY FISHERS, Washington
UNITED FLY TYERS, Massachusetts
UPPER FISHING CREEK FLY FISHERS, Pa.
WADERS OF THE WOLF, Wisconsin
WASATCH FLY CASTERS, Salt Lake City
WASHINGTON FLY FISHING CLUB, Seattle
WHITE CLAY FLY FISHERMEN, Pa.
WILDERNESS FLY FISHERS, California
WYNDHAM ANGLER'S CLUB, New Zealand
ZANESFIELD ROD & GUN CLUB, Ohio

State Tourist Office Listings

ALABAMA—Bureau of Publicity and Information, Room 116, State Capitol, Montgomery, Ala. 36104.

ALASKA—Travel Division, Department of Economic Development, Pouch E, Juneau, Alaska 99801.

ARIZONA—Arizona Department of Economic Planning and Development, 3303 N. Central Ave., Phoenix, Ariz. 85012.

ARKANSAS—Publicity and Parks Commission, State Capitol, Little Rock, Ark. 72201.

CALIFORNIA—State Office of Tourism, 926 J Building, Room 812, Sacramento, Cal. 95814.

COLORADO—Colorado Publicity Department, 600 State Services Building, Denver, Colo. 80203.

CONNECTICUT—Development Commission, State Office Building, Hartford, Conn. 06115.

DELAWARE—Bureau of Travel Development, State of Delaware, 45 The Green, Dover, Del. 19901.

DISTRICT OF COLUMBIA—Washington Convention and Visitors Bureau, 1616 K Street, N. W., Washington, D. C. 20006.

FLORIDA—Florida Development Commission, 107 W. Gaines, Tallahassee, Fla. 32304.

GEORGIA—Department of Industry and Trade, Tourist Division, 100 State Capitol, Atlanta, Ga. 30334.

HAWAII—Hawaii Visitors Bureau, 400 N. Michigan Ave., Chicago 60611.

IDAHO—Department of Commerce and Development, Room 108, State Capitol Building, Boise, Idaho 83702.

ILLINOIS—Department of Business and Economic Development Division of Tourism, 222 South College, Springfield, Ill. 62706. Also: Chicago Convention and Tourism Bureau, Inc., 332 S. Michigan Av., Chicago, Ill. 60604.

INDIANA—Tourist Division, Indiana Department of Commerce, 334 State House, Indianapolis, Ind. 46204.

IOWA—Iowa Development Commission, Tourism and Travel Division, 250 Jewett Building, Des Moines, Ia. 50309.

KANSAS—Department of Economic Development, State Office Building, Topeka, Kas. 66612.

KENTUCKY—Department of Public Information, New Capitol Annex, Frankfort, Ky. 40601.

LOUISIANA—Louisiana Tourist Development Commission, Box 44291, Baton Rogue, La. 70804.

MAINE—Department of Economic Development, State Office Building, Augusta, Me. 04330.

MARYLAND—Department of Economic Development, State Office Building, Annapolis, Md. 21401.

MASSACHUSETTS—Department of Commerce and Development, 100 Cambridge, Boston, Mass. 02202. .

MICHIGAN—Michigan Tourist Council, Stevens T. Mason Building, Lansing, Mich. 38936. Also: Southeast Michigan Tourist Association, 1404 Broderick Tower, Detroit; Upper Michigan Tourist Association, Box 1188, Iron Mountain, 49801; East Michigan Tourist Association, The Log Office, Bay City, 48706; West Michigan Tourist Association, 136 E. Fulton, Grand Rapids, 49502.

MINNESOTA—Vacation Information Center, State Capitol, St. Paul, Minn. 55101.

MISSISSIPPI—Travel Department, Mississippi Agricultural and Industrial Board, 1504 State Office Building, Jackson, Miss. 39201.

MISSOURI—Missouri Tourism Commission, Box 1055, Jefferson City, Mo. 65101.

MONTANA—Advertising Department, Montana Highway Commission, 204 Laboratory Building, MRC, Helena, Mont.

NEBRASKA—Game, Forestation and Parks Commission, Information and Tourism Division, State Capitol, Lincoln, Neb. 68509.

NEVADA—Nevada Department of Economic Development, Carson City, Nev. 89701.

NEW HAMPSHIRE—Department of Economic Development, 318 State House Annex, Concord, N.H. 03301.

NEW JERSEY—Promotion Section, Department of Conservation and Economic Development, Box 1889, Trenton, N.J. 08625.

NEW MEXICO—Tourist Division, Department of Development, State Capitol, Santa Fe, N.M. 87501.

NEW YORK—Department of Commerce, Travel Bureau, 112 State Street, Albany, N.Y. 12207. Also: New York Convention and Visitors Bureau, 90 E. 42nd Street, New York, N.Y. 10017.

NORTH CAROLINA—Travel and Promotion Division, Department of Conservation and Development, Raleigh, N.C. 27602.

NORTH DAKOTA—State Travel Department, Capitol Building, Bismarck, N. D. 58501.

OKLAHOMA—Oklahoma Industrial Development and Park Department, 500 Will Rogers Memorial Building, Oklahoma City, Okla. 73105.

OHIO—State of Ohio Development Department, Box 1001, Columbus, O. 43216.

OREGON—Travel Information Division, Oregon State Highway Department, 101 State Highway Building, Salem, Ore. 97310.

PENNSYLVANIA—Travel Development Bureau, Department of Commerce, South Office Building, Harrisburg, Pa. 17120.

RHODE ISLAND—Rhode Island Development Council, 49 Hayes Street, Providence, R. I. 02908.

SOUTH CAROLINA—Travel Division, Department of Parks, Recreation and Tourism, Box 1358, Columbia, S. C. 29202.

SOUTH DAKOTA—Publicity Division, Department of Highways, Pierre, S. D. 57501.

TENNESSEE—Division of Tourist Promotion, 2611 West End Avenue, Nashville, Tenn. 37203.

TEXAS—Tourist Development Agency, Box TT, Capitol Station, Austin, Tex. 78711. Also: Texas Highway Department, Travel and Information Division, Austin, Tex. 78701.

UTAH—Tourist and Publicity Council, Council Hall, State Capitol, Salt Lake City, Utah 84114.

VERMONT—Publicity Division, Vermont Development Department, Montpelier, Vt. 05602.

VIRGINIA—Department of Conservation and Development, Commonwealth of Virginia, Richmond, Va. 19232.

WASHINGTON—Tourist Promotion Division, Department of Commerce and Economic Development, General Administration Building, Olympia, Wash. 98501.

WEST VIRGINIA—Travel Development Division, West Virginia Department of Commerce, Capitol Building, Charleston, W. Va. 25305.

WISCONSIN—Wisconsin Conservation Department, Vacation and Travel Service, Box 450, Madison, Wis. 53701, or State of Wisconsin Vacation and Travel Service, 205 N. Michigan Ave., Chicago 60601.

WYOMING—Wyoming Travel Commission, 2320 Capitol Avenue, Cheyenne, Wyo. 82001.

(continued from inside front cover)
Service. The Federal Department of Transportation and agencies such as the Tennessee Valley Authority also are occasionally involved. Of the three major agencies, however, the one conducting the most extensive channelization projects is the Soil Conservation Service. This group is charged with "improving" conditions on small watersheds, and this is where the bulldozers are most active.

There is much the average fisherman and citizen can do to see that more of our valuable streams and rivers are not turned into fish-less ditches. They should write their representatives in Congress and in their state legislatures urging them to study carefully "flood control" proposals and to generally oppose reckless bulldozing and channelization of rivers and streams. Letters and petitions also should be filed with state conservation departments, regional offices of the U. S. Soil Conservation Service, and the Commanding General, Army Corps of Engineers, Washington, D.C.

Detailed information on the channelization problem, and what individual and organized sportsmen can do to help solve it, is available in brochure form from the National Audubon Society, R.R. 4, Roving Hills, Red Wing, Minnesota, 44066, or from the Society's national office, 950 Third Avenue, New York, New York, 10022.

Tom McNally

TWO VIEWS OF WYOMING'S FAMED SNAKE RIVER

Portion of the Snake River, in its natural state, has streamside cover, riffles, bend and deep pool—all of it good trout-supporting water.

After bulldozing for sake of "channelization" another nearby section of the Snake is destroyed. It produces no nymph or other bug life, contains no trout, and is a "dead area".

TOM McNALLY

is Outdoor Editor of *The Chicago Tribune* and one of the world's best-known and most popular outdoors writers. He has been a full-time, professional outdoor writer for 25 years, and has long been recognized not only as an authority on all phases of fishing but also an angler of great personal skill. He is considered, in fact, to be one of the very finest fly fishermen and fly casters alive.

In addition, Tom McNally is unique among the world's outdoor writers in that he is a qualified and fully professional writer. Thus he not only has experience and personal skill, but also the ability and training to put it in words for the benefit of others.

McNally is internationally known for his hundreds of magazine feature stories that appear regularly in *Outdoor Life, Field and Stream,* and other publications such as *Readers Digest, Life, Look,* and *Time.* In addition, McNally has authored many books and pamphlets on fishing, has starred in angling movies and made countless appearances on TV shows — including giving a casting demonstration "live" on an Arthur Godfrey TV production.

Tom McNally has matched wits with fish, both fresh and salt water species, all over the United States and Canada, throughout the Caribbean, Central and South America, in Europe, Africa, and much of the Pacific. In an "ordinary" year he will travel an average of 50,000 miles in pursuit of fish—and fishing stories, many of which are within the covers of this new *TOM McNALLY FISHERMEN'S BIBLE.*

Tom McNally admires a nine pound lake trout he took on ultralight spinning tackle (2 pound test line) at Great Bear Lake, Northwest Territories.

FISHERMEN! Here, in one original, accurate reference book, are features on:

Bass, pike, trout, tarpon, marlin, sailfish, mackerel, grayling, coho salmon, muskies and lots more

BONUS BOOK! The Complete Ultralight Spinning Story

SPECIAL FEATURES!

The only complete set of world and state-by-state angling records

Features on fly tying, custom rod building, Knot Tying, Fishing Frontiers, Directories (Tackle Manufacturers, etc.), Feature States and their fishing, Camping-Fishing Tips, New Angling Tricks, Latest in Tackle, and specials on boats, tackle, gear, lures, bait . . . and hundreds of descriptive, informative photographs.